TUDENT STUDY COMPANION

BIOLOGY
Life on Earth
Seventh Edition

Teresa Audesirk
Gerald Audesirk
University of Colorado at Denver

Bruce E. Byers
University of Massachusetts, Amherst

PEARSON

Prentice
Hall

Upper Saddle River, NJ 07458

Assistant Editor: Colleen Lee
Executive Editor: Teresa Ryu Chung
Editor-in-Chief, Science: John Challice
Vice President of Production & Manufacturing: David W. Riccardi
Executive Managing Editor: Kathleen Schiaparelli
Assistant Managing Editor: Becca Richter
Production Editor: Dana Dunn
Supplement Cover Manager: Paul Gourhan
Supplement Cover Designer: Joanne Alexandris
Manufacturing Buyer: Ilene Kahn
Photo Credits: Franz Lanting/Minden Pictures

© 2005   Pearson Education, Inc.
Pearson Prentice Hall
Pearson Education, Inc.
Upper Saddle River, NJ 07458

The author and publisher of this book have used their best efforts in preparing this book.
efforts include the development, research, and testing of the theories and programs to determine
effectiveness. The author and publisher make no warranty of any kind, expressed or implied
regard to these programs or the documentation contained in this book. The author and pub
shall not be liable in any event for incidental or consequential damages in connection with, or a
out of, the furnishing, performance, or use of these programs.

Printed in the United States of America

10   9   8   7   6   5   4   3   2

ISBN 0-13-145755-1

Pearson Education Ltd., *London*
Pearson Education Australia Pty. Ltd., *Sydney*
Pearson Education Singapore, Pte. Ltd.
Pearson Education North Asia Ltd., *Hong Kong*
Pearson Education Canada, Inc., *Toronto*
Pearson Educación de Mexico, S.A. de C.V.
Pearson Education—Japan, *Tokyo*
Pearson Education Malaysia, Pte. Ltd.

TABLE OF CONTENTS

CONTRIBUTING AUTHORS

James Hewlett, Finger Lakes Community College

Steven Kilpatrick, University of Pittsburgh at Johnstown

Kelli Prior, Finger Lakes Community College

Joanne Russell, Manchester Community College

Linda Smith-Staton, Pellissippi State Technical Community College

Teresa Snyder-Leiby, State University of New York at New Paltz

Mark Sugalski, New England College

David Tapley, Salem State College

Michelle Withers, Lousiana State University

David Zimmer, Cayuga Community College

TO THE STUDENT

Welcome to the *Student Study Companion* to accompany *Biology: Life on Earth 7e* by Teresa Audesirk, Gerald Audesirk, and Bruce Byers. This supplement has been constructed to help you review the major biological concepts that you will encounter during this course and ask you to think about them critically.

The *Student Study Companion* is divided into forty-two chapters that correspond directly to those in the textbook. Within each chapter you will find:

- **At-A-Glance–**an outline of the major concepts in the chapter.

- **Self Test–**multiple choice, short answer, and labeling questions that test your understanding of the chapter's major concepts.

- **Essay Challenge–**questions that require you to think in-depth about the biology in the world around you.

- **Media Activities–**a list and description of activities found on the Web site selected by your instructor. These activities range from animations that offer you a visual view of difficult processes to in-depth web investigations that extend and reinforce the concepts learned in the chapter case studies.

- **Issues in Biology–**web activities that allow you to explore biological issues that people face in their everyday lives.

- **Bizarre Facts in Biology–**exercises that allow you to explore the weird and quirky aspects of biology.

- **Key Terms–**a comprehensive list of important terms from the text.

- **Answer Key–**answers to the Self Test, Essay Challenge, Media Activities, Issues in Biology, and Bizarre Facts in Biology questions that allow you to gauge your understanding of a particular concept.

Not only will the *Student Study Companion* help you review important concepts, but it will also provide an opportunity to explore the biology in your life and in the world around you. For more practice with automated interactive coaching and access to the media activities, please visit http://www.prenhall.com/audesirk7 and log in to the Web site selected by your instructor.

CHAPTER 1: AN INTRODUCTION TO LIFE ON EARTH

AT-A-GLANCE

SELF TEST

1. A fundamental characteristic of life on Earth is that _____.
   a. living things have a complex, organized structure based on inorganic molecules
   b. living things passively acquire materials and energy from their environment and convert them into different forms
   c. living things grow and reproduce
   d. living things reproduce, using information stored in RNA
   e. none of the above
   f. The first, second, and third answers above are correct.

2. Homeostasis is the process by which _____.
   a. living things maintain their complex structure and the internal conditions needed to sustain life
   b. living things reproduce
   c. some organisms can enter a kind of suspended animation to survive harsh conditions
   d. like organisms associate with like organisms

3. Which of the following groups of organisms contains prokaryotic cells? Please select the most appropriate answer.
   a. Bacteria
   b. Archaea
   c. Plantae
   d. Bacteria and Archaea

4. Organisms that can extract energy from light are called _____; organisms that must obtain energy from molecules made by other organisms are called _____.
   a. herbivores, carnivores
   b. photosynthetic, herbivores
   c. heterotroph, autotroph
   d. autotroph, heterotroph

5. Science assumes that natural laws (such as the law of gravity) _____.
   a. apply uniformly through space and through time
   b. apply in the laboratory but not in nature
   c. change with time
   d. differ depending on the location of the observer

6. The process of evolution involves _____.
   a. natural selection of organisms that produce more offspring in certain environmental conditions
   b. changes in a species due to mutations
   c. adaptation of an organism to its environment
   d. all of the above
   e. the first and third answers above

7. You discover a new type of organism in the back of your fridge. Luckily, your roommate is a biology major and takes you to the lab where he works. You put a small piece of the fuzzy critter under the microscope and see that it is made of very simple, single cells with no nucleus. What type of organism might this be?
   a. Bacteria   b. Archaea
   c. Bacteria or Archaea   d. Fungus

8. A scientist is testing whether a new cancer drug will work on prostate cancer in humans. To properly interpret results of an experiment, control experiments are needed. Which of the following treatments would serve as a control in these experiments, so that the researchers can conclude that the changes that they see in the patients are due to the drug?
   a. Different doses of the drug are administered to patients.
   b. Some patients receive a "mock" injection that contains the same solution base and the same volume as the drug but does not actually contain the drug itself.
   c. At least 1000 individuals are treated with the drug.
   d. Patients at three different hospitals, each in a different state, are treated with the drug.
   e. Both the second and fourth answers are correct.

9. Your textbook lists seven characteristics that living organisms possess as a group. However, if you could distill these seven characteristics down to two general descriptive properties held in common by all living organisms, what would they be?
   a. macromolecular complexity and multiple levels of organization
   b. atoms and elements
   c. cellular structure and genetics
   d. chemical relationships and diversity

10. The organic complexity and organization characteristic of living organisms depends on the periodic capture of raw materials and energy. Ultimately, the source of these materials and energy is _____.
    a. metabolism   b. photosynthesis
    c. the sun   d. other life-forms

11. Energy, like gasoline for your car, is required for organisms to survive, and even thrive, in the face of diverse environments. An autotrophic organism _____.
    a. would be one who derived its energy from internalizing the cellular matter of other organisms (i.e., eats others)
    b. would be one who derived its energy from a renewable external energy source such as sunlight (i.e., photosynthetic organisms)
    c. would include cucumbers growing in your garden
    d. Both the second and third answers are correct.

12. Another way to describe the "scientific method" would be that it is _____.
    a. a conceptual and ethical framework that guides scientific inquiry
    b. dependent upon observations leading to a hypothesis and careful experimental design and scrutiny of experimental results (data), leading to a conclusion that refutes or supports the hypothesis
    c. dependent upon "getting the word out" to other scientists via peer-reviewed publications, including electronic journals
    d. all of the above

13. Experiments are carefully designed in an attempt to _____.
    a. test a single experimental variable
    b. test multiple experimental variables
    c. prove a hypothesis
    d. none of the above

14. Natural selection is best measured by _____.
    a. numerous adaptations
    b. reproductive success
    c. biodiversity
    d. rate of environmental change

15. A basic understanding of basic biological concepts _____.
    a. permits a deeper, and sometimes profound, appreciation of the world around us
    b. is just a set of facts and ideas about the world around us
    c. is necessary only for biology majors
    d. often decreases our appreciation (i.e., effectively dehumanizes) our appreciation of the world around us

16. Which of the following terms includes all of the others?
    a. molecule   b. atom
    c. subatomic particle   d. electron

17. The diversity of life is mainly due to _____.
    a. atoms   b. genetic variation
    c. prokaryotic cells   d. organ systems

18. You are a NASA scientist and have discovered an organism in outer space that contains its genetic material in the cytoplasm rather than in a nucleus. Given this characteristic, how might you classify this organism?
    a. heterotroph   b. eukaryote
    c. prokaryote   d. autotroph

19. Your baby starts crying. Since she hasn't eaten in two hours, you declare, "The baby must be hungry." Your statement is a(n) _____.
    a. hypothesis   b. experiment
    c. conclusion   d. observation

20. Natural selection would be best illustrated by which of the following?
    a. a bacterial cell in the human body that dies when a person takes antibiotics
    b. a bacterial cell in the human body with a genetic variation that allows it to survive when the person take antibiotics
    c. a bacterial cell in the human body that mutates itself when a person takes antibiotics

21. The units of heredity that provide information needed to control life are the _____.

22. A process called _____ allows organisms to keep conditions in their bodies fairly constant.

23. The most important force in evolution is _____.

24. In a scientific experiment, one must have a _____ in which all factors remain constant.

25. Structures, physiological processes, or behaviors that aid survival and reproduction in a particular environment are _____.

26. A _____ is a supposition of prediction, based on previous observations, that is given as a possible explanation for an observed phenomenon.

27. The diagram below indicates the levels of organization of matter found in the natural world. Identify each level of organization labeled below.

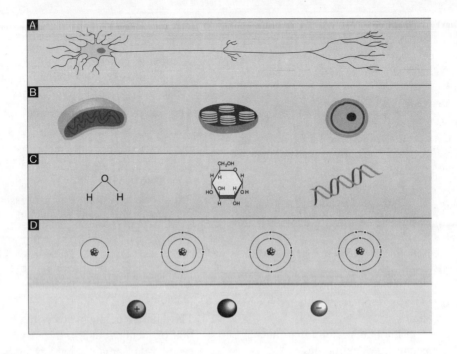

28. The diagram seen above is a continuation of the previous organization of matter diagram. Identify each level of organization labeled above.

29. Identify the structures indicated on this image of a plant cell.

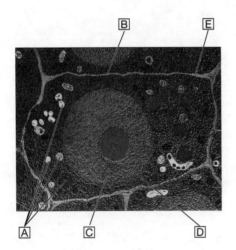

(Credit: Photo Researchers, Inc.)

30. Identify the structures indicated with A, B, and C on the micrograph below.

(c)

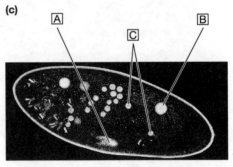

10 micrometers

The Kingdom Protista (domain Eukarya). This light micrograph of a *Paramecium* illustrates the complexity of these large, normally single, eukaryotic cells. Some protists photosynthesize, but others ingest or absorb their food. Many, including *Paramecium*, are mobile, moving with cilia or flagella. (Credit: Photo Researchers, Inc.)

ESSAY CHALLENGE

1. List the three natural processes that underlie evolution.

2. Compare and contrast prokaryotic and eukaryotic cells.

3. Imagine that you are a scientist and you observe a unique phenomenon. You are interested in determining the causes behind this phenomenon. Describe the process you would follow in order to accomplish this task.

4. Describe the characteristics that would make an organism an extremophile. Give an example.

5. Explain how the terms DNA and biodiversity are related.

6. Differentiate between inductive and deductive reasoning.

7. You observe two wishing wells at the mall. One of them contains many pennies and is clear while the other contains no pennies but looks cloudy and contaminated with bacteria. What are some of your hypotheses about why one well is cloudy and one isn't? Describe how you could test one of your hypotheses.

MEDIA ACTIVITIES

To access a Media Activity visit http://www.prenhall.com/audesirk7. Log in to the Web site selected by your instructor, navigate to this chapter, and select the appropriate Media Activity number.

1.1   Defining Life
Estimated time: 15 minutes

Explore the characteristics of life and the way we use the scientific method to ask questions about life.

1.2 Experimental Design
Estimated time: 10 minutes

This activity will introduce you to the scientific method, which is at the center of all scientific studies.

1.3 Web Investigation: Life on Earth – and Elsewhere?
Estimated time: 10 minutes

Most scientific discoveries are made by people who are just plain curious. The Internet can be a wonderful source of information for the novice scientist. Unfortunately not all of the information on the World Wide Web is correct. Good scientists not only evaluate their own experimental data but any other information resources they may access. In this exercise you will learn how to evaluate a Web site. Is the information provided on this Web page reliable? Follow the links to answer the questions below and evaluate the Tree of Life site (http://phylogeny.arizona.edu/tree/phylogeny.html).

1. Authority: Who is responsible for this page set? Is it maintained by an organization or group or is it a personal home page? What are the professional (scientific) qualifications of the author(s)? What is the stated purpose or function of the page?

2. Source and Quality: What is peer review (http://tolweb.org/tree/home.pages/peerreview.html)? Why is it important to the authors of the Tree of Life Web page that they state that their entries are now peer-reviewed? What is the significance of having a page on the Tree of Life Web page that is completed but not peer-reviewed?

3. Objectivity: Is this an impartial presentation of data or has the information been selected to present a specific viewpoint? Most sites have some bias, but how do the authors of this page make sure that all points of view are included?

4. Clarity and Presentation: Is the text easy to read and understand? Is the site easy to navigate? Does it load quickly? Do the buttons work?

ISSUES IN BIOLOGY

Extremophiles and Life on Other Planets
On July 20, 1976 (the bicentennial year of the Declaration of Independence), the Viking I Lander separated from the Mars vehicle and descended to the surface, landing in Plain of Chryse. This landing was followed a few months later

with the descent of Viking II to the Plain of Utopia, 4000 miles away from Viking I. Goals of the Viking Project (http://nssdc.gsfc.nasa.gov/planetary/viking.html) included obtaining high-quality images of the planet's surface and studying atmospheric conditions. Another goal was to test the Martian surface for signs of life.

How would you determine if life existed on another planet? In the Viking payload was a 15-kilogram apparatus that could carry out three separate tests. In the Labeled Release Experiment (http://www.biospherics.com/Mars/spie/spiehtml.htm), the Lander extended a mechanical arm and scraped up some soil. The soil was placed into a closed container and mixed with water and with radioactively labeled nutrients that had been brought from Earth, and the mixture was incubated at 10°C for 8 days. Then, the air above the moist soil was examined to see if it contained carbon dioxide gas, which could indicate the presence of microbes with a metabolism similar to much of the life on Earth's surface. The data that Viking I and II sent back were disappointing: None of the experiments provided strong evidence of life on Mars. However, recent discoveries back on planet Earth indicate that Viking was looking in the wrong place. If you want to find life on an inhospitable planet, you may need to know how inhospitable the surface is.

What might be wrong in thinking that Mars microbes would be physiologically like Earth microbes? Living things may or may not operate or be constructed in the same way as Earth life. Why would NASA scientists make this assumption? Even scientists are limited to what they know and what they can imagine as possibilities. We only know about Earth life.

What would be the characteristics of life forms on Mars? Many believe they could be similar to members of the Domain Archaea (http://www.ucmp.berkeley.edu/alllife/threedomains.html) and, thus, are prokaryotic, unicellular organisms as on Earth. In addition to dwelling in the deepest recesses of the planet, Archaea thrive in some places on Earth's surface, but in the most inhospitable conditions (http://www2.astrobiology.com/astro/extreme.html) imaginable. Their habitat ranges from the frozen ice seas of Antarctica to the boiling water geysers of Yellowstone National Park and the "black smokers" on the floor of the sea. Some live in environments equivalent to household ammonia or vinegar. It isn't just that they can manage to survive in these conditions, but for many, these harsh conditions are actually required for the cell to live and reproduce. This penchant for conditions that would kill most of the rest of us, Bacteria and Eukaryota alike, has earned for Archaea the nickname "Extremophiles," reflecting their preference (or requirement) for "life on the edge."

Most recently, a British team of exobiologists has pushed forward in the effort to search for life on Mars. Using all of the previous studies on Mars as a guide, the team designed and launched The British Beagle 2 lander (http://beagle2.open.ac.uk/index.htm) in 2003. One of their approaches (http://library.thinkquest.org/C003763/index.php?page=mars06) will be to test for the presence of methane in the atmosphere, as it is produced only by biological processes. They propose that the presence of any methane will finally provide proof of life on the Red Planet.

1. In the Viking experiments to test for life on Mars, what major assumptions were made about the basic characteristics of that life?

2. Where are extremophiles found on Earth?

3. Describe why NASA scientists have an interest in the study of extremophiles.

1. Why will the Beagle 2 team be searching for methane?

BIZARRE FACTS IN BIOLOGY

Hot Stuff

Many people enjoy the hot taste of chile peppers. Developing a deeper understanding of chile peppers has proven to be an important area of scientific research.

Many people often wonder what makes chile peppers so hot. Scientists at the Chile Pepper Institute (http://www. chilepepperinstitute.org/) describe the cause as a compound known as capsaicin. A PBS Special entitled, Life's Little Questions II (http://www.pbs.org/saf/1105/features/eureka.htm), explored the biological actions of capsaicin. The capsaicin in peppers initially burns the mouth. Eventually the taste and pain receptors on the tongue turn numb.

A scientist and anesthesiologist named Wendye Robbins observed this phenomenon and applied the scientific method to develop a medical treatment (http://www.ucsf.edu/pressrel/1998/03/0302caps.html) for patients with debilitating pain. She hypothesized that capsaicin could have similar numbing effects elsewhere in the body. She tested her hypothesis by adding the capsaicin compound, in certain concentrations, to a cream base and applied it to affected painful areas of the body of subjects with chronic pain. Just like in the mouth, that part of the body burned when the cream was first applied. To alleviate the pain of that initial burning, patients were given a local anesthetic. Once the initial burning wore off, the treatment numbed the pain receptors in the area, just as Dr. Robbins had hypothesized! The results of these studies showed that the capsaicin cream treatments were able to control the pain for patients, even when no other known medical treatment had been successful. Patients who had previously been unable to walk are now able to walk and even run, thanks to the "hot stuff" in chile peppers.

1. What is capsaicin?

2. Why would chile peppers actually produce capsaicin? What's the evolutionary advantage?

3. What does the compound capsaicin have to do with the field of medicine?

4. Many people who have bird feeders try to prevent squirrels from eating all of their bird food by sprinkling the bird food with hot chile pepper sauce. Based on what you've learned, how will this work to get rid of squirrels without harming the birds?

KEY TERMS

adaptation	domain	metabolism	organ system
atom	ecosystem	molecule	photosynthesis
autotroph	element	multicellular	plasma membrane
biodiversity	energy	mutation	population
biosphere	eukaryotic	natural causality	prokaryotic
cell	evolution	natural selection	scientific method
community	experiment	nucleus	scientific theory
conclusion	gene	nutrient	species
control	heterotroph	observation	subatomic particle
cytoplasm	homeostasis	organ	tissue
deductive reasoning	hypothesis	organelle	unicellular
deoxyribonucleic acid (DNA)	inductive reasoning	organic molecule	variable
	kingdom	organism	

ANSWER KEY

SELF TEST

1. c
2. a
3. d
4. d
5. a
6. d
7. a
8. e
9. a
10. c
11. d
12. d
13. a
14. b
15. a
16. a
17. b
18. c
19. a
20. b
21. genes
22. homeostasis
23. natural selection
24. control
25. adaptations
26. hypothesis
27. A. biosphere
    B. tissue
    C. organ system
    D. population
    E. community
28. A. cell
    B. organelle
    C. molecule
    D. atom

29. A. organelles
    B. cell wall
    C. nucleus
    D. nuclear membrane
    E. cell membrane
30. A. oral groove
    B. contractile vauole
    C. food vacuole

ESSAY CHALLENGE

1. 1) genetic variation among members of a population; 2) inheritance of those variations by offspring of parents who carry the variation; 3) natural selection, the survival and enhanced reproduction of organisms with favorable variations

2. Eukaryotic cells have a nucleus and membrane-bound organelles and are generally larger than prokaryotic cells. Prokaryotic cells do not have a nucleus or membrane-bound organelles and are generally smaller than eukaryotic cells.

3. 1) make an observation; 2) form a hypothesis; 3) conduct experiments; 4) form a conclusion

4. These characteristics include living in places that might be considered inhabitable, such as high temperatures, high acidity, and under high-pressure conditions. An example is organisms that can live in heated thermal vents in the ocean.

5. A change in DNA causes a mutation. This variability in populations results in biodiversity.

6. Inductive reasoning is creating a generalization based on observations that support that notion. Deductive reasoning is generating hypotheses based on well-supported and well-proven generalizations.

7. A potential hypothesis could be that the pennies prevent bacteria from growing. You could test this by placing some pennies on a plate of bacteria to see

if the presence of the pennies prevents bacteria from growing. There are many variables however!

MEDIA ACTIVITIES

1.3 Web Investigation: Life on Earth – and Elsewhere?

1. This is a Web page maintained by a consortium of scientists. It is not a personal Web page. It is maintained by a group of scientists. All of the authors are experts in their respective field of study. The purpose of the page is to provide a central place to access all information about classifying living things.

2. Peer review is the critical evaluation of manuscripts by professional colleagues, and is the traditional method of quality control in science. Scientific information that is peer-reviewed has been read by other experts in the field and deemed reliable. If a page is completed but not yet peer reviewed, then it has not gotten the "seal of approval" from a scientific expert yet!

3. Independent reviewers read over and evaluate all submissions to be sure that they are factual and reliable.

4. The text is easy to understand but there is a lot of information contained on this Web page. The site map helps you figure out where the information you're looking for is located!

ISSUES IN BIOLOGY

1. Life on the planet would be found on the surface of the planet.

2. They are found in inhospitable environments such as inside boiling water geysers and deep within the Earth's surface.

3. Extremophiles on Earth are probably most like what a life form on Mars would be like.

4. If methane is present, then a life form may be present. Methane is a by-product of the metabolisms of living things.

BIZARRE FACTS IN BIOLOGY

1. A compound found in chile peppers that makes the mouth burn and then causes numbness.

2. The Chile Pepper Institute site points out that it is believed that chiles evolved this feature to protect the fruits from being eaten by mammals. Capsaicinoids, the compounds that cause the burning sensation, are the only alkaloid chile produces. Birds, the natural dispersal agent of chiles, cannot feel the heat and thus disseminate the seeds. However, when mammals eat chiles, the seeds are destroyed in the digestive tract.

3. This compound can be used to numb the pain receptors of those with chronic pain.

4. The capsaicin will burn the mouths of the squirrels, but the birds will not feel the heat.

CHAPTER 2: ATOMS, MOLECULES, AND LIFE

AT-A-GLANCE

Case Study: Walking on Water

2.1 What Are Atoms?
Atoms, the Basic Structural Units of Matter, Are Composed of Still Smaller Particles

Scientific Inquiry: Radioactivity in Research

2.2 How Do Atoms Interact to Form Molecules?
Atoms Interact with Other Atoms When There Are Vacancies in Their Outermost Electron Shells
Charged Atoms Called *Ions* Interact to Form Ionic Bonds
Uncharged Atoms Can Become Stable by Sharing Electrons, Forming Covalent Bonds
Hydrogen Bonds Are Weaker Electrical Attractions Between or Within Molecules with Polar Covalent Bonds

2.3 Why Is Water So Important to Life?
Water Interacts with Many Other Molecules
Water Molecules Tend to Stick Together
Water-Based Solutions Can be Acidic, Basic, or Neutral
Water Moderates the Effects of Temperature Changes
Water Forms an Unusual Solid: Ice

Case Study Revisited: Walking on Water

Links to Life: Health Food?

SELF TEST

1. The basic structural units of chemistry and life are
   _____.
   a. atoms   **b.** electrons   **c.** protons
   d. neutrons   **e.** molecules

2. The atomic number of carbon is 6. A carbon atom has _____ protons and _____ electrons.
   a. 3, 3   **b.** 6, 6   **c.** 6, 12   **d.** 6, 3

3. Ions are atoms that have _____.
   a. different numbers of neutrons
   b. broken apart due to radioactive decay
   c. gained an electron
   d. lost an electron
   e. gained or lost an electron

4. Chemical bonds _____.
   a. are interactions between the outermost electron shells of atoms
   b. result when atoms share one or more electrons
   c. result when atoms gain or lose one or more electrons
   d. are the forces that hold atoms together in molecules
   e. all of the above

5. Ionic bonds form between atoms that have _____.
   a. empty outermost electron shells
   b. full outermost electron shells
   c. nearly empty and nearly full outermost electron shells
   d. equal numbers of protons
   e. equal numbers of neutrons

6. Covalent bonds _____.
   a. are interactions between the outermost electron shells of atoms
   b. result when atoms share one or more electrons
   c. result when atoms gain or lose one or more electrons
   d. are the forces that hold atoms together in molecules such as water
   e. all of the above
   f. all but one of the above

7. Chemical reactions _____.
   a. are interactions between the outermost electron shells of atoms
   b. result when atoms share one or more electrons
   c. result when atoms gain or lose one or more electrons
   d. are the forces that hold atoms together in molecules
   e. all of the above
   f. all but one of the above

8. How many single covalent bonds can the phosphorus atom form?
   a. 1   b. 2
   c. 3   d. 6
   e. 8

9. Nonpolar covalent bonds are different from polar covalent bonds because _____.
   a. electrons are shared unequally in nonpolar covalent bonds and are shared equally in polar covalent bonds
   b. electrons are shared equally in nonpolar covalent bonds and are shared unequally in polar covalent bonds
   c. electrons are lost in nonpolar covalent bonds and are gained in polar covalent bonds
   d. electrons are shared in nonpolar covalent bonds and are lost or gained in polar covalent bonds

10. Why is water so essential for life? Read all the choices carefully before selecting your answer.
    a. Water takes part in many biochemical reactions.
    b. Water is a good solvent.
    c. Water moderates the effects of temperature.
    d. When water freezes, it forms ice that floats.
    e. The atoms in water molecules are held together in polar covalent bonds.
    f. All of the answers are correct.

11. Oxygen atoms have an atomic number of 8. Neon atoms have 10 electrons. Predict whether or not these atoms are generally reactive (i.e., can form chemical bonds with other atoms). Explain your answer. (Note that this question is not asking whether oxygen can react with neon.)
    a. Both oxygen and neon are not reactive because their outermost electron orbitals are filled.
    b. Both oxygen and neon are reactive because their outermost electron orbitals are not filled.
    c. Oxygen is reactive because its outermost electron shell contains 6 electrons (is not filled); neon is not reactive because its outermost electron shell contains 8 electrons (is filled).
    d. Oxygen is not reactive because its outermost electron shell contains 8 electrons (is filled); neon is reactive because its outermost electron shell contains 2 electrons (is not filled).

12. Which of the following lists of terms is in the correct order of size, going from smallest to largest?
    a. electron, proton, atomic nucleus, electron shell, atom, molecule
    b. proton, electron, atomic nucleus, electron shell, atom, molecule
    c. molecule, atom, electron shell, atomic nucleus, proton, electron
    d. atomic nucleus, electron, proton, electron shell, atom, molecule
    e. electron, proton, atomic nucleus, electron shell, molecule, atom

13. Why are hydrophobic molecules such as fats and oils unable to dissolve in watery solutions?
    a. Water cannot interact with molecules that have polar covalent bonds, such as fats and oils.
    b. Water cannot interact with molecules with ionic bonds, such as fats and oils.
    c. Water cannot interact with hydrophobic molecules, such as fats and oils, because hydrophobic molecules form hydrogen bonds with each other, excluding the water.
    d. Water molecules form hydrogen bonds with each other, excluding the hydrophobic molecules.

14. You are waiting backstage for your cue to come onstage when you notice that you are breathing rapidly and beginning to feel light-headed. As you try to control your anxiety and slow your breathing, you think about what you learned in your biology class this week and realize that your hyperventilation is changing your blood pH. Explain.

    Reminder: Blood pH is maintained by carbonate buffer, which is related to the amount of CO_2 you breathe in or out. One way that your body controls the amount of carbonate in your blood is to change the rate of breathing. When you breathe out, you remove CO_2 and lower the amount of carbonic acid in the blood. As a result, the amount of H^+ ions in the blood decreases.

    Take your time on this one; relating pH to changes in H^+ concentration can be confusing.
    a. Rapid breathing decreases my blood's pH, making it more basic.
    b. Rapid breathing decreases my blood's pH, making it more acidic.
    c. Rapid breathing increases the pH of my blood, making it more basic.
    d. Rapid breathing increases the pH of my blood, making it more acidic.

15. Imagine that you wanted to make a time capsule in which you would seal important artifacts from your life (pictures, poems, a lock of your baby hair, etc.), to be opened by your heirs 1000 years from now. To prevent these artifacts from decaying, you want to fill the capsule with a gas that would be *least* reactive. Which of these gases would you choose: oxygen gas (O_2); carbon dioxide (CO_2); argon gas (Ar); hydrogen gas (H_2). (The atomic numbers of the atoms in these molecules are: oxygen = 8; carbon = 6; hydrogen = 2; and argon = 18.)
    a. oxygen gas   b. carbon dioxide
    c. argon gas   d. hydrogen gas

16. Atoms are the basic building block of elements. Each atom, and therefore the elements themselves, are made up of subatomic bits of matter that are electrically negative (electrons), electrically positive (protons), and electrically neutral or uncharged (neutrons). Which subatomic component defines (characterizes) the fundamental nature of each element?
    a. electrons   b. protons
    c. neutrons   d. isotopes

17. What allows one atom to physically interact with a second atom?
    a. properties of both nuclei
    b. properties of the electrons
    c. electron shells of both atoms
    d. external energy sources

18. One atom can form a chemical bond with a second atom as a result of _____.
    a. both atoms possessing incompletely filled outer electron shells
    b. both atoms possessing completely filled outer electron shells
    c. both atoms possessing empty outer electron shells
    d. all of the above

19. Covalent bonds _____.
    a. are strong compared to ionic bonds or hydrogen bonds
    b. share electrons with another atom
    c. may involve the unequal sharing of electrons between two atoms
    d. all of the above

20. Water's ability to act as a "universal" solvent is due to _____.
    a. the fact that there is so much of it in the world around us and in our own bodies
    b. its natural ability to interact with polar molecules such as ions and proteins
    c. the nature of oxygen, which pulls the hydrogen electrons a little closer to it than they are to the two hydrogen atoms
    d. both the second and third answers above

21. Why does water so greatly resist increases in temperature?
    a. It takes great energy to break the ionic bonds that hold water molecules together.
    b. It takes great energy to break the covalent bonds that hold water molecules together.
    c. It takes great energy to break the huge number of hydrogen bonds that hold water molecules together.
    d. none of the above

22. A solution of pH 7 has _____ times _____ H^+ ions than a solution of pH 9.
    a. 100; fewer
    b. 100; more
    c. 2; fewer
    d. 2; more

23. Which of the following is not a subatomic particle?
    a. proton
    b. neutron
    c. ion
    d. electron

24. Which of the following best explains why neon (Ne) atoms would not form bonds with other atoms?
    a. Neon atoms have no electrons.
    b. Neon has an empty outer shell.
    c. The outer shells of neon atoms are completely full with eight electrons.
    d. Neon atoms have 7 electrons in their outer shells.

25. The atoms Mg^+ and Cl^- would most likely be attached to each other by a(n) _____.
    a. ionic bond
    b. covalent bond
    c. hydrogen bond
    d. neutral bond

26. The atomic nucleus contains two types of subatomic particles; _____ are positively charged and _____ are uncharged.

27. Atoms of the same element with a different number of neutrons are called _____.

28. The results of losing, gaining, or sharing electrons are _____.

29. Atoms that have gained or lost electrons are called _____.

30. Atoms with partially filled outermost electron shells can become stable by sharing electrons with another atom, forming a _____.

31. Ions and polar molecules are termed _____ because of their electrical attraction to water; molecules that are uncharged and nonpolar are called _____.

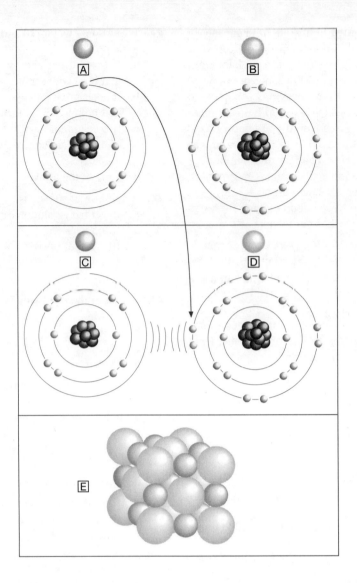

32. Indicate which of the figures above depict neutral atoms and which depict ions.

33. Find the protons, neutrons, and electrons in the depiction of helium below.

34. Identify the electrons, oxygen nucleus, hydrogen nucleus, and type of bond seen in the diagram below.

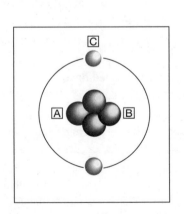

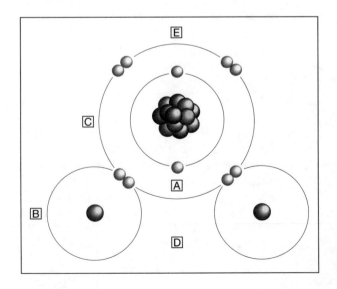

35. Hydrogen bonding is all based on a slight charge difference created when only 2 electrons circle the relatively larger nucleus of the hydrogen atom. Indicate on the figure below which end of the water molecule will be positive and which will be negative. The dashes indicate attractive forces.

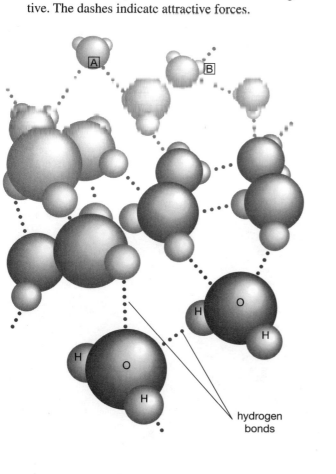

hydrogen bonds

36. Below is the pH scale. Indicate which area is acidic, which is basic, and which is neutral.

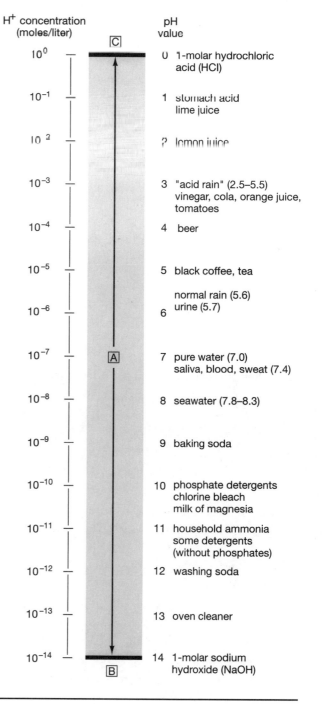

H⁺ concentration (moles/liter)	pH value	
10^0	0	1-molar hydrochloric acid (HCl)
10^{-1}	1	stomach acid lime juice
10^{-2}	2	lemon juice
10^{-3}	3	"acid rain" (2.5–5.5) vinegar, cola, orange juice, tomatoes
10^{-4}	4	beer
10^{-5}	5	black coffee, tea
10^{-6}	6	normal rain (5.6) urine (5.7)
10^{-7}	7	pure water (7.0) saliva, blood, sweat (7.4)
10^{-8}	8	seawater (7.8–8.3)
10^{-9}	9	baking soda
10^{-10}	10	phosphate detergents chlorine bleach milk of magnesia
10^{-11}	11	household ammonia some detergents (without phosphates)
10^{-12}	12	washing soda
10^{-13}	13	oven cleaner
10^{-14}	14	1-molar sodium hydroxide (NaOH)

ESSAY CHALLENGE

1. How does a polar covalent bond cause hydrogen bonding to occur?

2. List and describe two properties of water that are based on hydrogen bonding.

3. Compare and contrast the properties of acids and bases.

4. Why do cells need buffers? How do buffers accomplish their function?

5. Differentiate between inert and reactive atoms.

6. Free radicals have been described as dangerous because they steal electrons from the outer orbitals of atoms that make up the tissues of the body. Describe what antioxidants do to counteract the actions of free radicals.

7. You drop equal amounts of salt (NaCl) into two different beakers of water. One beaker of water is at room temperature, and the temperature of the second beaker is near its boiling point. Hypothesize which beaker of water will dissolve the salt faster and explain why.

8. A snake will preferentially choose a rock rather than a puddle of water to warm itself on a sunny day. Explain the property of water that is responsible for this phenomenon.

MEDIA ACTIVITIES

To access a Media Activity visit http://www.prenhall.com/audesirk7. Log in to the Web site selected by your instructor, navigate to this chapter, and select the appropriate Media Activity number.

2.1   Interactive Atoms
Estimated time: 5 minutes

An introduction to the basic chemistry needed to understand biological structures and processes.

2.2   Water and Life
Estimated time: 5 minutes

Explore the properties of water and why this molecule is essential for life.

2.3   Web Investigation: Walking On Water
Estimated time: 10 minutes

Water is central to life on our planet. This activity explores how the chemistry of water plays a central role in many different aspects of everyday life.

1. Most people find it easier to walk on wet sand rather than dry sand. How do adhesion and cohesion (http://www.pa.msu.edu/~sciencet/ask_st/081292.html) of water play a role in this phenomenon?

2. Most experts recommend using hot water for cleaning. Look at the graph on this Web site (http://hyperphysics. phy-astr.gsu.edu/hbase/surten.html#c3) and determine why the surface tension of water is important in this recommendation.

3. You may have noticed that you are unable to blow a bubble with pure water, but are able to form bubbles when soap is added. How does the surface tension (http://www.exploratorium.edu/ronh/bubbles/soap.html) of water play a role in this scenario?

4. While water can't form bubbles on Earth, International Space Station science officer Don Pettit recently discovered (http://science.nasa.gov/headlines/y2003/25feb_nosoap.htm) that water could form bubbles in zero gravity! The electrical attraction between water molecules, and thus the surface tension of water, is the same on Earth and in space. Explain what allowed water to form bubbles in space.

ISSUES IN BIOLOGY

How Might the Radioactive Decay of Isotopes Help Make Our Food Safer?

Each year about 50 million Americans will lose a day or two of their normal life activities due to consumption of contaminated food (http://www.nal.usda.gov/fnic/foodborne/foodborn.htm). Most commonly the organisms that cause these illnesses are bacteria, including *Staphylococcus*, *Salmonella*, *Listeria*, and *E. coli*. (http://www.fightbac.org/10least.cfm). Sometimes, particularly in young children, the infection that follows consumption of a contaminated food product causes serious symptoms that can lead to permanent organ damage or even death.

A relatively common source of foodborne illness is a strain of bacteria known as *E. coli* O157:H7. Our intestines—as well as the intestines of many vertebrates, including cattle and pigs—are inhabited by billions of *E. coli* cells that normally cause no trouble. In fact, they actually are beneficial in a number of ways, not least of which is that they produce vitamin K for us. Unfortunately, certain strains of *E. coli*, including the infamous 0157:H7 strain (http://www.doh.wa.gov/topics/ecoli.htm), are lurking in the environment, and this bacterial strain can cause serious illness. In the past few years, outbreaks of *E. coli* O157:H7 infections (http://vm.cfsan.fda.gov/~mow/chap15.html#updates) have occurred throughout the world. Often the culprit is contaminated meat, but vegetable and fruit products can also spread the bacteria. For example, contaminated apple juice, alfalfa sprouts, and radish sprouts have caused disease in hundreds and resulted in the deaths of at least several children, usually from hemolytic uremic syndrome (http://www.cheori.org/cpkdrc/what_is_hus.htm).

There are several common sense approaches to protecting yourself from *E. coli* infection (http://www.cdc.gov/ncidod/dbmd/diseaseinfo/escherichiacoli_g.htm), including cooking foods thoroughly and washing your hands properly. However, one treatment that might help to reduce contamination before it reaches consumers is sterilization of food by irradiation. In this process, the food is exposed to radioactive energy produced by the decay of radioactive cobalt (atomic symbol: Co). The major nonradioactive isotope of cobalt is Co-59, an atom with 27 protons and 32 neutrons. The radioactive isotope of cobalt used for food irradiation (and for cancer radiation therapy) is known as Co-60 and contains 27 protons and 33 neutrons. That 1 extra neutron makes the Co-60 nucleus unstable and, as in all radioactive isotopes, the Co-60 nucleus will break apart or change at a certain frequency. In the process of "radioactive decay" of this particular isotope, 1 neutron within the Co-60 nucleus is converted to a proton. This change in atomic structure converts the cobalt atom into a nonradioactive atom of nickel with 28 protons and 32 neutrons. The conversion also releases high-energy radiation known as gamma rays.

Gamma rays contain a considerable amount of energy. When they crash into another atom, they damage it, usually causing it to lose an electron (i.e., form an ion). The ionizing effects of gamma rays on molecules give gamma radiation the capacity to kill cells (http://whyfiles.news.wisc.edu/054irradfood/2.html), including bacteria. For example, gamma rays can break DNA molecules, preventing the cell from reproducing. Although it can damage and even kill cells, irradiation of food does not make the food itself radioactive, any more than having an X ray makes you radioactive. However, it does cause subtle changes to the food that make some opponents of the technology leery of its safety. Most studies indicate that these changes are similar to the changes produced by conventional cooking of the food. After considerable study, the Federal Drug Administration has found that the method is safe and effective (http://www.fda.gov/bbs/topics/NEWS/NEW00058.html). In addition, the American Dietetic Society, among other groups, has also endorsed the use of irradiation to help minimize foodborne illness. In fact, although you may not be aware of it, irradiation of certain foods such as grains and spices has been going on since the 1960s.

So, the next time you are having a nice salad at a salad bar or chomping a juicy cheeseburger, perhaps you will think about how the structure of atoms can be harnessed to make your food safer.

1. Explain the difference between radioactive and nonradioactive materials. Why can exposure to strong radiation damage cells?

2. What facts may convince you that it is safe to eat foods that have been exposed to radioactivity? Examine your answer to see whether your decision is based on scientific reasoning.

3. Imagine that a new sterilization method for food was discovered that was generally safe but slightly raised the risk of colon cancer. The scientists developing this method estimate that the treatment will save 10 lives and millions of health treatment dollars in the United States each year by preventing food poisoning but would cause 1 extra death from colon cancer per year. Should this method be approved? Explain your reasoning.

BIZARRE FACTS IN BIOLOGY

Carbon Copy?

Diamonds have long been prized as brilliant gemstones and the hardest known material on Earth. Diamonds are actually composed of a crystal lattice of carbon atoms. But did you know that one of the softest materials on earth, graphite, is simply a rearrangement (http://chemistry.about.com/gi/dynamic/offsite.htm?site=http://www.nyu.edu/pages/mathmol/textbook/carbon.html) of the carbon atoms in a diamond?

The lattice shape (http://www.pbs.org/wgbh/nova/diamond/insidediamond.html) of the carbon in diamonds contributes to its amazing properties, including strength, durability, and the ability to disperse light. In a diamond, each carbon atom is connected to four other carbon atoms by strong chemical bonds, creating diamond's rigid crystal structure. The Mohs scale (http://www.amfed.org/t_mohs.htm) is a hardness scale developed in 1822 by Austrian Friedrich Mohs that is often used to characterize gemstones. Diamonds rate highest on this scale, with a rank of a ten.

Graphite, however, is at the exact opposite end of the Mohs scale with a score of one. The carbon atoms in graphite are layered (http://www.sciam.com/askexpert_question.cfm?articleID=0001E803-BB40-1CEA-93F6809EC5880000), which forms a horizontal arrangement of stacked carbon. While the carbon atoms in a given stack are connected, the stacks themselves are not bonded together. This configuration explains why graphite is often used in pencils, as the layers of carbon atoms readily cleave off of the graphite molecule, allowing one to leave marks as they write with a graphite pencil. This alternative arrangement of carbon atoms in graphite, therefore, results in a completely different set of properties (http://www.bris.ac.uk/Depts/Chemistry/MOTM/diamond/diamond.htm), including its relative softness.

Scientists also investigate the unique properties of other less well known compounds (http://www.nsf.gov/od/lpa/nsf50/nsfoutreach/htm/n50_z2/pages_z3/08_pg.htm) composed solely of carbon. These studies have provided an insight into how identical carbon atoms can be arranged into so many distinctive materials.

1. How can graphite and diamond be different if they are both composed of carbon atoms?

2. Explain what makes graphite such a "soft" material.

3. Given your newfound knowledge of the Mohs scale, how would you rank the hardness of a copper penny?

KEY TERMS

acid	calorie	free radical	neutron
acidic	chemical bond	hydrogen bond	nonpolar covalent bond
antioxidant	chemical reaction	hydrophilic	pH scale
atom	cohesion	hydrophobic	polar covalent bond
atomic nucleus	compound	hydrophobic interaction	proton
atomic number	covalent bond	ion	radioactive
base	electron	ionic bond	solvent
basic	electron shell	isotope	surface tension
buffer	element	molecule	

ANSWER KEY

SELF TEST

1. a
2. b
3. e
4. e
5. c
6. f
7. e
8. c
9. b
10. f
11. c
12. a
13. d
14. c
15. c
16. b
17. b
18. a
19. d
20. d
21. c
22. b
23. c
24. c

25. a
26. protons; neutrons
27. isotopes
28. chemical bonds
29. ions
30. covalent bond
31. hydrophilic; hydrophobic
32. A. sodium atom (neutral)
    B. chlorine atom (neutral)
    C. sodium ion ($+$)
    D. chlorine ion ($-$)
    E. sodium chloride (an ionic compound)
33. A. proton
    B. neutron
    C. electron
34. A. electron
    B. hydrogen ion
    C. oxygen ion
    D. slightly positive end
    E. slightly negative end
35. A. negative end of the water molecule
    B. positive end of the water molecule
36. A. neutral
    B. basic
    C. acidic

ESSAY CHALLENGE

1. The answer at a minimum should include the following: Unequal sharing of electrons between atoms causes individual atoms in a molecule to have partial positive and negative poles. The attraction of these partial positive and partial negative poles is what forms a hydrogen bond.

2. Answer should at a minimum include two of the following: cohesion (water molecules have a tendency to stick to each other); surface tension (the tendency for a water surface to resist being broken); adhesion (the tendency of water molecules to stick to polar surfaces).

3. Answer should include the following: acids release hydrogen ions when dissolved in water; some acids have a sour taste; acids have a pH below 7; a base is a substance that combines with hydrogen ions, reducing their number; bases have a pH above 7.

4. Answer should include the following: cells conduct chemical reactions that release or take up hydrogen ions; they need buffers in order to maintain a specific pH; buffers accept or release hydrogen ions in response to small changes in hydrogen ion concentration.

5. Inert atoms have full outer orbitals (8 electrons) and do not form bonds. Reactive atoms do not have full outer orbitals and will form bonds with other atoms.

6. Antioxidants donate electrons to free radicals so that the free radicals become stable.

7. The hot water will dissolve faster because the water molecules are moving faster and will more rapidly surround the NaCl and dissociate it.

8. The specific heat of water is higher than the specific heat of the rock, so it takes longer for the water to heat up than the rock.

MEDIA ACTIVITIES

2.3 Web Investigation: Water Chemistry and Everyday Life

1. The cohesion between the water molecules and the adhesion between this layer of water and the grains of sand make each grain stick to its neighbor.

2. The warmer the water is, the lower its surface tension becomes. This lower surface tension makes it easier for the water to get into pores and fissures rather than bridging them with surface tension. Soaps and detergents further lower the surface tension.

3. Soap decreases the pull of surface tension. The surface tension in plain water is too strong for bubbles to last.

4. What is different is the competition between surface tension and gravity. On Earth, the pull of gravity causes the bubble to sag in the middle, it drains downward, and eventually the weight rips the bubble apart. In space, the bubble is weightless and doesn't get pulled downward, and therefore it doesn't break!

ISSUES IN BIOLOGY

1. A radioactive atom has an unstable nucleus. This causes changes in the nucleus, which results in production of high-energy radiation and gamma rays. Gamma rays can break molecules in cells, including DNA.

2. It has been approved by the Federal Drug Administration and endorsed by the American Dietetic Society. They have conducted scientific studies to reach their conclusions.

3. There are many answers to this question. Back up your answer with solid facts.

BIZARRE FACTS IN BIOLOGY

1. Diamonds are an interconnected lattice of carbon atoms and graphite is a stacked layer of carbon atoms.

2. Since the layers of carbon atoms are not bonded together, graphite is easily broken apart.

3. According to the Web link, a penny is a 3 on the scale.

CHAPTER 3: BIOLOGICAL MOLECULES

AT-A-GLANCE

SELF TEST

1. Functional groups are _____.
   a. groups of atoms in organic molecules that can participate in certain types of chemical reactions
   b. arrangements of cells into tissues
   c. classes of biological molecules with similar functions
   d. classifications of inorganic molecules based on their reactivity

2. In chemical reactions, the molecules that take part in the reaction are called *reactants*. Conversely, molecules produced by a chemical reaction are called *products*. During the process of polymerization (synthesis of biological polymers), water is a _____, and the reaction is consequently called a _____ reaction.
   a. reactant, dehydration
   b. reactant, hydrolysis
   c. by-product, dehydration
   d. product, hydrolysis

3. Carbohydrates are a class of biological molecules that include _____.
   a. sugars and polymers of sugars
   b. ring-shaped molecules that are soluble in water
   c. monosaccharides, disaccharides, and polysaccharides
   d. components of DNA and RNA
   e. The first, second, and third answers above are correct.
   f. All of the first four answers above are correct.

4. The general class of biological molecules that contains large, nonpolar regions that make these molecules insoluble in water is called _____.
   a. phospholipids
   b. fats
   c. lipids
   d. waxes

5. Saturated fats _____.
   a. have no double covalent bonds
   b. are solid at room temperature
   c. contain the maximum number of hydrogen atoms possible
   d. Both the first and second answers above are correct.
   e. The first, second, and third answers above are correct.

6. Phospholipids contain a "head group" that is _____ and two fatty acid "tails" that are _____.
   a. hydrophobic, hydrophilic
   b. hydrophilic, hydrophobic
   c. hydrolyzed, nonhydrolyzed
   d. hydrophilic, hydrophilic

7. Proteins are polymers of _____.
   a. peptides
   b. amino acids
   c. nucleotides
   d. sugars

8. Protein functions in cells include _____.
   a. storage and defense
   b. catalysis of biochemical reactions
   c. structure and movement
   d. transport and defense
   e. all of the above

9. A nucleotide is composed of _____.
   a. a sugar and a phosphate group
   b. a phosphate group and a nitrogen-containing base
   c. a sugar and a nitrogen-containing base
   d. a sugar, a phosphate group, and a nitrogen-containing base

10. Imagine that you see a diagram of molecular structures in which the atoms are shown as dots and covalent bonds are shown as lines between the dots. The molecules in the diagram have a variety of complex shapes, including long chains, branched chains, rings, and combinations of chains and rings. What type of molecules are these and what is the key atom in them?
    a. The complex structures of these molecules indicate that they are organic molecules and, therefore, contain carbon.
    b. The complex structures of these molecules indicate that they are inorganic molecules and, therefore, do not contain carbon.
    c. The complex structures of these molecules indicate that they are organic molecules and, therefore, do not contain carbon.
    d. The complex structures of these molecules indicate that they were created in a laboratory and, therefore, contain unnatural atoms.

11. At the gym one day, you notice a new "Energy Bar" being sold that advertises quick energy for your workout. To impress you further, it is claimed this bar contains only carbon, oxygen, and hydrogen atoms. What kind of biological molecule(s) would you be eating if you ate an "Energy Bar"?
    a. carbohydrates
    b. proteins
    c. DNA and RNA
    d. lipids
    e. carbohydrates and lipids
    f. carbohydrates and proteins

12. A scientist is studying the metabolism of proteins in yeast and wants to follow the formation of proteins from the earliest possible point. In her experiment, she will feed the yeast radioactive nutrients and follow the fate of the radioactivity in the cells. Which of the following atoms will allow her to exclusively follow proteins in the cell?
    a. radioactive carbon
    b. radioactive nitrogen
    c. radioactive oxygen
    d. radioactive sulfur

13. How are large organic molecules (macromolecules) synthesized?
    a. by hydrolysis of monomers
    b. by hydrolysis of polymers
    c. by a dehydration reaction utilizing monomers
    d. by a dehydration reaction utilizing polymers

14. Carbohydrates _____.
    a. can exist as monomers (monosaccharides), dimers (disaccharides), and polymers (polysaccharides)
    b. have the general chemical formula of $(CH_2O)_n$
    c. can function as a source of energy or can function as an extremely durable structural material, depending upon the specific nature of their chemical bonds between subunits (monomers)
    d. all of the above

15. A cell membrane is primarily composed of _____.
    a. oils, which are liquid at room temperature
    b. saturated fats
    c. phospholipids
    d. steroids

16. Proteins are macromolecules that can perform many different functions within an organism. This diversity of function for this macromolecule is due to the unique nature of one of its four functional groups that is bound to a central carbon atom. Which functional group is responsible for the wide diversity of function attributed to proteins?
    a. the carboxyl group   b. the amino group
    c. a hydrogen atom   d. the R group

17. The quaternary level of protein structure _____.
    a. refers to a functional (biologically active) complex of two or more three-dimensional proteins (e.g., hemoglobin)
    b. is demonstrated by the three-dimensional organization of a single polypeptide
    c. refers to the serial sequence, or arrangement, of amino acids that make up a protein
    d. none of the above

18. Nucleotides _____.
    a. are composed of a sugar, a salt, and a phospholipid
    b. are found only in nucleic acids, the molecules responsible for passing genetic information from generation to generation
    c. are found in nucleic acids, intracellular messenger molecules, and high-energy molecules
    d. Both the first and second answers above are correct.

19. All of the following are polysaccharides except _____.
    a. cellulose
    b. starch
    c. glycogen
    d. glucose

20. You have identified a protein that is unable to form disulfide bridges. This would affect which of the following?
    a. primary structure of the protein
    b. secondary structure of the protein
    c. tertiary structure of the protein
    d. dehydration synthesis

21. All of the following are proteins except _____.
    a. cholesterol
    b. enzymes
    c. antibodies
    d. All of the above are proteins.

22. What types of biological molecules transport fat molecules through the human bloodstream?
    a. complex carbohydrates
    b. cholesterol
    c. phospholipids
    d. lipoproteins

23. Which of the following is not found in DNA?
    a. adenine
    b. guanine
    c. uracil
    d. cytosine
    e. thymine

24. Individual subunits of large organic molecules are called _____; long chains of these molecules are called _____.

25. A carbohydrate consisting of just one sugar molecule is called a _____.

26. When two or more single sugars are linked together, they form a _____.

27. Oils, fats, and waxes are similar in that they all contain one or more _____.

28. Proteins are polymers of _____.

29. The _____ is the sequence of amino acids in a protein, while the _____ is the three-dimensional appearance of a protein.

30. Correctly identify the carbohydrate molecules labeled below.

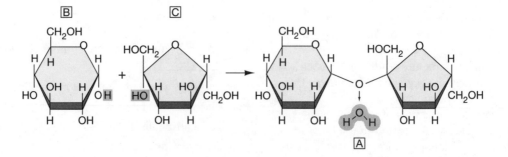

31. Identify the levels of protein structure as depicted below.

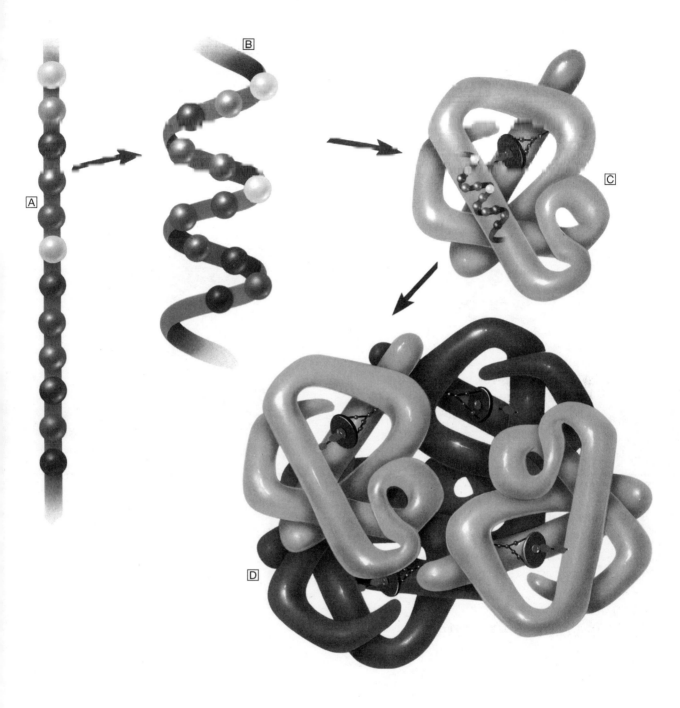

32. Identify each of the following functional groups.

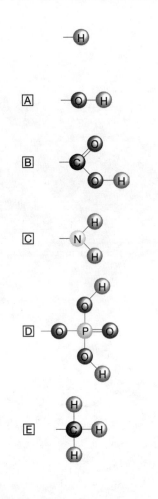

33. Identify the type of reaction indicated below. Also identify the molecules involved.

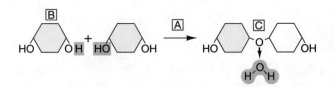

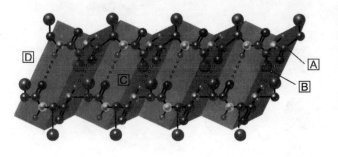

34. Label the portions of the molecule indicated below.

ESSAY CHALLENGE

1. What is the purpose of functional groups such as hydroxyl and carboxyl?

2. How do dehydration synthesis and hydrolysis differ?

3. List and describe three different types of carbohydrates and their functions.

4. List and describe the four levels of protein structure and how each level relates to the others.

5. Food scientists often work to find ways to produce healthier food choices. Explain why it is a challenge to produce a margarine that is solid at room temperature, but does not contain any saturated fat?

6. How is a phospholipid structurally different from a triglyceride?

7. Your friend is afraid of having a heart attack and has decided to eat a totally cholesterol-free diet. What would you say to your friend to try to convince him that no cholesterol is also harmful?

8. When a water system becomes contaminated with microbes, people are urged to boil their water before drinking it. Describe the effect that heating the water has on the proteins of the microbes and explain how this will make the water safe.

MEDIA ACTIVITIES

To access a Media Activity visit http://www.prenhall.com/audesirk7. Log in to the Web site selected by your instructor, navigate to this chapter, and select the appropriate Media Activity number.

3.1 Structure of Biological Molecules
Estimated time: 10 minutes

Review the chemical structures of the most important biological macromolecules.

3.2 Functions of Macromolecules
Estimated time: 5 minutes

Explore the functions of the major macromolecules.

Estimated time: 10 minutes

Let's take a closer look at olestra. While most artificial sweeteners, food colors, and fat replacers can be used for any food product, olestra is currently approved by the U.S. Food and Drug Administration (FDA) for use in "savory snacks" (e.g., potato chips) only. Some experts say that it is safe. Others think the side effects outweigh the benefits. In this exercise we will examine the pros and cons of the issue. Visit the sites below and answer the questions.

1. The Center for Science in the Public Interest (CSPI) opposes the use of olestra. Their reasons are listed on The Problems with Olestra site (http://www.cspinet.org/olestra/11cons.html). What are they?

2. Check out the manufacturer's site (http://www.olean.com/) for a more positive spin. What are the Olean (commercial name for olestra) benefits? Also check out the Digestive Effects and the page on vitamin absorption questions. Using the information from the links in Questions 1 & 2, make a comparison chart listing the positive and negative "facts" about olestra.

3. Take a final look at your olestra chart. Will you be eating olestra from now on? Would you recommend it to a friend? Optional: For more information on the complicated FDA approval process, look at government publication Olestra and Other Fat Substitutes (http://www.cfsan.fda.gov/~dms/bgolestr.html).

ISSUES IN BIOLOGY

What Are Vitamins and How Do They Affect Health?

Some of the most important decisions we make concerning our health involve our diets. Unfortunately, in our efforts to consume a healthy balance of foods http://www.nal.usda.gov:8001/py/pmap.htm), it can be difficult to sort out good information from that which is questionable or dangerous. This confusion does not only arise from "snake oil"-style advertisements that claim massive doses of vitamins can cure long lists of diseases. Scientists can also add to the confusion as their recommendations change to reflect new studies and new data. To illustrate the difficulty in judging information, we'll consider the case of vitamins—particularly vitamin A.

Humans have known for hundreds of years that a lack of fresh fruits and vegetables can cause serious, potentially fatal diseases such as scurvy (http://pc-78-120.udac.se:8001/WWW/Nautica/Medicine/Hutchinson(1794)a.html). However, until the early years of this century, it was thought that fruits and vegetables prevented disease by removing a toxic by-product produced by the body itself. Such ideas made bowel "cleansing" and other purging methods popular as a means of preventing disease, a concept that continues to be promoted. Experiments on the diets of rats in the early 1900s demonstrated that, instead of removing toxins, foods actually provide substances that are needed for health. These substances were called vitamin A and B, although the chemical nature of these molecules was not deciphered until much later. Vitamin C was subsequently discovered and was the first vitamin to be purified and whose chemical structure was revealed, earning a Nobel Prize for Albert Szent-Gyorgyi Von Nagyrapolt (http://nobelprizes.com/nobel/medicine/1937a.html) in 1937. Subsequent studies on human nutrition, usually using animal models, revealed that humans require a total of thirteen vitamins to remain healthy.

All vitamins are organic molecules that our bodies need in small amounts in order to perform essential enzyme reactions or to protect against damage caused by normal metabolic reactions. Because our cells lack the necessary enzymes to produce vitamins, we must consume them by eating the cells (or products of cells) from other organisms that can manufacture them. When we eat a carrot, we are eating carrot cells packed with carotene, which can be easily converted to vitamin A. Clearly, a molecule that is a vitamin for us is not a vitamin for all other organisms. For example, dogs do not need to consume vitamin C because their cells contain the necessary enzymes to manufacture it for themselves. And certainly, carrot plants do not need an external source of vitamin A.

Vitamin A is actually a member of a complex group of molecules that include retinoids and carotenoids. Carotenoids (http://dcb-carot.unibe.ch/carotint.htm), which include beta-carotene, are produced by plants (and many other organisms) and give certain fruits or vegetables their distinctive orange or yellow colors. Some carotenoids are needed for photosynthesis. In the human body the functions of vitamin A, a retinoid, are less well understood. One clear role of vitamin A is to produce retinal, which is the light receptor that binds to the protein rhodopsin and enables vision (http://science.howstuffworks.com/eye7.htm). Its role in vision explains one of the major symptoms of vitamin A deficiency: night blindness. Other symptoms of Vitamin A deficiency include xerophthalmia, or "dry eye," which is an inability to properly produce lubricating mucus in tears. This condition is currently the leading nonaccidental cause of blindness in the world. Vitamin A is also needed for proper function of the skin and other epithelial tissues as well as for proper growth and development. The biochemical nature of these functions of vitamin A are not known but are thought to result from its effects on gene expression.

What is so confusing about vitamin A? There appears to be a true consensus that eating high amounts of fruits and vegetables helps to lower the risk of cancers in humans. One reasonable hypothesis was that the protective molecules in fruits and vegetables were "antioxidant" vitamins such as vitamins A, C, and E. The CARET (Carotene and Retinol Efficacy Test) study was designed to test this idea by supplementing the diets of thousands of smokers with extra beta-carotene and vitamin A. As in all good epidemiological studies, the CARET study included controls. In this case some of the individuals were given supplements that appeared the same as the vitamin-containing capsules but actually lacked vitamins. The expectation was that individuals taking beta-carotene/vitamin A would develop cancers less frequently than the controls who were not taking additional beta-carotene/vitamin A. The CARET study was halted nearly 2 years early when it was discovered that individuals taking the supplements actually had a higher risk than controls of developing a cancer. Results of similar studies performed elsewhere were consistent with an enhancing role of beta-carotene in developing cancer. This new data forced scientists to do an apparent about-face on the advisability of taking beta-carotene supplements. Now, instead of supporting vitamin A supplements, many scientists urge against taking additional vitamin A at all and instead advise patients to obtain this vitamin directly from food.

Where does this leave the average consumer in the United States? First of all, we need to realize that we are all in a situation of "Let the Buyer Beware." The U.S. Food and Drug Administration (FDA) is charged with proving that a pharmaceutical company's claims for a particular drug are actually valid. However, the FDA *does not test* claims for the effects of dietary supplements. The bottom line is that, when it comes to vitamins, minerals, amino acids, herbs, bee pollen, and so on, suppliers do not have to provide evidence that their claims for longer life, higher energy, better outlook on life, more hair (or whatever) are true. All they are required to do is show that the items do not cause harm. However, when taken at high doses, even vitamin A can cause serious problems, including birth defects (http://www.fda.gov/bbs/topics/ANSWERS/ANS00689.html). Simply because a substance occurs naturally does not make it safe under all conditions.

Second, in order to make informed decisions about dietary supplements, it can do no harm—and potentially great good—to delve deeper into the claims of scientists and salespeople alike. Approach major changes to your diet or health treatments with skepticism and caution. Judge whether the source of the information you are evaluating is likely to be trustworthy. Consider whether the information is designed to entice you to purchase the item. Read and evaluate multiple points of view.

1. Does it surprise you that, nearly 90 years after the discovery of vitamin A, scientists still do not fully understand its role? Why do you think it might take even longer to figure this out?

2. What are the things you might look for in order to decide whether information is trustworthy or not?

3. On a small bottle of retinol—pure vitamin A—are a variety of warnings: "Toxic"; "Irritating to eyes, skin, and respiratory system"; "May cause birth defects"; and "If you feel unwell, show this label to your caregiver." How can a simple vitamin have such potential toxic effects? Do these warnings make you think differently about the idea of taking megadoses of vitamins? Should there be changes in the labeling systems for food additives to report their possible dangers?

BIZARRE FACTS IN BIOLOGY

X-Ray Vision

When doctors need to examine what is going on inside the human body, they often turn to X-rays to give them an answer. And now more than ever, when research scientists want an up-close look at the structure of different molecules of the body, they harness the short wavelengths of X-rays to help them as well.

The Human Genome Project gave scientists a wealth of information about the sequences of human genes and the proteins that they encode. However, knowing the sequence of a protein reveals little about its structure and function. The new Protein Structure Initiative (http://www.lbl.gov/Science-Articles/Archive/nigms-grant.html) is now aimed at determining the structure and function of thousands of proteins. This goal will depend largely on a technology known as X-ray crystallography (http://www-structure.llnl.gov/Xray/101index.html).

X-ray crystallography has been used to determine the structure of many biologically important molecules, including DNA (http://www.dnaftb.org/dnaftb/19/concept/index.html). In order to use this method, scientists must first synthesize a crystal form of the molecule to be tested. The X-rays that hit each atom of the crystal are diffracted and the diffraction pattern is interpreted by a computer to determine the actual arrangement of atoms in the molecule.

The applications of X-ray crystallography go beyond basic scientific interest in different protein structures. In 2002, X-ray crystallography provided "snapshots" of the structure of sodium channels (http://www.hhmi.org/news/mackinnon6.html) in the human body, giving scientists greater insight into their dynamic tasks in human physiology. These channels play a vital role in many body functions including heart pumping and nerve impulses. X-ray crystallography is also used as a means of understanding the complex interactions between tissues of the human body and new therapeutic drugs (http://www.yaleherald.com/archive/xix/2.17.95/news/crystallography.html). Researchers are hoping to use this method to design more effective treatments to combat HIV and other infectious diseases. This promising technology provides scientists with "X-ray vision" to look at the individual atoms of the human body. Many hope that it will be a stepping stone toward a better understanding of diseases and potential cures.

1. Outline the basic steps involved in X-ray crystallography.

2. What important feature of DNA did X-ray crystallography reveal?

3. How might X-ray crystallography help find a cure for diseases such as HIV?

KEY TERMS

adenosine triphosphate (ATP)
amino acid
carbohydrate
cellulose
chitin
coenzyme
cyclic nucleotide
dehydration synthesis
denatured
deoxyribonucleic acid (DNA)
disaccharide
disulfide bridge

enzyme
fat
fatty acid
functional group
glucose
glycerol
glycogen
helix
hydrolysis
inorganic
lactose
lipid
maltose
monomer

monosaccharide
nucleic acid
nucleotide
oil
organic
peptide
peptide bond
phospholipid
pleated sheet
polymer
polysaccharide
primary structure
protein
quaternary structure

ribonucleic acid (RNA)
saturated
secondary structure
starch
steroid
sucrose
sugar
tertiary structure
triglyceride
unsaturated
wax

ANSWER KEY

SELF TEST

1. a
2. c
3. f
4. c
5. e
6. b
7. b
8. e
9. d
10. a
11. e
12. d
13. c
14. d
15. c
16. d
17. a
18. c
19. d
20. c

21. a
22. d
23. c
24. monomers, polymers
25. monosaccharide
26. polysaccharide
27. fatty acids
28. amino acids
29. primary structure, tertiary structure
30. A. sucrose
    B. glucose
    C. fructose
31. A. primary structure
    B. secondary structure
    C. tertiary structure
    D. quaternary structure
32. A. hydroxyl group
    B. carboxyl group
    C. amino group
    D. phosphate group
    E. methyl group

33. A. dehydration synthesis
    B. monosaccharide
    C. disaccharide
34. A. peptide
    B. hydrogen bond
    C. pleated sheet
    D. primary structure

ESSAY CHALLENGE

1. Answer should include that functional groups determine the characteristics and chemical reactivity of the molecules to which they are bonded.
2. Answer should include the following: dehydration synthesis removes water from molecules and bonds them together; hydrolysis adds water to molecules and breaks them apart.
3. Answer should include the following: glucose is an energy source for cells; glycogen is the storage form of glucose in animal cells; cellulose is a structural element of cell walls in plant cells.
4. Answer should include the following: primary—the sequence of amino acids; secondary—the interactions within the chain of amino acids; tertiary—the three-dimensional structure of a protein; quaternary—subunits of proteins bonded together. Each level builds upon the previous levels.
5. When fatty acids are saturated, they can nestle closely together to form solids at room temperature. If a fatty acid is unsaturated, it contains double bonds which make it difficult for the chains to nestle together. Therefore, it does not form solid lumps at room temperature.
6. A triglyceride contains three fatty acid molecules bound to a glycerol. A phospholipid is similar except that one of the three fatty acids is replaced by a polar phosphate group.
7. Cholesterol is an important component of cell membranes. It is also used to produce bile in the liver, to make vitamin D, and is a component of different hormones in the body.
8. The high heat will alter the secondary and tertiary structure of the protein and it will be denatured. A protein can't function if it loses its shape. Without proteins to carry on their metabolisms, the microbes will die.

MEDIA ACTIVITIES

3.3 Web Investigation: Improving on Nature?

1. Olestra may cause nutrient deficiencies in the body and may cause digestive system problems.
2. Positive effects: less fat in diet; may have less risk of diseases such as heart disease, stroke, and diabetes. Negative effects: may cause poor nutrient absorption; may also cause stomach upset and diarrhea.
3. Possible answers: Yes, I would use Olestra products because they cut down on fat intake and may prevent heart disease. No, I would not use Olestra because they may cause digestive system problems. Instead, I will eat in moderation and cut fat in other ways.

ISSUES IN BIOLOGY

1. It takes many years to determine the role of different chemicals and vitamins. Since scientists are still learning about the human body itself, it will take even longer to learn about the effects of different chemicals on the human body.
2. Who has conducted the studies on this product? Who is making the claim about the product?
3. The body requires a certain, set level of vitamins. If more of those chemical are present, it can upset homeostasis in the body and cause harm.

BIZARRE FACTS IN BIOLOGY

1. Generate a crystal form of the molecule. Expose the crystal form to X-rays. The X-rays will form a diffraction pattern when they hit the different atoms of the crystal. A computer is used to interpret the diffraction pattern.
2. DNA is a double helix (like a twisted ladder).
3. If scientists can actually "see" how different molecules interact, they can design drugs that inhibit such an interaction, as in the example of HIV in the essay. They could block the ability of HIV to replicate by inhibiting its interaction with DNA.

CHAPTER 4: CELL MEMBRANE STRUCTURE AND FUNCTION

AT-A-GLANCE

SELF TEST

1. The fluid mosaic model describes membranes as fluid because _____.
   a. the phospholipids of membranes are constantly moving from one layer to the other layer
   b. the membrane is composed mainly of water
   c. the phospholipid molecules are bonded to one another, making them more moveable
   d. the phospholipids move from place to place around the motionless membrane proteins
   e. the phospholipids and proteins move from place to place within the bilayer

2. Which of the following types of molecules must pass through membranes via the aqueous pores formed by membrane proteins?
   a. gases such as carbon dioxide and oxygen
   b. small polar molecules such as water and ethanol
   c. large particles such as bacteria
   d. small charged ions such as Na^+ and Ca^{++}

3. Diffusion is the movement of molecules from _____.
   a. an area of higher concentration of that type of molecule to an area of lower concentration
   b. an area of lower concentration of that type of molecule to an area of higher concentration
   c. outside the cell to inside the cell

4. In osmosis, water diffuses from the side of the membrane with a higher concentration of water to the side with a lower concentration of water. What determines the concentration of water in a solution?
   a. the volume of the solution
   b. the amount of molecules other than water dissolved in the solution
   c. the size of the container

5. Which of the following processes does a cell use to take up molecules against their concentration gradient?
   a. simple diffusion   b. facilitated diffusion
   c. active transport   d. endocytosis
   e. Both the c and d are correct.

6. What is the difference between active transport and passive transport?
   a. Passive transport involves the movement of substances directly through the lipid portion of a membrane. Active transport requires an input of energy, whereas passive transport does not.
   b. Active transport requires energy and is unable to move substances against their concentration gradient. Passive transport does not require energy and can move substances against their concentration gradient.
   c. Active transport requires energy and can move substances against their concentration gradient. Passive transport does not require energy and can move substances only down their concentration gradient.

7. Of the following list of substances that can enter a cell, match the order with the correct mechanism by which they would enter cells: oxygen, water, sodium ions, potassium ions, bacterium. (Note that sodium ions are more concentrated outside cells than inside; potassium ions are more concentrated inside cells than outside.)
   a. simple diffusion, osmosis, facilitated diffusion, active transport, exocytosis
   b. osmosis, simple diffusion, facilitated diffusion, active transport, endocytosis
   c. passive transport, osmosis, simple diffusion, facilitated diffusion, active transport
   d. simple diffusion, osmosis, facilitated diffusion, active transport, endocytosis
   e. endocytosis, active transport, active transport, facilitated diffusion, exocytosis

8. Imagine that you are studying cell structure in various organisms in your biology lab. Your instructor gives you a microscope slide showing two types of cells that have been suspended in pure water. One type of cell swells up until it bursts. The other cell maintains its shape throughout the experiment. Suggest an explanation for these observations; assume that both cells were alive at the start of the experiment. Assume also that the concentration of water inside both types of cells is similar.
   a. The cell that burst lacked gap junctions, so water that entered the cell via osmosis could not leak back out through the junctions.
   b. The cell that burst lacked a plasma membrane for regulating osmosis.
   c. The cell that remained intact had plasmodesmata that allowed the excess water to leak out, thus balancing the tendency of water to enter the cell via osmosis.
   d. The cell that remained intact had a contractile vacuole for pumping out the excess water that entered the cell via osmosis.

9. The concentration of sodium ions is lower in the cytoplasm of a heart muscle cell than it is in the extracellular fluid. By what mechanism does the cell maintain this difference?
   a. active transport   b. osmosis
   c. facilitated diffusion   d. endocytosis

10. When placed in a certain sucrose solution, the volume of a cell decreases; therefore, the sucrose solution is _____ to the cell contents.
   a. isotonic   d. cannot determine from given
   b. hypertonic   information
   c. hypotonic

11. Choose the substance that will diffuse most rapidly across the plasma membrane.
   a. amino acid
   b. sodium ion
   c. small polar molecule such as water
   d. oxygen

12. Facilitated diffusion requires _____.
   a. a membrane transport protein
   b. a concentration gradient
   c. energy
   d. a membrane transport protein and a concentration gradient

13. During endocytosis, the contents of the endocytic vesicle _____.
   a. enter the cell
   b. exit the cell
   c. enter or exit the cell, always moving down a concentration gradient

14. Which of the following transport processes require(s) energy?
   a. facilitated diffusion
   b. osmosis
   c. endocytosis
   d. facilitated diffusion and osmosis
   e. facilitated diffusion, osmosis, and endocytosis

15. Membrane fluidity within a phospholipid bilayer is based upon _____.
   a. interactions among nonpolar (hydrophobic) lipid tails
   b. hydrophilic interactions among polar phospholipid heads
   c. the presence of transport proteins in the lipid bilayer
   d. the presence of water in the lipid bilayer

16. Recognition proteins function to _____.
   a. regulate the movement of ions across the cell membrane
   b. bind hormones and alter the intracellular physiology of a cell
   c. permit the cells of the immune system to distinguish between pathogens such as bacteria and cells of your own body
   d. all of the above

17. The point at which a substance is evenly dispersed within a fluid _____.
    a. is referred to as a *dynamic equilibrium*
    b. occurs when random movements of the substance cease
    c. happens when net diffusion is zero
    d. Both the first and third answers are correct.

18. Substances are able to cross the lipid bilayer of a cell at different rates that are unique for each substance. Which of the following characteristics would favor the simple diffusion of a substance across a cell membrane?
    a. low lipid solubility
    b. small molecule size
    c. small concentration gradients
    d. the number of membrane transport proteins for the substance

19. The term *tonicity* describes the solute concentration of the extracellular fluid relative to the solute concentration of the aqueous solution known as *cytoplasm*. In which direction would water flow according to the principles of osmosis if a cell were placed in a hypertonic solution?
    a. Water would flow out of the cell, leaving the cell shriveled and wrinkled.
    b. Water would flow into the cell, causing it to swell and perhaps even burst.
    c. The net flow of water would be zero because the solute concentrations inside and outside a cell are equal in a hypertonic medium.

20. Certain microorganisms have a high percentage of unsaturated fatty acids in their membrane. Because of this, these organisms _____.
    a. are able to withstand high temperatures because their membranes are firmer
    b. are able to withstand low temperatures because their membranes do not solidify as rapidly
    c. are able to carry out sodium ion transport more efficiently than most organsims
    d. are more rapidly recognized and destroyed by cells of the immune system

21. A hormone circulating in the bloodstream would most likely bind to _____.
    a. a recognition protein
    b. a receptor protein
    c. a channel protein
    d. protein filaments in the cytoplasm

22. Many metabolic poisons work by inhibiting ATP production. Which type of transport would be most affected?
    a. osmosis
    b. facilitated diffusion
    c. active transport
    d. simple diffusion

23. The antifungal drug nystatin combines with sterols in the plasma membrane of the fungal cell to disrupt the membrane and kill the cell. What other cell types might also be affected by nystatin?
    a. plant cells
    b. animal cells
    c. all cell types

24. When a drop of food coloring is placed in a glass of water, the spreading out of the molecules of food dye is caused by _____.
    a. the concentration of the molecules of dye
    b. the molecules trying to move to a lower concentration
    c. the random movement of molecules
    d. osmosis

25. Two types of connections between cells called "gap junctions" and "plasmodesmata" are specialized to _____.
    a. prevent the movement of molecules between cells that are tightly joined along ribbons of cell membrane
    b. tightly hold one cell against another at focal points, almost like a spot weld of superglue
    c. permit the passage of substances (e.g., ions) between cells through small passageways that directly link the cytoplasm of one cell to the cytoplasm of another cell
    d. None of these are correct.

26. All cells are surrounded by a thin _____.

27. The _____ consists of all of the internal contents of a cell, except the nucleus in eukaryotic cells.

28. The membrane components that spontaneously form a bilayer are _____.

29. Substances move from high to low concentration by a process called _____.

30. During _____, energy is used to move substances against their concentration gradient.

31. If a cell is placed in a _____ solution, there will be net water movement out of the cell.

32. The type of cell connection that makes the adjacent cells leakproof is a _____.

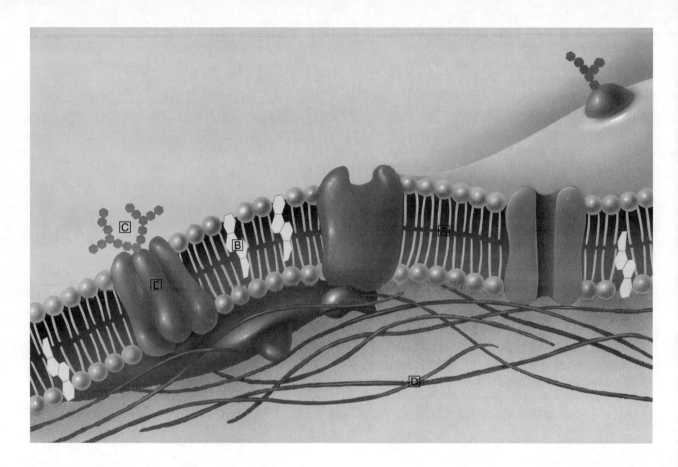

33. Label the parts of the cell membrane above.

34. This is a diagram of one phospholipid from the cell membrane. Label the individual parts.

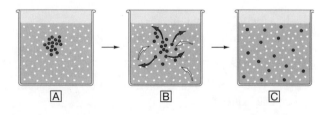

35. Match the steps in the process of diffusion with the sequence of images below:

36. Blood cells are used to demonstrate osmosis, since they show obvious shape changes in various solutions. Label the solution to which each of the following blood cells is reacting.

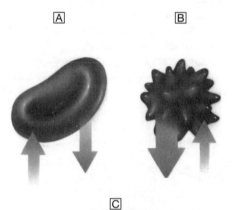

37. Identify the structures of a typical plant cell as seen in the image below.

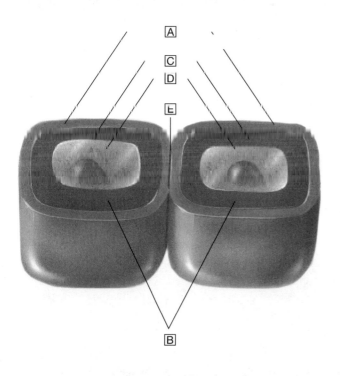

ESSAY CHALLENGE QUESTIONS

1. List and describe the three categories of membrane proteins and one function for each.

2. A cell with a 5% concentration of salt in it is placed in a solution with a 15% concentration of salt. Assume that the cell is permeable to water but not to salt. What will happen to this cell? How would you describe the condition of the outside solution?

3. Why is the plasma membrane referred to as a fluid mosaic model?

4. Insulin release following a meal triggers cells to transport glucose more rapidly into tissues, causing a decrease in blood glucose levels. Suggest two possible mechanisms for insulin action.

5. Explain why channel proteins can mediate much more rapid transport than carrier proteins can.

6. You have discovered a new membrane protein with the following characteristics: it has three regions: Regions A, B, and C. In your study, you notice that region A always faces the extracellular fluid and Region C always faces the cytoplasm. Region B is the part that spans the membrane. Describe the characteristics of Regions A, B, and C. Is this protein most likely a channel protein, carrier protein, or recognition protein?

7. If you were able to remove all cholesterol from the plasma membrane, what types of changes would you see in membrane characteristics?

8. Different types of cells have different percentages of proteins in their plasma membranes. For example, neurons contain only 18% proteins, whereas red blood cell membranes contain about 50% proteins. Even higher percentages of protein can be found in membranes of some intracellular organelles; for example, mitochondrial cell membranes contain 76% proteins. Discuss how the difference in composition of these membranes may be related to their function.

9. The bacterium, *Vibrio cholerae*, produces a protein toxin, cholera toxin. Cholera toxin binds to plasma membrane proteins in the cells of the intestinal lining and causes cells to actively secrete salts and water into the intestinal lumen. This leads to diarrhea and dehydration. The accepted treatment is oral rehydration therapy with dilute salts and glucose. Why does this work?

MEDIA ACTIVITIES

To access a Media Activity visit http://www.prenhall.com/audesirk7. Log in to the Web site selected by your instructor, navigate to this chapter, and select the appropriate Media Activity number.

4.1 Membrane Structure and Transport
Estimated time: 10 minutes

Explore how the cell membrane controls what enters and leaves a cell.

4.2 Osmosis
Estimated time: 5 minutes

Explore how osmosis affects cells.

4.3 Web Investigation: Vicious Venoms
Estimated time: 10 minutes

Many people are afraid of snakes. A person bitten by a poisonous snake might die without anti-venom treatment, yet venom components can also be life-saving drugs. This exercise takes a closer look at snake bites and venom.

1. For photos and information about snakes, view the *Snake Gallery* (http://www.manbir-online.com/htm2/snake. galle.htm). Click on Cobra to learn more about cobras. How does the spitting cobra deliver its venom? What type of substance is found in the venom of cobras and what does it do?

2. What exactly is snake venom (http://coloherp.org/cb-news/Vol-28/cbn-0103/Venom.html)? Describe the composition of venom. There are two general types of toxins known. What are they and what do they do?

3. There are two ways of making anti-venom (http://www.fda.gov/fdac/features/995_snakes.html). What is the traditional way of making anti-venom? What were the potential problems associated with it? What new method is being used to make anti-venom?

4. Read *Potions from Poisons* (http://www.time.com/time/pacific/magazine/20010115/poisons.html) and describe the drugs derived from the Thailand Cobra, Southern Copperhead, and Terciopelo snake.

ISSUES IN BIOLOGY

How Can Phospholipids Help Premature Babies Breathe?

A full-term baby develops (http://www.med.upenn.edu/meded/public/berp/) for 38 to 40 weeks in the protected environment of the mother's uterus before birth. In contrast, premature babies enter the world after only 23 to 37 weeks of development, making their appearance from less than 1 to more than 4 months early. Each year about 250,000 premature infants are born in the United States. About 40,000 of these babies will develop a serious lung disorder known as hyaline membrane disease or respiratory distress syndrome (RDS). Those babies born most prematurely have the highest risk of developing RDS. For example, about 60% of babies born after less than 28 weeks of gestation will suffer from the condition, but only 5% of those born after 34 weeks of gestation will have this condition. In the 1960s nearly every infant with RDS died. However, progress in neonatal care has raised the survival rate so that chances of survival are quite high: About 94% of them will survive.

Respiratory distress syndrome results from the inability of the baby's immature lungs to properly inflate. As a result, babies with RDS breathe rapidly but cannot take in sufficient amounts of oxygen to supply their tissues. Their tiny lips and nails turn blue from lack of oxygen. As a result of oxygen deprivation, additional complications arise, including stroke and bowel problems. See Nathan's Page (http://members.aol.com/ajoncs3224/awjones/family/nathan.htm) for information about what life is like for these tiny newborns. What makes it so difficult for the lungs to work properly in babies with RDS is the absence of a special slippery substance called surfactant (http://www.lungusa.org/diseases/rdsfac.html). This material is secreted by lung cells and forms a coat on the interior of the tiny alveoli in the lungs where oxygen enters the bloodstream. The coating enables the alveoli (http://edcenter.med.cornell.edu/CUMC_PathNotes/Respiratory/Respiratory.html) to expand, contract, and then re-expand with each successive breath. Without the surfactant, the alveoli have a hard time refilling once air is exhaled.

Surfactant is composed almost entirely of phospholipids. In fact, more than 60% of surfactant is a single phospholipid known as phosphatidylcholine. Interestingly, phosphatidylcholine is also a major substance in a commonly used kitchen aid that prevents food from sticking to pots and pans. The cooking spray, Pam™, contains lecithin, another name for phosphatidylcholine. You may be able to imagine a treatment for RDS. Why not simply expose the infant's lungs to a mixture of surfactant? In fact, in the late 1960s and 1970s that is exactly what physicians tried to do. Initial results were not very promising, but as surfactant preparations made from animal lungs became available, dramatic improvement in the survival of these tiny infants was observed. In 1990 an artificial surfactant was approved by the U.S. Food and Drug Administration (http://www.fda.gov/bbs/topics/NEWS/NEW00044.html). This is made of phosphotidylcholine mixed with two special types of alcohol that suspend the lipid and help it to spread across the surface of the lungs.

Delaying birth until the baby's lungs have matured is still preferred. A doctor can check if a baby has made surfactant by testing amniotic fluid collected by amniocentesis or sampled right after the mother's water breaks. If the baby has not yet made surfactant, the mother may be given betamethasone or dexamethasone (http://www.acs.ohio-state.edu/units/osuhosp/patedu/Materials/PDFDocs/medicatn/gendrug/corticos-fetal.pdf) to help the baby's lungs develop more quickly, as well as other drugs to try to stop labor and delay the birth. As you can see, phospholipids are not only important for membrane structure, but you owe each breath to their interesting properties—and they are saving thousands of premature infants each year from nearly certain death.

1. Review the structure of a phospholipid. Based on this structure, explain why alcohol instead of water is used to suspend the phospholipids in the artificial surfactant treatments for respiratory distress syndrome.

2. Before artificial surfactants were developed, surfactants for treatment of premature infants were prepared from lungs of animals or even human cadavers. What are potential risks of such materials?

BIZARRE FACTS IN BIOLOGY

When Egg Meets Sperm

The process of fertilization (http://arbl.cvmbs.colostate.edu/hbooks/pathphys/reprod/fert/fert.html) is really a chain of events, beginning with complex changes that occur in the plasma membrane of the sperm. Fertilization requires the specific recognition of the sperm by the egg, followed by fusion of the egg with only *one* sperm. But before it can fuse with the egg, the sperm must travel through the female reproductive tract and pass through outer layers of follicle cells, the corona radiata and zona pellucida, that surround the egg and form a barrier to sperm penetration (see chapter 36, *Animal Reproduction*, for a detailed discussion of reproduction). New strategies (http://www.nature.com/cgi-taf/dynapage.taf?file=/fertility/content/full/neb_nm_fertility57.html) for contraception and for treatment of infertility could be devised once the molecular processes of these complex events are understood.

When a sperm cell leaves the testis, no more new lipid synthesis occurs. While in the female reproductive tract, the sperm cell undergoes a series of changes called *capacitation*. One of the events that occurs during capacitation is a reorientation of the existing plasma membrane lipids and proteins and a depletion of cholesterol lipids in the sperm head membrane, causing membrane destabilization. At this point, the sperm is said to be *hyperactivated*. The destabilization that takes place in the sperm cell membrane prepares it for the *acrosome* reaction that occurs when it encounters the layers surrounding the egg. When the sperm comes in contact with the zona pellucida, it recognizes and binds to specific glycoproteins on the surface, releasing enzymes via exocytosis. The enzymes digest the zona pellucida in front of the sperm to make a pathway to the egg. The mechanism of sperm-egg binding is not fully understood, but may involve a transmembrane protein in the plasma membrane of the egg called *fertilin*, that specifically recognizes the sperm. After fusion, the egg releases enzymes that alter the zona pellucida and prevent fusion of additional sperm.

As the molecules that mediate the various steps of the fertilization process are better understood, it may be possible to immunize males or females with molecules that are necessary for reproduction. In this scenario, antibodies would be produced that would bind to and inactivate molecules needed for steps in the fertilization process. See a nice animation (http://brodylab.eng.uci.edu/cgi-bin/jpbrody/animation/files/16-980581646.html) of the fertilization process.

1. During capacitation, changes occur in the sperm head membrane. Among these changes are depletion of cholesterol. What function does cholesterol have in an animal cell membrane? What will occur if cholesterol is depleted?

2. What are the three categories of membrane proteins that exist in the plasma membrane? Binding of the sperm to the zona pellucida and fusion with the egg is very specific. Which category of membrane proteins would you expect to be involved in this process?

KEY TERMS

active transport	endocytosis	hypotonic	receptor-mediated
carrier protein	exocytosis	isotonic	endocytosis
cell wall	facilitated diffusion	osmosis	receptor protein
channel protein	fluid	passive transport	recognition protein
concentration	fluid mosaic model	phagocytosis	selectively permeable
concentration gradient	gap junction	phospholipid bilayer	simple diffusion
cytoplasm	glycoprotein	pinocytosis	tight junction
desmosome	gradient	plasma membrane	transport protein
diffusion	hypertonic	plasmodesmata	vesicle

ANSWER KEY

SELF TEST

1. e
2. d
3. a
4. b
5. e
6. c
7. d
8. d
9. a
10. b
11. d
12. d
13. a
14. c
15. a
16. c
17. d
18. b
19. a
20. b
21. b
22. c
23. b
24. c
25. c
26. plasma membrane
27. cytoplasm
28. phospholipids
29. diffusion
30. active transport
31. hypertonic
32. tight junction
33. A. phospholipid bilayer
    B. cholesterol
    C. carbohydrate
    D. protein filaments
    E. glycoprotein
34. A. hydrophilic head
    B. hydrophobic tail
35. A. A drop of dye is placed in water.
    B. Dye molecules diffuse into the water and water molecules diffuse into the dye.
    C. Both dye molecules and water molecules are evenly dispersed.
36. A. isotonic solution
    B. hypertonic solution
    C. hypotonic solution
37. A. primary cell wall
    B. secondary cell wall
    C. plasma membrane
    D. cytoplasm
    E. middle lamella

ESSAY CHALLENGE

1. 1) Transport proteins regulate the movement of hydrophilic molecules through the plasma membrane; examples are channel proteins, which form pores for ions, and carrier proteins, which grab specific molecules on one side of the membrane; 2) receptor proteins trigger cellular responses when specific molecules, such as hormones, bind to them; 3) recognition proteins serve as identification tags that allow cells to recognize each other, as in the immune system.

2. The cell will shrink as water flows out of it. The solution is hypertonic.

3. The "fluid" characteristic refers to the fact that the many components can move around in the membrane. Since there are many components, the membrane is considered a "mosaic." Analogous to a mosaic tile floor, the phospholipids form a "grout" for the proteins, which represent the "tiles."

4. Glucose transport can be accelerated by increasing the actual number of glucose transporters and by increasing the rate of glucose transport by the existing glucose transporters.

5. Channel proteins provide a pore through which the molecule or ion can travel. Once the channel is present, the movement of the substance is governed by the laws of diffusion. However, for a carrier protein to transport a substance, the substance must first bind to the carrier and a conformational change of the carrier occurs. This is an additional step that takes more time.

6. Regions A and C are hydrophilic because they face the aqueous extracellular and intracellular fluids, respectively. Region B is hydrophobic because it spans the region of the membrane that contains the hydrophobic fatty acid tails. Region A probably has a carbohydrate group attached to it, since it is always oriented to the outside, making this protein a glycoprotein. Most recognition proteins are glycoproteins, so there is a strong possibility that this is a recognition protein.

7. Removing cholesterol would make the membrane more fluid, less flexible, and more permeable to water-soluble substances. There would be more lateral movement of proteins in the membrane.

8. The plasma membrane of neurons with its high percentage of phospholipids most likely functions in insulating the cell. The mitochondrial membrane, with its abundant proteins, is most likely very active in transporting substances in and out of the mitochondria. The red blood cell membrane is intermediate in composition. A major function of the red blood cell membrane is to allow diffusion of oxygen into

and out of the cell, for which no transport proteins are necessary. However, the red blood cell membrane has other types of transport proteins as well as recognition proteins. The lipid composition of the red blood cell membrane contributes to its flexibility, enabling it to squeeze through small capillaries.

9. Intake of salt and sugar will restore vital solute concentrations in the bloodstream and lead to retention of fluids and less diarrhea. This is due to osmotic shifts in water. Untreated, water is moving by osmosis as salt is being excreted into the intestine. By restoring salts and sugars to the bloodstream, osmotic balance will be shifted back to a more normal state.

MEDIA ACTIVITIES

4.3   Web Investigation: Vicious Venoms

1. The spitting cobra can spray venom from a distance of about 8 feet. Cobra venom has an enzyme, lecithinase, that dissolves cell walls and membranes surrounding viruses.
2. Snake venom is toxic saliva made up of a mixture of enzymes. There are two general types of toxins known, neurotoxins and hemotoxins. A neurotoxic venom attacks the victim's central nervous system, whereas a hemotoxic venom attacks the circulatory system and muscle.
3. Anti-venom traditionally has been derived from antibodies created in the blood of a horse or sheep after the animal has been injected with snake venom (nonlethal doses). However, some people have allergies to horse or sheep proteins. A newer sheep antibody preparation has been synthesized in which the antibody preparation has been digested with enzyme to reduce allergic reactions.
4. A drug called Immunokine has been derived from the Thailand Cobra and is being tested for the treatment of multiple sclerosis. Contortrostatin is a protein from the Southern Copperhead that has been reported to retard growth and metastasis of tumors. Scientists are researching viper-venom antibiotics from the Terciopelo snake.

ISSUES IN BIOLOGY

1. Phospholipids have a polar (hydrophilic) head and a nonpolar (hydrophobic) tail region. Only the polar region of the molecule will interact well with the polar water molecule. Phospholipids will be more soluble in alcohol, which also has polar and nonpolar regions.
2. Using surfactants prepared from animal tissue carries the potential for disease transmission or allergic reactions.

BIZARRE FACTS IN BIOLOGY

1. Cholesterol stabilizes the membrane by wedging between and restraining the movements of the phospholipids. Removal of cholesterol will destabilize the membranes.
2. The three categories of membrane proteins are receptor proteins, transport proteins, and recognition proteins. Although the exact nature of the recognition and binding of the sperm to the egg is unclear, the binding appears to involve glycoproteins that act as sperm receptor proteins.

Chapter 5: Cell Structure and Function

AT-A-GLANCE

SELF TEST

1. Which of the following structures are found in all cells? Select the best answer.
   a. cell wall
   b. plasma membrane
   c. nucleus
   d. cytoplasm
   e. ribosomes
   f. b, d, and e

2. The cell theory states that _____.
   a. cells are generally small to allow for diffusion
   b. all cells contain cytoplasm
   c. cells are either prokaryotes or eukarotes
   d. all living things are composed of cells
   e. all cells arise from organic molecules such as DNA

3. Which of the following is an INCORRECT statement concerning the general characteristics of prokaryotic cells?
   a. Prokaryotic cells contain multiple molecules of DNA.
   b. Prokaryotic cells are enclosed by a cell wall.
   c. Prokaryotic cells contain cytoplasm.
   d. Prokaryotic cells do not contain a nucleus.
   e. Prokaryotic cells contain a nucleoid.

4. In what manner do molecules such as proteins and RNA enter into or exit from the nucleus?
   a. diffusion through the lipid bilayers of the nuclear envelope
   b. movement through pores in the nuclear envelope
   c. osmosis through the lipid bilayers of the nuclear envelope
   d. breakdown of the nuclear envelope

5. Chromosomes consist of _____.
   a. DNA
   b. proteins
   c. RNA
   d. proteins and RNA
   e. proteins and DNA

6. Which of the following correctly lists organelles that are part of the internal membrane system of eukaryotic cells?
   a. endoplasmic reticulum, Golgi apparatus, and lysosomes
   b. endoplasmic reticulum and mitochondria
   c. Golgi apparatus and nucleus
   d. endoplasmic reticulum, Golgi apparatus, and cell wall

7. The endoplasmic reticulum is needed for _____.
   a. synthesis of certain proteins
   b. hormone synthesis
   c. detoxification
   d. synthesis of lipids
   e. all of the above
   f. none of the above

8. Sorting and modification of proteins is an important function of _____.
   a. mitochondria
   b. chloroplasts
   c. lysosomes
   d. the Golgi complex
   e. the plasma membrane

9. Which of the following lists the correct order in which newly synthesized proteins are delivered to the plasma membrane?
   a. from the endoplasmic reticulum to lysosomes to the Golgi apparatus to the plasma membrane
   b. from the endoplasmic reticulum to the Golgi apparatus to the plasma membrane
   c. from the Golgi apparatus to the endoplasmic reticulum to the plasma membrane
   d. from the endoplasmic reticulum to the plasma membrane
   e. from the endoplasmic reticulum to the Golgi apparatus to lysosomes to the plasma membrane

10. Which of the following organelle(s) is (are) found in animal cells, but not in plant cells?
   a. mitochondria
   b. chloroplasts
   c. central vacuole
   d. cell wall
   e. cytoskeleton
   f. none of the above

11. In certain types of genetic engineering, DNA is injected into the nucleus of a recipient animal cell. What is the fewest number of membranes that must be pierced by the microscopic needle in order to inject the DNA? (Note that the needles used are not small enough to pass through a nuclear pore.)
   a. one
   b. two
   c. three

12. A researcher has discovered an unusual organism deep in the crust of Earth. She wants to know whether it is prokaryotic or eukaryotic. Imagine that she has rapid tests to determine whether the following molecules are present: DNA, RNA, and the proteins that form microtubules. Which test would you advise her to use and why?
   a. Test for DNA, because only eukaryotes have a nucleus.
   b. Test for RNA, because only eukaryotes have ribosomes.
   c. Test for microtubule proteins, because only eukaryotes have microtubules.

13. Imagine that you are late for a date and you reach your friend's door out of breath because you just ran the last three blocks from the bus stop. In a lame effort to impress and to try to make your date forget that you are half an hour late, you describe what oxygen is used for in your cells. Which of the following is correct?
   a. The lysosomes in my muscle cells need this extra oxygen to digest sugars and provide me with energy for running.
   b. The cellular enzymes in my leg muscles need this extra oxygen to repair the damage that occurs to my muscle cells as I run.
   c. The mitochondria in my muscle cells need this extra oxygen to produce sugars that, in turn, provide the energy I need to run.
   d. The mitochondria in my muscle cells need this extra oxygen to break down sugars and produce the energy I need to run.

14. Lysosomes contain very powerful digestive enzymes that can break down proteins, carbohydrates, and other molecules. Why don't these enzymes digest the cell itself?
   a. The enzymes will digest only foreign material.
   b. The enzymes are separated from the cytoplasm by the lysosomal membrane.
   c. The enzymes are inactive until secreted from the cell.

15. Why are living cells limited to remaining microscopic in size?
   a. cells produce a limited number of enzymes
   b. the energy needs of giant cells would outstrip available supply from the environment
   c. exchanges of substances at the membrane surface would take too long to diffuse throughout the interior of the cell
   d. both a and b

16. Prokaryotic cells _____.
   a. are large cells, typically greater than 10 mm in diameter
   b. include numerous membrane-enclosed structures known as organelles
   c. possess a single strand of DNA, but no definable membrane-enclosed nucleus
   d. all of the above

17. If the nucleus is the control center of the cell, how is information encoded and shipped to the cytoplasm?
   a. by RNA
   b. by chromosomes
   c. by nuclear pores
   d. by the nucleolus

18. The function of the endoplasmic reticulum is to _____.
   a. synthesize lipids and proteins
   b. modify and repackage newly synthesized lipids and proteins
   c. provide a barrier between the cytoplasm and extracellular fluid
   d. serve as a recycling and digestive center for the cell

19. Which of the following characteristics of mitochondria are true?
   a. They are able to take energy from food molecules and store it in high-energy bonds of ATP.
   b. All metabolic conversion of high-energy molecules (e.g., glucose) to ATP occurs within the mitochondria.
   c. They are able to directly convert solar energy into high-energy sugar molecules.
   d. They release oxygen during the process of aerobic metabolism.

20. Which of the following generalizations can you make about the cytoskeleton?
   a. The name implies a fixed structure like the bones of a vertebrate or 2 x 4 boards in the wall of a building.
   b. A variety of cytoskeletal elements are integral in the performance of numerous essential cellular functions.
   c. They provide a type of cellular armor on the outside of cells that serve a protective function.
   d. all of the above

21. The _____ surrounds the nucleus in eukaryotic cells.

22. All eukaryotic cells have _____, which convert energy stored in sugar to ATP.

23. The _____ forms membrane enclosed channels within the cell.

24. Both _____ and _____ are slender extensions of the cell membrane that move the cell through fluid or move fluid past the cell.

25. The _____ carry out the process of protein synthesis.

26. Plasmids are located _____.
   a. in the nucleus
   b. in the nucleolus
   c. in the cytoplasm
   d. continuous with the nuclear envelope

27. Suppose a *Paramecium,* a freshwater protist, was placed in salt water. What would occur (assume the salt water is hypertonic to the *Paramecium*)?
   a. The contractile vacuole would need to expel water more frequently.
   b. The cell would swell up and burst.
   c. The contractile vacuole would shrink.
   d. All of the above are correct.

28. Which organelle would you expect to be in abundance in the liver of a drug addict?
   a. Golgi complex
   b. smooth endoplasmic reticulum
   c. rough endoplasmic reticulum
   d. nucleolus
   e. ribosome

29. Which of the following is NOT consistent with the cell theory?
   a. A human is composed of trillions of cells.
   b. Bacteria are the smallest living organisms.
   c. Mitochondria and chloroplasts have their own DNA, and can reproduce.
   d. Embryos are a result of mitotic division of a single fertilized egg.
   e. Bacteria will multiply in food left out overnight on the counter.

30. Which of the following would NOT have originated by endosymbiosis?
   a. chloroplasts
   b. mitochondria
   c. flagella
   d. lysosomes
   e. The first two answers are correct.

31. The smallest type of cell are mycoplasmas, which have a diameter between 0.1 micrometer and 1.0 micrometer. Mycoplasmas most likely are _____.
   a. fungi
   b. viruses
   c. plant cells
   d. bacteria
   e. animal cells

32. In which of the following does one find ribosomes?
   a. plant cells
   b. animal cells
   c. bacterial cells
   d. mitochondria
   e. chloroplasts
   f. all of the above

33. The DNA in a eukaryotic cell is contained within the _____.

34. Prokaryotic cells do not contain _____.
   a. endoplasmic reticulum
   b. ribosomes
   c. cytoplasm
   d. DNA
   e. cell walls

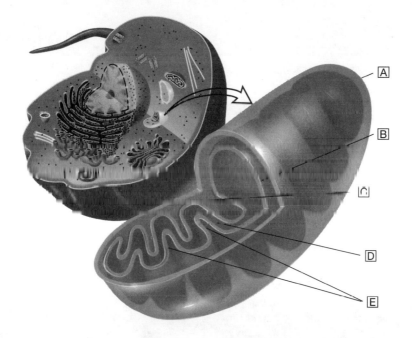

35. On this image of a mitochondrion above, identify the structures indicated.

36. Identify the indicated structures in the typical plant cell shown below.

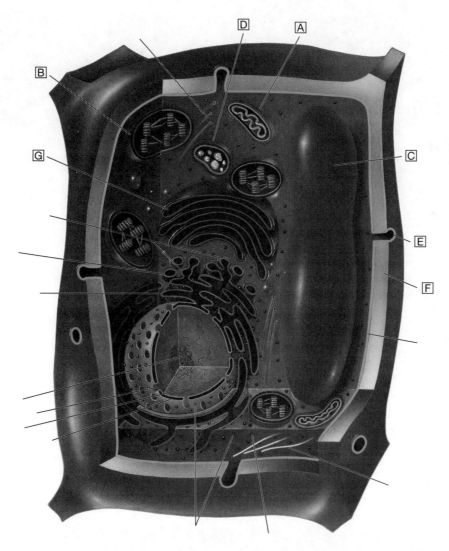

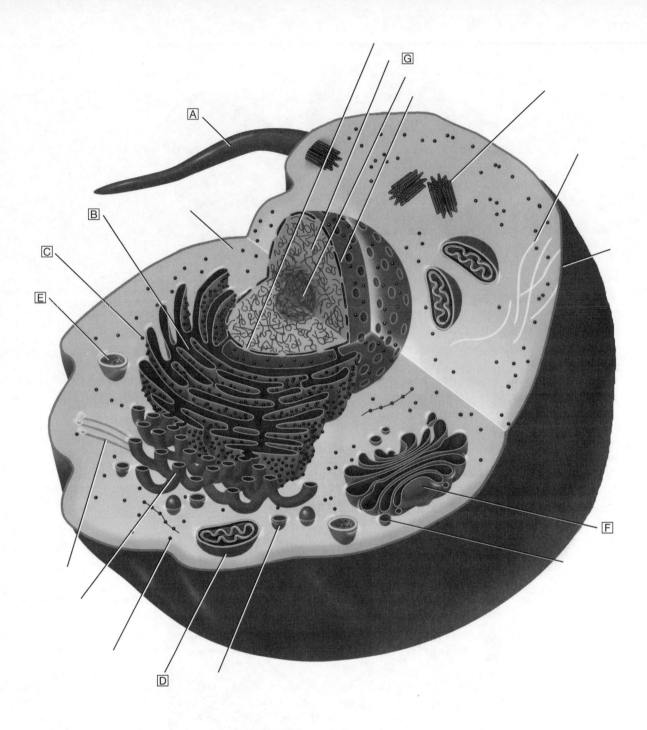

37. Identify the indicated structures on this eukaryotic cell.

38. Identify the structures indicated on this typical prokaryotic cell.

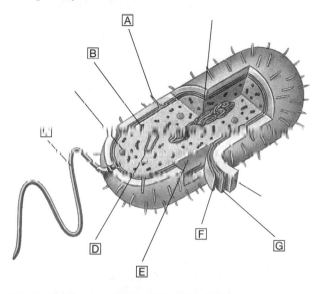

39. Label the structures of the cytoskeleton.

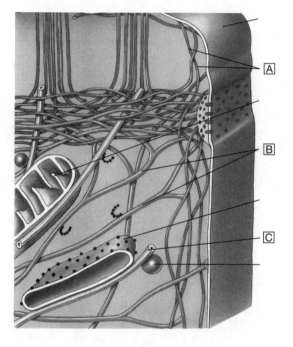

40. Identify the indicated structures on the image of a chloroplast below.

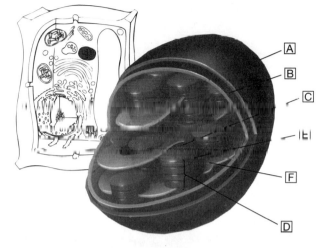

ESSAY CHALLENGE

1. List the three principles of the cell theory.

2. What are the major structural differences and similarities between prokaryotic and eukaryotic cells?

3. How do the ER and Golgi complex interact with each other?

4. Compare and contrast the structure and function of mitochondria and chloroplasts.

5. Antibiotics are effective in killing some bacteria by inhibiting cell wall synthesis. When you take antibiotics for an infection, why do they not cause harm to your cells?

6. Drugs that inhibit microtubule assembly are administered for some medical conditions. What will occur to the cell as a result? For what type of conditions would such a drug be given?

7. The main component of the red blood cell is hemoglobin, which is a protein responsible for carrying oxygen from the lungs to the tissues for use during aerobic metabolism. The red blood cell is small and has a biconcave shape. At maturity, it has no mitochondria or other organelles (they are expelled soon after the RBC enters the blood-stream). How does its structure suit its function as an oxygen carrier?

8. Low density lipoproteins (LDLs) are large complexes of proteins and lipids that carry cholesterol in the blood-stream. LDLs are broken down in the liver. For this to occur, the LDL is taken up by what mechanism? Explain the pathway it will take once it enters the cell.

9. Compare and contrast the structure and function of eukaryotic cilia and flagella.

10. Prokaryotic cells have only one chromosome and no nucleus or other organelles. Considering the complexity of cells and the functions a cell must perform to stay alive, give one reason why prokaryotic cells can be so efficient.

MEDIA ACTIVITIES

To access a Media Activity visit http://www.prenhall.com/audesirk7. Log in to the Web site selected by your instructor, navigate to this chapter, and select the appropriate Media Activity number.

5.1 Cell Structure
Estimated time: 5 minutes

Explore the structure of prokaryotic and eukaryotic cells.

5.2 Membrane Traffic
Estimated time: 5 minutes

This animation presents the details of membrane traffic in the cell, including transport of proteins, phagocytosis, and exocytosis.

5.3 Web Investigation: Spare Parts for Human Bodies
Estimated time: 10 minutes

In the case study that opened the chapter, you read about how researchers are attempting to grow new body parts in the laboratory by using cultured cells on scaffolding materials to grow skin, cartilage, heart valves, bone, and even entire organs. Researchers have been able to grow cells outside the body for quite some time, but have not, until recently, been able to create new organs. All of these methods began with undeveloped living cells called stem cells (http://stemcells.nih.gov/infoCenter/stemCellBasics.asp) that were able to multiply quickly and could be induced to become specialized cells that make up an organ. As the case study points out, the ability to take stem cells and grow new organs demonstrates advances in our ability to manipulate cells. What about going a step further, and actually building a cell from nonliving components? Has this ever been done? How close are researchers to achieving this goal? Could we ever manufacture cells for spare parts? This investigation looks at some of the research in this area.

1. In 1999, researchers reported the discovery of the minimum number of genes to support life (http://news.bbc.co.uk/1/hi/sci/tech/556984.stm#top) in an organism called *Mycoplasma genitalium*. How many genes does this organism have, and what was the minimum number necessary to sustain life?

2. Why did scientists choose *Mycoplasma genitalium* (http://jura.ebi.ac.uk:8765/ext-genequiz/genomes/mg9706/) for this research?

3. What is the estimated number of genes (http://www.er.doe.gov/production/ober/hug_top.html) in a human cell, a type of eukaryotic cell? How does this compare with the number of genes in *Mycoplasma genitalium*, a bacterial cell? What does this indicate about the difference in complexity between eukaryotic and bacterial cells?

4. In 2002, two researchers were awarded a grant by the Department of Energy to try to create life (http://news.bbc.co.uk/2/hi/science/nature/2499119.stm). How do they plan to accomplish this? If they are successful, what applications do they anticipate for their research?

5. If scientists are successful in building a cell, it would be a very simple bacterial-type cell. It would be a much more difficult task to create a human cell from nonliving components. There is controversy surrounding the attempt to create any life in the form of a cell. Some people feel that scientists are "playing God." What do you think?

ISSUES IN BIOLOGY

Why Is Taking All Doses of Prescribed Antibiotics Important for Worldwide Health?

What could 4000-year-old mummies possibly have to do with Christmas Seals? As strange as it seems, tuberculosis (TB), is the connection. Some Egyptian mummies dating from about 2400 B.C. display symptoms of tuberculosis infection (http://www.umdnj.edu/~ntbcweb/history.htm), a deadly disease that has plagued humans since that time. In the early 1900s, Christmas Seals (http://www.lung.ca/seals/) were invented as a way to raise money for treating children who suffered from tuberculosis. Although tuberculosis has not been a major cause of death in the United States in the past 45 years, it remains a serious illness in the developing world. Perhaps of more concern, the World Health Organization warns that drug-resistant strains of TB present a serious, worldwide threat to human health.

Tuberculosis is caused by *Mycobacterium tuberculosis* (http://www.uct.ac.za/depts/mmi/lsteyn/lecture.html), a bacterium first identified in 1882 by the great German microbiologist, Robert Koch. (Koch was awarded the 1905 Nobel Prize in medicine (http://www.nobel.se/medicine/laureates/1905/index.html) for this work.) The evidence of tuberculosis infection in Egyptian mummies indicates that this bacterium has been causing disease in human populations for more than 4000 years. At least 1 billion people have died from TB in the last 200 years alone, including many well-known individuals, such as Frederick Chopin, Robert Louis Stevenson, and Vivien Leigh. Currently, about one-third of the entire human population is infected with *Mycobacterium tuberculosis*. Although most of these people will not develop a full-blown case of TB, the disease will progress in about 8 million of these infected individuals to an active, infectious case of TB. About 3 million individuals will die this year as a consequence of the resulting damage to lungs or other organs.

A TB infection (http://www.mckinley.uiuc.edu/health-info/dis-cond/tb/TB.html) begins when a person inhales *Mycobacterium tubercuolosis* cells that have been encapsulated in the microscopic particles produced when a person with full-blown TB coughs or sneezes. The particles are so tiny that they get carried deep into the lungs, reaching the tiny alveoli. Usually, the bacteria are engulfed and destroyed by cells of the immune system known as macrophages. In some cases the bacteria are not destroyed but remain inside the macrophage, slowly reproducing. When the macrophage eventually dies, large numbers of bacteria are released, stimulating another immune reaction that walls off the bacteria in hardened nodules known as tubercules, the structures that give the disease its name. There are very few living bacteria in these tubercules; consequently, although a tuberculosis infection is present, the individual does not pass on the infection to others. If the infected person's immune system is weakened, the TB bacterium can begin to divide and multiply, eventually causing serious damage to the lungs (http://www.med.unsw.edu.au/pathology/Pathmus/m1114075.htm). The patient begins to lose weight, to cough, has a fever, and becomes increasingly weak. These symptoms explain why TB was known for many years as "consumption," since the disease appears to consume its victims.

A revolution in treatment of tuberculosis and other bacterial infections occurred in the middle of this century. Before the 1940s, the treatment of the TB was treated with different procedures in sanitariums for individual health. The sanitarium treatment allowed the body to rally and fight off the bacteria. For most, though, it did little to stem the course of the infection. In 1944 Selman Waksman (http://nobel.sdsc.edu/medicine/laureates/1952/) was able to isolate an antibiotic from a bacterium called *Streptomyces griseus*. Believe it or not, the bacterium itself originally came from a chicken coop! The antibiotic (http://www-micro.msb.le.ac.uk/Tutorials/dfwt/dfwt14.html), streptomycin, proved to be effective in treating TB, but bacteria that were resistant to streptomycin appeared almost immediately. Consequently, additional antibiotics were developed and used in combined therapy to treat patients with TB. This combined approach actually provided an effective cure for TB!

Today, the standard treatment for TB (http://www.vet.purdue.edu/bms/courses/bms445/chmrx/antitbhd.htm) is a combination of four antibiotics: isoniazid, rifampin, pyrazinamide, and ethambutol or streptomycin. Because each of these drugs targets a different enzyme or protein of the bacterium, it is unlikely that a strain can arise that is simultaneously resistant to all four antibiotics—provided the patient completes the entire 9 to 12 months of antibiotic treatment. This lengthy treatment is needed because *Mycobacterium tuberculosis* reproduces very slowly, dividing only once about every 20 days. Most antibiotics are effective only against actively growing and reproducing bacteria.

How is it that antibiotics are able to inhibit the growth of bacteria but usually have little effect on the cells of the human patient? Luckily for us, bacterial cells have fundamental differences from our own eukaryotic cells. Streptomycin, for example, targets bacterial ribosomes, thus inhibiting protein synthesis. Because eukaryotic ribosomes are slightly different, this drug is unable to bind to our ribosomes, thus protein synthesis in our cells continues in the presence of streptomycin. Many other antibiotics interfere with specific enzymes in the bacterium that are needed for cell wall production or other essential biochemical reactions. Examples of such antibiotics include penicillin, tetracycline, and vancomycin, as well as the anti-TB antibiotics, isoniazid, pyrazinamide, and ethambutol.

A serious concern is the advent of *Mycobacterium tuberculosis* strains that are resistant to the major antibiotics typically used for therapy. Multi-drug-resistant strains usually develop in individuals who do not complete their entire antibiotic therapy regime. After a few weeks or months of treatment, the patient feels much better—back to normal, in fact. During this time, the drugs have killed off normal bacteria, leaving only those few that have some degree of resistance to the antibiotics (http://www.fda.gov/fdac/features/795_antibio.html). If the patient stops taking the drugs prematurely, these resistant bacteria now can reproduce. Eventually, the growth of the bacteria cause the symptoms to return, but this time the standard drug cocktail is ineffective, and more toxic drugs must be used to control the infection. These drugs are also much more expensive, costing up to $250,000 for treatment of a single person! In the meantime, the individual may have passed the resistant strain to others. Such multi-drug-resistant bacteria have the potential to turn "conquered" foes such as TB and other bacterial infections into raging epidemics (http://www.thinkquest.org/library/site_sum.html?tname=11170&url=11170/) for which there are no effective treatments. It is ironic that, in our sophisticated age of computers and organ transplants, ancient scourges that have ravaged humans for thousands of years may return in new ferocity to once again claim billions of lives. Even more ironic is that our own cavalier attitudes toward bacteria and antibiotics will be the door through which these scourges emerge. Perhaps, next time you see a Christmas Seal, it will serve as a subtle reminder of these serious possibilities.

1. Some people advocate enforcible quarantine (http://biotech.law.lsu.edu/Books/lbb/x576.htm) to make certain that an individual completes the entire treatment for infectious diseases such as tuberculosis. Forcible detention, of course, may interfere with the civil rights of that individual. How do you think individual rights can be balanced with the society's need to prevent antibiotic-resistant diseases from developing? What about cases in which the individual rejects therapy due to religious reasons?

2. Doctors are under tremendous pressure to prescribe antibiotics to patients, even when there is no evidence of bacterial infections. For example, if a person is suffering from a cold, antibiotics will have no effect since colds are caused by viruses. Nevertheless, the patient feels better when handed a prescription. Do you think it is ethical for a doctor to prescribe antibiotics when the patient demands them? How might the doctor retain the patient's trust and business without giving in to inappropriate requests for antibiotics?

3. Researchers are taking a couple of different approaches to the antibiotic resistance issue. Some research is focused on what makes bacteria resistant to antibiotics, in hopes that by understanding this mechanism, better drugs can be developed. Recently, researchers from Lawrence Berkeley National Laboratory (http://www.sciencedaily. com/releases/2003/05/030512075547.htm)reported the discovery of a bacterial membrane protein that had the ability to bind and rid the cell of a variety of toxins in *E. coli*. They suggest that their research supports the development of drugs that inhibit this pump. Other researchers are developing a new class of antibiotics that work by inhibiting protein synthesis at the level of the bacterial ribosome. Linezolid (brand name Zyvox) (http://home.eznet.net/~webtent/linezolid.html), the first drug of this class to be approved by the Food and Drug Administration for limited situations, was recently shown to be effective in treating (http://www.med.nyu.edu/ communications/news/pr_19.html) five patients in New York suffering from an antibiotic-resistant form of tuberculosis. Both eukaryotic and prokaryotic cells contain ribosomes and carry out protein synthesis. Why is this class of antibiotics (http://puglisi.stanford.edu/research/pdf/pub48.pdf) effective against bacterial cells, but does not harm your own cells?

4. However, there is growing concern among some researchers that development of a new class of antibiotics, while offering great benefits to today's patients, may cause a future crisis (http://news.bbc.co.uk/1/hi/health/ 2994528.stm). Professor Graham Bell from McGill University in Canada warns that "regulatory authorities tend not to look many years ahead when deciding whether to grant licenses to new drugs." Do you think we should approve these new and effective antibiotics, without thinking of future repercussions? What if a member of your family was suffering from an antibiotic-resistant infection today?

BIZARRE FACTS IN BIOLOGY

The Blob?! Or Dog Vomit?

In 1973, firefighters in Dallas, Texas, were called to the scene to investigate a jelly-like mass (http://www.dnr.state. mn.us/volunteer/janfeb03/slimemolds.html) in a resident's backyard. Firefighters tried to restrain it, but it only became larger! This was a little too much like the 1958 Steve McQueen film, *The Blob* (http://www.imagesjournal. com/issue09/reviews/blob/pic2.htm), in which an alien glob streaks to earth on a meteor and begins to attack people. Just as Texans pleaded with the Governor to call in the National Guard, a local mycologist finally identified it as a fairly large slime mold, called *Fugligo septica*, or dog vomit slime mold (http://botit.botany.wisc.edu/toms_fungi/ june99.html).

What is a slime mold? Although quite slimy, it is not truly a mold (http://www.herb.lsa.umich.edu/kidpage/slimemold.htm). Molds are fungi, and fungi do not move during any stage of their life cycle, and have cell walls made of chitin. Slime molds can move (up to 1 mm per hour!), and do not have cell walls made of chitin.

Slime molds have both animal-like and plant-like characteristics. The plasmodium is the animal-like phase of the life cycle (http://bicmra.usuhs.mil/Physarum/LifeCycle.html). It is actually a large amoeba-like *synctium*, with multiple nuclei in a common cytoplasm. During damp weather, it forms a gelatinous blob with no cell wall and only a plasma membrane to hold its contents. Slime molds can exist in a variety of different colors, dependent on the pH. As long as the conditions are dark and moist, the plasmodium will move slowly in search of food. In fact, some researchers have shown that slime molds can negotiate the shortest way through a maze (http://news.bbc.co.uk/1/low/sci/tech/911790.htm)! If the conditions become too dry or no food is left, a stalked reproductive structure, called a sporangia, forms. This structure represents the plant-like phase. Spores are released from the sporangia and germinate when conditions are favorable. To view some images of slime molds, go here: http://botit.botany.wisc.edu:16080/images/130/Protista I/Plasmodial Slime Mold Images/.

1. Slime molds are often used in the laboratory to study *cytoplasmic streaming*. What is cytoplasmic streaming (http://www.indiana.edu/~q201bio/labs/lab2/cytoani.html)? What cell structure (http://www.biology.arizona.edu/cell_bio/tutorials/cytoskeleton/page3.html) is responsible for cytoplasmic streaming? Is it unique to slime molds? What purpose does it serve? You can view a movie of cytoplasmic streaming here: http://botit.botany.wisc.edu/toms_fungi/june99.html.

2. How does the slime mold obtain nutrients?

3. What is one fascinating thing about the nuclei (http://www.herb.lsa.umich.edu/kidpage/slimemold.htm) of plasmodial slime molds?

KEY TERMS

aerobic	contractile vacuole	food vacuole	nucleus
anaerobic	cytoplasm	Golgi complex	organelle
basal body	cytoskeleton	intermediate filament	plastid
central vacuole	deoxyribonucleic acid	lysosome	prokaryotic
centriole	(DNA)	microfilament	ribonucleic acid (RNA)
chlorophyll	endoplasmic reticulum	microtubule	ribosome
chloroplast	(ER)	mitochondrion	vacuole
chromatin	endosymbiont hypothesis	nuclear envelope	vesicle
chromosome	eukaryotic	nucleoid	
cilium	flagellum	nucleolus	

ANSWER KEY

SELF TEST

1. f
2. d
3. a
4. b
5. e
6. a
7. a, e
8. d
9. b
10. f
11. c
12. c
13. d
14. b
15. c
16. c
17. a
18. a
19. a
20. b
21. nuclear envelope
22. mitochondria
23. endoplasmic reticulum
24. cilia, flagella
25. ribosomes
26. c
27. c
28. b
29. c
30. e
31. d
32. f
33. nucleus
34. a
35. A. outer membrane
    B. inner membrane
    C. intermediate compartment
    D. matrix
    E. cristae
36. A. mitochondrian
    B. chloroplast
    C. central vacuole
    D. plastid
    E. plasmodesmata
    F. cell wall
    G. Golgi complex
37. A. flagellum
    B. rough endoplasmic reticulum
    C. ribosome
    D. mitochondrian
    E. lysosome
    F. Golgi complex
    G. nucleolus

38. A. pilus
    B. ribosomes
    C. prokaryotic flagellum
    D. plasmid (DNA)
    E. cytoplasm
    F. plasma membrane
    G. cell wall
39. A. microfilaments
    B. intermediate filaments
    C. microtubules
40. A. outer membrane
    B. inner membrane
    C. stroma
    D. granum
    E. thylakoid
    F. channel interconnecting thylakoids

ESSAY CHALLENGE

1. 1) every living organism is made up of one or more cells; 2) the smallest living organisms are single cells and the functional units of multicellular organisms; 3) all cells arise from preexisting cells
2. Prokaryotic cells lack a nucleus and membrane-bound organelles, while eukaryotic cells contain both of these. Both types of cells contain DNA, have a membrane, and have ribosomes.
3. The ER synthesizes proteins and lipids, which are then sent to the Golgi, where they are sorted, modified, and packaged into vesicles for export or to be kept inside the cell.
4. Mitochondria are the powerhouses of the cell, and convert the energy stored in food molecules into ATP. Chloroplasts are able to capture light energy and convert it into carbohydrate. Structurally, both are surrounded by a double membrane. However, the internal membrane of a mitochondria is highly folded and is called the cristae. Chloroplasts have a smooth internal membrane and a system of hollow membranous sacs called thylakoids. The fluid portion of the mitochondria is the matrix, whereas the fluid portion of the chloroplast is the stroma. Both mitochondria and chloroplasts can synthesize ATP, have ribosomes, and have their own DNA.
5. Animal cells do not contain a cell wall, so this type of antibiotic will have no effect on your cells.
6. Drugs that inhibit microtubule assembly can inhibit organelle movement in the cell, cause a change in shape, and stop cell division. In a cell that moves, such a drug will also prevent cell movement. These types of drugs are generally given as chemotherapeutic drugs because they stop cell division and inhibit the growth of a tumor.
7. Red blood cells have a good surface to volume ratio because of their small, biconcave shape. Because of

their good surface to volume ratio, diffusion of oxygen is efficient. They are small and flexible to move through the circulatory system. In addition, the cells do not have any mitochondria to consume the oxygen that is being carried.

8. Because it is large, the LDL is taken up by endocytosis. Once it enters the cell, the endocytic vesicle will fuse with a lysosome.

9. Both are slender extensions of the cell membrane. Flagella are longer than cilia and usually fewer in number. Both are made from a "9 + 2" array of microtubules, and both arise from centrioles that move to the plasma membrane to form basal bodies. Cilia provide a force that is parallel to the plasma membrane, and function in moving substances across the surface of the cell, and sometimes in movement of the entire cell. Flagella exert a force perpendicular to the plasma membrane and are involved in movement of the entire cell.

10. Prokaryotic cells are very small, so their surface to volume ratio makes them very efficient at diffusion. Because they are small and simple, they do not need to compartmentalize their functions into organelles.

MEDIA ACTIVITIES

5.3 Web Investigation: Spare Parts for Human Bodies

1. *Mycoplasma genitalium* has about 480 genes. These researchers determined that about 300 genes were required for life.

2. Mycoplasmas are a type of bacteria and are the smallest known organisms capable of growth and reproduction outside living host cells.

3. There are approximately 30,000 genes in a human cell compared to 480 in the bacterial cell. This indicates that eukaryotic cells are far more complex than bacterial cells.

4. Scientists will synthesize an artificial sequence of genetic material that contains the estimated minimum number of genes needed to sustain life. The artificial chromosome will then be inserted into a cell with no DNA, and tested for its ability to survive and reproduce. They anticipate that if they are successful, they will be able to create designer bacterial cells that may help to clean up the environment.

5. An expression of the pros and cons of creating life should be part of this answer. By building cells, scientists may be able to design cells that help to solve environmental and health problems. There is always the potential for unethical use of the technology, such as in the creation of new weapons for bioterrorism.

ISSUES IN BIOLOGY

1. This answer is based on individual opinion.

2. Answers may vary, but there should be some discussion of the problem of antibiotic resistance, the importance of the proper use of antibiotics, and the role of the doctor in patient education.

3. Bacterial ribosomes are slightly different from eukaryotic ribosomes.

4. Answers may vary, but you should demonstrate an awareness of the need to treat patients with the most effective medicines available today, while still safeguarding future generations.

BIZARRE FACTS IN BIOLOGY

1. The cytoskeleton is responsible for internal movement of organelles and cytoplasm, or cytoplasmic streaming. Cytoplasmic movement occurs in all cells, but it is very apparent in amoeboid types of cells. It helps to evenly distribute the contents of the cell.

2. The slime mold slowly crawls by amoeboid movement, consuming organic substances by the process of phagocytosis.

3. One fascinating thing about plasmodial slime molds is that the millions of nuclei in a single plasmodium all divide at the same time. Slime molds are ideal for scientists studying mitosis, the process of nuclear division.

CHAPTER 6: ENERGY FLOW IN THE LIFE OF A CELL

AT-A-GLANCE

SELF TEST

1. The laws of thermodynamics define the properties and behavior of energy. The first law states that energy _____.
   a. equals mass times the speed of light, squared (that is, $E = mc^2$)
   b. can be created by thermonuclear explosions
   c. cannot be created or destroyed but can be changed from one form into another
   d. is the basic structure of the universe

2. Which of the following does NOT illustrate kinetic energy?
   a. a car moving at 55 mph
   b. a 100-watt lightbulb, turned on
   c. a 9-volt battery
   d. a water droplet going down a waterfall
   e. the electrical current used to perk coffee

3. When electrical energy is used to turn on a lightbulb, the conversion from electrical energy to light energy is not 100% efficient. This loss of usable energy can be explained by _____.
   a. the first law of thermodynamics
   b. the second law of thermodynamics
   c. a destruction of energy
   d. a conversion to potential energy

4. The second law of thermodynamics relates the organization of matter to energy. It states that unless additional energy is acquired, the orderliness of a system tends to _____, whereas entropy _____.
   a. increase, decreases
   b. decrease, increases
   c. stay the same, increases
   d. decrease, stays the same

5. In a chemical reaction, the _____ are the atoms or molecules that enter into the reaction, and the _____ are the chemicals or atoms produced by the reaction.
   a. products, reactants
   b. reactants, products
   c. receptors, products
   d. catalysts, reactants

6. In endergonic reactions, _____.
   a. the products contain more potential energy than the products
   b. energy is released
   c. a net input of energy is not required
   d. all of the above
   e. none of the above

7. Activation energy _____.
   a. is required for endergonic reactions
   b. is produced by exergonic reactions
   c. is required for all chemical reactions
   d. is produced by chemical reactions

8. Energy from exergonic reactions is transferred from place to place in cells via _____.
   a. microscopic channels
   b. energy-carrier molecules such as ATP
   c. glucose
   d. mitochondria

9. The speed of a reaction is determined by its _____.
   a. reactants
   b. products
   c. activation energy
   d. potential energy

10. Enzymes are a class of proteins that catalyze chemical reactions in cells. Like all other catalysts, they speed up chemical reactions by _____.
    a. making the reaction endergonic
    b. releasing energy for the reaction
    c. lowering the activation energy of the reaction
    d. elevating the activation energy of the reaction

11. Which of the following are correct statements about how enzymes work?
    a. Enzymes catalyze specific chemical reactions because the shape of their active site allows only certain substrate molecules to enter.
    b. The substrate(s) enter the enzyme active site in specific orientations.
    c. The enzyme and the substrate(s) change shape, promoting a specific chemical reaction and then allowing the products to leave.
    d. The first three answers are all correct.
    e. Only the first two answers are correct.

12. The most important reason a particular enzyme can function only within certain limits of temperature, salt conditions, and pH is that _____.
    a. changes in temperature, salt, and pH change the shape of an enzyme
    b. changes in temperature, salt, and pH alter the amount of substrates
    c. changes in temperature, salt, and pH alter the amount of products
    d. changes in temperature, salt, and pH lower the activation energy of a reaction

13. ATP is well suited to its role as an energy-carrier molecule in cells because _____.
    a. the covalent bond between the last two phosphates can be broken to release substantial amounts of energy
    b. it contains covalent bonds
    c. it is small and can fit into a lot of places in the cell
    d. the covalent bonds between the last two phosphates are high-energy bonds that can absorb a substantial amount of energy when the bonds are broken

14. A substance that is acted upon by an enzyme to produce a product is called a(n) _____.
    a. allosteric inhibitor
    b. coenzyme
    c. substrate
    d. electron carrier

15. Which of the following situations illustrates the coupling of exergonic to endergonic reactions in cells?
    a. the production of ATP by breakdown of glucose
    b. the active transport of sodium into the cell
    c. the movement of a muscle powered by the hydrolysis of ATP
    d. All of the above are correct.

16. If all matter tends toward increasing randomness and disorder, how can life exist?
    a. Living things do not obey the second law of thermodynamics.
    b. There is a constant input of energy from the sun.
    c. Living things do not require energy.
    d. All of the above are true.

17. The amino acid threonine is converted to isoleucine by a sequence of five enzymatic reactions. When isoleucine levels are high, the first reaction in this sequence is "turned off." This is an example of _____.
    a. substrate activation
    b. feedback inhibition
    c. competitive inhibition
    d. coenzyme activation

18. The laws of thermodynamics _____.
   a. explain how energy is created and destroyed
   b. refer to fluctuating temperature changes
   c. define the basic properties and behavior of energy
   d. suggest that matter in a disorganized state requires energy to be constantly added to maintain the "disorganization"

19. Why do most reactions occur more rapidly at high temperature?
   a. Molecules move more rapidly at higher temperatures.
   b. Collisions between molecules are more frequent.
   c. Collisions will be hard enough to force electron shells to interact.
   d. All of the above are correct.

20. Pepsin is an enzyme that breaks down protein but will not act upon starch. This fact is an indication that enzymes are _____.
   a. catalytic
   b. hydrolytic
   c. specific
   d. temperature sensitive

21. Biological catalysts _____.
   a. are organic substances that lower the activation energy required to initiate a reaction that would normally take place at a slower rate
   b. are broken down and destroyed as part of the chemical process they help initiate
   c. are seldom regulated by the molecules that participate in the catalyzed reactions
   d. can speed up any reaction, even those that would not occur naturally

22. Which of the following is NOT used by an enzyme to promote a reaction?
   a. substrate orientation
   b. temporary chemical bonds
   c. electrical interactions
   d. increased kinetic energy of substrate
   e. bond distortion

23. Enzyme regulation can be precisely controlled through a variety of mechanisms such as _____.
   a. production of an inactive form of an enzyme that will become activated only when needed
   b. using a coenzyme that is necessary for function
   c. binding of a competitive inhibitor to the active site
   d. all of the above

24. Lysosomes have an acidic interior (pH = 5), unlike the rest of the cell (pH = 7). Lysosomal enzymes are most active at _____.
   a. pH = 4
   b. pH = 5
   c. pH = 7
   d. pH = 9

25. Which of the following is NOT true about enzymes?
   a. Enzymes are biological catalysts.
   b. Enzymes are proteins.
   c. Enzymes, like other reactants, are used up in the reactions that they catalyze.
   d. Enzymes are very specific for the reactions that they catalyze.

26. The energy of movement is called _____.

27. Without energy, processes that proceed spontaneously result in an increase in _____.

28. A _____ is a process that breaks and forms chemical bonds.

29. _____ is the most common energy-carrier molecule in cells.

30. The _____ of a cell is the sum of all of its chemical reactions.

31. _____ are biological catalysts synthesized by living organisms.

32. Identify the compounds in the diagram below indicating the equation for energy storage.

ATP synthesis: Energy is stored in ATP

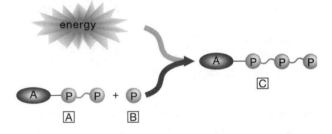

33. Identify the activation energy curves on the graph below.

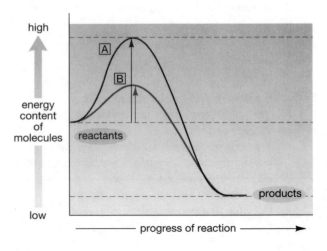

60

34. Label the structures associated with enzyme activity in the figure below.

35. Using the same image as in Question 34, place the sequence of enzyme–substrate activity in the proper order.

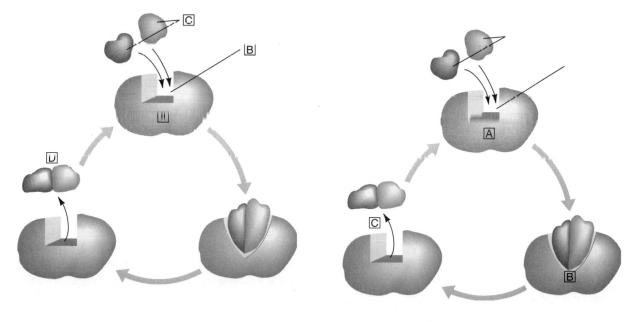

ESSAY CHALLENGE

1. How are exergonic and endergonic reactions linked?

2. What are the three important principles that relate to all catalysts?

3. How does an enzyme catalyze a reaction?

4. How do pH and temperature affect enzyme function?

5. Glycolysis is the metabolic pathway that breaks down some of the bonds in glucose to produce ATP from ADP. Glycolysis involves 10 biochemical reactions, each catalyzed by a different enzyme. The third step is catalyzed by the enzyme phosphofructokinase. This enzyme is stimulated by ADP but is inhibited by ATP. Explain how this effect can regulate the glycolysis pathway.

6. In recent years, archaebacteria have been found thriving under extreme conditions, some even in the hot springs at Yellowstone National Park. Most bacteria would be killed under these circumstances, but these thermophilic bacteria require temperatures as high as 100 degrees Celsius for life. What can you conclude about the enzymes found in these archaebacteria?

7. Most enzymes are susceptible to denaturation upon heating. However, many enzymes will be more stable in the presence of large quantities of its substrate. Explain why excess substrate may enhance enzyme stability and prevent denaturation.

8. Why can't you just take an ATP pill for quick energy?

9. Some mitochondrial poisons are classified as uncouplers. Suggest why these poisons are called uncouplers. What effect would they have on humans?

MEDIA ACTIVITIES

To access a Media Activity visit http://www.prenhall.com/audesirk7. Log in to the Web site selected by your instructor, navigate to this chapter, and select the appropriate Media Activity number.

6.1 Energy and Chemical Reactions
Estimated time: 5 minutes

Explore the basic concepts of thermodynamics and how they govern the life of a cell.

6.2 Energy and Life
Estimated time: 10 minutes

Explore the importance of ATP as the currency for work in the cell.

6.3 Enzymes

Estimated time: 5 minutes

Visualize the structure of an enzyme and explore how an enzyme's structure relates to its catalytic function.

6.4 Web Investigation: Energy Unleashed

Estimated time: 10 minutes

While biologists study the sophisticated biochemical processes organisms use to maintain relatively constant energy levels, dieters focus on two simple rules. Take in too much energy (i.e., too many calories) and you gain weight (or mass). Take in too few calories and weight loss, disability, and eventually death will result. But how much is too much? In this exercise we will use online calorie calculators to explore how different factors affect energy needs. Remember that this is only an exercise. The data obtained should not be used as the basis for any dietary or exercise program.

1. First enter your height, weight (no cheating), age, and sex into the Basal Metabolism Calculator (http://www.room42.com/nutrition/basal.shtml) to calculate your basic (non-exercising) energy needs.

2. It is time to start an exercise program. Enter the same numbers into the Energy Calculator (http://www.aces.uiuc.edu/~food-lab/energy/ec.html). Be patient; this calculator loads slowly. Choose "running, cross country, 20 minutes" as your activity. Calculate! How many calories did you burn while exercising?

3. Return to the Energy Calculator (http://www.aces.uiuc.edu/~food-lab/energy/ec.html) and change the weight value to 200 lbs. Calculate. Did you use more or fewer calories than before?

4. Look up the calorie content of your favorite fast food on the Food Finder (http://www.olen.com/food/). Use the Energy Calculator (http://www.aces.uiuc.edu/~food-lab/energy/ec.html) to estimate how many minutes of running it would take to burn off those calories.

5. If you are going to run, drinking the correct amount of fluids is critical, as was discussed in the Case Study, *Energy Unleashed*. What are the recommendations (http://www.usatf.org/news/showRelease.asp?article=/news/releases/2003-04-19-2.xml) for drinking if you are to enter a marathon?

ISSUES IN BIOLOGY

Why Is Maintenance of Protein Shape Important?

One of the most important truths about proteins is that their function absolutely depends on their three-dimensional shape (http://www.ks.uiuc.edu/Overview/gallery/biggifs/81.gif). Consequently, deciphering a protein's structure is a kind of "Holy Grail" for a biochemist interested in how a particular protein carries out its role in the cell. To approach this problem, biochemists frequently use a technique called X-ray crystallography (http://www.stolaf.edu/people/hansonr/mo/x-ray.html). In this technique (http://www-structure.llnl.gov/Xray/101index.html), the biochemist purifies a single protein, places it into a solution and then allows the solution to slowly evaporate. As the water or other solvent molecules diffuse out of the solution, the protein molecules become more and more concentrated. Hopefully, the protein molecules will then interact with each other to form a solid crystal of pure protein. If the scientists are able to produce a protein crystal, they can bounce X rays off of it to get information about the protein's three-dimensional shape. (This technique is not limited to proteins; the double helix nature of DNA was revealed by X-ray crystallography experiments carried out by Rosalind Franklin (http://www.physics.ucla.edu/~cwp/Phase2/Franklin,_Rosalind@841234567.html).) It is through such studies that we are beginning to understand the details concerning how a protein's shape is critical for its function.

The ultimate determinant of a protein's shape is the sequence of amino acids that make up the protein polymer (its primary structure (http://users.rcn.com/jkimball.ma.ultranet/BiologyPages/P/PrimaryStructure.html)). At critical sites in the amino acid chain, a single amino acid change can abolish the protein's function. Many human diseases, including sickle cell disease (http://www.scinfo.org/tutorial/Sickle_Cell/sld001.htm) and cystic fibrosis (http://www.cff.org/), result from the change of a single amino acid that prevents the protein from carrying out its normal function. In the case of cystic fibrosis (CF), the altered protein normally provides a channel for chloride ions to pass into or out of the cell, helping to regulate the amount of salt (http://www.people.virginia.edu/~rjh9u/cfsciam.html) and water inside and outside the cell. However, in most CF cases, the 508th amino acid (http://www.hosppract.com/genetics/9706gen.htm) (out of 1480 total) is missing from the CF protein. As a result, the CF protein's shape is slightly changed so that the cell sends it to the cellular equivalent of the recycling bin, rather than to the cell membrane. The absence of the CF protein in the cell's membrane leads to abnormal salt regulation, which in turn leads to other symptoms of the disease and ultimately to death.

Protein structure can also be exquisitely sensitive to changes in its environment. Even slight changes in pH, temperature, or salt concentration can diminish or eliminate a protein's activity. What does this mean for the proteins that we eat in our diet? If you do an Internet search using the keyword "enzyme," you are immediately plunged into a huge number of sites that espouse eating raw foods in order to maintain the "active enzymes" of the food. Recall that enzymes are simply a class of proteins that catalyze chemical reactions in cells. When foods are cooked, the increase in temperature causes proteins, including enzymes, to irreversibly unfold, losing their three-dimensional shape and inactivating them. To spare the enzymes in your food from this fate, the enzyme peddlers urge you to consume your foods raw. They suggest that the enzymes you eat are then free to carry out their functions in your stomach, thus saving your own body from producing digestive enzymes. Sounds intriguing, doesn't it? Of course, since most of us like at least some of our foods cooked, they are willing to sell us "enzyme supplements" for a rather substantial price, although what these enzymes are and what chemical reactions they catalyze are generally not revealed.

Considering what we know about enzymes, do these ideas make sense? A typical cell may have 10,000 different enzymes, each performing a specific role in the cell. For example, enzymes may be making a DNA polymer, breaking down glucose, producing hormones, or synthesizing cholesterol; just about everything a cell does is catalyzed by an enzyme. A large proportion of the enzymes in a cell are in the cytoplasm or nucleus, where the pH is around 7. What is going to happen to these enzymes when they complete their journey from our mouths to our stomachs? Parietal cells (http://arbl.cvmbs.colostate.edu/hbooks/pathphys/digestion/stomach/parietal.html) secrete hydrochloric acid, producing a pH of 2, which is 100,000 times more acidic than the cytoplasm. Only a few digestive enzymes, specifically made to function in this extreme condition, are able to work in the stomach. When the enzymes in raw food or in enzyme supplements reach the stomach, the acidic pH will unfold them and permanently inactivate them. Thus, they will suffer the fate of all of the proteins that you eat: digestive enzymes (http://arbl.cvmbs.colostate.edu/hbooks/pathphys/digestion/stomach/pepsin.html) that your cells secrete into the stomach and small intestine will break down the protein into amino acids that your cells can absorb and use to make their own proteins. The enzyme supplements might provide a source of dietary protein, but they are not going to be able to perform any enzymatic role. It would be much cheaper, and probably safer, to simply get the protein you need from a carton of yogurt or a can of beans.

Understanding biology not only makes the world around you more enjoyable as you begin to understand the intricacies of what it means to be alive. When it comes to "enzyme supplements," understanding the basic features of biology might just save you a bundle of cash!

1. Cystic fibrosis does not only affect lungs. Another characteristic of the disease is the inability to secrete digestive enzymes from the pancreas into the small intestine. Most digestion actually takes place there, rather than in the stomach, so cystic fibrosis patients take enzyme supplements to aid digestion. These enzymes are sealed in capsules that are enteric-coated, so that the capsule doesn't break down and release enzymes until it reaches the small intestine. Why is it essential that the capsules don't release the enzymes in the stomach?

2. From what you know about enzymes, why is it important to control a fever?

BIZARRE FACTS IN BIOLOGY

Firefly in a Test Tube

A test for bacterial contamination uses the glow produced in fireflies to look for possible "hot spots" of bacterial growth. Companies have even developed portable luminometers to check for bacterial growth in water, on food-handling surfaces, and following sewage remediation.

How does this work? This technology is known as ATP (adenosine triphosphate) bioluminescence. As you learned in this chapter, ATP is a high-energy molecule that is produced and used as "energy currency" in all types of cells. Bioluminescence refers to the production of light by living organisms, such as the firefly, certain bacteria, and many aquatic organisms. These organisms give off light for a variety of reasons—to escape predators, to attract prey, and to catch the attention of mates.

So what is ATP bioluminescence? How can the amount of bacteria on a surface or in water be measured quickly and economically? By using the same reaction that nature had developed for the firefly (http://iris.biosci.ohio-state.edu/projects/FFiles/frfact.html) and other bioluminescent organisms! The firefly uses a combination of a substrate, luciferin (http://www.lifesci.ucsb.edu/~biolum/chem/), and an enzyme, luciferase. Electrons are removed from luciferin by the enzyme, luciferase, to produce oxyluciferin and light. The reaction is dependent on ATP. All cells make and use ATP as a source of energy. The amount of light emitted in the reaction can be measured and is directly proportional to the amount of ATP, and therefore, the number of cells.

A luciferin is a general term used for compounds that have light-emitting capabilities. Bioluminescent organisms (http://www.hboi.edu/gallery/photoarchive/bio_gallery_1.html) produce diverse colors of light because their luciferin and luciferase are chemically different from each other.

An interesting fact is that this light-emitting reaction is very efficient. Very little energy is lost as heat, and so the production of light is referred to as "cold light" (http://www.inhs.uiuc.edu/chf/pub/surveyreports/autumn-01/firefly.html).

1. Normally, only about 10% of the energy in a lightbulb is emitted as light. The remainder is heat. What would happen if bioluminescent organisms were not efficient at producing light?

2. In a similar type of reaction, a protein called an aequorin (http://www.interchim.fr/bio/molprobes/cd/docs/sections/2005.htm) in jellyfish uses calcium instead of ATP for bioluminescence. In this reaction, what would high levels of bioluminescence indicate?

KEY TERMS

activation energy
active site
adenosine diphosphate (ADP)
adenosine triphosphate (ATP)
allosteric regulation
catalyst

chemical reaction
coenzyme
competitive inhibition
coupled reaction
electron carrier
endergonic
energy
energy-carrier molecule

entropy
enzyme
exergonic
feedback inhibition
first law of thermodynamics
kinetic energy
laws of thermodynamics

metabolic pathway
metabolism
potential energy
product
reactant
second law of thermodynamics
substrate

ANSWER KEY

SELF TEST

1. c
2. c
3. b
4. b
5. b
6. e
7. c
8. b
9. c
10. c
11. d
12. a
13. a
14. c
15. d
16. b
17. b
18. c
19. d
20. c
21. a
22. d
23. d
24. b
25. c
26. kinetic energy
27. entropy
28. chemical reaction
29. ATP
30. metabolism
31. enzymes

32. A. ADP
    B. phosphate
    C. ATP
33. A. activation energy without catalyst
    B. activation energy with catalyst
34. A. enzyme
    B. enzyme active site
    C. substrates
    D. product
35. A. substrates enter active site in a specific orientation
    B. substrates and active site change shape, promoting reaction between substrates
    C. substrates bound together, leave enzyme; enzyme ready for new set of substrates.

ESSAY CHALLENGE

1. Exergonic reactions provide the energy needed to drive endergonic reactions.
2. 1) they speed up reactions; 2) they can speed up only those reactions that would occur spontaneously anyway, but at a much slower rate; 3) they are not consumed in the reactions they promote
3. 1) the substrate enters the active site of the enzyme based on the structure of both; 2) the active site and substrate both change shape and react with each other; 3) when the final reactions are finished, the products are expelled and the enzyme reverts to its original shape
4. Most enzymes function best between pH 6–8 and at body temperature. Extremes in pH and temperature tend to break down the structure of enzymes, making them unable to bind to their substrates, and therefore useless.

5. Because phosphofructokinase catalyzes a reaction early in the glycolytic pathway, glycolysis will be "shut off" if cellular ATP levels are high. This is a form of allosteric inhibition. However, if ATP levels are low, and ADP levels are high, glycolysis will be "turned on" allosterically by ADP. This ability to precisely control glycolysis enables the cell to respond to changing conditions and use its resources efficiently.

6. Most enzymes will denature at high temperatures. These extreme bacteria have enzymes that are stable at high temperatures.

7. If the substrate is bound to the active site of the enzyme, the temporary bonds will help to maintain the enzyme's three-dimensional structure.

8. ATP does not cross cell membranes and is not stored by cells. Each cell needs to make its own supply of ATP. This is accomplished mainly by the process of cell respiration.

9. Recall that ATP is made by cell respiration in mitochondria. These poisons are uncouplers because they dissociate the endergonic reaction of ATP formation from the exergonic reaction of cell respiration. The lack of ATP production would have devastating effects on metabolism because ATP is the energy currency of the cell. If the uncoupler is in high enough concentrations, immediate death will result.

MEDIA ACTIVITIES

6.4 Web Investigation: Energy Unleashed

1. The answer is a number based upon a a student calculation that incorporates personal data.

2. The answer is a student calculation of calories that would be consumed during a running activity.

3. Answers will vary depending on student weight.

4. This is a student calculation of minutes of running needed to burn off calories consumed.

5. Long distance runners should consume 1 liter of fluid for every liter lost during a race. The rate of sweat loss by a runner can be determined before a race by using the USATF Self-Testing Program for Optimal Hydration.

ISSUES IN BIOLOGY

1. These enzymes would not function in the acidic environment of the stomach. Food would not be properly digested and absorbed.

2. Enzymes are very sensitive to changes in temperature. If the fever is too high, the enzyme will lose its three-dimensional shape and cease to function.

BIZARRE FACTS IN BIOLOGY

1. The organism would become too hot, possibly denaturing metabolic enzymes and causing death.

2. This aequorin is used in a similar way to determine the amounts of calcium present in a biological system.

CHAPTER 7: CAPTURING SOLAR ENERGY: PHOTOSYNTHESIS

AT-A-GLANCE

SELF TEST

1. In most land plants, photosynthesis occurs in cells of the _____ of the leaves, because these cells contain the largest numbers of chloroplasts.
   a. epidermis
   b. stomata
   c. cuticle
   d. mesophyll
   e. vascular bundles

2. Light energy is initially captured by "photosystems" within thylakoid membranes. Photosystems are organized arrays of _____.
   a. proteins
   b. chlorophyll molecules
   c. pigment molecules such as carotenoids
   d. all of the above
   e. none of the above

3. Why is carbon dioxide a key molecule in the light-independent reactions of photosynthesis?
   a. Carbon dioxide provides electrons to replace those lost by chlorophyll during the light-dependent reactions.
   b. Carbon dioxide, together with water, is the raw material for the synthesis of sugars, which are the key products of the light-independent reactions.
   c. Carbon dioxide inhibits the light-independent reactions of photosynthesis.
   d. Carbon dioxide is the major product of the light-independent reactions of photosynthesis.

4. What is photorespiration?
   a. Photorespiration is the process by which plants produce energy at night.
   b. Photorespiration is the process by which plant cells cool off in hot climates.
   c. Photorespiration is the process that prevents sugar production in C_3 plants when CO_2 levels are low and O_2 levels are high.
   d. Photorespiration is the process by which plants capture light energy and convert it into ATP.

5. In the light-dependent reactions of photosynthesis, ATP is produced by chemiosmosis. Describe this process.
   a. Chemiosmosis is the process by which water moves across a semipermeable membrane.
   b. As high-energy electrons move from carrier to carrier in the electron transport system of the thylakoid membrane, some of the energy is captured to pump hydrogen ions across it.
   c. When light strikes the chlorophyll molecules, water is moved via osmosis across the chloroplast membrane. When water moves back across the membrane, ATP is generated.

6. A lovely tree called the flowering plum has beautiful pink flowers in spring and deep-purple leaves in summer. What types of pigments are plentiful in this plant? Can photosynthesis occur in these purple leaves? Explain your answer.

   a. The leaves probably contain a high amount of phycocyanins and carotenoids and less chlorophyll than do plants with green leaves. They can still perform photosynthesis, because photosynthesis can occur to some extent at all wavelengths of light.

   b. The leaves probably contain a high amount of chlorophyll and carotenoids and lesser amounts of phycocyanins than do plants with green leaves.

   c. The leaves probably contain a high amount of carotenoids and lesser amounts of phycocyanins and chlorophyll than do plants with green leaves.

7. Take a deep breath and slowly exhale. The oxygen in that breath is being used by your mitochondria in reactions that produce ATP from sugars and other food molecules you ate. Where did that oxygen come from originally?

   a. The oxygen in the atmosphere is produced by the breakdown of carbon dioxide during photosynthesis.

   b. Plants produce the oxygen via the process of photorespiration when they break down sugars in their mitochondria.

   c. The oxygen in the air is produced by the splitting of water during the light-dependent reactions of photosynthesis.

   d. Plants produce the oxygen via the process of photorespiration, in which they break down sugars at night when photosynthesis cannot occur.

8. A scientist studying photosynthesis illuminated a culture of algae with bright visible light. She then turned out the light and simultaneously began to bubble radioactive CO_2 gas into the culture. After 30 minutes, she stopped the reaction and measured the amount of radioactivity inside the cells. What did she find? Explain your answer.

   a. There was no radioactivity inside the cells, because the CO_2 is used to produce O_2 in the light-dependent reactions. Thus, there was radioactivity in the air above the culture but not in the cells.

   b. There was radioactivity in the cells, because the CO_2 is used to synthesize sugar, even in the dark.

   c. There was no radioactivity in the cells, because light is required to produce sugars from CO_2 and water.

   d. There was radioactivity inside the cells, because CO_2 is used to replace the electrons that were lost by chlorophyll when the lights were turned on.

9. Imagine that you are trying to set up a large fish tank and want to select a colored light that will show off the fish to best advantage but will also allow the green plants in the tank to grow and stay healthy. You decide to measure the efficiency of photosynthesis by looking at the production of oxygen bubbles on the leaves (see Figure 7-5). At first, you use a white fluorescent lamp and see many oxygen bubbles on the leaves, indicating that photosynthesis is occurring normally. Next, you put a sheet of green cellophane between the white light and the water so that the light coming through to the tank appears green. Will the oxygen bubbles remain the same, increase, decrease, or disappear? Explain your answer.

   a. The bubbles will remain constant because photosynthesis can occur to some extent at all visible wavelengths of light.

   b. The bubbles will increase; because chlorophyll is green, photosynthesis will work best if leaves are exposed to green light.

   c. The bubbles will decrease, because green light cannot be absorbed by chlorophyll.

   d. The bubbles will disappear, because photosynthesis cannot occur in green light.

10. Which of the following is a true statement about photosynthesis?

    a. In photosynthesis, inorganic molecules such as carbon dioxide and water react to produce organic, energy-rich molecules such as glucose.

    b. In photosynthesis, oxygen is used to help break down glucose.

    c. Photosynthesis is an exergonic reaction.

    d. Photosynthesis is a process that is carried out primarily by autotrophic prokaryotic bacteria.

11. Leaves include a number of structural modifications for the purpose of photosynthesis, including _____.

    a. adjustable openings in the surface of the leaf that permit the passage of carbon dioxide, water, and oxygen

    b. a waxy covering on the surface of the leaf that is designed to reduce evaporation

    c. photosynthetic mitochondria

    d. Both the first and second answers are correct.

12. During photosynthesis, electrons are continuously lost from the reaction center of photosystem II. What source is used to replace these electrons?

    a. sunlight

    b. oxygen

    c. water

    d. carbon dioxide

13. The term *carbon fixation* refers to _____.
    a. the loss of carbon during glucose synthesis
    b. the incorporation of atmospheric carbon dioxide into a larger organic molecule
    c. the synthesis of glyceraldehyde-3-phosphate
    d. the regeneration of ribulose bisphosphate

14. Photorespiration occurs when _____.
    a. oxygen is combined with ribulose bisphosphate
    b. carbon dioxide is combined with ribulose bisphosphate
    c. stomata are closed
    d. Both the first and third answers are correct.

15. How have C_4 plants adapted to environmental conditions that would result in increased photorespiration?
    a. C_4 plants have substituted phophoenolpyruvate (PEP) for ribulose bisphosphate.
    b. PEP specifically combines with carbon dioxide even in the face of high oxygen concentrations.
    c. A molecule transports the fixed carbon into a cell type where the normal C_3 synthetic metabolism would be favored due to the now high concentrations of carbon dioxide.
    d. all of the above

16. The stomata _____.
    a. allow oxygen to exit
    b. allow carbon dioxide to enter
    c. allow light to enter
    d. allow excess heat to exit
    e. The first two answers are correct.

17. You have just discovered a new plant with red-orange leaves. What wavelengths of visible light are NOT being absorbed by this pigment?
    a. green, blue, and violet
    b. green and yellow
    c. green
    d. red and orange
    e. blue and violet

18. In the light-dependent reactions of photosynthesis the difference in hydrogen ion concentration across the thylakoid membrane is used to generate _____.
    a. NADPH
    b. glucose
    c. $FADH_2$
    d. ATP
    e. oxygen

19. Which of the following represents the products of the light-dependent reactions of photosynthesis? For what process are these products needed?
    a. ATP and oxygen; photosystem I
    b. NADPH and glucose; light-independent reactions
    c. carbon dioxide and water; Calvin-Benson cycle
    d. NADH and ADP; cellular respiration
    e. NADPH and ATP; Calvin-Benson cycle

20. Which of the following is NOT required for the light-independent reactions of photosynthesis?
    a. ATP
    b. stroma
    c. NADPH
    d. CO_2
    e. H_2O
    f. O_2

21. _____ converts the energy of sunlight into chemical energy.

22. _____ are organisms that can produce their own food in their cells.

23. Photosynthesis takes place within _____.

24. In the _____, light energy is converted to chemical energy in the form of ATP and NADPH.

25. In the _____, chemical energy is used to drive the formation of glucose.

26. _____ is the key light-capturing molecule found in chloroplasts.

27. Complete the following cycle of reactions.

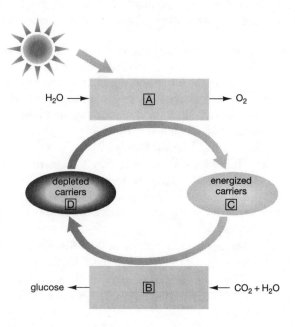

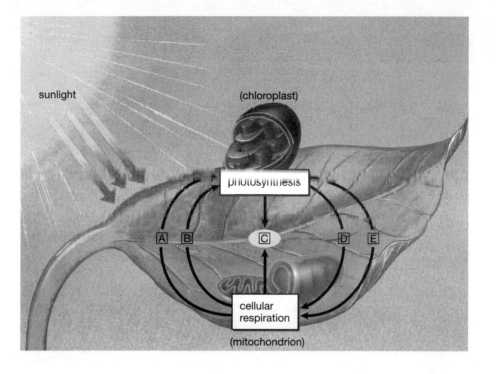

28. Using the image above, provide the connections between photosynthesis and cellular respiration.

29. Label the structures in this cross section of a leaf shown below.

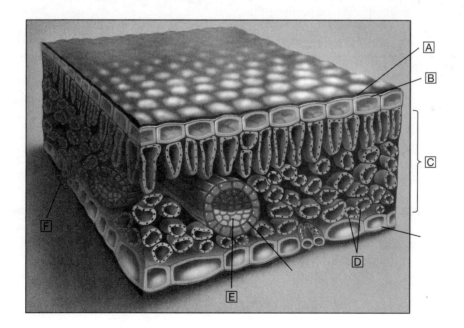

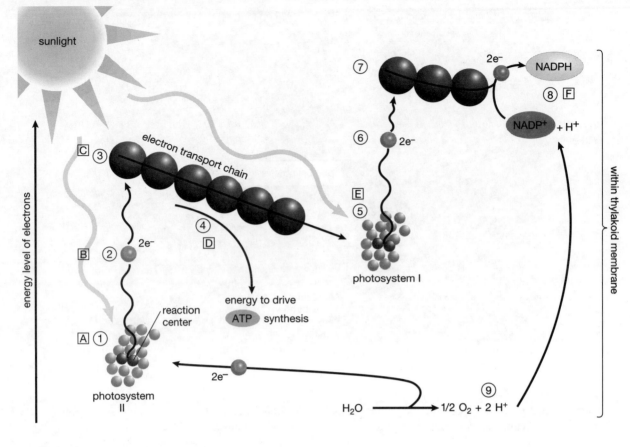

30. Above is a diagram of light-dependent reactions of photosynthesis. Place the descriptions of the steps in this process next to the appropriate portion of the diagram.

ESSAY CHALLENGE

1. When light strikes an object, what determines how our eyes perceive the color of that object?

2. How do the light-dependent reactions of photosynthesis convert solar energy to chemical energy?

3. Describe the Calvin-Benson cycle.

4. How are the light-dependent and light-independent reactions of photosynthesis related to each other?

5. Suppose you have a mutant plant that lacks the enzyme that is necessary to regenerate RuBP. What will occur?

6. Will photosynthesis continue indefinitely in the light with no CO_2? Why or why not?

7. If you were to examine the cells of an onion bulb you would find no chloroplasts. Will mitochondria be present? How do plant cells that do not contain chloroplasts survive?

8. You are performing an experiment in which you are collecting the products of photosynthesis. What reactant(s) would you need to begin with if you wanted to collect glucose that has radioactive carbon atoms?

9. You planted your seedlings in the early spring and went on vacation. Unfortunately, there was a hot, dry spell. Your neighbor forgot to water your new plants. Even though there was plenty of sun, the seedlings did not thrive. If you tested the seedlings for starch, what would you observe?

MEDIA ACTIVITIES

To access a Media Activity visit http://www.prenhall.com/audesirk7. Log in to the Web site selected by your instructor, navigate to this chapter, and select the appropriate Media Activity number.

7.1 Properties of Light
Estimated time: 5 minutes

Explore the properties of light and how light is captured by chloroplasts to power photosynthesis.

7.2 Photosynthesis
Estimated time: 10 minutes

Explore the process of photosynthesis in detail.

7.3 Chemiosmosis
Estimated time: 5 minutes

Review an elegant test of chemiosmotic hypothesis, which successfully demonstrated that a proton gradient can lead to ATP production.

7.4 Web Investigation: Did the Dinosaurs Die from Lack of Sunlight?
Estimated time: 10 minutes

While most people view the death of the dinosaurs as a unique biological disaster, geological records suggest that global mass extinctions have occurred several times. In the past 200 years more species have become extinct than in many previous millennia. This exercise will examine the causes of some modern extinctions in the hope that they might shed some light on the other mass extinctions, including the one that ended the age of dinosaurs.

1. What killed the dinosaurs? (http://www.ucmp.berkeley.edu/diapsids/extinctheory.html) There are two current theories. What do they have in common? How do they differ?

2. The Dodo Bird (http://www.bagheera.com/inthewild/ext_dodobird.htm) was hunted to extinction by men, pigs, and rats less than 100 years after it was first discovered (http://www.tombtown.com/bios/dodo.htm), but it has taken more than 300 years for some of the secondary biological repercussions to become apparent. What are they?

3. Even if all poaching was stopped, giant pandas (http://www.panda.org/resources/publications/species/threatened/giantpanda/index.htm) would still have a problem, and it is one that the dinosaurs might have faced too. What is it?

4. The Dwarf Wedgemussel (http://www.nwf.org/keepthewildalive/mussel/) may be only a small mollusc but it is threatened by pollution, loss of an obligate host, and habitat remodeling. What attempts have been made to save it? Have the attempts worked?

5. Consider the known causes of population decline for the modern species listed above. Could similar conditions have killed the dinosaurs? Has this exploration caused you to favor one of the current dinosaur extinction theories over the other?

ISSUES IN BIOLOGY

How Is Our Red Blood Related to Chlorophyll?

Chlorophyll is responsible for the beautiful green color of the plants around us, but did you realize that a molecule very similar to chlorophyll is also responsible for the red color of your blood? The chlorophyll molecule has a complex ring structure that binds a magnesium ion in its center. This basic structure is known as a porphyrin ring. A porphyrin ring is also at the heart of a molecule called heme, which carries oxygen from our lungs and delivers it to cells throughout our body. However, instead of magnesium, heme binds to an iron ion in its center. Heme also lacks the long "tail" that is present in chlorophyll (http://www.nyu.edu/pages/mathmol/library/photo/). In our red blood cells, each heme molecule is bound to a protein called globin, forming hemoglobin (http://www.psc.edu/MetaCenter/MetaScience/Articles/Ho/Ho-hemoglobin.html). Heme absorbs yellow and green light, so it appears red, giving our blood its characteristic deep crimson color.

Red blood cells live only about 120 days. Each day, about a billion red blood cells finish out their life span and are destroyed in the spleen, liver, and bone marrow. The globin in these cells is broken down to amino acids, to be used for making other proteins. The iron from the heme is rescued and conserved in the body's iron stores, so it is available to make more heme. Interestingly, the heme itself is broken down and excreted out of the body! A major intermediate in heme degradation (http://www-medlib.med.utah.edu/NetBiochem/hi7.htm), bilirubin, is produced by the liver. Instead of the red color characteristic of heme, bilirubin absorbs different wavelengths of light so that it appears yellowish. The excess production of bilirubin produces noticeable yellowing of the skin and whites of the eye in individuals with jaundice. You can also see the first stages of heme degradation when a bruise changes color (http://www.medicinenet.com/Script/Main/art.asp?li=MNI&ArticleKey=302&page=1#3whatdoes) from purple to yellow as the heme is broken down to bilirubin in the wounded tissue. If you have had a bruise that is greenish in color, the bilirubin has undergone alterations for biliverdin, which has a greenish color.

Bilirubin is normally secreted in the bile that the liver produces and dumps into the intestine to aid in digestion. Bacteria in the intestine further break down or modify the bilirubin, producing waste products that exit in feces and urine. In fact, the yellow or brown color of our wastes is produced by these products of heme digestion.

So what happens to the chlorophyll that we eat when we consume green vegetables? You can browse the Internet and come across dozens of claims for chlorophyll as a health food. For example, it is recommended that you consume chlorophyll in the juice or extracts from the young blades of green grasses such as wheat-grass or barley. Because of the similarity of chlorophyll and heme structure, the claims of the benefits of chlorophyll may seem plausible. Perhaps chlorophyll in our diet can save our cells some time and effort in making all those heme molecules to fill up the billions of red blood cells that our body produces every day. Among several assumptions, this idea presumes that increased heme production will result in production of more red blood cells, thus helping to treat conditions such as anemia. However, even the heme made in our own bodies is not reused but instead is broken down and excreted. Consequently, it is very unlikely that the chlorophyll we eat with our veggies does much more than pass through our system. In fact, consistent with this possibility, one warning about a potential side effect of chlorophyll supplements is that they can turn your feces green! This example illustrates how difficult it can be to separate fact from fiction, particularly when the fiction is mixed with truths. So when you need to make important decisions about your health and well-being, a distinct advantage can be a healthy dose of skepticism.

1. How can you determine whether or not to trust sources of information about health, diet, and disease treatments? For example, is an important consideration whether or not the information source is making money from selling the advised supplement or treatment?

2. Examine the structure of chlorophyll and heme. How can two molecules that do such apparently different tasks as chlorophyll and heme be so similar in structure?

3. Why do plant cells make chlorophyll, but not heme? Why do animal cells make heme, but not chlorophyll?

BIZARRE FACTS IN BIOLOGY

Striped Plants

Some plants are available, not only in solid green shades, but also in green and white "striped" or variegated forms. Home gardeners have a variety of opinions about variegated plants, but many people appreciate variegated varieties for their uniqueness and ability to add color to a landscape. One of the most common shade-loving plants, the hosta (http://users.bestweb.net/~habitat/Hosta.htm), is named for Dr. Nicholaus Tomas Host (1761–1834), physician to the Emperor of Austria. Hostas are easy to grow, thrive in the shade and are available in many sizes, textures, shapes, and colors, including variegated varieties. A common observation among gardeners is that variegated hosta have a slower growth rate and a greater tendency for pest infestations when compared to the solid green hosta.

1. Does any change in leaf color indicate variegation? What qualifies as variegation (http://www.plant-nurseries. com/Tony/variegated.html) in plants?

2. What causes variegation (http://faculty.ucc.edu/biology-ombrello/POW/variegated plants.htm) in a plant?

3. Sometimes a change in leaf color is due to a nutrient deficiency. What effect will a magnesium deficiency (http://www.ehs.calpoly.edu/ehs/ehs327/pages/nutbd.html) have on a plant? Study the structure of chlorophyll (http://www.tlchm.bris.ac.uk/motm/chlorophyll/chlorophyll h.htm) to understand why this deficiency affects leaf color.

4. Explain why variegated plants are slower growing (http://esa.confex.com/esa/2001/techprogram/paper 1793.htm) and more susceptible to pests.

5. A study has been done relating CO_2 levels to plant growth in both variegated and green varieties. If CO_2 levels continue to rise in the atmosphere, how would variegated plants respond (http://www.co2science.org/journal/2001/v4n16b2.htm)?

KEY TERMS

C_3 cycle
C_4 pathway
Calvin-Benson cycle
carbon fixation
carotenoids

chemiosmosis
chlorophyll
electron transport chain
grana
light-dependent reactions

light-independent
  reactions
photon
photorespiration
photosynthesis

photosystems
reaction center
stomata
stroma
thylakoid

ANSWER KEY

SELF TEST

1. d
2. d
3. b
4. c
5. b
6. a
7. c
8. b
9. c
10. a
11. d
12. c
13. b
14. d
15. d
16. e
17. d
18. d
19. e
20. f
21. photosynthesis
22. autotrophs
23. chloroplasts
24. light-dependent reactions
25. light-independent reactions
26. chlorophyll
27. A. light-dependent reactions
    B. light-independent reactions
    C. ATP, NADPH
    D. ADP, NADP+
28. A. water
    B. carbon dioxide
    C. ATP
    D. sugar
    E. oxygen

29. A. cuticle
    B. upper epidermis
    C. mesophyll cells
    D. chloroplasts
    E. stoma
30. A. light is absorbed by the light harvesting complex of photosystem II and energy is passed to the reaction center chlorophyll molecule
    B. electrons are ejected out of the energy center
    C. electrons are passed to the electron transport system
    D. due to the action of the electron transport system, a hydrogen gradient is created in thylakoids generating ATP
    E. light strikes photosystem I causing it to emit electrons
    F. the electrons from photosystem I are captured in an electron transport system and used to create NADPH

ESSAY CHALLENGE

1. The light that is reflected is the light that is seen, and therefore gives an object its color.
2. 1) The reaction center of each photosystem absorbs light energy and energizes electrons; 2) Photosystem II passes the energized electrons through a transport system which produces ATP; 3) Photosystem I uses the energized electrons to reduce $NADP^+$ into NADPH; 4) water is split to replace the electrons in the reaction center of each photosystem and oxygen is released.
3. 1) Carbon fixation: enzymes combine six RuBP molecules with CO_2 from the atmosphere; 2) synthesis of G3P: energy from ATP and NADPH is used to convert PGA to G3P; 3) regeneration of RuBP: ATP is used to regenerate the six RuBP molecules.

4. The light-dependent reactions produce the energy, in the form of ATP and NADPH, that is needed to fuel the light-independent reactions.

5. No RuBP will be available to fix carbon, and no sugar will be synthesized. The plants will die as seedlings, as soon as the stored starch in the seed is depleted.

6. The light-dependent reactions of photosynthesis will continue for awhile. However, no sugars can be synthesized in the light-independent reactions until carbon dioxide is present. Eventually, the light-dependent reactions will cease if NADP and ADP are not regenerated.

7. All eukaryotic cells, including plant cells, contain mitochondria. Plant cells that do not contain chloroplasts receive sugars from the green leafy part of the plant.

8. You will need to begin the reaction with carbon dioxide that is radioactively labeled on the carbon atom.

9. During hot, dry weather, stomata are closed and CO_2 cannot enter. Photorespiration occurs, and no glucose is produced. Little starch will be evident.

MEDIA ACTIVITIES

7.4 Web Investigation: Did Dinosaurs Die from Lack of Sunlight?

1. Both theories agree that there was a permanent global climatic change and most likely a massive terrestrial disturbance. Many organisms went extinct as a result. "Intrinsic Gradualists" believe that the cause of extinction was of an earthly nature and gradual. "Extrinsic Gradualists" believe that the cause of the extinction was of an extraterrestrial nature, and fairly sudden.

2. A particular species of tree was dependent on the dodo bird for reproduction. The dodo ate the fruit of this tree, and only by passing through the dodo's digestive system were the seeds able to grow.

3. Habitat destruction would be the greatest threat to the pandas if all poaching was stopped. Logging and forest clearance have significantly reduced the available habitat for the Giant Panda.

4. By planting and maintaining native floodplain forests on your riverside property, you can help to reduce the amount of silt and runoff that enter the waterways. Also, in preventing livestock and/or crops from encroaching on the riverbanks you can help to reduce erosion and pollution. Additionally, the U.S. Fish and Wildlife Service runs a Partners for Fish and Wildlife program that provides technical assistance to private landowners who would like to restore riverside habitat for the dwarf wedge mussel.

5. Loss of habitat as a result of a global climate change could have killed the dinosaurs. The remainder of the answer is based on individual opinion.

ISSUES IN BIOLOGY

1. The study may be biased if it is supported by a company or organization that may profit from the supplement or treatment. The best sources of information are primary sources that report on independent studies.

2. Both molecules contain a porphyrin ring. Chlorophyll has a magnesium atom at the center of the ring, and hemoglobin has an iron atom. Hemoglobin is a protein, whereas chlorophyll is a hydrocarbon. Both molecules are colored compounds.

3. The chlorophyll contained within plants cells absorbs light energy and converts it to chemical energy in the form of carbohydrate during photosynthesis. Oxygen is released in the process. Hemoglobin, found in the red blood cells of animals, has the ability to bind oxygen. The oxygen is transported throughout the bloodstream to the tissues, where it is used in the process of cell respiration to make ATP.

BIZARRE FACTS IN BIOLOGY

1. Variegation occurs in plants when the normal green portion of the plant is replaced by another color, generally white or off-white. The variegations may occur on the edge or center of the leaf, and be in the form of splotches or stripes.

2. Most often, variegation occurs as a genetically inherited trait in which the plant loses its ability to produce any pigment in an area of the plant.

3. A loss of chlorophyll, or chlorosis, is the result of a magnesium deficiency. Note that the magnesium atom is part of the chlorophyll molecule.

4. The lack of chlorophyll makes the plant less able to provide carbohydrates it requires. Because it is slower growing, it is unable to replace leaf tissue that has been damaged by pests.

5. If CO_2 levels accumulate, both green and variegated plants would respond with an increase in photosynthetic activity. Eventually, the green plants will acclimate to the increased CO_2 levels, and reduce the rate of photosynthesis. However, the variegated plants will continue to photosynthesize at high rates, perhaps because the leaf tissue sections that lack chlorophyll serve as substantial sinks for sugars produced in photosynthesis.

CHAPTER 8: HARVESTING ENERGY: GLYCOLYSIS AND CELLULAR RESPIRATION

AT-A-GLANCE

SELF TEST

1. Photosynthesis and glucose metabolism are related because _____.
   a. the products of photosynthesis are the raw materials for glucose metabolism
   b. the products of glucose metabolism are the raw materials for photosynthesis
   c. the products of photosynthesis are the same as the products of glucose metabolism
   d. the raw materials of photosynthesis are the same as the raw materials of glucose metabolism
   e. Both the first and second answers are correct.

2. Glycolysis is _____.
   a. the breakdown of starch to form glucose
   b. the synthesis of glucose from two molecules of pyruvate
   c. the breakdown of glucose to form two molecules of pyruvate
   d. the synthesis of pyruvate in mitochondria
   e. the lysis of glucose in chloroplasts

3. Which of the following statements concerning fermentation is (are) true?
   a. Fermentation occurs in either aerobic or anaerobic conditions.
   b. Fermentation, like glycolysis, occurs in the cytoplasm of cells.
   c. Fermentation produces additional ATP.
   d. The end product of fermentation in human cells is ethanol.
   e. all of the above
   f. none of the above

4. The energy-harvesting reactions of glycolysis produce two molecules of _____, two molecules of _____, and two molecules of _____.
   a. ATP, glyceraldehyde-3-phosphate, pyruvate
   b. ATP, NADH, pyruvate
   c. glucose, carbon dioxide, water
   d. pyruvate, glyceraldehyde-3-phosphate, water

5. In aerobic organisms growing in the presence of oxygen, the NADH produced by glycolysis ultimately donates its high-energy electrons to _____.
   a. electron transport chains in the mitochondria
   b. glucose
   c. pyruvate
   d. ATP

6. Respiration is the process of gas exchange (breathing in oxygen and breathing out carbon dioxide); cellular respiration is the process of _____.
   a. cellular gas exchange
   b. cellular cooling
   c. production of ATP via the electron transport system
   d. cellular reproduction

7. How is the oxygen that is breathed in during respiration used in cellular respiration?
   a. Oxygen is converted into CO_2 and breathed out.
   b. Oxygen is converted into ATP.
   c. Oxygen is the final electron acceptor of the electron transport system.
   d. Oxygen is used to produce glucose.

8. In eukaryotic cells, glycolysis occurs in the _____, and cellular respiration occurs in the _____.
   a. mitochondria, cytoplasm
   b. cytoplasm, mitochondria
   c. cytoplasm, chloroplasts
   d. chloroplasts, mitochondria

9. In eukaryotic cells, the enzymes for the Krebs cycle are located in the _____, and those for the electron transport system are located in the _____.
   a. cytoplasm, cell wall
   b. cytoplasm, mitochondrial matrix
   c. plasma membrane, cytoplasm
   d. mitochondrial matrix, inner mitochondrial membrane
   e. inner mitochondrial membrane, matrix

10. In eukaryotic cells, pyruvate produced by glycolysis is transported into the mitochondrial matrix, where _____.
    a. enzymes for the Krebs cycle break down the pyruvate, producing CO_2 as a waste product
    b. the electron transport system recombines pyruvate molecules to produce glucose
    c. enzymes for the Krebs cycle convert the pyruvate into alcohol or lactate
    d. the electron transport system breaks down the pyruvate, producing CO_2 as a waste product

11. As high-energy electrons are passed from carrier to carrier along the electron transport system in cellular respiration, the electrons lose energy. Some of that energy is *directly* used to _____.
    a. synthesize glucose
    b. break down glucose
    c. pump hydrogen ions across a membrane
    d. synthesize ATP

12. In eukaryotes, during the process of chemiosmosis, ATP is produced as hydrogen ions move from _____ to _____, passing through _____.
    a. the intermembrane compartment, the matrix, ATP synthase
    b. the matrix, the intermembrane compartment, ATP synthase
    c. the cytoplasm, the matrix, the electron transport system
    d. the matrix, the cytoplasm, the Krebs cycle

13. Why does death result from any situation that prevents a person from breathing?
    a. Oxygen is needed for cellular respiration, so lack of oxygen prevents cells from making sufficient ATP for essential cellular functions. Cells die as a result, eventually leading to death of the individual.
    b. Glycolysis requires oxygen in order to produce ATP, so lack of oxygen prevents cells from making sufficient ATP.
    c. Oxygen is necessary for both fermentation reactions and cellular respiration. so lack of oxygen prevents cells from making sufficient ATP.

14. The overall equation for glucose metabolism is $C_6H_{12}O_6 + 6O_2 \rightarrow 6CO_2 + 6H_2O + ATP$ and heat. The carbon atoms in the CO_2 molecules in this equation come from _____ during reactions of _____.
    a. O_2, glycolysis
    b. O_2, the electron transport system
    c. O_2, the Krebs cycle
    d. $C_6H_{12}O_6$, glycolysis
    e. $C_6H_{12}O_6$, the electron transport system
    f. $C_6H_{12}O_6$, the Krebs cycle

15. At the beginning of most recipes for bread, you are instructed to dissolve the yeast in a mixture of sugar (sucrose) and hot water, in some cases with a small amount of flour. Within a short time, this yeast mixture begins to bubble and foam, perhaps to the point of overflowing the container. What is happening?
    a. The bubbles are carbon dioxide that yeast produce as they break down the glucose and produce ATP via fermentation.
    b. The bubbles are oxygen produced by yeast as they grow.
    c. The bubbles are detergents that yeast produce to help them digest the proteins in the flour.
    d. The bubbles are water vapor produced as the hot water evaporates.

16. Where is the majority of ATP produced?
    a. in the aqueous fluid surrounding all cells
    b. in the cytoplasm of a cell
    c. in the mitochondria of a cell
    d. on the rough endoplasmic reticulum

17. Glycolysis can be broken down into what two parts?
    a. glucose activation and energy harvest
    b. fermentation and cellular respiration
    c. extracellular and intracellular events
    d. all of the above

18. How do cells recycle NADH back to NAD^+ during fermentation?
    a. by converting pyruvate to lactic acid
    b. by converting pyruvate to ethanol and carbon dioxide
    c. by converting pyruvate to acetyl CoA

19. The production of what molecule marks the end of glycolysis and the beginning of cellular respiration?
    a. Coenzyme A (CoA)
    b. acetyl CoA
    c. citrate
    d. pyruvate

20. What role is played by the electron transport chain during cellular respiration?
    a. The electron transport system takes energy from the high-energy electrons brought by electron carriers (e.g., NADH) and uses it to pump hydrogen ions against their concentration gradient from the matrix into the intermembrane compartment.
    b. The electron transport system allows hydrogen ions to diffuse down their concentration gradient from the intermembrane compartment to the matrix.
    c. The electron transport system produces ATP.
    d. all of the above

21. Why should anyone care about the importance of ATP production?
    a. Even though the production of ATP occurs within individual cells, a multicellular organism requires the energy produced to carry out vital functions essential for survival. Any organism would quickly die without constant production of ATP.
    b. The memorization of foreign-sounding biochemical terms was required by the instructor.
    c. Understanding glycolysis and cellular respiration permits insights into how different organisms manage their energy needs in different environments.
    d. Both the first and third answers are correct.

22. You are comparing two cultures of cells, one that is undergoing cellular respiration and one that is fermenting. Both cultures are producing ATP at the same rate. If this is true, what else would you observe about the fermenting culture?
    a. It would require more glucose per minute than the respiring culture.
    b. It would have a higher rate of glycolysis than the respiring culture.
    c. It would produce pyruvate at a faster rate than the respiring culture.
    d. It would require more oxygen than the respiring culture.
    e. The first three answers are correct.

23. Suppose that the reactions of mitochondria of a green plant were completely inhibited. What process would immediately stop?
    a. glycolysis
    b. fermentation
    c. photosynthesis
    d. ATP production
    e. lactate production

24. Which molecules are produced in glycolysis and used in fermentation?
    a. acetyl CoA and NADH
    b. pyruvate and NADH
    c. glucose, ATP, and NAD^+
    d. lactate, ATP, and CO_2
    e. pyruvate and ATP

25. Which pathway produces the most ATP per glucose molecule?
    a. fermentation
    b. glycolysis
    c. Krebs cycle
    d. cellular respiration
    e. electron transport and chemiosmosis

26. How many molecules of ATP would be produced from 20 molecules of glucose at the end of fermentation?

  a. 10

  b. 20

  c. 30

  d. 40

  e. 100

27. The initial reactions that break down glucose without the use of oxygen are called _____.

28. In the absence of oxygen, pyruvate acts as an electron acceptor in a process called _____.

29. _____ is a series of reactions, occurring under aerobic conditions, in which large amounts of ATP are produced.

30. If oxygen is present after glycolysis, pyruvate is transported to the mitochondria and broken down further in the _____.

31. Electrons from NADH and FADH$_2$ are deposited in the _____.

32. _____ is the process in which hydrogen ions move down their concentration gradient through ATP-synthesizing enzymes.

33. The figure below depicts an overview of glucose metabolism. Label the reactions indicated.

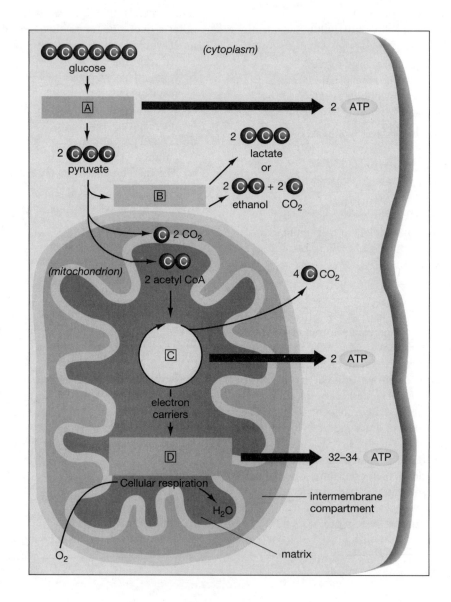

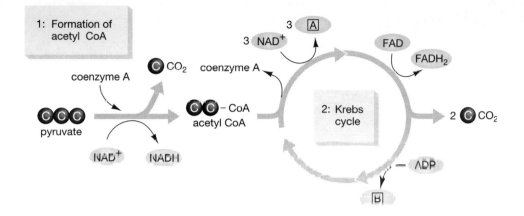

34. Two different molecules of energy storage are formed by the reaction depicted above. Match the molecule with its formation site in the reaction.

35. Glycolysis involves the breakdown of sugar. Put the correct compounds entering and exiting glycolysis in the diagram below.

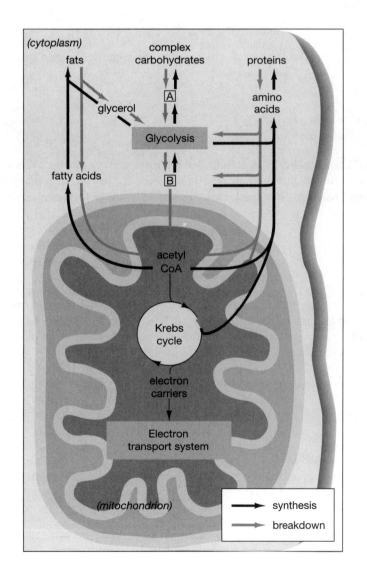

ESSAY CHALLENGE

1. In general, describe the process of glycolysis.

2. How does fermentation keep glycolysis going?

3. Compare and contrast fermentation and cellular respiration.

4. How are the three processes of glycolysis, the Krebs cycle, and the electron transport system connected to each other?

5. Suppose you are studying animal cells in culture that are metabolizing glucose. You are able to control exactly how much sugar is added to the culture. You add 50 molecules of glucose. How many molecules of ATP will be formed in the absence of oxygen? How many molecules of ATP will be formed if oxygen is available?

6. Type I diabetes results from too little circulating insulin. Insulin is a hormone that causes an increase in glucose transport into muscle and liver cells. For the patient with Type I diabetes, his/her body cells act as though they are starved of glucose, even though there are high levels of circulating glucose in the bloodstream. What is the effect of Type I diabetes on cell respiration? Be as specific as possible.

7. A patient with uncontrolled diabetes will often begin to break down fatty acids to acetyl CoA, and use acetyl CoA for cell respiration. During fat breakdown, carbon atoms are removed two carbons at a time and converted to acetyl CoA. How many NADH, $FADH_2$ and ATP will result from the breakdown of sixteen-carbon palmitic acid?

8. Suppose you are performing an experiment in which you are collecting the products of cell respiration from a culture of cells. If you begin with glucose that has radioactive carbon atoms, what product(s) from cell respiration would contain the radioactive carbon?

9. The chemiosmotic hypothesis explains the production of ATP in both photosynthesis and cell respiration as the result of a hydrogen ion gradient. Compare and contrast mitochondria and chloroplasts as to: (a) the location of the electron transport system connected to ATP production (b) the location of the buildup of H^+ ions and (c) the function of the ATP that is formed

---

MEDIA ACTIVITIES

To access a Media Activity visit http://www.prenhall.com/audesirk7. Log in to the Web site selected by your instructor, navigate to this chapter, and select the appropriate Media Activity number.

8.1   Glucose Metabolism
Estimated time: 10 minutes

Explore the mechanisms cells use to derive energy from the sugar glucose.

8.2   Interactions between Photosynthesis and Respiration
Estimated time: 10 minutes

In this exercise you will review how photosynthesis and respiration interact in a plant.

8.3   Web Investigation: The Flight of the Hummingbird
Estimated time: 10 minutes

Myth 1: Hummingbirds live on a strict diet of sugar water (nectar). Myth 2: They obtain this nectar by sucking it out of flowers using their beaks as straws. Fact: The feeding behaviors and diet of hummingbirds are perfectly adapted to their energy needs. What, how, and where do hummingbirds eat?

1. Hummingbirds draw up sugar solutions using the capillary action (http://www.cvco.org/science/audubon/hummers.html) of their unusual tongues (http://www.mschloe.com/hummer/huminfo.htm#tobill) and "filter-feeding" (http://www.portalproductions.com/h/eatinsects.htm) to trap insects. What other unique anatomical adaptation do they have that affects their feeding behavior?

2. Hummingbirds favor certain flowers (http://www.botgard.ucla.edu/html/MEMBGNewsletter/Volume3number3/Hummingbirds.html). What characteristics do these flowers have in common? How do they pick out their favorites (http://www.naturalinstinct.com/flowers.html)?

3. Baby hummingbirds (http://www.evwildlife.org/hummingbirds.htm) need a diet that is higher in protein than that of their parents. Why do you think that this is the case? Optional: For more information about hummers, check out the Interesting Facts About Hummingbirds site (http://www.humming-birds.com/facts.html).

ISSUES IN BIOLOGY

What Do Mitochondria Have to Do with Mother's Day?

Next time you are running to catch a bus, think about those wonderful mitochondria, nestled deep in the cytoplasm of nearly every cell in your body. Without them, you wouldn't be able to efficiently convert that bagel you had for breakfast into the ATP that your muscle cells need to contract properly and in the right direction. Even when you are sitting quietly on the bus, your cells require an input of energy simply to stay alive. In light of how important mitochondria are for your survival, it is perhaps startling to realize that mitochondria arose from an ancient truce between a predator cell and its prey. Our mitochondria, without which we could not survive, are actually the products of an enormously successful symbiosis (http://www.dc.peachnet.edu/~pgore/students/w96/joshbond/symb.htm) that began about 1.5 million years ago.

Look carefully at mitochondria (http://cellbio.utmb.edu/cellbio/mitoch1.htm) and you will find several clues that point to their original existence as independent, bacteria-like cells. For example, mitochondria reproduce by a type of division that appears similar to that used by bacteria (http://www.cellsalive.com/ecoli.htm). Like bacteria, mitochondria contain ribosomes (http://ntri.tamuk.edu/cell/ribosomes.html) and synthesize proteins from messages produced within them. Furthermore, each mitochondrion contains circular DNA molecules (http://cellbio.utmb.edu/cellbio/mitoch2.htm), as do bacterial cells. However, unlike bacteria whose chromosome contains several thousand genes, mitochondrial DNA contains just a few protein-encoding genes—about 13 in humans—and none of these genes are actually needed to build a mitochondrion or to help it reproduce! Instead, mitochondrial DNA encodes proteins that have essential roles in the Krebs cycle or in the electron transport system, which play key roles in harvesting the nutrients for the production of ATP. Thus, mitochondrial DNA is needed for mitochondrial function in cellular respiration, but not for mitochondrial existence.

Until fairly recently, no one would have imagined that defects in mitochondrial DNA could cause human disease. It was reasoned that, even if a mutation occurred in one of the DNA molecules, each mitochondrion has dozens of other copies that should mask the defect. Furthermore, even if all of the DNA in a single mitochondrion were mutated, cells contain many mitochondria and these should cover for the defective one sufficiently to prevent any symptoms. However, in 1988 it became clear that these assumptions were invalid when a human disease syndrome known as MERRF (http://www.ncbi.nlm.nih.gov/htbin-post/Omim/dispmim?545000.cs) was found to result from defects in mitochondrial DNA. Subsequently, a variety of human disease syndromes have been traced to defects in mitochondrial DNA (http://biocrs.biomed.brown.edu/books/Essays/MitochondrialDNA.html).

Mitochondrial diseases (http://www.neuro.wustl.edu/neuromuscular/mitosyn.html) are highly varied in terms of their onset and the range of symptoms they produce. For example, they can occur in infancy or develop later in life. They can cause symptoms ranging from muscle fatigue and weakness to death. They typically have their greatest effects on tissues with high energy demands. Consequently, symptoms of mitochondrial diseases are frequently related to brain function (stroke, epilepsy, mental retardation), to sight and hearing, and to muscle function (weakness, twitching).

However, mitochondrial DNA abnormalities have also been discovered in certain types of diabetes and are even suggested to be important for the symptoms of Alzheimer's disease and aging. Clearly, having mitochondria that function properly is essential for human health!

An interesting aspect of mitochondrial DNA is that we inherit it nearly exclusively from our mothers. Thus, your mitochondrial DNA was passed down to you from your mother, she received it from her mother, and so on. How is it possible to inherit mitochondrial DNA only from a single parent? The answer lies in the differences between your mother's and your father's cellular contribution to your initial existence. Eggs are enormous cells that are packed full of mitochondria. In contrast, sperm are tiny cells that have few mitochondria, and an egg may actively destroy (http://www.sciencenews.org/20000101/fob3.asp) the "invading" mitochondria. Evolutionary biologists have analyzed mitochondrial DNA to work out relationships between various populations of vertebrates, including humans. However, this DNA exclusively follows the maternal lineage. Some of these molecular analyses indicate that all human mitochondrial DNA in existence today can be traced back to a common maternal ancestor who lived in Africa about 100,000–200,000 years ago (http://www.actionbioscience.org/evolution/ingman.html). Of course, scientists don't think that "Mitochondrial Eve" was the ONLY woman alive at the time!

So, next time you run to catch that bus, think about mitochondria, and next Mother's Day, thank your Mom for her extra contribution to your genetic inheritance: your mitochondrial DNA (http://ahsc.arizona.edu/~msrgsn/gd/gdvol10b.htm).

1. Mitochondrial DNA can be used to trace the maternal lineage of humans and other vertebrates. What DNA would be a possible way to trace paternal lineages (at least in certain humans)?

2. During the military junta in Argentina that replaced the Peron regime, thousands of people were arrested and executed. These "disappeared" often had infants or small children who were given to various individuals, sometimes high-ranking individuals in the junta. Imagine that you wanted to reunite the children with their biological families. Could you use mitochondrial DNA analysis if only the paternal grandmother of the child in question survived? Explain.

3. Your red blood cells do not have mitochondria. Does this mean that they cannot make ATP? Explain.

BIZARRE FACTS IN BIOLOGY

Hot Plants

Estimated time: 15 minutes

There are several species of plants that not only have the ability to regulate their temperature, but also to cause it to increase, sometimes significantly higher than the environmental temperature! The ability to generate heat is called *thermogenesis*. How is the plant able to generate heat? As you have learned in Chapters 7 and 8, plants undergo both photosynthesis and cell respiration. These thermogenic plants carry out a modification of cell respiration, called the alternative respiration pathway (http://www.tau.ac.il/~ecology/virtau/2-elitsur/ey.htm#AlternativeRespiration%0D%0A) that allows them to generate a significant amount of heat energy. The ability to control temperature may give these plants several adaptive advantages (http://www.plantphysiol.org/cgi/content/full/132/1/25#Top%0D%0A). The warmth of the plant may cause the scent of its flower to become more volatile, thus attracting pollinators. The heat of the plant may promote flowering in cold weather. In some cases, thermogenesis may occur in order to provide a warm environment for pollinators.

Skunk cabbage (http://www.virtualinsectary.com/plants/plant_42.htm) is a good example of a thermogenic plant. These plants are among the first to bloom in the spring. The heat from the plant often melts the snow around them. Their flower is covered with a shell-shaped hood or spathe, and large leaves appear after the flowers have bloomed. The leaves have an odor that has been likened to decaying flesh, giving the plant its common name.

1. Read about thermogenecity (http://www.beardedman.net/science/aroids/) in skunk cabbage. What is the source of energy needed for this heat production?

2. How does the alternative electron transport pathway (http://www.acad.carleton.edu/curricular/BIOL/classes/bio359/studyguides/respiration/5respiration2.html) work? Is oxygen necessary?

3. Read about a relative to the skunk cabbage, the giant corpse flower (http://news.nationalgeographic.com/news/2003/07/0718_030718_stinkyflower.html#main). A recent specimen from the University of California-Davis Botanical Conservatory, "Ted," was studied by researchers. What was the highest temperature recorded in "Ted"? The smell of these plants is very strong. What chemicals are thought to cause the rotting corpse smell?

KEY TERMS

cellular respiration	glycolysis	Krebs cycle
chemiosmosis	intermembrane	matrix
electron transport chain	compartment	
fermentation		

ANSWER KEY

SELF TEST

1. e	10. a
2. c	11. c
3. b	12. a
4. b	13. a
5. a	14. f
6. c	15. a
7. c	16. c, d
8. b	17. a
9. d	18. d
	19. d

20. a
21. d
22. e
23. d
24. b
25. d
26. d
27. glycolysis
28. fermentation
29. cellular respiration
30. Krebs cycle
31. electron transport system
32. chemiosmosis
33. A. glycolysis
    B. fermentation
    C. Krebs cycle
    D. electron transport chain
34. A. NADH
    B. ATP
35. A. glucose
    B. pyruvate

ESSAY CHALLENGE

1. In glucose activation, glucose is "activated" by the addition of phosphates from ATP. In energy harvest, a series of reactions occurs in which the activated glucose is broken down to pyruvate, and ATP is synthesized.

2. During fermentation, pyruvate accepts electrons from NADH to produce ethanol or lactate. The regenerated NAD^+ is used to keep glycolysis going so that some ATP can be made even in the absence of oxygen.

3. Fermentation is anaerobic and produces a small amount of ATP. Cellular respiration is aerobic and produces a large amount of ATP. Both processes begin with glycolysis.

4. Pyruvate from glycolysis becomes the reactant in the steps leading to the Krebs cycle. Electron carriers from glycolysis and the Krebs cycle donate their high-energy electrons to the electron transport system. The energy from these electrons is used to generate a hydrogen ion gradient that results in the synthesis of 32-34 ATP. Oxygen acts as the final electron acceptor.

5. In the absence of oxygen, 50 glucose molecules will generate 100 ATP (2 per glucose molecule). In the presence of oxygen, 1806 (36 ATP per glucose) or 1900 (38 ATP per glucose) molecules of ATP will be generated from 50 molecules of glucose.

6. Cells will not have enough glucose for oxidation to ATP. Fatigue and mental confusion may result.

7. One acetyl CoA group will undergo one turn of the Krebs cycle, generating 3 NADH, 1 $FADH_2$, and 1 ATP. Palmitic acid breakdown will result in 8 molecules of acetyl CoA, which in turn will yield 24 NADH, 8 $FADH_2$, and 8 ATP.

8. All of the carbon atoms in glucose are converted to CO_2, so the cells will produce radioactive CO_2.

9. (a) The electron transport system for photosynthesis is located in the thylakoid membranes of the chloroplast, whereas the electron transport system used in cell respiration is located in the cristae of mitochondria. (b) Hydrogen ions accumulate in the thylakoid membrane space during photosynthesis, whereas in cell respiration, they accumulate in the intermembrane compartment of the mitochondria. (c) The ATP generated in photosynthesis is used in the light independent reactions to make carbohydrate. The ATP generated in cell respiration is used to power cell activities.

MEDIA ACTIVITIES

8.3 Web Investigation: The Flight of the Hummingbird

1. Hummingbirds have a unique anatomical wing structure that allows them to hover and fly both forwards and backwards.

2. Hummingbirds prefer brightly colored flowers, especially shades of red, and flowers with a high sugar content.

3. Baby hummingbirds need protein for proper growth and development.

ISSUES IN BIOLOGY

1. The paternal lineage can be traced in males by using the Y chromosome DNA. The Y chromosome can only be passed on from father to son. Because females have two X chromosomes, this method would not work with female offspring.

2. No. The paternal grandmother would pass on mitochondrial DNA to her son, the father of the child. However, the child would inherit mitochondrial DNA almost exclusively from his/her mother.

3. Red blood cells make ATP by using the reactions of glycolysis.

BIZARRE FACTS IN BIOLOGY

1. Large stores of carbohydrates provide the energy necessary for thermogenesis in skunk cabbage.

2. The alternative electron transport pathway is located on the inner mitochondrial membrane. In this pathway, the production of ATP is uncoupled from the flow of electrons. In these plants, heat is produced instead of ATP. This pathway still requires oxygen.

3. Ted's highest temperature was 90 degrees Fahrenheit. These plants use thermogenesis to heat up sulfur compounds that give the flower its corpse-like odor. This smell attracts pollinators, such as beetles and flies.

CHAPTER 9: DNA: THE MOLECULE OF HEREDITY

AT-A-GLANCE

Case Study: Sunshine Perils

9.1   How Did Scientists Discover That Genes Are Made of DNA?
Transformed Bacteria Revealed the Link Between Genes and DNA

9.2   What Is the Structure of DNA?
DNA Is Composed of Four Nucleotides
DNA Is a Double Helix of Two Nucleotide Strands
Hydrogen Bonds Between Complementary Bases Hold the Two DNA Strands Together
The Order of Nucleotides in DNA Can Encode Vast Amounts of Information

Scientific Inquiry: The Discovery of the Double Helix

9.3   How Does DNA Replication Ensure Genetic Constancy During Cell Division?
The Replication of DNA Is a Critical Event in a Cell's Life
DNA Replication Produces Two DNA Double Helices, Each with One Old Strand and One New Strand

A Closer Look: DNA Replication
Proofreading Produces Almost Error-Free Replication of DNA
Mistakes Do Happen

Case Study Revisited: Sunshine Perils

Links to Life: *Tyrannosaurus rex* Reborn?

SELF TEST

1. Except for eggs and sperm, different cells in your body are different because they have different _____.
   a. DNA   **b.** chromosomes
   c. proteins

2. The sugars and phosphates in the "backbone" of a DNA strand are held together by _____.
   a. covalent bonds   **b.** hydrogen bonds
   c. ionic bonds

3. The two strands of a DNA double helix are held together by _____.
   a. covalent bonds between the sugars of one nucleotide and the phosphates of the adjacent nucleotide
   b. hydrogen bonds between bases on opposite DNA strands
   c. ionic bonds between DNA and water

4. Following replication, each DNA double helix in a duplicated chromosome is organized by proteins into a structure called a _____.
   a. chromatid   **b.** chromatin
   c. chromosome

5. Mutations are changes in the_____.
   a. sugar-phosphate backbone of DNA
   b. base-pairing rules for DNA
   c. sequence of bases in DNA

6. Which of the following lists the correct order of events in DNA replication?
   a. Enzymes unwind the DNA double helix; DNA polymerase makes two new DNA strands complementary to the old ones; the two DNA molecules wind up into a double helix with one new strand and one old strand.
   b. Two DNA molecules wind up into a double helix with one new strand and one old strand; DNA polymerase makes two new DNA strands complementary to the old ones; enzymes unwind the DNA double helix.
   c. DNA polymerase makes the new DNA strands complementary to the old ones; enzymes unwind the DNA double helix; the two DNA molecules wind up into a double helix with one new strand and one old strand.

7. DNA structure can be described as a twisted ladder. Imagine you are climbing a model of DNA, just as if you were climbing a ladder. What parts of a nucleotide are your *feet* touching as you climb?
   a. the sugars   **b.** the bases
   c. the phosphates   **d.** the sugars and bases
   e. the sugars and phosphates
   f. the phosphates and bases

8. Human chromosomes range in size dramatically, with the smallest (chromosome Y) being many times smaller than the largest (chromosome 1). What is responsible for determining the size of a chromosome?
   a. the length of the DNA molecule in it
   b. the amount of protein associated with it
   c. the number of DNA molecules in it

9. How does the information carried in the sequence of bases in a DNA molecule specify a characteristic such as eye color?
   a. DNA makes a pigment that is stored in the cells of the eye.
   b. DNA encodes proteins that manufacture eye-color pigments.
   c. DNA can be blue, brown, or green, depending on the amount in the cell.

10. Imagine that you are studying a newly discovered bacterium from a hot springs in Yellowstone National Park. When you examine the nucleotide composition of this organism, you find that 10% of the nucleotides in its DNA are adenine. What percentage of nucleotides are guanine? Explain.
   a. 10%, because A pairs with G
   b. 90%, because 100% minus 10% equals 90%
   c. 40%, because A pairs with T (accounting for 20% of the bases), leaving 80% of the nucleotides as G-C base pairs; half of 80 is 40.

11. You might think that the amount of DNA should increase with the degree of complexity of an organism. If so, the total amount of DNA in a cell from an organism would be an indicator of how complex the organism is. However, organisms such as pumpkins and salamanders have more DNA than do humans, even though we are actually more complex. Propose an explanation.
   a. Salamanders and pumpkins have more DNA and therefore must encode more information in their DNA.
   b. Some of the DNA in an organism may not encode anything; salamanders and pumpkins have more of this noncoding DNA.
   c. Salamanders and pumpkins produce more types of proteins than do humans and therefore need more DNA to encode those proteins.

12. How can a cell, killed by heat in order to render it harmless, somehow still act to transform a second strain of bacterium from a noninfectious form into a disease carrier (i.e., a pathogen)?
   a. The second (noninfectious) strain of bacterium was changed into a disease carrier (i.e., pathogen) by something from the heat-killed cell.
   b. The heat-killed cell wasn't really dead.
   c. The second (noninfectious) strain spontaneously mutated into a deadly pathogen.
   d. Both the second and third answers above are correct.

13. Select the pairings of nucleotides determined by Chargaff's investigations.
   a. adenine-guanine / cytosine-thymine
   b. deoxyribose-phosphate / adenine-cytosine
   c. thymine-adenine / guanine-cytosine

14. To what does the phrase "ladder-like appearance" refer when considering the structure of DNA?
   a. double helix
   b. complementary base pairs (e.g., adenine and thymine) that are joined by hydrogen bonds
   c. DNA strand (i.e. "polymer") orientation
   d. the complementary base pairs as rungs and the sugar-phosphate backbone as the rails

15. Prior to cell division what does a "duplicated chromosome" contain?
   a. two chromatids
   b. two double helices of DNA held together at their middle
   c. a single double helix of DNA
   d. Both the first and second answers are correct.

16. Which of the following events occur within a DNA replication bubble?
   a. DNA polymerase helps to break hydrogen bonds between complementary base pairs.
   b. DNA helicase attaches the phosphate of a free nucleotide to the sugar of the previous nucleotide in the daughter strand.
   c. DNA helicase unwinds the double helix at each replication fork within a replication bubble.
   d. none of the above

17. Which of the following options would result from the actions of DNA polymerase during DNA replication?
   a. Two DNA polymerase molecules act to synthesize a long continuous daughter DNA strand from each parental strand; ligase is not needed.
   b. Two DNA polymerase molecules act to synthesize a short segment of daughter DNA strand from each parental strand; ligase is used to connect these short segments of both daughter strands.
   c. Two DNA polymerase molecules act to synthesize daughter DNA strands: one via a long continuous strand that moves in the same direction as the helicase, and a second polymerase synthesizes short segments of DNA that must be joined by ligase.
   d. none of the above

18. What is the name Watson and Crick gave to the physical structure of DNA? _____

19. _____ is the enzyme that splits the two original strands of DNA during replication.

20. Rosalind Franklin and Maurice Wilkins used _____ to help discover the physical structure of DNA.

21. As a DNA strand is duplicated, the newly created strand is called _____ to the original strand.

22. _____ light is one of the listed causes for skin cancer (melanoma).

23. Under normal circumstances, adenine will only be paired with _____ during DNA replication.

24. The four DNA nucleotides are subtly different, yet each is composed of similar subunits. On the diagram below, identify the three parts of a nucleotide.

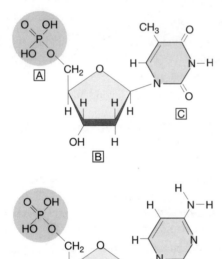

25. DNA is replicated within the nucleus. Enzymes are required to do this. Label the enzyme needed for each spot indicated on the image below.

26. Chromosomes are made of which of the following molecules?
  a. protein   **b.** DNA
  c. genes   **d.** protein and DNA
  e. protein, DNA, and genes

27. In Griffith's experiments, heating the S-strain bacteria killed them, but did not completely destroy their _____.

28. It is not the *number* of different nucleotides, but their _____ that is important in the ability of DNA to code for all the variability of organisms.

29. Why did many scientists have trouble believing that DNA could be the carrier of genetic information?
  a. DNA is a monotonous molecule with the same four nucleotides repeating over and over again.
  b. DNA has only four nucleotides, which seemed too few to encode the vast array of hereditary traits of organisms.
  c. Protein structure is innately more suited to carrying hereditary information.

30. The process by which a parent cell that is going to divide synthesizes an exact copy of its DNA is known as _____.

31. How many times is a cell's DNA replicated before it divides?
  a. once   **b.** twice
  c. three times

32. What is the approximate error rate for DNA polymerase?
  a. one error for every 100 bases added
  b. one error for every 10,000 bases added
  c. one error for every billion bases added

33. What is the approximate error rate for DNA replication?
  a. one error for every thousand nucleotides
  b. one error for every million nucleotides
  c. one error for every billion nucleotides

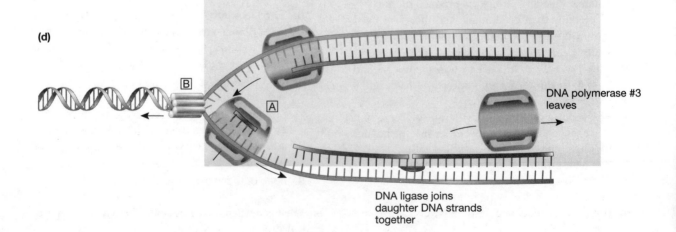

92

34. Which of the following can cause errors to accumulate in DNA?
  a. high levels of metabolic activity
  b. ultraviolet light
  c. cold temperatures
  d. None of the above are correct.

35. Which of the following can be caused by ultraviolet radiation in sunlight?
  a. Adjacent thymines become linked together.
  b. The DNA molecule is degraded from each end.
  c. DNA molecule becomes fragmented.
  d. All of the above can happen.

ESSAY CHALLENGE

1. What were some of the details that Franklin's and Wilkins's X ray diffraction experiments determined about the structure of the DNA molecule?

2. Given the information you now know about inheritance, what was responsible for the increased virulence in the R-strain of *Streptococcus pneumonia* seen by Griffith after it was mixed with heat-killed S strain?

3. Describe how the DNA replication process can be completed with such an extremely low error rate.

4. Describe the manner in which nucleotoide subunits are connected to each other to form the DNA strands.

5. If a colleague approaches you with information about the absolute amounts of adenine and cytosine in a DNA sequence, can you also determine the amounts of the other two nucleotides? Explain why, and give an example.

6. If your professor gives you a short piece of DNA with a particular sequence of nucleotides, such as (phosphate end)—TTGCTGTAGGTA—(deoxyribose end), what is the complementary strand's sequence? Identify the two ends (phosphate and deoxyribose) in your answer.

MEDIA ACTIVITIES

To access a Media Activity visit http://www.prenhall.com/audesirk7. Log in to the Web site selected by your instructor, navigate to this chapter, and select the appropriate Media Activity number.

9.1   DNA Structure
Estimated time: 5 minutes

The structure of the DNA double helix is the key to the ability of this molecule to store and transmit genetic information. In this activity, you will explore the structure of the DNA molecule.

9.2   DNA Replication
Estimated time: 5 minutes

This activity explores the process of DNA replication, which is crucial for the organism's growth and reproduction.

9.3   Web Investigation: Sunshine Perils
Estimated time: 20 minutes

Skin cancer is now the most common cancer in the United States. What is skin cancer? Who is most at risk? What are the treatment alternatives? How can it be prevented? This exercise explores the biochemical, medical, and psychological features of skin cancers.

1. There are three kinds of skin cancer (http://www.cancer.gov/cancerinfo/wyntk/skin#4): basal cell carcinoma, squamous cell carcinoma, and melanoma. What is the difference between a carcinoma and a melanoma? Which is the most invasive?

2. Use the Melanoma (http://www.cancer.gov/cancerinfo/wyntk/melanoma - National Cancer Institute) and MelanomaNet (http://www.skincarephysicians.com/melanomanet/welcome.htm - American Academy of Dermatology) fact sheets to answer the following questions. What are the signs and signals of melanoma?

3. What are the major genetic and behavioral risk factors for skin cancer?

4. What are the most common treatments for melanoma?

5. The number of skin cancer cases increases every year. What is the best way to avoid (http://www.mpip.org/prevention/06_06_00birth.html) skin cancer?

ISSUES IN BIOLOGY

Is There a Genetic Basis to Cancer?

Long before it was known that the DNA of chromosomes carries the genetic code, scientists had been studying chromosome structure in a variety of organisms. In the early 1900s, Boveri, a French scientist, examined chromosome structure in malignant cells (http://edcenter.med.cornell.edu/CUMC_PathNotes/Neoplasia/Neoplasia_08.html) derived from tumors. He, and others, noted that the chromosomes in these cells had two copies of several different chromosomes, had fragmented chromosomes, or had chromosomes with abnormal sizes or shapes. Boveri proposed that the presence of chromosome abnormalities might actually cause the cancer.

In 1960, Peter Nowell and David Hungerford, two researchers in Philadelphia, provided the first indication that Boveri was correct. These scientists were studying the chromosomes of people with a type of leukemia (http://www.leukemia.org/all_page?item_id=9346) called chronic myelogenous leukemia. This disease primarily affects adults and is characterized by the production of excess numbers of white blood cells known as granulocytes. In a one-paragraph report in the journal, *Science*, Nowell and Hungerford reported that all seven individuals they were examining had an unusually short chromosome 22. Echoing Boveri's earlier proposal, they hypothesized that the presence of this odd chromosome might be causing the cancer. They turned out to be right, at least partially, as you will see.

Because Nowell and Hungerford worked in Philadelphia, this tiny chromosome 22 came to be called the Philadelphia chromosome (http://www.pathology.washington.edu/galleries/Cytogallery/Bigframe_links/Ph1.html) by other researchers who began to investigate the possible link between this chromosome and the development of leukemia. On the basis of improved chromosome staining techniques, other researchers discovered that, in people with a Philadelphia chromosome, a portion of chromosome 22 had broken off and was joined to chromosome 9. Over many years of research by laboratories, it was found that the fusion between parts of chromosomes 9 and 22 creates a defective gene: Instead of quietly dying at the proper time, cells with this defect are unable to undergo the normal program of cell "suicide" that operates to regulate the levels of white blood cells. This observation was one of the first in which it was shown that cancers are diseases caused by defective genes. So, how is it that Nowell and Hungerford were only partly right about the Philadelphia chromosome causing cancer? Although the defect that results from the Philadelphia chromosome is important for developing chronic myelogenous leukemia, there are apparently other, as yet unknown genetic changes that must also happen for the disease to progress.

Researchers and physicians continue to study the Philadelphia chromosome to understand the molecular events involved in initiating a cancer. In addition, physicians around the world use the presence of the Philadelphia chromosome to diagnose chronic granulocytic leukemia and to monitor the effectiveness of treatments. For example, if a person is feeling exhausted, lacks an appetite, and has night sweats, the doctor will probably order a blood test to check a variety of things, including the numbers of red and white blood cells. If the presence of excess or immature white blood cells is seen, additional tests, such as bone marrow biopsies, may be performed to look for the presence of the Philadelphia chromosome (http://www.medterms.com/script/main/art.asp?articlekey=4870). If that chromosome is present, the patient is diagnosed with chronic granulocytic leukemia and proper treatment can begin. In many cases, the best option for treatment is a bone marrow transplant. Following the transplant, physicians will continue to monitor the patient's blood for cells that contain the Philadelphia chromosome. When cells containing this chromosome are no longer present, the patient is considered cured.

1. Why would scientists be interested in the gene that is present at the junctions of the Philadelphia chromosome?

2. Many conditions genetically predispose individuals to develop cancer, but these individuals contain no unusual chromosome(s). Does the lack of a visible chromosome defect make it unlikely that cancers in these individuals are caused by changes in the DNA? Explain your answer.

3. How might defects in a cell's ability to die via a cellular suicide program increase the risk for developing cancer?

BIZARRE FACTS IN BIOLOGY

Giant Chromosomes

In most organisms, the chromosomes are difficult to see. But some organisms have unusually large chromosomes (http://konops.imbb.forth.gr/AnoDB/Cytomap/chrom2.html) that can be seen even under low power with an ordinary microscope.

What makes these chromosomes so large? It turns out that these giant chromosomes consist of many copies of the chromosome that remain attached side-by-side. For that reason, they are called polytene chromosomes (http://msg.ucsf.edu:8100/~harmon/polytene.html) (poly = many; -tene = thread). They form when several bouts of DNA replication occur without the daughter strands separating, and without the cell dividing, a process called endoreplication (http://users.rcn.com/jkimball.ma.ultranet/BiologyPages/E/Endoreplication.html). The best-studied polytene chromosomes, which are found in the salivary gland cells in larvae of the fruit fly *Drosophila melanogaster* (http://www.ceolas.org/fly/intro.html), typically consist of over 2,000 copies of the DNA. Polytene chromosomes can also be found in other organisms, including beans (http://www.ba.cnr.it/Beanref/polytene.htm) and mosquitos (http://konops.imbb.forth.gr/AnoDB/Cytomap/Photos/photographs.html).

What might be the advantage of having so many copies of the DNA? As you will learn in Chapter 10, the information carried by the DNA must be transcribed into a message carried by RNA before it can be expressed. The cells with polytene chromosomes typically are busy manufacturing massive amounts of gene product. For example, the *Drosophila* salivary gland cells are producing much saliva, which contains several different proteins, particularly digestive enzymes. Having multiple copies of the chromosomes is one strategy for ensuring rapid synthesis of these gene products, since many RNA messenger molecules can be made simultaneously.

Preparing your own polytene chromosomes is easy to do in the biology lab. Here (http://www.woodrow.org/teachers/bi/1994/polytene_chromosomes.html) are some instructions in case you are interested in trying this for yourself.

1. How many bouts of replication do you think it would take to produce a polytene chromosome having at least 4,000 individual DNA molecules? Assume that each bout of replication involves all copies of the DNA molecuole that are present. Explain your answer.

2. Polytene chromosomes are characterized by distinct banding patterns that are characteristic of the particular chromosome being examined. For example, you can identify a *Drosophila* chromosome number one from any individual by its banding pattern. What do you think this consistent banding pattern tells you about the organization of the individual DNA molecules in that chromosome? Explain your answer.

3. Describe briefly how polytene chromosomes are formed.

KEY TERMS

adenine (A)	DNA	double helix	semiconservative
bases	DNA helicase	free nucleotides	replication
chromosome	DNA ligase	gene	sugar-phosphate backbone
complementary base pairs	DNA polymerase	guanine (G)	thymine (T)
cytosine (C)	DNA replication	nucleotides	

ANSWER KEY

SELF TEST

1. c
2. a
3. b
4. a
5. c
6. a
7. b
8. a
9. b
10. c
11. b
12. a
13. c
14. d
15. d
16. c
17. c
18. double helix
19. DNA helicase, helicase
20. X-ray diffraction
21. complementary
22. ultraviolet, UV
23. thymine
24. A. phosphate group
    B. deoxyribose sugar
    C. base

25. A. DNA polymerase
    B. DNA helicase
26. d
27. DNA, deoxyribonucleic acid
28. sequence, order
29. b
30. DNA replication, replication
31. a
32. b
33. c
34. b
35. a

ESSAY CHALLENGE

1. The X-ray diffraction images obtained by Franklin and Wilkins showed that DNA was a double helix. It also showed the distances between the turns of the helix and the distances between each nucleotide.
2. The living R-strain bacteria picked up piece of DNA from the dead S-strain bacteria that contained genes conferring virulence on the R-strain.
3. DNA polymerase relies upon base-pairing specificity to ensure that the correct nucleotide is added to the growing chain. However, errors do occur, and there are enzymes that can proofread and edit the newly synthesized strand and fix any errors.

4. The phosphate of one nucleotide is connected to the sugar of the next nucleotide through dehydration synthesis. This pattern is repeated along the length of the strand, creating the sugar-phosphate backbone of DNA.

5. The amount of adenine always equals the amount of thymine, and the amount of guanine always equals the amount of cytosine, in DNA. This is because of the double-helical nature of DNA. Adenine on one strand is always attached to a thymine on the other, so the amounts of these two bases are equal.

6. The strand complementary to the one in the question would be deoxyribose end—AACGACATCCAT—(phosphate end). The two strands are antiparallel, so the phosphate end of the complementary strand is at the same end as the deoxyribose end of the original strand. The nucleotides are complementary; that is, A is across from T and G is across from C, and vice versa.

MEDIA ACTIVITIES

9.3   Web Investigation: Sunshine Perils

1. Carcinomas are cancers that begin in cells that line organs. Melanomas are cancers of melanocytes, the pigment-producing cells of skin. Melanomas are the most invasive of these three cancer types.

2. Think ABCD: Asymmetry in the shape of a mole; Border of a mole being irregular; Color is uneven or blotchy; and Diameter of 1/4 inch or more.

3. Risk factors include dysplastic nevi (a type of mole), having 50 or more moles, fair skin, a personal or family history of skin cancer, especially melanoma, a weakened immune system, and blistering sunburns, especially as a child. Behavioral factors include suntanning, failing to cover up in bright sunlight, and exposure to UV light.

4. People with melanoma may receive surgery, chemotherapy, immunotherapy, or radiation therapy, or a combination of these treatments. Surgery removes the melanoma and surrounding tissues; chemotherapy involves administration of drugs that attack dividing cells, particularly cancer cells; immunotherapy involves providing drugs that boost the patient's immune system, making it more effective to fight the cancer; and radiation therapy involves exposure to radiation, which damages dividing cells.

5. The best overall strategy for avoiding skin cancer is to avoid exposure to UV rays in sunlight. Avoid exposure to midday sunlight, wear long sleeves and pants and a wide-brimmed hat. Use a sunscreen with an SPF of 30 or above. Finally, protect your eyes by wearing sunglasses that protect against both UV-A and UV-B.

ISSUES IN BIOLOGY

1. The most likely explanation for changes associated with chromosome translocations is that the gene at the point of a break was somehow altered during breakage and/or rejoining.

2. There are many ways in which a single gene can be altered with no visible effect on the chromosomes in which they are found. For example, a change in a single nucleotide is responsible for sickle-cell trait. Likewise, it is reasonable to expect that similar seemingly small changes might affect cancer-causing genes.

3. Cells whose metabolic machinery has become deranged, including cells in precancerous states, usually enter a suicide program, apoptosis. If there is a defect in the suicide program, then a cell that would normally have died can survive to give rise to a cancer cell.

BIZARRE FACTS IN BIOLOGY

1. Eleven rounds of replication will produce over 2000 copies of the DNA in a chromosome. (2, 4, 8, 16, 32, 64, 128, 256, 512, 1024, 2048).

2. The light regions in a banded chromosome appear to be regions where genes are being actively transcribed. Since the genes needed in a particular tissue at a particular stage in development are probably the same in different individuals, this would explain the consistency of banding patterns.

3. The DNA is replicated, but the DNA strands do not separate, and the cell in which the DNA is found does not divide. This process of replication without separation continues for several rounds until there are about 2000 strands of DNA.

CHAPTER 10: GENE EXPRESSION AND REGULATION

AT-A-GLANCE

SELF TEST

1. Which of the following is an accurate statement concerning the differences between DNA and RNA?
   a. RNA is usually double-stranded, but DNA is usually single-stranded.
   b. RNA has the sugar deoxyribose, but DNA has the sugar ribose.
   c. RNA contains three different nucleotides, but DNA contains four different nucleotides.
   d. RNA lacks the base thymine (which is found in DNA) and has uracil instead.

2. The process of RNA synthesis is called _____.
   a. transcription   b. translation
   c. replication   d. mutation

3. Information in DNA is carried in _____.
   a. the sugar-phosphate backbone of one DNA strand
   b. the base pairs between nucleotides in the two DNA strands
   c. the proteins that bind to the DNA double helix
   d. the order of the nucleotide bases in one DNA strand

4. Which of the following statements about the functions of RNA is correct?
   a. The information for protein synthesis is carried by tRNA.
   b. rRNA is an intermediate in the synthesis of mRNA.
   c. rRNA is an important component of ribosomes.
   d. Translation requires tRNA and mRNA, but not rRNA.

5. Which of the following correctly lists the items in order of their relative sizes?
   a. nucleotide, codon, base pair, promoter, hemoglobin mRNA, hemoglobin gene, ribosome, chromosome
   b. nucleotide, base pair, codon, promoter, hemoglobin gene, hemoglobin mRNA, ribosome, chromosome
   c. nucleotide, base pair, codon, promoter, hemoglobin mRNA, hemoglobin gene, ribosome, chromosome
   d. nucleotide, base pair, codon, promoter, hemoglobin mRNA, hemoglobin gene, chromosome, ribosome

6. Both transcription and translation occur in three steps. What happens during the elongation step of each process?
   a. During the elongation step of transcription, the RNA molecule is synthesized. During the elongation step of translation, the protein molecule is synthesized.
   b. During the elongation step of transcription, the RNA molecule is stretched out to full length. During the elongation step of translation, the protein molecule is stretched out to full length.
   c. During the elongation step of transcription, synthesis of an RNA molecule is started. During the elongation step of translation, synthesis of a protein molecule is started.
   d. During the elongation step of transcription, the mRNA molecule is completed. During the elongation step of translation, the protein molecule is completed.

7. The flow of genetic information in cells depends on specific base pairing between nucleotides. Which of the following correctly matches the type of base pairing with the process of translation?
   a. In translation, RNA base-pairs with DNA.
   b. In translation, rRNA base-pairs with mRNA.
   c. In translation, tRNA base-pairs with rRNA.
   d. In translation, tRNA base-pairs with mRNA.

8. During DNA replication, a mistake was made in which an A was changed to a G. This kind of mutation is called a(n) _____.
   a. point mutation   b. insertion mutation
   c. deletion mutation   d. neutral mutation

9. The DNA sequence of a codon in a gene was changed from AAT to AAC. This type of mutation is called a(n) _____. (Refer to Table 10-3 in your textbook.)
   a. point mutation
   b. insertion mutation
   c. deletion mutation
   d. neutral mutation

10. The cells in your skin have a different shape and different function from the cells in your liver because the two types of cells have different _____.
    a. DNA   b. proteins
    c. lipids   d. carbohydrates

11. Which genes are expressed in a cell depends on the cell's _____.
    a. environment   b. history
    c. function   d. all of the above
    e. All except one of the above answers are correct.

12. Which of the following is NOT a step at which gene expression can be regulated in eukaryotic cells?
    a. the rate of transcription
    b. the rate of translation
    c. the rate of DNA replication
    d. the types and rates of protein modification
    e. the rate of enzyme activity

13. In mammals, males have one X chromosome and one Y chromosome and females have two X chromosomes. How is the expression of genes on the X chromosome regulated so that there is equal expression of genes on the X chromosome in males and females?
    a. One X chromosome in females is inactivated so that females have only a single X chromosome capable of transcription.
    b. The genes on the X chromosome in males are transcribed twice as fast as in females.
    c. All of the X chromosomes are inactivated so that no genes are expressed from the X chromosome in either males or females.
    d. The Y chromosome contains balancing genes that help to raise the levels of mRNA produced by the X chromosome in males.

14. Imagine that a codon in the template strand of a gene has the sequence TAC. What sequence of the anticodon would decode this codon? Explain your answer.
    a. ATG, because the anticodon is complementary to the template strand
    b. AUG, because the anticodon is complementary to the template strand
    c. UAC, because the anticodon has the same sequence as the template strand (but it has U instead of T)
    d. TAC, because the anticodon has the same sequence as the template strand

15. Certain genes, sometimes called *housekeeping genes,* are expressed in all cells in your body. Other genes are expressed only in certain specialized cells. Which of the following genes is likely to be a housekeeping gene?
    a. hemoglobin
    b. milk proteins
    c. ribosomal proteins
    d. insulin

16. Imagine that a probe sent to Mars brings back a sample that contains a very primitive life-form that appears similar to bacteria. Scientists are able to revive it and begin to grow it in culture. Much to their amazement, they discover that the organism has DNA and that the DNA encodes proteins. However, the DNA of these Martian microbes contains only two nucleotides, and these nucleotides contain bases that are not present in the DNA of organisms on Earth. If the Martian microbe uses triplet codons, what is the maximum number of different amino acids that it can have in its proteins? Explain.
    a. 9, because $3^2 = 3 \times 3 = 9$
    b. 16, because $4^2 = 4 \times 4 = 16$
    c. 8, because $2^3 = 2 \times 2 \times 2 = 8$
    d. 7, because there are 8 possible codons ($2^3 = 2 \times 2 \times 2 = 8$) but at least one of the codons must be a stop.

17. Some people have eyes of two different colors. What is a possible explanation for this trait?
    a. A mutation occurred in the sperm that produced this individual's embryo.
    b. A mutation occurred in the egg that produced this individual's embryo.
    c. A chemical toxin inhibited production of pigment in one eye but not the other.
    d. During early stages of development, a mutation occurred in the cell that developed into one of the eyes, but not other cells in the embryo.

18. How did Beadle and Tatum use genetic mutations in strains of *Neurospora* as an investigative tool?
    a. They tested the hypothesis that a specific region of DNA (genes) could somehow encode a specific enzyme.
    b. They crossed mutant strains that required a specific dietary supplement to survive with normal *Neurospora.*
    c. They showed that strains with a dietary supplement requirement were defective in one or another enzyme in the biochemical synthetic pathway for that supplement but never to more than one enzyme from the same biochemical pathway.
    d. all of the above

19. mRNA complementary to DNA is produced via _____.
    a. replication
    b. transcription
    c. translation
    d. protein synthesis

20. The "genetic code" includes _____.
    a. units of three bases, each triplet (or codon) corresponding to a single amino acid
    b. specific base sequences in the nucleic acids that indicate where to "begin" and "end" the synthesis of a polypeptide
    c. only two bases per amino acid
    d. The first two answers are correct.

21. What is the promoter region?
    a. It is a region of RNA that binds to the RNA polymerase and initiates transcription.
    b. It is a component of each type of RNA.
    c. It is responsible for the selective nature of transcription.
    d. It is a region of a parent DNA strand that binds to the RNA polymerase and initiates transcription.

22. Which of the following is the first step in translation?
    a. bases of the tRNA anticodon bind with the bases of the mRNA codon
    b. the formation of a peptide bond between amino acids attached to the adjacent tRNAs on the ribosome
    c. the ribosomal subunits are disassembled
    d. stop codons on the mRNA bind to special proteins rather than tRNA molecules

23. Regulation of genetic expression _____.
    a. involves a limited number of molecules and steps and has been well understood for some time
    b. can be influenced by environmental conditions, including temperature changes
    c. can occur at any point during replication, transcription, or translation and involves many, many different molecules
    d. Both the second and third answers above are correct.

24. Cells produce molecules in a series of steps called _____ pathways.

25. Since DNA is in the nucleus, and protein synthesis takes place in the cytoplasm, there must be an intermediary that carries the DNA's message to the cytoplasm. This intermediary is called _____.

26. _____ consist of three bases. Each of these either initiates or stops translation or specifies a particular amino acid in DNA translation.

27. Three codons tell protein synthesis to cease. These codons are called _____ codons.

28. RNA _____ is the molecule that is responsible for synthesizing each form of RNA.

29. _____ is the type of RNA molecule that is created in the nucleus and then carries the genetic information to the cytoplasm.

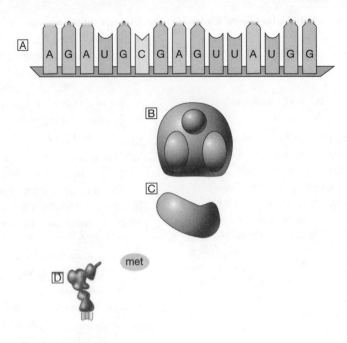

30. There are three different types of RNA, each with different functions. The image above depicts these different RNA types. Label the types and the portions of each as indicated.

31. Transcription and translation have many components. Label those indicated on the image below.

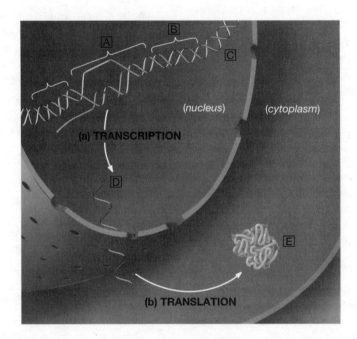

(nucleus) *(cytoplasm)*

(a) TRANSCRIPTION

(b) TRANSLATION

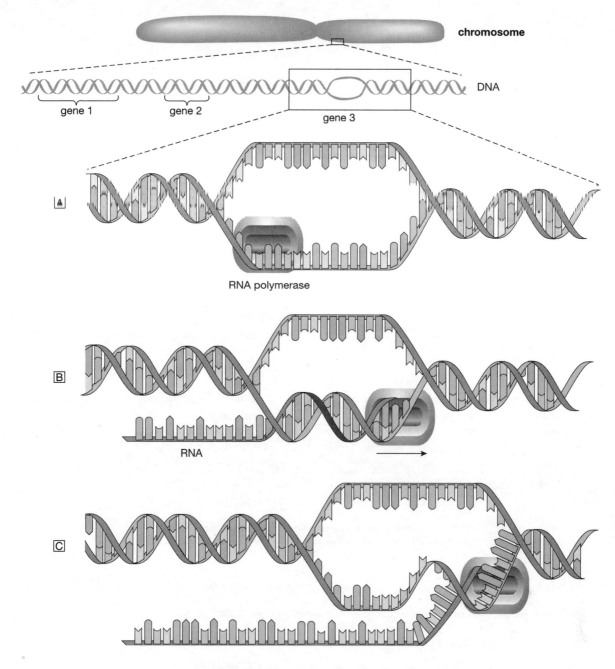

chromosome

DNA

gene 1

gene 2

gene 3

A

RNA polymerase

B

RNA

C

32. There are discrete steps in the process of transcription. Label these steps on the image above.

33. Identify each of the structures in the diagram below as they relate to transcription and translation.

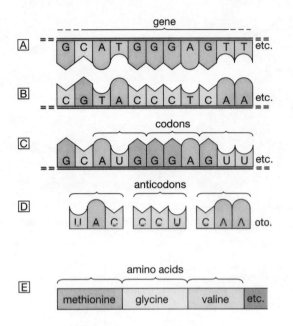

gene

A G C A T G G G A G T T etc.

B C G T A C C C T C A A etc.

codons

C G C A U G G G A G U U etc.

anticodons

D U A C   C C U   C A A etc.

amino acids

E methionine | glycine | valine | etc.

34. A typical DNA strand includes many portions that do not code for proteins. Label these structures on the diagram below. Follow the genetic material as it moves through the processes illustrated in Part b, labeling each step.

35. What does mRNA carry from the nucleus?
a. ribosomes **b.** information
c. amino acids **d.** tRNA

36. Unripe black walnuts contain a compound, juglone, that inhibits RNA polymerase. With which process would juglone most likely interfere?
a. mutation rate **b.** DNA replication
c. transcription **d.** translation

37. If you were to create a drug that recognized and bound irreversibly to the promoter region of a specific gene, thereby blocking it, what effect would you expect that drug to have?
a. There would be no effect on the gene.
b. Only transcription of that gene would halt.
c. Only translation of the gene would halt.
d. Both transcription and, eventually, translation of the gene would halt.

38. What kind of point mutation would have the most dramatic effect on the protein coded for by that gene?
a. a base substitution
b. a base insertion near the beginning of the coding sequence
c. a base insertion near the end of the coding sequence
d. deletion of three bases near the start of the coding sequence

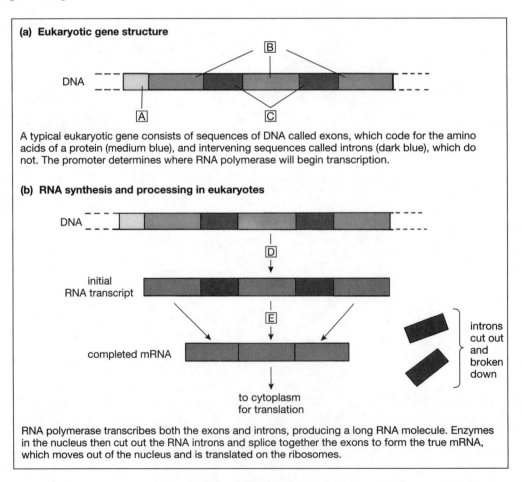

(a) Eukaryotic gene structure

DNA

A typical eukaryotic gene consists of sequences of DNA called exons, which code for the amino acids of a protein (medium blue), and intervening sequences called introns (dark blue), which do not. The promoter determines where RNA polymerase will begin transcription.

(b) RNA synthesis and processing in eukaryotes

DNA

initial RNA transcript

completed mRNA

introns cut out and broken down

to cytoplasm for translation

RNA polymerase transcribes both the exons and introns, producing a long RNA molecule. Enzymes in the nucleus then cut out the RNA introns and splice together the exons to form the true mRNA, which moves out of the nucleus and is translated on the ribosomes.

39. The codon that will be recognized by the anticodon GAU is _____.

40. _____ is the specific kind of nucleic acid found in ribosomes.

41. A mutation in which only one nucleotide in the DNA is changed is called a _____ mutation.

42. One kind of mutation that has a high probability of affecting the final protein is a _____ mutation.

43. In female mammals one X chromosome in each cell is inactivated, and the inactivated X forms a structure called a _____.

44. Gene _____ is the production of the protein (or RNA) coded for by a gene.

ESSAY CHALLENGE

1. Identify the three kinds of RNA and describe what each does in protein synthesis.

2. Identify and describe the three kinds of mutations discussed in Chapter 10.

3. What are the four different possible consequences that mutations may have for a protein?

4. Describe some of the evolutionary implications of mutations.

5. Identify and describe some of the levels at which genetic expression is regulated.

6 How is it possible for a man (who produces **no milk proteins**) to pass the ability to lactate to his daughters?

MEDIA ACTIVITIES

To access a Media Activity visit http://www.prenhall.com/audesirk7. Log in to the Web site selected by your instructor, navigate to this chapter, and select the appropriate Media Activity number.

10.1 Transcription
Estimated time: 10 minutes

The genetic information that is stored in the DNA found in the nucleus of a cell must be conveyed to the cytoplasm, where it can be translated into a specific sequence of amino acids. The intermediate molecule is RNA, synthesized by the process of transcription. This tutorial investigates the steps involved in transcription.

10.2 Translation
Estimated time: 10 minutes

Transcription provides a messenger RNA transcript of the gene. Now it is the task of the cell to take the information encoded in this messenger RNA and translate it into a specific sequence of amino acids. This process occurs on the ribosomes and involves a number of steps illustrated in this tutorial.

10.3 Web Investigation: Boy or Girl
Estimated time: 10 minutes

Everyone knows that chromosomes determine gender. Baby girls have two X chromosomes (XX) while baby boys are XY. But what about individuals with XO, XXY, or XYY genomes? Why are there female babies with XY karyotypes (chromosome sets)? Gender biology is much more complicated than one might think.

1. The SRY region of the Y chromosome has been shown to code for a factor that is "necessary and sufficient" for male physiological development. What is the experimental evidence for the essential role of SRY (http://www3.ncbi.nlm.nih.gov/htbin-post/Omim/dispmim?480000.mini)?

2. If an XY baby lacks the SRY gene, will the baby appear male or female? Will (s)he have a normal reproductive system?

3. Are individuals with XXY (http://www.nih.gov/health/chip/nichd/klinefelter), Klinefelter syndrome, male or female? How about Turner syndrome (http://www.turnersyndrome.ca/got_quest.html), XO, XYY (http://www.aaa.dk/turner/engelsk/xyy.htm#contents), or XXX (http://www.aaa.dk/turner/engelsk/triplex.htm#contents)? Are they capable of reproducing?

4. What biological errors of metabolism (http://www.med.jhu.edu/pedendo/intersex/sd4.html) result in XY females? Consider gene rearrangements and the SRY gene. How could an XX individual be physiologically male?

ISSUES IN BIOLOGY

What Can Flies with Eyes on Their Legs Tell Us About Gene Regulation?

From time to time, we hear reports of strange scientific experiments that make us wonder, "Why on earth would anyone want to do that?" One example occurred in 1995, when newspapers, magazines, and newscasts reported the existence of some very bizarre flies in Switzerland. Using genetic engineering techniques, Swiss researchers, led by Walter Gehring (http://www.biozentrum.unibas.ch/gehring.html), had produced flies with additional eyes. Instead of the normal situation in which the fly has two eyes (http://flybase.bio.indiana.edu/images/lk/Anatomy/Head/R_Turner_Micrographs/wild-type-head.jpg), each properly located on the side of the head, these genetic anomalies had eyes on their knees (http://www.biozentrum.unibas.ch/pictures/Gehring/Fly4_640.jpg), their antennae (http://www.biozentrum.unibas.ch/pictures/Gehring/eyeless1.jpg), their wings, and other strange places. One fly had fourteen "eyes" located in various positions on its body! When people heard this report, they imagined stories of Frankenstein and other mad scientists of Western literature—who else would attempt such a feat? However, the real question the researchers were asking had nothing to do with creating a "visually-endowed" fly. Instead, it dealt with the most fundamental nature of how genes determine the structure of body parts in organisms. And the way they answered the question was elegant and straightforward.

During development of a multicellular organism, whether it is a fly or a human, specific genes must be turned on in a temporally programmed series (http://www.pbs.org/wgbh/nova/odyssey/timing.html). This hierarchy of gene expression enables cells to adopt their ultimate location, shape, and function within the developing organism (http://www.pbs.org/wgbh/nova/odyssey/clips/). In the case of eye development, about 2,000 different genes must be "turned on" at the proper time and place for eyes to develop properly. Such genetic "pyramid schemes" underlie the formation of all tissues and organs in multicellular organisms. A good illustration of this process is to consider a complex array of dominoes, each poised to topple one or more other dominoes set up nearby. When one domino falls, a chain reaction occurs in which dozens or hundreds of other dominoes also fall, in a specified timing and order. When the whole event is over, the pattern of dominos that have fallen versus those that have been left standing depends on which initial domino was toppled.

In organisms, the first "dominoes" in a gene regulation pyramid are sometimes called master control genes (http://www.biozentrum.unibas.ch/report9899/gehring.html). These genes encode proteins that bind to the control regions of other genes and turn them on (i.e., activate transcription - http://www.stedwards.edu/science/quinn/p53page/basics32.htm). As a result, a second tier of genes is activated, many of which also activate expression of a third tier of genes. The process continues in a kind of genetic chain reaction until, ultimately, the set of proteins that are uniquely expressed in that particular cell is activated. For example, in red blood cells, hemoglobin (http://www.psc.edu/science/Ho/Ho-hemoglobin.html) must be produced since it carries oxygen and carbon dioxide. In eyes, the protein rhodopsin must be produced since it is the primary light receptor.

What are the master control genes that stimulate eye development? For such developmental questions, the fruit fly, *Drosophila melanogaster*, is a wonderful experimental organism. Mutant flies (http://www.exploratorium.edu/exhibits/mutant_flies/mutant_flies.html) had been discovered that lack eyes altogether (http://www.exploratorium.edu/exhibits/mutant_flies/eyeless.gif). The defective gene in these flies was identified and given the rather obvious name, "*eyeless*." The *eyeless* gene was cloned and its DNA sequence (http://www.ncbi.nlm.nih.gov/htbin-post/Entrez/query?uid=641809&form=6&db=n&Dopt=g) was determined. Now, the fun began in earnest. There are massive databases on the World Wide Web in which researchers throughout the world deposit information about the sequences of the genes they have discovered. In fact, it is typically a requirement of the publishers of scientific journals that information about a gene's sequence is placed in these amazing resources. The most common one is GenBank (http://www.ncbi.nlm.nih.gov/Genbank/GenbankOverview.html), a database managed by the U.S. National Center for Biotechnology Information (http://www.ncbi.nlm.nih.gov/). This information is an incredible boon to genetic research because it lets a researcher compare a gene sequence they are studying to that of ALL OTHER known genes on the planet. In many cases you can get clues about what your gene is doing by learning what it does in other organisms.

Here's where Gehring's group hit paydirt. They found other genes in the database that were similar to the *eyeless* gene of *Drosophila*. One is the *Pax-6 gene* (http://bioinfo.weizmann.ac.il/cards-bin/carddisp?PAX6&search=pax-6&suff=txt) from mice and the other is the *aniridia* gene from humans. Amazingly, both of these genes are involved in eye development. Mice with defects in the *Pax-6* gene have small eyes (http://www.hgu.mrc.ac.uk/Research/Devgen/AbnormDev/bobhill.htm) and humans with defects in their *aniridia* gene lack an iris. This information suggested the possibility that development of eyes in vertebrates might be similar to the development of eyes in flies, even though the basic design of their eyes is different (vertebrates have a simple eye and flies have a compound eye -). How can this hypothesis be tested?

The first step is to determine if *eyeless* itself is a master control gene. How can this idea be tested? In normal development, the *eyeless* gene is turned on only in cells that will become cells of the eye. If *eyeless* is truly a master control gene, turning it on in the wrong cells will produce eyes in the wrong places. This is exactly where the many-eyed flies came from. Using genetic engineering techniques, Gehring's team produced flies in which they could turn on the *eyeless* gene in cells that would normally just produce legs or wings or antennae. In all these cases, the developmental fate of at least some of the cells was short-circuited. For example, instead of becoming wing cells as unusual, some of the wing cells that were expressing the *eyeless* gene became eye cells instead. This result clearly showed that *eyeless* is one of the master control genes needed for eye cell differentiation.

Now, they can test the idea further. They took the mouse *Pax-6* gene and the human *aniridia* gene and expressed them in flies. These genes were also able to induce eyes in places that eyes don't normally exist. Thus, these genes are likely to be master control genes for eye development as well.

So, other than revealing more about the principles of gene regulation and its relationship to development, why are these experiments interesting? One possibility is that, by manipulating gene expression in the retina, scientists may be able one day to restore sight to people with damaged retinas. Normally, these cells do not divide, so damage to the retina is irreversible. However, if it were possible to transplant cells (http://www.blindness.org/publications/newsarticle.asp?id=143) and turn on the genetic program that will produce more retinal cells, some vision might be restored. So, the next time you hear about some apparent crazy experiments, perhaps you will delve deeper to find the real reason that the scientists devote their energy, as well as your tax dollars, to these studies.

1. Do you think that it is a good use of taxpayer dollars to maintain genetic databases that are accessible to anyone who has a modem and a computer? Why or why not? What are the advantages to scientists of being able to compare the sequence of their gene to that of other genes in other organisms?

2. How do the similarities between the sequence and the function of the *Drosophila eyeless* gene, the *Pax-6* gene of mice, and the *aniridia* gene of humans support the idea that all organisms on Earth are related by history and lineage (i.e., evolution)?

3. Injuries to tissues such as the heart, brain, and spinal cord are permanent because the cells making up these organs do not regenerate. Similarly, loss of a limb, an eye, or most other body parts is permanent because the cells at the wounds are unable to reinitiate the genetic program needed for regeneration. The cells simply divide until they fill in the wound with scar tissue. It is possible that experiments such as the ones described here may give scientists tools to reprogram cells so that they can be programed to regenerate a limb, a heart, and so on. Is this goal an ethical one that should be pursued? Do you envision any possible misuses of the technology? Who should be responsible for regulating how the technology is used?

BIZARRE FACTS IN BIOLOGY

Indy an' a Fly

Regular exercise and avoiding smoking and alcohol will reduce your risk of heart disease and increase the odds that you'll live to see your 70s or 80s, but how do you survive to be 100 or older (http://www.nmfn.com/tn/learnctr—lifeevents—longevity)? Restrict your food intake. Mice kept on calorie-restricted diets—20% to 30% fewer calories—live longer than their normal-calorie cagemates. But going through life in a state of near-starvation doesn't sound like a lot of fun, so what other options exist?

Changing the function of a single gene may be mimicking this near-starvation without the hard work. The partial loss-of-function mutation, *Indy*, has created a strain of fruit flies (*Drosophilia melanogaster*) that live, on average, twice as long as normal flies. *Indy* flies develop and reach maturity at the same rate as normal flies, and are just as fertile and produce just as many offspring. However, *Indy* flies produce offspring for a longer time period, so this mutation doesn't just permit old flies to live longer, it seems to truly extend the "productive" life span.

Indy, as in "I'm not dead yet" from the movie *Monty Python and the Holy Grail*, is a mutant form of a gene important for fuel metabolism. The scientists who isolated *Indy* believe that it slows down metabolism similar to the way calorie-restricted diets slow metabolism. Although we are still a long way from an anti-aging pill, understanding how *Indy* works to change the rate of metabolism may give us some insight into the relationship of energy production and use and aging (http://www.agingresearch.org/).

1. A partial loss-of-function mutation does not eliminate gene activity, only reduces it. What do you predict would be the consequence of a complete loss of function in the *Indy* gene?

2. Why is it significant that *Indy* flies develop and behave similarly to normal flies?

3. How could knowing about *Indy* help scientists interested in extending human life spans?

KEY TERMS

anticodon	insertion mutation	promoter	template strand
Barr Body	intron	ribonucleic acid (RNA)	transcription
codon	messenger RNA (mRNA)	ribosomal RNA (rRNA)	transfer RNA (tRNA)
deletion mutation	mutation	ribosome	translation
exon	neutral mutation	RNA polymerase	
gene	nucleotide substitution	start codon	
genetic code	point mutation	stop codon	

ANSWER KEY

SELF TEST

1. d
2. a
3. d
4. c
5. c
6. a
7. d
8. a
9. d
10. b
11. d
12. c
13. a
14. c
15. c
16. d
17. d
18. d
19. b
20. d
21. d
22. a
23. d
24. biochemical
25. RNA, mRNA
26. codons
27. stop

28. polymerase
29. mRNA, messenger RNA
30. A. messenger RNA (mRNA)
    B. ribosomal RNA large subunit
    C. ribosomal RNA small subunit
    D. transfer RNA (tRNA)
31. A. gene being transcribed
    B. gene not being actively transcribed
    C. DNA
    D. messenger RNA
    E. protein
32. A. initiation
    B. elongation
    C. termination
33. A. complementary DNA strand
    B. template DNA strand
    C. mRNA
    D. tRNA
    E. protein
34. A. promoter
    B. exons
    C. introns
    D. transcription
    E. RNA splicing
35. b
36. c
37. d
38. b
39. CUA
40. rRNA
41. point
42. insertion, deletion, insertion or deletion
43. Barr body
44. expression

ESSAY CHALLENGE

1. Messenger RNA, ribosomal RNA, and transfer RNA all play specific roles in protein synthesis.
2. Substitution, insertion, and deletion mutations either improperly match nucleotides, insert an extra nucleotide into a sequence, or delete a nucleotide from the sequence.
3. The mutation may 1) produce no change, 2) produce a change which has no effect, 3) change the function of the resulting protein, or 4) destroy the protein by producing an unexpected stop codon.
4. Mutations are the only way to create variation in populations. Otherwise, the correction functions of DNA transcription and protein translation would prevent all errors from propagating into the protein itself.

5. Cells can control gene transcription, mRNAs may be transcribed at different rates, proteins may rely on modification for proper function, or the life span of the protein may be controlled.
6. For a man to pass the ability to lactate to his daughters, the genes for that ability must be present. However, since he is not able to lactate himself, those genes are prevented from transcription by other factors.

MEDIA ACTIVITIES

10.3 Web Investigation: Boy or Girl?

1. Translocations in which the SRY region is placed on the X chromosome produce XX males. Also, mutations that inactivate the SRY region produce XY females.
2. The baby will be female with a normal reproductive system.
3. Kleinfelters and XYY individuals are male, whereas Turner and XXX individuals are female. All are capable of reproduction.
4. A mutant form of the SRY gene that does not produce gene product could cause XY females. Also, a defect in the testosterone receptor can cause XY females. An XX individual could be physiologically made if the SRY gene was translocated onto a male's X chromosome, and then passed on to his child.

ISSUES IN BIOLOGY

1. Whatever the position taken, the student should list the potential benefits of such access. One advantage of being able to compare sequences is to discern evolutionary relationships among different groups of organisms. Also, if the function of the new gene is unknown, comparing the sequence to known genes can provide useful information regarding the gene product's function.
2. The most plausible explanation for the highly conserved nature of these genes is that they share a common ancestry and their function is so crucial to the development of these animals that natural selection has resisted much change in their nucleotide sequence.
3. One potential down side (of several) of this technology might be that people would not be as concerned with, say, taking care of health problems that lead to organ failure (e.g., heart disease) if they know that they can merely regenerate a new one. Whatever positions students take should be supported with realistic and logical arguments based in fact.

BIZARRE FACTS IN BIOLOGY

1. Since the partial loss-of-function mutation exhibited by the *Indy* gene is to slow down metabolisms, it is likely that it changes an enzyme involved in metabolizing fuel molecules. If this enzyme were to lose its function completely, an inability to metabolize food molecules at all would likely result, and this would most likely be fatal.

2. If the *Indy* mutation changed behavior or development, any effects on metabolic rate and apparent aging might be due to behavioral or developmental effects, not directly because of altered metabolism.

3. Because ethical and procedural considerations make these kinds of experimental studies difficult or impossible in humans, biologists use experimental animals for this type of research. By first identifying genes of interest in experimental organisms and then studying them, scientists can learn a great deal about similar processes in humans, and develop methods for examining the same genes in humans in a practical and ethical manner.

CHAPTER 11: THE CONTINUITY OF LIFE: CELLULAR REPRODUCTION

AT-A-GLANCE

SELF TEST

1. When a cell divides, what must it pass on to its off-spring?
   a. a complete set of genetic instructions (that is, one copy of every gene)
   b. a complete set of messenger RNA molecules, so that the offspring cells can express every gene
   c. cytoplasmic components needed for survival, such as ribosomes, RNA polymerase, and organelles (in eukaryotic cells)
   d. all of the above
   e. Both the first and third answers are correct.

2. Which of the following statements about the chromosomes of prokaryotic and eukaryotic cells is true?
   a. Both prokaryotic and eukaryotic cells have multiple chromosomes.
   b. The chromosomes of prokaryotic cells contain a circular DNA double helix, but the chromosomes of eukaryotic cells contain a linear DNA double helix.
   c. The chromosome of prokaryotic cells is present in their nuclei, but the chromosomes of eukaryotic cells are in the cytoplasm.
   d. Chromosomes of eukaryotic cells are attached to the plasma membrane, but the chromosome of prokaryotic cells floats free in the cytoplasm.

3. A duplicated chromosome contains _____.
   a. two DNA double helices
   b. two sister chromatids
   c. four strands of DNA
   d. all of the above
   e. none of the above

4. Which of the following events occurs during the interphase portion of the eukaryotic cell cycle?
   a. cytokinesis
   b. DNA replication
   c. chromosome condensation
   d. metaphase

5. Which of the following correctly lists the order of the stages during mitosis?
   a. metaphase, telophase, anaphase, prophase
   b. anaphase, prophase, metaphase, telophase
   c. prophase, metaphase, anaphase, telophase
   d. telophase, metaphase, anaphase, prophase

6. During the process of cytokinesis in plants, _____.
   a. carbohydrate-containing vesicles fuse in the center of the cell, eventually splitting the cell in two
   b. microfilaments squeeze the cell in two
   c. the cytoplasm moves from one spindle pole to the other
   d. chromosomes move to opposite sides of the cytoplasm

7. Which of the following is NOT a function of mitosis in a multicellular organism?
   a. growth from a fertilized egg
   b. replacement of damaged cells
   c. maintenance of tissues
   d. production of gametes

8. A clone is _____.
   a. an unnatural creature fabricated by unscrupulous scientists
   b. any cell or organism that is genetically identical to another
   c. an exact duplicate of an organism
   d. produced by sexual reproduction

9. Alternate forms of a particular gene are called _____; they arise as a result of _____.
   a. alleles, meiosis
   b. mutations, mitosis
   c. alleles, mutation
   d. clones, sexual reproduction

10. *Meiosis* comes from a Greek word that means "to decrease." What decreases during the process of meiosis?
    a. the size of chromosomes
    b. the number of cells
    c. the length of the DNA double helices
    d. the number of chromosomes

11. During the process of meiosis, DNA is replicated _____, followed by _____ nuclear divisions.
    a. twice, two
    b. twice, one
    c. once, two
    d. once, one

12. During meiosis I, _____ separate; during meiosis II, _____ separate.
    a. homologous chromosomes, sister chromatids
    b. sister chromatids, homologous chromosomes
    c. sister cells, gametes
    d. DNA double helices, DNA double helices

13. Genetic recombination (crossing over) produces _____.
    a. new chromosomes
    b. mutations
    c. new combinations of alleles
    d. longer chromosomes

14. Sexual reproduction produces genetic diversity by _____.
    a. creating new combinations of homologous chromosomes
    b. creating new combinations of alleles
    c. fusing gametes to form the diploid organism
    d. all of the above

15. Some genes have more than two different alleles. For example, there are three alleles (I^A, I^B, and i) for the blood-type gene. How many alleles of the blood-type gene are in a human egg?
    a. one
    b. two
    c. three
    d. six

16. Imagine that you are looking at a eukaryotic cell in the microscope. When you examine the cell, you see that the nucleus is not present and that chromosomes are condensed and lined up independently in the center of the cell. What are the possible stages of division you might be observing in this cell?
    a. metaphase of mitosis
    b. metaphase of meiosis I
    c. metaphase of meiosis II
    d. metaphase of mitosis or meiosis I
    e. metaphase of mitosis or meiosis II

17. Imagine that you are looking at a eukaryotic cell in the microscope. When you examine the cell's nucleus, you see that the chromatin is spread uniformly through the nucleus—you cannot see chromosomes. Has the cell's DNA been replicated yet? Explain.
    a. The DNA has been replicated, because DNA replication occurs during interphase.
    b. The DNA has not replicated, because DNA replication occurs after chromosome condensation.
    c. You can't tell whether the DNA has replicated unless the DNA is condensed.

18. Which of the following chemicals would be potentially useful for treating cancer?
    a. a chemical that prevents recombination
    b. a chemical that prevents DNA synthesis
    c. a chemical that inhibits pairing of homologous chromosomes
    d. a chemical that induces mutations

19. Mating a male donkey to a female horse produces mules. Horses have 64 chromosomes and donkeys have 62 chromosomes. How many chromosomes do mules have? Why are they sterile?
    a. The mule has 126 chromosomes and is sterile because 126 chromosomes are too many to go through meiosis.
    b. The mule has 64 chromosomes, as does its mother. It is sterile as a result of mutations that prevent sperm production.
    c. The mule has 63 chromosomes and is sterile because the chromosomes cannot pair properly at metaphase of meiosis I.
    d. The mule has 63 chromosomes and is sterile because the chromosomes cannot pair properly at metaphase of meiosis II.

20. Seedless watermelons are very popular summertime treats. They taste great and you don't have to worry about where to spit the seeds. From the farmer's perspective, seedless watermelons are good products because they resist disease and have thick rinds that allow them to survive shipment well and to have a long shelf-life. However, purchasing seeds for seedless watermelons is expensive, about $150 for 1000 seeds. Since seedless watermelons don't produce seeds, where do these seeds come from?
    a. Crossing two different species of melon produces seedless watermelons, much like a mule is produced by crossing a donkey and a horse.
    b. Seedless watermelons are produced by crossing a haploid melon with a diploid melon, producing triploid seeds that can germinate and produce fruit but cannot make seeds properly.
    c. Seedless watermelons are produced by crossing a diploid ($2n$) melon with a tetraploid ($4n$) melon, producing triploid ($3n$) seeds that can germinate and produce fruit that cannot, itself, make seeds properly.
    d. The farmers spray a chemical on the watermelons to arrest meiosis so that the melons don't produce seeds.

21. Which of the following describes something that is unique to meiotic cell division?
    a. growth (adding mass) of an organism
    b. Genetically identical daughter cells are produced with each cell division.
    c. Daughter cells contain the same amount of DNA as the parent cell.
    d. Daughter cells contain half of the parental DNA.

22. To what does the term *haploid* refer?
    a. chromosomes that contain the same genes
    b. cells that contain a pair of each type of chromosome
    c. a complete set of chromosomes from a single cell that have been stained for microscopic examination
    d. cells that contain only one of each type of chromosome

23. During what part of the cell cycle are chromosomes duplicated?
    a. prophase
    b. metaphase
    c. anaphase
    d. interphase

24. If a diploid cell replicates its DNA so that it now contains an amount of DNA equal to $4n$, how does a haploid gamete get a $1n$ number of chromosomes and a $1n$ amount of DNA?

   a. There are two meiotic divisions and four daughter cells produced in meiotic cell division.

   b. There is only one meiotic division and two daughter cells produced in meiotic cell division.

   c. There is only one meiotic division and four daughter cells produced in meiotic cell division.

   d. none of the above

25. What events are responsible for the genetic variability seen in meiosis?

   a. The direction in which a parental chromosome faces during metaphase I is random.

   b. Homologous chromosomes exchange DNA with one another.

   c. Homologous chromosomes exchange RNA with one another.

   d. Both the first and second answers are correct.

26. What is *parthenogenesis*?

   a. replication of the DNA in a diploid cell, with the subsequent division of this DNA into two daughter cells

   b. replication of the DNA in a diploid cell, with the subsequent division of this DNA into four haploid daughter cells

   c. a type of reproduction that does not require the fusion of gametes from opposite sexes

   d. all of the above

27. Prokaryotic cells divide by undergoing a process called _____.

28. Eukaryotic cells undergo a cellular division process called _____.

29. Gametes are produced by a special cellular division process called _____.

30. During mitosis, sister chromosomes are connected to each other at the _____.

31. During metaphase, the paired chromatids are connected to opposite poles of the cell with structures called spindle _____.

32. _____ are alternate forms of a given gene.

33. This image depicts the steps involved in binary fission. Label those portions indicated.

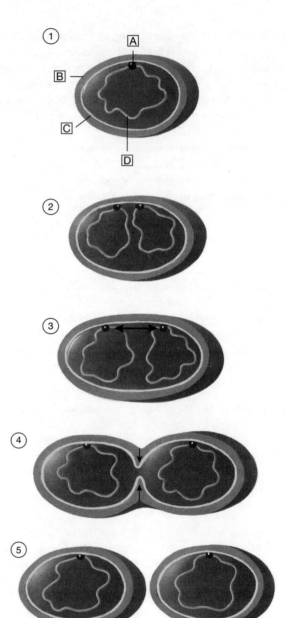

34. Add the missing cell cycle labels to the diagram below.

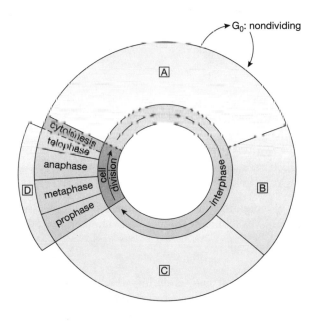

35. Identify the stages of mitosis depicted below.

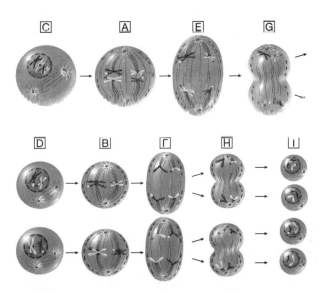

36. Mitosis differs from meiosis in some fundamental ways. Identify these differences by labeling the following diagram of meiosis.

37. Compare mitosis and meiosis by labeling the events below.

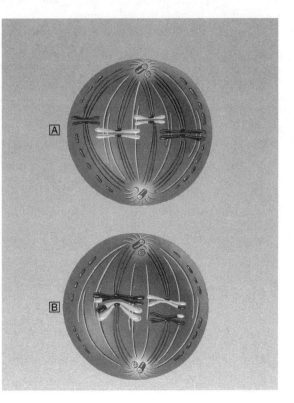

38. Which of the following is a difference between sexual and asexual reproduction?
   a. Asexual reproduction produces greater genetic variation than does sexual reproduction.
   b. Asexual reproduction allows genes to be shuffled more readily than does sexual reproduction.
   c. Asexual reproduction can occur more quickly than sexual reproduction.
   d. Asexual reproduction cannot contribute to the growth of multicellular organisms, whereas sexual reproduction can.

39. The specific place on a chromosome where a gene resides is called a(n) _____.
   a. allele
   b. centromere
   c. homologue
   d. locus

40. Which of the following would be an advantage of sexual reproduction?
   a. Sexual reproduction promotes genetic variability, thereby increasing the probability that an individual with new combinations of favorable traits may arise.
   b. Sexual reproduction ensures that individuals will inherit the most desirable genes from both parents.
   c. Sexual reproduction ensures that offspring are as similar as possible to their parents.
   d. There are no advantages to sexual reproduction; it is an evolutionary relic of an earlier stage.

41. What is the ultimate source of genetic variability in organisms?
   a. sexual reproduction
   b. DNA replication
   c. homologous chromosomes
   d. mutations in DNA

42. The two ends of a eukaryotic chromosome are called _____.

43. After a chromosome is duplicated, it consists of two _____ connected at the centromere.

44. If the diploid chromosome number of an organism is 24, its haploid chromosome number must be _____.

45. The phase of meiosis during which chromosomes condense, and homologous chromosomes pair up is called _____.

46. The phase of meiosis during which sister chromatids separate and move apart is called _____.

47. The phase of meiosis during which chromosomes are lined up individually at the cell's equator is called _____.

ESSAY CHALLENGE

1. How are binary fission and mitosis different? How are they similar?

2. What are the events that take place during the eukaryotic cell cycle?

3. Identify the phases of mitosis and the important actions of each phase.

4. Identify some advantages of sexual reproduction over asexual reproduction.

5. Identify the phases of meiosis.

6. How can meiosis help to encourage genetic variability?

MEDIA ACTIVITIES

To access a Media Activity visit http://www.prenhall.com/audesirk7. Log in to the Web site selected by your instructor, navigate to this chapter, and select the appropriate Media Activity number.

11.1 Cell Division in Humans
Estimated time: 5 minutes

This animation provides a brief overview of the cell cycle in humans.

11.2 Cell Cycle and Mitosis
Estimated time: 10 minutes

This activity describes the process of mitosis, and will help you to understand the steps into which mitosis is divided.

11.3 Meiosis
Estimated time: 10 minutes

In order for the fusion of sperm and egg to produce a cell with the correct number of chromosomes, the sperm and egg must each have one half the number of chromosomes as an adult cell. To accomplish this, certain cells in the body undergo a type of division, called meiosis, which reduces the chromosome number. This activity will lead you through the steps of meiosis.

11.4 How Meiosis Produces Genetic Variability
Estimated time: 5 minutes

Everyone is unique. How does the process of meiosis produce the amazing diversity we see around us? In this activity review the processes that produce such great genetic diversity.

11.5 Web Investigation: Cloning Conundrum
Estimated time: 20 minutes

The Missyplicity Project has raised questions about ethics and science. Explore some of these questions by answering the questions below.

1. The Case Study, Cloning Conundrum, mentions that the first animal cloned by the Missyplicity Project was a cat. This article from *The Scientist* (http://www.biomedcentral.com/news/20021127/03) discusses this project in some detail. Why is it much more difficult to clone dogs than cats and other mammals?

2. The idea behind the Missyplicity Project is to reproduce as closely as possible one beloved pet dog. But how identical (http://mediresource.sympatico.ca/health_news_detail.asp?channel_id=16&news_id=5560) will a cloned puppy be to the dog that provided its genes? Discuss this question in light of the linked article.

3. Should pets be cloned? The position (http://www.ri.bbsrc.ac.uk/news/articles/155.html) of the Roslin Institute, where Dolly, the first cloned mammal, was produced, is "no." Obviously, the people at Genetic Savings and Clone (http://www.savingsandclone.com/) disagree. Discuss the pros and cons of cloning pets.

4. There are vocal arguments in favor of (http://www.humancloning.org/) and opposed to (http://www.globalchange. com/noclones.htm) human cloning. Summarize these arguments, and support one side or the other.

ISSUES IN BIOLOGY

Why Can a Pause in Mitosis Be Crucial for a Cell's Health?

It is nearly a certainty that you or someone you know will develop a cancer at some point in your life. In fact, about 1 in 5 of us can expect to die as a result of a cancer (http://www.cancer.org/docroot/stt/stt_0.asp). Why is cancer so difficult to treat? The sad fact is that cancers result from defects in our own genes (http://www.people.virginia.edu/ ~rjh9u/cancgene.html), particularly the genes that regulate mitotic cell division. When these genes are defective, cells progress through the cell division cycle (http://www.biology.arizona.edu/cell_bio/tutorials/cell_cycle/cells2.html) without regard to the molecular messages that normally control (http://www.hhmi.org/news/elledge2.html) whether and how often a cell will divide. Inappropriate cell division is a serious problem. Even one extra division every few months (as in many breast cancers) is enough to produce a tumor within several years. Eventually, if not controlled, cells accumulate additional mutations that allow them to invade the surrounding tissue. At this point, a full-blown cancer exists: cells are undergoing unregulated cell divisions, refusing to do their proper jobs within the body, and moving into new locations.

To understand the series of genetic changes that convert a normal cell into a cancer cell, scientists have examined the DNA sequences of key cell-cycle regulation genes. In about 60% of the cancers they examine, a gene called p53 (http:// www.ncbi.nlm.nih.gov/books/bv.fcgi?call=bv.View..ShowSection&rid=gnd.section.107) is defective. The p53 gene is a member of the class of genes called "tumor-suppressor genes" (http://users.rcn.com/jkimball.ma.ultranet/ BiologyPages/T/TumorSuppressorGenes.html) whose normal function is to inhibit cell division. The role of the p53 protein is particularly important, because p53 is produced in response to DNA damage. If such damage exists, p53 is produced and activates genes that inhibit cell cycle progression. This pause allows time for the cell to repair the damage, thus helping to prevent mutations from being passed on to the daughter cells. This role has given p53 the nickname, "The Guardian of the Genome (http://www.mutationresearch.com/mutat/editorials/thompson.htt)." In cells that have mutations in the p53 gene (http://www.nci.nih.gov/intra/LHC/p53ref.htm), cell division progresses even though DNA damage has occurred. The resulting increase in mutation rate is undoubtedly very important in allowing cancers to develop.

In some cases, the DNA damage that occurs is too great to repair. Consequently, rather than simply pausing the cell cycle, p53 can alternatively activate a cell suicide program (http://www.hhmi.org/news/korsmeyer.html) called apoptosis. In this process, the cell gently releases its connections to neighboring cells, produces digestive enzymes that break its DNA into small fragments, and disintegrates into bite-sized pieces that are eaten and digested by other body cells. Following apoptosis (http://users.rcn.com/jkimball.ma.ultranet/BiologyPages/A/Apoptosis.html), the cell disappears without a trace. In addition to its importance in inhibiting potential cancerous cells from being produced, apoptosis is also important for removing unnecessary cells during development (http://www.acs.ucalgary.ca/~browder/ apoptosis.html). For example, you have fingers and toes instead of paddles because the cells between your fingers and toes underwent apoptosis.

Apoptosis is a major reason why cancer chemotherapy (http://www.oncolink.com/treatment/article.cfm?c=2&s=9& id=55) and radiation therapy work. Radiation therapy and many chemotherapy agents cause profound DNA damage— enough to induce apoptosis. Unfortunately, these treatments do not discriminate between cancer cells and normal cells. Any cell that is dividing is a potential target. In fact, the apoptosis of normal cells produces most of the side effects of chemotherapy (http://www.mayoclinic.com/invoke.cfm?id=HQ00401) and radiation therapy, including nausea and hair loss.

Given the connection between p53 and apoptosis, can you see a potential problem for physicians treating a patient who has cancer? In many cancers, the p53 gene is defective, but p53 is needed for efficient induction of apoptosis in response to DNA damage. Thus, for those cancers caused by cells with defective p53, chemotherapy and radiation therapy may be less effective than for other cancers. Indeed, examining the p53 gene in a particular cancer (http://www.kubler.com/newsp53.htm) can help physicians decide on appropriate courses of therapy. A recent approach to this problem involves gene-therapy (http://www.pslgroup.com/dg/296ca.htm). Experiments are being done in which normal p53 genes are injected into tumors (http://www.pslgroup.com/dg/2889e.htm). The idea is that the tumor cells will take up the p53 DNA and begin to express the p53 protein. It is hoped that restoring the "Guardian of the Genome" will activate the apoptosis pathway by itself or make the cancer cells once again sensitive to DNA damage.

1. If cancers are caused by mutations in our own genes, what changes might we make in our lives to help lower our risk of getting cancer?

2. What characteristics do you think would be needed in a theoretically perfect cancer therapy?

3. Why do you think cancer is more common in older people than in younger ones?

4. One possible side effect of chemotherapy or radiation treatment is development of new cancers. Thinking about the cause of cancer and how chemotherapy and radiation treatments work, explain why an increased incidence of new cancers might be expected.

BIZARRE FACTS IN BIOLOGY

The Cells That Ate the Mediterranean

Biology is a field rife with exceptions to the norm. You have learned that mitosis is the division of the nucleus, and that it is usually followed by cytokinesis, or cell division. But there's a reason that word "usually" is there. Sometimes mitosis happens, but cytokinesis is nowhere to be seen.

What happens when this occurs? Because there are two nuclei where once there was one, each of these cells now has two nuclei. And it doesn't stop there. Cells in which this occurs usually undergo several bouts of mitosis without cytokinesis, so they end up having numerous—sometimes thousands—of nuclei per cell, a condition referred to as being multinucleate.

In humans, there are a few types of tissues where this happens. The best known are cardiac (http://www.uoguelph.ca/zoology/devobio/210labs/muscle1.html#cardiac) and skeletal (http://www.uoguelph.ca/zoology/devobio/210labs/muscle1.html#skeletal) muscle tissue. But as a general rule, you can think of almost all of your cells as being regular cells with a single nucleus.

However, among fungi and algae, there are entire groups of species where the adult organism is one huge multinucleate cell. These are some of the most fascinating organisms, and many are beautiful as well. For example, there is an alga that is common in shallow tropical and subtropical waters called *Caulerpa*. This alga is surprisingly complex in structure, with different species having different forms, from grape-like clusters (http://www.globaldialog.com/~jrice/algae_page/grapecaulerpa.htm) to feather-like fronds (http://www.portofsandiego.org/sandiego_environment/images/caulerpa.jpg). It is hard to believe that these elaborate structures are composed of a single, large, multinucleate cell.

Why should multinucleate algae have evolved? One possibility is that they are capable of very rapid growth, which all these species seem to be capable of. In fact, one species, *Caulerpa taxifola*, has become a pest in several places where it is not native but has become introduced, most likely by escaping from aquaria. Large areas of the Mediterranean (http://www.pbs.org/saf/1204/features/caluerpa.htm) and of Southern California (http://swr.nmfs.noaa.gov/hcd/CAULERPA.htm) have become infested.

Fortunately, a solution may be at hand. Certain sea slugs have become specialized to feed on these multinucleate algae. If they can be introduced into the areas where *Caulerpa* has become a problem, they may help to control the outbreak. However, introducing yet another foreign species could potentially create other, as yet unforeseen problems, so scientists are debating whether to release these sea slugs or not. For an excellent summary of the *Caulerpa* problem, including the question of releasing these sea slugs, visit this site at the University of Salzburg (http://www.sbg.ac.at/ipk/avstudio/pierofun/ct/caulerpa.htm).

1. One possible advantage of being multinucleate for *Caulerpa* is that being multinucleate allows rapid growth. But by the time you are an adult, your muscle cells, both cardiac and striated, have completed growth. Why do you think these two kinds of muscle cells are multinucleate?

2. Can you think of any disadvantages to *Caulerpa* of being one large multinucleate cell?

3. Do you think it is likely that meiosis ever occurs without cytokinesis? If it does, what would this mean about the daughter cells?

KEY TERMS

allele
anaphase
asexual reproduction
autosome
binary fission
cell cycle
cell division
cell plate
centriole
centromere

chiasma (chiasmata)
chromatid
chromosome
clone
cloning
crossing over
cytokinesis
differentiation
diploid
duplicated chromosome

gamete
haploid
homologue
interphase
karyotype
kinetochore
locus
meiosis
meiotic cell division
metaphase

mitosis
mitotic cell division
prophase
recombination
sex chromosome
sexual reproduction
spindle microtubule
telomere
telophase

ANSWER KEY

SELF TEST
1. e
2. b
3. d
4. b
5. c
6. a
7. d
8. b
9. c
10. d
11. c
12. a
13. c
14. d
15. a
16. e
17. c
18. b
19. c
20. c

21. d
22. d
23. d
24. a
25. d
26. c
27. binary fission
28. mitosis, mitotic division
29. meoisis, meiotic division
30. centromere
31. microtubules, spindle microtubules
32. alleles
33. A. attachment site
    B. cell wall
    C. plasma membrane
    D. circular DNA
34. A. G_1 (growth)
    B. S (synthesis)
    C. G_2 (growth)
    D. mitosis

35. A. early prophase
    B. late prophase
    C. metaphase
    D. interphase
    E. anaphase
    F. telophase
    G. cytokinesis
36. A. metaphase I
    B. metaphase II
    C. prophase I
    D. prophase II
    E. anaphase I
    F. anaphase II
    G. telophase I
    H. telophase II
    I. gametes
37. A. mitosis
    B. meiosis
38. c
39. d
40. a
41. d
42. telomeres, telomere
43. sister chromatids, chromatids
44. 12, twelve
45. prophase I
46. anaphase II
47. metaphase II

ESSAY CHALLENGE

1. Both produce two cells with identical copies of the parental DNA. However, prokaryotes lack a nucleus and usually have a single circular chromosome, whereas eukaryotes usually have several linear chromosomes contained in a nucleus. See section 11.1 in your textbook.

2. There are two phases of the eukaryotic cell cycle: interphase and cell division, which includes mitosis (the division of the nucleus) and cytokinesis (the division of the cell). During interphase, the cell grows and the chromosomes are duplicated. During mitosis, the chromosomes are parceled out equally to the daughter nuclei. During cytokinesis, the cell divides. See section 11.1 in your textbook.

3. The phases are prophase, metaphase, anaphase, and telophase. Chromosomes condense during prophase, the chromosomes align along the equator of the cell during metaphase, sister chromatids are pulled to opposite poles of the cell during anaphase, and new nuclei form around each new collection of chromatids during telophase. See section 11.3 in your textbook.

4. Among other things, sexual reproduction allows for increased variation within populations, as long as the sexual reproduction occurs between unrelated individuals. Other advantages relate to the shuffling of genes that occurs during meiotic cell division. See section 11.4 in your textbook.

5. Meiosis consists of a type of modified mitosis, wherein chromosomes first replicate, then are divided twice. The first division is somewhat different from meiosis, in that the homologous chromosomes pair up and then separate. The daughter cells subsequently divide again by a mechanism very similar to mitosis, such that four daughter cells (gametes) result, each with a single chromatid for each chromosome. See section 11.5 in your textbook.

6. Mathematically, there are a dizzying number of possible combinations of alleles that can result from meiosis. Combined with sexual reproduction, this potential number of possibilities is further compounded and can virtually ensure a healthy amount of genetic variation in the population. See section 11.6 in your textbook.

MEDIA ACTIVITIES

11.5 Web Investigation: Cloning Conundrum

1. Dogs ovulate immature ova that cannot be cloned without first maturing them in an artificial oviduct, which requires advanced (and expensive) technology.

2. Genes are only one factor that determines an organism's characteristics. Envirnomental factors, including the environment in the womb, affect development. Other factors include family life, friends, and chance occurrences in the environment.

3. Whatever position the students take, they should fairly articulate the opposite position. Pro arguments include the freedom to choose your pet's characteristics, satisfying the desire to have a pet similar to a lost beloved one, and a sense of connection to a deceased pet. Anti arguments include the fact that a cloned pet will not be identical to the original, leading to possible disappointment, distress caused to the animals involved (surrogates and the original pet), and the high rate of death among cloned animals.

4. Whatever position the students take, they should fairly articulate the opposite position. Pro arguments include providing medical breakthroughs, organs for transplant, a type of "immortality," and a sense of freedom. Cons include the high risk of medical and emotional problems among clones as well as possible abuse of the technology.

ISSUES IN BIOLOGY

1. Avoiding environmental factors that increase mutation rate might lower the risk of cancer. Such factors include exposure to radiation, excess UV light in sunlight, toxic chemicals, and cancer-causing viruses.

2. Most cancer therapies damage any dividing cell, including non-cancerous ones. An ideal cancer treatment would attack cancerous cells but leave normal cells unharmed. It would also invariably destroy cancer-causing cells, since even a single surviving cancerous cell can cause a new tumor to form.

3. Because damage to DNA causes most cancers, people with more accumulated damage to their DNA will be more likely to develop cancer. DNA damage accumulates over time, so older people tend to have more cancers.

4. Radiation and chemotherapy both cause damage to DNA in dividing cells, ultimately activating p53 and triggering apoptosis in cancerous cells. Normal cells exposed to radiation or chemotherapy agents can also suffer damage to DNA, possibly without triggering apoptosis. This may result in a new cancer.

BIZARRE FACTS IN BIOLOGY

1. Because muscle cells (fibers) are so long, and because they are so metabolically active, they probably require nuclei interspersed along their length in order to provide enough capacity for synthesizing proteins (via mRNA produced in these nuclei) to the entire cell without the need to transport the large molecules from a single central nucleus.

2. *Caulerpa* cells cannot become differentiated into different cell types as can cells in multicellular organisms. Therefore, specialized structures at the tissue level and higher are impossible in these organisms.

3. Although it does not happen in animals, meiosis without cytokinesis does occur in some protozoans and plants. The result is a cell with more than one haploid nucleus.

CHAPTER 12: PATTERNS OF INHERITANCE

AT-A-GLANCE

SELF-TEST

1. Alleles are alternate forms of a gene. The alleles for the gene that determines blood type in humans are found at _____.
   a. different loci on homologous chromosomes
   b. different loci on the same chromosome
   c. the same locus on homologous chromosomes

2. Humans have about 35,000 genes. How many alleles of each of these genes are present in your muscle cells, disregarding genes on the X and Y chromosomes?
   a. 1   b. 2
   c. 23   d. 46

3. If a plant is true-breeding for a flower color, it is _____ for the flower-color gene.

   a. homozygous
   b. heterozygous
   c. dominant

4. A Punnett square is _____.

   a. a method of crossing pea plants
   b. a chart that can help you keep track of the alleles during genetic crosses
   c. named after an Augustinian monk in Brno, Moravia (currently part of the Czech Republic)

5. If a gene has alleles that are incompletely dominant, an individual that is heterozygous at this locus will have characteristics that are _____.

   a. the same as organisms that are homozygous for the recessive allele
   b. the same as organisms that are homozygous for the dominant allele
   c. intermediate between organisms that are homozygous for the recessive allele and organisms that are homozygous for the dominant allele

6. Which one of the following statements is true? (For extra practice, try to change the incorrect answers to make them correct statements. Also, give an example for each of the correct statements.)

   a. An allele is either dominant or recessive, not in between.
   b. A particular gene can have only two alleles.
   c. A single gene influences only a single trait.
   d. A single trait can be affected by many different genes.
   e. The environment is irrelevant to gene expression.

7. Cystic fibrosis is a recessive trait. Imagine that your friend Roger has cystic fibrosis but that his parents do not. What do you know about Roger's alleles and those of his parents at the cystic fibrosis locus of their DNA?

   a. This information is insufficient to allow me to conclude anything about the cystic fibrosis alleles in the DNA of Roger's parents.
   b. This information is insufficient to allow me to conclude anything about the cystic fibrosis alleles in Roger's DNA.
   c. Roger is heterozygous and his parents are homozygous at the cystic fibrosis locus.
   d. Roger is homozygous and his parents are heterozygous at the cystic fibrosis locus.

8. Anne Boleyn, King Henry VIII's second wife, was beheaded because she did not provide him with a son as an heir. Explain why King Henry should have blamed himself and not his wife.

   a. All of the sperm that males produce contain an X chromosome, so their genetic contribution to the child determines its sex.
   b. All of the eggs that females produce contain an X chromosome, so their genetic contribution to the child does not determine its sex.
   c. The eggs that females produce contain either an X or a Y chromosome, so their genetic contribution to the child is unrelated to its sex.

9. In many cases, conditions that occur more frequently in males than in females are due to sex-linked inheritance. Male pattern baldness is more common in males than in females, but that is not because of sex-linked inheritance. Suggest a possible explanation.

   a. An important gene for hair development must be on the X chromosome.
   b. An important gene for hair development must be on the Y chromosome.
   c. Male hormones affect expression of an important hair development gene.

10. Labrador retrievers may have yellow fur, chocolate brown fur, or black fur. Coat color is determined by two genes that have two alleles each. One gene, called E, determines whether the dog's fur is dark or light, with the dark allele (*E*) dominant to the light allele (*e*). The other gene, called B, determines whether the dark fur will be black or chocolate, with the black allele (*B*) dominant to the chocolate allele (*b*). If you mate two chocolate labs together, what color puppies can they have?

    a. Only chocolate puppies can be produced, because both parents must be *EEbb*.
    b. Chocolate or yellow puppies can be produced, because the parents can be either *Eebb* or *EEbb*.
    c. Chocolate, yellow, and black puppies will be produced, because both parents must be *EeBb*.
    d. Chocolate and black puppies will be produced, because both parents must be *EeBb*.

11. A couple brings home their new, nonidentical twin daughters, Joan and Jill. After several months, the father begins to suspect that there was a mix-up at the hospital, because Jill doesn't look much like either parent or like her sister. When the twins' blood tests come back, the father calls his lawyer to start a lawsuit against the hospital. The mother, father, and Joan have type A blood, but Jill has type O blood. Does the father have a case? Explain your answer. (The gene for blood type has three alleles: A, B, and O. The A and B alleles are codominant, and the O allele is recessive.)
    a. No, because parents with type A blood can have a child with type O blood.
    b. No, because parents with any blood type (A, B, AB, or O) can produce children with type O blood.
    c. Yes, because all of this couple's children will have type A blood.
    d. Yes, because people with type A blood can pass on only A alleles to their children.

12. What are alleles?
    a. specific physical locations of genes on a chromosome
    b. variations of the same gene (i.e., similar nucleotide sequences on homologous chromosomes)
    c. homozygotes
    d. heterozygotes

13. Consider this hypothetical example: If you were to apply Mendel's reasoning to the past presidential election, and hanging chads (C) were dominant to pregnant chads (c), which of the following genotypes would result in the expression of the dominant phenotype from a cross of F$_1$ offspring that are Cc?
    a. cc
    b. CC
    c. Cc
    d. Both the first and third answers above are correct.
    e. Both the second and third answers above are correct.

14. What does Mendel's law of independent assortment tell us about the behavior of genes during meiosis?
    a. Alleles of a particular gene will be distributed to gametes randomly, independent of other genes on different chromosomes.
    b. Alleles on the same chromosome will be distributed to different gametes independently.
    c. Independent assortment is synonymous with crossing over.
    d. all of the above

15. If an organism has only three chromosomes, how many chromosomes are autosomes?
    a. one   b. two
    c. three   d. none

16. A single gene capable of influencing multiple phenotypes within a single organism is said to be _____.
    a. codominant for that gene
    b. incompletely dominant for that gene
    c. polygenic for that gene
    d. pleiotropic for that gene

17. What is the root cause of sickle-cell anemia?
    a. mutations in the gene that directs the synthesis of the hemoglobin protein
    b. an amino acid substitution in the hemoglobin protein
    c. malaria
    d. abnormally shaped red blood cells

18. If the pea plants I planted this year all have red flowers, and the parent of those seeds also had red flowers, those seeds are said to be _____.

19. In Mendel's experiments, he first cross-bred true breeding purple-flowered peas with true breeding white-flowered peas. The first filial generation was found to consist entirely of _____-flowered pea plants.

20. Mendel found that the F$_1$ generation in his pea plant experiments looked like only one of the original parent plants, but that the flower color trait exhibited by the other parent showed up again in F$_2$. He suggested that purple flower color was _____ with respect to flower color in peas.

21. When one trait usually expresses itself in conjunction with another, and the genes which control that expression are found on the same chromosome, those two traits are genetically _____.

22. Sometimes, chromosomes will exchange stretches of DNA during a crossing-over event. This occurs at a _____.

23. When true breeding snapdragons with red flowers are cross-bred with true breeding white-flowered snapdragons, the progeny exhibit a color between white and red. This is because red and white have _____ dominance over each other.

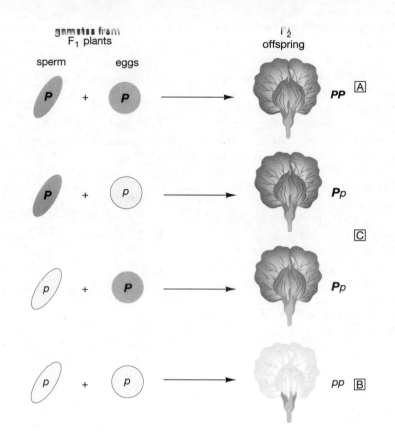

gametes from
F₁ plants

sperm   eggs   F₂ offspring

P + **P** → **PP** Ⓐ

P + **p** → **Pp**

Ⓒ

p + **P** → **Pp**

p + **p** → **pp** Ⓑ

24. In the diagram above, the capital *P* stands for purple, and the small *p* indicates white. This is an example of complete dominance. Label each of the F₂ offspring according to their color, as indicated by their genotype.

25. Fill in the missing genotype for each of the eggs across the top of the Punnett square below.

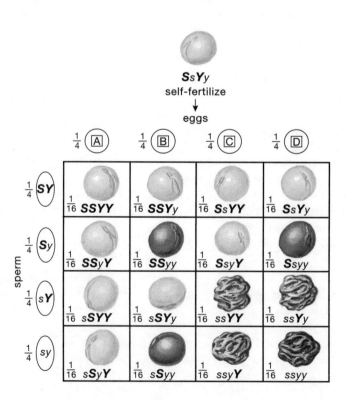

SsYy
self-fertilize
↓
eggs

	¼ Ⓐ	¼ Ⓑ	¼ Ⓒ	¼ Ⓓ
¼ **SY**	¹⁄₁₆ **SSYY**	¹⁄₁₆ **SSYy**	¹⁄₁₆ **SsYY**	¹⁄₁₆ **SsYy**
¼ **Sy**	¹⁄₁₆ **SSyY**	¹⁄₁₆ **SSyy**	¹⁄₁₆ **SsyY**	¹⁄₁₆ **Ssyy**
¼ **sY**	¹⁄₁₆ **sSYY**	¹⁄₁₆ **sSYy**	¹⁄₁₆ **ssYY**	¹⁄₁₆ **ssYy**
¼ **sy**	¹⁄₁₆ **sSyY**	¹⁄₁₆ **sSyy**	¹⁄₁₆ **ssyY**	¹⁄₁₆ **ssyy**

sperm

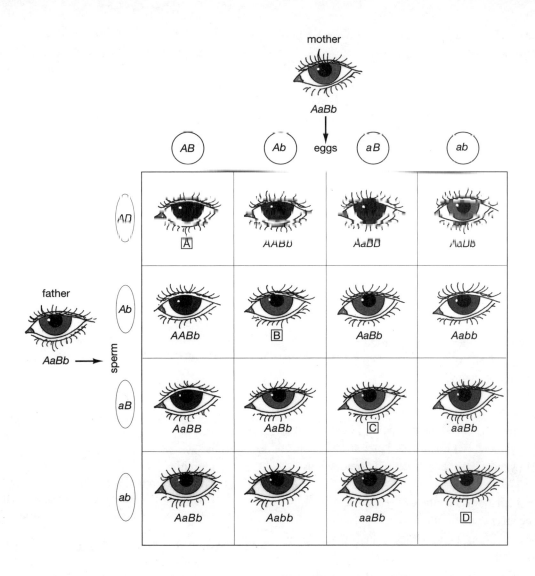

mother

AaBb

AB Ab eggs aB ab

father

AaBb →

sperm

AB | A | AABb | AaBB | AaBb
Ab | AABb | B | AaBb | Aabb
aB | AaBB | AaBb | C | aaBb
ab | AaBb | Aabb | aaBb | D

26. Human eye color is a trait that shows incomplete or mixed dominance. Using the clues given in the Punnett square above, complete the genotypes of the offspring on the diagonal.

27. Which of the following can account for a situation where Mendel's Law of Independent Assortment fails to hold?
   a. The genes are on the same chromosome.
   b. pleiotropy
   c. self-fertilization
   d. The genes have undergone recombination.
   e. crossing over

28. Some people are said to be "carriers" of genetic disorders. What does this mean?
   a. The individual is heterozygous for the disorder, and the allele for the disorder is recessive.
   b. The individual is heterozygous for the disorder, and the allele for the disorder is dominant.
   c. The individual is homozygous for the disorder.
   d. The individual is homozygous for the disorder, but is protected by the presence of an immunity gene.

29. Which of the following is true of a man with hemophilia?
   a. The man inherited the hemophilia gene from his mother.
   b. The man inherited the hemophilia gene from his father.
   c. The man could have inherited the hemophilia gene from either his mother or his father.

30. What happens if a baby has only one X chromosome, and no Y?
   a. Such a major chromosome deficiency is lethal, so the baby would be stillborn.
   b. This baby would be a female with Turner syndrome.
   c. The baby would be a male with Turner syndrome.
   d. The individual would have Klinefelter syndrome.

31. Which of the following is caused by an abnormal number of autosomes?
   a. Down syndrome   b. Klinefelter syndrome
   c. Turner syndrome   d. Marfan syndrome

32. Mendel's experiments with dihybrid crosses led him to develop his law of _____.

33. Geneticists study patterns of inheritance in human families to learn about genetic diseases. A chart showing how a trait is inherited over several generations of a family is called a _____.

34. Heterozygous individuals are _____ of recessive genetic disorders.

35. Errors in meiosis that cause a gamete to have too few or too many chromosomes are called _____.

36. A person with XO sex chromosomes has _____ syndrome.

37. An organism is described as Rr:red. The Rr is the organism's [A]; red is the organism's [B]; and the organism is [C].
    a. [A] phenotype; [B] genotype; [C] degenerate
    b. [A] karyotype; [B] hybrid; [C] recessive
    c. [A] genotype; [B] phenotype; [C] heterozygous
    d. [A] gamete; [B] linkage; [C] pleiotropic
    e. [A] zygote; [B] phenotype; [C] homozygous

38. The 9:3:3:1 ratio is a ratio of
    a. phenotypes in a test cross
    b. phenotypes in a cross of individuals that differ in one trait
    c. phenotypes in a cross of individuals that differ in two traits
    d. genotypes in a cross of individuals that differ in one trait
    e. genotypes in a cross of individuals that differ in two traits

39. A lawyer tells a male client that blood type cannot be used to his advantage in a paternity suit against the client because the child could, in fact, be the client's, according to blood type. Which of the following is the only possible combination supporting this hypothetical circumstance? (Answers are in the order mother:father:child.)
    a. A:B:O
    b. A:O:B
    c. AB:A:O
    d. AB:O:AB
    e. B:O:A

40. A heterozygous red-eyed female *Drosophila* mated with a white-eyed male would produce
    a. red-eyed females and white-eyed males in the F_1
    b. white-eyed females and red-eyed males in the F_1
    c. half red- and half white-eyed females and all white-eyed males in the F_1
    d. all white-eyed females and half red- and half white-eyed males in the F_1
    e. half red- and half white-eyed females as well as males in the F_1

41. Which is NOT true of sickle-cell anemia?
    a. It is most common in African Americans.
    b. It involves a one-amino-acid change in hemoglobin.
    c. It involves red blood cells.
    d. It is lethal in heterozygotes because it is dominant.
    e. It confers some resistance to malaria.

42. Sex-linked disorders such as color blindness and hemophilia are
    a. caused by genes on the X chromosome
    b. caused by genes on the autosome
    c. caused by genes on the Y chromosome
    d. expressed only in men
    e. expressed only when two chromosomes are homozygous recessive

ESSAY CHALLENGE

1. Describe how Mendel's initial cross-breeding and back-cross experiments helped to prove that genes are the component active in inherited traits.

2. Explain why Mendel's findings about flower color in peas do not explain all types of genetic trait inheritance.

3. Why are *Drosophila melanogaster* used so frequently in genetics exercises?

4. Describe how incomplete dominance (as in snapdragons) is different from complete dominance (as in peas).

5. Explain some reasons why polygenic inheritance provides a clearer explanation for human eye color than does single-gene inheritance.

6. Explain how the genetic disorders Turner syndrome, Trisomy X, Klinefelter syndrome, and XYY males are related.

MEDIA ACTIVITIES

To access a Media Activity visit http://www.prenhall.com/audesirk7. Log in to the Web site selected by your instructor, navigate to this chapter, and select the appropriate Media Activity number.

12.1 Monohybrid Crosses
Estimated time: 10 minutes

This tutorial will recreate one of Mendel's early experiments and show that a Punnett square can be used to determine how probability figures into genetic analysis.

12.2 Dihybrid Crosses
Estimated time: 10 minutes

In this tutorial, examine a set of crosses, focusing on two separate genetic traits. See how probability can help explain this situation also.

12.3 Web Investigation: Marfan Syndrome
Estimated time: 10 minutes

Marfan syndrome, a genetic disorder, afflicts one in every 3000 to 5000 people of all races and ethnicity. Marfan syndrome is one of many genetic disorders associated with a specific gene product, and the cellular and biochemical mechanisms underlying its many effects are relatively well understood. Read about these aspects of Marfan syndrome and answer the questions below.

1. Marfan syndrome is characterized by several seemingly unrelated disorders (http://www.marfan.org/pub/factsheet.html). Describe these disorders. What treatments are available?

2. How is Marfan syndrome inherited (http://www.yourgenesyourhealth.org/marfan/inherited.htm)? How can a child whose parents are not carriers get Marfan syndrome?

3. The gene for Marfan syndrome codes for a defective form of the protein fibrillin (http://www3.ncbi.nlm.nih.gov/htbin-post/Omim/dispmim?134797). What role does fibrillin play in the body? Why does a defect in this protein have so many different effects?

4. The Case Study in your textbook mentions that several historic figures, including Abraham Lincoln (http://www.marfan.org/pub/newsletter/vol01/nmf_16th.html) and the Egyptian pharaoh Akhenaten (http://www.marfan.ca/pharaoh.htm) had Marfan syndrome. How can we diagnose this disorder in people who lived long before the syndrome was even recognized?

5. The most serious symptoms of Marfan syndrome affect the heart (http://www.childrenheartinstitute.org/educate/marfan/marfan.htm). Describe the ways in which hearts of people with Marfan syndrome can be defective. What treatments are available?

ISSUES IN BIOLOGY

What Is the Most Common Genetic Disease in the United States?

The most common inherited fatal disease in the United States is an autosomal recessive condition called hemochromatosis (http://www.uphs.upenn.edu/news/News_Releases/july96/iron.html). Approximately 1 of every 10 Americans is a carrier (heterozygous for a normal allele and a defective allele) and almost 1 in 250 is homozygous for the defective allele. This means that about 1.5 million people in the United States alone are at risk of dying from complications caused by this disease. For comparison, 1 of 25 is a carrier of the cystic fibrosis allele, and 1 in 2500 is a homozygote who actually develops cystic fibrosis.

Hemochromatosis is caused by the uptake of excessive amounts of iron by the intestines. Although we all need iron, particularly in the hemoglobin (http://www.britannica.com/eb/article?eu=40808&tocid=0) that carries oxygen in our red blood cells, too much iron is extremely toxic. The excess iron becomes deposited into tissues such as the liver, heart, and pancreas, eventually interfering with the functioning of these vital organs. So much iron accumulates that some individuals with hemochromatosis have reportedly set off the metal detectors in airport security checks! Damage caused by the excessive iron accumulation causes complications such as cirrhosis (http://www.medlib.med. utah.edu/WebPath/LIVEHTML/LIVER013.html) and cancer of the liver, heart disease, and diabetes (http://www. familyvillage.wisc.edu/lib_diab.htm), normally beginning in middle age. However, years before they are diagnosed, people with hemochromatosis may display widely varying symptoms, including chronic fatigue, abdominal pain, and a bronzed skin coloration.

A simple blood test for hemochromatosis measures the amount of iron in the serum as well as the amount of blood proteins that bind to iron (ferritin (http://encarta.msn.com/dictionary_/ferritin.html) and transferrin (http://encarta. msn.com/dictionary_/transferrin.html)). A liver biopsy then can confirm the diagnosis. The good news is that, if the tests reveal you do have this disease, the treatment is simple: frequent blood withdrawal. When blood is removed, iron is also removed, eventually lowering the overall iron amounts in the body. After hemochromatosis (http://www. americanhs.org/) is diagnosed, the physician may prescribe removal of a unit (pint) of blood once or twice a week until the iron levels are reduced to normal ranges. To maintain these lower iron levels, an individual may then have blood withdrawn four to eight times each year. What happens to all that blood? The policy until recent years was to prevent people with hemochromatosis from donating blood. In fact, it COST them about $200 each time they gave up their unit of blood, which was subsequently destroyed. Recently, the FDA has approved the use of blood donated by people with hemochromatosis for transfusions, and these people can now have their blood removed for free.

Mercator Genetics recently reported in the prestigious journal *Nature* that the company had identified the gene for hemochromatosis. This gene, called HLA-H, is on chromosome 6 and appears to encode a protein that is related to those that determine tissue compatibility (these are the proteins tested to see if a person is a compatible tissue donor). They found that many people with hemochromatosis have a mutation that changes amino acid 282 in the HLA-H protein from cysteine to tyrosine. How this defect causes increased uptake of iron is not understood at present, but commercial genetic tests are now available for the disease. It is hoped that knowing the gene responsible for hemochromatosis will also provide new avenues for treatment.

1. What is the most common genetic disease in the United States?

2. Some people think that everyone should be routinely tested for hemochromatosis, since effective treatments are available. Can you think of reasons to support widespread testing? Can you think of problems that widespread testing for hemochromatosis might cause?

3. Why do you think that the public is so unaware of a common condition such as hemochromatosis but so well informed about much rarer conditions such as cystic fibrosis?

4. What would it be like to have hemochromatosis? You may also want to check out one family's story of their experience with hemochromatosis (http://web.tampabay.rr.com/shuzoo/webdoc6.htm).

BIZARRE FACTS IN BIOLOGY

Daddy's Little Girl

Sex: Everybody's got one. For mammals, sex is determined by the chromosomal "odd couple," the X and Y chromosomes. New evidence suggests that the set of sex chromosomes you own determines much more than if you can wear a skirt in public.

In sexually reproducing organisms, one member of each pair of chromosomes comes from the mother and one comes from the father. Each human egg cell carries 22 autosomes and one X chromosome. Sperm cells carry 22 autosomes and either an X or a Y chromosome. If the egg fuses with a sperm carrying an X chromosome, the embryo will be female (XX). Sperm carrying Y chromosomes produce male (XY) embryos. Whereas females get an X chromosome from both parents, males can get only an X chromosome from their mothers.

Occasionally, errors happen when chromosomes separate during mitosis or meiosis and an egg or sperm cell ends up without a complete set. If the lost chromosome is the X chromosome, the resultant embryo becomes a girl with the genotype of XO. We can see she is missing a chromosome by examining a karyotype (http://www.ornl.gov/hgmis/publicat/primer/karyotyp.gif), a picture of the chromosomes. This girl has Turner's syndrome (http://www.turner-syndrome-us.org/resource/med_info.html).

Because the error can happen in either the sperm or the egg cell, this girl's single X chromosome derives either from the mother (Xm) or the father (Xp). Surprisingly, if the girl has the Xm chromosome, she has considerably more trouble learning behavioral skills than if she had received an Xp chromosome, suggesting that some of the genes involved in learning self-control reside on the X chromosome. Furthermore, these genes must somehow give the message "behave yourself" if they are on the paternal X chromosome and the message "act up" if they are on the maternal one.

Boys, on average, are more likely than girls to have difficulty with language development and reading skills. Significantly more boys than girls suffer from autism, a disorder characterized by extreme, antisocial behavior. Observing typical "male" behavior in Turner's syndrome girls with Xm chromosomes suggest that chromosomes are "marked" and behave differently depending on whether they are of paternal or maternal origin.

This marking is called genomic imprinting (http://www.geneimprint.com/). Whereas both paternal and maternal genes are essential for normal development, they are not equivalent. Science may redefine what it means to be "a chip off the old block" or "daddy's little girl."

References

Iwasa, Y. 1998. The conflict theory of genomic imprinting: How much can be explained? *Curr Top Dev Bio* 40: 255–93.

Keverne, E. B., Martel, F. L., and Nevison, C. M. 1996. Primate brain evolution: Genetic and functional considerations. *Proc R Soc Lond B* 262: 689–96.

Pagel, M. 1999. Mother and father in surprise genetic agreement. *Nature* 397: 19–20.

Skuse, D. N., James, R. S., Bishop, D. V. M., Coppin, B., Dalton, P., Aamodt-Leeper, G., Bacarese-Hamilton, M., Creswell, C., McGurk, R., and Jacobs, P. A. 1997. Evidence from Turner's syndrome of an imprinted X-linked locus affecting cognitive function. *Nature* 387: 705–8.

Thornhill, A. R., and Burgoyne, P. S. 1993. A paternally imprinted X chromosome retards the development of the early mouse embryo. *Development* 118: 171–4.

1. Embyros that are genetically XO become girls with Turner's syndrome; what do you think would happen to a YO embryo?

2. What would be the advantage to the organism of genomic imprinting?

3. How could having "poor social skills" be an advantage to males such that the gene activity would be preserved during evolution?

A Typical Human: Brown Hair, Color Vision, Freckles, and Six Fingers!

Greg Harris, a pitcher for the Montreal Expos, upon his induction into the Baseball Hall of Fame in Cooperstown, New York, donated one of his two specially designed gloves for exhibition. Harris's glove is unique because it was made to accommodate his six fingers. Why do people look the way that they do? Where does the information come from to have six fingers rather than five? These human traits are passed down from parents to their children as genes on their DNA.

By studying the common pea plant, Gregor Mendel (http://www.accessexcellence.org/AB/BC/Gregor_Mendel.html)(a Czech monk) was the first to investigate how offspring inherit specific traits from their parents. When Mendel crossed two true-breeding plants with alternative traits—say, a purple-flowered plant with a white-flowered plant, the offspring showed only one of the two traits. Mendel observed that whenever he looked at a trait with two possible alternatives and used true-breeding plants, one trait was fully expressed (dominant) and the other had no noticeable effect (recessive). However, when Mendel crossed the offspring of these parents with each other, the recessive trait would reappear in one quarter of the new generation. The recessive trait had not been eliminated; it simply was not obvious in the presence of the dominant trait. We now know that dominant and recessive traits are products of the different alleles of a gene.

More than 100 human genetic disorders are known to be inherited as Mendelian traits (either as a dominant or recessive allele). Many dominant traits are not necessarily the "better" or "stronger" or most common in a population (for example, polydactyly (http://www.accessexcellence.org/AB/GG/polydactyly.html) —extra fingers and/or toes); it is simply the allele that produces a noticeable effect, a phenotype. The allele responsible for polydactyly occurs in one of the many genes responsible for directing the development of the embryo. When an allele causes such a gene product to be overexpressed, or expressed at an inappropriate time during development, then we see the effect—six fingers.

What makes an allele common or rare in a population? Again, it doesn't depend on whether the allele is dominant or recessive. An allele can become rare when the phenotype produced by the presence of the allele is selected against in the environment. In the extreme case, alleles become rare when the homozygous state (two of the same alleles) produces a lethal condition before those individuals can produce children. In the case of polydactyly, two dominant alleles probably prevents proper embryonic development, resulting in a miscarriage. One dominant allele provides extra fingers or toes, and, maybe, a Hall of Fame pitcher.

1. In your opinion, how much of who you are is based on the DNA that you carry and how much is based on the environment in which you were raised and live?

2. The symptoms of Huntington's disease do not appear until mid-life. There is no cure for this disease. Recent advances in human genetic molecular biology have identified the gene responsible for the disease. If one of your parents has the disease, you have either a 50 percent or a 100 percent chance of getting the disease. Would you want to know if you carried the gene for the disease? Why or why not?

3. Why are some dominant characteristics with no seeming advantage, such as the ability to curl your tongue, fairly common in human populations, whereas others, such as polydactyly, are more rare?

KEY TERMS

allele	genotype	law of segregation	recessive
autosome	hemophilia	linkage	self-fertilization
carrier	heterozygous	locus	sex chromosome
codominance	homozygous	multiple alleles	sex-linked
cross-fertilization	hybrid	nondisjunction	sickle-cell anemia
crossing over	incomplete dominance	pedigree	test cross
dominant	inheritance	phenotype	trisomy 21
Down syndrome	Klinefelter syndrome	pleiotropy	trisomy X
gene	law of independent	polygenic inheritance	true-breeding
genetic recombination	assortment	Punnett square method	Turner syndrome

---

ANSWER KEY

SELF TEST

1. c	8. b
2. b	9. c
3. a	10. b
4. b	11. a
5. c	12. b
6. d	13. e
7. d	14. a
	15. b

16. d
17. a
18. true breeding, true-breeding
19. purple
20. dominant
21. linked
22. chiasma
23. incomplete
24. A. purple homozygote
    B. white homozygote
    C. purple heterozygote
25. A. SY
    B. Sy
    C. sY
    D. sy
26. A. AABB
    B. Aabb
    C. aaBB
    D. aabb
27. a
28. a
29. a
30. b
31. a
32. independent assortment
33. pedigree
34. carriers
35. nondisjunction, nondisjunctions
36. Turner, Turner's
37. c
38. c
39. a
40. e
41. d
42. a

ESSAY CHALLENGE

1. Using these techniques, Mendel was able to show that single factors were responsible for flower color in peas.
2. Among other things, some traits require input from several genes or are transmitted disproportionately to members of only one sex.
3. Small size, short generation times, and relatively few chromosomes are all fairly good reasons why *Drosophila melanogaster* are used as genetic subjects.
4. Dominance relationships usually indicate how, or which, pigments are produced in a flower.
5. According to the diagram in Figure 12-12 in your text, there are too many different eye color shades to be explained by a single gene.
6. When sex chromosomes don't disjoin during meiosis, some gametes can end up with either zero or two sex chromosomes.

MEDIA ACTIVITIES

12.3   Web Investigation: Marfan Syndrome

1. Disorders include mitral valve prolapse, a weakened aorta leading to dissection, scoliosis, loose jointedness, disproportionate growth, myopia, and ocular dislocation. There are standard medical treatments for the above, but none address the underlying, genetic, cause.
2. Marfan syndrome is inherited as a simple dominant trait. About one quarter of Marfan cases are in children whose parents are normal. This is because a mutation occurred in the gene for fibrillin during formation of a gamete.
3. Fibrillin forms part of many different connective tissues in the body, such as tendons, bones, and the valves in your heart. Because fibrillin is a component of so many different tissues, it has many different effects on many different organs.
4. Medical historians refer to any historical accounts that mention the appearance or health of the person, as well as any images that are available, since Marfan individuals have characteristically long limbs. In the case of Aknehaten, the artwork produced during his reign seems to show people with Marfan-like features, which may reflect homage to the ruler.
5. Heart defects include weakening of the aorta and mitral valve prolapse. Marfan patients may receive beta blockers to reduce blood pressure, which might tear the aorta. It also helps prevent valve prolapse. Surgery can reinforce or replace the mitral valve, and can strengthen a weakened aorta.

ISSUES IN BIOLOGY

1. The most common genetic disease is hemochromatosis, which affects about 10% of all Americans.
2. Widespread testing would diagnose hemochromatosis in individuals who do not yet exhibit symptoms, thereby potentially enabling them to avoid organ damage. A possible negative consequence of widespread testing is discrimination by insurance companies as a result of testing.
3. The symptoms of hemochromatosis are usually subtle, gradually increasing as the person ages. They are often confused for other diseases, with the underlying hemochromatosis going undiagnosed. Conversely, cystic fibrosis usually presents severe symptoms in children, which makes it a much more visible disease in spite of its much rarer occurrence.
4. There is really no single correct answer to this question. However, the accompanying story linked to the question shows that these people experienced a great deal of frustration getting a proper diagnosis, as well as a lot of misunderstanding of this disease among their health care professionals.

BIZARRE FACTS IN BIOLOGY

Daddy's Little Girl

1. Because the X chromosome contains many genes that are required for life, a YO embryo would almost certainly not live.

2. From an evolutionary perspective, it is in the father's best interest to have the offspring demand as many resources as possible from the mother. This is not necessarily true for the mother. This may be the ultimate explanation for genomic imprinting in mammals, but in truth the research in this area is very preliminary.

3. In many mammals, the males are aggressive, defending territories and mates. The kinds of behaviors that such aggressive males exhibit might be considered "antisocial" in modern societies.

A Typical Human: Brown Hair, Color Vision, Freckles, and Six Fingers!

1. Individual answers will vary, but a correct response should point out that an individual's phenotype depends on both genetics and environmental factors.

2. Different students will have different opinions. However, they should all understand that there are advantages and disadvantages to both positions. Advantages may include making an informed decision about having children. Disadvantages include dealing with the sense of inevitable doom if you are, indeed, a carrier.

3. For some of these seemingly innocuous traits, the homozygous condition is, indeed, detrimental. For example, being homozygous for the polydactyly allele probably affects embryonic development enough so that some embryos die in the womb. Such alleles will become infrequent in a population.

CHAPTER 13: BIOTECHNOLOGY

AT-A-GLANCE

SELF TEST

1. Transformation is the process by which foreign _____ is taken up from a cell's environment, permanently changing the characteristics of a cell and its offspring.
   a. DNA   b. RNA
   c. protein

2. Antibiotic resistance can be passed among bacterial strains by _____.
   a. transformation   b. natural selection
   c. transplantation

3. Analysis of restriction fragment length polymorphisms (RFLPs) is a rapid way to examine differences in the _____.
   a. bacterial enzymes
   b. length of a DNA molecule
   c. number of genes on a chromosome
   d. DNA sequences of individuals

4. A pair of prospective parents is concerned about the risk of having a child with cystic fibrosis, because both the man and woman have a sibling who died from the disease. They undergo genetic testing and find that each carries one cystic fibrosis allele and one normal allele. What is the likelihood that their unborn child will have cystic fibrosis? (Recall that cystic fibrosis results from a recessive mutation.)

   a. 0% (None of their children will have cystic fibrosis.)

   b. 25% (The chance that this baby will have cystic fibrosis is 1 in 4.)

   c. 50% (The chance that this baby will have cystic fibrosis is 1 in 2.)

   d. 100% (All of their children will have cystic fibrosis.)

5. Imagine you are looking at a DNA fingerprint that shows an STR pattern of a mother's DNA and her child's DNA. Will all of the bands on the Southern Blot showing the child's DNA match those of the mother? Explain. (To help you answer this question, visit the Biology Animation Library (http://www.dnalc.org/resources/BiologyAnimation Library.htm) at Cold Spring Harbor Laboratory and play the tutorial about the Southern Blot technique.)

   a. Yes, because the child developed from an egg produced by the mother.

   b. Yes, because the DNA of mothers and children are identical.

   c. No, because a person's DNA pattern changes with age.

   d. No, because the father contributed half of the child's DNA.

6. Which of the following describes an example of DNA recombination?

   a. any organism that utilizes sexual reproduction

   b. the exchange of fluids between a cell's interior (cytoplasm) and its exterior (extracellular fluid)

   c. a viral infection resulting in a common cold

   d. Both the first and third answers are correct.

7. What are restriction enzymes?

   a. enzymes that are limited (i.e., restricted) in how big they can become

   b. vitamins such as vitamin A

   c. plasmids

   d. enzymes that cleave through a DNA helix wherever they encounter a specific sequence of nucleotides

8. What is a restriction fragment length polymorphism?

   a. different sizes of restriction fragments from two DNA molecules that are produced by a restriction enzyme

   b. a short sequence of single-stranded DNA that is able to bind with regions of interest along a DNA molecule

   c. Movement of DNA fragments varies according to size and electric charge through a gel when an electric current is applied.

   d. none of the above

9. What is the "polymerase chain reaction" (PCR) technique?

   a. a technique that incorporates repeated cycles of heating and cooling of DNA segments in the presence of primers and heat-resistant DNA polymerase

   b. an elegant chemical technique that utilizes the natural ability of DNA polymerase to synthesize DNA that is complementary to the parent DNA fragments

   c. a technique that allows investigators to determine the nucleotide sequence of a given gene

   d. a technique that has led to the development of genetic screening tests of newborns for genetic disease (e.g., cystic fibrosis) once the nucleotide sequence of disease-causing gene is known

   e. all of the above

10. What benefit does administration of genetically engineered human insulin provide to patients that pig/bovine insulin does not?

   a. There was no benefit; the nucleotide sequence that determines the structure of insulin is the same in all three species.

   b. Allergic reactions were avoided by using the recombinant human insulin.

   c. It could be produced in large quantities using bacteria/yeast genetically engineered to carry the human insulin gene.

   d. Both the second and third answers are correct.

11. What are some of the problems associated with the use of genetic screens for cystic fibrosis?

   a. Positive testing of a man and a woman each carrying a copy of the CF gene guarantees their offspring will have the disease.

   b. Ethical dilemmas: Individual carriers of the CF allele (Should they even attempt to conceive?), societal and insurance carriers (Should they be forced to bear the financial costs?).

   c. potential genetic discrimination by insurance companies

   d. Both the second and third answers are correct.

12. _____ is any commercial use or alteration of organisms, cells, or molecules to achieve specific goals.

13. Bacteria can pick up and utilize _____, which can change physical traits of bacteria.

14. Gel _____ uses physical properties of DNA fragments to help separate restriction fragments according to size.

15. An artificial gene reproduction technique that helps to produce human insulin is called the _____ chain reaction (PCR).

16. This image shows the sequence of viral infection. Complete the sequence by labeling the indicated steps.

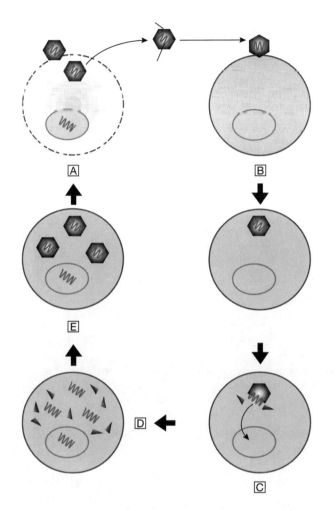

17. PCR requires the binding of both primers and DNA polymerase. One of these is a strand of DNA and the other is an enzyme. In the schematic of one PCR reaction shown below, label the primer and the polymerase.

18. The modification of genetic material to achieve specific goals is called _____.

19. To clone a gene, you first isolate the gene of interest and then you insert it into a _____, which then can be replicated inside bacteria.

20. Because potatoes engineered to produce vaccines must be eaten raw, researchers are now working to produce vaccine-containing _____.

21. Making transgenic animals usually involves injecting the desired DNA into a(n) _____.

22. In the first step of the polymerase chain reaction (PCR), _____ is used to separate the double helix of DNA into single strands.

23. Gel electrophoresis is used to _____.
    a. increase the amount of DNA of a particular sequence
    b. cleave DNA into small pieces
    c. separate DNA fragments by size
    d. extract DNA from tissue samples

24. Researchers must design short pieces of DNA that are complementary to DNA on either side of the segment to be amplified. These small pieces are called _____.
    a. primers
    b. DNA probes
    c. plasmids
    d. DNA fingerprints

25. STR polymorphisms can be used to identify individuals because _____.
    a. individuals are genetically unique
    b. restriction enzymes cut different recognition sequences in different people
    c. a given set of PCR primers works for only a small subset of individuals

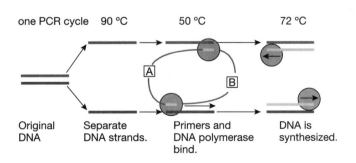

one PCR cycle   90 °C   50 °C   72 °C

Original DNA   Separate DNA strands.   Primers and DNA polymerase bind.   DNA is synthesized.

26. Which of the following sources of DNA could be used in DNA forensic analysis?

   a. semen
   b. saliva
   c. hair follicle
   d. blood
   e. all of the above

27. The primary goal of human gene therapy is _____.

   a. to correct genetic disorders by inserting normal genes in place of defective ones
   b. to provide counseling to affected people to help them live with their disorder
   c. to treat the symptoms of genetic disorders
   d. to correct genetic disorders in developing embryos

ESSAY CHALLENGE

1. Why is PCR (polymerase chain reaction) so important to people studying biotechnology?

2. Why do you think DNA fingerprinting is being used to analyze and compare fossils and living species?

3. Why is it advantageous to create corn and soybean plants that can produce their own kind of pesticide?

4. Daffodils were selected to donate genes to help rice produce vitamin A (section 13.6 in your textbook). Why?

5. Why is gene therapy so controversial if it is also so beneficial?

6. If there are tests available to find predispositions for certain genetic diseases, why don't more people have themselves tested prior to starting families?

MEDIA ACTIVITIES

To access a Media Activity visit http://www.prenhall.com/audesirk7. Log in to the Web site selected by your instructor, navigate to this chapter, and select the appropriate Media Activity number.

13.1 Genetic Recombination in Bacteria
Estimated time: 5 minutes

We often think of DNA and the genes it contains as being static and unchanging. In fact, it is anything but static. This activity will demonstrate some of the different ways that genetic recombination can occur in cells, both prokaryotic and eukaryotic.

13.2 Polymerase Chain Reaction (PCR)
Estimated time: 5 minutes

In this activity, you'll see the process of polymerase chain reaction (PCR), which allows minute amounts of DNA to be amplified into large amounts.

13.3 Human Genome Sequencing
Estimated time: 5 minutes

One strategy for sequencing the genome called map-based sequencing is the primary subject of this activity.

13.4 Manufacturing Human Growth Hormone
Estimated time: 5 minutes

In this activity, you'll see how human growth hormone can be produced cheaply and safely using recombinant DNA techniques.

13.5 Web Investigation: Guilty or Innocent?
Estimated time: 10 minutes

We usually think of molecular forensic evidence such as genetic "fingerprints" being used to convict a suspect. But the same molecular techniques are being used to free those wrongly convicted. The Innocence Project (http://www. innocenceproject.org/) is a nonprofit legal clinic whose sole purpose is identifying innocent people who were wrongly convicted of serious crimes. Learn about The Innocence Project and molecular forensic evidence by completing the following questions.

1. The Innocence Project has identified the factors leading to wrongful convictions. Describe some of the more common causes of wrongful convictions. Which of these factors can be corrected with molecular forensic evidence?

2. There are now several known genetic loci that can be used in molecular forensics that are located on the Y chromosome (http://ystr.charite.de/index_mkl.html). Why would such loci be useful in determining innocence? For what crimes might such loci be particularly well suited?

3. Several organizations representing the professions of criminal justice (http://www.ncjrs.org/nij/DNAbro/intro.html) are developing guidelines for handling and using molecular forensic evidence. Give several examples of the kinds of materials a police officer might look for and where in a crime scene they may be found. What precautions must a law enforcement official take when obtaining and storing samples for analysis?

4. The FBI (http://www.fbi.gov/) has developed a database (http://www.fbi.gov/hq/lab/codis/index1.htm) for storing DNA profiles of crime scenes and offenders. Currently, data from convicted felons and from crime scenes is collected. Do you feel it is justified to collect DNA samples from convicted felons? Would you object if samples were collected from the general population?

ISSUES IN BIOLOGY

Were Neanderthals Contemporary to Modern Humans?

Much of what we understand about human prehistory must be inferred from careful, painstaking analysis of artifacts and fossils. Each new discovery brings new ideas and may shatter old ones. The changes over the past 150 years in our ideas about human evolution are a particularly good example of how new information alters previous theories. In 1856 remains of unusual humanoids were discovered in the Neander Valley of Germany. These humanoids, which came to be known as Neanderthals (*Homo neanderthalensis*), were larger and heavier than modern humans (*Homo sapiens*) and had unusual skull features, including a prominent brow ridge. Subsequently, fossil remains of Neanderthals were found in many sites throughout Europe and Asia. Could these individuals be our ancestors?

One observation that seemed consistent with the idea that modern humans descended from Neanderthal ancestors is that the fossil record and dating information indicated that Neanderthals and *Homo sapiens* did not coexist. Instead, Neanderthal fossils appeared to be older than those of *Homo sapiens*. This finding led most paleontologists in the 1980s to believe that modern humans were descended from Neanderthal ancestors. The sophistication of Neanderthal tools seemed consistent with this idea. In fact, the recent discovery of a 43,000-year-old flute fashioned from a cave bear's thighbone even points to the possibility that Neanderthals made music!

However, the development of new dating methods shattered the confident assertion of the relationships between *Homo sapiens* and *Homo neanderthalensis*: These methods showed that, rather than preceding modern humans, Neanderthals lived at the same time and frequently in the same regions as *Homo sapiens*. Clearly, Neanderthals couldn't be our ancestors, but the new data raised new possibilities. Perhaps Neanderthals and modern humans had productive interactions, including mating and producing offspring. If so, present-day humans should contain genetic information derived from the Neanderthal lineage. Some scientists did not favor this idea, and, on the basis of other data, thought that modern humans migrated out of Africa about 100,000 years ago, replacing all humanoids in their paths. There appeared to be no direct way to determine which idea, interaction or extinction, was right—until now.

In July, 1997, (http://www.accessexcellence.org/WN/SUA10/neander797.html) scientists in the United States and Germany reported that they had succeeded in isolating a small fragment of mitochondrial DNA from a 30,000-year-old Neanderthal skeleton. This wasn't just any Neanderthal skeleton, but the very one first discovered in 1856 that gave the species its name! A tiny fragment of DNA, just 378 nucleotides long, was amplified from the skeleton by PCR and then sequenced. The Neanderthal sequence was compared with the sequences from 994 human lineages (including Africans, Europeans, Asians, and Native Americans) as well as with 59 chimpanzee sequences. The scientists doing the study found no evidence that Neanderthals contributed genetic information to modern humans.

A second study (http://cogweb.ucla.edu/Abstracts/Goodwin_00.html) on a precisely dated Neanderthal has confirmed this result. The answer appears clear: Neanderthals did not provide genetic contributions to modern humans. In fact, Neanderthals branched off the *Homo sapiens* lineage about 500,000 years ago!

1. How can DNA analysis reveal information about human history?

2. The analysis of Neanderthal DNA is one example in which the polymerase chain reaction technique was used to carry out an experiment that would have been impossible just a few years ago. Explain why PCR is so useful for the analysis of samples that contain very little DNA.

3. Mitochondrial DNA is an interesting molecule for many reasons. One reason is that we inherit it only from our mothers and not from our fathers. This means that the mitochondrial DNA in you and all of your siblings came from your mother and the mitochondrial DNA in her and her siblings came from her mother, and so on. Thinking about the size and complexity of egg and sperm cells, can you think of a reasonable hypothesis for why males do not pass on mitochondrial DNA to their progeny?

4. Sometimes it is very frustrating to hear about scientific research because the answers seem to change. For example, one day we learn that vitamin A protects us from cancer; a short time later, we learn that vitamin A is not protective, but may actually make an existing cancer worse. How does the history of our understanding of human evolution illustrate why science itself is an evolving process, in which the answers change as new data become available?

BIZARRE FACTS IN BIOLOGY

Monkeyshines

He's only 3 months old, but Andi is the most notorious primate on the planet. His name says it all; it's a turned-around acronym for "inserted DNA." This little rhesus monkey has within every cell of his body a gene that came from a jellyfish, and he's the first transgenic animal that is also a near-relative to humans.

Why a jellyfish gene? This particular gene encodes a protein that glows called green fluorescent protein (http://www.rcsb.org/pdb/molecules/pdb42_1.html) (GFP). Any cell that carries the gene and makes GFP should glow green. GFP is a marker; it shows the researchers which cells do and don't have this introduced gene. Andi doesn't glow, yet he might as he gets older, but using other methods to identify the GFP DNA sequence has detected the gene in Andi's hair, toenails, mouth cells, and white blood cells.

Andi got his GFP gene before he was a glimmer in anyone's eye. Mature egg cells, 224 of them, were injected with a high dose of a retrovirus (http://www.accessexcellence.org/AB/GG/diagram.html) carrying the GFP gene. A retrovirus forces the host cell to make a DNA copy of its genes that can incorporate into the host cell's DNA. The infected egg cells are then injected with a single sperm, increasing the odds that fertilization will be successful. Of the 224 starting eggs, three healthy monkeys were born and one was Andi (http://abcnews.go.com/sections/us/DailyNews/monkey010111.html).

147

Making transgenic monkeys is a difficult and inefficient proposition but promises great returns on the effort. The cloning techniques that made Andi could be used to make a primate model for human disease, such as Parkinson's disease, that we cannot mimic in mice. Techniques developed to make transgenic primates may improve the effectiveness of human gene therapy treatments. One thing is certain: Andi shows that it is possible to "monkey around" with any genome.

Reference

Chan, A. W. S., Chong, K. Y., Martinovich, C., Simerly, C., and Schatten, G. 2001. Transgenic monkeys produced by retroviral gene transfer into mature oocytes. *Science* 291:309–12.

1. Why is Andi, the first transgenic primate, so remarkable?

2. Why are scientists trying to make primates carrying genes from other organisms?

3. If we can introduce a novel gene into a monkey, can we do the same for humans?

Frankenplants?

Imagine preventing blindness by supplying an RDV of vitamin A in a bowl of rice—not sprayed on but part of the rice kernel. Imagine someone being vaccinated against diarrheal disease by eating a potato or banana. Imagine producing twice as much corn in an acre of land. Would these crops be miracles or monsters?

Transgenic, or genetically modified (GM), crops (http://www.consecol.org/Journal/vol4/iss1/art13/) seem to be a little of both. GM crops carry one or more genes from another, distinct, organism. Some crops have been modified to have superior resistance to insect damage or viral disease, or to supply more nutrients, or to grow in poor soil. These "miracles" happen thanks to a plant bacterium.

The bacterium, *Agrobacterium tumefaciens* (http://helios.bto.ed.ac.uk/bto/microbes/crown.htm), can have part of its DNA replaced by other genes. A plant stock can be infected with the modified bacterium, which then incorporates its DNA into the DNA of the plant's cells. The novel gene is expressed and the growing plant expresses new features: slower ripening, freeze-tolerance, insect resistance, and so forth. New plants can be propagated from the leaves or stems of the infected plant, and these new plants will carry the introduced gene in every cell, including the seeds.

GM crops raise several major concerns. One is that these novel proteins will cause allergic reactions in human consumers. Second, these proteins might sicken friendly insects and interfere with the pollination of unrelated plants. Third, these genes might "jump" to noxious weeds and create nuisance plants immune to our chemical herbicides. Some evidence suggests that these scenarios are unlikely. However, we just don't have enough data to make a confident decision. Monsters or miracles? Maybe more miracle than monster, but the jury is still out.

References

Rommens, C. M., and Kishore, G. M. 2000. Exploiting the full potential of disease-resistance genes for agricultural use. *Curr Op in Biotechnol* 11: 120–5.

Tacket, C. O., Mason, H. S., Losonsky, G., Clements, J. D., Levine, M. M., and Arntzen, C. J. 1998. Immunogenicity in humans of a recombinant bacterial antigen delivered in a transgenic potato. *Nat Med* 4:607–9.

Wal, J. M. 1999. Assessment of allergic potential of (novel) foods. *Nahrung* (Food) 43:168–74.

Ye, X., Al-Babili, S., Beyer, C., and Zhang, J. 2000. Engineering the provitamin A (b-carotene) biosynthetic pathway into (carotenoid-free) rice endosperm. *Science* 287:303-5.

1. Why would we want to introduce novel genes into crop plants?

KEY TERMS

amniocentesis	DNA probe	plasmid	restriction fragment length
biotechnology	gel electrophoresis	polymerase chain reaction	polymorphism (RFLP)
chorionic villus sampling	genetic engineering	(PCR)	stem cell
(CVS)	genetically modified	recombinant DNA	transformation
DNA fingerprinting	organism (GMO)	restriction enzyme	transgenic

---

ANSWER KEY

SELF TEST

1. a
2. a
3. d
4. b
5. d
6. d
7. d
8. a
9. e
10. d
11. d
12. biotechnology
13. plasmids, DNA, DNA fragments
14. electrophoresis
15. polymerase
16. A. host cell bursts, releasing newly assembled viruses
    B. virus attaches to susceptible host
    C. virus releases genes into cytoplasm of host
    D. viral genes encode synthesis of viral proteins and duplication of viral genes
    E. new viruses assemble
17. A. primer
    B. DNA polymerase
18. genetic engineering
19. plasmid
20. bananas, banana
21. fertilized egg, egg
22. heat, high temperature
23. c
24. a
25. a
26. e
27. a

ESSAY CHALLENGE

1. The ability to clone many millions of copies of a gene sequence in a short time frame can help scientists make discoveries faster.
2. Much like fingerprints in humans, no two individuals are exactly alike, but all individuals of a species are highly similar in almost all ways.
3. Keeping pests away from plants can help increase production on open lands that are becoming more scarce.
4. Rice that can produce its own vitamin A is a valuable addition to diets that often lack this vital nutrient.
5. Human gene therapy has wide-ranging implications, not only for the individual benefiting from the therapy, but for his or her children and for the species.
6. There are several ethical issues that remain to be worked out with regard to what information can be or should be known about another person.

MEDIA ACTIVITIES

13.5 Web Investigation: Guilty or Innocent?

1. Factors leading to wrongful convictions include: DNA Inclusions, Other Forensic Inclusions, False Confessions, Informants/Snitches, False Witness Testimony, Microscopic Hair Comparison Matches, Bad Lawyering, Defective or Fraudulent Science, Prosecutorial Misconduct, Police Misconduct, Serology Inclusion, Mistaken I.D. There is at least one incident for each factor where DNA evidence has exonerated the convicted person.

2. Loci on the Y chromosome can determine the sex of the person whose DNA is being fingerprinted, in addition to increasing the reliability of sexual assault or kinship testing.

3. Police officers look for any object that might carry genetic material: weapons, clothing, eyeglasses, facial tissues, cotton swabs, laundry, toothpicks, cigarette butts, stamps and envelopes, bottles, cans, glasses, condoms, bedding, bullets, bite marks, and fingernails. These might contain sweat, skin, blood, tissue cells, hair, dandruff, mucus, semen, earwax, saliva, vaginal or rectal cells, or urine. Evidence should be handled to avoid contamination, such as by the investigator's own DNA. It should be stored and handled in a manner that prevents degradation of the sample.

4. Students will have their own opinions on this subject. A thoughtful answer should address the question of a right to privacy, and what limitations on that right are both appropriate and constitutional.

ISSUES IN BIOLOGY

1. The more closely two species or individuals are related (or the more recent their common ancestor), the more similar their DNA sequences will be.

2. PCR can rapidly and relatively easily increase the amount of DNA available from a sample, thereby making its analysis possible.

3. Sperm generally contain a single large, specialized mitochondrion associated with the tail, which does not enter the egg cell at fertilization.

4. Scientific understanding is always provisional, in the sense that if better information becomes available, theories and hypotheses are subject to revision or even outright rejection.

BIZARRE FACTS IN BIOLOGY

Monkeyshines

1. Because Andi is a primate, it may be possible to create primate models for human conditions for which there are no good laboratory model systems, such as mice or rats. Also, this is much closer to producing genetically modified humans and other transgenic models, which some find promising and others find alarming.

2. Scientists can learn much about primate, and therefore, human, biology from transgenic primates.

3. Although theoretically this will be possible, the methods currently used to introduce genes into primates would be clearly unethical if applied to humans.

Frankenplants

1. Introduced genes can confer resistance to herbicides or to insect pests, among other things.

CHAPTER 14: PRINCIPLES OF EVOLUTION

AT-A-GLANCE

SELF TEST

1. The ability of organisms to pass on to their offspring physical changes that the parents developed during their own lifetimes is known as _____.
   a. genetic drift
   b. natural selection
   c. artificial selection
   d. adaptive radiation
   e. inheritance of acquired characteristics

2. Structures that may differ in function but that have similar anatomy, presumably because of descent from common ancestors, are called _____.
   a. analogous structures
   b. homologous structures
   c. vestigial structures

3. Structures that serve no apparent purpose but are homologous to functional structures in related organisms are called _____.
   a. analogous structures
   b. homologous structures
   c. vestigial structures

4. Structures that have similar functions and superficially similar appearance but very different anatomy, such as the wings of insects and birds, are called _____. The similarities are due to similar environmental pressures rather than to common ancestry.
   a. analogous structures
   b. homologous structures
   c. vestigial structures

5. The ostrich is a large, flightless bird. Its wings, therefore, represent _____.
   a. analogous structures
   b. homologous structures
   c. vestigial structures

6. Which of the following lines of evidence support(s) the idea that evolution occurs?
   a. the fossil record
   b. genetic and biochemical analyses
   c. comparative anatomy and embryology
   d. artificial selection
   e. all of the above

7. All vertebrate embryos resemble each other during the early stages of development. For example, fish, turtles, chickens, mice, and humans develop tails and gill slits during early stages of development. This suggests that _____.
   a. early embryonic development is conservative
   b. ancestral vertebrates possessed genes that directed the development of tails and gill slits, and all of their descendants still retain those genes
   c. genes that modify the developmental pathways in vertebrates arose later in evolution
   d. all of the above

8. Which of the following is NOT one of the main points of Darwin's theory of evolution?
   a. Life on Earth is quite old.
   b. Evolution is gradual and continuous.
   c. Contemporary species share a common descent.
   d. Species are formed and adapt by the process of natural selection.
   e. All of the above are true.

9. Which of the following is a basic requirement for natural selection to be an effective evolutionary force?
   a. Mutation must occur frequently.
   b. Individuals reproduce at a rapid rate.
   c. Each population is limited to a small size.
   d. A population exhibits some genetic variability.
   e. all of the above

10. What does the idea of "uniformitarianism" suggest about the geological record and the age of Earth?
    a. Earth was only 6000 years old.
    b. Species were evidence of acts of divine creation.
    c. Earth's species were created initially but many were destroyed by successive catastrophes.
    d. Natural processes (e.g., sedimentation due to river flow) occurring over long stretches of time accounted for the thick layers of rock where fossils are found, rather than cataclysmic events.

11. What was the untested weakness in Darwin's manifest *On the Origin of Species*?
    a. organisms evolved through the inheritance of acquired characteristics
    b. natural selection
    c. the passage of traits from generation to generation, and that variations in these traits occurred randomly
    d. all of the above

12. Which of the following would be considered to be an example of analogous structures?
    a. molar teeth in a vampire bat
    b. superficially similar structures in unrelated species
    c. internally similar structures (e.g., of birds and mammals) that are used for many different functions
    d. Both the first and third answers are correct.

13. Which of the following would describe artificial selection?
    a. breeding organisms for the purpose of generating certain features or traits (e.g., dog breeds)
    b. coloration changes in guppy populations in the absence of predators
    c. increased frequency of roaches that avoid sugar-baited poison traps
    d. all of the above

14. Which of the following people allowed for species to change over time?
    a. Plato
    b. Aristotle
    c. Cuvier
    d. Lamarck

15. Charles Darwin was NOT influenced by which of the following people in formulating his ideas about natural selection?
    a. Thomas Malthus
    b. Charles Lyell
    c. William Smith
    d. Gregor Mendel

16. Which of the following is an incorrect statement about mutation?
    a. Mutation introduces variation into a population.
    b. Mutations can be inherited from parents to offspring.
    c. Mutations may have no effect on the organism.
    d. Mutations that are favored by selection are more likely to occur.

17. You are a biologist studying a natural population of mice, and you observe that in one area the proportion of darker colored mice is greater than the proportion of lighter colored mice. In another area, the opposite is true. You find that only the area with more dark mice has predators. Therefore, you hypothesize that darker mice are favored in areas with predators, perhaps because they are more difficult to see. If your hypothesis is true, what would you expect to happen in the few generations after predators are introduced to an area with a population of mice that previously did not have predators?
    a. The proportion of darker colored mice will decrease.
    b. The proportion of darker colored mice will not change.
    c. The predators will evolve to be able to better see the darker mice.
    d. The proportion of darker colored mice will increase.

18. In what way does the human population influence evolution?
    a. Human development changes the habitats of many species, influencing natural selection on those species.
    b. Use of antibiotics by humans has selected for antibiotic-resistant bacterial populations.
    c. Humans are responsible for the many breeds of dogs found today.
    d. all of the above

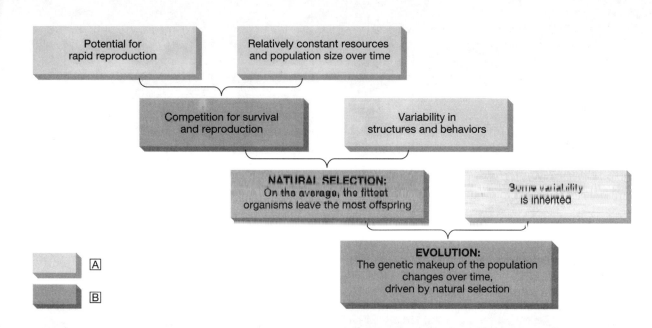

Potential for
rapid reproduction

Relatively constant resources
and population size over time

Competition for survival
and reproduction

Variability in
structures and behaviors

NATURAL SELECTION:
On the average, the fittest
organisms leave the most offspring

Some variability
is inherited

EVOLUTION:
The genetic makeup of the population
changes over time,
driven by natural selection

A

B

19. The diagram above indicates a flowchart of evolutionary reasoning. After reading and understanding the information, label the key to indicate which boxes are observations and which are conclusions based on those observations.

20. Three major changes can be concluded from the evolutionary tree of the modern horse. Using the clues from the diagram below, label the points where these three changes occurred.

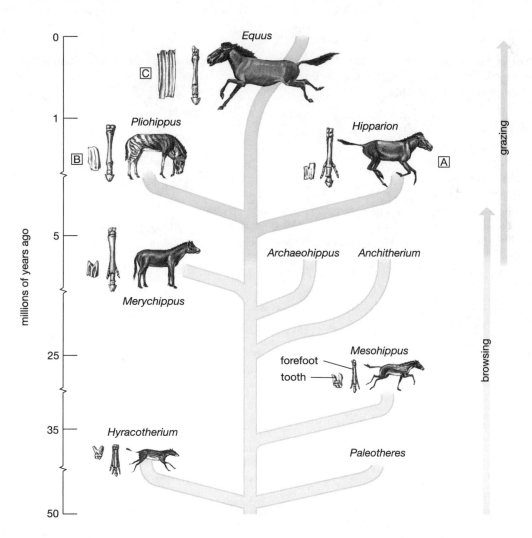

153

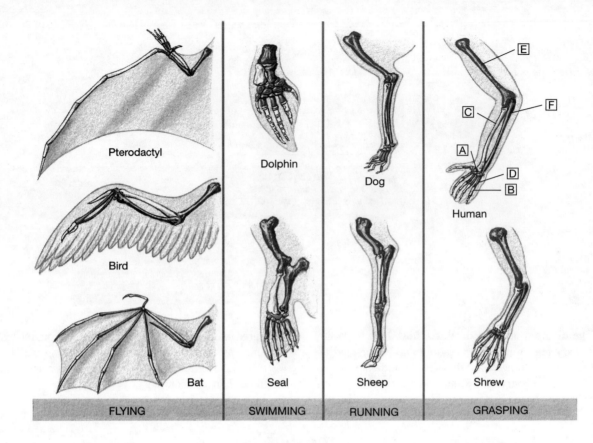

Pterodactyl	Dolphin	Dog	Human
Bird			
Bat	Seal	Sheep	Shrew
FLYING	SWIMMING	RUNNING	GRASPING

21. Each of the limbs above shows the same set of bones (homologous structures). Using the human forearm as the key, label each of the bones.

22. Outwardly similar body parts that serve a similar function in unrelated organisms (such as the wings of insects and birds) are _____.
    a. analogous structures
    b. homologous structures
    c. vestigial structures
    d. evidence of convergent evolution
    e. evidence of divergent evolution
    f. Both the first and fourth answers are correct.

23. Who, or what, was Charles Darwin?

    a. a physician

    b. a theologian

    c. a naturalist

    d. Both the second and third answers are correct.

    e. all of the above

24. Natural selection acts on _____, while evolution occurs in _____.

ESSAY CHALLENGE

1. Explain how the discovery of fossils has helped to strengthen support for the theory of evolution.

2. Darwin suggested natural selection as the mechanism by which species evolve over geologic time. Describe how natural selection is more plausible than other descriptions of evolution, such as "catastrophism" or Lamarck's "Inheritance of Acquired Characteristics" hypothesis.

3. Describe how embryological similarities across vertebrate species give some evidence of those species having descended from a common ancestor.

4. What are vestigial structures and why are they found in some species?

5. Describe how biochemical analyses have helped provide support for a generalized theory of evolution.

6. How are artificial selection and natural selection similar? How are they different?

7. Despite his view that species are unchanging, Aristotle's "ladder of Nature" superficially resembles a modern version of the "tree of life" from an evolutionary perspective, with plants evolving before animals, and more "complex" animals evolving later than more "primitive" ones. Explain why the two views correspond even though one does not allow for evolution.

8. How do fossils of extinct species suggest that evolutionary change occurs?

9. How was Lamarck's contribution to evolutionary biology important? Why was his theory abandoned? How is his theory different from Darwin's theory of natural selection?

10. List several examples of how Darwin was influenced by his own observations on the voyage of the *Beagle*, and by the work of his contemporaries in science, while developing his theory of evolution by natural selection.

11. Explain the phrase "natural selection acts on individuals but affects populations."

12. Suppose a biologist discovered a bacterial species that uses one additional amino acid (21 instead of the usual 20) in its proteins. Would you conclude that this species is unrelated to all other species? Explain.

13. Insects may evolve to become resistant to pesticides. What problems does this cause? How could this insect adaptation be avoided?

MEDIA ACTIVITIES

To access a Media Activity visit http://www.prenhall.com/audesirk7. Log in to the Web site selected by your instructor, navigate to this chapter, and select the appropriate Media Activity number.

14.1 Analogous and Homologous Structures
Estimated time: 5 minutes

This exercise will help you to learn the difference between structures that are similar because of common origin or because of similar evolutionary pressures.

14.2 Natural Selection for Antibiotic Resistance
Estimated time: 5 minutes

This activity demonstrates the mechanism of natural selection using the example of evolution of an antibiotic resistance trait in a population of the bacteria that cause the human disease tuberculosis.

14.3 Web Investigation: A Missing Link Unearthed
Estimated time: 10 minutes

Finding fossils and analyzing the fossil record is hard work. Sometimes the results are quite unexpected. This exercise will explore the fossil record of birds.

1. *Archaeopteryx* (http://www.ucmp.berkeley.edu/diapsids/birds/archaeopteryx.html) is considered the oldest known fossil bird. What features does it share with dinosaurs? Why is it considered a bird?

2. *Confuciusornis* is another fossil bird. It is almost as old as *Archaeopteryx* but shares one feature with birds that *Archaeopteryx* lacks (http://www.carnegiemuseums.org/cmnh/exhibits/feathered/confuciusornis.html). What is it?

3. Several years ago scientists were excited to discover *Archaeoraptor* (http://www.enchantedlearning.com/subjects/dinosaurs/news/Archaeoraptor.shtml) "the first flying dinosaur." *Archaeoraptor* is now more frequently referred to as the "Piltdown chicken." Why?

4. **Optional:** The centerpiece of "The Centaur Excavations at Volos" (http://web.utk.edu/~blyons/centaur.html) exhibit on display in the C. Hodges Library at the University of Tennessee is a centaur skeleton. Can you come up with an alternative nickname?

ISSUES IN BIOLOGY
What Is the Evolution Debate?
No other concept in biology has been as controversial as the idea of organic evolution. As everybody knows, you just don't argue about religion or politics, and evolution strikes right at the heart of religious belief for many people. The idea that humankind has had a long history of evolutionary change, sharing common descent with other primates, is seen as a direct challenge to a literal interpretation of the Bible. In fact, in 1925 John T. Scopes, a biology teacher from

Dayton, Tennessee, was placed on trial and convicted for teaching evolution in his high school class. This famous trial, known as the Scopes "Monkey Trial," was the subject of various stage and film productions of *Inherit the Wind* (http://xroads.virginia.edu/~UG97/inherit/contents.html), each version reflecting the social context of its time.

The issue of legality in the teaching of evolution did not end with the Scopes trial. In 1965 a teacher in Little Rock, Arkansas, filed a lawsuit against the Little Rock school board contending that an anti-evolution law on the books in Arkansas violated her constitutional right to freedom of speech. The case lasted nearly two years, ending when the Arkansas Supreme Court, in a 6-to-1 decision, upheld the 1928 law prohibiting the teaching of evolution. The Supreme Court of the United States, however, struck down the Arkansas law in 1968. In 1967 two events returned the evolution vs. creationism spotlight to Tennessee. A Knoxville man filed suit against the state Attorney General and the local board of education, claiming that his son's education was being restricted by not introducing him to evolution; and like Scopes, another teacher, this time from Jacksboro, lost his job for teaching evolution, which still violated Tennessee law. So, 42 years after the Scopes trial, the Tennessee legislature finally repealed that law. Still, this was not the end of the legal battle over the teaching of evolution. In 1987 the U.S. Supreme Court ruled 7-to-2 against a Louisiana law requiring creationism to be taught as a science along with evolution in public schools. The two Supreme Court rulings against anti-evolution legislation have not dampened the fires of the creationists (http://emporium.turnpike.net/C/cs/), and there continue to be attempts by the lawmakers of a number of states (including Alabama, Georgia, and Tennessee) to either weaken the presentation of evolution (taught as only theory, not fact) or introduce the creationist viewpoint into the classroom.

Not all Christians view evolution as a threat to their religious beliefs. Although evolution remains a problem for many modern-day fundamentalist Christians, many other Christians are able to assimilate evolution and the workings of the natural world into their religious framework. In fact, some Christians attempt to incorporate the views of both creationism and evolution directly into one mutual construct known as theological evolution. The Catholic Church has always taken a more liberal stance on the position of evolution. For example, Pierre Teilhard de Chardin (http://www.cruzio.com/~cscp/teilhard.htm), a Jesuit priest and philosopher, spent nearly 20 years in China, where he conducted research at the "Peking Man" site at Zhoukoudian. In his philosophy of "neohumanism," he synthesized evolution with a metaphysical understanding of humans. More recently, the Pope has declared that "fresh knowledge leads to recognition of the theory of evolution as more than just a hypothesis" and that evolution offers no challenge to the church's teachings. In the final analysis, individuals must decide for themselves what makes sense for them. The Ultimate Creation vs. Evolution Resource (http://www.apokolips.com/evolution.html), although biased toward creationism, has a multitude of links to information on both sides of this ongoing debate. A more balanced point of view about whether religion and evolution are compatible is presented in an essay, God and Evolution (http://www.talkorigins.org/faqs/faq-god.html).

1. In what ways does the biblical account of creation differ from the concept of organic evolution?

2. Is "creation science" really science? Consider the scientific method and the role of falsifiable hypotheses.

3. Do you believe that religious beliefs and belief in the process of evolution can coexist? If yes, how? If not, why not?

4. In what ways does the biblical account of creation differ from the concept of organic evolution?

BIZARRE FACTS IN BIOLOGY

Winged Wooing in Hawaii

Many people are familiar with the tiny common fruit fly, *Drosophila melanogaster*, which is common worldwide in temperate areas. Most people don't know that the Hawaiian islands are home to hundreds of unique close relatives of this "weed" species, and that they show an incredible degree of diversity. Many species remain undescribed by researchers, so there may be as many as one thousand different *Drosophila* species in Hawaii alone.

About 100 species of Hawaiian *Drosophila* belong to a group called the "picture-wings" (http://www.biology.duke.edu/rausher/hawdros.htm) because of elaborate pigmentation patterns on their wings. Some of these species are much larger than the common *D. melanogaster*, and many have highly modified mouths or legs. Some species are even flightless! Perhaps they should be called "fruitless flies."

Many of the more unusual features of males in these species may be due to the flies' courtship practices. In order to successfully mate with a female, a male fly may need to directly compete with other males (and have evolved specific modifications, like a "hammerhead," to do so). Then, to attract the female, he may need to dance, sing (vibrate the wings), or douse his intended with perfume (pheromones).

It is believed that all of these diverse species are descended from one ancient colonizing species (http://www.hawaii-forest.com/essays/9810.html) from the mainland, at a time when there was only one Hawaiian island. This species diversified into many by the process of adaptive radiation (http://www.meta-library.net/evolution/oppor-body.html), natural selection to adapt to specific environmental conditions. As the new islands formed by volcanic activity, there was further colonization and diversification into the many species observed today.

1. What are some of the different habitats to which the various fruit fly species of Hawaii have evolved?

2. What are some of the ways that males of Hawaiian *Drosophila* species compete with each other for females?

3. What does it mean to say that natural selection is an "opportunistic process"? How does this help to explain the diversity of Hawaiian *Drosophila*?

KEY TERMS

analogous structures
artificial selection
catastrophism
convergent evolution
evolution

fossil
homologous structures
inheritance of acquired
    characteristics
natural selection

population
uniformitarianism
vestigial structure

ANSWER KEY

SELF TEST

1. e
2. b
3. c
4. a
5. c
6. e
7. d
8. e
9. d
10. d
11. c
12. b
13. a
14. d
15. d
16. d
17. d
18. d
19. A. observation
    B. conclusions based on observation
20. A. teeth became larger and harder, noticeably changing the diet from those of the earliest horses
    B. body size increased, perhaps in response to predation
    C. Stout strong legs and large strong hooves developed, perhaps in response to life on the open plains
21. A. carpals
    B. phalanges
    C. radius
    D. metacarpals
    E. humerous
    F. ulna
22. f
23. d
24. individual organisms, populations

ESSAY CHALLENGE

1. See sections 14.1 (Fossil Discoveries Showed That Life Had Changed Over Time) and 14.3 (Fossils Provide Evidence of Evolutionary Change over Time) for discussions of the importance of the discovery of fossils. Your answer should at a minimum indicate that fossils reflect the existence of species that are now extinct. Furthermore, the fossil record fails to show examples of many currently existing species. This evidence tends to argue against a single creation event that resulted in all current species simultaneously. Also, fossil sequences may show long term skeletal changes in lineages of organisms.

2. See section 14.1 (Some Scientists Devised Nonevolutionary Explanations for Fossils; Some Pre-Darwin Biologists Proposed Mechanisms for Evolution) for discussions of catastrophism and Lamarck's hypothesis. Your answer should describe the processes involved in each of the three theories and should also provide evidence of why those theories are less able to describe the process of evolution. For example, catastrophism proposes that all species were originally created, but those species that are now extinct were destroyed by major catastrophes. This theory fails to describe why mammal fossils and dinosaur fossils are rarely found in rocks of the same geologic age. Lamarck's theory predicted that all physical changes to an organism could be inherited, resulting in evolution. His main example is in the evolution of giraffes from having short necks to the long necks of the present animals. Present-day animals were supposed by Lamarck to have resulted from constant, steady increases in the length of the species' neck until the giraffes of today were seen. Lamarck's theory, if true, would predict much more variation in physical forms than we presently have. Also, experiments show that physical changes to an organism are not inherited; a man who loses an arm in an accident does not have children born without that arm.

3. See section 14.3 (Embryological Similarity Suggests Common Ancestry) for a discussion of this idea. Karl von Bauer suggested that the similarities between various vertebrate embryos may be explained by common genes that were shared by a distant common ancestor. For example, the gill slits found in human embryos and those seen in fish embryos have very different adult expressions. Gills are nonexistent in human adults but are very prominent features of adult fish.

4. See section 14.3 (Comparative Anatomy Gives Evidence of Descent with Modification) for a discussion of vestigial structures. Your answer should

identify that vestigial structures serve no purpose for members of the current species. At the same time, these structures must have no negative effect on reproductive success. An example given in the text is the pelvic structure found in some whales.

5. See section 14.3 (Modern Biochemical and Genetic Analyses Reveal Relatedness among Diverse Organisms) for a discussion of the importance of DNA sequence comparisons. Your answer should include a description of the large number of DNA gene sequences that perform the same function in, and are shared among, species from widely different kingdoms and phyla

6. See section 14.2 (Natural Selection Modifies Populations over Time) for a description of how natural selection works, and section 14.4 (Controlled Breeding Modifies Organisms) for a description of how artificial selection works. Both types of selection act on variations seen in the current population. Both types of selection predict that individuals with more favorable features will survive to reproduce. One difference is that natural selection occurs in a natural (i.e., without human interference) environment, whereas artificial selection is done by humans. One example is the selection for plants that produce very large flowers. This trait may be attractive to humans, but in a natural environment, large flowers may weigh down a plant and thus prevent it from being pollinated.

7. Section 14.1.A (Early Biological Thought Did Not Include the Concept of Evolution) presents Aristotle's "ladder of Nature." Aristotle arranged the ladder according to biological complexity, with plants being more simple than some animals, and some animals more complex than others. Since more complex species tended to evolve later than less complex ones, Aristotle's categorization roughly corresponds to the order of evolution.

8. Section 14.1.C (Fossil Discoveries Showed That Life Had Changed Over Time) describes the importance of the discovery of fossils of extinct species in influencing thought about evolutionary change. In finding that there were species in the past that no longer exist, scientists realized that different groups of species existed at different times in the past, suggesting that species have changed over time.

9. Section 14.1.G (Some Pre-Darwin Biologists Proposed Mechanisms for Evolution) discusses Lamarck. He was significant in that he proposed a mechanism for evolutionary change, the inheritance of acquired characteristics. This mechanism was incorrect, as organisms do not generally inherit physical changes acquired during the lifetimes of their parents, so his theory was abandoned. In Lamarck's theory, environmental pressures would directly influence evolutionary change, while Darwin's theory has the environment affecting change only indirectly, by

favoring individual variants that already exist. The environment does not create those variants, as in Lamarck's theory.

10. Section 14.1.H (Darwin and Wallace Proposed A Mechanism of Evolution) and the Scientific Inquiry box (Charles Darwin—Nature Was His Laboratory) discuss Darwin's influences. Students might mention a number of things. Darwin had studied the natural world firsthand in his own observations as a young man, during the voyage of the *Beagle*, and following his return to England. In the Galapagos islands, he had seen many species that were similar, but different from, mainland species. He collected fossils of extinct species similar to living ones. Hutton and Lyell's concept of uniformitarianism suggested an old Earth with plenty of time for slow evolutionary processes to result in significant changes. Malthus' writings about human populations kept in check by limited resources strongly influenced Darwin's suggestion of the analogous process of natural selection in natural populations.

11. Section 14.2.B (Natural Selection Modifies Populations over Time) discusses how natural selection favors individuals, allowing some to reproduce more offspring than others. This has an effect on the population, however, by influencing the genetic composition of the next generation of offspring. Individuals themselves cannot evolve, but populations can evolve, as defined by changes in allele frequencies over time. (There is more on this in Chapter 15.)

12. Section 14.3.D (Modern Biochemical and Genetic Analyses Reveal Relatedness among Diverse Organisms) discusses how all organisms are biochemically similar. The student should recognize that the use of an additional amino acid may be an adaptation in that particular species, and does not necessarily indicate a lack of relatedness to all other species. The other 20 amino acids are the same, and presumably there is a great amount of similarity to other species in other ways. The overall similarity still suggests relatedness.

13. One part of Section 14.4.B (under the heading Natural Selection Can Lead to Pesticide Resistance) mentions the problems associated with this phenomenon. As insect pests become more resistant to one chemical pesticide, farmers have to switch to other chemicals to try to control the insects. This is expensive, leads to more chemical pollution of the environment, and may result in insects resistant to all pesticides. Students may suggest various solutions; one may be to alternate pesticides from year to year so that the insect population cannot adapt to one in particular. Any answer should be a biologically reasonable way of avoiding adaptation of the insect population.

MEDIA ACTIVITIES

14.3 Web Investigation: A Missing Link Unearthed

1. *Archaeopteryx*, like dinosaurs, had teeth, a flat sternum, a long bony tail, "belly ribs," and claws. However, unlike dinosaurs and like birds, it had feathers, wings, a "wishbone," and reduced fingers.
2. *Confuciusornis* had no teeth.
3. The *Archaeoraptor* fossil was found to be a fake constructed by combining two other fossils, much like "Piltdown man," which purportedly showed an ape-human transitional form, was a fake.
4. An obvious answer is the "Piltdown centaur," but the student's answer will depend on his or her creativity.

ISSUES IN BIOLOGY

1. The biblical account of the origin of life describes separate creation of each individual species, while evolution suggests that new species originate from biological changes in existing species. Also, biblical creation takes place in seven "days," while organic evolution suggests an old Earth and long periods of time for biological change.
2. By most professional definitions of science, "creation science" is not really science. A scientific approach to asking and answering questions about the natural world usually involves proposing testable hypotheses, with predictions that can support or refute the hypotheses if they are empirically observed. Because the existence of God and the supernatural creation of species cannot be supported or refuted by observable natural evidence, they cannot be investigated scientifically, but are accepted as a matter of faith.
3. The answer to this question will vary with the student, but the student should be clear in supporting his or her position.

BIZARRE FACTS IN BIOLOGY

1. Different species may lay their eggs in rotting trees, fermenting bark, or slime. Some species live in high altitude rain forests, others in drier lowlands.
2. *D. heteroneura* males butt heads like bighorn sheep. Males of one species wrestle with each other, while in another species a male will produce a very loud buzzing from the abdomen until his competitor is driven off.
3. This means that natural selection does not force a species to evolve toward some eventual goal, but is a result of the many (often random) factors in the immediate environment of the organism. Those that are better able to survive and reproduce at that time and place will be selected. Since Hawaii has a great diversity of microhabitats and climates, particularly for a tiny fly, natural selection in numerous variable environments can result in a great many fly adaptations, and eventually separate species.

CHAPTER 15: HOW ORGANISMS EVOLVE

AT-A-GLANCE

SELF TEST

1. Which of the following is a mechanism or cause of evolution?
   a. mutation   b. gene flow
   c. genetic drift   d. natural selection
   e. all of the above

2. Selection against individuals at both ends of a phenotypic distribution for a character, favoring those in the middle or average of the distribution, is an example of _____.
   a. kin selection   b. sexual selection
   c. directional selection   d. disruptive selection
   e. stabilizing selection

3. Body size varies among individuals in a species of lizard in the genus *Aristelliger*. Small lizards have a hard time defending a territory, and thus mating, but large lizards are more likely to be preyed on by owls. Therefore, natural selection favors individuals with an average body size. This is an example of _____.
   a. kin selection
   b. sexual selection
   c. directional selection
   d. disruptive selection
   e. stabilizing selection

4. The process by which two species evolve adaptations in response to one another, such that evolutionary change in one species produces an evolutionary change in the other is called _____.
   a. coevolution
   b. natural selection
   c. directional selection
   d. balanced polymorphism

5. Which of the following selective processes did Darwin suggest to explain the evolution of the conspicuous structures and courtship behaviors that male animals use to attract a mate?
   a. kin selection
   b. sexual selection
   c. natural selection
   d. directional selection
   e. disruptive selection
   f. stabilizing selection

6. Which of the following is most likely to result in the evolution of altruistic behavior?
   a. kin selection   b. sexual selection
   c. natural selection   d. directional selection
   e. disruptive selection   f. stabilizing selection

7. Which of the following is a correct statement?
    a. Natural selection is a mindless, mechanical process.
    b. Darwin had no knowledge of the mechanics of heredity.
    c. Heredity plays an important role in the theory of evolution by natural selection.
    d. Evolution is a property not of individuals but of populations.
    e. The changes that we see in an individual as it grows and develops are not evolutionary changes.
    f. all of the above

8. Natural selection acts (through predation) against banded water snakes on certain Lake Erie islands, favoring the uniformly light-colored snakes. The banded form is very common on the nearby mainlands. Yet banded snakes are maintained in the island populations and not eliminated completely. This is probably due to _____.
    a. mutation   b. gene flow
    c. genetic drift   d. natural selection

9. Genetic drift will tend to _____.
    a. increase genetic variability both within and between populations
    b. decrease genetic variability both within and between populations
    c. increase genetic variability within populations but decrease genetic variability between populations
    d. decrease genetic variability within populations but increase genetic variability between populations

10. The Hardy-Weinberg equilibrium represents an idealized, evolution-free population in which the allele frequencies and genotype frequencies will not change over time. In order for this to happen, five conditions must be met: 1) there must be no mutation; 2) there must be no gene flow between populations; 3) the populations must be very large; 4) all mating must be random; and 5) there must be no natural selection. If one of these five conditions was violated, genetic change, and thus evolution, would occur in the populations of subsequent generations. Suppose that only condition 3 were violated—that the population was very small. In this situation, the evolution would probably be due to _____.
    a. mutation
    b. migration
    c. genetic drift
    d. natural selection
    e. all of the above

11. What is a gene pool?
    a. a region of DNA found at a specific position on a chromosome
    b. the number of copies of an allele for a specific gene in a population
    c. the total number of all the genes in a population
    d. none of the above

12. What is the Hardy-Weinberg principle?
    a. a model of population genetics that shows that evolution will occur if all of the conditions of the principle are met
    b. a model of population genetics that shows that evolution will occur if even one of the conditions of the principle is violated
    c. a model of population genetics that describes how evolution occurs in nature
    d. Both the first and third answers are correct.

13. Which of the five conditions of the Hardy-Weinberg principle describe how never-before-seen DNA can enter a population?
    a. mutations   b. gene flow
    c. decreasing   d. nonrandom mating
       population size   e. natural selection

14. Genetic drift, population bottlenecks, and founder populations all illustrate _____.
    a. decreasing population size has a greater effect on changing allele frequencies than increasing the population size
    b. that reducing population size will likely decrease genetic variability within the population
    c. the strong role played by very small isolated populations in the creation of new species
    d. all of the above

15. Which phrase best describes the concept of natural selection?
    a. survival of the fittest
    b. reproductive success
    c. long life
    d. Both the first and third answers are correct.

16. What type of natural selection favors individuals with rarely encountered traits over individuals with traits that are frequently encountered?
    a. disruptive selection   b. stabilizing selection
    c. directional selection

17. Evolution is best defined as a change in _____.
    a. number of species   b. physical traits
    c. DNA sequence   d. allele frequencies

18. Gene flow _____.
    a. cannot influence the evolution of a population
    b. prevents the spread of alleles through a species
    c. causes populations to diverge from each other
    d. makes populations more genetically similar

19. In a mainland bird population, most individuals are black in color, and gray is a rare variation. A small group of these birds is carried by strong winds to a distant island, where they establish a new population. After a few generations, the gray phenotype is very common. What is most likely to be responsible for this?
    a. natural selection   b. mutation
    c. gene flow   d. nonrandom mating
    e. genetic drift

20. A population of insects, newly introduced to a forest, is adapting to different breeding sites: females can lay their eggs either on mushrooms on the forest floor or on the fruits of trees. In time, one group has adapted to the mushrooms, and another to the fruit. What type of selection drove these adaptations?

a. sexual selection

b. stabilizing selection

c. directional selection

d. disruptive selection

21. Why is the sickle cell allele found at a high frequency in African human populations?

a. Individuals with sickle cell anemia are resistant to malaria, which has historically been prevalent in Africa.

b. Heterozygote carriers of the allele are susceptible to malaria, which has historically been absent in Africa.

c. Individuals with sickle cell anemia are susceptible to malaria, which has historically been absent in Africa.

d. Heterozygote carriers of the allele are resistant to malaria, which has historically been prevalent in Africa.

22. _____ are sequences of DNA located at specific positions of a chromosome.

23. Individuals with two identical copies of a given allele are called _____ for that allele.

24. When populations get very small, the danger of losing genetic variability is high. This is called a _____

25. Chance effects can change an allele's frequency in a population. This phenomenon is called _____.

26. Natural selection acts on phenotypes, which are the physical representation of an individual's _____.

27. _____ selection is a type of selection that favors individuals with average values of traits.

28. Selection can be stabilizing, directional, or disruptive. Look at the diagram below and label each of these types of selection as they appear.

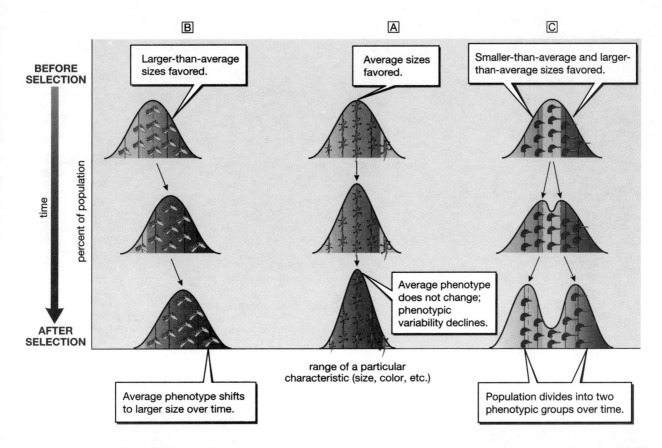

29. This diagram indicates the heredity pattern for sickle cell anemia. The H indicates normal hemoglobin; the h indicates sickling hemoglobin. Analyze the image and label the circles appropriately. Indicate which individual will survive, which will die of malaria, and which will die of sickle-cell anemia.

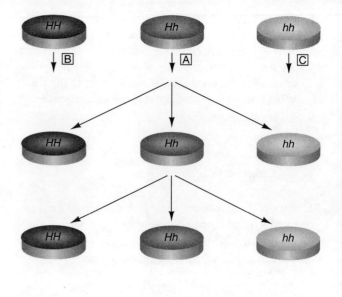

ESSAY CHALLENGE

1. Explain how genes and alleles are related.

2. Describe how a population bottleneck can be detrimental to a population.

3. Explain two effects of gene flow on populations.

4. How are genotype and phenotype related?

5. Give brief descriptions of the terms *directional, stabilizing,* and *disruptive selection.*

6. Explain altruism and how it can be beneficial to species that exhibit altruistic behaviors.

7. The Hardy-Weinberg principle states that if a population meets a set of conditions, it will be at equilibrium and no evolutionary change can occur. However, these conditions are rarely met in natural populations. Why, then, is this principle useful?

8. What does it mean to say that a mutation is not goal-directed?

9. A neutral mutation is one that does not affect the organism's fitness; it is no better or worse for the organism to have it. What types of DNA mutations are likely to be neutral?

10. If female peacocks prefer to mate with males with longer, showier tails, sexual selection will guide the evolution of even longer, more showy tails in males. Although it may become extreme, the trait must stop evolving at some point. What factors may halt the evolution of a sexually selected trait?

11. Populations with little genetic diversity may be at risk of extinction without the ability to adapt to changing environmental conditions. What might scientists do to help increase the genetic variation of an endangered population?

MEDIA ACTIVITIES

To access a Media Activity visit http://www.prenhall.com/audesirk7. Log in to the Web site selected by your instructor, navigate to this chapter, and select the appropriate Media Activity number.

15.1 Agents of Change
Estimated Time: 10 minutes

Natural selection is one agent of microevolution. Explore four other agents that can change allele frequencies in a population.

15.2 The Bottleneck Effect
Estimated Time: 5 minutes

Genetic drift is one of the major mechanisms of evolutionary change and has significant implications for small natural populations. This activity illustrates the bottleneck effect, which involves genetic drift, in a population of amoebas.

15.3 Three Modes of Natural Selection
Estimated Time: 5 minutes

Natural selection can produce three different effects on the genetic variation of a population. These three modes known as directional, stabilizing, and disruptive selection are demonstrated in this activity.

15.1 Natural Selection at Work: Alpine Skypilots
Estimated Time: 10 minutes

The size of alpine skypilot flowers differs between the bare alpine and forested sub-alpine environments. What factors contribute to this difference? Is it natural selection or some other factor at work? This activity will allow you to walk through Candace Galen's experiments as she uncovered this mystery.

15.5 Web Investigation: Evolution of a Menace
Estimated time: 15 minutes

Antibiotic resistance is reaching crisis proportions. Diseases that were all but eradicated only a few years ago are back and resistant to all known treatments. This exercise will take a brief look at the basic biology, medical repercussions, and social implications of bacterial antibiotic resistance.

1. There are two main categories of antibiotics and five Mechanisms of Antibiotic Resistance (http://www.geocities.com/krbushcalgary/types.htm). What are they?

2. First, a DNA mutation(s) leads to a functional antibiotic resistance gene. Then the gene is passed from bacterial strain to bacterial strain. Which of the four Methods for Movement of Resistance Genes (http://www.foodsafetynetwork.ca/animal/ab-res-ppr wjp.htm#Methods%20for%20movement%20of%20res%20ge) has the greatest clinical impact?

3. What are the two biggest contributors to the development of resistant bacterial strains (http://www.cmaj.ca/cgi/reprint/159/9/1129)? How does the use of antibiotics in livestock affect humans (http://www.agric.gov.ab.ca/livestock/pork/baconbits/9905a.html)?

4. Optional: Read *Staphylococcus aureus* - Isolation of Various Strains and Antibiotic Sensitivity Testing (http://www.springerlink.com/.../Perry/2.2.9.p03/eaview.html). Is this a description of evolution?

5. What steps can individuals take to combat the resistance epidemic (http://www.chiro.org/LINKS/FULL/Challenge_of_Antibiotic_Resistance.html)? Can government action help?

ISSUES IN BIOLOGY

Spiraling Towards Extinction

What factors contribute to the extinction of a population? In what researchers have called the "extinction vortex" (http://cas.bellarmine.edu/tietjen/images/no_need_to_isolate_genetics.htm), the genetic diversity of a natural population is increasingly diminished by a feedback loop of genetic consequences that may eventually drive the population extinct. It starts when the habitat of a large, healthy population is fragmented into smaller pockets as a result of human development or the introduction of new species from other areas (often unwittingly by human activity). This leaves a number of smaller subpopulations. Genetic drift can play a role in randomly eliminating genetic variants, but inbreeding depression (http://biodiversity-chm.eea.eu.int/CHMIndexTerms/Glossary/I/inbreeding_depression) also takes its toll. Inbreeding is a type of nonrandom mating in which individuals mate with close relatives. In populations that are kept small over a period of generations, inbreeding is inevitable, and it has the effect of increasing the proportion of individuals that are homozygous for recessive deleterious alleles. These homozygotes are less fit than the population average, and more likely to be eliminated by natural selection. The result is inbreeding depression, a decrease in the average fitness of the population. As selection culls the less fit individuals, the size of the population further shrinks, and the problems of genetic drift, inbreeding, and natural selection are magnified. The population spirals into extinction.

The case of the greater prairie chicken (http://nature.org/magazine/summer2002/unlucky13/animals/art7428.html) in Illinois is an unfortunate example of the extinction vortex in action. In a study (http://www.shanmonster.com/chicken/news/news011.html) conducted over the course of 35 years, the prairie chicken population was monitored by researchers who observed some startling changes. Because of habitat fragmentation, the size of the population decreased from over 2000 to less than 50, with a corresponding loss of genetic diversity. There was measurable inbreeding depression, as hens produced fewer eggs, and those chicks that did hatch had lower survival rates.

Researchers hoped to save the Illinois population by somehow restoring some of the lost genetic variation. Fortunately, prairie chicken populations in several other states, such as Kansas and Minnesota, are large and healthy. In the early 1990s, researchers transplanted prairie chickens from these states into Illinois, which increased the size of the population as well as provided a boost of alleles that had been lost. Within a few years, the Illinois population was growing, and fertility and survival rates were increasing.

A species related to the greater prairie chicken, the Attwater's prairie chicken in Texas (http://www.npwrc.usgs.gov/resource/othrdata/sheyenne/populate.htm), has also suffered from a loss of habitat and the problems of inbreeding. However, there are no large natural populations, and the species is considered close to extinction. Biologists are now trying to supplement the natural population with birds reared in captivity. The last individual of another related species, the heath hen, died in 1932. The natural range of this species was limited by human development on Martha's Vineyard, and hunting reduced the size of the population. The heath hen's habitat was devastated by a fire in 1916. New predators, such as goshawks and feral cats and dogs, were introduced to the island. Finally, domestic turkeys brought to the island carried a poultry disease, and many of the remaining heath hens died from it. In short, a series of catastrophic events sealed the fate of the heath hen.

Although the Illinois prairie chickens seem to be recovering, it's not yet clear whether they'll persist. Biologists don't know how much genetic variation is needed for long-term sustainability, or what the minimum population size for genetic "health" really is, though it has been proposed that at least one hundred cocks (males) would be necessary. For now, though, the prairie chicken has a second chance.

1. What are biologists doing to try to rescue the Attwater's prairie chicken from extinction?

2. What is the estimate for the minimum prairie chicken population size needed to remain viable?

3. What factors contributed to the extinction of the heath hen?

BIZARRE FACTS IN BIOLOGY

No Sibling Rivalry Here

The evolution of eusocial systems in the animal kingdom was once a mystery. Meaning "truly social," eusociality (http://es.rice.edu/projects/Bios321/eusocial.insect.html) is characterized by a reproductive division of labor, overlapping generations, and having a class of workers (usually sisters of the offspring) cooperate in care of the young . Only one or a few females (the "queens") actually reproduce with only a few of the males. There are "sterile castes" of males and females that do not reproduce, but perform the necessary tasks of the colony, including helping to raise the offspring of those that do reproduce. At first glance, it seems that this system is doomed from an evolutionary perspective. Why would the majority of the colony sacrifice their own reproductive fitness to benefit those that do reproduce? Assuming this altruistic behavior is genetically based, it should be quickly eliminated by natural selection, since those altruistic genes would not be directly passed on to future generations.

For some eusocial species, the key to the mystery is in the genetic relatedness of the individuals. Most eusocial species are insects belonging to the orders Hymenoptera (which includes bees, wasps, and ants) and Isoptera (termites). Hymenopterans are haplodiploid (http://cellmath.med.utoronto.ca/TELEPOLIS/FootNote_Hap.html), meaning that males mature from unfertilized eggs and are haploid, while females mature from fertilized eggs and are diploid.

Fathers cannot have sons, only daughters. Fathers pass along *all* of their genes to their daughters, and sisters share 100% of the genes from their father and 50% from their mother, for an average of 75% relatedness. (Contrast this with more common diploid animals, in which full siblings have 50% relatedness to each other and to each of their parents.) Since females in haplodiploid systems are 50% related to their own daughters and 75% related to their sisters, they actually ensure survival of more of their own genes by helping their sisters to survive rather than having their own offspring. The males, on the other hand, are 100% related to both their mothers and their daughters, so it benefits them just as much to aid their mothers as to reproduce. In other words, the inclusive fitness of both males and females is higher than their individual fitnesses, and the altruistic behavior is favored.

Strangely enough, there are eusocial mammals, specifically the African naked mole rat (http://www.qmw.ac.uk/~ugbt991/CGFNMR.htm), which lives in underground colonies much like ants. Unlike other mammals, they are ectothermic (http://www-personal.umich.edu/~cherger/syllabusfolder/animaldiversity/Heterocephalus_glaber.html): they warm themselves by basking in the shallow surface tunnels during the day. One queen reproduces with a few males, while the rest of the males and females are either "workers" maintaining the colony or "soldiers" defending the colony. Researchers believe that behavioral interactions with the queen cause the nonbreeders to suppress their own hormone production, rendering them infertile. Unlike eusocial insects, naked mole rats are not haplodiploid, so why would such a system be favored? It has been suggested that because environmental conditions in the naked mole rats' habitat are so harsh, it is nearly impossible for one or a few individuals to dig a burrow and find enough food to survive. Working cooperatively, the colony survives. The inclusive fitness of nonbreeders is high, because at least some of their genes are shared by the breeders, and there is little hope of reproducing independently.

1. What are the three major criteria (http://courses.washington.edu/insects/444Students/LecOutlines/Sociality.htm) for eusociality?

2. Assuming that the evolutionary goal of reproduction is to have as many of your own genes in the next generation as possible, what is the potential parent-offspring conflict in haplodiploid eusocial insects? (Think about the perspectives of the mothers and their sons and daughters. Would it be better for each of them if the mothers were producing more sons or more daughters?)

3. Naked mole rats differ from other mammals in one important physiological mechanism. What is this?

4. Explain how the eusocial system of naked mole rats may have evolved by selection.

KEY TERMS

adaptation
allele frequency
altruism
coevolution
competition
directional selection

disruptive selection
equilibrium population
fitness
founder effect
gene flow
gene pool

genetic drift
Hardy-Weinberg principle
kin selection
mutation
natural selection
population

population bottleneck
predation
sexual selection
stabilizing selection

ANSWER KEY

SELF TEST

1. e
2. e
3. e
4. a
5. b
6. a
7. f
8. b
9. d
10. c
11. c
12. b
13. a
14. d
15. b
16. a
17. d
18. d
19. e
20. d
21. d
22. genes
23. homozygous
24. population bottleneck
25. genetic drift
26. genotype
27. stabilizing
28. A. stabilizing selection
    B. directional selection
    C. disruptive selection
29. A. lives and reproduces
    B. dies of malaria
    C. dies of sickle-cell anemia

ESSAY CHALLENGE

1. Your answer should indicate that alleles are different forms of the same gene. Diploid (or polyploid) organisms may have multiple copies of a gene, and may have copies of the same allele (homozygous) or different alleles (heterozygous).

2. Your answer should include a description of the variability found in a large population. When population sizes get smaller, the amount of genetic variability also becomes smaller. Under certain circumstances, some genes may lose all variability (become fixed for one allele) in the now smaller gene pool.

3. Your answer should include descriptions of the following ideas: potential for spread of advantageous alleles throughout the population and maintenance of a species' variability over a larger geographic area. Gene flow also tends to make different populations more alike.

4. Genotype is the description of an individual's allele set. Individuals are either homozygous or heterozygous for each gene. Phenotype is the physical expression of a given genotype, and may also be influenced by the organism's environment.

5. Directional selection is selection that favors individuals with a certain value of a trait over others who have average values of the same trait. If the trait is height, directional selection will consistently favor the tallest (or smallest) individuals over others. Stabilizing selection is selection that favors individuals with average values of a given trait. If the trait is height, stabilizing selection will favor individuals who are of average height over those who are shorter or taller. Disruptive selection is selection that favors individuals with extreme values of a given trait. If the trait is height, disruptive selection will favor individuals who are very tall and very short over individuals who are of average height.

6. Your answer should identify that altruism is a strategy that can result in an increase of the altruistic individual's own alleles in the general population, even if that individual does not survive or reproduce. This strategy often means that the individual is endangering its own chances of successfully reproducing in the process. One example of altruism is kin selection. This means that certain individuals will give up their own reproductive chances to assist the development of other closely related individuals in their community, allowing their own alleles that are shared with their relatives to be retained.

7. Though it is unlikely that an equilibrium population will exist in nature, the principle provides

evolutionary biologists with a baseline for comparison. In observing real populations, they can check to see how the conditions may be violated, and what patterns of evolutionary change may result. For example, if the population is small, genetic drift is likely to be important in changing allele frequencies. If a population is isolated, gene flow may not be important. The Hardy-Weinberg principle indicates what conditions will result in evolutionary change.

8. This statement means that mutations do not happen because they are needed now or may be needed at some point in the future. A mutation occurs randomly, and may be eliminated by natural selection if it is detrimental at that time. Alternatively, it may increase in frequency by selection if it is beneficial at that time, or if it is neutral and genetic drift results in a chance increase. A neutral mutation may be beneficial or detrimental if the environment of the organism changes.

9. There are several types of DNA changes that are likely to be neutral. Mutations in DNA sequences that lie outside of genes, or those in introns (which do not contain protein-coding information) cannot change proteins. Mutations outside of genes may affect the transcription of genes, but those that do not would be selectively neutral. Also, a mutation from one codon to another for the same amino acid will not change the resulting protein and is likely to be neutral.

10. Selection favors some alleles over others, and by eliminating some alleles will reduce genetic variation. Once genetic variation is reduced, further evolution cannot occur. Also, these exaggerated male traits may endanger them by making them more visible to predators and easier to catch. When natural selection against the trait balances sexual selection for it, the trait will stop evolving. Finally, it may simply be physiologically impossible to evolve beyond a certain point because of developmental constraints; it may be impossible to invest the amount of energy needed to grow the tail.

11. If there are other, variable populations of the same species elsewhere, scientists may be able to introduce new alleles by forcing gene flow: taking a sample of the diverse population to the genetically depauperate one.

MEDIA ACTIVITIES

15.3 Web Investigation: Evolution of a Menace

1. The two main categories of antibiotics are those that cause inhibition of cell wall synthesis, and those that cause inhibition of synthesis of nucleic acids or proteins. The five mechanisms of resistance are to modify the target of activity, pump out the antibiotic, prevent the antibiotic from getting into the cell (by modifying the membrane or using proteins), or enzymatically destroying the antibiotic.

2. Plasmids are responsible for most movement of resistance genes between cells.

3. The two biggest contributors to the development of resistant bacterial strains are the use of antibiotics in human medicine and in livestock feed (to promote health and growth). Resistant strains from livestock can be transferred to humans through the meat (rarely) or by eating vegetables exposed to manure fertilizer from treated livestock.

4. No, the study involved selecting for strains of bacteria that had already evolved antibiotic resistance.

ISSUES IN BIOLOGY

1. There is an effort to introduce birds raised in captivity into the natural population.

2. The historical data suggest that 100 cocks (males) are the minimum number necessary for persistence of the population.

3. It is believed that a combination of human activity and fires limiting habitat, predation from several introduced species, and disease contributed to the extinction of heath hens.

BIZARRE FACTS IN BIOLOGY

1. There must be a reproductive division of labor, generations must overlap so that there is some parental care of offspring, and there must be cooperative brood care such that sisters help with the care of siblings.

2. Mothers do not benefit any more from having daughters or sons, because they are 50% related to both. Daughters, however, would "prefer" that their mothers have more daughters (their sisters), to whom they are 75% related, than sons (their brothers), to whom they are only 25% related. Sons, however, have no such "preference" because they are 50% related to both brothers and sisters.

3. Naked mole rats cannot thermoregulate; they are essentially ectotherms ("cold-blooded"), like reptiles. They maintain body temperature by huddling together and basking in tunnels near the surface warmed by the sun.

4. Individual couples who tried to reproduce on their own were more likely to fail, as they could often not be able to make a sufficient burrow. Those that carried genes for more cooperative behavior worked together to make a large burrow to support all offspring, who carried these "cooperative" genes, ensuring that these genes would be passed to the next generation. Because the colony was a small group of related individuals, those that did not themselves reproduce still had many of their genes in the next generation, carried by those they had helped to raise.

CHAPTER 16: THE ORIGIN OF SPECIES

AT-A-GLANCE

Case Study: Lost World

16.1 What Is a Species?
Biologists Need a Clear Definition of Species
Species Are Groups of Interbreeding Populations
Appearance Can Be Misleading

16.2 How Do New Species Form?
Geographic Separation of a Population Can Lead to Allopatric Speciation
Ecological Isolation of a Population Can Led to Sympatric Speciation
Changes in Chromosome Number Can Lead to Sympatric Speciation
Change over Time Within a Species Can Cause Apparent "Speciation" in the Fossil Record
Under Some Conditions, Many New Species May Arise

16.3 How Is Reproductive Isolation Between Species Maintained?
Premating Isolating Mechanisms Prevent Mating Between Species
Postmating Isolation Mechanisms Limit Hybrid Offspring

16.4 What Causes Extinction?
Localized Distribution and Overspecialization Make Species Vulnerable in Changing Environments
Interaction with Other Organisms May Drive a Species to Extinction
Habitat Change and Destruction Are the Leading Causes of Extinction

Earth Watch: Hybridization and Extinction

Evolutionary Connections: Scientists Don't Doubt Evolution

Case Study Revisited: Lost World

Links to Life: Biological Vanity Plates

SELF TEST

1. According to Ernst Mayr, speciation depends on _____.
   a. competition
   b. extinction
   c. isolation
   d. genetic divergence
   e. population growth
   f. Both the third and fourth answers are correct.

2. Populations of two species living in the same areas (for example, chorus frogs and wood frogs living in the same ponds of Ohio woodlots) are said to be _____.
   a. allopatric
   b. sympatric
   c. convergent
   d. divergent
   e. symbiotic

3. Which of the following is a premating reproductive isolating mechanism?
   a. ecological isolation
   b. temporal isolation
   c. behavioral isolation
   d. mechanical incompatibility
   e. all of the above

4. The rapid speciation of Darwin's finches on the Galapagos Islands is an example of _____.
   a. coevolution
   b. sympatric speciation
   c. adaptive radiation
   d. branching of an evolutionary tree
   e. convergent evolution

5. Which of the following is the first step in the process of allopatric speciation?

   a. genetic drift

   b. interspecies contact

   c. geographic isolation

   d. evolution of two species independently

   e. reproductive isolation

6. Which of the following is (are) likely to promote sympatric speciation?

   a. gene flow

   b. genetic drift

   c. geographic isolation

   d. ecological isolation

   e. chromosomal aberrations

   f. Either the fourth or fifth answers are correct.

7. The rapid evolution of many new mammalian forms following the extinction of the dinosaurs 65 million years ago is an example of _____.

   a. coevolution

   b. adaptive radiation

   c. convergent evolution

   d. allopatric speciation

   e. sympatric speciation

8. If a haploid egg from a diploid plant is fertilized by a haploid sperm from a diploid plant, and the fertilized egg duplicates its chromosomes but does not divide into two cells, the resulting cell may then divide normally, producing an individual plant that will be _____.

   a. haploid

   b. diploid

   c. triploid

   d. tetraploid

   e. none of the above

9. Which of the following is (are) true of the biological-species concept?

   a. Asexually reproducing organisms use the same criteria as sexually reproducing organisms.

   b. Naturally occurring populations must actually interbreed to be considered as the same species.

   c. Different appearance is sufficient justification to categorize overlapping, naturally occurring populations as different species.

   d. None of the above

10. Which of the following is considered to be a requirement for speciation to occur?

    a. Populations must be isolated (geographically or in some other manner) from one another.

    b. Isolated populations must become genetically distinct from one another.

    c. Exchanges of genetic information must be restricted between populations.

    d. all of the above

11. Matings among which organisms with the following sets of chromosomes would not produce offspring with the same number of chromosomes?

    a. haploid

    b. diploid

    c. tetraploid

    d. triploid

12. Genetic divergence is required for speciation to occur, but how can speciation be guaranteed?

    a. There are mechanisms preventing interbreeding between developing species.

    b. Individuals from developing species are kept from being able to mate with each other.

    c. Offspring produced from the mating of individuals from developing species are unable to pass along their genes to a subsequent generation.

    d. all of the above

13. Which of the following may cause a species to become extinct?

    a. habitat encroachment (e.g., urbanization)

    b. seasonal changes in the weather

    c. an inability to successfully compete for limited resources (e.g., food, water, habitat)

    d. Both the first and third answers are correct.

14. Which of the following is most characteristic of populations of *different* species?

    a. Members of the two populations resemble each other.

    b. Members of the two populations can be distinguished by their appearance.

    c. The two populations are geographically separated from each other.

    d. The two populations are adapted to different habitats.

    e. A fertile female from one population mated with a fertile male from the other population produces no offspring.

175

15. Which of the following is NOT an example of speciation?

   a. A small group from a large mainland population colonizes a remote island.

   b. A river that has long divided two populations of mice is diverted by an earthquake, and the two mouse populations come into contact and breed together. The hybrid offspring, however, are sterile.

   c. In a bird population, there is disruptive selection for habitat: one group adapts to the tree-tops, while another adapts to the lower branches and ground. The two groups rarely interbreed, but when they do the hybrid offspring do not live long because they have a mixture of both kinds of adaptations and are not adapted to either habitat.

   d. Over a period of several million years, a deer-like species evolves from being very small and feeding on grasses and small shrubs to being much larger and feeding on the lower branches of trees.

   e. Due to meiotic error, a diploid plant capable of self-fertilization produces a self-fertilizing tetraploid offspring.

16. Which species is at least risk of extinction?

   a. The species has many geographically isolated populations, all of them small.

   b. The species is composed of one large, continuous, genetically variable population.

   c. The species lives only in a tree that is itself endangered.

   d. The species' major food source is an insect population that is declining because of pesticide use.

   e. A native plant species lives in an area where a newly introduced nonnative plant is adapted to the same type of habitat but grows more quickly.

17. Biologists sometimes combine two groups previously considered different species into the same species because _____.

   a. they may be physically divergent, but they are found to interbreed in nature

   b. the two species have evolved to lose premating reproductive isolating mechanisms

   c. the two species have evolved to lose postmating reproductive isolating mechanisms

   d. the two species have evolved to be more physically similar

   e. the two species have expanded their ranges and now encounter each other

18. _____ speciation can occur when two populations are separated by geographic space and then diverge genetically.

19. _____ speciation can occur if two populations share the same geographic area but do not share habitats.

20. One feature of plants that can allow them to speciate at a higher rate than other organisms is their ability to tolerate _____. This means that their gametes can contain more than one copy of each chromosome.

21. _____ radiation is what can occur when one species develops into many. Usually, this occurs when a single species invades an area with many underutilized niches.

22. When a species has no surviving members, it is said to be _____.

23. Loss of or damage to an endangered species' _____ is one of the chief threats of extinction for these species.

24. In both allopatric and sympatric speciation, identifiable steps occur. Label each of these steps on the following diagram.

25. Interpreting an evolutionary tree involves special graphical understandings. Label the generic evolutionary tree below with the proper interpretations.

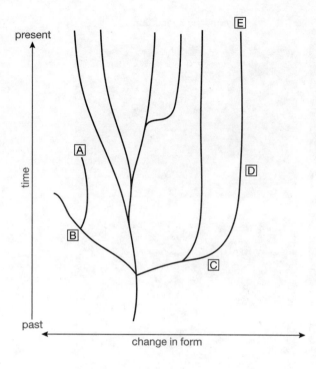

26. How many ways can reproductive isolation be maintained between two species?

a. in two basic ways

b. in four ways

c. in at least eight ways

d. in an infinite number of ways

27. The concept that evolutionary change is not slow and continuous but rather occurs in comparatively brief bursts, separated by longer stable intervals with less evolutionary change, is known as _____.

a. coevolution

b. adaptive radiation

c. convergent evolution

d. allopatric speciation

e. sympatric speciation

f. punctuated equilibrium

ESSAY CHALLENGE

1. Provide a definition for the term *species* that describes how two populations of the same species can become two separate species.

2. Describe the biological-species concept, and identify any reasons why it cannot be generalized to all species.

3. What are some criteria for deciding if two individuals are from different species?

4. Identify one of the postmating mechanisms and how it prevents two species from successfully interbreeding.

5. Identify one of the premating mechanisms and how it prevents two species from successfully interbreeding.

6. Describe how changes in a local habitat can cause species to go extinct.

7. Why can't the biological-species concept be used to assign fossils to species categories? What criteria can be used?

8. What processes lead to the genetic divergence of isolated populations?

9. Describe how adaptive radiation may have led to the many species of finches on the Galapagos Islands.

10. Several species of fruit flies live at the same altitude on a mountainside in Hawaii. Each species is found in its own range, and there is little overlap with the ranges of other species. These species ranges are distributed in a circle around the mountain. Flies from adjacent species can usually interbreed somewhat, but not enough to be considered the same species. However, on one side of the mountain, the two adjacent species are anatomically different and cannot interbreed at all. Explain how these species probably evolved.

11. Ernst Mayr believes that allopatric speciation is much more likely to occur than sympatric speciation. Why would you expect this to be true?

12. Explain how interactions with another species, such as a competitor or a prey species, may cause a species to become extinct.

13. Humans are presently causing many extinctions of rain forest species due to habitat destruction for development of land for farming. Suggest a few ways that further rain forest extinctions may be prevented.

14. The Earth Watch for Chapter 16 discusses how hybridization between an endangered species and a close relative species can lead to the endangered species' extinction. How might the opposite happen (hybridization with another species may help prevent extinction)?

15. Is a new human species likely to evolve by allopatric speciation? Why or why not?

MEDIA ACTIVITIES

To access a Media Activity visit http://www.prenhall.com/audesirk7. Log in to the Web site selected by your instructor, navigate to this chapter, and select the appropriate Media Activity number.

16.1 What is Speciation?
Estimated Time: 2 minutes

The animation provides a brief overview of the concept of speciation through reproductive isolation.

16.2 Allopatric Speciation
Estimated Time: 5 minutes

This activity demonstrates how a single population may be separated geographically into two populations, and one or both may evolve into new species.

16.3 Sympatric Speciation
Estimated Time: 5 minutes

This activity demonstrates how a single population may split into two different populations, without being separated geographically, and one or both may evolve into new species

16.4 Speciation by Polyploidy
Estimated Time: 5 minutes

In this activity, explore how new plant species can form through changes in ploidy, which is the number of chromosome sets in an organism.

16.5 Web Investigation: Lost World
Estimated time: 20 minutes

Is the great age of exploration over? Think again. Thousands of new organisms, ecosystems, and other natural wonders remain to be discovered. This exercise looks at a few recently discovered animal species and how they were found. Answer Questions 1 through 3 for each animal. After you have finished, use your answers to complete Question 4.

The Annamite Mountains of Vietnam/Laos are the home of three recently discovered species: the saola (http://www.animalinfo.org/species/artiperi/pseunghe.htm), the giant muntjac (http://forests.org/archive/asia/newdeer.htm), and a strange striped rabbit (http://news.bbc.co.uk/1/hi/sci/tech/422674.stm). At least ten new species of monkeys have been discovered in Brazil since 1990. They include the black-faced lion tamarin (http://www.thewildones.org/Animals/bflt.html), the dwarf marmoset (http://forests.org/archive/brazil/newmonke.htm), and the two latest additions, the manicore (http://members.tripod.com/uakari/callithrix_manicorensis.html) and acari marmosets (http://members.tripod.com/uakari/callithrix_acariensis.html). The Peruvian (a.k.a. lesser) beaked whale (http://www.wdcs.org/dan/publishing.nsf/(allweb)/4E7BBE375EF0EE5D802568F8004E6097) was the first new whale species discovered in 28 years.

1. How was it discovered (if this information is available in the linked sites)?

2. What is its normal habitat?

3. What is its survival status?

4. What do these "new" species have in common? Do you think they will still be around in 100 years?

ISSUES IN BIOLOGY

What Is a Species?

The concept of the species (http://sorrel.humboldt.edu/~klll/speciesdef.html) is one of the most fundamental and important concepts in all of biology, yet it is also one of the most problematic. As your textbook points out in the Introduction to Chapter 16, throughout most of human history, "species" was a poorly defined concept (Some scientists would say that is still the case). "Species" normally referred to one of the originally created "kinds" mentioned in the Bible; the word *species* is Latin for "appearance." So, in a very simple sense, *species* refers to a specific kind of organism with a specific appearance. Although this is a very simplistic definition of species, it does reflect what most people observe around them—that organisms come in discrete kinds that appear to be different from other kinds.

The classic *biological-species concept* that is presented in most general biology textbooks, including this one, defines species as "groups of actually or potentially interbreeding natural populations, which are reproductively isolated from other such groups." This definition was given by Ernst Mayr (http://www.aaas.org/spp/dser/evolution/history/mayr.shtml), an ornithologist who made important contributions to our understanding of the process of speciation. Mayr's definition of *species*, based on reproductive isolation, reinforces our impression that species are distinctive types; they are, after all, reproductively isolated (incapable of reproducing with other species). This definition has some problems and limitations. For example, there is the problem, mentioned in the text, of discerning boundaries among asexually reproducing organisms. However, this definition seems to be, at least, the starting point for discussions about what constitutes a species.

In our attempt to classify organisms into a hierarchical scheme of organization, from kingdoms down to species, we realize that the higher taxonomic levels, from genera on up, are merely abstractions and that our current classification may not reflect biological reality perfectly (see the Issues in Biology section for Chapter 18). That is why taxonomists are always tinkering with their classifications. Many biologists, however, believe that the species is a biologically meaningful grouping, perhaps the only biologically meaningful taxonomic category. But there are examples in nature that sometimes make us wonder about that.

Although we think of species as being distinct kinds of organisms, clearly separated in some important biological way from other kinds, we must remember that new species evolve from existing species and also that populations evolve adaptations to local conditions. We should, then, be able to find populations that are intermediate between other populations that are apparently distinct species. We should also expect to find populations that show significant geographic variation (presumably adaptations to local conditions) but that are not different species. With respect to geographic variation within species, we need to consider only the various human "races" to appreciate the fact that populations within species can and do vary significantly.

Rat snakes, *Elaphe obsoleta*, show different patterns of geographic variation in body color (black, brown, orange, or yellow) and pattern (plain, blotches, or stripes). The geographic distribution of subspecies (a term we use to denote geographical variants within a species) would differ, however, depending on whether we described them on the basis of color or pattern.

The red crossbills (http://research.amnh.org/ornithology/crossbills/species.html) are an interesting example. Crossbills are seed-eating finches that use their unique crossed bill to open conifer cone scales in order to extract seeds. A number of different types of red crossbills, which vary only slightly in physical characteristics (such as body size and color) and can be difficult to distinguish, have been included in the same species, *Loxia curvirostra*. There are many areas where the different forms overlap, but individuals mate only with their own kind, even though the physical differences seem slight. It appears that these birds use differences in vocal patterns to distinguish among themselves and that the types should be considered separate biological species.

Finally, consider ring species (http://www.don-lindsay-archive.org/creation/ring_species.html): two distinct, reproductively isolated species in one locality that grade into each other through a series of intermediate forms distributed around a geographic barrier. One of the best examples of this phenomenon is the herring gull (*Larus argentatus*) and the lesser black-backed gull (*Larus fuscus*), both of which live throughout the region of the Arctic Ocean. The herring gull is larger and has a gray mantle (wing plumage) and pink legs; the lesser black-backed gull has a nearly black mantle and yellow legs. On the coasts of northern Europe, these two species may be found together in the same nesting colonies, but they rarely hybridize. In North America we generally find only the herring gull; as we follow populations around the pole from North America to Asia, these birds become decreasingly like the European herring gull and increasingly like the European lesser black-backed gull. In Siberia, about half way around, these birds are called the vega gull but are classified as the same species as the herring gull (*L. argentatus*), even though they have almost yellow legs and a noticeably darker mantle.

So, some populations that look different *are* different species, some populations that look different *aren't* different species, and some populations that don't look different *are* different species. Also, some species are "connected" to each other by intermediate populations.

1. What is a species (That is, what do you think should define a species)?

2. The morphological (or phenotypic) species concept would assign individuals to the same species on the basis of physical similarity. When would applying this concept lead to a different conclusion than the biological-species concept?

3. Are species real, in a biological sense, or are they just an abstraction devised by biologists to help us understand the organization of life?

BIZARRE FACTS IN BIOLOGY

Teaching Old Genes New Tricks

One of the great puzzles in evolution is how do new, exotic features appear? Darwin's natural selection process takes time, lots of it, and how useful would a "pre-eye" or "pre-wing" structure be? The evolutionary record (fossils) is light on "missing link"-type creatures. Some scientists think this is because novel features arise suddenly and that evolution proceeds through punctuated equilibria (http://talkorigins.org/faqs/punc-eq.html). Whether new features arise slowly or suddenly still doesn't explain how it happens. Maybe old genes just learn new tricks.

Butterfly wings are large, brightly colored, and patterned—much different from the wings of flies and other insects. Surprisingly, the jump from bargain wings to designer wings may just involve turning on an existing gene in a new spot.

The distalless gene controls the process of limb development in many different animals and insects, suggesting that it is, evolutionarily, very old. In butterflies, distalless is turned on in a novel spot, the developing wing cells, and produces the colorful eyespots characteristic of butterfly wing patterns.

Another collection of fly genes, the achaete-scute family, have also been taught new tricks in the butterfly genome. The achaete-scute genes in flies direct certain cells to make the sensory cells that will make the fly's bristles. Butterflies have a similar family of genes, called ASH-1 that also direct specific cells to become sensory cells. But the ASH-1 genes stay active in developing butterflies longer than in flies and direct these sensory cells to make the colored scale cells of the butterfly wing surface instead of bristles.

Old genes learning new tricks may explain how life on Earth advanced by leaps and bounds.

References

Carroll, S. 1997. Genetics on the wing or how the butterfly got its spots. *Nat Hist* 106(1):28–32.

Galant, R., Skeath, J. B., Paddock, S., Lewis, D. L., and Carroll, S. B. 1998. Expression pattern of a butterfly achaete-scute homolog reveals the homology of butterfly wing scales and insect sensory bristles. *Cur Bio* 8:807–13.

Takayama, E., Motoyama, M., and Yoshida, A.. 1997. Color pattern formation on the wing of a butterfly *Pieris rapae*. 2. Color determination and scale development. *Develop Growth Differ* 39:485–91.

1. Describe how the punctuated equilibria model of evolution differs from the model proposed by Darwin.

2. Are brightly colored wings an evolutionary advantage?

3. How can we explain the variety of patterns seen on butterfly wings?

KEY TERMS

adaptive radiation
allopatric speciation
extinction
isolating mechanism
polyploidy

postmating isolating
  mechanism
premating isolating
  mechanism
reproductive isolation

speciation
species
sympatric speciation

ANSWER KEY

SELF TEST

1. f
2. b
3. e
4. c
5. c
6. f

7. b
8. d
9. d
10. d
11. d
12. d
13. d

14. e
15. a
16. b
17. a
18. allopatric
19. sympatric
20. polyploidy
21. adaptive
22. extinct
23. habitat
24. A. original population
    B. reproductive isolation
    C. genetic divergence
    D. isolation, either geographical or ecological
25. A. extinct species
    B. speciation events
    C. rapid phenotypic change
    D. slow phenotypic change
    E. existing species
26. c
27. f

ESSAY CHALLENGE

1. Two populations of the same species may become separate species if, say, they are separated by large physical distance or if the two populations begin to exploit different niches. However, to be considered true species according to the biological-species concept, there must be some mechanism preventing successful interbreeding of the two populations, either by preventing mating or preventing survival and successful reproduction of hybrids of the two populations.

2. The biological-species concept is that two populations belong to different species if they cannot successfully interbreed. This theory does not explain how to tell asexual species apart.

3. If individuals from different populations cannot successfully reproduce together, they may be from different species. They may be able to successfully mate, but cannot produce viable or fertile offspring. They may also be from different species if they cannot or will not mate. For example, they may have different mating displays, they may be receptive to mating at different times, they may have adaptations that prevent them from encountering each other, or they may not be able physically to mate.

4. One of the best examples of postmating incompatibility is the mule. Donkeys and horses can produce offspring called mules. However, since those offspring are sterile, horses and donkeys are considered separate species. In other cases, offspring of members of two different species cannot survive to reproductive age, a situation called hybrid inviability. Also, the two species may be gametically incompatible, meaning that the sperm of one species cannot fertilize the eggs of another.

5. One example described in the text was of two species that had evolved into having slightly different breeding seasons. Even several days' difference in pollen production and reception can be significant in plant species. Other examples would be if the two species were adapted to different habitats such that they do not encounter each other to mate, if they have different courtship behaviors, or if their sexual organs are physically incompatible.

6. Losing habitat to development or having a habitat destroyed by pollution, especially to a species with a very small range, can have devastating effects. If the population cannot move elsewhere or adapt to the changing conditions in time, they can become extinct. Habitat fragmentation may break a formerly large population into a number of smaller isolated groups, each of which is now more likely to become extinct than the original large population. Once all of the populations of a species are gone, the species itself is extinct.

7. The biological-species concept (BSC) cannot be used for fossils because it is impossible to tell if fossils could interbreed or not, the basis for the BSC. Species assignments for fossils must be based on anatomical similarity.

8. If both populations are small, random genetic drift in each of them will result in the loss of different alleles for various genes, resulting in genetic differences. Different selection pressures in the two populations can also cause them to adapt differently. Also, given enough time, different mutations can accumulate in the two populations.

9. Millions of years ago, a small group of finches (or even a single mated female) may have accidentally traveled from the mainland, perhaps aided by a strong storm, to found a colony on one of the islands. As they adapted to the new habitat, they evolved into a new species. A small group may have then colonized another island. In another example of allopatric speciation, a new species evolved as this founder population adapted to a new set of environmental conditions. The process repeated a number of times, leading to a diversity of species on the islands.

10. Probably, the distribution comes from an ancient population of flies that colonized and adapted to one area on the side of the mountain. Over many years, the population began spreading around the mountain in both directions, and evolving to new species along the way. When the two expanding branches met at the opposite side, they had greatly diverged and were no longer capable of any interbreeding.

11. Both types of speciation require some barrier to reproduction between two groups to evolve. Allopatric groups are completely separate, preventing gene flow and allowing divergence over time, and eventually the evolution of reproductive barriers. Sympatric groups, on the other hand, are not

separated, and any gene flow between them may prevent them from diverging and forming reproductive barriers. It is only if adaptations of the two sympatric groups prevent them from mating with each other that speciation can result.

12. In a competitive situation, a species may be driven to extinction if its competitor is better adapted and can better utilize the resources provided by the local habitat. In a predator-prey relationship, the predator may become extinct if it overharvests its prey and has no other source of food. In fact, the latter situation could result in the extinction of both predator and prey species.

13. There are a number of possible answers to this question, including making use of better farming practices to minimize the need for land (and taking steps to slow the growth of the human population) or setting aside areas to be left pristine and untouched by human development.

14. If a species is endangered, then populations may be small and/or lack genetic diversity. An influx of genes from another species may help restore genetic diversity, allowing increased potential for future adaptation, and increase the population size, lessening the risk for loss of diversity by genetic drift. As long as the hybridization is not extensive, the endangered species can retain its separate identity.

15. For a new human species to evolve by allopatric speciation, a population would have to be completely isolated from breeding with other humans for a very long time. Given the increasing rates of gene flow among previously separate groups of people, this possibility is becoming less likely.

MEDIA ACTIVITIES

16.5. Web Investigation: Lost World

1. The saola was discovered when three pairs of horns were found in Vietnam in May 1992. The muntjac was discovered through skulls found in Vietnamese villages and descriptions by hunters. The striped rabbit was discovered as dead specimens in a Laotian market. A skull of the Peruvian beaked whale was discovered in a Peruvian fish market in 1976, and an adult male was found stranded on a Peruvian beach in 1988. The links do not provide detailed information on the discovery of the black-faced lion tamarin, dwarf marmoset, manicore marmoset, or acari marmoset.

2. The saola, muntjac, and striped rabbit are found only in Vietnam and Laos in areas of high altitude and dense vegetation. The black-faced lion tamarin is found only in the Atlantic coastal forests of Eastern

Brazil. The dwarf, manicore, and acari marmosets live in small areas near rivers in Brazil. The Peruvian beaked whale is limited to the mid- and deep waters of the eastern tropical Pacific, near Peru.

3. The species found in Vietnam and Laos are endangered because of increasing loss of the forests where they live. The links do not specifically indicate the status of the primates. It is not known whether the Peruvian beaked whale is rare or whether there is a large population in deeper waters.

4. These species are found in areas that are either very inaccessible, small, or both. Some (such as the Vietnamese species) may be extinct in 100 years because of habitat destruction, but others (particularly the whales) may still be around then if human activity in that time does not impact their habitats.

ISSUES IN BIOLOGY

1. Although this is a somewhat subjective question, Mayr's biological-species concept of interbreeding populations is a good one. You should defend their answer if it differs from this.

2. If two groups are physically similar but do not interbreed, they would be "biological" species but not "morphological" species. Also, if two populations diverge physically but can still interbreed, they would not be "biological" species but might be classified as "morphological" species.

3. Species designated by the biological-species concept are real in a biological sense, because they represent a potentially common gene pool. In theory, all populations of the same species could exchange genes and together contribute to the future evolution of the species.

BIZARRE FACTS IN BIOLOGY

1. Darwin's model of evolution is that evolution occurs gradually over a long period of time. The punctuated equilibria model is that some physical characteristics of fossil lineages do not change for a very long time, then quickly evolve to a new form.

2. Presumably they are an advantage, or natural selection would have eliminated individuals with brightly colored wings from the population.

3. The origin of the variety of patterns can be explained by the expression of a similar set of genes at different times or in different ways in the different species. The persistence of the variation in these patterns is likely to be due to natural selection favoring the individual patterns found in different species.

CHAPTER 17: THE HISTORY OF LIFE

AT-A-GLANCE

SELF TEST

1. Which of the following was NOT a common component of Earth's early atmosphere?
   a. hydrogen   b. oxygen
   c. methane   d. ammonia
   e. carbon dioxide

2. The most fundamental difference between prokaryotes and eukaryotes is that eukaryotes have _____.
   a. a cell wall
   b. a plasma membrane
   c. a membrane-bound nucleus
   d. genetic material
   e. multiple cells

3. The first animals to "invade" the land were probably _____.
   a. arthropods   b. fish
   c. amphibians   d. reptiles

4. Which of the following was an evolutionary advancement that allowed reptiles to exploit life on land fully?
   a. improved lungs
   b. internal fertilization
   c. shelled, waterproof eggs
   d. scaly, waterproof skin
   e. all of the above

5. The reptiles gave rise to _____.
   a. fish   b. amphibians
   c. birds   d. mammals
   e. Both the third and fourth answers are correct.

6. Which of the following was a likely characteristic of the early primates?
   a. color vision
   b. long, grasping fingers
   c. a proportionally larger brain
   d. forward-facing eyes with binocular vision
   e. all of the above

7. Which of the following represents the modern scheme of protein synthesis?
   a. DNA → RNA → protein
   b. RNA → DNA → protein
   c. DNA → protein → RNA
   d. RNA → protein → DNA
   e. protein → DNA → RNA
   f. protein → RNA → DNA

8. Which of the following would be an advantage of multicellularity?
   a. a better chance for escaping predation
   b. the potential for capturing and eating larger prey
   c. the ability to specialize different body parts for different purposes
   d. all of the above

9. The hominids belonging to the genus *Australopithecus* first evolved in _____.
   a. Asia   b. Africa
   c. Australia   d. Europe

10. Given the following list, which is the correct numbered sequence from earliest to most recent hominid development?
    1. bipedalism
    2. cave paintings
    3. first stone tools made
    4. first migration out of Africa
    5. buried dead and "religious" rites

    a. 1, 2, 3, 4, 5   b. 3, 1, 2, 4, 5
    c. 1, 3, 4, 5, 2   d. 3, 2, 1, 5, 4
    e. 1, 4, 3, 5, 2

11. Which of the following would have prevented the development of conditions favorable for the evolution of life after Earth was formed?
    a. complex organic molecules
    b. energy in the form of lightning and energy from the sun
    c. unbound, or free, oxygen molecules
    d. carbon dioxide and sulfur dioxide

12. What organic macromolecule do scientists believe was the first one able to generate more copies of itself during prebiotic conditions?
    a. DNA   b. RNA
    c. protein   d. none of the above

13. What experimental evidence suggests that eukaryotic cells formed symbiotic relationships with bacteria?
    a. Both chloroplasts and mitochondria contain DNA that is distinct from that found in the nucleus of the eukaryotic cell.
    b. There are similarities in both structure and function between the cilia and flagella of eukaryotes and the coiled/spiral form of bacteria.
    c. There are present-day examples in which a eukaryotic organism contains either a population of bacteria or a different form of algae.
    d. all of the above
    e. none of the above

14. Which of the following characteristics is believed to be an evolutionary advantage of multicellular eukaryotic organisms?
    a. Multicellular organisms are easily ingested by single-celled predators.
    b. Multicelled organisms were able to let certain cells specialize to carry out functions that single-celled organisms could not.
    c. Multicellularity allowed cells to remain small and able to efficiently exchange carbon dioxide and oxygen, despite increasing the size of the organism.
    d. Both the second and third answers are correct.
    e. none of the above

15. If a species first evolved in the seas, which of the following would NOT be an obstacle to its effort to colonize land?
a. dehydration of cells and tissues
b. the external skeleton of arthropods
c. exchange of gametes between individuals
d. locomotion

16. Which of the following features distinguish the hominid line from the lineage of apes?
a. binocular vision
b. large brain
c. hands with opposable thumbs
d. dependence upon an upright posture for locomotion

17. Which statement best describes the pattern of extinction throughout biological history?
a. The rate of extinction has steadily increased over the entire history of life.
b. The rate of extinction has steadily decreased over the entire history of life.
c. There has been very little extinction except during mass extinction events.
d. There has been a relatively constant turnover of species with occasional mass extinction events.

18. Alexander Oparin and John Haldane suggested that organic matter could arise from nonliving matter through a series of chemical reactions. This is called _____ evolution.

19. The first structures that could enclose genetic material in a protective environment are called

_____.

20. If an organism lives in the absence of oxygen, it is called an _____.

21. Some researchers suggest that the first eukaryotes were actually various different prokaryotes living in cooperation within the same cellular membrane. This belief is called the _____ hypothesis.

22. A sperm cell enclosed in a watertight container is called _____.

23. Humans have their skeletons inside their bodies, but arthropods have theirs on the outside. This is called an _____.

24. Stanley Miller and Harold Urey attempted to re-create life using basic chemicals and the setup below. Label the parts to this apparatus.

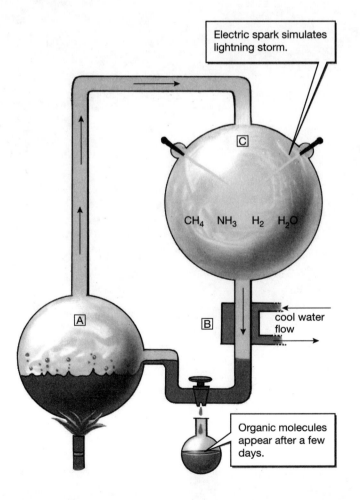

Electric spark simulates lightning storm.

C

CH₄ NH₃ H₂ H₂O

A

B

cool water flow

Organic molecules appear after a few days.

25. The diagram below is meant to depict the history of Earth on a 24-hour clock face. Using this analogy, place the events below at their proper "time" in history.

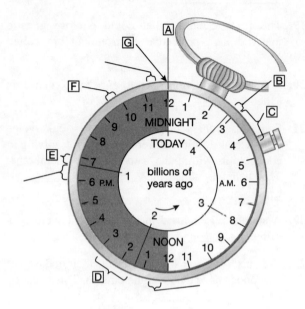

Earth's history projected on a 24-hour day

26. The diagram below indicates the probable origin of mitochondria and chloroplasts. Label each of the steps in this process.

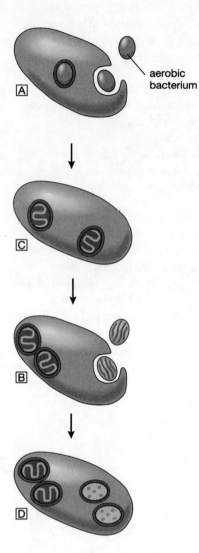

aerobic bacterium

27. Using the evolutionary tree below as a guide, label
the indicated species of human.

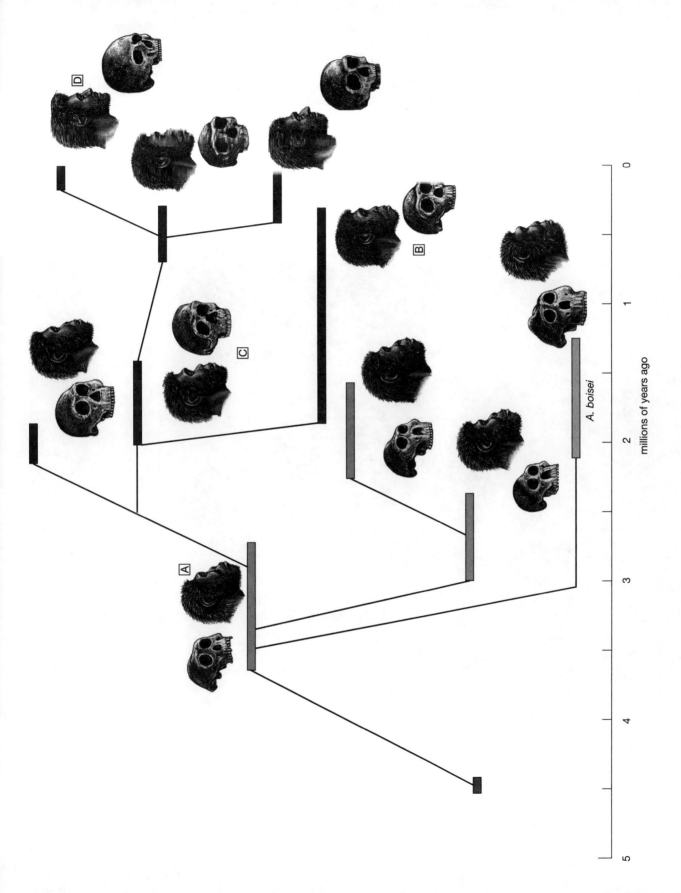

A. boisei

millions of years ago

28. As humans evolved, their use of tools became more sophisticated. Identify the genus and species of human that is responsible for the creation of each of these tools.

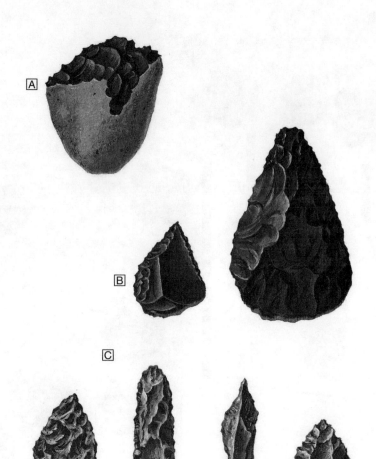

29. There are two theories on the evolution of *Homo sapiens*. Label these two correctly using the diagrams below.

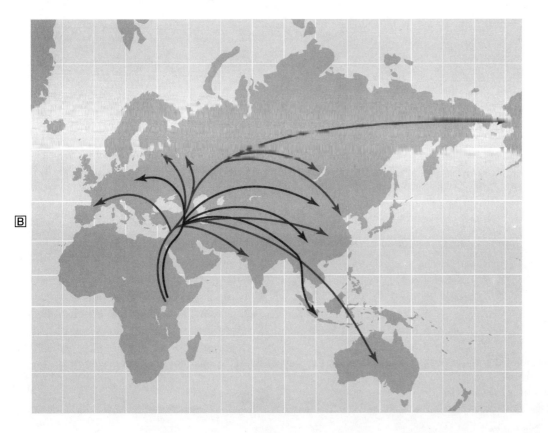

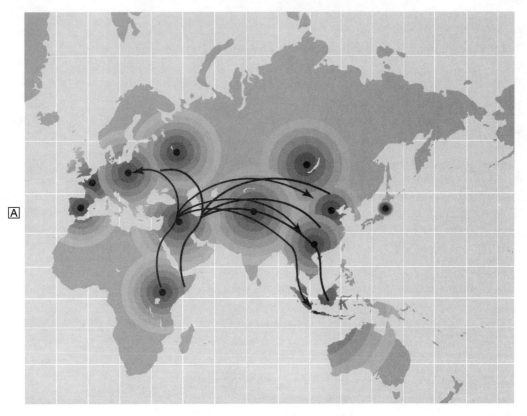

ESSAY CHALLENGE

1. Describe how Miller and Urey's experiments with a hypothetical early Earth atmosphere helped to propose how life formed on Earth.

2. Describe how eukaryotes could have arisen, given that Earth was inhabited only by prokaryotic cells.

3. Why might it be more advantageous for an organism to be multicellular than unicellular?

4. What were some of the major obstacles that stood in the way of living beings moving onto dry earth?

5. What are some of the bodily features that humans share with early primates?

6. Explain why the scenario of prebiotic evolution leading to the origin of life is plausible.

7. How do we know that the earliest organisms were anaerobes?

8. What are ribozymes, and what does their existence suggest about the role of RNA in the prebiotic world?

9. What are microspheres, and what does their existence suggest about the origin of the first living cells?

10. What were the first photosynthetic organisms like?

11. Does the demonstration that spontaneous generation does not occur regularly mean that life on Earth did not arise from nonliving systems?

12. Beginning about 2.2 billion years ago, the concentration of oxygen gas in the Earth's atmosphere rose significantly. Where did the oxygen come from, and how did it get there?

13. Why was the rise of oxygen in the Earth's atmosphere both a crisis and an opportunity for life at the time?

14. What were the first multicellular organisms, and what specific advantages did their multicellularity have?

15. Why do biologists believe that the early evolution of animals produced many types that have no current descendants?

16. What was the importance of the evolution of plant pollen?

17. Explain how amphibians are only partially adapted to a terrestrial existence.

18. What are some of the causes of mass extinctions that have been proposed? Do they all have the same cause?

19. Why does human cultural evolution occur more rapidly than biological evolution?

20. What purpose does a mass extinction play in evolution and speciation?

MEDIA ACTIVITIES

To access a Media Activity visit http://www.prenhall.com/audesirk7. Log in to the Web site selected by your instructor, navigate to this chapter, and select the appropriate Media Activity number.

17.1 Endosymbiosis
Estimated Time: 5 minutes

This activity demonstrates how cellular symbiosis may have resulted in the complex organelles of mitochondria and chloroplasts.

17.2 Evolutionary Timescales
Estimated Time: 5 minutes

In this activity, you will explore the evolutionary history of three important types of organisms: land plants, terrestrial vertebrate animals, and primates.

17.3 Plate Tectonics
Estimated Time: 5 minutes

This activity demonstrates how the continents have moved over the course of time and points out some important effects of continental drift on the distribution and evolutionary histories of organisms.

17.4 Web Investigation: Life on a Frozen Moon?
Estimated time: 10 minutes

What are the origins of life? Since water is one of the basic elements of life as we know it, many astrobiologists believe that the best way to detect life in space is to look for liquid water. Recent observations suggest that there may be liquid water on Europa, one of the moons of Jupiter. This exercise will take a closer look at the fourth largest satellite of Jupiter.

1. First, define astrobiology (http://astrobiology.arc.nasa.gov/overview.html).

2. What is the evidence (http://www.spaceref.com/news/viewpr.html?pid=2474) that Europa has a liquid water layer under its icy crust?

3. Does Europa have an atmosphere (http://www.pbs.org/lifebeyondearth/alone/europa.html) likely to support life?

4. How does the discovery of sulfuric acid on Europa (http://spacescience.spaceref.com/newhome/headlines/ast30sep99_1.htm) affect the astrobiologists' view of Europa?

5. Astrobiologists are also studying the subglacial Lake Vostok (http://www.smithsonianmag.si.edu/smithsonian/issues00/jul00/vostok.html) in Antarctica. How is it similar to Europan bodies of water?

ISSUES IN BIOLOGY

Who Were Our Early Human Ancestors?

Homo sapiens is the species with the big brain, and we want to know everything. We especially want to know about ourselves. Who are we, and from where have we come? We like to think of our species as being unique in the biological world. Indeed, we classify ourselves in a genus (*Homo*) in which we are the only species, and our genus in a family (Hominidae) that until recently contained only that genus. (Chimpanzees, gorillas, and orangutans are now also classified as Hominidae.) But it wasn't always so. As the textbook points out, there was a time when a number of hominid types (assumed to be distinct species) existed simultaneously—first in Africa, then later in Europe, the Middle East, and Asia. We are interested not only in the evolutionary relationships among these contemporaneous hominids, but also in their ecological and social relationships. Did they come in contact with each other? Did they compete for resources? Did they act aggressively toward each other? Did they interbreed? And finally, which of these many hominid forms are in our own direct ancestry?

The story of our origin, of hominid evolution, is a tale with many chapters, and each new edition of the story has many revisions. The story has unfolded slowly, because much of the information on which it is based comes from fossils and artifacts thousands to millions of years old. We uncover these treasures from our past slowly and, quite literally, in bits and pieces; it has been difficult to gain a full understanding of their meanings. Now, however, more accurate dating techniques and other new technologies, especially in molecular biology, can be brought to bear on this evidence from our past, and the story is becoming clearer.

Humans have long wondered about the possibility of an evolutionary relationship with other animals, and apes seemed the most likely candidates for our nearest "relatives." Because our large brain seems to be our most unique characteristic, it was believed that a larger brain was what would have distinguished our earliest ancestors from the other apes. Thus it was expected that the "missing link" would have a large brain but would otherwise be apelike. This expectation was reinforced when, in 1912, a skull with a large cranium and apelike jaw was supposedly discovered in a gravel bed at Piltdown, England. Although this specimen contradicted fossil remains from Java, which indicated that the body had evolved more rapidly than did the brain, it was accepted as a human ancestor. It wasn't until some 40 years later that "Piltdown Man" was shown to be a hoax (http://www.pbs.org/wgbh/aso/databank/entries/do53pi.html); a relatively modern cranium had been planted in the gravel bed with the jaw of an orangutan.

Our story started to get back on track in 1924, when a South African anatomy professor, Raymond Dart, was given a box of rocks collected from the local quarry at Taung. To Dart's delight, the collection contained the remains of a child's skull and preservation of the fossilized brain. This "Taung child" (http://www.talkorigins.org/faqs/homs/taung.jpg) (links to image of the skull), as it came to be known, clearly was not an ape, at least in Dart's mind. The skull suggested that the creature walked upright (bipedal), and the teeth were not apelike. Dart named his specimen *Australopithecus africanus*, African southern ape. But the cranium was small, and the Piltdown hoax had not yet been exposed; also, the find was far south in Africa, where no apes had been found. So, Dart's discovery met with considerable skepticism. It wasn't until Robert Broom's several discoveries of fossils (cranial and post-cranial remains) of adult specimens in South Africa that *Australopithecus africanus* was widely accepted as a true hominid approximately 2 million years old.

The next great discovery was made by Donald Johanson, working in the Afar Badlands, near Hadar, Ethiopia. In 1973 Johanson discovered a knee joint from a bipedal creature that was dated to be more than 3 million years old. The following year, Johanson's team discovered what has probably become the most famous hominid fossil in all of anthropology—Lucy (http://www.talkorigins.org/faqs/homs/lucy.html). Named for the Beatles' song "Lucy in the Sky with Diamonds," which was a camp favorite, these fossil remains constituted nearly 40% of the skeleton of a small female. Lucy, dating back to about 3.2 million years, was a completely bipedal creature but with a small cranium. Lucy and her kind are more primitive than *A. africanus* and have been given the scientific name *Australopithecus afarensis*. Farther south in Africa, at a place called Laetoli in Tanzania, Mary Leakey discovered fossil remains of *A. afarensis* and fossilized footprints (http://www.pbs.org/wgbh/aso/tryit/evolution/footprints.html) in a volcanic layer dating to 3.7 million years ago. For many years, Lucy's kind held the distinction of being the oldest hominid, but that has now changed. Recent finds push the date of hominid origin (http://news.nationalgeographic.com/news/2001/07/0712 ethiopianbones.html) back as far as 6 million years.

Looking back toward our earliest point of origin, we must also ask when modern forms began and what was the origin of the genus *Homo*. In 1959 Richard and Mary Leakey discovered a new kind of hominid at Olduvai Gorge in Tanzania. They associated this new species, which had a much larger brain than did any australopithecine, with the primitive tools they had been finding in that area. The age of this fossil and these tools was 1.8 million years; the fossil came to be called *Homo habilis*, meaning "handy man." A number of other specimens have been discovered and assigned to this genus, pushing the date of the origin of the genus *Homo* back to about 2.5 million years. About 1.7 million years ago, a newer, more advanced form with an even larger brain came on the scene. The African fossils of this species were related to the fossils found earlier at sites in Java and Peking, China, and this species came to be called *Homo erectus*. *Homo erectus* was thought to be the first hominid to migrate out of Africa, but that idea is currently being challenged.

Since the migration of *Homo erectus*, there have been other migrations out of Africa (http://www.sciam.com/article.cfm?articleID=00062D52-ABB0-1C72-9EB7809EC588F2D7&ref=sciam), and the relationship of the these migrant groups to modern humans (http://www.mc.maricopa.edu/~reffland/anthropology/anthro2003/origins/hominid_journey/earlyasian/Larick-/.html) is one of the most controversial topics in all of anthropology. One of these migrations out of Africa gave rise to the first hominids to move into Europe and remain there during exceedingly cold periods. These cave-dwelling populations were the Neanderthals (http://sapphire.indstate.edu/~ramanank/). As a group, the Neanderthals have an undeserved poor reputation. In 1856 a skeleton found in the Neander Valley of Germany (*thal* or *tal* means "valley" in nineteenth-century German) was the first hominid to become widely known. This discovery was made 3 years before Darwin published *On the Origin of Species*, however, and people were generally unprepared to accept a primitive creature in our ancestral closet. So, the skeleton was reconstructed as a bent-knee, shuffling, apelike brute. But the Neanderthals were an intelligent group with a cranial capacity as large or larger than that of modern humans: They survived in truly cold climates, they were the first people known to bury their dead (which accounts for why we find so many Neanderthal remains); and they probably practiced spiritual rituals as well. What happened to the Neanderthals is a real mystery (http://www.archaeology.org/9709/newsbriefs/dna.html). Some anthropologists believe that they were replaced by more modern forms, but others argue that they were simply absorbed into more-modern populations and that modern Europeans show some Neanderthal characteristics.

By 30,000 years ago the Neanderthals had disappeared and the hominids were essentially modern humans, having spread throughout Africa, Europe, the Middle East, and Asia. The tool cultures had advanced through several stages of refinement, and hominids were embarking on a new cultural revolution—symbolic expression (http://www.culture.gouv.fr/culture/arcnat/chauvet/en/index.html).

1. What characteristics do you think make humans unique, and in what ways are humans like other primates?

2. The Neanderthals are an interesting puzzle; they disappear from the fossil record fairly abruptly about 30,000 years ago. Do you think that they were replaced by another, more modern hominid line or absorbed by interbreeding with a more modern form?

3. Did modern humans evolve from many regional groups already established throughout the world, or did a final wave of migration out of Africa replace more-primitive forms everywhere?

BIZARRE FACTS IN BIOLOGY

Out of Africa, or Not

Out of Africa they came, 100,000 years ago. Modern humans (*Homo sapiens*) moved into Europe and Asia, displacing the native populations of *Homo erectus*. The local populations, Neanderthals in Europe and Ngandong in Asia, failed to compete with the larger-brained invaders and died out. That's the scenario painted by the replacement model of human evolution, and the evidence supporting the model lies within our mitochondria. Mitochondria have their own DNA, mtDNA (http://www.talkorigins.org/faqs/homs/mtDNA.html), a 16,000-base-pair, double-stranded circle that is all that remains of their existence as free-living organisms before the evolution of eukaryotic cells. Most sexually reproducing organisms inherit mitochondria only from their mothers, so mtDNA is a record of our ancestry through the maternal line because mitochondria reproduce clonally and the recombination rate of mtDNA is extremely low.

Many studies have shown that the mtDNA of living humans shares sequences found in the ancient African *H. sapiens* fossils but not with mtDNA samples from Neanderthal or other archaic human fossils, supporting the replacement model. However, scientists comparing mtDNA from fossil human skeletons from Australia (2,000 to 60,000 years old) found DNA sequences not present in either modern humans or the African fossils, suggesting that these Australian hominids had mtDNA sequences from another source, possibly an archaic indigenous population. This DNA evidence is supported by a comparison that shows the skull shape of these archaic Australian humans is more similar to the skull of an ancient, indigenous population from Java (http://www.talkorigins.org/faqs/homs/java.html) than the skulls of the ancient Africans. This evidence supports a multiregional model of evolution.

The multiregional model represents a minority opinion among paleobiologists. This new evidence, however, has raised some questions about what happened long ago on the fringes of the human world. Maybe not all of our mothers came out of Africa.

References

Adcock, G. J., Dennis, E. S., Easteal, S., Huttley, G. A., Jermiin, L. S., Peacock, W. J., and Thorne, A. 2001. Mitochondrial DNA sequences in ancient Australians: Implications for modern human origins. *PNAS* 98:537–42.

Holden, C. 2001. Oldest human DNA reveals Aussie oddity. *Science* 219:230–31.

Wolpoff, M. H., Hawks, J., Frayer, D. W., and Hunley, K. 2001. Modern human ancestry at the peripheries: A test of the replacement theory. *Science* 219:293–97.

1. How do the replacement model and multiregional model of human evolution differ?

2. Why is mtDNA a useful tool to explore evolutionary questions?

3. Why does it matter which theory is correct?

KEY TERMS

amphibian	exoskeleton	microsphere	reptile
arthropod	hominid	plate tectonics	ribozyme
conifer	lobefin	primate	spontaneous generation
endosymbiont hypothesis	mammal	prokaryote	
eukaryote	mass extinction	protocell	

ANSWER KEY

SELF TEST

1. h
2. c
3. a
4. e
5. e
6. e
7. a
8. d
9. b
10. c
11. c
12. b
13. d
14. d
15. b
16. d
17. d
18. prebiotic
19. microspheres
20. anaerobe
21. endosymbiont
22. pollen
23. exoskeleton
24. A. boiling chamber
    B. condenser
    C. electric spark chamber
25. A. formation of Earth
    B. first Earth rocks
    C. first prokaryotes
    D. first eukaryotes
    E. first animals
    F. first land plants
    G. first humans
26. A. anaerobic, predatory prokaryotic cell engulfs an aerobic bacterium
    B. mitochondria-containing cell engulfs a photosynthetic bacterium
    C. descendants of engulfed bacterium evolve into mitochondria
    D. descendants of photosynthetic bacterium evolve into chloroplasts
27. A. *Australopithecus afarensis*
    B. *Homo erectus*
    C. *Homo ergaster*
    D. *Homo sapiens*

28. A. *Homo habilis*
    B. *Homo ergaster*
    C. *Homo neanderthalensis*
29. A. multiregional hypothesis
    B. African replacement hypothesis

ESSAY CHALLENGE

1. Miller and Urey helped to describe how the components of the early atmosphere could have given rise to simple organic compounds, like ATP, amino acids, and so on.

2. Some scientists suggest that one type of prokaryote consumed but was unable to digest certain kinds of prokaryotes. This was a great advantage to the early cells, especially if they consumed a cell that could produce its own energy, as a mitochondrion can.

3. Among other things, multicellular organisms can become larger, thus making it easier to get food or acquire other resources, such as light or water.

4. Among the possibilities are moving around without the support of water, difficulty in obtaining and maintaining water, greater exposure to UV radiation, and reproducing without a water environment to allow gametes to encounter each other.

5. Some possible answers are long, grasping fingers, binocular vision, and a large brain.

6. Miller and Urey's experiment and its variations have shown that fairly complex precursors of biological molecules could have easily formed in conditions found on the early Earth, including simple catalysts and membranes. A very long period of time was available from the time the Earth cooled to the time the first organisms appeared (as documented by fossil remains), so that by a process of chemical natural selection more efficient systems of replication and metabolism could have evolved in a stepwise manner.

7. Chemical analyses of rocks dated to the time of the first organisms show that there was a much smaller concentration of oxygen gas in the early atmosphere than there is now, indicating that these early organisms must have been anaerobes. After the evolution of photosynthetic organisms, oxygen concentrations increased as a consequence of photosynthetic activity, and aerobic metabolism evolved.

8. Ribozymes are RNA molecules that, like protein enzymes, are capable of catalyzing chemical reactions. This means that RNA is capable of information storage (like DNA) and catalytic activity. Some scientists have suggested that an "RNA world" may have existed as a precursor to true life, in which the replication of RNA molecules was catalyzed by other RNA molecules in a system that is a simpler form of the DNA replication (catalyzed by protein enzymes) that exists in living cells.

9. Microspheres are chemical structures of protein and lipid, formed by wave action, that resemble living cell membranes in their chemical structure. Some can pass materials, grow, and divide. In prebiotic times, microspheres might have protected ribozymes from the surrounding environment and allowed the evolution of protocells (nonliving cell-like structures), and eventually living cells.

10. The first photosynthesizers were probably much like the purple photosynthetic bacteria of today, using H_2S (hydrogen sulfide) as a source of hydrogen for forming more complex organic molecules from CO_2. As H_2S was depleted, they evolved to be able to use water (H_2O) as a source of hydrogen, as most photosynthesizers do today.

11. Spontaneous generation, life arising from nonliving material, was shown to not occur regularly by the experiments of Louis Pasteur and others. However, this does not mean that it did not occur at least once in the past by a long process of chemical prebiotic evolution, just that it does not frequently occur.

12. Oxygen atoms are present in many inorganic compounds, particularly water and carbon dioxide. The action of photosynthetic organisms of using these two chemicals along with light energy to produce organic compounds produced molecular oxygen gas as a by-product.

13. The organisms at the time were strict anaerobes, not only unable to metabolically use oxygen, but actually poisoned by it. As organisms evolved an aerobic metabolism that uses oxygen, they were able to produce more energy from the same compounds than with anaerobic metabolism.

14. The first multicellular organisms were probably algae, as seen in the fossil record dated to about one billion years ago. Being larger than their unicellular predators, they would have been more difficult to be preyed upon. Also, different tissues of the organism could evolve to specialize in their functions, such as roots for anchorage or leaves for photosynthesis.

15. The fossil evidence reveals many animal body plans that are not represented in any current animal phylum. They appear rather "suddenly" in the fossil record, suggesting that many evolutionary innovations preceding their appearance were simply not preserved as fossils.

16. Pollen represented a gamete that did not require water to survive and fertilize another gamete, so that plants could evolve to become completely adapted to a terrestrial existence, rather than an aquatic one.

17. Although amphibians may possess lungs for breathing oxygen gas, and legs for locomotion on land, many still need to obtain oxygen partially through their skin, and must remain wet to do so. Also, the external fertilization of amphibian sperm and eggs requires a water medium.

18. Although the precise causes of mass extinctions are still a matter of debate, it seems that catastrophic climatic shifts are the major heralds of mass extinction events. Such changes may have various causes, such as volcanic activity or the impact of a large meteor.

19. Biological evolution results from genetic changes from generation to generation, so is limited by the rate of origin of new biological features and the rate of reproduction of the population. Cultural evolution results primarily from learning, and new cultural features can be passed from person to person almost immediately.

20. Mass extinction has typically meant that most species of some taxonomic families or genera suddenly go extinct. This sudden loss of competition for resources can allow other organisms to fill the niches left empty by the now extinct species.

MEDIA ACTIVITIES

17.4 Web Investigation: Life on a Frozen Moon?

1. Astrobiology is the study of the origin, evolution, distribution, and destiny of life in the universe. It uses multiple scientific disciplines and space technologies to address fundamental questions: * How does life begin and develop? * Does life exist elsewhere in the universe? * What is life's future on Earth and beyond?

2. Magnetic readings are consistent with there being a layer of electrically conductive liquid, such as salt water.

3. Europa does have a thin oxygen atmosphere, but it is not known whether it can support life.

4. The presence of sulfuric acid confirms that Europa is an unusual place, but does not necessarily rule out the possibility of life there. Sulfuric acid is an oxidant that may be used as a source of energy for Europan organisms, if they exist.

5. Lake Vostok is similar to a Europan sea in that it is a body of water capped by ice but kept liquid by heat from the planet's interior.

ISSUES IN BIOLOGY

1. Humans share most anatomical features of other primates, and DNA sequences are also very similar. Humans are unique in having a large brain, walking upright, communicating in complex ways, and having general high intelligence.

2. Evidence suggests they coexisted with individuals indistinguishable from modern humans for some time. There are cultural and genetic differences that suggest that Neanderthals were not assimilated into the modern human population, but were outcompeted.

3. Recent evidence supports the multiregional hypothesis, with genetic and cultural exchange between various different human populations at different times.

BIZARRE FACTS IN BIOLOGY

1. The replacement model says that modern humans originated in Africa relatively recently and migrated from there to the rest of the Old World, replacing the more archaic human populations. In contrast, the multiregional model says that ancient humans originated in Africa and spread through the Old World, but that modern humans evolved in many areas, with genetic exchange among different populations contributing to this evolution.

2. Mitochondrial DNA is transmitted from mother to offspring, without recombining with paternal mtDNA, so the maternal genetic lineage can more easily be traced than lineages of other genes. The occasional mutation causes different lineages to differentiate. By comparing the similarities between the mtDNA of different populations, knowing the rate of mtDNA mutation, the date of the common ancestor can be estimated.

3. If the multiregional hypothesis is correct, it may mean that some human populations (such as aboriginal Australians) may be more distantly related to the rest of the species than previously thought.

CHAPTER 18: SYSTEMATICS: SEEKING ORDER AMIDST DIVERSITY

AT-A-GLANCE

SELF TEST

1. What is the most inclusive of the major taxonomic categories?
   a. genus
   b. order
   c. phylum
   d. kingdom
   e. domain

2. What is the least inclusive of the major taxonomic categories?
   a. species
   b. order
   c. phylum
   d. division
   e. class

3. Which kingdom comprises eukaryotic organisms that are typically unicellular?
   a. Animalia
   b. Fungi
   c. Archaea
   d. Plantae
   e. Protista

4. Which kingdom comprises eukaryotic organisms that are multicellular and autotrophic and possess cell walls?
   a. Animalia
   b. Fungi
   c. Bacteria
   d. Plantae
   e. Protista

5. Which kingdom comprises eukaryotic organisms that are multicellular and heterotrophic and do not possess cell walls?
   a. Animalia
   b. Fungi
   c. Archaea
   d. Plantae
   e. Protista

6. Which of these scientific names of species is correctly written?
   a. *Aneides Aeneus* (the green salamander)
   b. *Crotalus horridus* (the timber rattlesnake)
   c. *falco peregrinus* (the peregrine falcon)
   d. Marmota monax (the woodchuck)
   e. *Salmo* (the rainbow trout)

7. In the following sequence what is missing from the hierarchy of major taxonomic categories (please list in order): species–_____–family–_____–class.
   a. genus, domain
   b. genus, order
   c. kingdom, order
   d. order, genus
   e. order, division
   f. phylum, genus

8. Pretend that you could divide a funnel into seven horizontal layers and then you put all of the taxonomic categories into the funnel. Which taxonomic categories, representing individual species, would trickle out of the bottom of the funnel, one at a time?
   a. kingdoms and phyla
   b. phyla and classes
   c. classes and families
   d. families and genera
   e. genus and species (or genus species, i.e., the scientific name)

9. Which of the following is NOT used by taxonomists (biologists who classify organisms) to distinguish one species from another?
   a. genetic characteristics
   b. similar features due to convergent evolution acting on distantly related species
   c. distinguishing features seen in organisms during the development of an organism
   d. external anatomical features

10. What is a domain?
    a. the broadest taxonomic category, of which there are three
    b. the taxonomic category that contains insects, birds, and mammals
    c. the taxonomic category that contains all living species of humans
    d. a synonym for the taxonomic category, kingdom

11. Why can classification schemes (taxonomies) change from year to year?
    a. A population of individuals of one species evolves into a new species.
    b. New species are discovered.
    c. New data about previously described species is discovered.
    d. all of the above
    e. Both the second and third answers are correct.

12. Which of the following statements about biodiversity is (are) true?
    a. Bottled water is more biodiverse than pond water.
    b. Tropical forests are more biodiverse than temperate forests.
    c. Arthropods exhibit more biodiversity than mammals.
    d. Both the second and third answers are correct.

13. How does molecular genetics help us to distinguish and evaluate the degree of evolutionary relatedness among species?
    a. by allowing us to compare nucleotide sequences of DNA from the same chromosomal regions from different species
    b. by allowing us to compare DNA sequences from different chromosomal regions between two closely related species
    c. The first two answers are both correct.
    d. Neither of the first two answers are correct.

14. Anatomical features of species may not always be useful for determining species relationships because of _____.
    a. convergent evolution
    b. homologous structures
    c. adaptation
    d. common ancestry

15. Changes at the domain or kingdom levels of classification _____.
    a. never occur
    b. rarely occur
    c. occur about every five years
    d. occur very frequently

16. The phylogenetic species concept stresses _____ as the criterion for assigning individuals to the same species.
    a. anatomical similarity
    b. recent common ancestry
    c. potential for interbreeding
    d. similarity in behavior

17. Some systematists would like to remove the class Reptilia from the classification system because _____.
    a. reptiles have evolved since the classification was established
    b. reptiles have been found to consist of distantly related groups
    c. reptiles are now extinct
    d. there are other closely related groups that are currently not classified with the reptiles

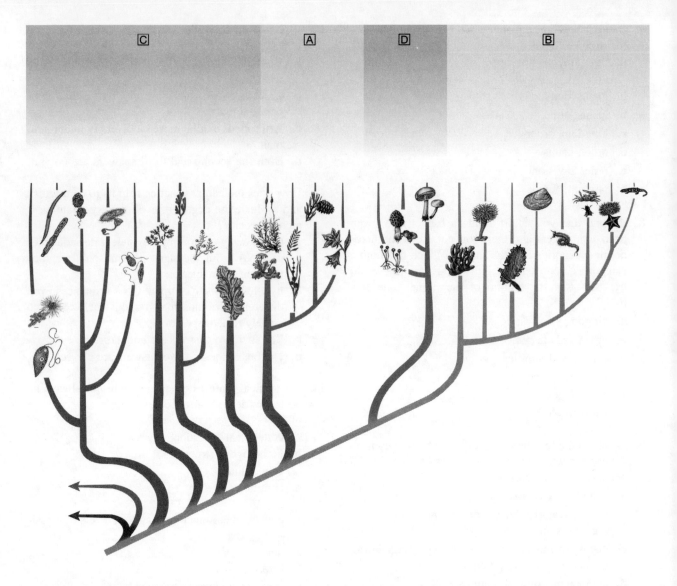

18. Identify the four kingdoms illustrated in the branch of the evolutionary tree seen above.

19. The evolutionary tree below demonstrates the term *monophyletic*. Identify that portion that is monophyletic and that which is not monophyletic.

(b)

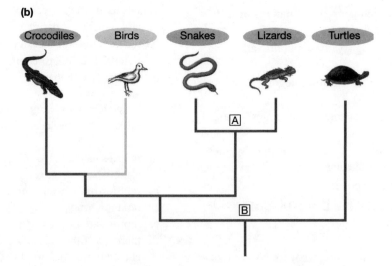

20. Using the evolutionary chart below as a guide, indicate which species of primate are most closely related. Start with the chimp as number 1 and continue to number the rest of the primates in descending order as they diverge farther and farther from the chimp.

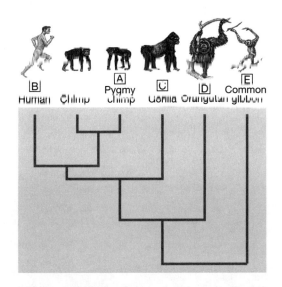

ESSAY CHALLENGE

1. What is the scientific reasoning behind shifting from a two-domain to a three-domain classification?

2. Under what conditions is the "biological species definition" difficult or impossible for systematists to apply to a population of organisms?

3. What does the phrase "phylogenetic species concept" mean?

4. Why can't systematists use physical similarity as the only criterion for inferring relatedness between species?

5. What anatomical features are useful to systematists in determining relationships between species?

6. What inherited features of a species are useful to systematists in determining relatedness?

7. Why was the five-kingdom system of classification proposed by Whittaker in 1969 an improvement over the older two-kingdom system?

8. There are currently four kingdoms in the domain Eukarya. Why are systematists now considering adding more kingdoms to the classification system?

9. Why is it that most of the species described by biologists are animals?

10. What problems are there in trying to determine the number of species of bacteria?

11. Do you think that birds should be categorized apart from reptiles? Why or why not?

12. What does the genetic variability among human populations suggest about the place of origin of humans?

MEDIA ACTIVITIES

To access a Media Activity visit http://www.prenhall.com/audesirk7. Log in to the Web site selected by your instructor, navigate to this chapter, and select the appropriate Media Activity number.

18.1 Taxonomic Classification
Estimated Time: 5 minutes

Classification is a means of categorizing all organisms on Earth. This activity will help you understand the hierarchy of taxonomic groups used by biologists.

18.2 Tree of Life
Estimated Time: 10 minutes

In this animation you will explore the Tree of Life, how molecular genetics are used to establish evolutionary relationships, and why there is so much disagreement about how the Tree of Life should be structured.

18.3 Web Investigation: Origin of a Killer
Estimated time: 20 minutes

The search for the origins of the HIV viruses involves the often conflicting activities of evolutionary biologists, epidemiologists, clinicians, and social activists. Alternate theories, intricate data analyses, and contradictory conclusions are common. This exercise will explore popular theories and recent developments in HIV studies.

1. Most researchers agree that both HIV viruses were originally transmitted from primates to humans. What they disagree about is how and when (http://www.avert.org/origins.htm) the transfer took place. What primate species were the "original" hosts?

2. Edward Hooper has popularized the iatrogenic (medically caused) oral polio vaccine theory, i.e., HIV was passed to humans when HIV-1-contaminated chimpanzee cells were used to prepare vaccines (http://www.uow.edu.au/arts/sts/bmartin/dissent/documents/AIDS/River/Prospect.html). According to this theory, when should the first cases of HIV-1 have occurred?

3. After extensive testing, researchers identified an African HIV-1-infected plasma sample (http://www.aegis.com/news/ads/1998/ad980242.html) originally collected in 1959. However these researchers think that HIV-1 evolved much earlier. Why?

4. In 2000, Belgian researchers presented evidence for an even earlier viral origin (http://www.aegis.com/news/newsday/2000/ND000710.html). How does this affect the polio vaccine theory?

5. The Hunt for the Origin of AIDS (http://www.theatlantic.com/issues/2000/10/cohen2.htm) summarizes various theories and recent research, including HIV-2 data and possible chimp-to-human transmission mechanisms. How and when do you think HIV-1 and HIV-2 first infected humans?

ISSUES IN BIOLOGY

Classification Conundrums—What Is a Kingdom, Anyway?

As your textbook explains, the hierarchical classification system now used by biologists originated with Aristotle and was arranged in its modern format by Carolus Linnaeus (http://www.ucmp.berkeley.edu/history/linnaeus.html). The seven major categories of the hierarchy below the domain level—kingdom, phylum/division, class, order, family, genus, and species—are sometimes referred to as Linnaean categories.

Systematics involves naming organisms and categorizing them on the basis of their evolutionary relationships (that is, their phylogeny). As is true of any scientific discipline, systematic conclusions are only tentative. Whenever newer and more complete data on phylogeny are available, the systematic status of taxonomic groups will change. Why should anyone be surprised that a system developed at least a century before Darwin's time might be having problems? Both the techniques of data acquisition available to systematists and the procedures of their discipline have changed dramatically since even the 1950s, when Whittaker introduced the five-kingdom system that is now being challenged.

Why this is so important, and why it has such a dramatic effect on which classification scheme you learn, requires some knowledge of taxonomic philosophy. There are three currently available schools of taxonomy. Classical, or traditional (sometimes called evolutionary), taxonomy attempts to meld information on past evolutionary branching patterns with the degree of divergence of the considered taxonomic groups. Phenetic taxonomy is classification on the basis of morphological similarity. Cladistic (often called phylogenetic) taxonomy is based solely on what can be discerned of the past evolutionary branching patterns.

As the name implies, the traditional school was the dominant view of systematics for a long time. Currently, the cladistic school predominates. That this has consequences for the taxonomy and systematics of organisms can be illustrated by the classification of birds. Traditionalists have no problem with the vertebrate class Aves (birds), especially considering the novel features that birds evolved compared to most reptiles. Cladists, who are concerned only with branching patterns, recognize the birds as only one evolutionary lineage of dinosaurs and thus as unworthy of recognition as their own class (see "Dinosauricon" http://dinosauricon.com/taxa/avialae.html).

210

Is it time to acknowledge that the goals of the science of systematics do not entirely correspond to the needs of an informed public (or of an introductory biology class)? In general, the goals of systematics are to have stability (that is, names that do not change over time), to demonstrate uniqueness (that is, one taxonomic category, one name), and to indicate relationships (named groups at a given taxonomic level should be closer relatives than are groups at other levels). These goals allow for maximum information retrieval capability. Traditionalists have long admitted the lack of correspondence between different taxonomic levels (consider two genera: the genus *Solidago*, goldenrods, has more than 100 species, whereas genus *Pandion*, the osprey, has only one species). Even allowing for extinctions over time, there can be little branching-sequence equivalence to these genera, although there may be an equivalent amount of divergence. As professional systematists place more significance on branching relationships, the Linnaean categories have less usefulness. However, perhaps it is no more reasonable to expect the general public to follow the currents in professional systematics, or to learn each new category or branching sequence that is uncovered, than it was to expect the general public to keep up with each twist and turn of biological nomenclature (http://www.inform.umd.edu/PBIO/nomcl/indx.html).

Given the current concerns about biodiversity and its loss, perhaps it is most reasonable to adopt a standardized taxonomy of common names—one based on reasonable and apparent properties of the organisms. This does not necessarily void the goals of the professionals, but it adds a goal of accessibility for the nonprofessional. It is not really a novel idea; it has had a long tradition in ornithology. The American Ornithologists' Union (http://www.aou.org/) is responsible for maintaining a list of standardized common names of the birds of North America. The Society for the Study of Amphibians and Reptiles (http://www.ssarherps.org/) has been doing the same for North American species for years. Standardized common names can be reasonable for indicating relatedness, too (for example, woodpeckers or water snakes), and such names are more widely used and understood outside the profession. It would also allow for the reasonable consideration of, for example, the algae within the plant kingdom, with no apologies. What is a kingdom, indeed?

1. What other examples of classification problems can you think of?

2. In what way is domain-level and kingdom-level organization useful? How does knowledge of an organism's domain differ from knowledge of its genus or species?

3. Do you think that a standardized classification of common names could be more stable than the scientific classifications have become?

BIZARRE FACTS IN BIOLOGY

Branches of the Tree of Life

Once, the classification of organisms (phylogeny) was simple: living things were either plants or animals. Classification became a little more complex when microorganisms were discovered, but scientists just grafted another branch, the protists, to the phylogenic tree. Another discovery—that there are only two kinds of cells, prokaryotic and eukaryotic—simplified things again and let us prune the tree back to two branches. Because scientists still tended to classify organisms based on physical characteristics, most found the two-branch tree too limiting, so the most commonly used phylogenetic tree actually had five branches: Animals, Plants, Protists, Bacteria, and Fungi. However, a group of bacteria newly recognized as a separate group, the Archaea, have us again asking how many branches there are on the Tree of Life.

Archaeans were first isolated from the hot sulfur springs of Yellowstone National Park but have since appeared in some unexpected places, including 3.5-billion-year-old rocks from Australia and Africa. These fossils suggest that the Archaea are among the oldest organisms on Earth, even older than other bacteria. But this is very puzzling, because when scientists examined Archaean ribosomal RNA (http://www.fossilmuseum.net/Tree_of_Life/Domains_Archaea_Bacteria/Domains_Archaea_Bacteria.htm), they found them much more like the ribosomes of eukaryotic cells, which were thought to be evolutionarily "younger" organisms, rather than prokaryotic (bacterial) ribosomes. A dilemma arose: How could these Archaea be "older" than the other bacteria but have a "modern" ribosome?

Based on the analysis of ribosomes, Dr. Carl Woese (http://www.life.uiuc.edu/micro/woese.html) suggests that the Archaea should be their own branch on the tree, which is called a domain. The bacteria would constitute a separate domain, as would the eukaryotes, bringing the number of branches back to three. This suggestion is controversial because using ribosomal RNA information to place other organisms, such as whales, on the phylogenetic tree doesn't always give the same placement as when scientists use traditional methods, such as body structure. Until scientists learn how to reconcile molecular information with physical information, the Tree of Life will continue to be pruned and grafted.

1. Why may the analysis of ribosomes be a better means of classifying organisms than the analysis of organism structures?

KEY TERMS

Archaea	domain	monophyletic	species
Bacteria	Eukarya	order	systematics
biodiversity	family	phylogeny	
class	genus	phylum	
DNA sequencing	kingdom	scientific name	

ANSWER KEY

SELF TEST

1. e
2. a
3. e
4. d
5. a
6. b
7. b
8. e
9. b
10. a
11. e
12. d
13. a
14. a
15. b
16. b
17. d

18. A. plantae
    B. animalia
    C. protista
    D. fungi
19. A. monophyletic
    B. monophyletic
20. A. 2
    B. 3
    C. 4
    D. 5
    E. 6

ESSAY CHALLENGE

1. Prokaryotes are very different from eukaryotes for a variety of reasons. Researchers have found genetic differences among the prokaryotes as profound as the differences between prokaryotes and eukaryotes. Much of the new evidence of these differences

comes from DNA sequence comparisons. Many researchers now split the prokaryotes into two distinct domains, Bacteria and Archaea, even though the members of these two domains resemble each other when viewed under a microscope.

2. The basis of the biological species concept used in this text depends upon organisms interbreeding, something sexually reproducing organisms do. However, this criterion provides no basis for distinguishing species that reproduce asexually. Therefore, the biological species definition is not all-inclusive and must be broadened to include asexually reproducing organisms.

3. An evolutionary tree is supposed to represent relatedness among species. Depending upon how you define the term *species,* you can get very different evolutionary trees, or classifications. Characteristics determine relatedness under a phylogenetic definition of species: physical characteristics, physiological characteristics, biochemical characteristics, and genetic characteristics, for example. Applying the phylogenetic species definition would dramatically increase the current numbers of "species" in the world.

4. Some species may evolve characteristics that are superficially similar because they are in similar environments; this is called convergent evolution. For example, dolphins are generally shaped the same as fish are, because both are adapted to an aquatic existence, but the two are not closely related. These similarities would not reflect true relationships between species.

5. In addition to looking at both external and internal anatomical characteristics, systematists must examine features very closely, sometimes microscopically, to determine whether similarity among species is due to convergent evolution or whether the features are truly homologous.

6. Systematists may compare the chromosome structures of species using a microscope, or isolate and sequence homologous DNA fragments, in order to assess the evolutionary relationships among species.

7. The two-kingdom system classified all microscopic organisms in the same kingdom as plants, but it became clear that they were very different. The new system was a recognition of these differences. Under the newer system, most single-celled eukaryotes were placed in their own kingdom (Protista), as were all prokaryotes (Monera). Also, the cellular and anatomical differences between plants and fungi warranted the establishment of a separate kingdom for the fungi.

8. Many systematists recognize that groups that diverged early in evolutionary history should be considered as kingdom status, and by this logic several groups within the current kingdom Protista may

be elevated to kingdom status. The suggestion comes as a result of recent information about the evolutionary history of protists.

9. Biologists generally first describe species that are easy to find and see, such as large animals in temperate regions. There are probably a large number of non-animal species in the tropics, but biologists have not yet made the effort to formally identify most of them.

10. Bacteria reproduce asexually, so the biological species concept cannot be used to distinguish between bacterial species. Biologists have suggested other criteria, such as a minimum amount of genetic divergence, to distinguish species. By this criterion, there are nearly as many species in a single soil sample as have been formally identified, so the number of species (if this criterion is accepted) would be very high and take a large amount of time and effort to identify and classify.

11. Students in favor of including birds with reptiles may argue that this is better because birds are descended from reptiles and are just as closely related to some groups of reptiles as are other groups of reptiles. Those against classifying birds with reptiles may believe that they have diverged enough in their anatomy, physiology, and behavior to warrant separate classification.

12. Recent studies have indicated that there is much less genetic diversity in the human species than most other species, and that the greatest diversity is found among African populations. Because genetic variation is expected to increase over time, older populations should have greater variation. This suggests that African populations are the oldest human populations, and that Africa is the birthplace of the human species.

MEDIA ACTIVITIES

18.3   Web Investigation: Origin of a Killer

1. It is believed that two types of simian immunodeficiency virus (SIV), one originally from red-capped mangabeys and one from greater spot-nosed monkeys recombined in a chimpanzee host to form HIV, which is capable of infecting humans. At some point, there was a zoonosis (cross-species infection) from chimpanzees to humans, possibly as a result of humans killing and eating chimpanzees.

2. The first cases of HIV-1 should have occurred during and after 1957, when (allegedly) polio vaccines prepared using chimpanzee cell cultures would have been used.

3. The great amount of genetic divergence between the HIV-1 and HIV-2 viruses suggests that they diverged much earlier than the 1940s; more time would be necessary for random mutations to accumulate and result in such divergence.

4. If this scenario is true, the "polio vaccine theory" would have to be incorrect, because the suggestion is that the HIV virus originated over 300 years ago.

5. The available evidence suggests that HIV made the jump from chimpanzees to humans sometime early in the 20th century, perhaps after having evolved much earlier in chimpanzees. Whether the polio vaccine campaign of the 1950s contributed to the origin or the spread of HIV is still in debate.

ISSUES IN BIOLOGY

1. You may answer with various examples. Many might question the classification of humans apart from chimpanzees and gorillas, given the close evolutionary relationship between them.

2. The higher levels of classification allow recognition of broad similarities between many organisms. Members of the same domain or kingdom will be similar in major ways (such as cellular structure), but may be very different in many other ways. Members of the same lower-level category, such as genus or species, will be much more similar and vary much less for most traits.

3. This is an opinion question, but you may answer that anyone attempting classification of organisms, whether based on scientific or common names, will be faced with the same problems and difficulties.

BIZARRE FACTS IN BIOLOGY

1. Some ribosomal RNA genes are similar among all living organisms, and can be used as a basis for comparison among them. There are no physical structures that are homologous among all types of organisms and cells.

CHAPTER 19: THE DIVERSITY OF VIRUSES, PROKARYOTES, AND PROTISTS

AT-A-GLANCE

SELF TEST

1. A particle between 0.05 and 0.2 microns containing genetic material enclosed in a protein coat is called a _____ .

2. Identify the category of each cell type seen in the image below.

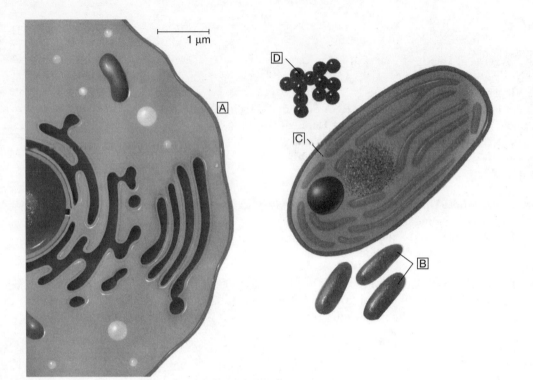

3. Viruses are not cellular and are often considered to be nonliving. Which of the following characteristics supports this conclusion?

   a. Viruses cannot reproduce on their own.

   b. Viruses are unable to grow or divide.

   c. Viruses have no membranes of their own.

   d. Viruses have no ribosomes for protein synthesis.

   e. All these choices support this conclusion.

4. A _____ is a kind of virus that can infect bacteria.

5. Which of these is a viral disease?

   a. botulism

   b. strep throat

   c. syphilis

   d. herpes

   e. plague

   f. Lyme disease

6. What are viruses, viroids, and prions?

   a. nonliving, infectious agents or pathogens that can cause disease in organisms

   b. small sequences of nucleotides or amino acids that are devoid of their own cell membrane

   c. substances that can cause disease only after entering a host cell and taking over the nuclear machinery

   d. all of the above

7. What are viruses that attack bacteria called?

   a. prions

   b. bacteriophages

   c. herpes viruses

   d. mosaic viruses

   e. viroids

8. Identify the structures indicated on the following image of a virus particle.

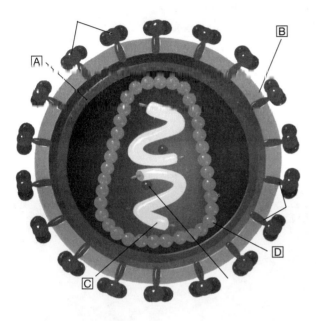

9. Label each step in HIV's invasion into the cell pictured below.

10. _____ is the substance that differentiates a bacterial cell from an archaeal cell.

11. Classification of prokaryotes may use many kinds of traits. Which of these are NOT used in prokaryotic classification?
   a. cell shape   **b.** means of locomotion
   c. nutrient sources   **d.** staining properties
   e. type of nucleic acid

12. Which of the following traits allows some bacteria to survive extreme conditions for millions of years?
   a. aerobic respiration   **b.** endospore formation
   c. conjugation   **d.** binary fission

13. Hospitals must sterilize surgical instruments at very high temperatures and pressure because some bacteria can survive harsh conditions by making _____.
   a. zygotes   **b.** endospores
   c. seeds   **d.** fruiting bodies
   e. basidiospores

14. The technique that helps to classify bacteria based on their cell-wall construction is _____.

15. What type of bacteria are photosynthetic?
   a. prokaryotic methanogens
   b. cyanobacteria
   c. sulfur bacteria
   d. Both the first and third answers above are correct.
   e. Both the second and third answers above are correct.

16. Which of the following enable plants to obtain a usable form of nitrogen?
   a. bacteria   **b.** viruses
   c. prions   **d.** zooflagellates

Herpes virus, a double-stranded DNA virus, invades a skin cell.

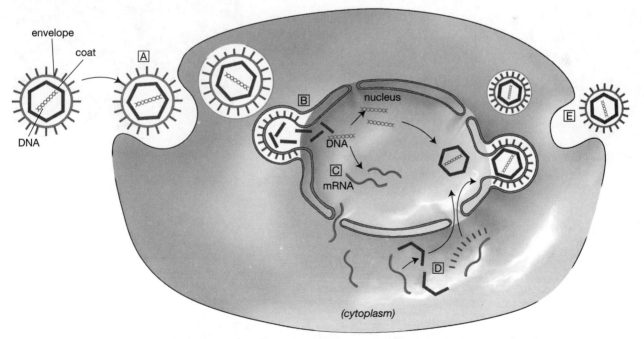

217

17. Which of these is a bacterial disease?
  a. influenza **b.** common cold
  c. AIDS **d.** genital warts
  e. tetanus

18. The simple form of cell division by which prokaryotic cells reproduce is called _____.
  a. binary fission **b.** conjugation
  c. endospore formation **d.** mitosis

19. Which of the following is a producer in its ecosystem because of the photosynthesis it performs?
  a. prions **b.** viruses
  c. cyanobacteria **d.** zooflagellates
  e. sporozoans

20. Which of the following is associated with cyanobacteria?

  a. plasma membrane

  b. DNA or RNA surrounded by a protein coat

  c. chloroplasts

  d. DNA inside a nucleus

  e. cell walls with cellulose

21. Label each stage in the slime mold life cycle shown below.

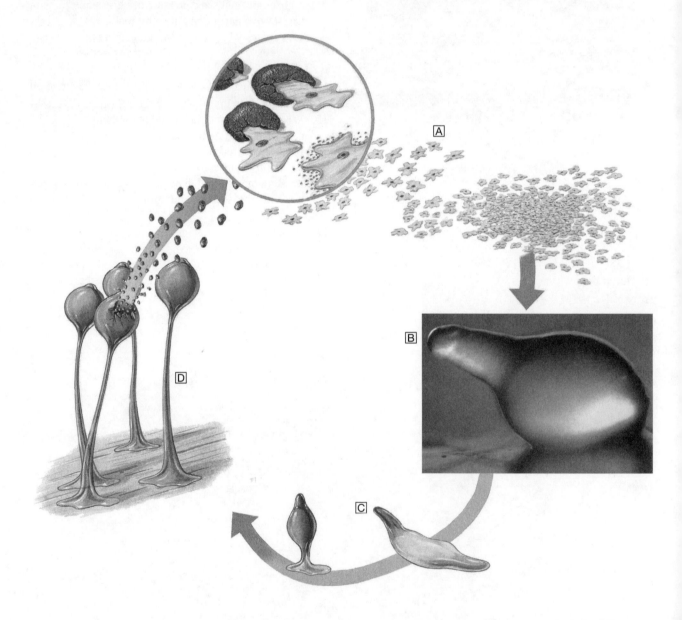

22. Trypanosoma is a unicellular, eukaryotic blood parasite that causes African sleeping sickness. Into which of the following groups is it classified?
    a. Archaea
    b. Viruses
    c. Bacteria
    d. Plantae
    e. Protista

23. Which protists are entirely parasitic and have no means of locomotion?
    a. cellular slime molds
    b. ciliates
    c. amoebas
    d. sporozoans
    e. zooflagellates

24. Identify the structures indicated below.

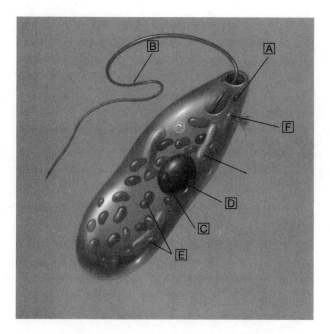

25. What phytoplankton group can reproduce so prodigiously that they can cause "red tides," killing large numbers of fish because the gills are clogged?
    a. red algae
    b. brown algae
    c. diatoms
    d. dinoflagellates

26. Which protists use flagella for locomotion?
    a. cellular slime molds
    b. ciliates
    c. diatoms
    d. euglenoids
    e. zooflagellates
    f. both euglenoids and zooflagellates

27. Correctly identify the structures indicated on this image.

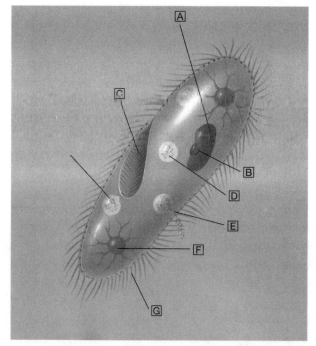

28. Which of these is a component of phytoplankton and supports aquatic food chains via its photosynthesis?
    a. sporozoans/apicomplexans
    b. diatoms
    c. brown algae
    d. amoebas
    e. slime molds

29. Which of the following shares a common ancestor with plants and is most like the earliest plants?
    a. cyanobacteria   b. slime molds
    c. green algae   d. amoebas
    e. viroids

30. Which of the following correctly describes the organism that causes equine protozoan myeloencephalitis?
    a. prokaryotic
    b. heterotrophic
    c. photosynthetic
    d. cell wall with peptidoglycan

31. Which of the following is an important recycler of nutrients (decomposer) in its ecosystem?
    a. slime molds
    b. sporozoans/apicomplexans
    c. cyanobacteria
    d. viruses
    e. green algae

219

32. The tests below are performed on an unidentified organism, and the results are as noted. How should you classify the organism?

> Chemical A glows when it binds to a plasma membrane. Results = glowing.
>
> Chemical B turns blue in the presence of chloroplasts. Results = blue color develops.
>
> Chemical C fizzes when it binds to a nuclear membrane. Results = fizzing.
>
> Chemical D produces a bad odor when the organism is multicellular. Results = no bad odor.

a. cyanobacteria   b. red algae
c. viruses   d. ciliates
e. diatoms

ESSAY CHALLENGE

1. Contrast the three noncellular infectious agents.

2. How are viruses able to reproduce when they lack the organelles needed to create new genetic material and protein coats?

3. Compare and contrast the organisms of the two prokaryotic domains.

4. Of what importance to a food chain are the algae?

5. How does the ability of bacteria to perform conjugation benefit bacteria? Of what concern to humans is the ability of bacteria to perform conjugation?

6. You've been given a beaker of water containing unidentified microbes and are charged with determining what kind of microbes are present in the water.

   You perform the following tests:

   Add solution A which glows when it binds to a nuclear membrane.

   Add solution B which fizzes in the presense of DNA.

   Add solution C which turns blue in the presence of chloroplasts.

   Add solution D which creates a bad odor when peptidoglycan is present.

   Your results are: no glow, fizzing, no color change, and a bad odor.

   What kind of microbes are present in the water? Explain your answer. Of what importance are these microbes to other organisms?

7. How are cyanobacteria and algae similar to and different from each other?

MEDIA ACTIVITIES

To access a Media Activity visit http://www.prenhall.com/audesirk7. Log in to the Web site selected by your instructor, navigate to this chapter, and select the appropriate Media Activity number.

19.1 Retrovirus Replication
Estimated Time: 5 minutes

The Closer Look Essay in this chapter describes the structure of retroviruses and illustrates the process by which they reproduce. This activity demonstrates the uptake of a retrovirus (in this case HIV) by its host cell (a helper T cell) and the process by which new HIV components are produced and assembled into new viruses.

19.2 Herpes Virus Replication
Estimated Time: 5 minutes

The herpes virus uses a different mechanism to invade human cells. Explore the details in this animation.

19.3 Bacterial Conjugation
Estimated Time: 5 minutes

This animation shows how some prokaryotes are able to exchange genetic information through the process of conjugation.

19.4 Web Investigation: Agents of Death
Estimated time: 10 minutes

While biological weapons are not new, the bacterial strains, delivery mechanisms, and toxins have become much more sophisticated. In this exercise we will study biological weapons from a biological, functional, and social perspective. Have biological weapons been effective in the past? How dangerous are current designs, and what can be done to defend against them?

1. Take a look at Biological Weapons: A Historical Perspective (http://jama.amaassn.org/cgi/content/short/278/5/412) or the List of Biological Weapons (http://whyfiles.org/059bio_war/history.html). There are several instances where biological weapons were used in warfare prior to the 20th century. What organisms were used and how were they dispersed?

2. In recent years, many biological weapons programs have focused on anthrax (http://www.cdc.gov/ncidod/dbmd/diseaseinfo/anthrax_t.htm), which is caused by *Bacillus anthracis*. Which people exposed to anthrax-contaminated mail in 2001 were more likely to die from the resulting infection—people who touched the mail or people who inhaled the bacterial spores from the mail?

3. Anthrax may be prevented by vaccination (http://www.hopkinsbiodefense.org/pages/agents/agentanthrax2002.html). Why is the use of anthrax as a weapon still of great concern?

4. The U.S. military has instituted a mandatory Anthrax Vaccine Immunization Program (http://www.ngwrc.org/news/content/MonNov011000001999.asp). Do you think this is an effective defense strategy? Can you think of additional or alternative strategies?

ISSUES IN BIOLOGY

Why That Prescription for Antibiotics May Be Useless

Bacteria develop resistance to antibiotics when mutations to their DNA occur. If a mutation is favorable and allows bacteria to survive exposure to antibiotics, then that trait can be selected for by the misuse and abuse of antibiotics. Conjugation allows bacteria to pass on resistance to antibiotics to bacteria of the same or even different species: The Battle of the Bugs: Fighting Antibiotic Resistance—How Resistance Occurs (http://www.fda.gov/fdac/features/2002/402_bugs.html). There are a number of antibiotics that are no longer as useful as they once were for fighting bacterial infections. Bacterial diseases that no longer respond as well to antibiotic therapy include tuberculosis, gonorrhea, and staph infections that often occur following surgery. A more extensive list of microbes now resistant to antibiotics can be found at Fact Sheet: Antimicrobial Resistance (http://www.niaid.nih.gov/factsheets/antimicro.htm).

What's causing the increasing number of antibiotic-resistant bacteria? There are a number of reasons for the increases: The Battle of the Bugs: Fighting Antibiotic Resistance—Preserving Antibiotics' Usefulness and From Farm to Fork. Solving the problem of antibiotic-resistant bacteria will need to involve doctors, the general public Miracle Drugs vs Superbugs—Too Much of a Good Thing (http://www.fda.gov/fdac/features/1998/698_bugs.html), and the agricultural industry.

1. What are some of the antibiotics to which bacteria have become resistant?

2. How have physicians contributed to the increase in the number of antibiotic-resistant bacteria?

3. How are antibiotics misused by the agricultural industry?

4. What can the general public (patients) do to prevent further increases in antibiotic-resistant bacteria?

BIZARRE FACTS IN BIOLOGY

Life on the Extreme Edge

Imagine life in the most inhospitable of environments, an environment without oxygen or with extremely high salt concentration, boiling temperatures, or strong acid. How could any organism live there? How could a cell's plasma membrane and large molecules remain functional under these conditions? A unique group of microorganisms, the Archaea, have mastered the art of living on the edge.

Archaeans were first isolated from the hot sulfur springs of Yellowstone National Park. They are classified into three main groups, depending on their habitat: methanogens (http://www.space.com/searchforlife/life_methane_020116. html), halophiles, and thermoacidophiles (http://www.microbe.org/microbes/thermophiles.asp). The methanogens are rod-shaped, live in strictly anaerobic environments, and produce large quantities of methane (CH_4) from carbon dioxide and hydrogen. They live in marshes, lake bottoms (causing the rotten egg smell that occurs when you poke a stick into the mud at the bottom), and feces (from the intestines of animals—the cause of intestinal gas). The halophiles require high concentrations of salt, such as in the Great Salt Lake, Utah. The thermoacidophiles normally grow in hot (100 ˚C), acidic (pH 1.0) environments.

Researchers are interested in finding out how organisms can live at temperatures that would destroy most biological molecules, especially enzymes, that are required for all the metabolic processes within a cell. Some of these enzymes have been exploited for biotechnology. For example, a thermally stable DNA polymerase (used to copy DNA molecules) was isolated from a thermoacidophile in a hot spring in Yellowstone. This enzyme allowed for the development of the technique polymerase chain reaction (PCR). The PCR (http://www.encyclopedia.com/searchpool. asp?target=@DOCTITLE%20polymerase%20chain%20reaction) method allows scientists to amplify minute amounts of DNA for analysis (for example, from a drop of blood or from a prehistoric mosquito trapped in amber). This technique has revolutionized the field of forensics and cut the time for the Human Genome Project from decades to years.

1. If archaeans are the most ancient of organisms on the planet, what do their habitats tell us about the conditions on Earth 3.5 billion years ago?

2. From what you know about cellular metabolism and about how enzymes function in the cell, how do you think thermophiles are able to survive at such high temperatures?

KEY TERMS

acellular slime mold
algae
alveolate
amoeba
anaerobe
apicomplexan
bacteriophage
cellular slime mold
chromist
cilia

ciliate
conjugation
diatom
dinoflagellate
endospore
euglenoid
flagellum
foraminiferan
Gram stain
heliozoan

host
nitrogen-fixing bacterium
pathogenic
phytoplankton
plasmid
plasmodial slime mold
plasmodium
prion
protist
protozoa

pseudoplasmodium
pseudopod
radiolarian
viroid
virus
water mold
zooflagellate

ANSWER KEY

SELF TEST

1. virus
2. A. eukaryotic cell (animal)
   B. prokaryotic cell (rod)
   C. eukaryotic cell (plant)
   D. prokaryotic cell (round)
   E. viruses
3. e
4. bacteriophage
5. d
6. d
7. b
8. A. protein coat
   B. envelope (lipid bilayer)
   C. genetic material (viral RNA) coated with protein
   D. core proteins
9. A. virus enters host nucleus
   B. viral envelope merges with nuclear membrane; protein coat disintegrates and viral DNA enters nucleus and is copied
   C. viral DNA is transcribed into mRNA, which moves to the cytoplasm

D. mRNA makes coat and envelope proteins, which enter the nucleus
E. newly formed viruses leave the cell by exocytosis.
10. peptidoglycan
11. e
12. b
13. b
14. Gram stain
15. e
16. a
17. e
18. a
19. c
20. a
21. A. single amoeba-like cells emerge from spores, crawl, and feed
    B. when food becomes scarce, cells aggragate into sluglike mass called a *pseudoplasmoidium*
    C. *pseudoplasmoidium* migrates toward light
    D. *pseudoplasmoidium* forms fruiting bodies which release spores
22. e

23. d
24. A. eyespot
    B. flagellum
    C. nucleolus
    D. nucleus
    E. chloroplasts
    F. contractile vacuole
25. d
26. f
27. A. macronucleus
    B. micronucleus
    C. oral groove
    D. food vacuole
    E. anal pore
    F. contractile vacuole
    G. cilia
28. b
29. c
30. b
31. a
32. e

ESSAY CHALLENGE

1. Prions consist only of protein. Prions have no DNA or RNA associated with them. Viroids are bare strands of RNA. Viruses are genetic material (DNA or RNA) surrounded by a protein coat.

2. Viruses "borrow" the replication machinery from their host cells to produce more copies of viral genetic material and new protective coats.

3. Archaea are distinguished from bacteria by their unique cellular membrane composition and their unique RNA subunit sequences. Bacteria and Archaea are similar because the organisms classified as such are unicellular prokaryotes. They lack membrane-bound organelles characteristic of eukaryotic-celled organisms.

4. Since algae are able to perform photosynthesis, they create food for themselves and for organisms that consume the algae. They would be described as the producers in a food chain (more details about food chains in Chapter 41).

5. Bacteria gain genetic variability during conjugation and may acquire genes for antibiotic resistance from other bacteria. Their ability to gain antibiotic resistance in this manner is of concern to humans because existing antibiotics may no longer effectively treat bacterial diseases.

6. Bacteria are the microbes present in the water. The tests indicate the presence of DNA that is not contained in a nucleus and a cell wall that contains peptidoglycan. Bacteria have many jobs of importance to other organisms. Some fix nitrogen for plants, some digest cellulose for ruminants, like cows, and some are decomposers and recycle nutrients from dead/discarded tissues.

7. They are both autotrophs and transform energy via photosynthesis. Both are producers in a food chain. Cyanobacteria are prokaryotes, while algae are eukaryotes. Cyanobacteria lack chloroplasts. Algae have chloroplasts.

MEDIA ACTIVITIES

19.4   Web Investigation: Agents of Death

1. Water supplies were contaminated by dead bodies. Soldiers who'd died from the bubonic plague were catapulted into a city under attack, thereby spreading the plague to the city's residents and the locations to which they fled. British soldiers gave Native Americans blankets used by people with smallpox, which may have caused the huge outbreaks of smallpox among the Native American tribes.

2. People who inhaled the spores from the contaminated mail were more likely to die because inhalation anthrax is more difficult to treat than cutaneous anthrax. Very few people die from cutaneous anthrax.

3. Although the anthrax vaccine appears to be safe and effective some vaccines may cause the disease that they're intended to prevent. The supply of anthrax vaccine is limited (like the vaccine for influenza in 2003) so it may not be possible to vaccinate a large number of people. Additionally 6 inoculations are currently recommended.

4. Vaccinations have traditionally been effective ways to prevent infections. During the contaminated mail scare of 2001, many people took the antibiotics prescribed for anthrax as a preventative measure. This may prevent infection by anthrax, but may also contribute to the escalating problem of antibiotic-resistant bacteria. Alternate strategies could include a method of detecting the presence of an aerosol form of anthrax, which might minimize exposure. Improved methods of destroying anthrax spores might help minimize the spread of infection.

ISSUES IN BIOLOGY

1. Methacylin, vancomycin, penicillin, and tetracycline are some that are mentioned.

2. Doctors are pressured by time and patient demands and often prescribe antibiotics as a time-saving measure.

3. Antibiotics are used to prevent diseases in fruit crops. They are used to prevent diseases in, and increase production by, food-producing animals. The exposure of bacteria to these antibiotics is contributing to the increase in antibiotic-resistant bacteria.

4. Patients should demand prescriptions for antibiotics, should complete the course of antibiotic treatment instead of stopping when they feel better, and should not borrow antibiotics from someone else. Washing hands well with soap and water and proper cooking and storage of food can contribute a lot to the prevention of bacterial infections.

BIZARRE FACTS IN BIOLOGY

1. The conditions on Earth 3.5 billion years ago were likely to be quite hot (from volcanic activity and UV radiation). There would have been little/no atmospheric oxygen.

2. Enzymes are sensitive to pH and temperature and will function effectively only when conditions are optimal. Less than optimal conditions may cause proteins to unfold, making them nonfunctional. Thermophiles' enzymes are more tightly folded than the enzymes of organisms living at moderate temperatures. The amino acid glycine is more uncommon in the enzymes of the thermophiles, which makes the enzymes more rigid and difficult to unfold. The thermophiles may also have a protein which refolds the enzymes as they become unfolded by the extreme heat.

CHAPTER 20: THE DIVERSITY OF FUNGI

AT-A-GLANCE

SELF TEST

1. Which of these characteristics are typical of the fungi?

   a. autotrophic

   b. possess cell walls of chitin

   c. have cytoplasmic connections between the cells

   d. diploid

   e. Both the second and third answers are correct.

2. Which of the following is characteristic of, or associated with, fungi?

   a. prokaryotic cells

   b. cell walls with peptidoglycan

   c. photosynthesis

   d. extracellular digestion

   e. production of embryos

3. The tests below have been performed on a cell from an unidentified organism. Based on the results that follow, how would you classify this organism?

   Tests:

   Chemical A turns green when a nucleus is present.
   Chemical B bubbles when chloroplasts are present.
   Chemical C pops when chitin is present.

   Results:

   Chemical A turns green.
   Chemical B doesn't bubble.
   Chemical C pops.

   a. plant
   b. fungus
   c. bacterium
   d. diatom
   e. virus

4. What is the tangled mass of branched filaments that typically forms the fungal body?
   a. conidia
   b. hyphae
   c. mycelia
   d. rhizoids
   e. sporangia

5. Label the structures seen on this cross section through fungal hyphae.

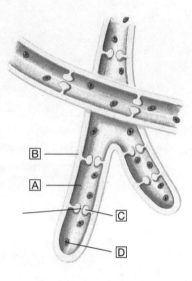

6. Which of the following is most likely to happen if there is a sudden change in temperature?
   a. asexual reproduction
   b. sexual reproduction

7. What distinguishes fungal reproduction from that of plants and animals?
   a. There is no asexual reproduction.
   b. There is no sexual reproduction.
   c. There is no embryo produced when fungi reproduce.

8. _____ allow the fungus to reproduce and are usually released to be carried on the wind.

9. A haploid asexual spore is formed by a haploid mycelium via _____.
   a. fertilization
   b. meiosis
   c. mitosis
   d. pollination

10. Which of the following is associated with the mostly aquatic chytrids?
   a. flagellated spores
   b. cell walls of chitin
   c. eukaryotic cells
   d. haploid body
   e. All of these are associated with the chytrids.

11. Soft fruit rot and black bread mold belong to which division of Fungi?
   a. Ascomycota
   b. Basidiomycota
   c. Deuteromycota
   d. lichens
   e. Zygomycota

12. A zygospore undergoes _____ to produce haploid spores.
   a. germination
   b. meiosis
   c. fertilization
   d. mitosis
   e. transcription

13. Label the stages in the life cycle of a typical zygomycete shown on the next page.

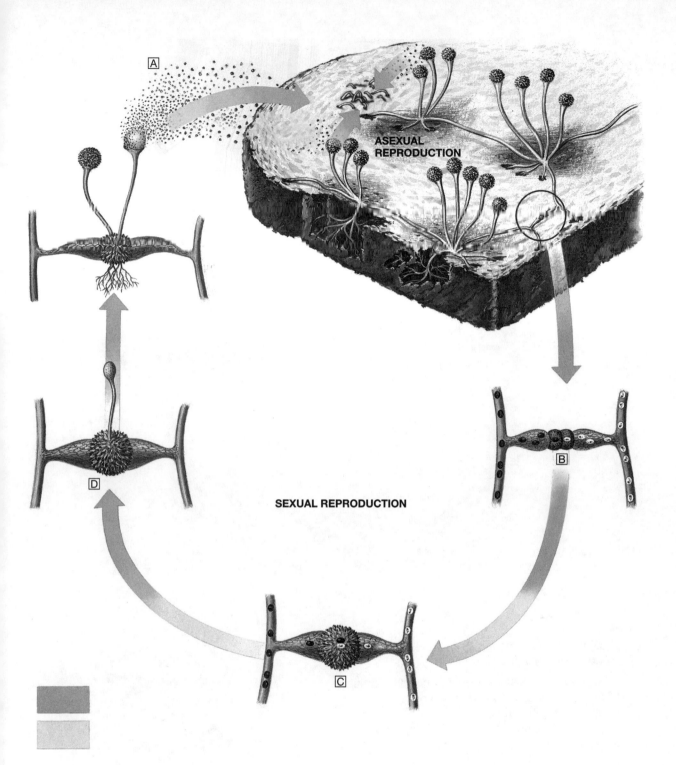

ASEXUAL REPRODUCTION

SEXUAL REPRODUCTION

14. Which group of fungi are known as the sac fungi because of the shape of the spore-containing diploid reproductive structures?

    a. Basidiomycetes   **b.** Ascomycetes

    c. Zygomycetes   **d.** Chytrids

15. Yeasts, truffles, and Dutch elm disease belong to which division of Fungi?

    a. Ascomycota   **b.** Basidiomycota

    c. Deuteromycota **d.** lichens

    e. Zygomycota

16. The clublike structure producing the spores of typical mushrooms is called _____.

    a. ascus

    b. basidium

    c. conidia

    d. sporangia

    e. mycorrhizae

17. Basidiomycetes are also known as _____.

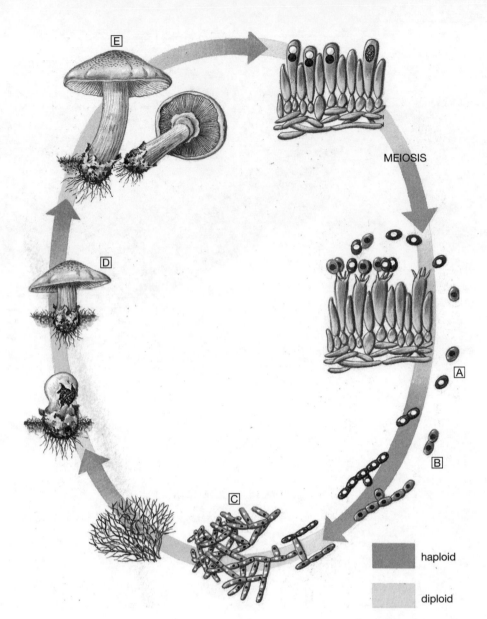

MEIOSIS

haploid

diploid

18. Label the stages in the life cycle of a typical basidiomycete shown above.

19. Which of the following is associated with the group of fungi known as the deuteromycetes?
    a. asexual reproduction
    b. flagellated spores
    c. zygospores
    d. closely related organisms
    e. embryos

20. Which of the partners in the symbiotic relationship known as a lichen gains food (sugars) from the other partner?
    a. alga   b. fungus
    c. plant roots   d. cyanobacteria

21. A _____ is a symbiotic interaction between a fungus and a cyanobacterium.

22. Lichen is a symbiotic organism. Label the structures associated with this partnership in the figure to the right.

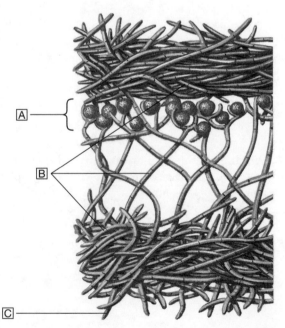

23. A test reveals that a lichen contains a prokaryotic symbiont. What kind of organism is this prokaryotic symbiont?
    a. fungus
    b. heterotrophic bacterium
    c. plant
    d. cyanobacterium
    e. arthropod

24. The sugar-producing symbiont in a mycorrhiza is a(n) _____.
    a. plant
    b. fungus
    c. cyanobacterium
    d. alga

25. What beneficial agricultural role is played by fungi?
    a. Fungal pathogens are used as fungal pesticides to protect numerous crop species from various insect species.
    b. Application of rusts and smuts alter the coloration of crops, confusing potential insect predators.
    c. The American elm and American chestnut have benefited from application of ascomycete fungi.
    d. none of the above

26. Which of the following is/are (an) example(s) of the economic significance of the Fungi?
    a. animal disease agents
    b. commercial foods
    c. plant disease agents
    d. symbiosis with plants
    e. All of these are economically significant.

27. Which of the following is a fungal disease?
    a. AIDS
    b. athlete's foot
    c. botulism
    d. Lyme disease
    e. malaria
    f. polio

28. Which of these economic problems or diseases is NOT caused by a fungus?
    a. corn smut
    b. Dutch elm disease
    c. histoplasmosis
    d. Mad Cow disease
    e. mushroom poisoning
    f. ringworm

29. In what ways do some fungi directly affect human health?
    a. as parasites causing disease
    b. as producers of toxins that act as poisons
    c. as a source of antibiotics
    d. all of the above
    e. none of the above

30. Aflatoxins are carcinogenic compounds that can be produced by molds of the genus _____.

31. If yeasts are responsible for the alcohol in wine and beer, why don't we get a little tipsy from eating bread?
    a. Alcohol is not produced by yeast inoculated into bread dough.
    b. Fermentation is impaired by the dough.
    c. Baking the bread evaporates the alcohol produced by the fermenting yeasts.
    d. Yeasts are actually not used in breads, but an ascomycete mold is.

32. Beer is produced through the use of a fungus called _____.

33. Arthrobotrys species capture _____ for a source of protein.

34. Which of the following is the most important role fungi have in their ecosystems?
    a. recyclers of nutrients like carbon and nitrogen from dead animal and plant bodies
    b. parasites on crops like corn, tobacco, and apples
    c. symbionts with algae or cyanobacteria
    d. pathogens that cause diseases like ringworm, athlete's foot, and yeast infections
    e. edible fungi such as truffles, morels, and mushrooms

ESSAY CHALLENGE

1. In the previous chapter, you learned about organisms in the domain bacteria and the kingdom protista. Compare and contrast those organisms with the fungi covered in this chapter. Your answer should include physical characteristics and the importance of them to other living things.

2. What is the advantage to making spores as a reproductive strategy?

3. What are the four phyla of fungi? How are they similar? Different?

4. With what other organisms can fungi live in mutually beneficial relationships? How does the fungus benefit from these relationships?

5. Based on the discovery that in lichens with algal symbionts the fungal hyphae penetrate the algal cell walls just like fungi that parasitize plants, and on the knowledge that fungi may use up to 90% of the algae's sugars, is it reasonable to refer to lichens as mutually beneficial relationships?

6. While scratching his athlete's foot, a friend says that fungi are aggravating and that humans would be better off without them around. What will you tell your friend to convince him/her that the loss of fungi would be devastating to humans?

7. What fungal activities support the notion that your muscle proteins may contain nitrogens that were once a part of the muscle proteins of a *Tyrannosaurus rex*?

8. In this chapter and the previous one, you learned about the organisms that do the incredibly important job of decomposition (breaking down dead bodies). What organisms from this chapter and the previous one perform this all-important job of decomposition? Why would the ecosystems in which these organisms are found cease to function without them?

MEDIA ACTIVITIES

To access a Media Activity visit http://www.prenhall.com/audesirk7. Log in to the Web site selected by your instructor, navigate to this chapter, and select the appropriate Media Activity number.

20.1 Fungi Structure and Reproduction
Estimated Time: 5 minutes

Explore the major structures and reproductive life cycles of the fungi.

20.2 Classification of Fungi
Estimated Time: 5 minutes

Explore the major divisions of the fungi and their distinguishing characteristics.

20.3 Web Investigation: Humongous Fungus
Estimated time: 10 minutes

The case study that begins this chapter features the humongous fungus *Armillaria ostoyae*. The finding of these giant fungi (Oregon, Washington, and Michigan all tout their humongous fungi!) has provided forest management (http://www.sciencedaily.com/releases/2003/03/030327074535.htm) people with new insights into how humans impact forests and the management of forests. The *Armillaria* fungus is now known to be a natural participant in a forest ecosystem. Its spread is not worsened by the suppression of forest fires by humans as was once believed.

The Oregon fungus was not the first humongous fungus to be identified. In 1992, the fungus *Armillaria bulbosa* (http://botit.botany.wisc.edu/toms_fungi/apr2002.html) (now more correctly classified as *Armillaria gallica*) was identified in Michigan. Extensive genetic comparisons showed conclusively that the 37-acre fungus was in fact one organism. Although the Michigan humongous fungus is really located in a different township, Crystal Falls, MI (http://www.crystalfalls.org/humongou.htm), claims it as their own. Every September, Crystal Falls celebrates its famous fungus with a Fungus Fest where you can get a fungus burger or fungus fudge! If you plan to see the fungus while you're there, prepare to be disappointed because it is mostly underground and out of sight.

1. What tree species should be considered for replacement of trees removed during harvesting?

2. What type of genetic information was examined to demonstrate the Michigan fungus was one organism?

3. What late night show host had some fun with the Michigan humongous fungus? According to the host in question, what does the fungus taste like?

ISSUES IN BIOLOGY

Where Have All The Fungi Gone?

In the Earth Watch of this chapter the issue of disappearing fungi is addressed. Lest you shrug this off as of little concern, consider that many of the fungi that are disappearing live symbiotically with plants (mycorrhizae). The relationship between plants and fungi benefits both organisms. The heterotrophic fungi obtain sugars produced by the photosynthetic activities of the plants. In turn, the fungi provide the plants with additional nutrients from the soil. Plants involved in mycorrhizae grow better than plants that are not (see figure 24-20 in your textbook). Some plants, like orchids (http://users.sunbeach.net/users/lec/orchid.html), are dependent on their fungal partners for survival. Cultivation of some plants like the Pink Ladyslipper orchid (http://www.uga.edu/~botgarden/GEPSN2b.html) is futile because of the poorly understood relationship between the orchid and its fungal partner. Attempts to restore endangered plant species (http://www.hawaii.edu/scb/docs/science/scinativ_mycor.html) may fail without the presence of the proper fungal species.

Plants aren't the only organisms dependent on their fungal partners. Some animals like the endangered northern flying squirrel (http://www.srs.fs.usda.gov/pubs/viewpub.jsp?index=2056) rely on mycorrhizae for food. The truffles that the squirrels consume form mycorrhizae with specific plant species.

1. If the fungi involved with orchid seeds are eliminated, what do you predict will happen to the seeds? How will the population of orchids be affected?

2. Will fungi form mycorrhizae with just any kind of plant?

3. If the spruces in the Southern Appalachians were removed and replaced with pines, what do you predict would happen to the northern flying squirrels?

BIZARRE FACTS IN BIOLOGY

Just When You Thought It Was Safe . . .

Right now in soil near you, a microscopic biotic drama is being played out. In the lead role is a predaceous fungus, and the supporting role belongs to its prey, the nematodes (http://nematode.unl.edu/wormgen.htm) (roundworms).

Predaceous fungi (http://botit.botany.wisc.edu/toms_fungi/aug2000.html) spread their mycelium throughout the soil like a tangle of octopus arms. Nematodes slither blindly through the soil, occasionally bumping into the mycelium—a chance meeting in total darkness. It could be a chemical in the soil that attracts the nematodes or just a chance encounter; nonetheless, once the nematode encounters the fungus, the worm becomes entrapped. These predaceous fungi have several methods, depending on the species, by which to snare their next meal. Some species have rings on their mycelia that constrict their prey. The constricting rings are like tiny lassos through which an unknowing nematode crawls. Cells in the ring swell, closing the noose. Other species use branched hyphae with adhesives for capturing prey. As you can see, not all predators have teeth, sharp claws, hooked talons, or even vision.

After capture, the fungus sends threads of hyphae into the nematode's body and begins the process of digestion. The mode of nutrition in which an organism obtains its food from another source is called heterotrophy. The nematode's proteins, carbohydrates, and fats are broken down into usable products for the fungus. Life thus recycles.

1. There is an ever-escalating "arms race" in nature; for example, a plant produces a chemical to deter being eaten by an insect—the insect evolves a chemical to detoxify the plant. How might nematodes avoid predatory fungi? What would need to take place from an evolutionary perspective?

2. Speculate as to how a fungus, which normally processes material that is no longer living (such as a dead tree), could become so specialized as to feed on nematodes?

3. What are some downsides to this fungal specialization?

KEY TERMS

asci	hyphae	mycorrhizae	spore
basidia	imperfect fungus	sac fungus	zygospore
basidiospore	lichen	septa	zygote fungus
club fungus	mycelium	sporangium	

ANSWER KEY

SELF TEST

1. e
2. d
3. b
4. c
5. A. cytoplasm
   B. cell wall
   C. septum
   D. haploid nuclei
6. b
7. c
8. spores
9. c
10. e
11. e
12. b

13. A. spores
    B. opposite mating strains meet and nuclei fuse
    C. diploid zygospore
    D. germinating zygospore
14. b
15. a
16. b
17. club fungi
18. A. mating strains
    B. germinating mating strains
    C. compatible hyphae fuse and grow into mycelium
    D. mushroom develops from aggregated hyphae
    E. gills bear reproductive basidia
19. a
20. b
21. lichen

22. A. algal layer
    B. fungal hyphae
    C. attachment structure
23. d
24. a
25. a
26. e
27. b
28. d
29. d
30. Aspergillus
31. c
32. yeast
33. nematodes
34. a

ESSAY CHALLENGE

1. Fungi are unlike bacteria because bacteria are prokaryotic and unicellular, while fungi are eukaryotic and multicellular (exception = yeasts). They both have cell walls surrounding their plasma membranes, but the fungal cell wall contains chitin while that of the bacteria contains peptidoglycan. Fungi and the organisms in the kingdom protista are similar because they're eukaryotic. Some protists are similar to fungi (exception = yeasts) with regards to the number of cells (many) while some protists are different, since many protists are unicellular. Some bacteria, the slime molds, and some fungi are similar because they perform the important job of decomposition. Some bacteria and many protists are very different from fungi because they are photosynthetic autotrophs, while fungi are all heterotrophs.

2. Spores are produced in large numbers, ensuring that some will find favorable conditions in which to germinate. Spores can be wind blown or distributed by animals to places far from the fungus that produced them.

3. Chytridiomycota (chytrids), Zygomycota (zygote fungi), Ascomycota (sac fungi), and Basidiomycota (club fungi). Similarities: heterotrophs, multicellular (exception is yeast), cell walls with chitin, asexual spores. Differences: Chytrids - produce flagellated spores; Zygomycota - form zygospores; Ascomycota - form asci; Basidiomycota - form basidia.

4. Some fungi form lichens when they live with unicellular algae or cyanobacteria. Some fungi live symbiotically with the roots of plants. The fungi gain food from their photosynthetic partners.

5. Since the algae are gaining protection from harsh environmental conditions and if the algae are not harmed by the fungi, it is still reasonable to refer to the lichen as mutually beneficial. If the algae are harmed by the fungi's use of such a high percentage of the sugars produced, then it may be better to refer to the relationship as parasitic.

6. Without fungus, there would be no cheese, beer, wine, or mushrooms on pizza. Many antibiotics are produced by fungi and the transplant drug cyclosporin, derived from a fungus, helps to reduce rejection risks.

7. A hugely important job of some fungi is to break down dead plant and animal bodies which releases carbons, nitrogens, and other nutrients. These nutrients can be taken up by plants and used to make a variety of plant molecules. When a plant is eaten, the same nutrients are released during digestion and used to make a variety of molecules in the consumer. Without the decomposition performed by fungi, nutrients would stay locked up inside the dead bodies.

8. The organisms that act as decomposers are fungi, slime molds, and some of the heterotrophic bacteria. The decomposers are incredibly important to proper functioning of their ecosystems because they release nutrients from the dead bodies of plants and animals. If the nutrients remained locked up in the dead bodies, eventually there'd be none left with which to make the molecules needed by living things.

MEDIA ACTIVITIES

20.3 Web Investigation: Humongous Fungus

1. Western larch, western white pine, and ponderosa pine are trees less susceptible to root disease caused by the fungus.
2. Mating type loci and mitochondrial DNA restriction patterns.
3. David Letterman. Chicken!

ISSUES IN BIOLOGY

1. Since the fungi enable the seeds to germinate, the seeds are not likely to sprout without their fungal partners. If the orchid seeds can't germinate, baby orchids will not develop and replace old orchids that die. Ultimately, the population of orchids could disappear.
2. The fungi in the most common type of mycorrhizae are not known to be specific to a certain kind of plant. However, the climate and soil conditions can influence the extent to which the fungus benefits the plants.
3. Since the article says that high production of truffles was associated with spruce-fir or spruce-mixed hardwood stands, it is likely that the fungus does not develop mycorrhizae with pines. Therefore, replacing the spruces with the pines may eliminate the truffles on which the squirrels feed.

BIZARRE FACTS IN BIOLOGY

1. A mutation might occur that inhibits adhesive hyphae from sticking to the nematodes, allowing them to escape the predatory fungus, or some nematodes may wiggle more vigorously and escape the nooses of the fungal hyphae. The nematodes that

escape predation will be the ones who reproduce, and they should have offspring capable of escaping predation as well. Over time the nematodes should become a population that is more capable of escaping predation.

2. There may have been a large number of nematodes in the soil, making it easy to encounter them. Fungi that were able to entrap nematodes might have gained nutrients more easily than fungi that had to grow long filaments in order to encounter a dead tree. The ease of gaining nutrients would give those fungi more energy to spend on reproduction.

Over time there would be a selection for those fungi able to trap nematodes.

3. Organisms that rely on one type of food or one source of nutrients are vulnerable because if the source of food or nutrition is eliminated, the other organisms are at great risk for extinction. Species that rely on a variety of nutrient sources are not likely to be adversely affected if the population of one nutrient source is adversely affected. The panda is an example of a species that is threatened because the only type of food it consumes is bamboo. Less bamboo results in fewer pandas

CHAPTER 21: THE DIVERSITY OF PLANTS

AT-A-GLANCE

SELF TEST

1. Which of the following supports the hypothesis that plants evolved from green algal ancestors?

   a. Plants and green algae both store food as glycogen.

   b. Plants and green algae both have cell walls made of chitin.

   c. Plants and green algae both use the same type of chlorophyll and accessory pigments during photosynthesis.

   d. Plants and green algae both have true roots, stems, and leaves and complex reproductive structures.

2. Early plant evolution most likely occurred in freshwater habitats because _____.

   a. most green algae are freshwater organisms

   b. water temperature can fluctuate seasonally or daily

   c. freshwater habitats may dry up periodically

   d. all of the above

3. _____ algae presumably gave rise to land plants.

4. Sporophytes produce haploid spores via _____.
   a. meiosis
   b. mitosis
   c. fertilization
   d. pollination

5. When haploid spores divide by mitosis, multicellular haploid plants called _____ form.

6. In the diploid generation, the plant body is known as the _____.

7. Which plant generation is responsible for the production of haploid gametes?
   a. sporophyte
   b. gametophyte
   c. zygote
   d. spore

8. All plants produce _____.
   a. spores
   b. seeds
   c. pollen
   d. swimming sperm
   e. fruits

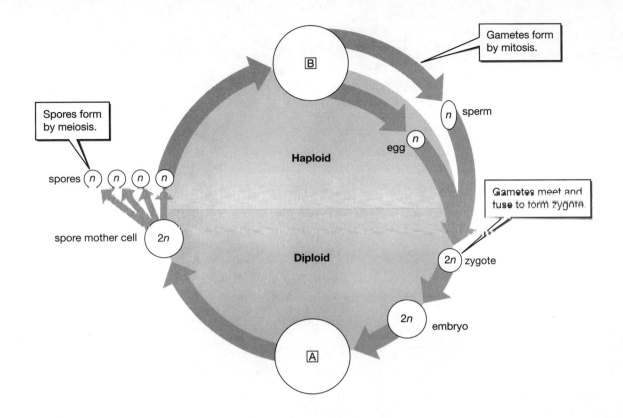

9. Plants show an alternation of generation between sporophytes and gametophytes. Label these generations correctly on the diagram above.

10. The presence or production of _____ distinguishes plants from their nearest relatives, the green algae.

    a. cell walls with cellulose

    b. multicellular, dependent embryos

    c. starch

    d. a nucleus

11. Based on the characteristics of plants, which of the following "jobs" in an ecosystem is performed by plants?

    a. producer

    b. decomposer

    c. primary consumer

12. The rigors of the terrestrial environment led to many adaptations among terrestrial plants. Which of these is NOT a necessary adaptation to dry land?

    a. conducting vessels

    b. cuticle and stomata

    c. lignin

    d. roots or rootlike structures

    e. separate gametophyte stage

13. What structural adaptation of land plants functions to deliver water and minerals from the roots to the rest of the plant?

    a. cuticle

    b. stomata

    c. conducting vessels

    d. lignin

14. Photosynthesis stops during very hot and dry weather because _____.

    a. the stomata close, which cuts off the plant's supply of carbon dioxide needed to perform photosynthesis

    b. plants don't make lignin when it's hot and dry

    c. most plants lack vascular tissue that would enable them to absorb water from the soil

    d. the waxy cuticle melts in the hot weather

15. Which of the following is NOT an example of the sporophyte stage of the alternation of generations?

    a. oak tree

    b. moss

    c. pine tree

    d. tomato plant

239

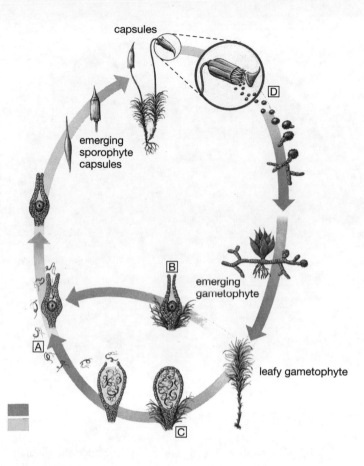

capsules

emerging
sporophyte
capsules

D

B

emerging
gametophyte

leafy gametophyte

A

C

16. What is the reproductive structure of bryophytes and of seedless vascular plants that encloses eggs and protects them from drying out?

 a. antheridium
 b. archegonium
 c. gametophyte
 d. rhizoids
 e. sporangia

17. The relatively small size of the bryophytes is probably due to _____.

 a. the absence of vascular tissue
 b. the dependence on water for reproduction
 c. their habitat
 d. the lack of true leaves
 e. a unique but conservative pattern of reproduction

18. Bryophytes have _____, which are similar to roots.

19. Label the indicated structures of the life cycle of a typical moss in the diagram above.

20. Even though they are vascular plants, and thus moderately advanced terrestrially, the ferns have not solved all of the problems of terrestrial life. How is this so?

 a. Their zygotes remain unprotected from desiccation.
 b. They are broad leafed.
 c. They do not possess a gametophyte stage.
 d. They lack advanced vascular tissue.
 e. Typically, they lack erect stems.

21. The silica deposits in the outer layer of cells in *Equisetum* gave it its nickname: _____.

240

22. Label the parts of the life cycle of a typical fern in the diagram below.

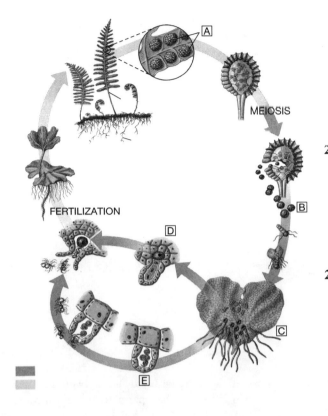

23. Seed plants produce male gametophytes known as
_____.

   a. fruit
   b. flower
   c. pollen
   d. seed
   e. sporangium

24. Which of the following is best adapted to a dry habitat?

   a. moss
   b. ferns
   c. horsetails
   d. crabgrass

25. Why has the evolution of reproductive adaptations, the development of pollen and seeds, proven so successful for the gymnosperms and angiosperms?

   a. Both adaptations permit the storage of water for later use.
   b. Both adaptations eliminate the need for dissemination by water.
   c. Both adaptations permit dissemination over long distances through the actions of wind or animals.
   d. Both the second and third answers are correct.
   e. All of the above are correct.

26. Which of the following protects the plant embryo?

   a. seed
   b. spore
   c. waxy cuticle
   d. stomata
   e. lignin

27. Label the structures indicated on these two seed types.

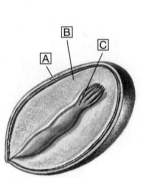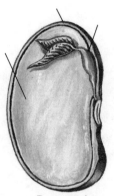

Pine seed
(gymnosperm)

Bean seed
(angiosperm)

(a)   (b)

28. The sperm of conifers _____.

   a. swims to an egg
   b. is carried in a pollen grain that has tiny wings
   c. is transported to an egg by a bee
   d. are triploid
   e. are found in the ovary of a flower

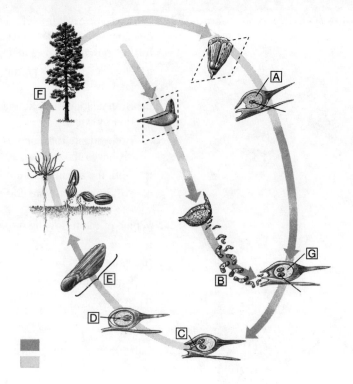

29. Label the indicated portions of the life cycle of a typical conifer.

30. The adaptations that attract potential pollinators are _____.

31. Which of the major adaptations does your textbook suggest is most vulnerable to herbivore attack, especially by insects?

    a. broad leaves

    b. fruits

    c. flowers

    d. roots

32. Successful (with regards to land dwelling) and accurate delivery of the sperm to the egg occurs when land dwelling plants produce _____.

    a. swimming sperm

    b. pollen grains with wings

    c. attractive, sweet-smelling flowers

    d. a long, green, dangling flower

33. Flowering plants such as roses and geraniums belong to which group of plant?

    a. angiosperms

    b. conifers

    c. seedless vascular

    d. bryophytes

    e. gymnosperms

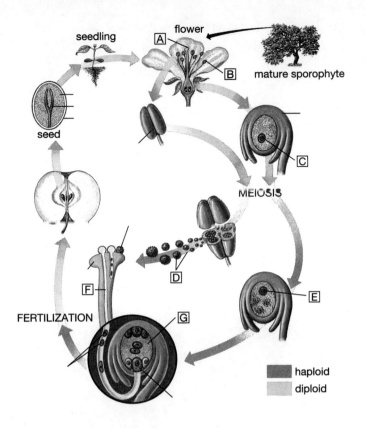

seedling

flower

A

B

mature sporophyte

seed

C

MEIOSIS

D

E

F

FERTILIZATION

G

haploid

diploid

34. Label the indicated portions of the life cycle of a typical flowering plant in the diagram above.

ESSAY CHALLENGE

1. Give a few reasons why green algae and ancestral plants are so similar.

2. Meiosis produces haploid cells. In animals (life cycles we tend to be most familiar with, since we are animals), meiosis occurs to produce the gametes used to perform sexual reproduction. Why are plants' gametes produced via mitosis?

3. What are some of the adaptations that plants had to accumulate to survive on land?

4. Why are mosses often referred to as the amphibians of the plant kingdom?

5. What is the most important feature of ferns, one that makes them so successful?

6. How have land plants adapted to reproduction outside of water?

7. What structural feature(s) would you expect to see on a pollen grain that is dependent upon the wind for dispersal? Why do plants that produce windblown pollen make TONS of it?

8. Identify three major adaptations that led to the proliferation of angiosperms (flowering plants).

9. Why do most angiosperm plants drop their leaves when the weather turns cold?

MEDIA ACTIVITIES

To access a Media Activity visit http://www.prenhall.com/audesirk7. Log in to the Web site selected by your instructor, navigate to this chapter, and select the appropriate Media Activity number.

21.1 Evolution of Plant Structure
Estimated time: 10 minutes

This animation illustrates the evolutionary changes that have occurred in plant structures and how the changes have allowed the plants to exploit different habitats.

21.2 Fern Life Cycle
Estimated time: 5 minutes

View the stages of and structures involved in the fern life cycle.

21.3 Web Investigation: Queen of the Parasites
Estimated time: 10 minutes

The queen of the parasites, Rafflesia, discussed in the chapter case study is only one of several plants that produce very stinky flowers (http://biology.fullerton.edu/facilities/greenhouse/amorphophallus/index.html). Many may wonder "why stinky, putrid-smelling flowers?" Flower characteristics tend to correspond with pollinator characteristics so that a specific pollinator visits one kind of flower, which increases the accuracy of pollen transport. Rafflesia's stinky flowers may help it overcome some of the huge problems the plant has ensuring successful pollination (http://unix.cc.wmich.edu/~tbarkman/rafflesia/Rafflesia.html). If pollination of a female Rafflesia flower occurs, a small round fruit containing thousands of seeds develops. The fruit ensures the seeds are dispersed (http://www.szgdocent.org/ff/f-praff.htm), thereby increasing the distribution of Rafflesia plants.

A parasitic lifestyle is not unique to Rafflesia. Dodder (http://www.colostate.edu/Depts/CoopExt/TRA/dodder.html), a pest plant, is non-photosynthetic like Rafflesia. Mistletoe (http://www.forests.qld.gov.au/educat/btl/mistle.htm) which most people think of only at Christmas, is considered a semi-parasitic plant because it retains the ability to do photosynthesis.

1. What is another kind of plant that makes putrid-smelling flowers? Geographically, what does this plant have in common with Rafflesia?

2. What Rafflesia flower characteristics hinder the plant's ability to ensure successful pollination?

3. How are Rafflesia seeds dispersed?

4. What does mistletoe obtain from its host plant?

ISSUES IN BIOLOGY

Where Have All the Food Plants Gone?

You are probably aware that the loss of biodiversity is a major environmental problem today, due primarily to habitat degradation and deforestation (see Issues in Biology for Chapters 23 and 42), but did you know that we face an equally serious loss of biodiversity in our food supply? Today, 97% of food plants that were available in 1900 are extinct, leaving the world to rely on 150 food plants, of which 20 make up 90% of our food supply. Agriculture really has two options: either cultivate crops that are adapted to local conditions, or change the conditions to suit the plants. The modernization of agriculture that began in the 1950s and '60s has taken us down the second path. Today hybrid varieties of plants are produced for high yield, uniform harvesting time, and durability for shipping across the country; and they are supported by the agrichemical industry in the form of herbicides, pesticides, and fertilizers. The result is that our food supply now depends upon a few hybrid varieties: six varieties constitute about 90% of our corn crop, four varieties about 60% of our wheat crop, and two varieties about 80% of our potato crop. The situation is similar among livestock, where, for example, Holsteins constitute about 80% of our dairy cattle and our beef cattle are mostly Angus and Hereford.

This monoculture approach to agriculture is not without problems. When a disease or pest is successful with a particular variety, the result can be disastrous. The classic example occurred when Ireland planted a single variety of potato that was susceptible to a virus. The result was the great potato famine of 1846 that drove waves of immigrants to this country. More recently, and closer to home, a fungus blighted our corn crop in 1970. Beginning in Florida, and spreading through the corn belt, it destroyed 20% of our yield that year, up to 50% in some states. So, how did we get into this situation? Prior to the Industrial Revolution, about 150 years ago, the majority of Americans lived and worked on small farms. Industrialization, however, has had such an impact on agriculture that now only about 3% of the American workforce produces enough food for our nation and for trade on the world market. In order for an increasingly smaller labor force to sustain the agricultural needs of a growing nation, changes had to be made, and technology stepped in. Now, American agriculture is largely controlled by large corporations, with the result that a few high-yield varieties of hybrid and engineered seeds, which are dependent upon the use of agrichemicals, are the standard. Hybrid seed offers a great advantage for the seller, as hybrid plants are usually either sterile or will not breed true and cannot be saved for the next planting, so the seed must be purchased again each year. Moreover, hybrid varieties can be patented so commercial developers have proprietary control over their use. This practice has led to revolt in India, where farmers are exercising methods of protest dating back to the Indian independence movement, spearheaded by Gandhi, in order to defend their rights to grow, breed, and exchange crops without control by transnational corporations.

One solution to the problem of diminishing diversity in our food supply is the preservation of heirloom varieties of plants (http://www.metroactive.com/papers/metro/09.05.96/produce-9636.html), local varieties of plants that have been grown in family gardens for generations. Probably no one in this country has done more to preserve heirloom varieties than Kent Whealy (http://csf.colorado.edu/perma/diversity/whealy.html). Kent and his wife, Diane, had been given seeds from a couple of garden varieties of plants by Diane's grandfather. These seeds had been brought over from Bavaria by his father. When the grandfather passed away that year, the Whealys decided that if these heirloom varieties were to survive, they would have to cultivate them. One of the plants was a large pink German tomato that they have grown to up to nine inches across (compare that with what you find in stores these days). In 1975 Kent began to locate others who had heirloom varieties, and since then this effort has grown into a network, known as the Seed Savers Exchange (http://www.seedsavers.org/), of some 8,000 people who are working to collect, maintain, and distribute heirloom varieties. To date, they have cataloged 17,000 varieties, including more than 4,000 of tomatoes, 700 of peas, 700 of lettuce, 600 of potatoes, and 120 of watermelons. Other seed saver organizations have also emerged, as people are beginning to appreciate native plants as part of their cultural heritage (http://fadr.msu.ru/rodale/agsieve/txt/vol5/4/art1.html).

The preservation of heirloom varieties offers many benefits for our agricultural system. First, these varieties are often adapted to local growing conditions, so that some varieties may be particularly useful in certain areas. Secondly, these varieties represent genetic diversity, a genetic library from which we can borrow information. For example, a gene resistant to the fungus that spread throughout our 1970 corn crop was found in an heirloom variety that had been kept in a farm museum. And finally, the heirloom varieties just taste better and continue to grow to be harvested over a longer season. So while most people are looking to the technologies of the future to sustain our agricultural productivity, some people are also looking to the past.

1. Why do some people feel that our current food supply is vulnerable to disaster?

2. In what ways has modern agriculture improved our ability to feed growing populations, and what problems have we inherited with these technological advancements?

3. What are heirloom varieties of plants, and how might they be important to the future of our agricultural system?

BIZARRE FACTS IN BIOLOGY

When Is A Moss Not Really A Moss?

The common names of some organisms may imply they're something entirely different from what they really are. Two such examples are reindeer moss and Spanish moss. Based on the common names, one might conclude the organisms in question are in the plant group of bryophytes and are therefore nonvascular plants with dominant gametophytes. Lace lichen (http://www.hastingsreserve.org/OakStory/LaceLichen2.html), which is sometimes mistakenly called Spanish moss, only adds to the confusion.

Reindeer moss (http://www.nps.gov/bela/html/reinmoss.htm) is like lace lichen because it is actually a lichen. It is also formed by the symbiotic relationship between a fungus and an alga. The range of this lichen is quite extensive, but it is an especially important component of the tundra biome.

Spanish moss (http://www.co.beaufort.sc.us/bftlib/spanish.htm) is actually an angiosperm. It produces tiny flowers and after fertilization a seed-containing pod forms. The seeds have a winglike structure which allows them to be caught by the wind and blown to another tree branch. Spanish moss is an epiphyte, meaning it grows on the surface of other plants. If you're still wondering how an angiosperm came to be called a moss, it's because the French and their rival Spanish explorers taunted each other with names based on the Native American name for the plant that eventually were shorted to "graybeard" and "Spanish moss."

1. What kind of organism is a lace lichen?

2. For what animals is reindeer moss an important source of food? How are these animals able to digest the reindeer moss?

3. How is a plant that is an epiphyte different from a plant that is a parasite?

KEY TERMS

alternation of generations	conifer	gymnosperm	sporophyte
angiosperm	cuticle	lignin	stoma
antheridium	flower	ovule	vascular
archegonium	fruit	pollen	vessel
bryophyte	gametophyte	seed	zygote

ANSWER KEY

SELF TEST

1. c
2. d
3. green
4. a
5. gametophytes
6. sporophyte
7. b
8. a

9. A. sporophyte
   B. gametophyte
10. b
11. a
12. e
13. c
14. a
15. b
16. b

17. a
18. rhizoids
19. A. sperm
    B. archegonium
    C. antheridium
    D. spores
20. a
21. scouring rushes
22. A. masses of sporangia
    B. haploid spores
    C. gametophyte
    D. archegonium
    E. antheridium
    F. sporophyte
23. c
24. d
25. d
26. a
27. A. seed coat
    B. stored food
    C. embryo
28. b
29. A. ovule
    B. pollen
    C. fertilization
    D. embryo
    E. seed
    F. mature sporophyte
    G. female gametophyte
30. flowers
31. a
32. c
33. a
34. A. stigma
    B. anther
    C. spore-forming cell
    D. pollen
    E. spore
    F. pollen tube
    G. female gametophyte

ESSAY CHALLENGE

1. Green algae store food as starch, use all of the same chlorophyll and accessory pigments as land plants, and also have cellulose in their cell walls.
2. Meiosis occurs during a plant's life cycle to produce spores. The spores then germinate to form haploid gametophytes which then produce gametes. As the gametophyte is already haploid, meiosis cannot be performed to produce gametes.
3. Roots to anchor the plant, a waxy cuticle to limit evaporation of water, and stomata to regulate gas exchange during photosynthesis.
4. Moss and amphibians are terrestrial groups of organisms but typically must live their lives close to water. Mosses are dependent upon nearby water because they are nonvascular plants and unable to transport water over long distances. Water is also required for fertilization, since they produce flagellated male gametes.
5. Only ferns have broad leaves, which allow them to capture more sunlight than other seedless vascular plants.
6. Pollen disperses male gametes without water, and seeds keep plant zygotes/embryos from drying out.
7. Pollen grains that are carried by the wind have wing-like structures that facilitate their transport by the wind. You should see the wings in Figure 21-7. Since most of the pollen that is windblown lands in/on places other than its intended destination (on your car or up your nose!), the plants make TONS of it to ensure that some pollen is transferred successfully.
8. Flowers help to attract pollinators, fruits attract herbivores that carry the seeds over large distances, and broad leaves give temperate-climate plants a larger surface area for photosynthesis.
9. Colder days mean an end to long sun-filled days. Shorter, colder days mean less photosynthetic activity.

MEDIA ACTIVITIES

21.3   Web Investigation: Queen of Parasites

1. Another kind of plant that makes stinky flowers is the *Titum arum*. It too is found on the Indonesian island of Sumatra.
2. Rafflesia produces unisex flowers, so a male flower must be in proximity to a female flower if pollination is to occur. High flower bud mortality minimizes the chances of male and female flowers blooming near one another. Flower blossoms last only 5-7 days. Habitat destruction means the plants are increasingly separated from each other, making it unlikely that a male and female flower will bloom near one another.
3. Squirrels and tree shrews eat the fruits and then disperse the seeds in their stools.
4. Mistletoe does its own photosynthesis but gets water and mineral nutrients from its host plant.

ISSUES IN BIOLOGY

1. Our food supply is dependent upon a limited number of strains/breeds of plants and animals. That means the genetic variability in those populations is fairly limited.
2. Today's crops are high yield and can be harvested in a minimal amount of time. The harvested materials can be shipped over long distances without being adversely affected. The problem associated with limited variation is the increased risk that an entire crop might be wiped out if the plants are or become susceptible to disease or pests. The Irish potato

famine is a great example of the problem associated with depending upon one variety of plant as a primary food source.

3. Heirloom plants are varieties of plants that have been grown locally in family gardens for years. The importance of heirloom plants is that they're adapted to the local climate and its growing conditions. There is also a great deal of genetic diversity found in heirloom plants that may ensure a species's survival. Heirloom plants tend to produce better tasting fruits and vegetables and can be harvested for a longer period of time.

BIZARRE FACTS IN BIOLOGY

1. Lace lichen is a symbiotic relationship between a fungus and an alga.
2. Reindeer moss makes up 60-70% of the winter diets of reindeer and caribou. These animals have microorganisms in their digestive systems (much like those of cows) capable of digesting the lichen.
3. An epiphyte grows on the surface of other plants without doing harm to the other plants. Epiphytes don't get nutrients from the plants on which they live. Parasitic plants draw nutrients from and may harm the plants on which they live.

CHAPTER 22: ANIMAL DIVERSITY I:
INVERTEBRATES

AT-A-GLANCE

SELF TEST

1. Which of the following is NOT a characteristic of most animals?
   a. heterotrophism
   b. capable of movement at some point in the life cycle
   c. delayed response to external stimuli
   d. sexual reproduction

2. Which of the following characteristics is NOT shared by plants and animals?
   a. multicellular
   b. eukaryotic
   c. sexual reproducers
   d. heterotrophs

3. Which of the following distinguishes animals from fungi?
   a. Animals are multicellular.
   b. Animals are heterotrophs.
   c. Animal cells lack a cell wall.
   d. Animal cells are eukaryotic.

4. How does "radial symmetry" differ from "bilateral symmetry"?
   a. A radially symmetrical animal has dorsal and ventral surfaces. Bilaterally symmetrical animals do not.
   b. Radially symmetrical animals can be divided into symmetrical halves with any plane through the central axis. Bilaterally symmetrical animals can be divided into equal halves by only one specific plane through a central axis.
   c. Radially symmetrical animals possess three embryonic germ layers, while bilaterally symmetrical animals only possess two.
   d. Most radially symmetrical animals are active, free-moving organisms throughout their lives, while bilaterally symmetrical animals are not.

5. How many planes through the central axis will divide an organism with bilateral symmetry into roughly equal halves?
   a. one   b. two
   c. many

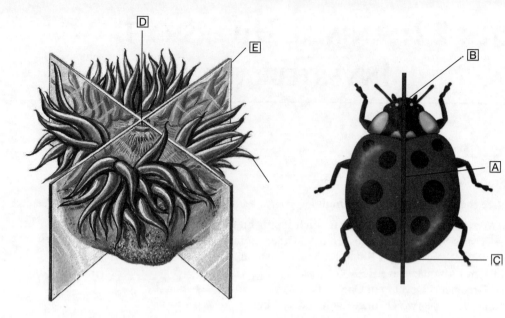

6. Body symmetry is an important criterion for classification purposes. Label the diagrams above indicating plans of symmetry and orientation.

7. Among animals with a fixed body shape, those that are elongated, such as earthworms or scorpions, have which type of symmetry?

   a. none

   b. bilateral symmetry

   c. anterior

   d. radial symmetry

   e. ventral

8. Animals that have concentrations of sensory organs (or even brains) in a well-defined head are a result of the evolutionary process called _____.

9. An animal with cephalization will have which of the following?

   a. a cephalic vein

   b. an anus

   c. sensory cells/organs and nerve cells clustered at the anterior end of the animal

   d. a completely lined fluid-filled body cavity

   e. all of the above

10. Which of the following is NOT a function associated with a body cavity?

    a. support

    b. digestion

    c. protection of internal organs

    d. allowing internal organs to operate independently of the body wall

11. Which of the following is an example of a coelom?

    a. an air-filled cavity

    b. a fluid-filled cavity

    c. a fluid-filled cavity around the digestive tract that is not surrounded by tissues that are mesodermal in origin

    d. none of the above

12. Species of which of these phyla have a pseudocoelom?

    a. Annelida

    b. Arthropoda

    c. Mollusca

    d. Nematoda

    e. Platyhelminthes

13. Species of which of the following animal phyla are deuterostomes?

    a. Annelida

    b. Arthropoda

    c. Chordata

    d. Echinodermata

    e. All except the first answer above are correct.

    f. Both the third and fourth answers are correct.

14. Which of the following is NOT associated with sponges?

    a. epithelial cells

    b. connective tissue

    c. oscula

    d. collar cells

    e. active larvae

15. What is a spicule?

    a. the basic building block of the sponge internal skeleton

    b. a type of epithelial cell

    c. an ameboid cell

    d. the structure responsible for asexual reproduction

16. The phylum Porifera shares a similar body plan throughout. Label the structures of this body plan in the diagram below.

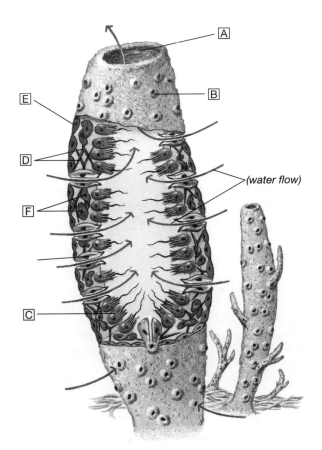

17. Although Cnidarians have both a polyp and a medusa body form, these two share common structures. Label these structures in the figure below.

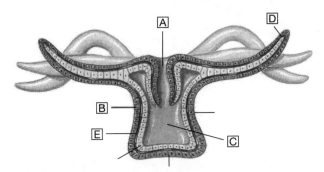

18. What are the two functions of the gastrovascular cavity of a cnidarian?
  a. digestion and prey capture
  b. respiration and sexual reproduction
  c. digestion and distribution of nutrients
  d. movement and response to threats
  e. filter blood and remove waste

19. A gastrovascular cavity, with a single opening, is the characteristic digestive system of animals in which phylum?
  a. Arthropoda   **b.** Nematoda
  c. Mollusca   **d.** Platyhelminthes
  e. Porifera

20. Which of the following is associated with or characteristic of a parasitic flatworm like a tapeworm?
  a. hooks and suckers
  b. eyespots
  c. a respiratory system
  d. cilia
  e. a complex digestive system

21. Flatworms have bunches of nerve cells that act as a simple brain. The bunches of nerve cells are called

_____.

22. Some worms (such as flukes) possess both male and female reproductive organs. Flukes are considered _____ because of this trait.

23. What is the excretory structure in annelid worms?
  a. flame cells   **b.** kidney
  c. crop   **d.** nephridium
  e. gizzard

24. Animals in which of the following phyla are segmented?
  a. Annelida   **b.** Arthropoda
  c. Echinodermata   **d.** Mollusca
  e. Both the first and second answers are correct.
  f. Both the first and fourth answers are correct.

25. Annelids (segmented worms) have many structures comparable to those observed in vertebrates (like you). Which of the following is a vertebrate structure to which there is nothing comparable in an annelid?
  a. heart   **b.** kidney
  c. lung   **d.** teeth

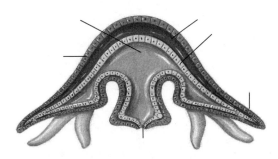

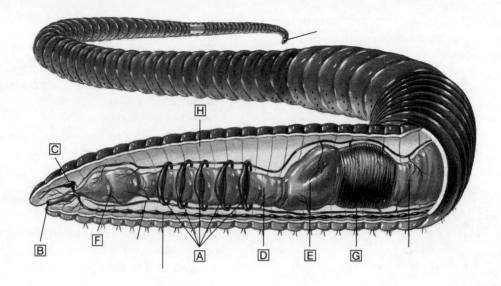

26. Label the typical annelid structures on the earthworm shown above.

27. Which of the following is NOT a mollusk?
   a. barnacle
   b. clam
   c. octopus
   d. slug
   e. snail

28. The success of the cephalopods as predators is supported by the presence of _____.
   a. beaklike jaws
   b. a complex eye
   c. a large and complex brain
   d. tentacles
   e. all of the above

29. Below is a diagram of a typical mollusk. Label the structures indicated.

30. Arthropods are a highly diverse, successful, and fairly complex group of invertebrates. Which of the following evolutionary trends is associated with the arthropods?

   a. an absence of tissues

   b. a gastrovascular cavity

   c. a pseudocoelom

   d. cephalization

31. Shedding an old, small exoskeleton to allow a larger one to grow is called _____.

32. Insects have a stage that is non-feeding and persists through metamorphosis. An insect in this stage is called a _____.

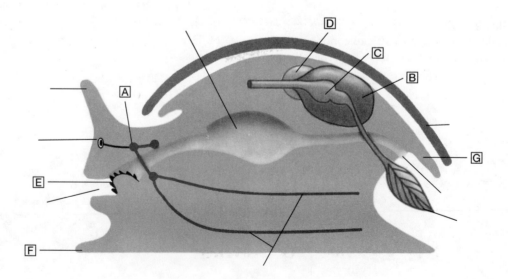

33. Arthropods have a typical body structure exemplified by the grasshopper below. Label the structures indicated.

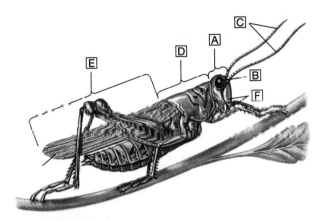

34. A starfish is an example of an animal with radial _____.

35. The water vascular system unique to echinoderms allows them to _____.
   a. move
   b. do gas exchange
   c. capture food
   d. all of the above

ESSAY CHALLENGE

1. What are some advantages and disadvantages of exhibiting radial symmetry?

2. Why do some species of worms and other animals have both male and female reproductive organs?

3. Explain why a free-living flatworm like a Planarian has cilia, eyespots, and a pharynx which are structures that are absent from a parasitic flatworm like a tapeworm.

4. Why do earthworms die on the dry sidewalks when it stops raining?

5. Most mollusks have open circulatory systems. However, the organisms in the class of cephalopods have closed circulatory systems. Explain why this difference exists.

6. What causes the supply of soft-shelled crabs (for eating purposes) to vary throughout the year?

MEDIA ACTIVITIES

To access a Media Activity visit http://www.prenhall.com/audesirk7. Log in to the Web site selected by your instructor, navigate to this chapter, and select the appropriate Media Activity number.

22.1 Architecture of Animals
Estimated time: 10 minutes

This chapter describes the anatomical features associated with the various animal phyla that indicate branching of the animal evolutionary tree. This activity will allow you to explore those features and the associated animal phyla.

22.2 Web Investigation: The Search For a Sea Monster
Estimated time: 10 minutes

Many fascinating creatures can be found in the oceans' depths. This exercise looks at the relatively limited information available about a few, better-known species.

1. The first whole giant squid specimen was discovered more than 100 years ago. Why are they so difficult to study (http://seawifs.gsfc.nasa.gov/squid.html)? One fact is well known. Giant squid are a favorite food of (http://nmml.afsc.noaa.gov/education/cetaceans/sperm2.htm) _____.

2. Probably the most famous deep-sea resident is the coelacanth. Why is it called a "living fossil" (http://www.seasky.org/monsters/sea7a1b.html)? Is it the ancestor of mammals (http://www.dinofish.com/biol.htm)? The coelacanth has two biological features (http://www.amnh.org/exhibitions/expeditions/treasure_fossil/Treasures/Coelacanth/coelacan.html) more characteristic of mammals than fish. What are they?

3. What is the most unusual feature of the gulper eel? Like many deep water species, gulpers have distinctive markers (http://www.mbayaq.org/efc/living_species/default.asp?hOri=0&hab=9&inhab=186) on their tails. What are they?

4. Many rare deep-sea species are threatened by fishing, habitat destruction, or other human interventions. What can you do to help?

ISSUES IN BIOLOGY

Heartworms—Prevention Is The Best Medicine

Dirofilaria immitis (http://www.biosci.ohio-state.edu/~parasite/dirofilaria.html) is a widely distributed organism that causes heartworm in dogs. *Dirofilaria immitis* may also parasitize cats, ferrets (http://www.afip.org/ferrets/htworm.html), and a number of other species including humans. Heartworms are classified as Nematodes (http://nematode.unl.edu/wormgen.htm) or roundworms.

Heartworms are not transmitted from one dog to another or from dogs to humans. The mosquito (http://www.avma.org/careforanimals/animatedjourneys/pethealth/canine.asp) is the vector (transmitting agent) for the parasite. When an infected dog is bitten by a mosquito, immature heartworms (microfilariae) are taken in by the feeding mosquito. In a couple weeks when the mosquito feeds again, it can pass on infective larvae to a healthy dog. The infective larvae migrate to the heart of the newly infected dog and mature into adult heartworms. The mature heartworms mate and produce new microfilaria which circulate in the infected dog's blood. A blood test (http://www.heartwormsociety.org/CanineHeartwormInfo.htm) can be done to check for the presence of circulating microfilaria and antigens from the female heartworms.

Treatment of a heartworm infection requires medications that kill both adult worms and the microfilaria. Unfortunately, the dead/dying worms often clog blood vessels, which may result in the dog's death. Minimal activity may be required for a complete recovery. The prevention (http://muextension.missouri.edu/explore/agguides/pets/g09930.htm) of heartworms is much easier and cheaper than the treatment of the disease.

1. On what continent would your dog be safe from heartworm infection (the organism is not found there)?

2. Why are ferrets likely to experience heart failure with an infection of only two worms?

3. Could your dog get heartworms even if it is an indoor dog?

4. What other major organ besides the heart is greatly affected by a heartworm infection?

5. Why would intolerance of exercise be one of the earliest detectable symptoms of heartworm infection?

BIZARRE FACTS IN BIOLOGY

Blue Bloods Aren't Just British

Blue-colored blood is found in most arthropods and mollusks. A molecule in their blood called hemocyanin transports oxygen. Hemocyanin differs from the more familiar hemoglobin because of the copper in the molecule that turns blue (http://www.mbl.edu/animals/Limulus/blood/bang.html) when exposed to oxygen.

One particular organism that has this blue blood is the horseshoe crab (http://www.photolib.noaa.gov/coastline/line0592.htm). Horseshoe crabs are more closely related to spiders than real crabs and one species (*Limulus polyphemus*) is commonly found along the Atlantic coast, especially between Virginia and New Jersey, and in the Gulf of Mexico. Horseshoe crabs feed on a variety of organisms like clams, marine worms, and algae and are in turn fed upon by immature Atlantic loggerhead turtles.

Ecologically (http://www.horseshoecrab.org/nh/eco.html), the crabs are of importance to migrating shorebirds that lay over in the Delaware Bay area en route to the birds' Canadian breeding grounds. The birds feast on the energy-rich horseshoe crabs' eggs, enabling the birds to continue their journey northward. Many other species eat the eggs and larvae of horseshoe crabs, or live symbiotically (http://www.brookdalecc.edu/staff/sandyhook/dgrant/field/limulus.htm) with the adult crabs.

Economically, the crabs are of great importance to humans. They've been used in eye research, suture material production, the development of wound dressings, and are the primary bait used by eel and conch fisheries. One of the most important uses of the crabs has been for the testing of bacterial contamination of pharmaceutical products. A substance called Limulus Amebocyte Lystate (LAL) (http://www.horseshoecrab.org/med/med.html) can be isolated from the blood of the crabs and used to detect bacterial endotoxins. The LAL assay replaced the expensive and time-consuming use of rabbits to detect bacterial contamination.

1. When hemoglobin is exposed to oxygen, what color does it become? What mineral is associated with the color of hemoglobin?

2. Since horseshoe crabs are arthropods, what process must they perform in order to grow in size? What is a disadvantage to growing in this fashion?

3. In the 1980s, horseshoe crabs began to recover from a period of overharvesting. How was the Delaware Bay ecosystem impacted by the overharvesting prior to the 1980s and how did the recovery of the crabs affect this ecosystem?

4. What kind of symbiotic relationship does the horseshoe crab appear to have with the *Limulus* leech, *Bdelloura*?

5. What specific class of bacteria produces the endotoxins for which the LAL assay tests?

KEY TERMS

bilateral symmetry	endoderm	invertebrate	protostome
budding	endoskeleton	larva	pseudocoelom
cephalization	exoskeleton	mesoderm	pupa
closed circulatory system	ganglion	metamorphosis	radial symmetry
coelom	gill	molt	segmentation
compound eye	hemocoel	nerve cord	tissue
deuterostome	hermaphroditic	open circulatory system	vertebrate
ectoderm	hydrostatic skeleton	parasite	

ANSWER KEY

SELF TEST

1. c
2. d
3. c
4. b
5. a
6. A. plane of symmetry
   B. anterior
   C. posterior
   D. central axis
   E. plane of symmetry in a radially symmetrical animal

7. b
8. cephalization
9. c
10. b
11. d
12. d
13. f
14. b
15. a
16. A. osculum
    B. pore
    C. collar cell

D. spicules
E. epithelial cell
F. amoeboid cell

17. A. mouth
   B. body wall
   C. gastrovascular cavity
   D. tentacle
   E. mesoglea

18. c
19. d
20. a
21. ganglia
22. hermaphrodites or hermaphroditic
23. d
24. e
25. c
26. A. hearts
   B. mouth
   C. brain
   D. esophagus
   E. crop
   F. pharynx
   G. gizzard
   H. coelom
27. a
28. e
29. A. ganglia (brain)
   B. coelom
   C. heart
   D. gland
   E. radula
   F. foot
   G. mantle
30. d
31. molting
32. pupa
33. A. head
   B. compound eye
   C. antennae
   D. thorax
   E. abdomen
   F. mouth parts
34. symmetry
35. d

ESSAY CHALLENGE

1. The animal often is free to move in any direction, but may be unable to control those movements well (such as jellyfish).

2. Hermaphrodites have both male and female reproductive organs and can often self-fertilize. The ability to perform self-fertilization would be an advantage to a parasite like a tapeworm that may never encounter another tapeworm while living in the intestine of its host.

3. A free-living flatworm has to get its own food, so it will use its eyespots to "find" its food, its cilia to get to its food, and its pharynx to take in its food. Since a parasitic flatworm gets its food from its host, it has no need for those structures.

4. Earthworms lack specialized respiratory structures, depending instead on moist skin for exchanging gases. When the sidewalks dry after it stops raining, the earthworm's skin dries out, and it is unable to do gas exchange. No gas exchange = no ATP production.

5. Cephalopods are especially active mollusks. An open circulatory system (less efficient than a closed) wouldn't supply the cells with enough glucose and oxygen to meet the demands for energy. Other mollusks are not especially active, so an open circulatory system's less efficient delivery of glucose and oxygen is sufficient.

6. Soft-shelled crabs are crabs that recently molted (shed their old exoskeleton). Since crabs don't molt year round, the supply of soft-shelled crabs varies depending upon the molting of the crabs.

MEDIA ACTIVITIES

22.2 Web Investigation: The Search for a Sea Monster

1. Giant squid are difficult to study because they live in such deep waters, and a live one has never been observed in its natural habitat nor has one been maintained in an aquarium. Giant squid are a favorite food of sperm whales.

2. Coelacanth fossils that date back over 410 million years have been found, and then in 1938 a live coelacanth was caught. Coelacanths may be the ancestors of the tetrapods (including the mammals), but evidence also points to the possibility that lungfish may be the ancestors of the tetrapods. Coelacanths have bony, fleshy fins and produce eggs that hatch internally, which are features more characteristic of mammals than fish.

3. Gulper eels can unhinge their jaws and stretch their stomachs enough to consume a fish the size that they are. The tips of their tails have a bioluminescent organ.

4. Use public transportation, carpool, recycle, and choose seafood that is not threatened.

ISSUES IN BIOLOGY

1. Antarctica. The parasite is found in at least some part of all the other continents.

2. Ferret hearts are quite small and unable to handle a large worm load.

3. Yes, because the female mosquito that transmits the microfilaria is very small and easily slips through cracks around openings like doors and windows.

4. Lungs.
5. Since the heart and lungs are the major organs affected by heartworm, the exchange and distribution of oxygen are compromised, which limits the production of ATP needed for exercise.

BIZARRE FACTS IN BIOLOGY

1. Hemoglobin turns red in the presence of oxygen. Iron is the mineral that gives hemoglobin its red color.
2. They must shed their exoskeleton to grow. This process is known as molting. After molting, the organism is vulnerable to predators until its new exoskeleton hardens.
3. Prior to the crabs' recovery, species which relied on the crabs and their eggs for food would have turned to other food sources (impacting their numbers) or declined in numbers themselves. After the recovery of the crabs, the species that rely on them for food should have experienced population increases. A greater number of migratory birds should have been attracted to the bay area (which was the case and that's how scientists made the connection between the birds and the crabs).
4. Biologists now seem to think that *Bdelloura* has a parasitic relationship with *Limulus*, given the damage done to the book gills by the larvae of the leech.
5. Gram negative bacteria.

CHAPTER 23: ANIMAL DIVERSITY II: VERTEBRATES

AT-A-GLANCE

Case Study: Fish Story

23.1 What Are the Key Features of Chordates?
Invertebrate Chordates Lack a Backbone
Vertebrates Have a Backbone

23.2 What Are the Major Groups of Vertebrates?
Some Vertebrates Lack Jaws
Jawed Fishes Rule Earth's Waters
Earth Watch: Frogs in Peril
Amphibians Live a Double Life
Reptiles and Birds Are Adapted for Life on Land
Mammals Provide Milk to Their Offspring

Evolutionary Connections: Are Humans a Biological Success?

Case Study Revisited: Fish Story

Links to Life: Do Animals Belong in Laboratories?

SELF TEST

1. Which of the following is a characteristic of chordates?
   a. ventral, hollow nerve cord
   b. radial symmetry
   c. protostome development
   d. a true body cavity (coelom)
   e. all of the above

2. Species of which of the following animal phyla are deuterostomes?
   a. Annelida
   b. Arthropoda
   c. Chordata
   d. Echinodermata
   e. All except the first answer above are correct.
   f. Both the third and fourth answers are correct.

3. All members of the phylum Chordata, whether human or lancelet, share certain key features. Which of the following traits is NOT characteristic of all chordates?
   a. dorsal, hollow nerve cord
   b. notochord
   c. pharyngeal gill slits
   d. tail
   e. bony endoskeleton

4. The only chordate feature present in adult humans is the _____.
   a. post-anal tail
   b. dorsal, hollow nerve cord
   c. pharyngeal gill slits
   d. notochord

5. The invertebrate chordates lack _____.
   a. pharyngeal gill slits
   b. a post-anal tail
   c. a backbone
   d. a dorsal, hollow nerve cord
   e. all of the above

6. Which of the following enables you to identify the lamprey species that are parasitic?
   a. suckerlike mouths lined with teeth
   b. complex eyes
   c. fleshy fins
   d. bony skeletons
   e. jaws with rows of razor-sharp teeth

7. Cartilaginous fish are characterized by _____.
   a. a three-chambered heart
   b. poorly developed lungs
   c. a skeleton formed entirely of cartilage
   d. milk-producing mammary glands

8. Which of the vertebrate groups is the most diverse, but often overlooked because of humans' habitat bias?
   a. bony fish   b. jawless fish
   c. mammals   d. birds

9. The range of amphibian habitats on land is limited by _____.
   a. eggs protected by a jellylike coating
   b. use of their skin as a supplementary respiratory organ
   c. external fertilization
   d. All of these are correct.

10. Amphibians are most like _____.
   a. mosses
   b. flowering plants
   c. conifers
   d. ferns
11. Reptiles are well adapted to living in drier habitats because of their _____.
   a. hollow bones
   b. production of a shelled amniotic egg
   c. two-chambered heart
   d. moist skin used as a supplemental respiratory organ
   e. external fertilization
12. The ability of birds to fly is facilitated by their _____
   a. four-chambered heart
   b. lungs supplemented by air sacs
   c. external development in a shelled egg
   d. hollow bones
   e. All of these are correct.
13. Which of the following characteristics are shared by both arthropods and mammals?
   a. a well-developed nervous system
   b. a closed circulatory system
   c. an internal skeleton
   d. compound eyes
14. What defines, or distinguishes, a mammal from other vertebrates?
   a. its hairless exterior
   b. its primitive, simple brain
   c. milk-producing glands
   d. the fact that most mammals complete the great majority of their development outside the uterus
15. A long period of uterine development and gas, nutrient, and waste exchange between the mother and embryo are characteristic of _____.
   a. all mammals
   b. birds
   c. marsupials
   d. placental mammals
   e. monotremes
16. The group of terrestrial vertebrates that may be indicators of environmental degradation is the _____.
   a. amphibians
   b. bony fishes
   c. lancelets
   d. reptiles

ESSAY CHALLENGE

1. Identify four features of chordates and explain why these features are important.

2. Explain why it might be important for an animal to be amphibious.

3. Mosses are often referred to as the amphibians of the plant kingdom. What are the similarities between mosses and amphibians that cause people to say that?

4. Why do some scientists believe that birds are recent descendants of reptiles?

5. Why are lungs supplemented by air sacs and a four-chambered heart essential to a bird's ability to fly?

6. Why are birds and mammals warm-blooded?

7. What are some benefits and disadvantages of being "warm-blooded?"

MEDIA ACTIVITIES

To access a Media Activity visit http://www.prenhall.com/audesirk7. Log in to the Web site selected by your instructor, navigate to this chapter, and select the appropriate Media Activity number.

23.1 Web Investigation: Fish Story
Estimated time: 10 minutes

If you read the case study in Chapter 23, you know the coelacanth (http://www.dinofish.com/) was once believed to be extinct. The scientific community was amazed when one was discovered (http://www.austmus.gov.au/fishes/fishfacts/fish/coela.htm) in the waters off South Africa in 1938. Fourteen long years went by before a second coelacanth was found. Now there are estimated to be 1000 or fewer coelacanths living in the waters off South Africa. The most recent find (http://www.scienceinafrica.co.za/2003/october/coelacanth.htm) in September, 2003 was off southern Tanzania, so the range of coelacanths off the coast of Africa may be more extensive than previously believed.

In 1997 a coelacanth was noticed at a fish market by Dr. Mark Erdmann who was honeymooning in Indonesia (http://www.washingtonpost.com/wp-srv/national/horizon/nov98/fishstory.htm) 6000 miles from where coelacanths were known to live. Dr. Erdmann spoke briefly with the fisherman and photographed the fish, but did nothing else because he thought he must have missed the announcement about a second group of coelacanths off Indonesia. When he returned to Berkeley (http://www.ucmp.berkeley.edu/vertebrates/coelacanth/coelacanths.html) a week later he realized that he'd made an important new find in Indonesia. Genetic analysis of a second Indonesian fish indicated that the Indonesian coelacanth was indeed a different species of coelacanth.

Today many people may only be familiar with the coelacanth thanks to the attention it received in a Volkswagen commercial (http://www.priweb.org/ed/ICTHOL/ICTHOL02_peer_review_papers/32.html). In the commercial the coelacanth was compared by an auto mechanic to the "extinct" full-size tire. However, the scientific community is very interested in the coelacanths because there are many unanswered questions about them and further study of them may provide insight into the evolution of the tetrapods (four-legged animals).

1. How are the paired fins of coelacanths similar to our arms and legs?

2. What did scientists believe the fleshy fins of the coelacanths indicated about the fish?

3. Coelacanths are ovoviviparous meaning they give birth to live offspring (known as pups). What advantage is there to bearing live offspring as opposed to practicing external development, which is typical of many fish?

ISSUES IN BIOLOGY

What Is Happening to the Frogs?

The spectacular golden toad, once found in the montane preserve of Monte Verde, Costa Rica, has not been seen since 1989. The gastric brooding frog of Queensland, Australia (http://cgee.hamline.edu/frogs/science/declines.html), whose bizarre parenting activity involved the female swallowing her fertilized eggs (her stomach stopped secreting digestive enzymes and she brooded her eggs there until they were tiny, but fully formed froglets, capable of life on their own), disappeared about the same time. In California a recent search for frog populations first studied 75 years before found that there were only four of seven species at 26 of 70 documented locations. Similarly, at various South American sites, once abundant species have become rare or extinct. In Minnesota, deformed frogs (http://www.pca.state.mn.us/hot/frogs.html) are becoming common. All over the world, it appears, amphibians are in trouble. What catastrophe is responsible? Are the frogs vanishing?

Scientists first became aware of a problem in the late 1980s. Presentations at international conferences in 1989 and 1990 made it clear that there might be a problem. (Remember that in any scientific query, the answers are no better than the data, and in 1990 good, quantitative data were in short supply.) Although many herpetologists—those who study amphibians and reptiles—believed that they had witnessed declines in amphibian populations, there were very few long-term studies to address the issue. The result was that herpetologists organized a response to the perceived loss of the animals that they studied. An international organization, the Declining Amphibian Populations Task Force (http://www.open.ac.uk/OU/Academic/Biology/J_Baker/JBtxt.htm), and a North American organization, the North American Amphibian Monitoring Program (http://www.pwrc.usgs.gov/naamp), were established to coordinate research efforts.

First, there was the question of whether or not the numbers of amphibians really were declining. Of course, it is pretty hard to argue that extinction is not a decline and that the golden toads and the gastric brooding frogs were not species that were merely being overlooked. But the losses of these species were not enough on which to base an argument for the existence of a worldwide decline of amphibian populations. The problem is that amphibians, especially most salamanders (but many frogs as well) are secretive animals that are not regularly or frequently seen by very many people unless they are closely observed (studied). The argument was made that populations being studied were probably quite abundant when they were chosen, and that there is evidence that at least some amphibian populations undergo dramatic size fluctuation, remaining small for several years. Therefore, herpetologists ought to expect decline in some of their study populations. That argument did not really explain why impressions of decline were so widespread among herpetologists, nor did it explain the California study.

Currently, we are getting better data. Recent studies of the frog fauna of the Monteverde Cloud Forest Preserve in Costa Rica found that it was "highly improbable" that the 20 species (of an original fauna of 50 species) that disappeared after 1987 population crashes that claimed the golden toad could be the result of normal population changes. Even those previously abundant species that survived the crash do not appear to be recovering. Another study of a nearby montane ecosystem in Costa Rica also found "atypical population fluctuations" (declines) of aquatic breeding amphibian species.

Why should we care about what is happening to amphibians? One reason to care is that amphibians have been compared to the canaries miners took with them into mines. When oxygen levels declined too far, the sensitive canaries quit singing, thus warning the miners to leave. Amphibians, with their dual lives on land and in water and their thin permeable skins, may be very sensitive to degradation of their habitat. Although many populations of amphibians have disappeared as a result of habitat loss (the United States has lost more than 50% of its wetlands; some states like California and Ohio have lost nearly 95%), the population declines and extinctions that have occurred in montane areas of the western United States, Costa Rica, South America, and Australia have occurred in preserved habitats. Pollution is suspected as one cause of the Minnesota frog deformities. Some evidence exists that UVB radiation, increasing as a result of ozone loss, may harm sensitive amphibians (http://www.sciam.com/article.cfm?articleID= 000D5DCC-CA4A-1E1C-8B3B809EC588EEDF&catID=2), though not all populations are sensitive and some are not exposed to much sunlight. Similarly, some amphibian populations have demonstrated a sensitivity to waters acidified by acid deposition. Therefore, another reason to care is that, since human fingerprints seem to be all over the mystery of the amphibian declines, humans have a moral obligation to figure out the problem and correct it—before the amphibians are all gone!

1. Why are amphibians "caught between two worlds," namely aquatic and terrestrial habitats?

2. Why do amphibians have thin, permeable skins?

3. How do environmental changes to their habitats actually threaten the life or health of amphibians?

BIZARRE FACTS IN BIOLOGY

Busy Birds

Most birds fly and flying requires LOTS of energy (remember your study of ATP synthesis back in Chapter 8?). If you've already read Chapter 23, you know that birds have many adaptations like hollow bones, four-chambered hearts, and lungs supplemented by air sacs that enable them to fly.

The energy to fly requires high metabolism, and high metabolism requires lots of food and oxygen. The metabolism of hummingbirds (http://www.learner.org/jnorth/tm/humm/EnergyTorpor.html) is especially high, so they spend a great deal of time eating. They will visit hundreds of flowers a day in search of nectar. If the hummingbirds are unable to collect enough food, they must do something to conserve energy.

The hummingbirds' four-chambered heart prevents oxygenated and deoxygenated blood from mixing, so more oxygen can be delivered to the tissues that use it to make ATP. More oxygen can also be delivered if the heartbeat (http://www.rubythroat.org/RTHUAnatomyMain.html) is faster and the respiratory rate is high. When a hummingbird is flying, its heart rate may increase to 1220 beats per minute.

1. Hummingbirds weigh 1/10 of an ounce and need 10 calories per day. That equates to 100 calories per ounce. So that you can better relate to the hummingbird's eating dilemma, complete the following activity.

   A. Indicate the number of calories per serving in your favorite food. Be sure to share what your favorite food is too.
   B. Indicate the number of calories per day you would need if you burned energy at the same rate as a hummingbird. Show all your work.
   C. Indicate the number of servings of your favorite food you'd have to consume per day if you burned energy at the same rate as a hummingbird. Show all your work.

2. What do hummingbirds do to conserve energy when they have a bad food-finding day or when the weather is not conducive to feeding?

3. How does the ruby-throated hummingbird's resting heart rate and respiratory rate compare with the average human's resting heart rate and respiratory rate?

KEY TERMS

amnion	mammary gland	notochord	post-anal tail
amniote egg	marsupial	pharyngeal gill slit	vertebral column
cartilage	monotreme	placenta	vertebrate
endoskeleton	nerve chord	placental	

ANSWER KEY

SELF TEST

1. d
2. f
3. e
4. b
5. c
6. a
7. c
8. a
9. d
10. a
11. b
12. e
13. a
14. c
15. d
16. a

ESSAY CHALLENGE

1. The notochord, dorsal nerve cord, pharyngeal gill slits, and post-anal tail all exist in chordates and show a specialization of function that is important for chordates. For example, the notochord allows the animal to develop strong muscles, which are anchored to the notochord.
2. If conditions are particularly bad in one habitat, the amphibian can move to the other. For short periods of time, this strategy is effective.
3. Amphibians and moss both need water for reproduction. Moss produce swimming sperm, so water is required for fertilization. Amphibians perform external fertilization and development, which means water is required. Amphibians must keep their skin moist in order to use it for respiration.
4. Feathers appear to be very specialized types of scales, and birds also have scales on their legs.

5. Lungs supplemented by air sacs enable a bird to acquire the large amounts of oxygen needed for the ATP synthesis which supports flying. A four-chambered heart prevents oxygenated and deoxygenated blood from mixing, which ensures cells receive lots of oxygen and are able to synthesize lots of ATP.
6. The high metabolic rate of birds and mammals means they generate a lot of ATP. When the energy in glucose is transformed into ATP, a great deal of energy is lost as heat (the second law of thermodyamics). The loss of energy as heat maintains a high body temperature.
7. "Warm-blooded" creatures can regulate their own body temperature, but this ability consumes large amounts of energy.

MEDIA ACTIVITIES

23.1   Web Investigation: Fish Story

1. The movement of coelacanths' paired fins is similar to the movement of our arms and legs.
2. Scientists believed that the coelacanths might use their fleshy fins to "walk" along on the ocean floor, but none have been observed exhibiting such behavior. The fleshy fins were also thought to indicate a relationship between the coelacanths and the ancestor(s) of the tetrapods. Now the lungfish are thought to be more closely related to the tetrapods than are the coelacanths.
3. Internal development should provide the offspring with greater protection against predation. A female with offspring developing internally will take the offspring with her when a predator approaches. Organisms that practice external development may protect their offspring (eggs) to some extent, but will generally save their own neck when there is real danger from a predator. Many organisms (like sea turtles) that practice external development lay their eggs and leave, which means the offspring are really vulnerable to predation.

ISSUES IN BIOLOGY

1. Amphibians reproduce externally which means water is needed to prevent drying out of the gametes and embryos. They use gills (which require water) for gas exchange during the larval stage of their lives. The lungs they use for gas exchange as terrestrial adults are small and saclike which means they must also rely on using their moist thin skin for gas exchange.
2. Amphibians do gas exchange with their thin permeable skin, which is also typically moist. The ability to do gas exchange with their skin supplements that gas exchange they do with their small saclike lungs.
3. Exposure to greater UV radiation may kill or harm amphibian embryos, cause eye damage and limb deformities in adults. Pollutants may be responsible for limb deformities or may make amphibians more susceptible to parasitic infections.

BIZARRE FACTS IN BIOLOGY

1. These answers will vary from student to student, since personal information about their weight and favorite food is required to complete the activity.
2. Hummingbirds go into torpor to conserve energy. Torpor is a sleep-like state in which their body temperature and heart rate drop dramatically.
3. The hummingbird resting heart rate is 250 beats per minute, which is ~3.5 times that of the human. The hummingbird resting respiratory rate is 250 breaths per minute, which is almost 18 times that of the human.

CHAPTER 24: PLANT ANATOMY AND NUTRIENT TRANSPORT

AT-A-GLANCE

SELF TEST

1. The primary function of the vascular tissue system in plants is to _____.
   a. transport water, minerals, and sugars throughout the plant
   b. store mineral and food reserves for the plant
   c. cover and protect the outer surfaces of the plant
   d. perform photosynthesis within the plant body

2. The evaporation and loss of water vapor through the leaves of a plant is called _____.
   a. photosynthesis
   b. respiration
   c. cohesion
   d. transpiration

3. In plants a region of actively dividing cells (such as there is at the tip of the root or stem) is referred to as _____.
   a. parenchyma
   b. vascular tissue
   c. ground tissue
   d. a meristem

4. The primary photosynthetic cells of dicot leaves are _____.
   a. epidermal cells
   b. guard cells
   c. mesophyll parenchyma cells
   d. collenchyma cells

5. An association between a plant root and a fungus that helps the plant attain nutrients from the soil is called _____.
   a. mycorrhizae   b. root nodules
   c. root hair   d. lichen

6. The location of leaf attachment on a stem is called a _____.
   a. branch   b. node
   c. petiole   d. internode

7. Vascular tissue of plants is composed of _____.
   a. xylem for moving water and minerals, and phloem for moving products of photosynthesis
   b. xylem for moving products of photosynthesis, and phloem for moving water and minerals
   c. stomata for moving water, and guard cells for moving products of photosynthesis
   d. cortex for moving water, and root hairs for moving products of photosynthesis

8. The cohesion-tension mechanism of water movement occurs when _____.
   a. the buildup of water pressure in the roots forces water up the stem through the xylem
   b. the water is loaded into vessel elements by active transport at the source and unloaded at the sink to ensure a constant movement of water through the xylem
   c. the transpiration of water from the leaf surface pulls water up the xylem as a result of hydrogen bonding between water molecules
   d. the stem contracts and decreases its diameter to force the water molecules through the tracheids and vessels

9. During secondary growth, the vascular cambium _____.
   a. divides to form xylem toward the center and phloem toward the outside
   b. divides to form the cortex and pith
   c. is crushed by the rapidly dividing xylem and phloem cells
   d. produces cork and cork parenchyma cells to form the periderm

10. While visiting your aunt in Michigan, one morning you find a beaver gnawing on a birch tree. You scare it off but not before it has removed a strip of bark all the way around the tree. Despite erecting a fence around the tree to prevent additional damage, the tree dies after a few months. The first event that would occur in this tree's death would be _____.
    a. death of the leaves of the tree, because they stopped receiving water from the soil
    b. death of the leaves of the tree, because they could no longer produce sugars by photosynthesis
    c. death of the roots of the tree, because they would no longer be able to absorb water from the soil
    d. death of the roots of the tree, because they would no longer be able to receive carbohydrates from the leaves

11. A tree trunk increases in size. What is this process called, and what are the mechanisms responsible for such growth?
    a. primary growth; mitotic cell division and cell differentiation
    b. secondary growth; mitotic cell division and cell differentiation
    c. differentiated cells; undifferentiated meristem
    d. apical meristem; mitosis alone

12. What main type of ground tissue would you be ingesting if you ate a carrot?

a. parenchyma

b. collenchyma

c. sclerenchyma

d. parenchyma, collenchyma, and sclerenchyma in equal parts

13. Which of the following is NOT a step by which minerals become absorbed by roots?

a. diffusion of minerals into root hairs

b. diffusion through cytoplasm to pericycle cells

c. active transport into the extracellular space around the xylem

d. diffusion into the xylem

14. How do plants overcome the force of gravity and make water flow upward?

a. transpiration of water from the leaves

b. tension

c. hydrogen bonds between water molecules

d. cohesion

e. all of the above

15. How do plants balance the need to photosynthesize, which requires carbon dioxide from the atmosphere, with the water loss that comes from transpiration?

a. by regulating the opening and closing of the stomata

b. by regulating the potassium ion concentration within the guard cells

c. Potassium concentrations are increased when photosynthesis outstrips cellular respiration due to the influence of low carbon dioxide levels under these conditions.

d. all of the above

16. _____ are located at the ends of roots and shoots.

17. _____ tissue consists of cells with hardened and thick secondary cell walls.

18. _____ transports water and minerals from roots to the rest of a plant.

19. _____ transports water, sugars, amino acids, and hormones throughout a plant.

20. Most land plants form symbiotic relationships with fungi to form root-complexes called _____.

21. _____ is the process in which water evaporates through the stomata in a leaf.

22. Identify the anatomy of the plant as indicated below.

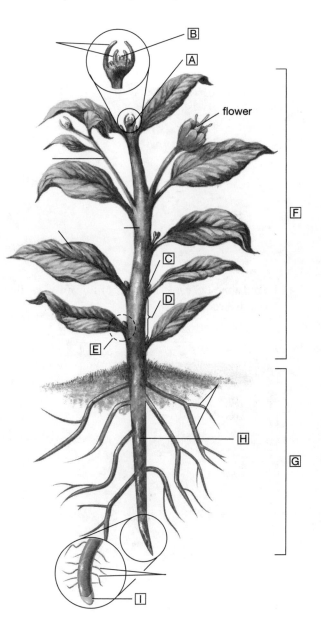

271

23. Identify the structures seen below on this typical root.

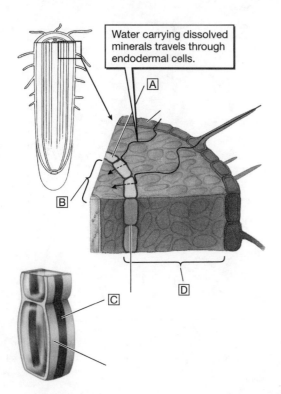

C

A

B

D

E

F

24. Identify the indicated portions of this cross section through a root.

Water carrying dissolved minerals travels through endodermal cells.

A

B

C

D

25. Label the layers of a typical tree trunk.

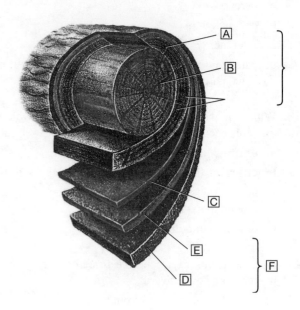

A

B

C

E

D

F

26. The typical dicot leaf has structures that are easily identifiable. Label these structures in the diagram below.

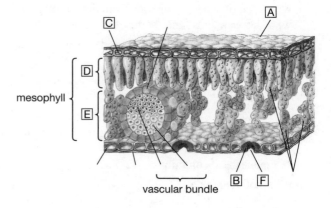

C

A

D

mesophyll

E

B   F

vascular bundle

27. You have a species of oak tree that is known to produce anthocyanins. What could you measure that would indicate if the tree is going to produce bright red instead of a dark purple color in the fall?

a. a cell sap with pH 6.5

b. a cell sap with pH 3.0

c. the concentration of carotenes

d. sugar concentration of the cell sap

e. anthocyanin concentration of the cell sap

28. You are on an expedition through a tropical rain forest and find a plant that has woody growth, parallel leaf venation, and flower parts in multiples of four. Why is the botanist of the group incredulous?

a. It is a newly discovered monocot.

b. It is a newly discovered dicot.

c. It doesn't fit either of the major categories for flowering plants and may represent a lost link in evolution.

d. It represents a hybrid between monocot and dicot plants.

29. Maple syrup is produced from fluid taken from sugar maple trees in the late winter or very early spring. Why are these trees tapped only during this time of the year?

a. This is when roots serve as a source, and young buds are the sink.

b. This is the time of year roots are a sink.

c. This is the only time when sugars are transported.

d. Sapwood requires cold temperatures to transport fluids.

30. Which tissue in the above ground portion of a plant body contains the least densely packed cells? What is the function of these air spaces?

a. collenchyma; serves as a source of oxygen for photosynthesis

b. pith; helps with support

c. xylem; allows pressure for transport

d. spongy and palisade parenchyma; serves as a source of carbon dioxide for photosynthesis and oxygen for cellular respiration

31. When a tree is girdled, there is often a slight increase in diameter just above the region where the bark was removed.

Select one: True   False

32. Why would one NOT expect to find root hairs in the area between the region of cell elongation and the root cap?

a. There are no epidermal cells in this area.

b. The root cap is pushed down between soil particles by cells undergoing elongation. Root hairs would be torn off. Root hairs are formed later in development in the mature region.

c. There is no vascular cylinder in these regions.

d. These regions of the root do not require water.

33. Absence of ATP would not have any impact on mineral uptake, since minerals are transported in xylem, and transpiration is a passive process.

Select one: True   False

34. Most of the biomass in plants is due to uptake of minerals from nutrient-rich soils.

Select one: True   False

35. One would expect water transport to be the same in the xylem if water was not a polar molecule.

Select one: True   False

36. Pressure-flow theory explains sugar movement in phloem from _____, where sugars are actively made, toward _____, where sugars are used or converted to starch.

a. sink; source

b. sink; sink

c. source; sink

d. source; source

e. none of the above

ESSAY CHALLENGE

1. How do roots acquire minerals from the soil?

2. Compare and contrast primary and secondary growth in a plant.

3. What purpose do the bacteria-filled nodules on the roots of legumes serve?

4. Every parenchyma cell of a leaf is within 1–2 cells of a vein. What systems would be affected in a mutant individual with parenchyma cells that are 6–7 cells away from a vein. How would the(se) system(s) be affected?

5. What is the difference between sapwood and heartwood?

6. How do branched roots develop?

7. Which type of beneficial microbe can enhance forest health? What benefits does this association provide to the microbe and the trees?

8. When a tree is girdled, it still has functional xylem to bring water and minerals up the trunk. Why does it eventually die?

9. Why is it essential that water molecules are polar for the cohesion-tension theory of movement in xylem?

10. How do guard cells open and close stomata?

11. (a) What are three environmental factors that affect potassium transport into/out of guard cells? (b) What effect do they have? (c) Which one will override the other two?

12. List the steps involved in the pressure-flow theory of sugar movement in phloem.

13. Associations with nitrogen-fixing bacteria are one way some plants can thrive in nitrogen-poor soils. Some bog plants have a different adaptation to increase nitrogen availability. How do they accomplish this? Why are nitrogen-fixing bacteria not an option for these bog plants?

MEDIA ACTIVITIES

To access a Media Activity visit http://www.prenhall.com/audesirk7. Log in to the Web site selected by your instructor, navigate to this chapter, and select the appropriate Media Activity number.

24.1 Plant Anatomy
Estimated time: 5 minutes

This tutorial allows you to move about the plant body. Click on the plant structure to zoom in on it and learn more details about its function.

24.2 Primary and Secondary Growth
Estimated time: 5 minutes

Explore the relationship between primary and secondary growth in a plant stem.

24.3 Nutrient Up-take
Estimated time: 5 minutes

Explore how roots take up nutrients from the soil.

24.4 Plant Transport Mechanisms
Estimated time: 5 minutes

Explore the structures and mechanisms plants use to transport water, minerals, and sugars throughout the plant body.

24.5 Web Investigation: Why Do Leaves Turn Red in the Fall?
Estimated time: 10 minutes

We are fortunate to be able to enjoy the fall leaf color changes. Fall "leaf peeper" season is not only enjoyable, but it also provides thousands of dollars of income from tourists to the Northeastern USA. But what does all of this accomplish for the trees? And how are the colors developed? The first question is still under very active investigation. Visit this site on fall leaf colors (http://scifun.chem.wisc.edu/chemweek/fallcolr/fallcolr.html) to answer the following questions about the chemistry and environmental factors involved in fall leaf color.

1. Chlorophyll is not a very light-stable compound. How does the leaf maintain chlorophyll amounts during the summer?

2. Carotenes are more stable and persist in leaves even as chlorophyll breaks down and exits the leaf. What is the function of carotenes?

3. Anthocyanins are water-soluble pigments that produce the red leaf colors. What is the role of pH in determining whether the anthocyanins appear bright red or purple?

4. What role do cold temperatures play in fall leaf color?

5. How does dry weather affect red leaf color?

ISSUES IN BIOLOGY

How Is Hydroponics Possible?

Prior to the sixteenth century it was generally accepted that plants grow by acquiring or feeding from some substance in the soil, which caused them to increase their mass, a point of view that is still attractive to many today. From the sixteenth-century plant growth experiments of van Helmont to those of the present day, we now know that plant growth is not so easily explained as a plant "eating soil." Today we understand that plants acquire the resources necessary for their growth from several sources. From the atmosphere comes carbon dioxide and oxygen, which supplies the carbon used to build organic molecules and the oxygen needed for cellular respiration. The hydrogen needed to build carbohydrates is derived from water. From the sun comes the energy necessary to convert atmospheric carbon dioxide and water into plant sugars. (Review Chapter 7, "Capturing Solar Energy: Photosynthesis.") And from a source such as the soil come the inorganic elements that are essential to the proper growth and development of the plant.

While the source of these essential elements in most natural systems is from the breakdown of material in the soil, in fact any solution containing the essential elements may serve as the plant's source for these substances. Thus was born the plant-growing technique of hydroponics, in which plants are raised in soilless conditions, their roots bathed in a water solution containing those nutrients required for plant growth (http://archimedes.galilei.com/raiar/histhydr.html).

Experiments in which plants were grown in water solutions containing known quantities of various elements have led to the classification of certain elements as essential for plant growth. (See section 24.6 "How Do Plants Acquire Nutrients?" in your textbook.) Further, some of these elements were found to be required in relatively large quantities, the macronutrients, while others were found to be required in very small amounts, the micronutrients. If one or more of these essential nutrients are lacking, plant growth suffers and the plant commonly displays characteristic deficiency symptoms (http://www.ag.uiuc.edu/~vista/html_pubs/hydro/symptoms.html).

With this information and the experimentally determined needs of specific plant species, a large number of "recipes" for plant nutrient solutions have been devised. One of the earliest of these, and one that can still be successfully used today, was developed by Knop and is known as Knop's nutrient solution. Its formulation is as follows:

Compound	g/l
KNO_3	0.2
$Ca(NO_3)_2$	0.8
KH_2PO_4	0.2
$MgSO_4 - 7H_2O$	0.2
$FePO_4$	0.1

This and other nutrient solution formulations are currently being used to grow plants in soilless conditions not only for plant research purposes, but also to raise plants commercially.

1. What advantages do you see in using hydroponics for growing commercial crops? Any disadvantages?

2. Besides carbon, oxygen, and hydrogen, the macronutrients required for plants include nitrogen, potassium, phosphorus, and magnesium. How are these elements used in the plant's physiology? Why are these required in relatively large amounts?

3. Some would say that growing plants out of soil is not natural, that using a source of minerals that is not organic or natural results in plants that are deficient and unnatural. What is the difference between organic and hydroponic gardening? Is one better than the other? Which would you select to use as a source of food?

BIZARRE FACTS IN BIOLOGY

Plants That Remind Us of Leaches?

Most plants produce their food through photosynthesis (see Chapter 7). There are some intriguing exceptions—parasitic plants. These plants attach themselves to a host plant and obtain sugars by sinking rootlike structures into the host plant. They are ecto-parasites, similar to leaches and ticks in the animal kingdom. Some of the common parasitic plants include dodder, mistletoe, and *Rafflesia*, which produces the world's largest flower. Dodder and mistletoe (http://www.sarracenia.com/faq/faq5970.html) can be very destructive to their hosts. Dwarf mistletoe (http://www.fs.fed.us/r4/boise/field_trip/meadow/bugscrud.html) is much more damaging to the host than other types of mistletoes, because it is not capable of photosynthesis. *Rafflesia* (http://www.senckenberg.uni-frankfurt.de/private/gwinter/rafl.htm) is extremely rare and found only in limited regions of the world. The common name is the corpse lily—guess what type of pollinator is attracted to these flowers?

1. Which is more destructive, mistletoe or dodder? Why?

2. If mistletoe has leaves and is photosynthetic, why is it considered a parasite?

3. What are witches' brooms?

4. *Rafflesia* is the largest flower. Unlike the other parasitic plants discussed in this section, it does not grow in trees. Select one: True   False

278

KEY TERMS

abscisic acid	epidermal tissue	nodule	sieve plate
annual ring	epidermis	nutrient	sieve tube
apical meristem	fibrous root system	parenchyma	sieve-tube element
bark	ground tissue system	pericycle	sink
blade	guard cell	periderm	source
branch root	heartwood	petiole	stem
bulk flow	internode	phloem	stoma
cambium	lateral bud	pit	taproot system
Casparian strip	lateral meristem	pith	terminal bud
cohesion–tension theory	leaf	pressure-flow theory	tracheid
collenchyma	leaf primordium	primary growth	transpiration
companion cell	legume	primary root	vascular bundle
cork cambium	meristem cell	root	vascular cambium
cork cell	mesophyll	root cap	vascular cylinder
cortex	mineral	root hair	vascular tissue system
cuticle	monocot	root system	vein
dermal tissue system	mycorrhizae	sapwood	vessel
dicot	nitrogen fixation	sclerenchyma	vessel element
differentiated cell	nitrogen-fixing bacterium	secondary growth	xylem
endodermis	node	shoot system	

ANSWER KEY

SELF TEST

1. a
2. d
3. d
4. c
5. a
6. b
7. a
8. c
9. a
10. d
11. b
12. a
13. a
14. e
15. d
16. apical meristems
17. sclerenchyma
18. xylem
19. phloem
20. mycorrhizae
21. transpiration
22. A. terminal bud
    B. apical meristem
    C. lateral bud
    D. internode
    E. node
    F. shoot system
    G. root system
    H. taproot
    I. root cap

23. A. xylem
    B. phloem
    C. cortex
    D. vascular cylinder
    E. apical meristem
    F. root cap
24. A. endodermis
    B. vascular cylinder
    C. Casparian strip
    D. cortex
25. A. sapwood
    B. heartwood
    C. vascular cambium
    D. cork and cork cambium
    E. secondary phloem
    F. bark
26. A. cuticle
    B. guard cell
    C. upper epidermis
    D. palisade layer
    E. spongy layer
    F. stoma
27. b
28. c
29. a
30. d
31. True
32. b
33. False
34. False
35. False
36. c

ESSAY CHALLENGE

1. 1) active transport of minerals into root hairs; 2) diffusion of minerals through cytoplasm to pericycle cells; 3) active transport in the extracellular space of the vascular cylinder; and 4) diffusion of minerals into the xylem

2. Primary growth occurs by mitosis of the apical meristem cells, increases the length of a plant, and aids in the development of specialized plant structures. Secondary growth occurs by mitosis of cells in the lateral meristems and is responsible for increases in diameter of roots and shoots.

3. These nodules contain nitrogen-fixing bacteria that convert nitrogen gas into ammonium nitrate, which plants can use. The bacteria feed the plant and the plant feeds the bacteria.

4. Student's answer should include: 1) systems affected will be water/mineral availability to the parenchyma and sugar transport out of the parenchyma 2) both of these systems will be slowed down because diffusion through several additional cells is needed to transport material to and from the vein.

5. Heartwood is older and at the center of the trunk. It does not conduct water and minerals but does accumulate wastes and contributes to strength and resistance to rot. The sapwood is younger, conductive tissue located closer to the vascular cambium.

6. Answers should include information about the pericycle, hormones, and the apical meristem.

7. The beneficial microbe association is mycorrhizae. The fungus provides increased availability of phosphorus and other minerals to the tree, and the tree provides the fungus with sugars, amino acids, and vitamins. The mycorrhizae are also able to link trees by forming an underground connection. Trees that are shaded or limited in nutrients can receive photosynthesis products from adjacent trees through fungal connection.

8. The roots will not be able to receive sugars that they require for energy. Part of bringing minerals into the roots requires active transport.

9. Water moves up through the xylem as a column. The attraction of the polar molecules to each other allows a continuous chain of water molecules to be drawn up through the xylem.

10. When potassium is actively transported into the guard cells, the water concentration decreases. This produces a concentration gradient with higher water concentration outside the cell, and water enters the guard cells by osmosis. The guard cells close when potassium is released from the guard cell, reversing the water concentration gradient.

11. (a) Light, carbon dioxide concentration, and water are three environmental factors that affect potassium transport in guard cells. (b) Light and low carbon dioxide levels stimulate active transport of potassium into the guard cells. Water enters the guard cells and the stoma opens. Loss of water causes cells to wilt and release abscisic acid, which stops potassium pumps. (c) Water loss will override the other two environmental triggers to protect the plant from desiccation.

12. The six steps include: sucrose source, phloem sieve-tube loading, osmosis into leaf sieve tube, sucrose sink, osmosis out of the sieve tube, and bulk flow driven by hydrostatic pressure gradient.

13. Leaves of some of these plants are modified to trap and digest insects. The insect proteins provide nitrogen. Nitrogen-fixing bacteria are limited to legumes and cannot survive in the acidic soils of bogs.

MEDIA ACTIVITIES

24.5 Web Investigation: Why Do Leaves Turn Red in the Fall?

1. Active synthesis of chlorophyll is possible with sunlight and warm temperatures. Chlorophyll constantly is broken down and synthesized during the summer.

2. Carotenes extend the useful wavelengths of light for photosynthesis. They are considered to be accessory pigments that transfer energy from absorbed light to chlorophyll.

3. An acidic pH results in bright reds, and less acidic pH results in purples.

4. 1) Chlorophyll synthesis requires warm temperatures. Cold temperatures result in the chlorophyll not being replaced as it is in the warm summer months. There is a decrease in nutrient transport to the leaves, and less chlorophyll is synthesized. Carotenes are light stable, and so the yellow/orange light reflected by the carotenes appears as fall leaf color. 2) Anthocyanin production is enhanced by cool temperatures.

5. There are more anthocyanins produced during dry days. Sugars are more concentrated in cells that have less water. The sugars react with specific proteins to form anthocyanins.

ISSUES IN BIOLOGY

1. Advantages include: Soil-borne pests and diseases are immediately eliminated, as are weeds. And the labor involved in tending your plants is markedly reduced. More important, raising plants in a non-soil medium will allow you to grow more plants in a limited amount of space. Food crops will mature more rapidly and produce greater yields. Water and fertilizer are conserved, since they can be reused. In addition, hydroponics allows you to exert greater control over your plants, to unsure more uniform results. Two principal advantages are high crop yields and its special utility in non-arable regions of the world.

Disadvantages include: Poor rooting media, the use of unsuitable materials, particularly in constructing the troughs used as growing beds, and crude environmental control.

The early systems had little or no environmental control, and with no control of temperature or humidity, there was a constant fluctuation in the growth rate. Mold and fungi in the grasses were an ever-present problem. The use of thoroughly clean seed grain with a high germination ratio was found to be completely essential if a good growth rate was to be achieved.

2. C, O, H are used in large amounts in carbohydrate structure. N is a key component of amino acids that are the building blocks for proteins. K is essential for ion balance, stomatal opening/closing. P is used in DNA and cell membrane structure. Mg is found at the center of every chlorophyll molecule.

3. Organic gardening utilizes natural sources of nutrients, soil and no artificial chemicals. Over the past few decades one important breakthrough in hydroponics was the development of a completely balanced plant food. Work in this area is still continuing, but there are many ready made formulas available. Most of them are good, but very few, if any, will work consistently without the use of various additives at different stages of the crop. The choice of using organic farming or hydroponics is up to the individual.

BIZARRE FACTS IN BIOLOGY

1. Dodder is more destructive because it is not photosynthetic and draws much more of the host's resources than the mistletoe.

2. Even though it is photosynthetic, the mistletoe penetrates host dermal tissue with rootlike structures and requires a host.

3. These are branches of host trees that have died back due to mistletoe parasites. The lateral buds break after death of the apical bud and cause branches to form. These are then attacked by the dwarf mistletoe, die back, and the pattern continues to repeat itself. It results in clumps of bushy, dead branches at the site of infection.

4. True

CHAPTER 25: PLANT REPRODUCTION AND DEVELOPMENT

AT-A-GLANCE

SELF TEST

1. The principal function of the petals of a flower is to _____.
   a. produce the female gametophyte
   b. produce pollen grains
   c. attract pollinators
   d. protect the flower body

2. Which of the following is a method flowers may use to attract pollinators?
   a. the production of nectar
   b. the production of a rotten odor
   c. the production of pollen
   d. All of the above may be used to attract pollinators.

3. The embryo sac is contained within the _____, which is located inside the _____.
   a. anther; stamen
   b. stigma; carpel
   c. ovule; ovary
   d. ovary; ovule

4. A seed contains each of the following except a(n) _____.
   a. embryonic plant
   b. food source
   c. seed coat
   d. stoma

5. In the life cycle of a plant, spores are produced by the _____.
   a. gametes
   b. sporophyte
   c. eggs
   d. gametophyte

6. The male gametes of flowering plants are contained within the _____.
   a. seed
   b. stigma
   c. ovule
   d. pollen grain

7. Which of the following is true of double fertilization?
   a. One sperm fuses with the egg to form a zygote, and a second sperm fuses with the polar nucleus to form the endosperm.
   b. One sperm fuses with the tube cell to form the embryo, and a second sperm fuses with a generative cell to form the endosperm.
   c. The first fertilization event results in the production of a zygote, and a second fertilization event occurs several days or weeks later to produce a second zygote, which degenerates to the endosperm.
   d. Double fertilization is a rare event in flowering plants that results in the production of two identical embryos.

8. The principal role of a mature, fleshy fruit is to _____.
   a. aid seed dispersal by animals or other means
   b. provide nutrients for the germinating seeds
   c. produce cytokinins so that the surrounding buds stay dormant
   d. make the plant attractive so that humans will care for it

9. The function of the cotyledons in most dicot seeds is to _____.
   a. store food for the embryo and growing seedling
   b. protect the embryo
   c. transfer the stored food to the embryo
   d. help with seed dispersal

10. If an area is burned with a fire hot enough to kill all of the existing plants in an area, we will typically find new plant life established in the area within a year. The first plants are commonly grasses and annual dicots. How can the rapid establishment of these plants be explained?
   a. The seeds of these plants were present in the soil all along and were released from their dormancy by the heat of the fire.
   b. The fruits of these plants were transported into this area from outlying, unburned regions.
   c. The seeds of these plants were near the surface of the soil at the time of the fire and were protected by their seed coat and dormancy. Their dormancy was broken by their new exposure to the light when the covering plants were burned away.
   d. All three explanations probably contributed to the presence of these plants after the fire.

11. All plant life cycles consist of two unique stages, one in which the chromosomal number of cells is haploid and the other in which the chromosomal number of all cells is diploid. What haploid plant cell undergoes repeated mitotic divisions to produce a haploid adult organism?
   a. sporophyte   b. gametophyte
   c. spore   d. gamete

12. Flowers are made of modified _____.
   a. sepals   b. leaves
   c. stigmas   d. fruits

13. What happens to the megaspore mother cell contained inside an ovary?
   a. Nothing. The megaspore is eventually fertilized by a pollen grain.
   b. The megaspore cell develops into a series of layers called *integuments*.
   c. The megaspore cell divides meiotically to produce four haploid megaspores.
   d. none of the above

14. To what does the phrase "double fertilization" refer?
   a. pollination and fertilization
   b. production of a triploid endosperm
   c. the fusion of a sperm with both polar nuclei
   d. the fusion of a sperm with the egg cell
   e. Both the second and third answers are correct.
   f. Both the third and fourth answers are correct.

15. What advantage does dormancy (characterized by decreased metabolic activity and resistance to adverse environmental conditions) provide many recently matured seeds?
   a. It provides an enforced delay before germination can begin upon maturation of the seed.
   b. It can provide sufficient time for the dispersal of seeds from the parent plant by weather and/or animals.
   c. It can provide an enforced delay until environmental conditions exist that are favorable for the growth of the seed.
   d. all of the above
   e. none of the above

16. What are some of the mechanisms that plants have developed to protect growth of structures during germination?
   a. cover the delicate tips of structures growing through soil with protective caps
   b. extend the period of dormancy
   c. allow the delicate tip of a growing shoot to "trail in the wake" of another structure that is "armored" against the abrasive effects of soil particles
   d. Both the first and third answers are correct.
   e. Both the second and third answers are correct.

17. _____ contain anthers and a carpel.

18. _____ are male reproductive structures in flowers.

19. _____ lack either anthers or a carpel.

20. _____ occurs when a pollen grain lands on a stigma.

21. _____ are the parts of a plant embryo that absorb food molecules from the endosperm.

22. _____ is the process in which two interacting organisms force natural selection of each other.

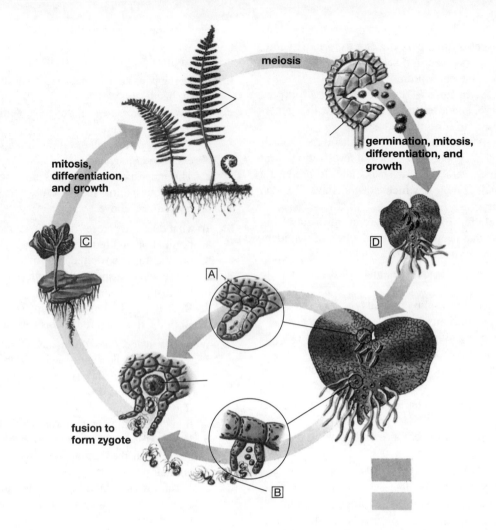

23. Label the structures indicated on the life cycle of a fern shown above.

24. Label the parts of the flower indicated on the diagram below.

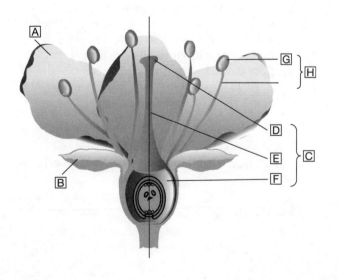

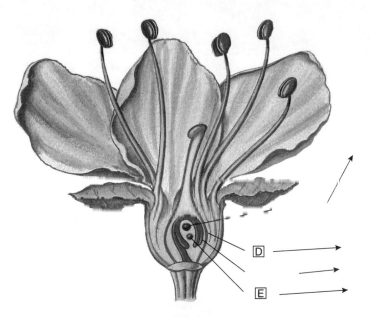

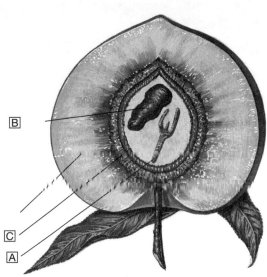

25. Fruit develops from fertilized flowers. Label the portions of these images above.

26. Monocots and dicots share characteristics in their seeds. Label these shared items in the diagram below.

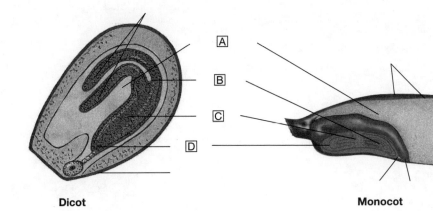

Dicot

Monocot

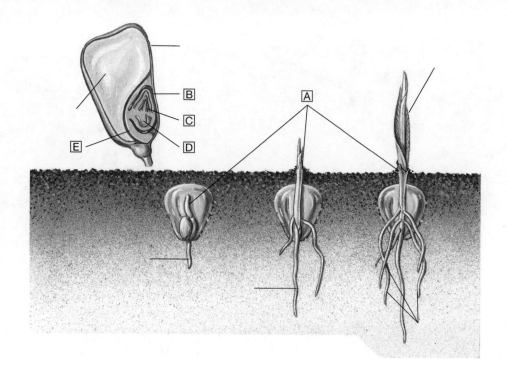

27. Label the portions of the developing monocot (corn) shown above.

28. Similar to the monocot question above, label the structures indicated below in the developing dicot.

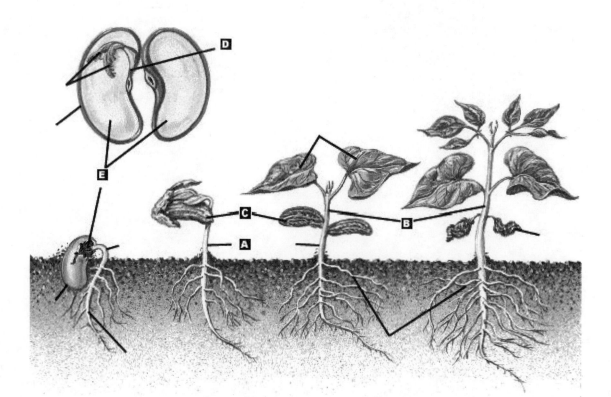

ESSAY CHALLENGE

1. Describe the alternation of generations in plants.

2. What three mechanisms break dormancy in seeds?

3. How do flowers and insects help each other?

4. In what ways do fruits aid in the dispersal of seeds?

5. How do scientists think flowers evolved?

6. Compare and contrast pollen and embryo sac formation.

7. Describe how double fertilization occurs and what is formed as a result of this process.

8. You are shopping in the produce section with one of your roommates who happens to be a plant science major. Your roommate comments that all the fruits and vegetables are really fruits, and in actuality are ripe ovaries. You need to explain these statements to a third roommate who is totally weirded out.

9. Bean seeds have very large, fleshy cotyledons. What will happen to the young seedling if you remove the cotyledons as soon as the shoot emerges from the ground?

10. Why does the forest service allow small fires to burn and even start some prescribed burns in certain areas?

MEDIA ACTIVITIES

To access a Media Activity visit http://www.prenhall.com/audesirk7. Log in to the Web site selected by your instructor, navigate to this chapter, and select the appropriate Media Activity number.

25.1 Reproduction in Flowering Plants
Estimated Time: 5 minutes

Explore the basic reproductive structures in flowering plants and learn their function.

25.2 Fruits and Seeds: Structure and Development
Estimated Time: 5 minutes

Examine the basic structures of fruits and seeds and then explore the process of fruit and seed development.

25.3 Web Investigation: Time Capsules, Smoke Signals and Seed Sprouting
Estimated time: 15 minutes

Most of us are familiar with Smokey Bear (http://www.smokeybear.com/) and the need to prevent rampant fires caused by careless human activity. But we are also learning fire is a natural selective force that has shaped many ecosystems (http://www.experiencewyoming.com/yellowstone-teton.whyfires.htm). Suppression of small fires in these regions has often resulted in more severe fires due to a buildup of fuel. Other ecosystems have evolved without this selective force (http://www.findarticles.com/cf_dls/m1200/n14_v154/21213729/p1/article.jhtml).

In addition to shaping plant populations, fires also impact global temperatures (http://earthobservatory.nasa.gov/Library/GlobalFire/). Fires release particulates and carbon into the atmosphere and remove biomass that would otherwise decrease carbon levels via photosynthesis. Global collaborations allow us to better understand the complex role of fires in the environment.

1. Give some examples of habitats that have coevolved with fire. What are the fuel sources for each?

2. What are the beneficial effects of frequent smaller fires in regions like the northwestern USA?

3. Small fires in tropical rain forests have the opposite effect and make more destructive fires more likely later. Why?

4. What are the major emissions from forest fires?

ISSUES IN BIOLOGY

How Are Plants Vegetatively Propagated?

Have you ever wondered how apple farmers are able to plant acres and acres of apple trees and know that each tree will produce the same type of high-value fruit? The answer is that they don't grow the trees from seeds. Instead the farmers plant saplings that were vegetatively produced from a known variety of tree. If a farmer grows plants from seed, each seed represents a separate sexual reproductive event. (Review section 25.5 "How Do Seeds and Fruits Develop?" in your textbook.) Consequently, each seed has the potential of possessing genetic differences that may make the crop less valuable. (Review Chapter 11, "The Continuity of Life: Cellular Reproduction.") For annual crops, which come and go in a single season, this may not be too much of a problem. But with some crop plants, such as grape vines and fruit trees, which require a considerable investment of time and resources before they begin producing, having a "bad" type of grape produced after five or more years of care could be disastrous.

To avoid these problems created by the uncertainty of sexual reproduction, the agriculture industry has relied on the vegetative propagation of plants with desirable traits. In vegetative propagation, a portion of the parent plant is cloned to produce offspring that have the same genetic characteristics as the parent plant. By this cloning process we are able to produce orchards in which all the plants produce McIntosh apples or a specific variety of grape for a wine. Some of these cloned varieties of plants have an ancient history. For example, the common orange day lily has been vegetatively propagated from an original parent for more than 400 years, while some grape varieties can trace their origins to an original parent that lived more than 2000 years ago!

There are a variety of methods that can be used to vegetatively propagate a plant with desirable qualities (http://www.ces.ncsu.edu/hil/hil-8701.html). One ancient method, called layering, is to bring a portion of the stem into contact with the soil. Then many plants will spontaneously produce an adventitious root along this section of stem. Once the roots have become established, that stem portion can be pruned from the parent plant, leaving two genetically identical plants. In cases where bending the stem to the soil is impractical, creating a wound in the stem followed by wrapping the wound with damp moss usually works just as well to establish a new root system on the stem.

Many plants will produce offspring if a portion of the plant body is separated, either naturally or by humans, from the parent plant. This form of vegetative reproduction is used extensively in the cultivation of plants such as potatoes, bananas, and plants that produce bulbs or corms. You may also be familiar with establishing new plants by "planting" the leaf of a parent plant. For many species, especially those with fleshly leaves, roots will form at the base of the leaf or along the leaf's margins if the leaf is placed in contact with moist soil after it is removed from the plant. The application of a rooting hormone to the cut leaf facilitates this process (http://ag.arizona.edu/pubs/garden/mg/propagation/asexual.html).

Grafting is another way in which the desired characteristics of a plant can be passed on to future generations. When grafting plants, a portion of one plant, the scion, is "attached" to and becomes part of another plant, the stock. Grafting has the advantage of being able to combine the desirable characteristics of two or more plants into a single individual. For example, if one variety of plant has a particularly hardy or disease-resistant root system while another variety produces the desired type of fruit, grafting the two together often achieves the benefits of both.

A final method of vegetative propagation that is increasing in popularity is called tissue culturing. In this method a very small portion of plant tissue can be removed from the parent and placed in sterile conditions with the appropriate plant hormone, and it will grow to produce a mature plant. This method has the advantage of using a smaller amount of the parent plant and the potential of "assembly line" production. However, it calls for a specialized environment and growing conditions that are not readily available to every individual.

1. What commercially produced plants, used for either food or ornamental purposes, can you think of that are probably reproduced vegetatively? What kind of advantages do these growers realize?

2. Which methods of vegetative propagation would be best suited to someone wanting to produce a small number of plants for their flower bed at home? Which methods of vegetative propagation would be best suited to produce these plants commercially on a large scale?

3. While vegetative propagation of plants for agricultural purposes has the distinct advantage in that you know what type of plant product you are going to get, it also has several disadvantages. Can you think of some of the disadvantages?

BIZARRE FACTS IN BIOLOGY

Walk Through a Meadow

To most people, pollen is just a part of a plant, but for allergy sufferers, it's trouble! Why does such a small biological object cause so many problems? The topic here is pollen and pollen allergies (http://www.niaid.nih.gov/newsroom/focuson/allergy99/allergyspot.htm).

1. What are the two major methods for pollen distribution (http://www.bbg.org/gar2/topics/botany/repro_flowers.html)? What is the technical term for pollination by bats?

2. What is an allergic reaction (http://www.aafaflorida.org/features/answers/)? What characteristics are shared (http://museum.gov.ns.ca/poison/ragweed.htm) by plants most likely to produce allergic reactions?

3. Some scientists consider Cry9C, a protein genetically engineered into the Starlink strain of corn, a possible allergen (http://www.biotech-info.net/altered_food.html). Why?

4. Although Starlink was not approved for human consumption, Cry9C has been found in some products on grocery store shelves. What role did pollination (http://web.aces.uiuc.edu/faq/faq.pdl?project_id=28&faq_id=590) play in this contamination?

5. Recently Cry9C contamination was found in a second variety (http://www.biotech-info.net/2nd_variety.html) of corn. How did it get there?

6. Starlink has been removed from the market. In the future it is likely that no new genetically engineered agricultural product will be licensed for sale if it is not approved for human consumption. Do you think that this is a good policy?

KEY TERMS

alternation of generations
anther
carpel
coleoptile
complete flower
cotyledon
dormancy
double fertilization
egg
embryo sac
endosperm

epicotyl
fertilization
filament
flower
fruit
gametophyte
generative cell
germinate
hypocotyl
incomplete flower
integument

megaspore
megaspore mother cell
microspore
microspore mother cell
ovary
ovule
petal
polar nucleus
pollen grain
pollination
seed

seed coat
sepal
spore
sporophyte
stamen
stigma
style
tube cell
zygote

ANSWER KEY

SELF TEST

1. c
2. d
3. c
4. d
5. b
6. d
7. a
8. a
9. a
10. d
11. c
12. b
13. c
14. f
15. d
16. d
17. complete flowers
18. stamens
19. incomplete flowers
20. pollination
21. cotyledons
22. coevolution
23. A. egg
    B. sperm
    C. young sporophyte
    D. young gametophyte
24. A. petal
    B. sepal
    C. carpel
    D. stigma
    E. style
    F. ovary
    G. anther
    H. stamen
25. A. embryo
    B. endosperm
    C. seed coat
    D. ovary
    E. zygote

26. A. endosperm
    B. shoot tip
    C. embryo
    D. root tip
27. A. coleoptile
    B. coleoptile in seed
    C. leaves in seed
    D. root in seed
    E. cotyledon
28. A. hypocotyl
    B. epicotyl
    C. coyledons
    D. root in seed
    E. cotyledons in seed

ESSAY CHALLENGE

1. Diploid structures alternate with haploid ones. The diploid form is called the *sporophyte* and produces haploid spores that germinate into the gametophyte. The gametophyte can produce sperm and eggs.

2. 1) drying: many seeds must dry out before they can germinate; 2) cold: many seeds will not germinate unless exposed to prolonged cold temperatures; 3) disruption of the seed coat: some seeds are impermeable to water and oxygen or contain chemicals that prohibit germination; only a hard rainfall can sometimes disrupt the seed coat

3. Flowers provide food in the form of pollen for many insects. When insects feed on the pollen, they unknowingly spread pollen from flower to flower, thus assisting in reproduction for the plant.

4. When animals eat fruits, the seeds inside are usually not digested. When the animal excretes its wastes, seeds are dispersed to various locations. Some fruits explode and propel seeds out. Other fruits are lightweight and are distributed by wind, some float and are distributed by water, and others cling to animal fur and are then distributed.

5. Gymnosperms (early seed plants) were present before angiosperms. Some of the cone-bearing gymnosperms have pollen that is highly nutritious and serves as a food source for beetles. The female cones of the same species secrete sugars that also provide food for the beetles. Pollen is transferred from male to female structures by the beetle. Plants that inherited mutations that would provide a food source or in some way attract pollinators, reproduced with more success, and these traits continued to be passed to more plants in the next generation. The end result is a large variety of flowering plants.

6. Both pollen and the embryo sac are very small gametophytes (composed of a few haploid cells). A diploid mother cell undergoes meiosis and is the precursor of both (microspore mother cell for pollen and megaspore mother cell for embryo sacs). Differences are that the pollen grain is smaller (three nuclei versus eight for the embryo sac), all cells resulting from the microspore go on to divide by mitosis to form a pollen grain, and only one of the four cells formed by meiosis of the megaspore mother cell go on to divide by mitosis to form the embryo sac (the other three degenerate).

7. When the pollen tube successfully grows and joins with the base of the embryo sac, the tube ruptures. One of the sperm joins with the egg to form the zygote. The zygote will divide by mitosis and form the embryo. The second sperm joins with the two polar bodies. The union of three haploid nuclei results in the formation of triploid endosperm tissue.

8. Fruit develops from the flower's ovary wall after double fertilization takes place. The tissue usually enlarges and forms a protective covering around the seeds. The edible parts of most fruits and vegetables started as ovary tissue in the flower of the plant that produced the fruit.

9. Cotyledons provide nutrition to the emerging seedling. If the cotyledons are removed very early, the seedling will be deprived of nutrition. It is possible that the embryonic leaves will produce enough sugar to allow the plant to continue to grow— although not as much as would be available with the cotyledons. The plant may grow slowly or it may not be able to survive long enough to be able to fully support itself through photosynthesis.

10. Fires are a natural part of the ecosystem in temperate areas, and trees have thick bark to withstand small fires. Some species even depend on fire to remove germination inhibitors from the seeds, allowing the next generation to develop. Dead branches and needles are dropped by trees throughout their development and accumulate on the forest floor. If these are not consumed on a regular basis, large amounts of fuel accumulate and produce much hotter, more destructive fires in the future.

MEDIA ACTIVITIES

25.3 Web Investigation: Time Capsules, Smoke Signals and Seed Sprouting

1. Lodgepole pines drop branches and twigs that serve as fuel. Open meadow areas dry out during the summer and the grasses are fuel sources. Sage brush and shrubs in open areas contain creosote that is flammable even when wet.

2. Frequent fires use up accumulated fuel and burn out before becoming excessively hot. This helps to prevent occurrence of large extremely hot fires that consume the seeds and hinder new plant growth. Frequent fire allows release of nutrients that were locked up in the dead biomass of the fuel, removal of germination inhibitors from some seeds, and production of open areas with light exposure for photosynthesis of young growth.

3. The northern forests evolved with fire, and plants are adapted to surviving fire (thicker bark) and even depending on fire (requiring it for germination). Tropical forests do not have these adaptations. The sources of fire in the tropics are also very recent in evolutionary history—human use of fire to clear land.

4. Greenhouse gases such as carbon dioxide, carbon monoxide, nitrous oxides, and methane.

ISSUES IN BIOLOGY

1. Examples of plants propagated by simple layering include climbing roses, forsythia, rhododendron, honeysuckle, boxwood, azalea, and wax myrtle. Examples of plants propagated by tip layering include purple and black raspberries, and trailing blackberries. Compound layering works well for plants producing vine-like growth such as heart-leaf philodendron, pothos, wisteria, clematis, and grapes. Mound layering works well on apple rootstocks, spirea, quince, daphne, magnolia, and cotoneaster. Plantlets at the tips of runners may be rooted while still attached to the parent or detached and placed in a rooting medium. Examples include strawberry and spider plant. Plants produced by vegetative means have the advantage that the grower gets continuity in ornamental and fruit characteristics.

2. Layering and rooting of cuttings are low-tech examples that are easily done at home. Grafting takes more expertise and is used in industry. Tissue culture requires high investment but also produces large numbers of clones for commercial use.

3. Any time there is a large group of genetically identical plants, a monoculture, any change to the environment can have drastic impacts. For example, if the plants are all susceptible to a type of disease or insect pest and that pest comes into the area, high crop losses will occur.

BIZARRE FACTS IN BIOLOGY

1. Wind and animals: Chiropterogamy
2. Hooks on the exterior of some pollen grains attach to mucus membranes of the human respiratory lining. Some people inherit the response of producing histamines as a reaction to the pollen irritation. Wind dispersal and rough/sharp exterior are shared characteristics of pollen that causes allergic reactions.
3. The gene for the protein comes from bacteria and is not a normal part of the human diet. There are no antibodies available to test if people could be allergic to this protein, so it is unknown if it is an allergen.
4. Wind carries pollen over distances, and the Starlink pollen can pollinate corn in nearby fields.
5. The company that created the biotech corn, Aventis CropScience, said that the gene that was spliced into its StarLink corn—Cry9C—had been found in another corn hybrid produced by the company licensed to produce StarLink. "Aventis CropScience performed the tests after several farmers stated that corn with no known connection to StarLink was testing positive for Cry9C," the company said in a statement. "Aventis CropScience does not know how Cry9C protein came to be present in a variety other than StarLink brand seeds."
6. Support your answer with information on the role of pollination in transferring genes from one field to another.

CHAPTER 26: PLANT RESPONSES TO THE ENVIRONMENT

AT-A-GLANCE

SELF TEST

1. The downward growth of roots into the ground is an example of _____.
   a. phototropism   b. gravitropism
   c. abscission   d. senescence

2. Which hormone is responsible for stimulation of cell division and cell differentiation as lateral buds are released from dormancy?
   a. cytokinin   b. auxin
   c. ethylene   d. abscisic acid

3. Which statement about gibberellins is false?
   a. Gibberellins promote the development of fruit.
   b. Gibberellins activate enzymes that stimulate seed germination.
   c. Gibberellins stimulate stem elongation.
   d. Gibberellins delay the process of senescence (aging).

4. Long-day plants flower specifically when the _____.
   a. light period is less than some critical length
   b. light period is greater than some critical length
   c. dark period is less than some critical length
   d. dark period is greater than some critical length

5. Gravitropism in roots is a response to _____ and to the hormone_____.
   a. gravity; auxin
   b. Earth's rotation; cytokinin
   c. altitude; ethylene
   d. the biological clock; phytochrome P_r

6. Rapid stem elongation and larger fruit size are promoted by _____.
   a. auxins   b. gibberellins
   c. cytokinins   d. abscisic acid

7. One rotten apple spoils the whole barrel because the rotting apple produces _____.
   a. auxin   b. cytokinin
   c. gibberellin   d. ethylene

8. One of the possible consequences for a plant with a defective gene for the production of abscisic acid would be _____.
   a. an increased rate of senescence of the plant's tissues
   b. an increased rate of lateral root development
   c. the development of fruit without fertilization
   d. a decreased dormancy period for the plant's seeds

9. Why do the coleoptiles of oats bend toward the light?
   a. Oat coleoptiles exhibit negative phototropism.
   b. Gibberellins stimulate growth on the illuminated side of the shoot.
   c. Auxins are found at highest concentrations and stimulate growth on the darker side of the shoot.
   d. Changes in turgor pressure in cells on the darker side of the shoot cause the shoot to bend toward the light.

10. If a plant were strapped upside down to the wall of a rapidly rotating drum (like the ones you might ride on at an amusement park), which of the following would you expect to happen?
   a. The artificial G forces would cause the roots to grow toward the middle of the drum and the stem to grow away from the middle.
   b. The artificial G forces would cause the roots to grow away from the middle of the drum and the stem to grow toward the middle.
   c. The roots and stem would curl around such that the roots would grow toward Earth and the stem would grow toward the sky.
   d. The roots and stem would grow in the direction they were oriented, because they could no longer be influenced by Earth's gravitational forces.

11. Which of the five classes of plant hormones mentioned is most likely to play a prominent role in the maintenance of dormancy?
   a. auxins   b. gibberellins
   c. cytokinins   d. ethylene
   e. abscisic acid

12. How does auxin control the direction of root growth so that roots grow down into the ground, rather than up out of the ground?
   a. Roots respond to light penetrating the soil in a manner known as *positive phototropism*.
   b. Auxin accumulates along the side of the growing root furthest from the ground surface. This inhibits cell elongation on the lower side of the root, and the root bends and grows downward.
   c. Auxin stimulates a negative gravitropism.
   d. all of the above

13. What is believed to be responsible for the detection of gravity in roots and shoots?
   a. Plastids settling onto the lowest surface of the root/shoot (i.e., furthest away from the surface of the soil) initiate a series of steps that end with auxin triggering an unequal elongation in the root/shoot.
   b. Auxin itself is able to detect the direction of gravity.
   c. Both the first and second answers are correct.
   d. none of the above

14. What is responsible for ensuring that the relative growth rate of the roots does not overwhelm the growth rate of the shoots and vice versa?
   a. auxin
   b. cytokinin
   c. the phenomenon known as *apical dominance*
   d. Both the first and second answers are correct.

15. Plants that flower whenever a plant has undergone enough growth and maturation regardless of how long the sun is up are called _____.
   a. day-neutral plants   b. long-day plants
   c. short-day plants

16. Phytochromes are believed to be play a role in _____.
   a. inhibition of the elongation of seedlings in the case of P_{fr}
   b. detection of light wavelengths that control the metabolic "biological" clock of plants
   c. chlorophyll synthesis
   d. all of the above

17. _____ promotes the elongation of cells in parts of the shoot of a plant.

18. _____ is the tendency for plant parts to grow toward gravity.

19. _____ is the tendency for plant parts to grow toward light.

20. _____ are a group of molecules similar to auxin that promote the elongation of cells in stems.

21. _____ is the process by which the growing tip of a plant suppresses lateral growth.

22. _____ is the process in which plants undergo rapid aging during autumn.

23. Auxin causes directed shoot and root growth. Label the boxes below in the proper order.

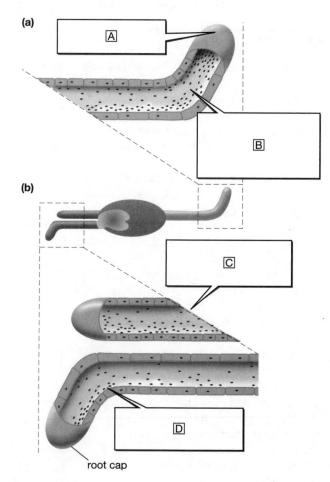

(a)

A

B

(b)

C

D

root cap

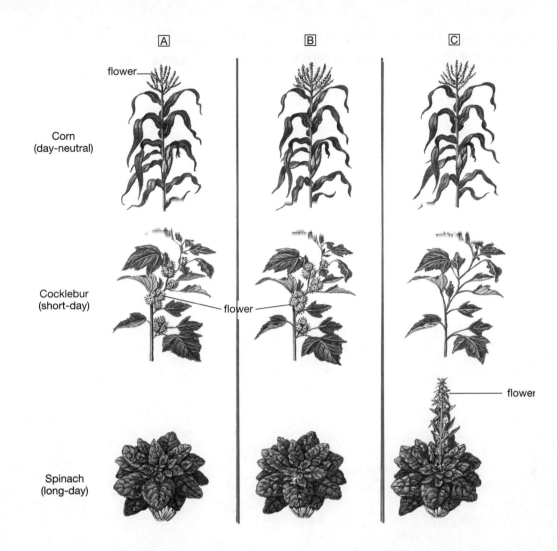

flower

Corn
(day-neutral)

A   B   C

Cocklebur
(short-day)

flower

Spinach
(long-day)

flower

24. Plant growth and reproduction is affected by daylength. In the chart above, you are given some information about the requirements of each plant type. Correctly label the columns of the diagram.

25. When leaves fall off, they do so at the abscission layer. Label this layer in the photomicrograph of a maple leaf cross-section to the right.

26. Although different from animal antibody-producing immune systems, plants produce many chemicals that aid in protection from insects, herbivores, and diseases.
Select one: True   False

(Credit: Photo Researchers, Inc.)

27. What may occur to plants that are downwind from a plant of a different species that is under insect attack?

a. Nothing will be different, since they are a different species from the one under attack.

b. The downwind plant may respond to some of the volatile signal compounds produced by the plant under attack, increasing production of protective compounds before being attacked.

c. The plant undergoing attack will produce additional auxins and replace the tissues under attack, but the adjacent plants will not be affected.

d. The plant downwind from the plant under attack will most likely be swarmed with insects before any compounds can be produced by the plant under attack.

28. What type of signal is responsible for the rapid movement of some plant leaves such as the mimosa or the Venus flytrap?

a. electrical

b. auxin

c. cytokinin

d. ethylene

29. When the Venus flytrap snaps shut around a small insect, what is the response of the plant to the initial electrical fluctuation?

a. Electrical potential from the hair movement stimulates cells of the outer layer to rapidly pump hydrogen ions into the cell walls. This creates an acidic condition that activates enzymes which loosen fibers in the cell walls, weakening them. High osmotic pressure inside the cells causes them to absorb water and rapidly increase in size while the inner layer doesn't. This snaps the leaf closed.

b. "Motor cells" increase their permeabililty to potassium ions, water flows by osmosis, and the cell shrinks as water is lost from the leaflets and petiole, and they wilt rapidly.

c. Potassium and hydrogen ions are pumped across the cell membrane, resulting in a rapid increase in water from osmosis. The leaf snaps shut with the increase in turgor pressure.

d. The insect is held in place by sticky substances until the leaf can respond to the electrical signal in a manner similar to an animal nerve cell.

30. What was the FlavrSavr tomato?

a. This was an early attempt to genetically engineer fruit to not produce an enzyme involved in fruit softening, so the tomatoes would be harder and ship more readily while having the flavor advantage of longer time on the vine.

b. This was a genetically engineered tomato with the master gene for fruit ripening blocked to allow longer time on the vine for better flavor to be followed with ethylene treatment after shipment to finish the ripening process.

c. This was a genetically engineered tomato that had much larger concentrations of lycopene, an antioxidant with potential cancer fighting abilities.

d. This was a genetically engineered tomato that was dark purple, adding to its flavor intensity.

ESSAY CHALLENGE

1. Compare and contrast the effects of abscisic acid and gibberellin on seeds.

2. Describe how plants are classified with respect to flowering

3. In general, how do phytochromes function and what do they do?

4. Describe two processes that are caused by auxin.

5. Discuss similarities and differences between plant hormones and animal hormones.

6. How does the interaction of auxins and cytokinins affect the shape of mature plants?

7. What would happen to a short-day plant like cocklebur, when it is exposed to a light flash during the night a few days before it would normally have flowered?

8. Why is senescence and dormancy preparation essential for deciduous tree/shrub survival in temperate climates? Which hormone(s) is (are) involved and what functions do they stimulate?

9. How do plants under insect or pathogen attack "warn" neighboring plants?

10. Why do tomatoes picked green and ripened later with ethylene not taste as good as their vine-ripened counterparts?

MEDIA ACTIVITIES

To access a Media Activity visit http://www.prenhall.com/audesirk7. Log in to the Web site selected by your instructor, navigate to this chapter, and select the appropriate Media Activity number.

26.1 Hormones
Estimated time: 5 minutes

In this activity you will view the basic principles of hormone structure, transport, and activity. See how hormones produce the effects of phototropism and gravitropism.

26.2 Plant Responses to Phytochrome
Estimated time: 5–15 minutes

In this simulation, experiment with the effects of daylength and different wavelengths of light on plant flowering.

26.3 Plant Response to Stimuli
Estimated time: 5 minutes

Explore some of the unique mechanisms used by plants to respond to outside stimuli.

26.4 Web Investigation: Predacious Plants
Estimated time: 15 minutes

Remember the plant Seymour in *The Little Shop of Horrors?* Now that's a carnivorous plant! Real carnivorous plants may not be quite as flashy, but they have evolved fascinating mechanisms for attracting, catching, and digesting their prey. This exercise takes a brief look at Seymour's "relatives."

1. Each genus has its own technique(s) for trapping prey. How do Venus Flytraps (Dionaea - http://www.sarracenia.com/faq/faq5200.html), Sundews (Drosera - http://www.sarracenia.com/faq/faq5240.html), American pitcher plants (Sarracenia - http://www.sarracenia.com/faq/faq5520.html), and Portuguese Dewy Pine (Drosophyllum - http://www.sarracenia.com/faq/faq5280.html) do it?

2. List the four mechanisms carnivorous plants use to digest (http://www.sarracenia.com/faq/faq1260.html) prey?

3. Most carnivorous plants live in wetlands (http://www.sarracenia.com/faq/faq4040.html). Why?

4. Still looking for Seymour? Here is some information on the largest carnivorous plants (http://www.sarracenia.com/faq/faq1160.html). Can they eat mammals?

ISSUES IN BIOLOGY

What Is the Commercial Use of Plant Growth Regulators?

The ability to influence the growth and development of plants has become more important as the agricultural industry has become increasingly mechanized and as the public has demanded more high-quality produce. If one is going to mechanically remove all the fruit from a plant at a given point in time, it is desirable that as many of the fruits be mature and of desirable appearance as possible. If the harvesting process occurs over a period of days or weeks, it also would be desirable to hold the crop in a good condition over that time. If larger leaves add to the economic value of the crop, then it is desirable to treat the plants in such a way as to reduce the production and growth of lateral branches with smaller leaves. In many cases, naturally occurring plant hormones or synthetic substitutes have been found to have effects beneficial to the agricultural industry in their efforts to deliver the types of high-quality produce to the consumer. Of the five major plant hormones (Review section 26.1 "What Are Plant Hormones and How Do They Act?" in your textbook), only abscisic acid or similar synthetic compounds have not found practical uses, largely because of the high cost to synthesize these compounds and because of their sensitivity to UV light.

Auxins (Review section 26.2 "How Do Hormones Regulate the Plant Life Cycle?" in your textbook) and auxin-like compounds are the oldest substances and probably the most abundantly used substances in agriculture. While the naturally occurring auxin indol acetic acid (IAA) is too unstable to be useful in an agricultural situation, a large number of synthetic compounds have been found to behave in a similar fashion in the plant and have the properties necessary to be useful in the fields. Indolebutyric acid (IBA) and naphthalene acetic acid (NAA) are commonly used to promote root development in stem cuttings. Treating apple and pear trees with NAA just after their full bloom will cause a thinning of up to 80% of the developing fruit, a situation that is desirable because fewer large fruit have a greater market value than many small fruit. Later in fruit development, NAA, 2,4-dichlorophenoxyacetic acid (2,4-D), and 2,4,5-trichlorophenoxypropionic acid (2,4,5-TP) may be used to delay fruit drop, extending the harvest season. Many farmers, as well as many homeowners, will use 2,4-D as an herbicide to kill broadleaf weeds in their fields or lawns (http://pmep.cce.cornell.edu/profiles/extoxnet/24D-captan/24D-ext.html).

Of the more than 90 forms of gibberellin that have been identified in higher plants and in the fungus Gibberella (http://www.biologie.uni-hamburg.de/b-online/e31/31d.htm), only the forms GA_4 and GA_7 have been found to have commercial value. These gibberellins are used extensively to increase the size and quality of seedless grapes. They are used to delay the ripening of lemons so that these can be harvested during the months with the greatest demand. Application of gibberellins to artichokes promotes the production of flower buds and allows for earlier harvesting dates. These gibberellins are also used to increase the yields of malt from barley and sucrose from sugarcane.

The cytokinin-like compounds, benzyladenine and tetrapyranylbenzyladenine, are used to promote lateral branching in white pine and carnations, respectively. A combination of benzyladenine, GA_4, and GA_7, called Promalin, is used to promote the elongation of the Delicious apple varieties so that they have the elongated shape expected by the public, rather than a rounder shape. Promalin is also applied to young fruit trees to increase lateral branching, producing a tree with the desired shape for mechanical harvesting.

Several treatments or compounds that increase ethylene concentrations in or around the plants have found commercial uses. Among the oldest of these treatments is the burning of fires or running of gas engines adjacent to fields of pineapple and mango, helping to synchronize flowering in these plants. The incomplete combustion of fuels in both of the cases adds ethylene to the environment to achieve the desired effect. A compound commonly applied to *Hevea brasiliensis* (the tree that produces natural rubber) is 2-chloroethylphosphonic acid or ethephon. Ethephon degrades to ethylene within the plant, which in Hevea has been found to increase the flow of latex, raising rubber yields as much as 100%. Another use of ethephon is its application to cherry trees prior to harvest, decreasing the force required and subsequent tree damage from mechanical harvesters. Ethephon treatment of walnuts has also increased their market value. In grapes, ethephon is used to promote color development and reduce acidity in the fruits (http://www.actahort.org/books/120/120_31.htm).

1. Reviewing the actions of abscisic acid given in the textbook, if you were to develop a synthetic abscisic acid that could be used commercially, how would you expect it to affect crop plant development? Can you think of any crop plants that could benefit from these effects?

2. If you were a grower of a crop not mentioned above—anything from apricots to yams—which of the available hormone treatments do you think could be of value to your crop? How would this treatment affect the crop and how would that increase the crop's value?

3. Many individuals express a desire for "chemical-free" food. What benefits can you think of for "chemical-free" farming? What would be the disadvantages to the farmer and the consumer?

BIZARRE FACTS IN BIOLOGY

Some Like It Hot

Consider the chili pepper. A native of tropical climates, it is widely cultivated in the Caribbean, South and Central America, and Mexico. To shield its leaves from the sun's ultraviolet radiation, it grows in the shade of other bushes. Its fruit is bright red-orange, so it's attractive to birds. That's good because the chili needs to disperse its seeds and birds can travel long distances. Why, then, do chilies burn? If you want a bird to eat the fruit and carry the seeds, either on its feathers (birds are sloppy eaters) or in its digestive tract, to a new site, then why fill the fruit with fiery capsaicins (http://student.biology.arizona.edu/honors98/group12/pepper.html)?

Because birds have a poor sense of smell and taste, the fiery fruit does not discourage them. Mammals, small and large, tend to avoid eating the chilies because of the burn, saving the fruits for the birds. Chilies contain beta-carotene, vitamin C, and fats, so it is possible that the burn might signal a nutritious meal to the birds. The fats are especially important because they provide a source of concentrated energy, something most fruits don't do.

Birds also move food through the digestive tract quickly; the seeds of a fruit may be "in transit" for as little as 20 minutes. Consequently, seeds are not damaged and will germinate after the bird has dropped them. In the case of the chili, a plant that likes to find shade, seeds are dropped while a bird visits another fruit-bearing bush, providing an ideal environment for the new chili plant. The chili plant succeeds in dispersing (http://www.zoo.ufl.edu/gpryor/hot.peppers.html) its seeds and the birds get essential nutrients, a definite "win-win" situation for bird and plant.

References

Nabhan, G. P. 1997. Why chilies are hot. *Nat His* 106(5):24–9.

Surh, Y-J., and Sang, S. L. 1995. Capsaicin, a double-edged sword: toxicity, metabolism, and chemopreventive potential. *Life Sci* 56:1645–55.

1. How would you define the interaction between the bird and the chili plant?

2. Why doesn't the seed get digested when the bird eats the fruit?

3. Nutritionally, which is more beneficial, eating mild peppers or hot peppers?

KEY TERMS

abscisic acid	cytokinin	gravitropism	plant hormone
abscission layer	day-neutral plant	hormone	senescence
apical dominance	ethylene	long-night plant	short-night plant
auxin	florigen	phototropism	
biological clock	gibberellin	phytochrome	

ANSWER KEY

1. b
2. a
3. d
4. c
5. a
6. b
7. d
8. d
9. c
10. b
11. e
12. b
13. a
14. d
15. a
16. d
17. auxin
18. gravitropism
19. phototropism
20. gibberellins
21. apical dominance
22. senescence
23. A. shoot tip produces auxin
    B. auxin accumulates on lower side of shoot, causing cell elongation there and bending shoot upward
    C. auxin enters the root, and root cap cells direct auxin to the lower side
    D. root cell elongation is inhibited by auxin, so root bends downward.
24. A. equal day and night length
    B. short days, long nights
    C. long days, short nights
25. A. abscission layer
    B. petiole
    C. bud
26. True
27. b
28. a
29. a
30. a

ESSAY CHALLENGE

1. Both hormones affect dormancy of seeds. Abscisic acid enforces dormancy by slowing down metabolism in the seed embryo. Gibberellin stimulates germination by initiating the synthesis of enzymes that digest the food reserves of the endosperm and cotyledons.

2. 1) a day-neutral plant flowers as soon as it has grown sufficiently, regardless of daylength; 2) a long-day plant flowers when the daylength is longer than some critical value and the corresponding dark period is uninterrupted, which is species-specific; 3) a short-day plant flowers when the daylength is shorter than some critical value and the corresponding dark period is uninterrupted, which is species-specific.

3. Phytochromes detect light. One form absorbs red light, and the other form absorbs far red light. These molecules detect daylength based on how much of each phytochrome is present in a plant.

4. Auxin controls the orientation of the sprouting seedling, stimulates shoot elongation away from gravity and toward light, and may control the direction of root growth.

5. Plant and animal hormones are both chemical signals that are transported from one part of the body to another. Hormones have specific effect(s) on target cells that may vary from species to species. Animal hormones include hormones produced only by one or the other sex. Sex hormones are not produced by plants.

6. Auxins are produced in the shoot tips, move down the stem and allow growth of the plant shoot upward. Cytokinins produced in roots move upward and stimulate side buds to grow. The high ratio of auxins and cytokinins stimulates shoot growth. As roots grow larger they produce more cytokinins, which further stimulates lateral shoot growth so shoot growth keeps up with root growth. Conversely, growing stems produce more auxins which stimulate root branching, allowing the root growth to keep up with the shoot growth.

7. The flowering would be delayed. The phytochrome detects the light flash that has interrupted the long night period. Short-day plants require an uninterrupted period of a certain length for flowering to occur.

8. Part of the preparation for dormancy includes ripening and drop of fruits that are dispersed by animals. This distributes the seeds in preparation for the next generation. Cool temperatures decrease the amounts of cytokinins and auxin production, so shoot and root growth slows (see answer to Question 6 above). Ethylene stimulates the breakdown of proteins, starches, and chlorophyll for transport to the roots for storage. This provides the tree/shrub with a food source to be mobilized in the spring to provide energy to sprouting buds. Ethylene is also involved in formation of the abscission layer at the base of petioles to allow leaf drop after the proteins, starches, and chlorophyll have been transported to the roots.

9. Plants produce many compounds to provide protection from insects and diseases. Some of these compounds stimulate production of additional protective compounds. Some of the protective compounds are volatile and can diffuse to nearby plants, stimulating their defense responses.

10. As fruit develops, it is a sink for sugars and many compounds involved in flavor from the parent plant. The longer the fruit remains attached to the plant, more of these flavor components can be transported to the ripening fruit.

MEDIA ACTIVITIES

26.4   Web Investigation: Predacious Plants

1. Insect capture by Venus Fly Trap is performed by attracting the insects with nectar to bilobed leaves, which snap shut upon the prey. Sun Dew plants bear stalks or tentacles on their leaves, and these stalks are tipped with glands (which are often brightly colored). The glands exude attractive nectar, adhesive compounds, and digestive enzymes. Insects that land on the leaves stick fast and are digested. Often nearby glandular tentacles are stimulated and also adhere to the insect, and on many species the entire leaf coils around the prey. American Pitcher Plants capture insects by not letting them escape from their pitchers once the prey topple in. Some species exude an amazing variety of chemicals, including digestive enzymes, wetting agents, and insect narcotics! Others rely on bacterial action to digest the prey. It appears that while the glands of Drosera (Portugese Dewy Pine) hold fast to their prey, the glands of Drosophyllum mostly function to coat the prey with mucous. In its struggles to escape, the prey becomes completely immersed in mucous and drowns.

2. Enzymes, bacteria that produce enzymes, assassin bug frass (poop) and bird droppings.

3. In the types of wetlands that house carnivorous plants, there are very few nutrients available for plants. Noncarnivorous species that live there have a difficult time obtaining necessary nutrients and so do not thrive. Meanwhile, carnivorous plants have found a different way to obtain nutrients, and so can survive. Catching bugs gives the carnivorous plants a competitive advantage over the non-carnivorous plants.

4. Nepenthes–these large vines can grow up to tens of meters long. Plants in this genus also have traps that have evolved to capture some of the largest prey, including creatures as large as frogs. Very rarely, captures of birds or rodents have been reported, but these cases probably involved sick animals and certainly do not represent the norm.

ISSUES IN BIOLOGY

1. One of the functions of abscisic acid is to promote transport of food from leaves to developing seeds. Increases in abscisic acid could increase availability of food to developing seeds and would be beneficial for increasing yields in grain crops like corn, wheat, oats, and others. Abscisic acid also promotes dormancy in some seeds and could be beneficial in increasing storage of grains.

2. This is an open question, with many possible answers. Auxins will suppress lateral bud growth, mediate response to light direction, induce development of vascular tissue, induce formation of roots on cuttings, inhibit leaf and fruit drop, or cause defoliation in high doses. Cytokinins are used commercially to promote cell division in roots, delay leaf aging, and influence development of vascular tissues. Ethylene promotes fruit ripening, leaf and flower aging, and release of fruits. Gibberellins promote seed germination and stimulate flowering in some plants.

3. As a consumer most people agree that the fewer foreign chemicals in the diet the better. Many of the chemicals used will have different effects at different concentrations and will accumulate in bodies over a lifetime. The use of agrochemicals is also a major source of pollution (fertilizer runoff from fields, insecticides, herbicides—the above site on 2,4-D indicates toxicity levels, fungicides). Advantages for the farmer include not having the cost of buying and applying the chemicals. Disadvantages to the consumer and farmer include potential increase of disease and insect damage, production on a smaller scale (if pests are not controlled chemically they are controlled by physical approaches that are more time consuming). Use of herbicides allows no-till practices that decrease erosion. Chemical-free farming relies on plowing and hoeing to disrupt weeds. This results in some soil loss to erosion.

BIZARRE FACTS IN BIOLOGY

1. Both benefit from the interaction. The fruit of the hot pepper provides nutrients to the bird. The bird doesn't chew up the seeds and the seed moves quickly through the digestive tract for dispersal.

2. The hot pepper fruit has compounds that act as laxatives and result in the seeds passing quickly (about 20 minutes) through the digestive tract and excreted.

3. In addition to beta carotene and vitamin C (also found in sweet red peppers), the hot peppers are a source of fat. This is a very high-energy food form.

CHAPTER 27: HOMEOSTASIS AND THE ORGANIZATION OF THE ANIMAL BODY

AT-A-GLANCE

SELF TEST

1. Negative feedback responses _____.
   a. tend to counteract the changes to which they respond
   b. tend to magnify the changes to which they respond

2. Positive feedback systems _____.
   a. magnify or enhance changes that are occurring in a physiological variable
   b. counteract or negate changes that are occurring in a physiological variable

3. The constancy of an animal body's internal environment is maintained by _____.
   a. a single feedback mechanism
   b. a few independent feedback systems
   c. a coordinated, integrated network of systems

4. Which of the following is NOT one of the major categories of animal tissue?
   a. endocrine tissue   b. connective tissue
   c. epithelial tissue   d. muscle tissue
   e. nerve tissue

5. Which of the following is NOT a type of connective tissue?
   a. fat   b. blood
   c. bone   d. tendons
   e. glands

6. Organs are _____.
   a. formed of all four tissue types
   b. formed of two or more tissues that operate independently of one another
   c. formed of two or more tissues that function together

7. Special sensory nerve endings in the skin of the hand are responsive to temperature. When an extremely hot object is encountered, nerves conduct this information to the spinal cord, which, in turn, sends a signal to skeletal muscle, causing it to contract and pull the affected part of the body away from the stimulus (often before the sensation of a burn is felt).

   In this scenario, the control center is _____.

   a. the nerve endings in the skin

   b. the spinal cord

   c. the skeletal muscles of the hand

   d. the nerves conducting impulses from the sensory nerves to the spinal cord

8. Desert lizards rely on energy from the sun to regulate their body temperatures. Heat from the sun penetrates the skin and warms the blood, which is then circulated to the body core and other regions, warming them. When they need to cool their bodies, they move out of the sunlight until body temperatures drop. They must also, of course, be able to maintain water balance in extremely dry environments. Which of the following features would you NOT expect to find in reptilian skin?

   a. sweat glands

   b. a thick layer of heavily keratinized cells

   c. a relatively thin dermis

9. Fish do not maintain whole-body temperatures different from the temperature of the water in which they live. However, many fish, if given a choice of water temperatures from which to choose (say, in an experimental aquarium that offers a gradient of water temperatures), will select a narrow range of water temperatures in which to live. Thus, they exhibit a "preferred temperature" that they can maintain by controlling the amount of time they spend in water of different temperatures.

Does this represent true homeostasis in the fullest sense of the term? Justify your answer.

   a. Yes. This qualifies as homeostasis because a constant body temperature is maintained.

   b. Yes. This qualifies as homeostasis because body temperature is actively regulated such that internal physiological variables are kept within the range that cells need to function.

   c. No. This does not qualify as homeostasis because, even though the fish are maintaining relatively constant internal conditions, they are not using a feedback system in order to maintain these conditions.

   d. No. This does not qualify as homeostasis because homeostasis involves the control of a physiological variable within very narrow limits so that cells can function. The body temperature of a fish fluctuates with the temperature of the external environment.

10. How do animals regulate their physiology so that the physiological parameters (e.g., regulation of pH, body temperature, electrolyte balance) stay within narrow limits?

   a. homeostasis

   b. dynamic equilibrium

   c. negative feedback systems

   d. all of the above

   e. none of the above

11. Consider a scenario in which your core body temperature drops to 91°F. If a negative feedback mechanism responded to this change, what would it do to that core temperature?

   a. It would drop the body temperature further toward a negative, or colder value.

   b. There would be no change in the body temperature due to negative feedback.

   c. It would reverse the drop in temperature so that the body begins to warm toward its normal operating temperature.

   d. none of the above

12. Pretend that your body would respond to a decrease in body temperature using positive feedback. In this hypothetical example, in what way would positive feedback alter your core body temperature if it were to drop from 98.6°F to 97°F?

   a. The body temperature would continue to drop.

   b. The body temperature would reverse its dropping temperature and begin to warm again.

   c. The body temperature would remain at 97°F with no further changes.

   d. none of the above

13. Arrange the organizational levels that make up the body of an animal from the most simple to the most complex.

   a. cell—tissue—organ—organ system

   b. organ system—organ—tissue—cell

   c. tissue—cell—organ system—organ

   d. tissue—organ—cell—organ system

14. Which of the following is NOT a property, or characteristic, of epithelial tissue?

   a. It can form associations with some types of connective tissue, resulting in a continuous sheet of membrane.

   b. It can restrict the movement of substances across it (i.e., epithelial tissues can act as barriers).

   c. Epithelial cells are rapidly dividing cells that are continuously replaced.

   d. Epithelial-lined membranes are really cell membranes.

15. What type of connective tissue are the tendons and ligaments?

   a. loose connective tissue

   b. fibrous connective tissue

   c. specialized connective tissues

   d. none of the above

16. _____ is the term that describes the constancy of the body's internal environment.

17. _____ are groups of structurally similar cells that perform a particular function.

18. _____ is a process involved in homeostasis that works to return a physiological variable to a set point.

19. _____ tissues form continuous sheets called *membranes*.

20. _____ tissues serve mainly to support and bind other tissues.

21. _____ tissue has the ability to sense and respond to the world.

307

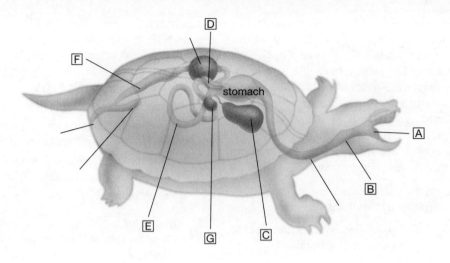

22. Identify the organs of the digestive system on the image of a turtle shown above.

23. The stomach is a key organ to the digestive system. Label the tissues of the stomach indicated on the diagram below.

24. Bone is one of the connective tissues. Label the structures seen on the photo of bone below.

Organ:
Stomach

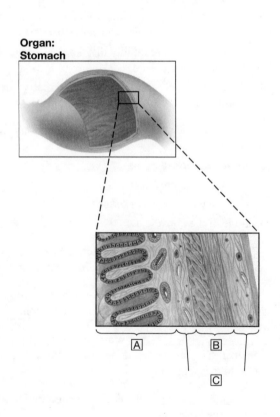

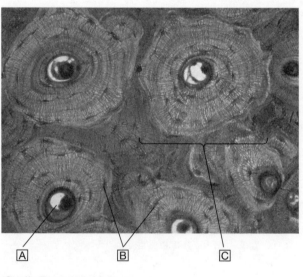

(Credit: Peter Arnold, Inc.)

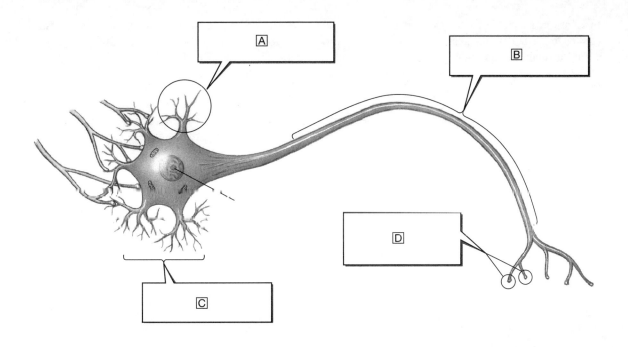

25. Nervous tissue is made up of neurons like the one pictured above. Label the portions of the neuron indicated, giving a function where appropriate.

26. Label the structures visible on the image of skin shown below.

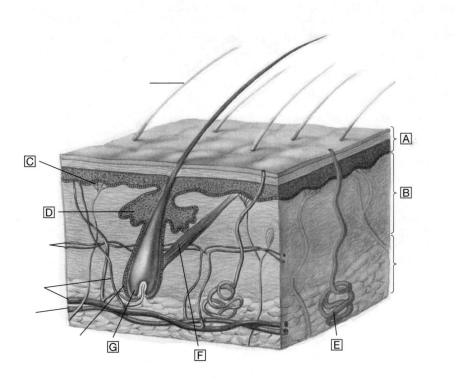

27. In an unfortunate accident, a young man is struck in the leg by a bullet that tears through the femoral artery just above his right knee. The subsequent blood loss leads to a rapid drop in blood pressure. Baroreceptors in the aorta monitor blood pressure and send signals to the vasomotor center of the brain. In this case, the vasomotor center will increase its sympathetic stimulation of the blood vessels which will cause them to constrict. This constriction leads to an increase in blood pressure. This is a description of _____.

   a. a positive feedback system

   b. a negative feedback system

   c. both a positive and a negative feedback system

28. Refer to the scenario described in Question 27. What is the variable, or physiological parameter, being controlled by this system?
   a. blood pressure
   b. blood volume
   c. blood vessel diameter
   d. sympathetic nerve activity

29. Refer to the scenario described in Question 27. What represents the control center in this feedback system?
   a. blood pressure   **b.** vasomotor center
   c. blood vessel diameter   **d.** baroreceptors

30. Refer to the scenario described in Question 27. What represents the effector in this feedback system?
   a. blood vessel diameter   **b.** baroreceptors
   c. vasomotor center   **d.** blood pressure

ESSAY CHALLENGE

1. What are the similarities and differences between endocrine and exocrine glands?

2. List and describe three types of connective tissues and their functions.

3. Compare and contrast the three different types of muscle tissue.

4. Compare and contrast negative and positive feedback systems.

5. You are measuring a physiological parameter that you know is under the control of a negative feedback system. By measuring the value of this variable at regular intervals, you are able to collect enough data to display it in graphical form. Describe what this graph would look like when you produce it and explain why it looks the way it does.

6. Explain how a snowball rolling down a hill could be considered an example of a positive feedback system. In this system, identify the variable and the effector.

7. The human body has the ability to control blood pH using a negative feedback system. In emergency situations, doctors will often put a buffer into an IV fluid to help restore the patient's pH back to normal. As a doctor, explain what information you would like to know about this system before you decide to make a decision to supplement your body's natural ability to control this variable.

8. The dermis of the skin and a tendon are both examples of connective tissue. Explain why you would not want your tendons to have the same structure as the dermis.

MEDIA ACTIVITIES

To access a Media Activity visit http://www.prenhall.com/audesirk7. Log in to the Web site selected by your instructor, navigate to this chapter, and select the appropriate Media Activity number.

27.1 Homeostasis
Estimated time: 5 minutes

In this activity, you will discover how feedback systems help maintain stable equilibrium in animals.

27.2 Web Investigation: From Nightmare to Medical Miracle
Estimated time: 25 minutes

Erika Nordby's diaper-clad body withstood the frigid blasts of –20°C temperatures. As the human body cools, serious life-threatening problems arise. How did Erika withstand these conditions? What did she experience as her core body temperature dropped before being warmed up by the doctors? In this investigation we will explore some of these issues.

1. What is shock (http://www.mayohealth.org/home?id=FA00056)? Why is untreated shock a potential medical emergency (http://www.merck.com/pubs/mmanual/section16/chapter204/204a.htm)? How common is shock (http://www.vnh.org/StandardFirstAid/chapter4.html)?

2. What is hypothermia (http://www.mayoclinic.com/invoke.cfm?id=DS00333)?

3. What is mild (http://www.princeton.edu/~oa/safety/hypocold.shtml) hypothermia and how can it be treated in the field? What is post-rescue collapse (http://hypothermia.org/hypothermia.htm)? How can it be minimized (http://www.experts.com/features/alan_steinman.asp)?

4. Dr. Peter Cox of the Toronto Hospital for Sick Children was quoted in an article by the Canadian Press (http://www.canoe.ca/Health0102/27_tot2-cp.html) as saying "In our world, we don't declare somebody dead until they're warm and dead." Why does this appear to be especially true for small children (http://abcnews.go.com/sections/living/DailyNews/coldrevival010302.html)?

ISSUES IN BIOLOGY

How Do Animals Cope with Environmental Change?

Strange as it may seem at first, the ability of organisms to maintain homeostasis in the face of changing environments lies at the heart of one of the major causes of loss of biodiversity: human-induced environmental degradation. Although we are increasingly able to document the nature, extent, and general consequences of the changes human activity has brought about, we are only beginning to explore the mechanisms responsible for those consequences. If we are to make the kinds of sound policy decisions that will allow us to maintain a balance between human activity and biodiversity, we need to improve our understanding of the phenomena that lie at the intersection of physiology and ecology. Your understanding of the basic chemistry of life as well as of the nature and importance of homeostatic systems should be enough for you to begin to ask—maybe even begin to answer—questions about this area of concern. The ability of organisms to maintain homeostasis is not infinite: over evolutionary time, natural selection has resulted in each species having a specific range of environmental conditions (e.g., temperature, moisture, salinity, pH, etc.) over which it can maintain its internal environment. When environmental conditions exceed those limits, organisms can respond in one of three ways. If change is relatively slow and the appropriate kinds of genetic variation exist, natural selection may result in a change of tolerances; the organisms may adapt to the new conditions. If change is too fast, or if the appropriate kinds of genetic variation don't exist, options are more limited: Individuals may be able to migrate to areas where conditions are better, or individuals die. When change is rapid, when it extends over a species' range, and when migration isn't an option, extinction may well be the result.

We know that environmental conditions are changing all over the planet. On the largest scale, the increase in atmospheric carbon dioxide levels is predicted to cause a change in global climate. An international team of scientists, the Intergovernmental Panel on Climate Change (http://www.ipcc.ch/), has been studying this issue and trying to develop scientifically sound predictions and policy recommendations. According to their 2001 report, the consequences of our current emission patterns will be felt in many of our most important ecosystems; at this scale, though, our current knowledge allows us to make only the most general of predictions. Ecosystems, and the species that inhabit them, are vulnerable to environmental stresses, and some will be irreversibly damaged or lost. Climate change is predicted to have a detrimental effect on the genetic and species diversity of aquatic and terrestrial ecological systems. The geographic distribution of wetlands will change as changes in temperature lead to changes in precipitation patterns. The coastal systems at greatest risk of major change include coastal wetlands, coral reefs, and river deltas. These are the very systems with high levels of biodiversity and great economic importance. On a more local scale, acid precipitation (http://www.epa.gov/airmarkets/acidrain/) and acid mine drainage are causing major changes to the pH of surface waters. Acid precipitation and acid mine drainage have two important potential effects on water chemistry: they can lower pH dramatically and they can increase the concentration of heavy metals, such as iron. Because they use highly permeable body tissues to exchange gases with water, fish, amphibians, crustaceans, and aquatic insects (http://www.epa.gov/airmarkets/acidrain/effects/surfacewater.html) are especially sensitive to these changes. The high permeability of their gas-exchange tissues means they cannot entirely prevent harmful chemicals from entering their bodies; by definition, they cannot maintain homeostasis. Many surface waters of the eastern United States have seen drastic declines in some fish and other animal species, some to the point of local extinction. Unfortunately, correcting the problems (http://www.dep.state.pa.us/dep/deputate/minres/bamr/amd/science_of_amd.htm), especially of acid mine drainage, is something we're only beginning to learn how to do.

1. You suspect that the national forest nearest you is being affected by acid precipitation and/or acid mine drainage. What kind of information would you need (what kinds of research would be necessary) to make a case that acidification was a problem? To whom would you make the case?

2. Although the idea of ecosystems as delicately balanced machines in which a single lost piece can cause the entire system to crash is exaggerated, these systems are built of numerous parts that interact in complex ways. How many realistic consequences can you envision for a forest system affected by acid mine drainage?

3. Policy makers, whether at local, national, or international levels, often make decisions based on cost-benefit analyses. Unfortunately, it is often easier to predict the costs of mitigating environmental damage (by, e.g., imposing limits on carbon emissions or building passive acid reclamation devices for mountain streams) than it is to put a dollar value on the benefit of doing so. Why is this so? (In other words, why is it hard to place dollar amounts on the benefits of maintaining healthy ecosystems with all their biodiversity?) How can this problem be addressed?

BIZARRE FACTS IN BIOLOGY

Frog-cicles and Super-cool Squirrels?

Try freezing a fresh strawberry and then thaw it out: What have you got? A squishy strawberry. The strawberry's cells are more than 70% water, so as the berry freezes, the water molecules form the lattice structure typical of ice crystals. Because this lattice needs more room than liquid water, the cells expand, damaging intracellular structures and the plasma membrane and making the strawberry squishy.

So how do animals, whose cells are also 70% water, survive in climates where freezing temperatures are common? Some aquatic animals, such as wood frogs and the gray tree frog, actually freeze solid (http://www.naturenorth.com/winter/frozen/frozen.html) in winter! The lenses of their eyes turn white when they freeze. But when spring arrives, these same frogs thaw out and hop away to get on with their lives! How do they avoid the damage that freezing causes for most creatures? The answer is both simple and elegant. Their cells concentrate sugars, which lower the freezing point for the cytoplasm and prevent freezing. It's the extracellular fluid in these animals that freezes around the tissues, thereby avoiding cellular damage.

Using a similar mechanism, some warm-blooded mammals also have made adaptations to deal with extreme cold. Arctic ground squirrels (http://www.state.ak.us/adfg/wildlife/geninfo/game/ff_squir.htm) hibernate in burrows that reach temperatures well below zero. However, during hibernation, their heart rates drop from 200 beats per minute to 2 to 4 beats per minute, and their body temperature drops from 37.0°C (98.6°F) to −2.3°C (26.4°F). They don't actually freeze, they supercool! The water in their bodies goes below freezing but doesn't form ice. Researchers think they accomplish this feat by eliminating molecules that serve as a foundation for the formation of ice crystals. In essence, these animals freeze without becoming solid.

1. How could discoveries about protecting cells from freezing affect the way food is grown and preserved?

2. What impact would this antifreezing technology have on surgical procedures such as organ transplants or on space travel?

KEY TERMS

adipose tissue	endocrine gland	ligament	positive feedback
blood	epidermis	lymph	skeletal muscle
bone	epithelial tissue	membrane	smooth muscle
cardiac muscle	exocrine gland	negative feedback	tendon
cartilage	gland	nerve tissue	tissue
collagen	glial cell	neuron	
connective tissue	hair follicle	organ	
dermis	homeostasis	organ system	

ANSWER KEY

SELF TEST

1. a
2. a
3. c
4. a
5. e
6. c
7. b
8. a
9. b
10. d
11. c
12. a
13. a
14. d
15. b
16. homeostasis
17. tissues
18. negative feedback
19. epithelial
20. connective
21. nerve
22. A. mouth
    B. pharynx
    C. liver
    D. pancreas
    E. small intestine
    F. large intestine
    G. gallbladder
23. A. epithelial tissue
    B. muscle tissue
    C. connective tissue
24. A. central canal
    B. bone cells
    C. concentric rings of matrix
25. A. dendrites (signal receivers)
    B. axon (signal transporter)
    C. cell body
    D. synaptic terminals (impulse transmission)

26. A. epidermis
    B. dermis
    C. sensory nerve ending
    D. sebaceous gland
    E. sweat gland
    F. muscle
    G. hair root
27. b
28. a
29. b
30. a

ESSAY CHALLENGE

1. Both of these glands are derived from epithelial tissue and secrete substances. Endocrine glands secrete substances (such as hormones) into the spaces around cells. These substances may then diffuse into nearby capillaries where they will then be carried to distant sites. Exocrine glands remain connected to the epithelium by a passageway called a *duct*. Substances secreted from these glands travel in these ducts directly to their site of action.

2. 1) Loose connective tissue is composed of a loose arrangement of fibers and combines with epithelial tissues to form membranes; 2) fibrous connective tissue contains densely packed collagen, includes tendons and ligaments, and is used primarily for support; 3) specialized connective tissues include cartilage, bone, fat, blood, and lymph and have many functions.

3. Skeletal muscle has an orderly arrangement of muscle fibers, is under voluntary control, and moves the skeleton. Cardiac muscle is an involuntary muscle with an orderly arrangement of muscle fibers. Cardiac muscle fibers are interconnected by gap junctions which leads to a coordinated contraction that is needed for the heart to act as a pump. Smooth muscle is involuntary, lacks the orderly arrangement of muscle fibers, and is found in the walls of many internal organs.

4. Negative feedback systems reverse the initial stimulus, and positive feedback systems enhance the original stimulus. Both respond to internal or external stimuli.

5. The value of the variable would be plotted on the *y*-axis (the dependent variable) with time on the *x*-axis (the independent variable). The graph would show the variable increasing and decreasing within some narrow limits. Negative feedback causes the variable to reverse its direction of change, so any time the value of the variable increases, it will subsequently decrease. This reversal would also be seen when the variable is decreasing.

6. As the snowball rolls down the hill, it picks up more snow and then its speed increases. As it moves faster, it picks up snow at a faster rate and continues to accelerate. The amplification of the speed of the snowball is the net result and is what defines this as positive feedback. In this system, the speed of the snowball is the variable that is being amplified and the effector is the snow because the addition of new snow is what causes a change in the variable.

7. In homeostasis controlled by negative feedback systems, a physiological variable will change naturally within certain narrow limits. Doctors make decisions on when to "step in" based on knowledge of those limits. These acceptable limits may be different from person to person and are affected by things such as age and gender.

8. The dermis is an example of loose connective tissue. The protein fibers in this tissue are very loosely arranged in a diffuse network. Tendons have very orderly arrangements of dense collagen fibers which gives them their strength and helps them with their job of attaching muscle to bone. If tendons had the structure of dermis, they would tear very easily.

MEDIA ACTIVITIES

27.2 Web Investigation: From Nightmare to Medical Miracle

1. Shock is a collection of symptoms associated with a reduced ability of the heart and circulatory system to deliver adequate amounts of oxygen and nutrient-rich blood to the vital organs and tissues of the body. The degree of shock that a person experiences depends on the type of illness or injury. Since some degree of shock is related to most insults on the body, signs and symptoms of shock are very common. In an emergency situation, shock must be dealt with immediately because a lack of oxygen and nutrients to the vital organs (such as the brain and heart) could lead to multiple organ failure, coma, and death.

2. Hypothermia is usually associated with prolonged exposure to low external temperatures. Hypothermia occurs when your body fails to maintain its normal core temperature. Your normal core body temperature may fluctuate from around 98 to 99°F, but when it falls below 95°F, you experience hypothermia.

3. A person with mild hypothermia (95 to 98°F) can be treated by moving the person to a warmer temperature, providing dry clothing, an external heat source (e.g., fire or "cuddle"), and food and warm drinks. Even after a person is rescued from the conditions that produced their hypothermia, their body temperature may continue to fall in what is called *after-drop*. In order to minimize this serious condition, it is important to reduce their activity. A patient should not be asked to participate in their own rescue by climbing, walking, or moving. Although movements produce body heat, they also help bring blood that was cooled at the surface of the body to the core where further cooling may occur and contribute to the after-drop.

315

4. The key to surviving severe hypothermia is a slow metabolism. When vital internal organs cool, their metabolic demand for oxygen decreases. The rapid cooling, along with symptoms related to shock, lead to a decreased heart rate and respiration rate. This means that the body has a decreased ability to deliver oxygen and nutrients to vital organs. If those organs have a low metabolic demand, then this problem is less likely to lead to organ damage. This delicate balance is more likely to occur in smaller bodies. Small children have a very large surface area relative to their volume, so core cooling occurs more rapidly. In addition, shivering is a mechanism that is less likely to occur in very small children, which means that core temperatures can drop more rapidly. Taken together, the result is that vital organs will cool more rapidly and reach a depressed metabolic state in which there is very low oxygen demand. This helps preserve those organs until the child can be rewarmed.

ISSUES IN BIOLOGY

1. Acidification of water and soil will change its pH. One of the major pieces of evidence that will need to be collected is the pH levels of affected regions. In addition, it will be important to correlate the known damaging effects of acidification with those changes. The presence, absence, or decreased abundance of certain organisms that are highly sensitive to environmental stress (indicator species) can be measured. This information will have to be compared to areas believed to be unaffected by the stress (a control). National Forests are managed by the federal government, and therefore an agency such as the EPA (Environmental Protection Agency) would be an appropriate place to report these results.

2. Because ecosystems are so complex, a complete list of consequences would be difficult to describe. Examples of such consequences can be the loss of sensitive species. Certain organisms are very sensitive to environmental stress and could be lost from an ecosystem affected by acid mine drainage. If these organisms are a prey species for a specific predator, the predator could suffer as a result. If the lost species is an important predator, then the ecosystem might become overpopulated with its prey if it is tolerant to the pH stress. The acid mine drainage could select only for those organisms that can withstand the stress, and this could lead to a loss of biological diversity. Diverse ecosystems are more stable and would be able to withstand further stress. The loss of biological diversity will weaken the ecosystem to the point where it becomes more vulnerable to other environmental stresses.

3. When industries are asked to adhere to regulations that protect the environment, they are able to calculate the effect that these changes will have on profits. The link between the change and the measurable outcome (profit) is often easy to see. With the environment, changes often lead to a wide variety of connected outcomes due to the complexity of an ecosystem. Many of these outcomes are difficult to measure, and therefore, comparing them to profit is not an easy task. In addition, much of the value we place on ecosystems is qualitative (not a measurable quantity). In order to deal with this issue, it is important to identify quantitative changes that can be measured in the environment. In some cases, the consequences of an environmental insult can be tied back into an economic cost. An example would be in the case of tourism. In many areas of the world, tourism makes up a large percentage of the economy, and natural attractions such as diverse ecosystems are a major part of this segment of their tourism industry. For many of these regions, it is in their best interest to strike a delicate balance between industrial needs and the health of their ecosystems.

BIZARRE FACTS IN BIOLOGY

1. Crop damage from extreme cold costs farmers millions of dollars. The National Weather Service estimated that in 1996, frost and freezing temperatures caused $260 million of crop damage in the United States and its territories. With discoveries about how cells are protected from freezing, scientists might look for ways to incorporate those protective mechanisms into crop plants. Genetically modified plants might be better able to handle the stress of extreme cold. Freezing foods for transport so that they can be preserved often damages the structure of the food and changes its properties. If foods could be frozen without this structural damage, then freezing could be used as a natural preservation method without the loss of food quality.

2. When an organ is harvested for transplant, it must be chilled with ice to preserve it. This preservation process is limited and the organ will only be viable for a short time. It is crucial that the organ is quickly transported to an operating room where it can be transplanted into the organ recipient. These limitations could be reduced if organs could be frozen for long periods of time and then used at a future date. Freezing an organ would cause catastrophic damage on the cellular level, so currently this is not an option. If antifreezing technology could be applied to the cryopreservation of organs, then this damage could be avoided. Space travel to distant parts of our solar system and beyond would require very long periods of time. The astronauts sent on these missions might reach a very old age before reaching their destination. One way to prevent this is to put the astronauts into a "suspended state of animation" which would require freezing them (cryopreservation). As with freezing organs, this process would produce massive damage on the cellular level. Antifreezing technology would help facilitate this process for space travel.

CHAPTER 28: CIRCULATION

AT-A-GLANCE

SELF TEST

1. The _____ is an organism with an open circulatory system.
   a. snail   b. sponge
   c. octopus   d. frog
   e. human

2. Mixing of oxygenated and deoxygenated blood within the heart occurs in the _____.
   a. bird   b. fish
   c. dog   d. frog
   e. flatworm

3. The most important factor in the return of blood flow back to the heart is _____.
   a. the pumping of the heart
   b. high pressure
   c. skeletal muscle contraction
   d. valves in the veins

4. The cardiac cycle is _____.
   a. the time period between the two heart sounds
   b. the action of the heart in a minute's time
   c. the blood leaving the heart and returning to the heart
   d. the synchronous contraction of the two atria followed by the contraction of the two ventricles

5. Erythroblastosis fetalis is a disease in newborns which is caused by _____.
   a. low blood oxygen level
   b. the mother's immune system recognizing fetal Rh factor and making Rh antibodies
   c. fetal Rh antibody attacking maternal red blood cells with Rh factor
   d. lack of Rh proteins in the fetal blood
   e. the clotting mechanism

6. Why are people with excessive cholesterol deposition at risk for clotting disorders?
   a. Plaques in the walls of arteries may cause the lining of the vessel to rupture.
   b. Cholesterol acts as an enzyme and converts prothrombin into thrombin.
   c. Antibodies react with cholesterol, causing agglutination of the blood.
   d. Cholesterol reacts with fibrin.

7. The _____ is NOT part of the lymphatic system.
   a. thyroid   b. thymus
   c. spleen   d. tonsils
   e. lymphatic capillaries

8. Epinephrine is given as treatment for shock victims because _____.
   a. it is an anticoagulant
   b. it eliminates excess water and salts from the body, reducing blood pressure
   c. it increases heart rate and blood pressure
   d. it dilates the coronary artery carrying oxygenated blood to the heart muscle

9. People with kidney damage, particularly those who are on hemodialysis, tend to be severely anemic. Why?
   a. The damaged kidneys are excessively destroying red blood cells.
   b. There is a lack of erythropoietin.
   c. The bone marrow cannot get enough cholesterol to make the necessary red blood cells.
   d. Excessive urea excreted by the kidneys into urine prevents the bone marrow from making blood cells.

10. Jane Doe, a woman with type B– blood, delivers a healthy baby girl who is O+. One year later she delivers another baby girl who is B+ but is suffering from erythroblastosis fetalis. Why is the first child not affected, but the second child is?
    a. As a woman gets older, she makes elevated levels of anti-Rh antibodies.
    b. The second child has a B blood type. The mother has produced anti-B antibodies that are causing the disease.
    c. It is the first Rh+ fetus that actually sensitizes the mother's immune system to the Rh factor.
    d. By the time that she became pregnant with the second baby, Jane Doe had formed anti-O antibodies.

11. Which of the following is NOT a part of all circulatory systems?
    a. a fluid that acts to transport substances throughout the body
    b. a system of passageways that carry the fluid
    c. an open region inside the body where internal organs are immersed directly in the fluid
    d. a muscular pump for pushing the fluid through the passageways

12. What is the overriding main function of the vertebrate circulatory system?
    a. to transport substances
    b. to cool the body
    c. to regulate the pH of fluids in the body
    d. to fight against invading pathogens

13. What do you call the muscular chambers in a heart?
    a. capillaries
    b. atria
    c. partitions
    d. ventricles
    e. Both the second and fourth answers are correct.

14. Uncoordinated and irregular contractions of one of the chambers of the heart are referred to as _____.
    a. fibrillations
    b. a delay of the atrioventricular node
    c. a pacemaker
    d. a stroke

15. What is the determining factor that stimulates erythropoietin release from the kidney?
    a. too much carbon dioxide in the blood
    b. too little carbon dioxide in the blood
    c. too much oxygen in the blood
    d. too little oxygen in the blood

16. Which of the following people would have the HIGHEST blood pressure during ventricular relaxation?
    a. a person with a systolic pressure of 130
    b. a person with a blood pressure of 110/70
    c. a person with a blood pressure of 100/80
    d. a person with a diastolic pressure of 90

17. The evolution of the cardiovascular system in vertebrates involved several important changes. Which one of the following represents the order of a major change that occurred?
    a. a closed to an open circulatory system
    b. 3-chambered to a 2-chambered and then a 4-chambered heart
    c. 4-chambered to a 3-chambered and then a 2-chambered heart
    d. an open to a closed circulatory system

18. Which of the following blood pressures has the highest *systolic* reading?
    a. 120/80
    b. 140/70
    c. 90/55
    d. 150/90
    e. 130/95

19. What would happen if a person received a drug that acted as a thrombin inhibitor?

   a. His heart rate would drop.

   b. His heart rate would increase.

   c. He would become anemic because of a decrease in the number of red blood cells.

   d. His ability to produce blood clots would be inhibited.

20. The liver is responsible for producing a variety of proteins found in plasma. When a person suffers from liver failure, a common symptom is edema (swelling) of the tissues. Why does this occur?

   a. The person is making smaller proteins that diffuse into the tissues. Water then follows these proteins into the tissues.

   b. The person is making fewer plasma proteins, but the few that remain are diffusing into the tissues. Water then follows these proteins into the tissues.

   c. The liver is overproducing plasma protein. The excess protein displaces water and forces it into the tissues.

   d. The liver is making fewer plasma proteins and a weak osmotic gradient is produced. Water that has entered the tissue begins to accumulate there.

21. How are capillaries specialized for the exchange of respiratory gases?

   a. The capillary walls are only one cell thick.

   b. The capillary walls are wrapped in a layer of smooth muscle.

   c. They allow the passage of fluids through spaces between the cells.

   d. They have one-way valves.

   e. Both the first and third answers are correct.

22. Megakaryocytes are responsible for the production of _____.

23. Animals have one of two major types of circulatory systems: _____ and _____.

24. The _____ cycle takes about 0.8 seconds to complete.

25. In a typical blood pressure reading, the higher of the two numbers is considered the _____ pressure.

26. _____ causes the red color in erythrocytes.

27. There are five common types of white blood cell that are all referred to as _____.

28. _____ carry blood away from the heart.

29. Label the structures indicated on this diagram of a human heart.

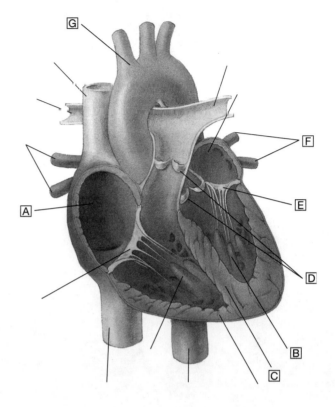

30. In order for the human heart to beat efficiently, the impulse to contract must follow a specified pathway. Label this pathway in the diagram below.

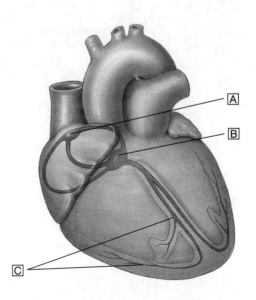

319

31. Label the four vessels indicated on this diagram of the circulatory system of a typical human.

aorta

superior vena cava

inferior vena cava

liver

D

C

lung capillaries

pulmonary artery

heart

kidney

intestine

B

A

33. Label the structures of the lymphatic system on the illustration below.

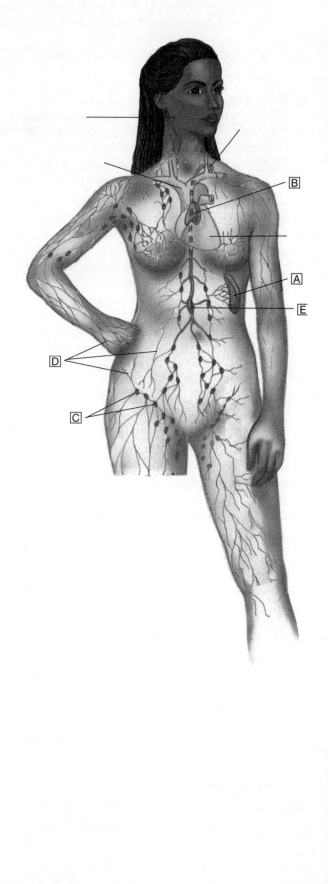

B

A

E

D

C

32. Label the anatomical structures associated with capillary beds as depicted below.

D

C

B

A

endothelium

capillary

connective tissue
(external layer)

smooth muscle
(middle layer)

connective tissue

endothelium
(inner layer)

artery

vein

ESSAY CHALLENGE

1. Compare and contrast an open and closed circulatory system. What type of organisms possess each type?

2. During the course of vertebrate evolution, the heart has become increasingly more complex. In going from simple to complex, describe the changes that have occurred in the heart over evolutionary time.

3. Describe the events that take place in the cardiac cycle. In your description, include both the electrical and muscular events.

4. Describe the role that the nervous system plays in controlling heart rate.

5. When an Rh-negative mother has an Rh-positive child, a subsequent fetus will be at risk while in the uterus. Explain this risk.

6. How do red blood cells form and what is their life span?

7. Describe the process of blood clotting.

8. Describe how the function of the lymphatic system involves an interaction with the circulatory system?

MEDIA ACTIVITIES

To access a Media Activity visit http://www.prenhall.com/audesirk7. Log in to the Web site selected by your instructor, navigate to this chapter, and select the appropriate Media Activity number.

28.1 Circulatory Systems
Estimated time: 10 minutes

Explore the structure, function, and evolution of circulatory systems in animals.

28.2 Heart Structure and Function
Estimated time: 5 minutes

Explore the various structures and functions of the vertebrate heart.

28.3 The Cardiac Cycle
Estimated time: 5 minutes

View a brief animation of the steps of the cardiac cycle.

28.4 Blood Pressure
Estimated time: 10 minutes

See what blood pressure is, learn how to measure it yourself, and explore the effects of various chemicals on blood pressure.

28.5 Web Investigation: Sudden Death
Estimated time: 20 minutes

In the United States, more people die from heart disease than from any other illness. When healthy young adults are tragically struck down by this powerful killer, we are reminded of the factors that put us at risk and the lifestyle changes that help reduce that risk. Darryl Kile's father died of a heart attack at the age of 44, which suggests that some degree of risk may be inherited. In this investigation, you will explore the nature of Coronary Artery Disease (CAD) and uncover some of the risk factors that may have contributed to Darryl's death.

1. Describe the relationship between Coronary Artery Disease (CAD) and atherosclerosis (http://www.heartpoint. com/coronartdi.html).

2. Risk factors for CAD are often categorized as "controllable" or "uncontrollable." What are the major risk factors (http://www.mayoclinic.org/coronaryartery-rst/risks.html) for CAD and how are they categorized?

3. Several different physiological systems (http://my.webmd.com/content/article/2/1675_50290.htm?lastselectedguid= {5FE84E90-BC77-4056-A91C-9531713CA348}) are involved in producing the characteristic narrowing of the arteries associated with CAD. What are these systems and how do they interact with each other to produce this narrowing?

4. High levels of LDL, often referred to as the "bad cholesterol," are a strong risk factor for the development of CAD. The levels of LDL (http://www.1uphealth.com/health/ldl_info.html#definition) in a person's system are determined by a combination of genetic and lifestyle factors. Familial Hypercholesterolemia (FH) (http://www. medped.org/MEDPED-What-is-FH.html) is an inherited condition that puts a person at risk for very high levels of LDL. Describe the structure and function of LDL and why a person with FH often has high levels of LDL in his system.

5. In many cases, a person's cholesterol level cannot be managed with lifestyle changes such as dietary restrictions. Their only option may be to turn to cholesterol-lowering drugs such as statins (http://www.intelihealth.com/IH/ ihtIH/WSIHW000/8775/23591.html). How do these drugs help lower a person's cholesterol?

ISSUES IN BIOLOGY

Is Congestive Heart Failure an Epidemic?

Almost 5 million Americans have congestive heart failure (CHF). It is a common end stage of various cardiovascular diseases: valve disorder, chronic hypertension, myocardial infarction, viral cardiomyopathies, and coronary artery disease, just to name a few. Consider the following points: cardiovascular diseases are the #1 killer in the United States, and the population is getting older as well as living longer with cardiovascular disease. Most of the audience reading this essay right now will be impacted by CHF—parents, grandparents, friends, and so on.

The statistics (http://www.ncbi.nlm.nih.gov/entrez/query.fcgi?holding=npg&cmd=Retrieve&db=PubMed&list_uids= 8376698&dopt=Abstract) of congestive heart failure are alarming. CHF is present in 2% of persons aged 40 to 59, 5% of persons aged 60 to 69, and 10% of persons over the age of 70. The incidence, or newly diagnosed cases, of CHF in men and women is equal over the age of 65, about 10 in 1000. However, there is a racial difference: 25% more African Americans have the disease than do Caucasians.

Congestive heart failure is caused by weakened heart muscle that cannot effectively pump blood out. When the ventricles contract, less blood is ejected and the blood will be under less pressure. Depending on whether the CHF involves damage in the left ventricle or the right ventricle, the effect can involve pulmonary congestion, poor systemic circulation, or both if the muscular weakness encompasses both ventricles.

Signs of CHF (http://www.americanheart.org/presenter.jhtml?identifier=339) are fatigue, shortness of breath, rapid heart rate, swelling in legs and ankles, excessive urination, cold and sweaty skin, a cough (particularly with bloody sputum), and weight gain.

The treatments for CHF include weight loss, restriction of fluid intake, moderate physical activity, medications, and a possible heart transplant. Of course, the first treatment needs to address the original cause of the CHF; these treatments might include a valve replacement or a coronary artery bypass. The medications commonly used are diuretics, which eliminate excess water and salts in urine; vasodilators, which expand the arterial diameters and reduce the resistance that reduces blood flow; and angiotensin-converting enzyme inhibitors, which block the activation of a powerful vasoconstrictor, called angiotensin, normally produced in the body. Mild to moderate congestive heart failure can be treated. If the heart is severely damaged, a transplant may be the only choice (assuming the overall health of the person is good). The fatality rate for CHF is high, with one in five persons dying within a year. Many people will go in and out of congestive heart failure repeatedly over a 5- to 10-year period.

One of the more interesting potential treatments is a small mechanical pump called a left ventricular assist device, or LVAD. It is now used as a temporary device for patients who are awaiting a heart transplant. Studies have shown that there may be a long-term benefit to the LVAD since patients who use them show an increase in their existing heart efficiency. Perhaps reducing the workload on the left ventricle by having a supplemental mechanical left ventricle allows the heart muscle to grow stronger and pump more effectively.

The best control of CHF is by preventing the contributing cardiovascular diseases to CHF. Faster therapies and earlier diagnoses of these other diseases will decrease the potential epidemic of congestive heart failure.

1. Why or how is CHF an outcome of other cardiovascular diseases?

2. Why would giving a vasodilator to reduce resistance help in the treatment of CHF?

3. Early signs of CHF are shortness of breath and pulmonary edema. Explain these symptoms.

BIZARRE FACTS IN BIOLOGY

Growing New Blood Vessels

The coronary arteries form a network of vessels around the heart. These vessels deliver a steady cargo of oxygenated blood to the heart muscle so that normal heart function can be maintained. Coronary Artery Disease (CAD) involves a blockage or narrowing of these vessels which cuts down the flow of blood to the muscle. One of the treatments for this disease is bypass surgery (http://yourmedicalsource.com/library/cardiacbypass/CB_whatis.html). In this procedure, a vessel is harvested from some other part of the body (e.g., leg vein). One end of this harvested vessel is grafted "upstream" of the blockage while the other end is attached to the downstream side. Blood can now flow through this new vessel and "bypass" the diseased portion of the coronary artery. This complex and highly invasive surgery can be very risky and involves many potential complications. What if the heart could simply grow new vessels that could bypass the coronary disease to restore circulation? This process, called angiogenesis, could help restore blood flow to areas affected by clogged or narrowed arteries. The challenge for scientists and doctors is to find ways to encourage the heart (http://www.sciencedaily.com/releases/2001/11/011115071858.htm) to establish this new circulation. It has long been known that tumors (http://press2.nci.nih.gov/sciencebehind/angiogenesis/angio04.htm) could perform this angiogenic "trick" with incredible efficiency. By establishing a more advanced circulation, tumors are able to receive the necessary nutrients and oxygen to sustain their growth. The new vessels also offer a way for tumor cells to break off and travel through the circulation to a distant site in a process called metastasis (http://press2.nci.nih.gov/ sciencebehind/cancer/cancer09.htm).

1. With knowledge of how angiogenesis occurs, how might scientists and doctors use this information to treat cancer patients?

2. Coronary artery disease and tumor development are two areas of angiogenesis research. Can you think of other ways that scientists and doctors might apply their knowledge of how angiogenesis works?

KEY TERMS

angina	closed circulatory system	lymph	semilunar valve
arteriole	erythrocyte	lymphatic system	sinoatrial (SA) node
artery	erythropoietin	lymph node	spleen
atherosclerosis	fibrin	lymphocyte	stroke
atrioventricular (AV) node	fibrinogen	macrophage	thrombin
atrioventricular valve	heart	open circulatory system	thymus
atrium	heart attack	pacemaker	tonsil
blood	hemocoel	plaque	vein
blood clotting	hemoglobin	plasma	ventricle
blood vessel	hypertension	platelet	venule
capillary	interstitial fluid	precapillary sphincter	
cardiac cycle	leukocyte	Rh factor	

ANSWER KEY

SELF TEST

1. a
2. d
3. c
4. d
5. b
6. a
7. a
8. c
9. b
10. c
11. c
12. a
13. e
14. a
15. d
16. d
17. d
18. d
19. d
20. d
21. e
22. platelets
23. open, closed
24. cardiac
25. systolic

26. hemoglobin
27. leukocytes
28. arteries
29. A. right atrium
    B. left ventricle
    C. ventricular septum
    D. semilunar veins
    E. atrioventricular valve
    F. pulmonary veins
    G. aorta
30. A. SA node
    B. AV node
    C. excitable fibers
31. A. femoral artery
    B. femoral vein
    C. carotid artery
    D. jugular vein
32. A. venule
    B. arteriole
    C. precapillary sphincters
    D. capillaries
33. A. spleen
    B. thymus
    C. lymph nodes
    D. lymph vessels
    E. thoracic duct

ESSAY CHALLENGE

1. In section 28.1: "Animals Have Two Types of Circulatory Systems," you will find a discussion on these two types of circulatory systems. An open circulatory system involves one or more hearts pumping blood through a network of vessels that open up to a space within the body called a hemocoel. Blood in the hemocoel will bathe the tissues before being picked up by the vessels again. This type of system is typical of many arthropods (e.g., spiders and insects) and mollusks such as snails and clams. Although closed circulatory systems are found in some invertebrates such as the earthworm and some active mollusks such as the squid, it is typically associated with the vertebrates. In a closed system, the blood is confined to the heart and a continuous network of vessels that transport blood from the heart and return it to this organ without leaving the circulation.

2. Review section 28.2 for more information on the evolution of the vertebrate heart. The fishes possess an example of the first vertebrate heart to evolve. This simple heart consisted of a single atria and a single ventricle. In amphibians and many reptiles, you will find the three-chambered heart that consists of two atria and one ventricle. The addition of the second atria meant that vertebrates could have two separate circulations: one for obtaining oxygen and one for distributing it to the tissues. In some reptiles, this separation is enhanced by a partial wall between the right and left side of the ventricle. In mammals, the heart consists of two atria and two ventricles. Along with the separate circulations, the fourth chamber meant that deoxygenated blood returning from the tissues could not mix with the oxygenated blood returning from the lungs.

3. In section 28.2: "The Vertebrate Heart Consists of Muscular Chambers," you will find a discussion on the cardiac cycle. During the cycle, the sinoatrial node (SA node) sends an electrical impulse that travels through the muscles of the right and left atria, which then contract in synchrony. Next, the atrioventricular node (AV node) is excited by the previous impulse. The impulse is delayed here but then travels down tracts of excitable fibers to the ventricles, which will contract about 0.1 seconds after the atria.

4. The autonomic nervous system consists of the parasympathetic and the sympathetic nervous system. Signals from the parasympathetic nervous system cause the heart rate to slow to about 70 beats per minute in an average adult. The sympathetic, or "fight or flight" system is responsible for the acceleration of heart rate.

5. In Section 28.3: "Blood Type Is Determined by Specific Proteins on Red Blood Cell Membranes," you will find a discussion on Rh factor and its role in determining risks during pregnancy. When an Rh-negative mother has an Rh-positive child, the mother will have produced Rh antibodies against the child's blood cells because her immune system "sees" these cells as foreign. If a subsequent fetus is Rh-positive, her antibodies can cross the placenta and attack her child's blood which leads to a very dangerous form of anemia in the child.

6. In section 28.3: "Red Blood Cells Have a Relatively Short Life Span," you will find a discussion on red blood cell formation. Red blood cells are formed in the bone marrow of certain bones found in the chest, upper arms, upper legs, and hips. During their development, they lose their nuclei which means that they cannot replace themselves. The result is a very short life span for a cell, which lasts only approximately 4 months.

7. In section 28.3: "Platelets Are Cell Fragments That Aid in Blood Clotting," you will find a discussion on how a clot is formed. Clotting starts when platelets and other factors in the plasma contact an irregular surface like a damaged blood vessel. Platelets adhere to the damaged area and partially block the opening. A complex series of events is then initiated, resulting in the production of thrombin. Thrombin causes the conversion of fibrinogen into fibrin, which then produces a fibrous network that stops the bleeding. Platelets adhere to the fibers and a clot (or scab) forms.

8. Review Section 28.5 in your text for more information on this interaction. The lymphatic system has vessels that are like veins and capillaries and are found in close association with these vessels. Lymphatic vessels pick up excess fluid that accumulates in the tissues and return it to the circulatory system. Lymphatic vessels are also responsible for transporting digested fats that are too large to diffuse through the walls of capillaries around the small intestine. These fats are eventually transported back into the circulatory system as lymph dumps into major veins that make their way back to the heart via the superior vena cava. Finally, the lymphatic system plays a major role in immunity. Pathogens transported by blood may make their way into the lymphatic circulation where they are destroyed by white blood cells such as macrophages and lymphocytes.

MEDIA ACTIVITIES

28.5 Web Investigation: Sudden Death

1. Coronary Artery Disease is a condition in which blockages in the major coronary vessels prevent oxygenated blood from reaching the cardiac tissue. Often referred to as "hardening of the arteries," atherosclerosis is the process through which the blockages that define CAD are created. Atherosclerosis describes the deposition of fat and cholesterol in the arterial walls. This deposition causes the vessel to narrow, which leads to a reduction in blood flow.

2. Risk factors that are uncontrollable include gender, family history, and age. Males are at greater risk than females, and when you age, your risk for CAD increases. In addition, people with a family history of heart disease are at a much greater risk for developing this disease. Many of the controllable risk factors are considered lifestyle factors such as smoking, exercise, diet, high blood pressure, high cholesterol, and stress.

3. Narrowing of a vessel may begin when the vessel is damaged by factors such as high blood pressure. An inflammatory response to this damage involves components of the blood clotting system. If the vessel does not heal properly, it begins to thicken. In addition, cholesterol gets deposited into the wall of the vessel as the vessel continues to narrow. The damage and underlying deposits weaken the vessel wall which can crack or break and stimulate the formation of blood clots. If these clots are large enough, they may completely block the vessel and produce a heart attack.

4. Your body requires cholesterol for important functions such as the synthesis of cell membranes and steroid hormones. Because cholesterol is not water soluble, it needs to be transported to the tissues in particles called lipoproteins. LDL is one type of these particles that appears to have the important job of delivering cholesterol to body tissues. In order for cells to obtain the cholesterol contained in an LDL particle, it must construct a receptor on its membrane that the LDL particle can bind to. In Familial Hypercholesterolemia, the individual has inherited a defective form of this receptor. The result is that cells have difficulty taking up the LDL particles and therefore the levels of LDL in the blood become elevated.

5. Statins work by inhibiting an enzyme that helps the liver produce cholesterol. By inhibiting cholesterol production, the amount of cholesterol in a person's system can be lowered. Taken in combination with lifestyle changes such as a low-fat diet and exercise, they have been shown to be very effective at lowering a person's cholesterol level.

ISSUES IN BIOLOGY

1. When the heart is failing, it is usually because it has been damaged by some chronic underlying problems such as clogged arteries, high blood pressure, valve defect, or some other medical condition. It is the constant stress produced by these other conditions that weakens the heart.

2. In CHF, the heart is weak and is unable to produce the forceful contractions necessary to maintain proper circulation. Vasodilators cause blood vessels to relax, which reduces the amount of resistance the blood faces as it travels through these vessels. With less resistance, the weaker contractions will be able to move blood more efficiently. In addition, since high blood pressure is often the cause of CHF, the vasodilators will help reduce the blood pressure and relieve some of the stress that produced the condition.

3. As oxygenated blood returns to the left side of the heart from the lungs, it is sent out by the left ventricle to the body tissues. In CHF, the contractions are weak. This causes the blood to "back up" in the lungs. As blood is unable to return to the heart, it builds up in the pulmonary (lung) circulation where the pressure rises. As the blood pressure builds up around the lungs, fluid is forced from the blood into the lung spaces, which causes swelling (edema). This swelling causes the shortness of breath that CHF patients experience.

BIZARRE FACTS IN BIOLOGY

1. Tumor angiogenesis leads to an increase in blood flow to the site of the tumor. This new circulation helps bring nutrients and oxygen to the tissue. Tumor cells grow and divide very rapidly and require this nutrient delivery in order to maintain their rapid development. In addition, metastasis of tumor cells leads to the formation of new tumors at

distant sites. The inhibition of angiogenesis near tumors could be a way to starve the tumor and prevent metastasis. This inhibition is currently a very active area of medical research and a new suite of drugs appear promising in the fight against cancer.

2. There are many diseases that can be blamed on too much or too little angiogenesis. There are more than 70 diseases that relate to excessive angiogenesis, including diseases such as diabetic blindness, age-related macular degeneration, rheumatoid arthritis, and psoriasis. Treatments for these diseases will involve shutting down or inhibiting the signals that produce the new blood vessels. In complications related to diabetes, stroke, delayed wound healing, and coronary artery disease, the challenge is to stimulate the growth of new vessels to restore lost circulation.

CHAPTER 29: RESPIRATION

AT-A-GLANCE

SELF TEST

1. Figure 29-9 shows gas exchange occurring in a _____.

   a. lung of a mammal

   b. gill of a fish

   c. tracheae in an insect

   d. trachea of a mammal

   e. gill of an arthropod

2. An advantage of gas exchange in aquatic habitats, as compared to terrestrial, is that _____.

   a. water contains more dissolved oxygen than air

   b. gills are more protected from environmental damage

   c. keeping respiratory membranes moist is easy

   d. body heat is more easily maintained

3. The major criterion that determines rate of breathing is _____.

   a. blood oxygen level

   b. blood carbon dioxide level

   c. nitrogen in the atmosphere

   d. blood carbon monoxide level

   e. blood glucose level

4. When you perform a strenuous exercise, _____.

   a. respiratory muscles accessory to the diaphragm and rib muscles will contract to increase chest volume

   b. excess carbon monoxide will stimulate the respiratory center of the brain so the rate of breathing increases

   c. oxygen will diffuse into the capillaries around the alveoli in addition to diffusion through the walls of the bronchi

   d. additional oxygen and carbon dioxide are exchanged through the skin to support the increase in metabolism

5. *Carcinogenic* means _____.
   a. mutation of cells   **b.** cancer-causing
   c. toxin-producing   **d.** cell death

6. The Heimlich maneuver is seen in Figure 29-8. What happens?

   a. There is a neural pressure point where the hands are placed, and this stimulates the brain's respiratory center.

   b. The person gasps for air when the maneuver is performed, thereby displacing the food with air.

   c. The arm contraction squeezes or massages the food upward.

   d. The diaphragm is forced upward by the pressure of the arms pulled upward against the chest.

7. Carbon monoxide poisoning kills by _____.
   a. preventing the production of neurotransmitters in brain cells
   b. binding to oxygen, thereby preventing it from getting to hemoglobin
   c. depriving cells of oxygen by competing with it for the hemoglobin in the red blood cells
   d. enzymatically destroying the cells of the body

8. Take a huge breath while sitting up straight in your chair, and then do this again while slumped over. Compare the air volume entering the lungs in each situation. Why is there a difference?
   a. The chest and rib cage cannot be increased in size effectively when you are slumped over in a chair.
   b. You cannot contract your chest muscles when slumped in a chair.
   c. There is less air moved into the lungs when you are slumped because the tissues need less oxygen for cellular respiration.
   d. The rib cage stays locked in an upward and outward orientation.

9. Compare the lungs to other respiratory structures such as gills and skin. What is the major advantage of the lungs?
   a. Oxygen diffuses faster across lung respiratory membranes than gill respiratory membranes.
   b. The lungs have more surface area, with accompanying greater respiratory membrane for gas exchange.
   c. Lungs are easier to inflate than gills.
   d. The alveoli of lungs are more protected than other respiratory membranes.

10. Sleep apnea is a cessation of breathing that can result in lack of sleep, irritability, lack of concentration, tiredness, and, in severe cases, heart attacks. The apnea is prompted either by a failure of the brain to communicate with the respiratory muscles or an obstructed airway associated with the tongue or muscles of the pharynx or larynx. The more efficient treatment, although one that many people prefer not to use, is the CPAP—continuous positive airway pressure. Fitting over the nose, the mask is attached to a tube that is connected to a portable low-pressure generator. How is this breathing different from normal breathing?
   a. There is no difference between the breathing mechanics. The generator produces negative pressure breathing, causing the air to be sucked into the lung in a similar way to normal breathing.
   b. The generator increases the air pressure so that the air is actually forced into the lungs. This is the opposite of what happens in a normal breath.
   c. The generator sucks the air out of the lungs actively, whereas in a normal expiration it is passively accomplished.

11. Why is breathing so important?
   a. A fresh supply of oxygen must be constantly provided so that cells are able to metabolize glucose efficiently.
   b. The constant production of carbon dioxide by cells must be constantly removed from the body.
   c. Because respiration, also called *breathing,* is synonymous with cell respiration.
   d. all of the above
   e. Both the first and second answers are correct.

12. What features that facilitate diffusion of respiratory gases are shared by all animals with some type of respiratory system?
   a. The surface across which the exchange of respiratory gases is made is exceedingly thin.
   b. The respiratory surface is always moist.
   c. The respiratory surface is very big.
   d. The respiratory surface is an internal lung.
   e. all of the above
   f. The first three answers are all correct.

13. Which of the following stages in the process of respiratory gas exchange occurs by diffusion?
   a. the movement of respiratory gases across the respiratory surfaces of the lung
   b. the movement of respiratory gases between the tissues of the body and the circulatory system
   c. the movement of atmospheric gas into and out of the lungs
   d. the movement of respiratory gases within the blood of the circulatory system
   e. Both the first and second answers are correct.
   f. Both the third and fourth answers are correct.

14. Which of the following represents an evolutionary adaptation that terrestrial animals have to aid in improving the efficiency of their respiratory systems?
   a. keep the respiratory exchange surfaces outside the body to expose them to the oxygen in the air
   b. moisten the respiratory exchange surface only when necessary
   c. thicken the membrane lining the body surface to reduce water loss and promote the diffusion of gases through the skin
   d. development of complex internal lungs with massive amounts of surface area for gas exchange

15. Through what sequence of structures would a volume of air have to travel from the mouth into the lungs?
   a. mouth—pharynx—bronchi—bronchioles—alveoli
   b. mouth—pharynx—bronchioles—bronchi—alveoli
   c. mouth—larynx—trachea—pharynx—alveoli
   d. none of the above

16. What mechanism is used to transport both carbon dioxide and oxygen in the blood?
   a. hemoglobin
   b. dissolved in the blood plasma
   c. sodium bicarbonate ions
   d. all of the above

17. _____ are chambers that contain moist, delicate respiratory surfaces that are protected within a body.

18. The _____ are a system of branching internal tubes that insects use to convey air to their body cells.

19. The _____ is a flap of tissue that guards the opening to the larynx.

20. _____ are the tiny air sacs in the lungs where gas exchange occurs.

21. The _____ is a dome shaped muscle that is found under the lungs.

22. _____ is the process by which air is actively drawn into the lungs.

23. Label the steps involved in oxygen transport through the body by correctly filling in the boxes below.

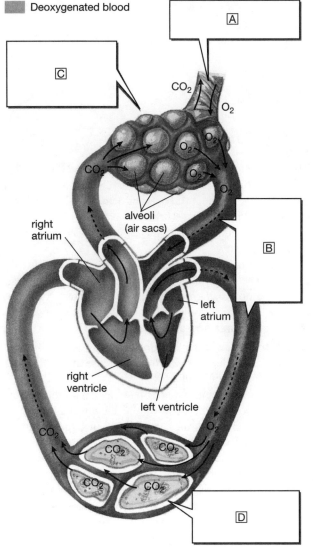

■ Oxygenated blood
■ Deoxygenated blood

A

C

CO_2
O_2

O_2
O_2
CO_2
O_2
O_2

alveoli (air sacs)

right atrium

B

left atrium

right ventricle

left ventricle

O_2

CO_2

CO_2
CO_2
CO_2
CO_2

D

24. Identify the structures of the arthropod respiratory system by labeling the image below.

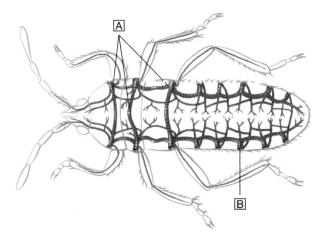

A

B

25. Label the structures of the typical Aves respiratory system below.

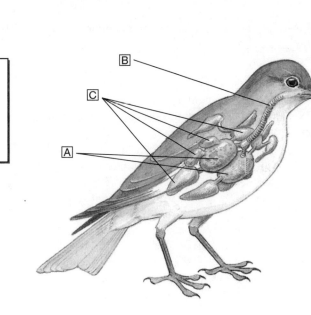

B

C

A

331

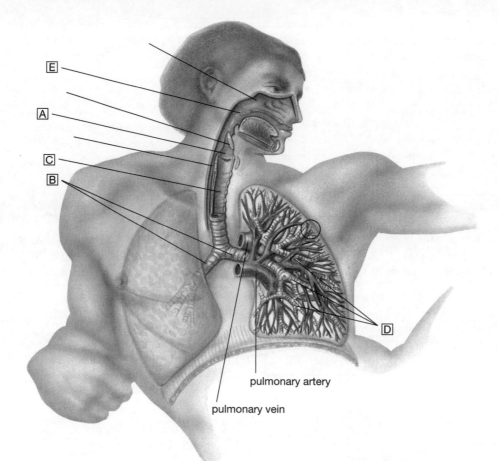

pulmonary artery

pulmonary vein

26. Label the structures indicated on the typical human respiratory system shown above.

27. Once the gas reaches the alveoli, it comes into contact with the respiratory membrane, where gas exchange occurs. Label the structures found at this end of the respiratory system.

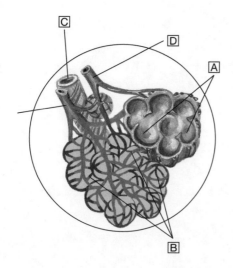

28. If humans did not have lungs, but instead their skin was thin and moist for gas exchange, they would struggle to meet the oxygen demand of the tissues. Why does this not work?
   a. The connection to the circulatory system would be lost.
   b. Temperature control would become very difficult.
   c. The external air does not contain a sufficient amount of oxygen for sufficient gas exchange.
   d. The skin would not provide a great enough surface area for gas exchange.

29. Why do many emphysema patients voluntarily contract muscles that help them increase their chest volume when they inhale?
   a. Emphysema patients have less respiratory surface area because of the damaged alveoli. To compensate, they must bring in larger volumes of air when they inhale.
   b. Emphysema patients have a higher metabolism. In order to meet the higher oxygen demand of the tissues, they must bring in larger volumes of air.
   c. The diaphragms of emphysema patients become paralyzed. The voluntary actions used to increase chest volume help compensate for this problem.
   d. The tumors associated with this disease obstruct the airways. The expansion of the chest cavity helps draw air past these obstructions.

332

30. A patient is rushed to the hospital unconscious. The doctor notes that the lips, extremities, and nail beds of this patient have turned blue. The patient's friend tells the doctor that he thinks it is carbon monoxide poisoning. Why should the doctor be skeptical of this diagnosis?

   a. The doctor should be skeptical because carbon monoxide would cause harm to humans only if it were at extremely high concentrations in the air we breathe.

   b. The doctor should be skeptical because carbon monoxide breaks apart into carbon and oxygen. The oxygen can then bind to the hemoglobin in the red blood cells.

   c. The doctor should be skeptical because the blue color in the nail beds and lips means that the person has either lost a large amount of blood, or blood is just not reaching these areas of the body.

   d. The doctor should be skeptical because when carbon monoxide binds to hemoglobin, it produces the bright red color seen when oxygen binds to this molecule.

31. The surface tension in the alveoli of the human lung is reduced by the production of _____.

32. When oxygen and carbon dioxide are carried in the blood, very little is carried in the plasma in a dissolved form. How does this help facilitate gas exchange at the lungs and tissues?

   a. This helps the blood pull oxygen into the blood from the air and carbon dioxide into the blood from the tissues.

   b. The gases travel faster when they are bound to hemoglobin.

   c. By competing for hemoglobin, the carbon dioxide can force the oxygen into the tissues. At the lungs, the oxygen forces the carbon dioxide off of this molecule so that it can be released into the air.

   d. By removing the oxygen and carbon dioxide from solution in the plasma, a gradient for these gases can be maintained to favor diffusion.

ESSAY CHALLENGE

1. Compare and contrast the respiratory systems in insects and terrestrial vertebrates.

2. How does gas exchange occur in the alveoli?

3. How are oxygen and carbon dioxide transported through the blood?

4. How is the respiratory rate controlled in a human?

333

5. Describe the forces involved in drawing air into the lungs during inhalation.

6. Explain why moist skin is important for respiration in earthworms, frogs, and salamanders?

7. Premature babies often have difficulty producing surfactants. Explain why these babies often struggle to produce a breath.

8. Bicarbonate ions (HCO_3^-) play an important role in maintaining blood pH. Explain how your respiration rate can have an effect on this important physiological relationship.

9. When a person is suffering from asthma, bronchiole spasms and mucus secretions can reduce the amount of space for air to move through the lungs. Asthma patients must learn to control their breathing during these "attacks" so that they do not hyperventilate. Why is hyperventilation an appropriate response when a person with normal lungs is starved for oxygen, but not in the case of the asthma patient?

MEDIA ACTIVITIES

To access a Media Activity visit http://www.prenhall.com/audesirk7. Log in to the Web site selected by your instructor, navigate to this chapter, and select the appropriate Media Activity number.

29.1 Gas Exchange
Estimated time: 5 minutes

Watch an overview of the stages of gas exchange in the animal respiratory system.

29.2 Human Respiratory Anatomy
Estimated time: 5 minutes

Explore the structures and function of the human respiratory system.

29.3 Oxygen and Carbon Dioxide Transport
Estimated time: 5 minutes

Explore mechanisms for transporting oxygen and carbon dioxide to and from the respiratory system.

29.4 Web Investigation: Lives Up in Smoke
Estimated time: 10 minutes

Everyone knows that smoking causes cancer, heart problems, emphysema, and other respiratory ailments. Unfortunately, secondhand smoke remains controversial. This exercise will survey the scientific evidence for the harmful effects of environmental tobacco smoke.

1. In 1993 the Environmental Protection Agency published an extensive report on the "Respiratory Health Effects of Passive Smoking: Lung Cancer and Other Disorders." What were the major conclusions (http://www.epa.gov/iaq/pubs/etsfs.html) of this study?

2. Cigarette smoke contains more than 50 harmful substances (http://www.hc-sc.gc.ca/hppb/regions/ab-nwt/tobacostinks/facts#Whatharmful), including several known carcinogens. What is the biological effect of carbon monoxide?

3. One argument used by tobacco supporters is that secondhand smoke is not a health risk because it is not inhaled. Is this true? What are the physiological effects of even short-term exposure (http://www.pslgroup.com/dg/7e57a.htm) to secondhand smoke?

4. Based on the information above, do you think that smoking should be banned in schools? In all public buildings? Why or why not?

ISSUES IN BIOLOGY

What Are the Physiological Stresses of Deep Diving?
Francisco Pipin Ferreras has logged more than 550 free dives without the use of scuba equipment. In 1994 he completed the world record depth of 127 meters (about 385 feet) on a single breath of air! How is this possible? Since he had more than 20 years of preparation for this event, his respiratory system and nervous system were well prepared for the physiological changes which would occur as he moved quickly deeper and deeper into the blackness.

His real difficulties began at around 300 feet, when he found it almost impossible to equalize his ears. When a person moves from lower atmospheric pressure down to a higher pressure—as in descending in an airplane, for example—the pressure pushes the eardrum inward toward the middle ear. This can cause a rupture of the eardrum and subsequent hearing loss. This is a real problem in scuba diving, and in fact, prevents many people with ear and sinus problems from diving. To avoid the problem, as you descend you take air into the nasal passageways (using compressed air in the scuba tank), force air up the Eustachian tubes (http://www.physlink.com/Education/AskExperts/ae37.cfm) (which connect the nasal cavities and middle ear), and equalize the pressure on both sides of the eardrum (the middle ear side and the external ear side). Since Ferreras had very little air left in his lungs at that point, and he did not want to waste it on equalization, he did something remarkable. He took seawater into his nasal passages, forcing air from the sinuses in his skull into the middle ear, thereby balancing the pressure across the eardrum.

The other real trouble with which Ferreras had to contend was potential nitrogen narcosis (http://www.scubadiving.com/training/instruction/narced.shtml). Seventy-eight percent of the air we breathe is nitrogen gas, although it is not used by our cells. Nitrogen gas is insoluble at sea level, but gases go into solution faster as the outside pressure increases. So as the diver gets down to about 80 feet or lower, the amount of dissolved nitrogen in the blood is increasing to the point that the nitrogen may have an effect on the brain. The effects have been compared to the euphoria associated with being drunk—lightheadedness, impaired motor skills, inability to think rationally. Although there are no lasting effects of the narcosis upon return to land, the problem is returning back to land when one is that severely impaired. People have been known to become so disoriented that they will dive deeper instead of ascending.

The third problem that a diver may have is decompression sickness (http://www.hyperchamber.com/decompression illness/) upon ascent. As the outside pressure decreases, the nitrogen gas which was soluble in the tissues and plasma begins to come out of solution in the form of small bubbles. These bubbles can block blood circulation, causing brain damage, joint pain (the "bends"), paralysis, and even death. This did not worry Ferreras because he knew that he would be going into a decompression chamber as soon as he hit the surface; he had planned on that. The normal diver avoids this by adhering to dive tables, which tell you the maximum amount of time to stay at a particular depth. If the diver goes below this depth or for a longer than suggested time, a recommended "decompression stop" (15 or so feet below the surface) is used to allow the extra nitrogen gas to slowly come out of solution in the tissues. If the diver has really overstayed the depth and/or time, a decompression chamber, also called a hyperbaric chamber, will be recommended.

These are but a few of the problems related to diving. However, the training that one goes through before ever taking the first dive is extensive, and you are required to pass a certification test. But the joys of being underwater, of seeing "fairy" landscapes that are unseen by most, and identifying organisms that you've only seen in a coffee-table book on the underwater world, more than makes up for the discomforts. As you are studying the respiratory system, keep in mind how respiratory physiology is involved in sports activities, and in fact, everyday activities.

1. How can nitrogen cause two very different problems of narcosis and decompression sickness?

2. Why is decompression sickness also called the "bends"?

3. How does a hyperbaric chamber treatment work?

4. One solution that SCUBA divers rely on to reduce the dangers of deep diving is to breathe a mixture of helium and oxygen. Why does this help reduce the risks?

BIZARRE FACTS IN BIOLOGY

The Aquatic Lung—Breathing Liquid

The 1989 movie *The Abyss* (20th Century Fox) popularized the idea that animals could breathe liquid as long as it had oxygen carrying properties similar to the air we breathe. In the movie, a mouse is shown submersed in a mysterious pink liquid. After recovering from the initial shock of inhaling a fluid, the mouse begins to breathe as it normally would in standard room air. Although water does contain dissolved oxygen, it does not have enough carrying capacity to be able to deliver a sufficient amount of oxygen to support our tissues. The human lung evolved to exchange gases with the air we breathe. When filled with water, the gas exchange surface is unable to meet the demands of the body and our tissues begin to starve for oxygen. At the same time, our ability to expel carbon dioxide as a waste product becomes compromised. The mystery behind the pink liquid is that it contains a molecule called perfluorooctyl bromide (http://members.cox.net/gmgroat/perfluorooctyl_bromide.htm).

The concept of liquid breathing was first explored by Dr. J. Kylstra at the State University of New York at Buffalo. By "forcing" oxygen into a simple saline solution, Dr. Kylstra was able to significantly increase the amount of oxygen carried by this liquid. The mice in Dr. Kylstra's lab were able to breathe the liquid and receive adequate amounts of oxygen. Problems arose when it was discovered that the saline was unable to effectively remove carbon dioxide from the mice. Carbon dioxide levels quickly rose to lethal levels in his test subjects. Many different formulations have been tested, but the current use of liquid breathing mediums involves the employment of the perfluorocarbons. In addition to being able to carry 20 times more oxygen than Dr. Kylstra's saline, these compounds also have excellent carbon dioxide carrying capacities. The oxygen and carbon dioxide carrying capacities of these compounds are only a couple of the many unique characteristics (http://classes.kumc.edu/cahe/respcared/liquidventilation/wikeper.html) that make perfluorocarbons useful in liquid ventilation and oxygenation of tissues.

When most divers drop below the surface, they rely on a tank that has been filled with compressed air. Sometimes this air has been modified to reduce the amount of nitrogen which has been shown to be the source of a wide variety of diving injuries and sicknesses (http://www.marinemedical.com/articles/diving.htm). While it may be many years before SCUBA tanks are routinely filled with a liquid breathing medium, the medical applications (http://www.allp.com/LiquiVent/Graphics/sld001.htm) of this technology are becoming realized.

1. If the human lung has evolved to exchange oxygen and carbon dioxide with air, how is it possible that this exchange can occur when the lung is bathed in a liquid?

2. Why would liquid breathing be beneficial to a SCUBA diver?

3. How might this technology be useful for organ transplants?

KEY TERMS

alveoli	diaphragm	inhalation	trachea (in
bronchiole	emphysema	larynx	birds/mammals)
bronchi	exhalation	lung	trachea (in insects)
bulk flow	gas-exchange portion	pharynx	vocal cord
chronic bronchitis	gill	respiratory center	
conducting portion	hemoglobin	spiracle	

ANSWER KEY

SELF TEST

1. a
3. c
3. b
4. a
5. b
6. d
7. c
8. a
9. b
10. b
11. e
12. f
13. e
14. d
15. a
16. a
17. lungs
18. tracheae
19. epiglottis
20. alveoli
21. diaphragm
22. inhalation
23. A. gases move in and out of the lungs by bulk flow
    B. gases dissolved in blood are transported by bulk flow
    C. oxygen and carbon dioxide are exchanged in the lungs by diffusion
    D. oxygen and carbon dioxide are exchanged in the tissues by diffusion
24. A. tracheae
    B. spiracle
25. A. lungs
    B. trachea
    C. air sacs

26. A. larynx
    B. bronchi
    C. trachea
    D. bronchioles
    E. pharynx
27. A. alveoli
    B. capillary network
    C. bronchiole
    D. branch of pulmonary artery
28. d
29. a
30. d
31. surfactant
32. d

ESSAY CHALLENGE

1. Insects have tracheae that bring air directly to the body cells. Air enters the tracheae through the spiracles. Some insects use muscular pumping movements to enhance air movement through the tracheae. Most terrestrial vertebrates have lungs that have delicate respiratory surfaces that exchange gas. Breathing is carried out through contraction of a muscle called the *diaphragm,* which brings air in and gets rid of waste. Both insects and terrestrial vertebrates use muscular pumping to bring air into their bodies.

2. The alveoli have thin walls that are kept moist, which aids in gas exchange. Gases dissolve in the fluid that keeps the alveoli moist and then diffuse through the alveolar membranes into the capillaries.

3. In the blood, oxygen binds reversibly to hemoglobin, a protein found in red blood cells. Carbon dioxide is transported in three ways: 1) it reacts with water to form bicarbonate ion, which then diffuses into the plasma; 2) it binds to hemoglobin; and 3) it stays dissolved in the plasma.

4. The respiratory center in the brain receives input from several sources and adjusts breathing rate and volume to meet the body's needs. Changes in carbon dioxide levels in the blood stimulate receptors that signal the respiratory center. Changes in oxygen in the blood are also sensed, but the respiratory center is less sensitive to these changes.

5. During inhalation, the diaphragm contracts and is drawn downward. At the same time, the rib muscles also contract and the chest wall expands. When the chest cavity expands, it draws the lungs with it. The expansion of the lungs creates a vacuum (negative pressure) inside that draws air in.

6. A moist surface is crucial to facilitate the exchange of gases by diffusion across any respiratory surface. The earthworm relies entirely on gas exchange through its skin. Frogs and salamanders use their moist skin as a supplement to exchange at the lungs.

7. The surface tension produced by the moist surfaces of the alveoli can cause these small air sacs to collapse. Surfactants help reduce this surface tension. With low levels of surfactant, premature babies must struggle to inflate their lungs by forcing air into the collapsing alveoli.

8. When carbon dioxide combines with water in the blood, it forms bicarbonate. If you hold your breath, carbon dioxide levels in the blood increase. When you hyperventilate, the levels of carbon dioxide drop. Both of these will have an effect on bicarbonate ion levels and blood pH.

9. During exhalation, the reduced amount of air in the airway of an asthma patient allows the mucus-clogged passageways to collapse more readily. Forced exhalations while hyperventilating can cause the airway to collapse. This exacerbates the problem caused by the reduced airway space and the "signal" to hyperventilate becomes stronger. By breathing slowly and under control, the asthma patient can maintain the airway and ensure an adequate supply of oxygen to the tissues.

MEDIA ACTIVITIES

29.4   Web Investigation: Lives Up in Smoke

1. The EPA has concluded that the widespread exposure to environmental tobacco smoke in the U.S. is a serious and substantial public health risk. Exposure to this environmental pollutant increases the risk of developing upper and lower respiratory tract infections in children and has been shown to be involved in the development of symptoms related to chronic middle ear disease. In addition, exposure increases the frequency and severity of asthmatic episodes and plays a role in the development of new cases of asthma in children. In adults, exposure to tobacco smoke increases the risk of developing lung cancer.

2. Carbon monoxide competes with oxygen for binding sites on hemoglobin molecules contained in red blood cells. This competition leads to a reduced ability of your body to deliver oxygen to metabolically active tissues such as the brain and heart.

3. Short term exposure to secondhand smoke can reduce the levels of antioxidants circulating in the bloodstream. Antioxidants (such as vitamin C) are important for neutralizing dangerous free radical molecules. These free radicals are produced during normal metabolism, but are also found in tobacco smoke. Free radicals can damage DNA (which can lead to tumor formation) and can combine with cholesterol to produce a form of this molecule known to cause plaques in arteries (atherosclerosis).

4. One of the arguments used for banning smoking in public places is that individual decisions to smoke have an impact on the rights of others. Should a person be forced to "smoke" by inhaling secondhand smoke? On the other side of the argument, the decision to smoke is a personal one and should not be regulated.

ISSUES IN BIOLOGY

1. When diving to great depths, the amount of nitrogen dissolved in the blood increases. This increase in dissolved nitrogen causes the impairments associated with nitrogen narcosis. As you return to the surface, the dissolved nitrogen can form nitrogen gas bubbles if you return too quickly. These air bubbles are what produce the symptoms associated with decompression sickness.

2. The aches and pains produced in the joints as a result of decompression sickness often make it difficult for the person to stand up straight. This "bent" stature is what led to the term "bends."

3. Hyperbaric chambers simulate the pressures of deep diving. When a person returns to the surface with symptoms of decompression sickness, the chamber can repressurize their body. This helps remove some of the nitrogen gas bubbles by returning some of the nitrogen to the dissolved state. By slowly bringing the body back to atmospheric pressure, the body is able to dump this nitrogen safely from the lungs.

4. Nitrogen is about four times more toxic than helium. By preparing a mixture of helium and oxygen, the diver is able to avoid the problems associated with nitrogen gas.

BIZARRE FACTS IN BIOLOGY

1. Animal respiratory systems are designed to facilitate gas exchange through the process of diffusion, in which molecules move from areas of higher concentration to areas of lower concentration. In the case of liquid breathing, the medium through which

the lung is exposed to the gases is different, but the actual concentration gradients can be maintained. The "trick" is in finding a fluid that will support a gradient that is similar to the air we breathe.

2. When a diver descends, the pressure of the water collapses the air-filled lungs. In order to prevent this collapse, divers breathe compressed air, which delivers the needed oxygen and keeps the lungs inflated. Unfortunately, other gases such as nitrogen are delivered to the body under pressure. This excess nitrogen is responsible for problems such as nitrogen narcosis and decompression sickness. A liquid would not be as compressible and would match the pressure of the surrounding water. The problems associated with breathing compressed gas can now be avoided.

3. The preservation of a harvested organ is crucial for the success of a transplant. Once an organ is procured, it is quickly transported on ice to an awaiting surgical team where it is transplanted. Without its blood supply, the organ would quickly begin to starve for oxygen unless it is cooled on ice. To help preserve the organ, oxygen-saturated liquids could be circulated through as a temporary blood substitute, or the organ might be bathed in the liquid for transport.

CHAPTER 30: NUTRITION AND DIGESTION

AT-A-GLANCE

SELF TEST

1. Why is it that vitamins A, D, E, and K can be toxic, but not C and B?
   a. Fat-soluble vitamins are stored in the body.
   b. Vitamins B and C do not affect brain chemistry.
   c. Those vitamins are used faster than C and B.
   d. Humans get more A, D, E, and K than C and B in their diets.

2. Essential amino acids are those that _____.
   a. are the 10 or so required to make proteins
   b. can be synthesized in the body given the right fatty acid building blocks
   c. are not synthesized in the body; they must be taken in with food

3. The major nutrient group used for quick energy production is _____.
   a. vitamins
   b. proteins
   c. lipids
   d. carbohydrates
   e. electrolytes

4. _____ refers to physically grinding up, then chemically breaking down, food.

5. Label these structures of the avian digestive system.

6. Label the following image of a hydra digesting a food particle.

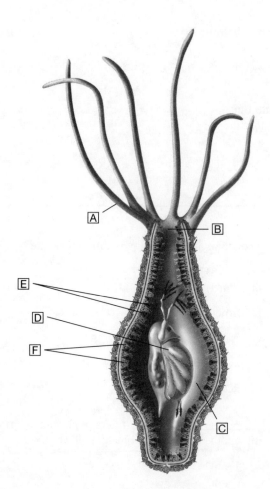

7. Digestion in the Cnidaria, as in hydra, occurs in a
_____.
   a. crop
   b. coelom
   c. digestive tract
   d. gastrovascular cavity
   e. pharynx

8. Collar cells (Figure 30-5) are found in
_____.
   a. sponges
   b. fish
   c. insects
   d. tapeworms
   e. hydra

9. Below is a diagram of a typical collar cell of a sponge. The shaded objects are food items. Label the remaining structures to demonstrate how sponges digest food.

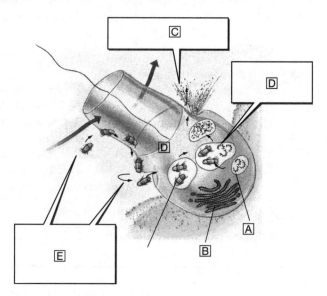

10. _____ is the process by which food is pushed through the esophagus.

11. _____is the human storage form of carbohydrate.

12. Chyme is _____.
   a. a protein-digesting enzyme
   b. the thickened food material after digestion in the stomach
   c. enzymatic juice secreted by the small intestine
   d. the fatty material absorbed into lacteals, also called *chylomicrons*
   e. an enzyme that breaks down complex carbohydrates into disaccharides

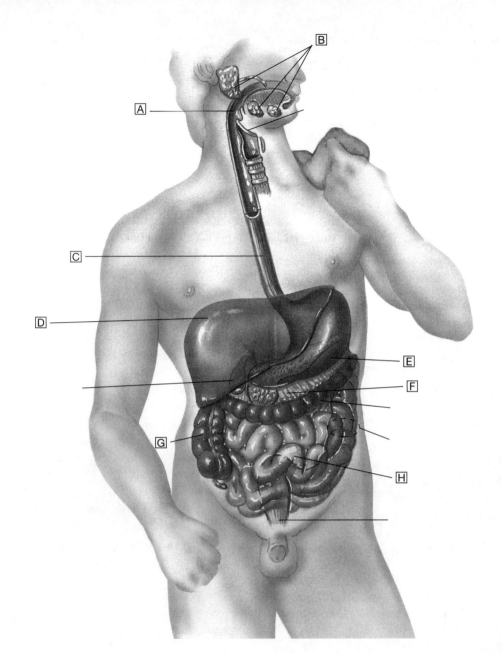

13. Label the indicated structures in the human digestive system above.

14. Label the structures indicated on the diagram of a stomach shown below.

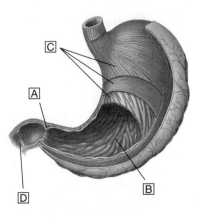

15. The _____ is a tube that propels food from the mouth to the stomach.

16. The cause of ulcers is _____.
   a. *Helicobacter pylori*
   b. stress
   c. alcoholism
   d. allergies
   e. smoking

17. The function of bile is the _____.
   a. facilitation of sugar and amino acid absorption
   b. mechanical breakdown of fats for better breakdown with lipase, a lipid-digestive enzyme
   c. production of bile pigments
   d. production of glucose
   e. maintenance of blood glucose level

343

18. The nasal cavities and oral cavity merge into the pharynx. What keeps food and drink from going into the nasal cavity rather than down the esophagus?
   a. The tongue blocks the upper pharynx leading into the nasal cavities.
   b. The soft palate moves up against the opening to the nasal cavities, blocking the entryway.
   c. Breathing is temporarily stopped so that the nasal cavities can close when swallowing.
   d. The esophagus constricts at the upper end of the pharynx so the entry to the nasal cavities is blocked.

19. Weight loss, anemia, and fatigue are symptoms of what problem?
   a. Gallstones. The hardened bile in the gallbladder affects lipid metabolism, causing weight loss and fatigue. The anemia is due to a lack of bile pigments available to produce red blood cells.
   b. Peptic ulcer. The bleeding ulcer causes loss of blood, resulting in anemia and fatigue. The weight loss is caused by the inability of the stomach to absorb nutrients.
   c. Intestinal cancer with subsequent loss of function of part of the small intestine. There is less surface area for nutrient absorption, hence the weight loss. The lack of nutrients also accounts for the inability to make the hemoglobin and red cells, for the anemia, and for the lack of oxygen-carrying capacity, fatigue.
   d. Colitis. The inflammation of the colon makes it impossible for nutrients to be properly absorbed, hence the weight loss and fatigue. The inflammation also disrupts the absorption of various vitamins required to make hemoglobin and red blood cells and reduces oxygen-carrying capacity.

20. What is it that "raises the temperature of a gram of water by 1 degree Celsius"?
   a. a Calorie   b. a calorie
   c. a fat gram   d. an ATP

21. What is the correct sequence of events that all digestive systems must follow in the processing of foodstuffs?
   a. ingestion—chemical breakdown—mechanical breakdown—absorption—elimination
   b. ingestion—mechanical breakdown—chemical breakdown—absorption—elimination
   c. ingestion—absorption—mechanical breakdown—chemical breakdown—elimination
   d. ingestion—absorption—chemical breakdown—mechanical breakdown—elimination

22. What triggers the swallowing reflex?
   a. food entering the mouth
   b. food entering the larynx
   c. food entering the pharynx
   d. food entering the trachea

23. Which of the following is NOT a function of the stomach?
   a. It is the site where protein digestion begins due to the actions of pepsin.
   b. Rhythmic contractions known as *peristaltic movements* move food into the stomach and aid in the mixing of the partially digested contents and the gastric secretions (chyme) of the stomach.
   c. It produces a thick mucus secretion along the stomach lining that protects the stomach from being digested by its own secretions (e.g., pepsin).
   d. It is one of the primary sites for the absorption of digested protein fragments.

24. Why does the small intestine absorb more nutrients than any other region of the digestive tract?
   a. because it is the site of segmentation movements
   b. because the exposed surface area approaches that of a tennis court in size
   c. because of the concentrated supply of capillaries that lie in intimate contact with this region of the digestive tract
   d. all of the above

25. Starch (amylose) digestion is complex and involves several different parts of the digestive anatomy. Which of the following represents the places in the human body where starch is chemically digested?
   a. mouth and liver
   b. salivary gland and pancreas
   c. mouth and large intestine
   d. mouth and small intestine

26. Which of the following is the active form of an enzyme that chemically digests proteins in the stomach?
   a. pepsin   b. pepsinogen
   c. lipase   d. secretin

27. The role of the liver in the digestion of food is _____.
   a. to produce lipase for the digestion of fat
   b. to produce bile for the emulsification of fat
   c. to produce pepsin for the digestion of protein
   d. to produce bile for the digestion of carbohydrates

28. An earthworm's digestive anatomy is designed so that this animal can feed more frequently than an animal such as a sea anemone. Which of the following explains this relationship?
   a. A sea anemone does not produce any digestive enzymes.
   b. A sea anemone cannot ingest its food.
   c. An earthworm has a highly efficient ruminant stomach.
   d. An earthworm has a tubular digestive tract, while a sea anemone has a digestive system with only one opening.

344

29. Which of the following explains why the average herbivore has a longer intestine than the average carnivore?
   a. Carnivores do not have to mechanically digest their food.
   b. Carnivores absorb much of their nutrients from the stomach.
   c. The cell walls in plants are difficult to digest. For herbivores, the longer intestine provides more opportunity to extract nutrients from plant material.
   d. Carnivores produce the enzyme cellulase. This enzyme helps in the digestion of cellulose found in the cell walls of plant cells. This efficient digestion of plant material means that carnivores can have shorter intestines.

ESSAY CHALLENGE

1. What basic needs do the five major nutrients fulfill for the body?

2. Compare and contrast intracellular and extracellular digestion.

3. What tasks do all digestive systems carry out regardless of the type of organism?

4. What adaptations have ruminants developed to assist in the digestion of cellulose?

5. Explain how the human mouth takes part in both the mechanical and chemical digestion of food.

6. Explain why "never drink on an empty stomach" is sound advice when you are consuming alcoholic beverages.

7. The mechanical digestion of food, the role of the villi and microvilli in the small intestine, and bile salts all take advantage of a similar principle to help facilitate the process of digestion. Describe this principle and explain how it is involved in each of these digestive concepts.

8. Explain how a person on a long-term course of antibiotics to treat a chronic infection can develop a vitamin K deficiency.

9. There are three different types of enzymes secreted by the pancreas. What are these enzymes and what role do each of them play in digestion?

MEDIA ACTIVITIES

To access a Media Activity visit http://www.prenhall.com/audesirk7. Log in to the Web site selected by your instructor, navigate to this chapter, and select the appropriate Media Activity number.

30.1 The Digestive System
Estimated time: 5 minutes

Explore the anatomy and function of the human digestive system.

30.2 Physical and Chemical Digestion
Estimated time: 5 minutes

See how major nutrients are broken down in each portion of the digestive system and transported to the body's cells.

30.3 Web Investigation: Fat in the Family?
Estimated time: 10 minutes

The media message is simple: "thin is beautiful," "50 steps to lose weight," "the instant weight-loss diet," and so on. Still the number of overweight Americans grows every year. Yet some people can eat several thousand calories a day and never gain a pound. This exercise will examine the roles of heredity, biochemistry, and behavior in obesity.

1. The body mass index is a frequently used measure of obesity. Calculate your own BMI (http://www.cdc.gov/nccdphp/dnpa/bmi/calc-bmi.htm). Is your BMI in the normal range (http://www.nhlbi.nih.gov/health/public/heart/obesity/lose_wt/risk.htm)?

2. Morbid obesity is common in individuals with the genetic disorder Prader-Willi. Give two reasons why (http://www.pwsausa.org/faq.htm#6). How does the Prader-Willi food pyramid differ from the standard USDA food pyramid?

3. Several obesity-related genetic markers have been discovered in mice. What genes do they code for (http://www.hhmi.org/genesweshare/d130.html)? How do the products (http://arbl.cvmbs.colostate.edu/hbooks/pathphys/endocrine/bodyweight/leptin.html) of these genes affect obesity?

4. Scientists frequently study twins and/or adoptive families in order to distinguish between environmental and genetic influences. What is the heritability (http://www.findarticles.com/cf_0/m0841/1_35/59644082/print.jhtml) (genetic component) of obesity as calculated from twin study data? Using adoptive family data? Which is considered the more accurate number? Is a shared environment (http://grammashouse.net/obesity4.htm) a good predictor of obesity?

ISSUES IN BIOLOGY

What Are the Side Effects of Eating Chocolate?

Psychoactive drug? Stimulant? Antidepressant? Chocoholics claim all of these titles (plus more) for chocolate. Some are unfounded, but many of the effects have some truth to them. The major nutrient groups that chocolate comprises are fats (cocoa butter and cocoa paste) and carbohydrates (starch and various sugars, like saccharose). There is a minute amount of protein. There are also a variety of minerals—potassium, magnesium, calcium, sodium—and vitamins—A, D, E, B_1, B_2. However, there are some very interesting chemicals (http://www.exploratorium.edu/exploring/exploring_chocolate/choc_8.html) that may have psychological and neurological effects as well.

Anandamide stimulates brain cells the same way as the active ingredient in marijuana, tetrahydrocannibinol (THC). However, the National Institutes of Health claims that a 130-pound person would have to eat 25 pounds of chocolate to obtain a marijuana-like effect. This same chemical is also present naturally in the brain: anandamide and THC seem to use the same target cells. Anandamide has been found in dark chocolate, but not in white chocolate which is made by a different process. In addition, chocolate has a couple of other chemicals, one of which is n-acylethanolamine, that prevent the breakdown of anandamide. It may be that it helps to retain the concentration of anandamide, which prolongs a mild sense of euphoria.

Theobromine, particularly associated with dark chocolate, stimulates the nervous system, producing an increase in appetite, increased muscle fitness, and increased heart muscle tone. In fact, evidently it is this particular compound that is dangerous for dogs—it causes cardiac arrhythmias and possible heart attacks.

Cocoa beans have caffeine, and there can be quite a bit of it depending on the form of the chocolate. Here is a comparison of caffeine amounts in various chocolate products.

6 milligrams, cocoa beverage (8 ounces)

5 milligrams, chocolate milk beverage (8 ounces)

6 milligrams, milk chocolate (1 ounce)

20 milligrams, dark chocolate, semi-sweet (1 ounce)

26 milligrams, baker's chocolate (1 ounce)

44 milligrams, chocolate-flavored syrup (1 ounce)

Compare these to 100 milligrams of caffeine in an 8-ounce cup of coffee or 40 milligrams in an 8-ounce cup of tea. Caffeine has a wide variety of effects: stimulation of the nervous system, increased urination, and attentiveness.

Phenylethylamine is similar to amphetamines and therefore contains psycho-stimulating properties. It is sometimes called the "love molecule" and is suspected of being the molecule related to the "high" experienced by lovers. Scientists suspect that touching of hands, caresses, and a stare across the room all can trigger the production of phenylethylamine in the brain. The effects of this chemical (http://www.monash.edu.au/pubs/montage/Montage_9601/lovedrug.html) might be a quickened heart rate, sweaty palms, a flush on the skin, and increased breathing rate.

Serotonin is a neurotransmitter in the brain that facilitates nerve impulse transmission associated with well-being. A deficiency of serotonin or excess breakdown of it appears to be related to depression. In fact, there are a variety of antidepressants on the market—Prozac® and Paxil®—that inhibit serotonin uptake, making serotonin more available at the neural junction. Perhaps serotonin in chocolate acts in a similar way. Of course, all of this is conjecture. First, these chemicals are in minute amounts in chocolate. Second, these chemicals may be broken down or changed by various enzymes and pH extremes as they move along the digestive tract. Third, just because all of these chemicals are found in chocolate does not mean that they end up in your body in significant amounts. Perhaps the claimed effects of chocolate are only wishful thinking!

1. Which chemical in chocolate is called the "love drug"? Why?

2. How would chocolate possibly work as an antidepressant?

3. Give one reason why all of these claims might just be talk.

BIZARRE FACTS IN BIOLOGY

Termites of the Sea—A Nutritional Mystery

On May 11, 1502, Christopher Columbus set sail from the port of Cadiz on his fourth voyage to the new world with four old ships and 140 men. One year later, Columbus and his entire crew found themselves marooned on the island of Jamaica without a ship to carry them home. It would be another year before they could commission a trip home to Spain. Columbus and his ships became the victims of a scourge familiar to many mariners of the time. Shipworms had eaten a large portion of the hulls of those four old ships, and their only choice was to abandon or beach the vessels out of desperation. A shipworm (*Toredo navalis*) is actually not a worm (http://www.crmonline.de/English/Services/ Marine_Research/Teredo_/teredo_.html). Shipworms are part of the Teredinidae family of mollusks which places them closer to clams than to worms. This seemingly magical mollusk has the unique ability to live entirely off the energy it extracts from a complex carbohydrate called cellulose (http://www.visionlearning.com/library/module_ viewer.php?mld=61). Cellulose is a structural molecule that is used by a plant to construct the rigid cell wall that surrounds all of its cells. The ability to digest cellulose is not unique. Although humans lack the ability to accomplish this chemical feat, ruminant animals such as cows, sheep, and goats have elaborate digestive systems that can break down the cellulose with the help of microorganisms (http://www.mun.ca/biology/scarr/Ruminant_Digestion.htm).

The mystery of this digestive tale revolves around the normal nutritional requirements of animals. Although cellulose provides an excellent source of energy for the shipworm, it lacks the element nitrogen. Nitrogen is an essential component of proteins. Because proteins perform a wide range of vital functions, animals cannot survive without this essential molecule. In humans, protein deficiencies are responsible for debilitating diseases such as kwashiorkor (http://phoenity.com/diseases/kwashiorkor.html). In addition to having the rare ability to live off a pure cellulose diet, shipworms are somehow able to produce proteins from a diet that lacks the essential element required for their production. Shipworms owe all of their nutritional magic abilities to a symbiotic bacteria (http://aem.asm.org/cgi/ content/full/68/12/6292). In addition to providing enzymes for digesting cellulose, this oxygen-dependent (aerobic) microorganism is able to extract an unusable form of nitrogen from the air and seawater and convert it to a form that organisms can use. This process, called *nitrogen fixation*, is similar to the task performed by bacteria that reside in the roots of leguminous plants, such as beans, peas, clover, and alfalfa. Of all of the known aerobic bacteria, none combine both celluose-digesting and nitrogen-fixing skills like the bacteria that live in harmony with the shipworm.

1. Explain why humans have a difficult time digesting plant material.

2. Our large intestine houses a wide variety of symbiotic bacteria. Although it might be useful to have a symbiont that could digest cellulose, explain why the bacteria found in the shipworm would not be a good candidate.

3. Biotechnology can be broadly defined as the technology used in the commercial utilization of living organisms and their products. Can you think of any biotechnological uses for the shipworm?

KEY TERMS

absorption	epiglottis	large intestine	protease
amylase	essential amino acid	lipase	pyloric sphincter
bile	essential fatty acid	liver	rectum
bile salt	extracellular digestion	lysosome	ruminant
body mass index	feces	microvillus	secretin
calorie	food vacuole	mineral	segmentation movement
Calorie	gallbladder	mouth	small intestine
carnivore	gastric inhibitory peptide	nutrient	stomach
cellulase	gastrin	nutrition	urea
cholecystokinin	gastrovascular cavity	omnivore	villi
chyme	glycogen	pancreas	vitamin
colon	herbivore	pancreatic juice	
digestion	intracellular digestion	peristalsis	
digestive system	lacteal	pharynx	

ANSWER KEY

SELF TEST

1. a
2. c
3. d
4. digestion
5. A. esophagus
   B. crop
   C. liver
   D. stomach (gizzard)
   E. small intestine
   F. rectum
6. A. tentacle
   B. mouth
   C. gastrovascular cavity
   D. food
   E. gland cells
   F. nutritive cells
7. d
8. a
9. A. lysosome
   B. Golgi apparatus
   C. waste products are expelled by exocytosis
   D. food vacuole merges with lysosome
   E. food particles are filtered by collar and enter cell via endocytosis
10. peristalsis
11. glycogen
12. b
13. A. pharynx
    B. salivary glands
    C. esophagus
    D. liver
    E. stomach
    F. pancreas
    G. large intestine
    H. small intestine

14. A. pyloric sphincter
    B. folds
    C. muscle layers
    D. beginnings of small intestine
15. esophagus
16. a
17. b
18. b
19. c
20. b
21. b
22. c
23. d
24. d
25. d
26. a
27. b
28. d
29. c

ESSAY CHALLENGE

1. The five major nutrients provide 1) energy to fuel metabolism and activities; 2) the chemical building blocks to construct complex molecules in the body; and 3) minerals and vitamins that participate in various metabolic reactions.

2. In intracellular digestion, digestion occurs after a cell has engulfed food particles. The particles are enclosed in a food vacuole, which then fuses with a lysosome, which then digests the food particles. In extracellular digestion, chunks of food are broken down outside of cells by enzymes, and then the cells absorb the smaller particles. Both processes break down food, but the location of the breakdown is different.

3. 1) ingestion: food must be brought into the digestive tract, usually through a mouth; 2) mechanical breakdown: food must be physically broken down into smaller pieces; 3) chemical breakdown: particles of food must be exposed to digestive enzymes and fluids that break down large molecules into small ones; 4) absorption: the small molecules must be transported out of the digestive cavity and into cells; and 5) elimination: indigestible materials must be expelled from the body.

4. Ruminants regurgitate food and rechew it. They have stomachs with many chambers that contain microorganisms that digest the cellulose into a usable form.

5. Mechanical digestion occurs when chewing breaks down the ingested food into smaller pieces. The first phase of chemical digestion also occurs here as salivary amylase begins the breakdown of starch into simple sugars.

6. Although the small intestine is responsible for the absorption of the majority of the products of digestion, alcohol can enter the bloodstream through the stomach wall. On an empty stomach, alcohol can produce a very strong and rapid effect that can lead to impaired judgment. Food in the stomach absorbs some of the alcohol and slows down its passage into the bloodstream.

7. In all three cases there is a maximization of surface area to help facilitate digestion. In the mechanical digestion of food, the physical breakdown of the food into smaller particles helps produce more surface area for the digestive enzymes to begin the chemical digestion process. In the small intestine, the villi and microvilli help to dramatically increase the surface area of the intestinal wall. This increased surface area leads to a more efficient absorption of the products of the chemical digestion of food. Bile salts act as an emulsifying agent, dispersing large globs of fat into smaller fat droplets. These smaller droplets expose a larger surface area to facilitate chemical digestion by lipase enzymes.

8. Many of the antibiotics used to treat infection are nonselective. This means that they not only kill the bacteria responsible for the infection, but they may destroy a wide range of bacteria that reside in the body. Our bodies contain a variety of different types of beneficial bacteria. One of these beneficial types lives in the large intestine where it lives off unabsorbed nutrients. This intestinal bacteria is beneficial because it synthesizes a variety of vitamins, including vitamin K. A person on long-term antibiotic treatment can become vitamin K deficient if the drugs destroy these helpful bacterial residents.

9. Pancreatic juice is a digestive secretion produced by the pancreas. This juice contains three different digestive enzymes. Amylase helps break down starch, lipases are involved in fat digestion, and several different proteases are involved in the chemical attack on proteins.

MEDIA ACTIVITIES

30.3 Web Investigation: Fat in the Family?

1. Keep in mind that the BMI is not a diagnostic tool. Your BMI does not give you information about disease. In addition, because the BMI is calculated simply from your height and weight, it can be misleading when looking at the ranges. For example, a 5'10" bodybuilder weighing 210 pounds would fall into the obese range, even if this person had a very small percentage of body fat.

2. The disease has an effect on the hypothalamus of the brain. This part of the brain is what controls your feeling of hunger. In this disease, patients never feel full and have a continuous urge to eat. In addition, patients with this disease tend to have less muscle mass, which means they are burning fewer calories. The two primary changes in the food pyramid for this disorder is a general reduction in total servings (fewer calories) and the shifting of the bread group up the pyramid.

3. Researchers discovered that mice that lacked a gene called *ob* were unable to produce a molecule called leptin. Leptin is a chemical that helps signal the brain to create the feeling of being full. Another gene found lacking in obese mice was responsible for producing a leptin receptor. This receptor is important for the brain to have the ability to receive the leptin signal.

4. The genetic component of obesity risk is very large. Adoptive family data suggests that 30–50% of the variation in BMI can be accounted for by the heritable component of obesity. Twin studies suggest that this number is more like 50–80%. The environmental risk factor is difficult to measure. It is believed that children who share an environment with two obese parents are four times more likely to be obese than children without obese parents. Adoptive studies suggest that the biological parent's weight is a stronger predictor of child's weight than the environment of the adoptive parent. Although environment does play a role in obesity, measuring the shared environment risk component is difficult due to the strong genetic factors that are involved.

ISSUES IN BIOLOGY

1. Phenylethylamine is a molecule in chocolate that has an effect similar to amphetamines, which are a strong stimulant. The "high" experienced by lovers is believed to resemble the effect of this molecule.

2. Several chemicals in chocolate are associated with the good feeling produced from consuming this confectionary treat. For example, anadamide is a chemical isolated in chocolate that works as a neurotransmitter in the brain to produce feelings of

well-being. The "feel good" effects of the various chemicals in chocolate can be used to explain how it might possibly work as an antidepressant.

3. Simply isolating various compounds from chocolate does not mean that they have the biological effect associated with those compounds. The amount of a substance is important for understanding its effect. For some of these compounds, the effect might be realized only by consuming unhealthy amounts of chocolate. In addition, the human body metabolizes and breaks down molecules fairly quickly. This means that many substances are not given the chance to produce their effect after they are consumed.

BIZARRE FACTS IN BIOLOGY

1. Cellulose is a rigid structural carbohydrate that makes up plant cell walls and gives the plant its strength. When we consume plant material, we must rely on mechanical digestion to break the material apart. Chemical digestion is difficult because humans lack the essential enzyme cellulase that is important for breaking down cellulose.

2. There are many different reasons why the shipworm bacteria would not be a good candidate. Shipworms live in saltwater conditions that the bacteria are adapted to. The gut conditions do not mirror a saltwater environment. In addition, the human gut is highly anaerobic (no oxygen) and this bacteria is oxygen-dependent (aerobic). The process of evolution provides another consideration. The shipworm and symbiotic bacteria have developed their relationship over long periods of evolutionary time. This relationship is highly specialized and the probability of transferring this relationship to a human is unlikely.

3. Just as bacteria in sewage treatment plants are able to convert sewage into simple compounds, the shipworm might be useful to the recycling industry. Wood and wood products such as paper take up large amounts of landfill space and their breakdown is slow. Shipworms could be used to accelerate this process. While the worms break down the cellulose, they are also fixing nitrogen. As the worms die off, their bodies could be used as a fertilizer which is now rich in nitrogen.

CHAPTER 31: THE URINARY SYSTEM

AT-A-GLANCE

SELF TEST

1. Which organ converts ammonia to urea?
   - **a.** liver
   - **b.** pancreas
   - **c.** gallbladder
   - **d.** kidney

2. Flame cells are the specialized excretory structures found in _____.
   - **a.** flatworms
   - **b.** earthworms
   - **c.** protozoa
   - **d.** insects

3. In the human urinary system, the kidneys _____ the urine.
   - **a.** store
   - **b.** transport
   - **c.** produce
   - **d.** excrete

4. Tubular reabsorption is _____.
   - **a.** the process by which wastes and excess substances that were not initially filtered out into Bowman's capsule are removed from the blood
   - **b.** the concentration of the filtrate due to the concentration of salts and urea
   - **c.** the passage of blood cells and proteins from the glomerulus
   - **d.** the process by which cells of the proximal tubule remove water and nutrients and pass them back into the blood

5. The hormone ADH _____.
   - **a.** controls the concentration of the urine
   - **b.** controls the amount of blood that enters the kidney
   - **c.** controls the reabsorption of nutrients
   - **d.** determines the pH of the blood

6. Angiotensin is a hormone that _____.
   - **a.** causes arterioles to constrict
   - **b.** regulates the amount of water reabsorbed from the urine
   - **c.** catalyzes the formation of angiotensin
   - **d.** stimulates the production of red blood cells

7. What initiates glomerular pressure filtration?
   - **a.** the permeability of the glomerular walls
   - **b.** the inability of large proteins to pass through the capillary walls
   - **c.** diameter differences between the incoming and outgoing arterioles
   - **d.** osmotic pressure differences between the glomerulus and Bowman's capsule

8. Why does urea diffuse from blood into dialysis fluid during hemodialysis?

   a. The dialysis membrane is permeable only to urea.

   b. Urea molecules are more concentrated in blood than in dialysis fluid.

   c. This prevents the loss of essential water during hemodialysis.

   d. Special diets in the hemodialysis patients increase urea concentrations.

9. In what ways is blood plasma that exits the kidney by way of the renal vein different from plasma that enters the kidney by way of the renal artery?

   a. The exiting plasma is the same as the entering plasma.

   b. The exiting plasma contains more dissolved nutrients.

   c. The exiting plasma contains fewer dissolved wastes.

   d. The exiting plasma contains more dissolved wastes.

10. What effect would constriction of the incoming arteriole have on the filtration pressure in the glomerulus?

    a. The glomerular pressure and the amount of filtrate produced would increase as a result of the constricted afferent arteriole.

    b. The constricted afferent arteriole would not change the already smaller size of the outgoing arteriole, thus the glomerular pressure and amount of filtrate would not change.

    c. The glomerular pressure would decrease and the amount of filtrate produced would decrease as a result of the constricted afferent arteriole.

    d. The glomerular pressure would decrease and the amount of filtrate produced would increase as a result of the constricted afferent arteriole.

11. What similar functions do the protonephridia of flatworms and the nephridia of roundworms have in common with each other?

    a. Almost none; the species are too different.

    b. Both act to filter out wastes for subsequent excretion.

    c. Both act to filter out nutrients to retain them inside the body.

    d. Both the second and third answers are correct.

    e. none of the above

12. Freshwater trout are urinating all of the time and producing many times their own blood volume over the course of a 24-hour day, while the desert-dwelling kangaroo rat might excrete only a few milliliters over the same time period. What do these two very different outcomes have in common?

    a. Both mechanisms are attempting to regulate the water volume within the body.

    b. Both mechanisms are attempting to maintain a constant level of acidity within the body.

    c. Both mechanisms are attempting to govern the levels of the same ions (e.g., Na^+ and K^+).

    d. all of the above

    e. none of the above

13. What physiological advantage does the ability of some species to excrete uric acid have over the ability of other species to excrete urea?

    a. Fewer electrolytes (ions) are lost.

    b. Excretion of uric acid enables a greater volume of urine to be produced.

    c. More electrolytes are lost.

    d. Very little water loss occurs as a result of excreting uric acid.

    e. Both the first and fourth answers are correct.

14. What happens to a substance that is not filtered, nor reabsorbed, but secreted?

    a. The body retains it.

    b. It is excreted from the body.

    c. Its concentration in the blood gradually decreases.

    d. Its concentration in the blood gradually increases.

    e. Both the second and third answers are correct.

    f. Both the first and fourth answers are correct.

15. Where is blood filtered?

    a. between the proximal tubule and the distal tubule

    b. between the descending limb of the loop of Henle and the ascending limb of the loop of Henle

    c. between the collecting duct and Bowman's capsule

    d. between Bowman's capsule and the capillary bed known as the *glomerulus*

16. Under which of the following conditions would you expect the production and secretion of the hormone, ADH, to increase?
    a. trapped, unharmed, under the rubble that used to be your house after a large storm
    b. You've just suffered your first loss of the 4th of July softball tournament, and now your team will need to play six games in one day with only two 1-hour breaks to reach the championship game.
    c. A plumber came out early in the morning and shut off the water supply to your new house so that a new water main could be put in. All that you've been doing is sitting around the house in the shade waiting for the water to come back on and for the delivery of your new dishwasher and refrigerator. The water to the house isn't turned on until 7 p.m. that evening.
    d. all of the above
    e. none of the above

17. _____ are kidney-like structures found in many invertebrates.

18. The _____ is a hollow muscular chamber that collects and stores urine.

19. The process of _____ results in many substances being forced through capillaries in the glomerulus.

20. In _____, substances in the filtrate are brought back into the blood circulation.

21. In _____, substances in the blood are actively transported directly into the filtrate.

22. _____ is a hormone released by the kidneys when blood pressure falls.

23. The flatworm has a simple excretory system. Label the structures indicated on the following diagram of a flatworm.

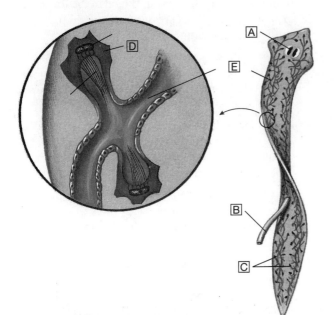

24. Annelids have a slightly more sophisticated excretory mechanism than flatworms. Label the structures of the annelid system below.

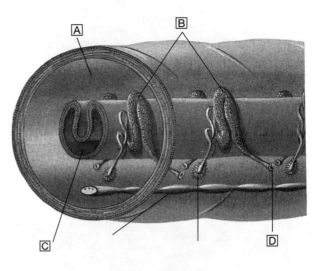

25. Below are the structures of the human excretory system. Label the organs indicated..

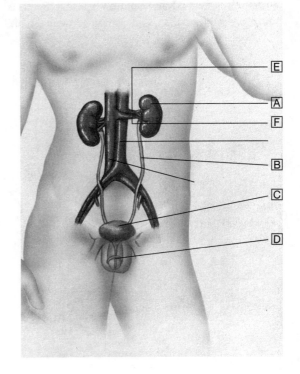

26. The kidney is the functional unit of the human excretory system. Label the areas of the kidney in the diagram below.

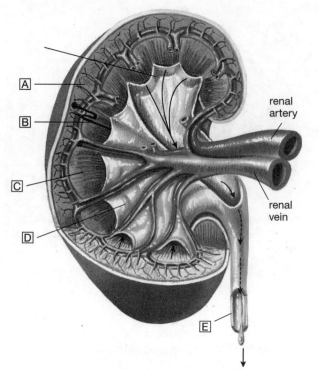

renal artery

renal vein

27. The nephron is the functional unit of the excretory system in humans. Each nephron has specific parts, with specific functions. Label these parts on the diagram below.

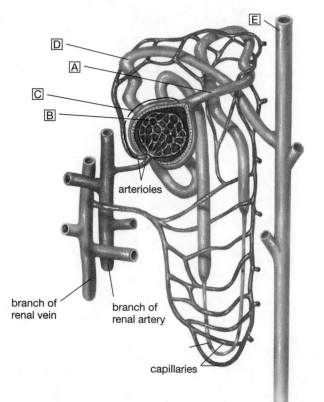

branch of renal vein

branch of renal artery

arterioles

capillaries

28. A diuretic is any substance that causes an increase in urine output. Which of the following can explain why alcohol acts as a diuretic?

  a. Alcohol causes the release of endorphins from the brain. The endorphins help stimulate ADH release.

  b. Alcohol causes the release of endorphins from the brain. The endorphins inhibit ADH release.

  c. Alcohol stimulates the production of angiotensin in the blood.

  d. Alcohol stimulates the release of erythropoietin from the kidney.

29. Which of the following could explain why a person might have an elevated amount of nitrogen in their urine?

  a. The glucose concentration of the urine is elevated.

  b. The protein concentration of the urine is elevated.

  c. There is an abnormally high amount of glucose in the blood due to a diet rich in carbohydrates.

  d. The person has a diet that is very high in protein.

30. Which of the following could be a sign of a failing kidney?

  a. a drop in the number of red blood cells

  b. dramatic changes in systemic blood pressure

  c. water retention and swelling in the tissues

  d. all of the above

31. A very common type of drug used to control high blood pressure is an ACE inhibitor. These drugs inhibit an enzyme involved in the production of a hormone called angiotensin. Which of the following explains why blood pressure would drop if you were taking this drug?

  a. By inhibiting the enzyme, angiotensin production drops and more water is retained in the blood. The increase in blood volume helps lower blood pressure.

  b. By inhibiting the enzyme, angiotensin production drops and more water is removed from the blood. The decrease in blood volume helps lower blood pressure.

  c. By inhibiting the enzyme, there is less angiotensin traveling to the kidneys. This leads to a constriction of the blood vessels leading to the kidneys and a lower filtration rate.

  d. By inhibiting the enzyme, there is less angiotensin traveling to the kidneys. This leads to a constriction of the blood vessels leading to the kidneys and a higher pressure in the glomerulus.

32. When a person takes a drug, the drug will eventually be eliminated from the body. One of the primary mechanisms for this removal is tubular secretion. Which of the following would produce the greatest reduction in the ability of our kidneys to remove drugs?
   a. a reduction in the salt gradient within the renal medulla
   b. damage to Bowman's capsule
   c. damage to the wall of the urinary bladder
   d. damage to the distal tubule of the nephron

ESSAY CHALLENGE

1. How does the mammalian urinary system help maintain homeostasis?

2. Describe the structure and function of the nephron.

3. If a person drinks more water than their body can handle, what happens to their ADH output?

4. When blood pressure in a person falls, what do the kidneys do?

5. If red blood cells are produced in bone marrow, explain why someone with damage to the kidney could become anemic.

6. Explain why animals that live in very dry conditions have very long loops of Henle.

7. Explain why the blood vessels that carry blood to the nephrons in the kidney constrict when your blood pressure falls.

8. How does the glomerulus differ from other capillary beds found in the human body?

MEDIA ACTIVITIES

To access a Media Activity visit http://www.prenhall.com/audesirk7. Log in to the Web site selected by your instructor, navigate to this chapter, and select the appropriate Media Activity number.

31.1 Urinary System Anatomy
Estimated time: 5 minutes

Explore the structure and function of the urinary system.

31.2 Urine Formation
Estimated time: 10 minutes

Examine how the nephron cleans waste and toxins from the blood.

31.3 Web Investigation: Family Ties
Estimated time: 10 minutes

Each year in the U.S., tens of thousands of people lose kidney function. While about 20,000 receive kidney transplants from compatible donors, over 46,000 patients currently await kidney transplants and about 200,000 are kept alive by hemodialysis (more commonly referred to simply as "dialysis"). What is hemodialysis and how does it work? What other "medical miracles" might help people with urinary system problems in the future?

1. What are the most common causes of kidney failure (http://www.kidneypatientguide.org.uk/site/fail.html)? What are some of the things you can do to maintain healthy kidneys (http://www.diabetesselfmanagement.com/article.cfm?aid=1205&char=527)?

2. There are three major treatment choices: hemodialysis, peritoneal dialysis, and kidney transplantation (http://www.niddk.nih.gov/health/kidney/pubs/esrd/esrd.htm). What are the major benefits and disadvantages (http://www.kidneydirections.com/us/patients/choices/index.htm) of each?

3. Scientists have identified the causes of three diseases in mice that mimic human kidney diseases (http://www.niddk.nih.gov/health/kidney/Research_Updates/winter99_00/1.htm#mayor). Why are these results significant?

4. How does dialysis work (http://www.kidney.ca/hem-e.htm) to remove the wastes that the kidney would normally remove for you?

5. Why is it not uncommon for people with kidney failure to develop anemia (http://kidney.niddk.nih.gov/kudiseases/pubs/anemia/index.htm) as part of their disease?

ISSUES IN BIOLOGY

Performance Enhancing Drugs

The World Anti-Doping Agency (http://www.wada-ama.org/en/t1.asp) is involved in coordinating the fight against the use of performance enhancing drugs in all forms of sport. One of their primary missions is to establish standards for testing and analysis of samples from athletes to screen for these drugs and then establish standards for controlling their use in competition. The gold standard for drug testing continues to be a screen of a urine sample which can detect a variety of substances (http://www.fpnotebook.com/PSY108.htm). When an athlete takes part in a doping regimen to boost performance, his body will metabolize the drug and clear it from his system. This is why a person needs to take several doses of a specific drug to realize its effects. In some cases, the drug is excreted in its original form in the urine. In other cases, the drug is broken down or modified before being excreted. Tests for these drugs have to be designed to detect the metabolic breakdown products and not the original drug itself.

In October 2003, it was announced that 40 high-profile athletes were being subpoenaed by a federal grand jury to investigate a company that was supplying nutritional supplements to athletes to help boost their performance and enhance their strength and conditioning programs. Of particular concern was information regarding the distribution and use of a previously undetectable form of an anabolic steroid (http://165.112.78.61/SteroidAlert/Steroidalert.html) called tetrahydrogestrinone or THG. Only recently was a test developed to detect this synthetic hormone in urine, and the fear is that THG has been widely used by athletes at all levels of sport. The issue has revealed what many had previously suspected; there is a race going on between those who can modify performance enhancing drugs to escape detection and those who are developing new tests that can uncover these chemical tricks to reveal their presence in urine.

1. Briefly describe the two processes that occur in the kidney to explain how a drug might end up in the urine where it can be detected.

2. In some drug tests, what is being detected is a metabolite (chemical modification) of the drug and not the drug itself. Why do you suppose that some drug substances need to be broken down or modified before we excrete them?

3. One of the more common chemical modifications that your body makes to a drug molecule during drug metabolism is to attach a polar molecule to the drug. How does this help ensure that once a drug enters the kidney tubule that it will remain in the filtrate for excretion?

BIZARRE FACTS IN BIOLOGY

Dry as a Rat

Imagine the nightmare of being stranded in the middle of the desert with only a small canteen of water to get you through a day of hiking. As you begin your journey back to civilization, you begin to rapidly lose water as you sweat in an attempt to control your escalating body temperature. Your increased respiratory rate only adds to the water loss. Just when you think that you might be able to make it home, you take your last sip from the canteen. From this point forward, your water loss begins to exceed your water gain. In an attempt to conserve water, your kidneys start producing a concentrated urine (http://science.howstuffworks.com/kidney6.htm). As you begin to struggle, your attention is drawn to a small rodent (http://nasa.utep.edu/chih/theland/animals/mammals/dime.htm) that darts out of a small burrow in front of you. As you walk by, you are amazed at how this rodent appears to survive so well in an environment that is ravaging your own body. When you eventually make your way out of the desert, you are extremely dehydrated and require medical intervention. As soon as you recover, you track down a local biologist to find out more about your rodent encounter. The biologist tells you that you most likely crossed paths with a Kangaroo Rat (*Dipodomys merriami*) (http://www.desertusa.com/aug96/du_krat.html). You find out that not only does this animal survive in the desert, but it does so without consuming any water. How is this possible? Why was your body not able to adapt to the desert condition when you ran out of water?

1. Briefly explain the mechanism involved in the production of the concentrated urine that you were producing as you began to dehydrate. What was your body measuring to know when it needed to begin conserving water through the production of concentrated urine?

2. Describe how Kangaroo Rats are adapted to the desert environment.

3. The Kangaroo Rat produces some of the most concentrated urine in the animal kingdom. This urine can reach solute concentrations that are more than twice what you would find in seawater. It was discovered that much of this ability can be attributed to having nephrons with extremely long loops of Henle. How does this feature help the Kangaroo Rat produce concentrated urine?

KEY TERMS

ammonia	excretory pore	nephron	tubular reabsorption
angiotensin	filtrate	nephrostome	tubular secretion
antidiuretic hormone	filtration	protonephridium	tubule
(ADH)	flame cell	renal artery	urea
bladder	glomerulus	renal cortex	ureter
Bowman's capsule	hemodialysis	renal medulla	urethra
collecting duct	homeostasis	renal pelvis	uric acid
erythropoietin	kidney	renal vein	urinary system
excretion	nephridium	renin	urine

ANSWER KEY

SELF TEST

1. a
2. a
3. c
4. d
5. a
6. a
7. c
8. b
9. c
10. c
11. d
12. d
13. e
14. e
15. d
16. d
17. nephridia
18. bladder
19. filtration
20. tubular reabsorption

21. tubular secretion
22. renin
23. A. eyespot
    B. extended pharynx
    C. excretory pores
    D. flame cell
    E. tubule
24. A. coelom
    B. nephridia
    C. intestine
    D. excretory pore
25. A. kidney
    B. ureter
    C. urinary bladder
    D. urethra
    E. renal artery
    F. renal vein
26. A. cortex
    B. nephron
    C. renal medulla
    D. renal pelvis
    E. ureter

27. A. proximal tube
    B. glomerulus
    C. Bowman's capsule
    D. distal tube
    E. collecting duct
28. b
29. d
30. d
31. b
32. d

ESSAY CHALLENGE

1. 1) it regulates blood levels of ions; 2) it regulates the water content of the blood; 3) it maintains blood pH; 4) it retains important nutrients; 5) it secretes hormones; and 6) it eliminates cellular wastes

2. The nephron has three major parts: 1) the glomerulus, a knot of capillaries that collect fluid from the blood; 2) Bowman's capsule; 3) a long twisted tubule with three parts (proximal and distal tubules, and loop of Henle), which reabsorbs and secretes substances.

3. The concentration of the blood will decrease, which will in turn reduce ADH output. Water will then be secreted.

4. The kidneys release the hormone renin, which catalyzes the formation of angiotensin, which in turn causes arterioles to constrict. This constriction causes an increase in blood pressure.

5. The kidneys release a hormone called erythropoietin that travels in the blood to the bone marrow, where it stimulates the marrow to produce more red blood cells, whose function is to transport oxygen. When a person's kidneys become damaged, the loss of this stimulus could lead to anemia.

6. The loop of Henle passes deep into the medulla of the kidney where the salt gradient increases in strength. The salty medulla produces an osmotic gradient that helps facilitate the movement of water out of the filtrate. With a greater force for the removal of water, the animal is able to produce a more concentrated urine and retain more water in the tissues. In very dry conditions, this water conservation strategy is extremely important for survival.

7. When blood pressure falls, the constriction of the vessels carrying blood to your kidneys leads to a lower rate of filtration and less filtrate production. This means that less water will be removed from the blood. Water retention causes an increase in blood volume and, consequently, an increase in blood pressure.

8. Blood flows into and out of the glomerulus through an arteriole. In other capillary beds, the blood leaves through a venule. In addition, the glomerular capillaries are much more permeable to allow for filtration of the blood as it passes through Bowman's capsule.

MEDIA ACTIVITIES

31.3 Web Investigation: Family Ties

1. The most common causes of kidney failure are diabetes, high blood pressure, and glomerulonephritis (inflammation of the kidneys). There are many risk factors that can be controlled with lifestyle changes. Controlling blood pressure and dietary intake of glucose, salt, and protein can help reduce the risk of kidney damage and the progression of kidney disease.

2. Hemodialysis usually involves a treatment that must be conducted at a clinical center. These regular visits can be restrictive to a person's lifestyle. Peritoneal dialysis (PD) gives the patient more freedom because the person can undergo treatment at home. This also means that, for PD, the patient is more involved in their own care. In PD, your blood never leaves your body as it does in hemodialysis, but PD can put stress on the peritoneal membrane, and it involves a permanent catheter in the abdomen, which increases the risk for infection. For a kidney transplant, the major benefit is that the new kidney releases the patient from the daily dialysis treatments. Since this treatment involves an invasive surgical procedure, all of the risks associated with surgery must be considered, and there is always the risk of organ rejection in any transplant surgery.

3. By identifying the disease mechanisms in animal models, scientists will have a better understanding of how to treat these diseases in humans.

4. In hemodialysis, your blood is circulated through a machine outside of your body. As the blood passes through the machine, waste products travel out of the blood across a selectively permeable membrane that makes up the tube carrying the blood. These wastes can then be discarded. In peritoneal dialysis, the process is similar, except that the membrane that is utilized for the transport of waste is located in your abdomen (the peritoneal membrane).

5. The kidney produces an important hormone called erythropoietin, or EPO. This hormone stimulates the bone marrow to produce red blood cells. When the kidneys fail, you can become deficient in this hormone and begin to show a decline in the number of red blood cells. This decline can lead to anemia.

ISSUES IN BIOLOGY

1. Urine production is a combination of glomerular filtration, reabsorption, and secretion. In order for a drug to become detectable in the urine, it must enter the filtrate through the glomerulus during glomerular filtration or directly through tubular secretion. Any of the drug that is not reabsorbed can become detectable in urine during a drug test.

2. In many cases, the chemical properties of the drug molecule make it difficult for the kidney to incorporate the drug into the filtrate for excretion. Drugs

that are very large may never make their way into the filtrate through glomerular filtration. If the drug is bound to plasma proteins or other blood components, it may be difficult to incorporate them into the filtrate through secretion. By modifying the drug through metabolism of the molecule, it can be converted into a form that can be more easily incorporated into the filtrate for eventual excretion.

3. Once the drug enters the filtrate through glomerular filtration or secretion, it can only make its way back to the blood through the process of reabsorption. For a majority of drugs, the kidney tubule does not have a transport mechanism to transport the molecules out of the filtrate. By having a polar molecule attached to the drug, the drug has difficulty diffusing through the lipid bilayers of the cells that line the tubule. In addition, their polar nature makes them hydrophilic and more likely to remain in the filtrate, which has a high water content.

BIZARRE FACTS IN BIOLOGY

1. When you began to dehydrate, your pituitary released larger amounts of ADH which traveled to the kidney and made the collecting ducts more permeable. As the collecting duct passed through the "salty" medulla, water was drawn out of the filtrate. This process helped the body retain water as it produced a concentrated urine. As your body lost water, the blood solute concentration began to rise. Specialized neurons in the brain, called osmoreceptors, measured this change and initiated the release of ADH from the pituitary.

2. The Kangaroo Rat gets all of its daily intake of water from its food. In order to conserve that water, it produces an extremely concentrated urine. In addition, this rodent spends its days in burrows that are moist and humid, and they do not sweat or pant like other animals when they want to cool their bodies. They are able to dump heat because they are very small and have a large surface area relative to their volume.

3. In the descending loop of Henle, water leaves the kidney tubule as it moves down its gradient from the filtrate to the salty medulla. In the Kangaroo Rat, the extra length of the tubule allows for more water movement out of the filtrate. In addition, as the long loop dips deeper into the medulla, it encounters a much stronger salt gradient. This produces a much stronger osmotic gradient that helps facilitate the movement of water from the filtrate and eventually a concentrated urine.

CHAPTER 32: DEFENSES AGAINST DISEASE

AT-A-GLANCE

SELF TEST

1. Most microorganisms ingested in food are destroyed by _____.
   a. stomach acid
   b. cilia
   c. saliva
   d. mucus
   e. interferon

2. Major histocompatibility complex (MHC) antigens are _____.
   a. antigenic determinants on microorganisms
   b. proteins produced by newly formed cancer cells
   c. a type of antibody molecule
   d. the binding sites of the HIV virus
   e. recognition markers on cells used for identification by one's own immune system

3. Which of the following statements regarding antibody is true? An antibody _____.
   a. has one binding site for antigens
   b. is found in a variety of body fluids and organ systems
   c. can be given to treat bacterial infections as an antibiotic
   d. is produced by platelets
   e. once produced, protects for the rest of one's life

4. If a microorganism is able to invade the internal tissues, bypassing physical and chemical barriers, it will likely be destroyed by _____.
   a. the skin
   b. the inflammatory response
   c. mucous membrane
   d. protein-digesting enzymes
   e. ciliary action

5. Since allergies are such a nuisance and allergens aren't harmful to us, why do we even make allergy antibodies?
   a. Allergens used to be harmful, but we have evolved resistances to them, so allergy antibodies are just evolutionary baggage.
   b. Allergy antibodies help defend us against parasites that typically enter the body through the mouth, nose, and throat by increasing mucus secretions and coughing or sneezing to expel the parasites.
   c. Allergy antibodies are just a mistake of the immune system and have no real use.
   d. Allergens are harmful to us and allergy antibodies protect us from them.

6. AIDS and the infectious agent HIV are difficult to treat because _____.
   a. HIV reproduces more quickly than any other virus known to humans
   b. HIV can mutate rapidly into drug-resistant forms
   c. no antibiotics can destroy HIV
   d. HIV spreads from organ to organ

7. Why is chemotherapy but not radiation therapy used to treat cancers that have spread throughout the body?
   a. Radiating the entire body would cause too much healthy tissue damage.
   b. Chemotherapy kills rapidly dividing cells regardless of location in the body.
   c. Cancerous cells become resistant to radiation once they have begun to spread through the body.
   d. Both the first and second answers are correct.
   e. Both the second and third answers are correct.

8. In order for transplanted organs to be successfully accepted by the recipient's body, the donor and recipient must be matched and the recipient must be placed on medication, even for a long period after the transplant. Why are organ transplants such a problem?
   a. We don't have the technology yet to successfully transplant organs.
   b. Unless every donor and recipient are close relatives, their MHC proteins are bound to differ.
   c. Although scientists can move cells into a recipient body, they cannot do this with an entire organ.
   d. The recipient's disease may have progressed to such an extent that the transplant cannot succeed even when matched properly.

9. Nosocomial diseases are infectious diseases that are obtained in a hospital (or related) setting. The most common type of nosocomial infection is a urinary tract infection (UTI) associated with catheters. A catheter is a hollow tube apparatus that is inserted up the urethra of the urinary tract into the otherwise sterile urinary bladder. It is used to eliminate urine in people who have lost (either permanently or temporarily) the ability to void urine. Why are UTIs and catheters so often associated?
   a. The catheters are not sterilely packaged. Bacteria on the catheters then ascend up the urethra to the bladder.
   b. Improper handling of the catheters contaminates them and they become conduits for bacteria from the outside to the inside, thereby bypassing the host defenses such as skin and mucous membranes.
   c. The catheters cause injury to the mucous membrane of the urethra, making the tissue very susceptible to inflammation.
   d. The insertion of the catheter produces small breaks in blood vessels lining the urethral membrane, allowing bacteria from the blood to enter the urethra and eventually the urinary bladder.

10. Your 5-year-old daughter has just come home from day care feeling poorly and not eating. The next day, she has vomiting, a rash, diarrhea, and some neurological symptoms. The diagnosis is bacterial meningitis, a contagious bacterial infection, usually not life-threatening. Within a week, she is up and about again, apparently healthy. The little boy who lives next door to you gets this same disease 3 months later, and you become worried that your daughter will again get meningitis. They play together all the time, and he could easily transmit the bacterium to her during play. Is this a potential problem?
    a. Yes, your daughter is at risk for contracting meningitis again. Kids under the age of 10 years have immature immune systems that will not protect them. Maternal antibodies have long since dissipated in her body, leaving her exposed to all sorts of pathogenic microorganisms.
    b. Yes, your daughter is at risk for meningitis again. Bacteria do not elicit as strong an immune response as viruses do, and her immune system will not be able to contain the infection.
    c. No, your daughter is not at risk for contracting meningitis again, particularly since the time span between the first exposure and second exposure to this infectious agent is not very long. Upon "seeing" the bacteria again, her memory cells from the previous exposure will become activated very quickly, again making large amounts of protective antibody.
    d. No, your daughter is not at risk for meningitis again. Once you have contacted an infectious agent and memory cells have been produced, that infectious agent will always be identified and eradicated before the infection can take place.

11. You and your friend each have a little boy. The kids are always playing in dirt, climbing trees, falling off bikes, and generally getting into everything. When your little Johnny comes home with a runny nose or a small cut, your philosophy is to clean the wound well or give him a decongestant and then let it take its own course. Your friend's philosophy is the exact opposite of yours. When her little Tommy comes home with similar problems, she takes him immediately to the doctor for antibiotics. Who is right and who is wrong? Why?
    a. Your friend is right to take him for antibiotics. One can never know how pathogenic an infectious microorganism can be.
    b. You are. It is probably better to allow his immune system to take care of these minor infections.
    c. Neither of you are doing the best thing. Both of you should vaccinate the boys with every known immunization, thereby protecting them from everything.

12. Which of the following descriptive terms generally describe the human immune system?
    a. complex
    b. simple
    c. multifaceted
    d. one-dimensional
    e. both complex and multifaceted
    f. both simple and one-dimensional

13. What is the purpose of the inflammatory response?
    a. to combat large-scale infections in the body
    b. to attack the body's own cells that have been taken over by microbes
    c. to attack microbes that have surmounted the body's initial defenses
    d. none of the above

14. How do antibodies recognize microbes or toxins?
    a. There is a lock-and-key type fit between the shape of the antibody and the shape of the antigen.
    b. "Constant regions" on the antibodies interact with microbes that bear morphological features that mirror the constant region of the antibody.
    c. Heavy and light chains of the antibody "constant" region detect chemical odors from the microbes.
    d. all of the above

15. Which of the following is a limitation of the humoral response to microbial invasion?
    a. B cells are capable of attacking only microbial invaders that have taken over host cells.
    b. The humoral response is only capable of effectively attacking invading microbes before they enter a host cell.
    c. B cells have a limited ability to stop the immune response once the microbes have been neutralized.
    d. B cells indiscriminately devour invading microbes.

16. Which of the following is designed to confer immunity to a particular disease?
    a. antibiotics
    b. neuraminidase inhibitors
    c. vaccines
    d. all of the above

17. Why is cancer so hard to cure?
    a. because cancer cells started as normal body cells that then lost control of cell division, so they are very hard to distinguish from healthy body cells
    b. because cancer cells are more resistant to toxins than normal cells
    c. because cancer cells are genetically different from all of the other cells of the body
    d. None of the answers is correct.

18. _____ is a chemical that damaged cells release into a wounded area.

19. The _____ arises from interactions among various types of lymphocytes in order to eliminate foreign invaders from the body.

20. _____ recognize and bind to foreign molecules in the body.

21. In _____, protection is provided by B cells and antibodies in the bloodstream.

22. In _____, T cells attack invaders that have entered cells.

23. An _____ is a disease in which the immune system attacks components of one's own body.

24. Identify the structures indicated on the figure below.

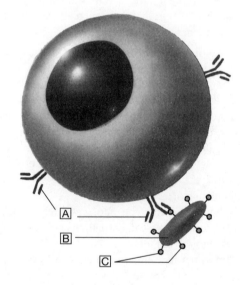

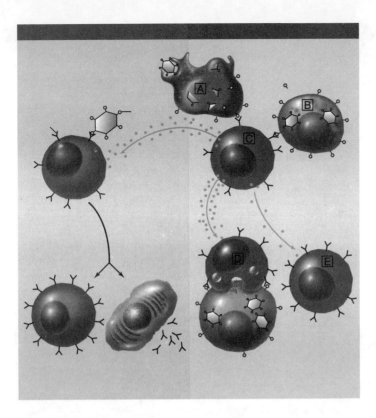

25. Identify the labeled cell types in the image above.

26. Identify the indicated portions of the HIV virus particle below.

27. Identify the indicated portions of the antibody below.

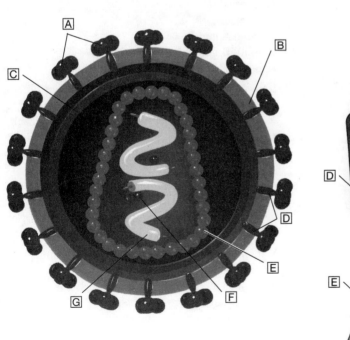

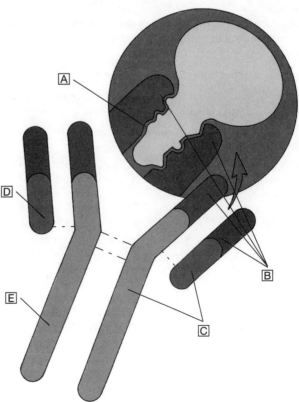

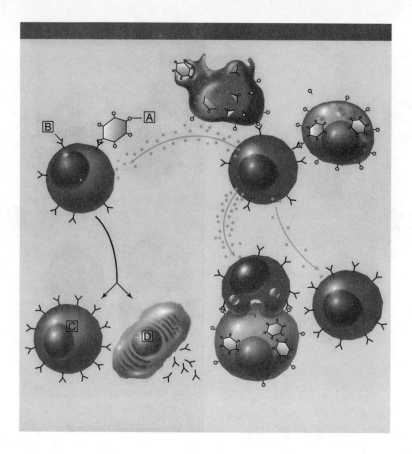

28. Identify the labeled cells and structures in the image above.

29. Can you have immunity to a microbe that you haven't encountered before?

   a. Yes. If you have encountered the same or very similar antigen of another microbe.

   b. Yes. Your immune system has as many memory cells as it has antibodies.

   c. No. You must encounter an entire microbe before you can become immune to it.

   d. No. You cannot establish immunity against any microbes.

30. Do antibiotics work on viruses? Why or why not?

   a. Yes, antibiotics can disrupt the cellular membranes of bacteria, protists, and viruses.

   b. Yes, antibiotics kill cells that use DNA to reproduce.

   c. No, viruses must enter the body's cells to reproduce and are "protected" from antibiotics.

   d. No, viruses use RNA to replicate; therefore, antibiotics do not affect them.

31. Vaccinations are good at providing immunity against _____.

   a. bacteria

   b. protists

   c. viruses

   d. both A and B

   e. both B and C

   f. all of the above

32. If allergic reactions are caused by antibodies binding to allergens, why are the responses localized (limited to a given tissue like a runny nose or upset stomach)?

   a. Antibodies that respond to allergens are attached to mast cells, which are located in tissues, not circulating through the bloodstream.

   b. Allergens interact directly with tissues and cause inflammatory response wherever they fall.

   c. Allergic responses aren't tissue specific.

   d. None of the answers is correct.

33. Which of the following is a valid treatment for autoimmune diseases?

   a. replacement of the lost or damaged tissue

   b. antibiotics

   c. immune suppression therapy

   d. both A and B

   e. both A and C

ESSAY CHALLENGE

1. List and describe the human body's two types of external barriers to invasion.

2. How does the inflammatory response assist in defense of the body after injury?

3. How does the immune system distinguish between self and non-self?

4. Once a person gets chicken pox, he or she typically doesn't get the disease again. Why?

5. If allergies are immune responses against harmless organisms, why do we even have them?

6. Why can children with SCID survive for up to a year after birth?

MEDIA ACTIVITIES

To access a Media Activity visit http://www.prenhall.com/audesirk7. Log in to the Web site selected by your instructor, navigate to this chapter, and select the appropriate Media Activity number.

32.1 Defense Against Infectious Agents
Estimated time: 5 minutes

View the body's defenses against infectious agents.

32.2 Inflammation
Estimated time: 5 minutes

Review the details of the inflammatory response.

32.3 Clonal Selection
Estimated time: 10 minutes

Explore how B cells are activated to produce antibodies by foreign antigens.

32.4 Effects of HIV on the Immune System
Estimated time: 5 minutes

In this animation, you will explore how HIV enters host cells, how it replicates and destroys the host, and why the loss of HIV-infected cells compromises the immune response.

32.5 Web Investigation: Fighting the Flu
Estimated time: 10 minutes

Fifty years ago, childhood diseases (measles, mumps, chicken pox, etc.) were just part of growing up. Everyone knew of people who had died of whooping cough (pertussis) or were crippled by polio. Today, despite extensive vaccination programs, some individuals still get polio, rubella, and the rest. Why?

1. What are the four types of vaccines (http://www.immunizationinfo.org/parents/howVaccines_work.cfm)? There are two polio vaccines (http://www.polioeradication.org/vaccines/polioeradication/all/background/vaccines.asp). Which is safer? Which is more effective? Explain your answers.

2. What percentage of American children were vaccinated (http://www.nt.who.int/vaccines/globalsummary/ pGS2000.cfm) against measles in 2001? How many cases of measles were reported? How many more cases of measles were reported in 1990, than in 2001?

3. So far smallpox is the only viral disease that has officially been eradicated by international public health action. Due to recent concerns about the use of this virus by terrorist groups, the president has put out a vaccination plan (http://www.bt.cdc.gov/agent/smallpox/vaccination/vaccination-program-statement.asp) for the United States. According to this plan, who should be vaccinated? Is it recommended for the general public to be vaccinated?

ISSUES IN BIOLOGY

What Is an Allergy?

In some people, the immune system launches attacks against antigens, such as pollen or shellfish proteins, that are not a danger to the person. These abnormal reactions by the immune system are called allergies (http://people.ku.edu/~jbrown/allergy.html) or hypersensitivities. The antigens that evoke these responses are called allergens. There are two basic categories of allergies: 1) immediate hypersensitivity where the reaction occurs within minutes, or 2) delayed hypersensitivity where the reaction typically doesn't show up for a couple of days. Immediate hypersensitivities are caused by abnormal B cell responses, while delayed hypersensitivities are caused by abnormal T cell responses. Of the five classes of antibodies produced by B cells (IgA, IgD, IgE, IgG, IgM), the IgE antibodies are responsible for immediate hypersensitivity reactions. The mechanism for this reaction is explored in section 32.5 of this chapter "What Happens When the Immune System Malfunctions?" (also, see Fig. 32-13). When IgE antibodies (produced from an earlier sensitizing exposure) encounter their allergen, they stimulate mast cells to release histamine, thus initiating the inflammatory response and leading to the symptoms common to allergies.

Different allergens produce different symptoms because they meet up with the immune system in separate sites of the body. Inhaled allergens, such as pollen and cat dander, generate upper respiratory tract symptoms similar to a bad cold—congestion, difficulty breathing, and sneezing. Ingested allergens, from foods like chocolate or strawberries, evoke gastrointestinal symptoms, such as diarrhea, vomiting, nausea, and hives. If the allergen is injected into the bloodstream, as happens with insect stings, a variety of very severe symptoms can result because the allergen is carried rapidly throughout the body. An early description of a severe allergic reaction to an insect sting was recorded in 2641 B.C. on an Egyptian tablet describing the death of a king. A severe allergic reaction like this is called anaphylaxis (http://www.nationaljewish.org/medfacts/anaphalaxis.html). The word *anaphylaxis* means "away from protection."

In an anaphylactic reaction, the major problems are a drop in blood pressure and the resulting reduction in blood flow, defined as shock. Dizziness, seizures, and loss of consciousness can occur as a result of drop in blood flow to the brain. Swelling of the lips, tongue, and throat, and constriction of the bronchioles in the lungs can impede breathing and swallowing. Gastrointestinal symptoms, such as diarrhea, vomiting, and nausea can occur. Severe hives—itchy, fluid-filled eruptions all over the body, is another common symptom.

Inhaled allergens do not normally elicit severe anaphylactic reactions, but some food allergens can: peanuts, seafood, nuts, eggs, and cow's milk in particular.

Treatment is directed at reversing the most serious symptoms—respiratory distress and drop in blood pressure. The preferred medication is epinephrine, or adrenaline, which increases the heart rate and the strength of heart contractions, thereby increasing blood pressure and restoring circulation. In addition, a bronchodilator might be given to reduce the difficulty in breathing.

Because anaphylactic shock is so severe, swift, and potentially deadly, it is best if an allergic person stays away from the allergen. For this reason, physicians ask patients about their possible allergies to penicillin before starting therapy for an infection, or to eggs, before giving a flu shot (the inactivated virus in the shot is grown in eggs). Individuals who have had an anaphylactic reaction carry an epinephrine syringe designed for self-administration—particularly important when traveling or camping. These kits (http://www.lung.ca/asthma/allergies/lifethreat.html) are sold by prescription only. Physicians also recommend that anyone at risk of anaphylaxis wear an emergency notification bracelet.

1. Describe the mechanism of allergies, from the first contact with the allergen to the onset of symptoms.

2. Since allergies give us such problems and IgE antibodies mediate these responses, why do we have IgE antibodies?

3. People who suffer from anaphylaxis are encouraged to carry a vial of adrenaline with them if they are in danger of coming into contact with their allergen—for example, when going camping, if they are allergic to bee stings. How does adrenaline alleviate the symptoms of a severe allergic reaction?

4. There has been a rise in allergic reactions to latex. What population is at highest risk for these allergies?

BIZARRE FACTS IN BIOLOGY

Blue Babies

Newborns suffering from erythroblastosis fetalis (http://www.infoplease.com/ce6/sci/Ao817644.html) are commonly referred to as "blue babies" because a lack of red blood cells (RBCs) gives a bluish color to their skin. Why do these babies have too few RBCs? Their mother's immune system attacked and destroyed them. This destruction by the mother's immune system is caused by Rh incompatibility (http://demeter.hampshire.edu/~rhinfo/whatis.html).

Rh (http://anthro.palomar.edu/blood/Rh_system.htm) or Rhesus factor, named after its initial discovery in rhesus monkeys, is an antigen on the membranes of RBCs. Rh incompatibility occurs when the baby expresses this antigen (Rh positive), but the mother does not (Rh negative). This antigen is inherited as a dominant allele, so if an Rh positive (Rh+) father and an Rh negative (Rh-) mother have a child, there is at least a 50% chance that the baby could be Rh+. Under normal conditions, an Rh- mother does not have circulating antibodies against the Rh antigen. However, if during birth, fetal blood mixes with the mother's blood, the mother's B cells will recognize the Rh factor as foreign and mount an immune response against it. This is referred to as Rh sensitization (http://demeter.hampshire.edu/~rhinfo/pathogenesis.html). Since there is a delay between the initial exposure to an antigen and the immune response, the first baby is in no danger of attack from the mother's immune system. However, after Rh sensitization has occurred, the RBCs of subsequent Rh+ fetuses will be attacked and destroyed.

Treatment for erythroblastosis fetalis is typically to give the newborn a blood transfusion. However, measures preventing Rh sensitization from occurring have dramatically reduced the occurrence of this problem in developed countries. Prevention is simple. Within 72 hours after the birth of an Rh+ baby, the Rh- mother is given antibodies against the Rh antigen (http://www.rhogaminfocenter.com/information.php). This leads to the destruction of the fetal RBCs before the mother's immune system can mount an immune response to them.

1. B cells in the mother's blood can recognize the fetal Rh antigen as a result of the mixing of blood during birth. What keeps the mother's B cells from recognizing the fetal Rh antigens during pregnancy?

2. Rh isn't the only antigen on RBCs. RBCs can also express A antigens (type A blood), B antigens (type B blood), both A and B antigens (type AB blood), or neither antigen (type O blood). As with the Rh factor, if an individual does not express a particular antigen on their RBCs, their immune system will mount an attack against that antigen when exposed to it. For example, an individual with type O blood cannot accept types A, B, or AB blood, because their immune system will attack it. In contrast to Rh incompatibility, blood type incompatibility between a mother and second child does not typically result in erythroblastosis fetalis. Why (http://users.rcn.com/jkimball. ma.ultranet/BiologyPages/B/BloodGroups.html#The_Rh_System)?

KEY TERMS

acquired immune
   deficiency syndrome
   (AIDS)
allergy
antibody
antigen
autoimmune disease
B cell
cancer
cell-mediated immunity
clonal selection

complement system
constant region
cytokine
cytotoxic T cell
fever
helper T cell
histamine
human immunodeficiency
   virus (HIV)
humoral immunity
immune response

immune system
inflammatory response
lymphocyte
macrophage
major histocompatibility
   complex (MHC)
mast cell
memory B cell
memory T cell
microbe
natural killer cell

neutrophil
phagocytic cell
plasma cell
severe combined immune
   deficiency (SCID)
T cell
T-cell receptor
tumor
vaccination
variable region

ANSWER KEY

SELF TEST

1. a
2. e
3. b
4. b
5. b
6. b
7. d
8. b
9. b
10. c
11. b
12. e
13. d
14. a
15. b

16. c
17. a
18. histamine
19. immune response
20. antibodies
21. humoral immunity
22. cell-mediated immunity
23. autoimmune disease
24. A. antibody
   B. microbe
   C. antigen
25. A. macrophage
   B. infected cell
   C. helper T cell
   D. cytotoxic T cell
   E. memory cytotoxic T cell

26. A. glycoproteins
    B. envelope
    C. protein coat
    D. spikes
    E. core proteins
    F. reverse transcriptase
    G. viral RNA coated with protein
27. A. antigen binding site
    B. variable regions
    C. constant regions
    D. light chains
    E. heavy chains
28. A. antigen on microbe
    B. antibody on B cell
    C. memory B cell
    D. plasma cell
29. a
30. c
31. f
32. a
33. e

ESSAY CHALLENGE

1. 1) The skin is a barrier to entry by foreign invaders and prevents bacterial growth through various secretions. 2) Mucous membranes secrete antimicrobial agents to kill invaders, secrete mucus to trap any foreign invaders, and use cilia to expel mucus and foreign invaders from the body. 32.2.A: Skin and Mucous Membranes Form External Barriers to Invasion

2. The inflammatory response attracts phagocytic and natural killer cells to the area to kill any local invasion by microbes and walls off the injured area, isolating it from the rest of the body. 32.2.B: Nonspecific Internal Defenses Combat Disease

3. The surfaces of the body's cells contain proteins, the major histocompatibility complex (MHC), that are unique to each individual. When immune cells mature during development, any cells that recognize "self"—bind to their own MHC antigens—are destroyed and thus cannot attack the body once the immune system matures. All other immune cells that do not recognize "self" remain. 32.3.A: The Immune System Recognizes the Invader

4. Exposure to an antigen which stimulates a humoral or cell-mediated immune response generates memory cells that may survive for many years. Upon subsequent exposure to that antigen, the remaining army of memory cells will mount a large, rapid immune response that will fend off the attack before it can make you get sick. 32.3.C: The Immune System Remembers Past Victories

5. The type of antibodies that cause allergic responses also give us protection against parasitic infection.

6. Right after birth, babies still have leftover antibodies from their mother's blood. In addition, neonates that breastfeed can continue to get antibodies through the mother's milk.

MEDIA ACTIVITIES

32.5   Web Investigation: Fighting the Flu

1. The four types of vaccines are: 1) live bacteria or viruses that have been altered so that they cannot cause disease; 2) killed bacteria or inactivated viruses; 3) toxoids (bacterial toxins that have been made harmless); 4) parts of bacteria or viruses. The two types of polio vaccines are: 1) the attenuated, oral polio vaccine (OPV) and 2) the killed, injected polio vaccine (IPV). The IPV is safer because it is a killed virus and carries no risk of vaccine-associated polio paralysis, although the risk of this is still very low with the OPV. Both vaccines are effective at producing antibodies in the blood (serum immunity) but only the OPV offers strong localized immunity in the intestines where polio viruses reproduce. Thus, the OPV is the vaccine of choice for eradication of polio, because it not only provides individual immunity but it also helps to stop transmission from person to person.

2. 91% of American children were vaccinated for measles in 2001. There were 109 reported cases of measles during 2001. There were 27,677 more reported cases of measles in 1990, than in 2001.

3. According to the president's plan, volunteers for Emergency Smallpox Response Teams, health care workers, and other critical personnel will be asked to volunteer to receive the smallpox vaccine. No, it is not recommended that the general public receive the smallpox vaccine.

ISSUES IN BIOLOGY

1. 1) The allergen is recognized by a B cell with an antibody to the allergen. 2) The B cells divide and differentiate to produce plasma cells, which crank out antibodies to the allergen. 3) The stems of the antibodies attach to mast cells. 4) Upon subsequent exposure, binding of the antibodies to allergen stimulates the mast cells to release histamine, which initiates the inflammatory response.

2. There is some evidence that IgE antibodies help protect us against parasitic infection.

3. Adrenaline halts the release of adrenaline by mast cells. In addition, it contracts blood vessels, preventing further leaking and helping to increase blood pressure, increases heart rate which increases the amount of oxygen to the brain and other tissues, and relaxes airways, making it easier to breathe.

4. Health care workers use latex gloves as part of their daily work, so this population is at the highest risk for latex allergies.

BIZARRE FACTS IN BIOLOGY

1. B cells do not cross the placental barrier. As long as the placenta is intact, B cells can't get to the fetus's RBCs. However, during pregnancy, rupturing of the placenta is common, allowing mixing of fetal and maternal blood.

2. The class of antibodies responsible for recognizing Rh antigens can cross the placental barrier between mother and child, while the class of antibodies responsible for recognizing blood type (AB) antigens cannot. So, even if a mother has circulating antibodies against the blood type antigen expressed on the fetus's RBCs, they cannot cross the placenta. Thus, the fetal RBCs are not destroyed.

CHAPTER 33: CHEMICAL CONTROL OF THE ANIMAL BODY: THE ENDOCRINE SYSTEM

AT-A-GLANCE

SELF TEST

1. Hormone specificity is determined by receptors on _____.
   a. target cells
   b. endocrine glands
   c. exocrine glands
   d. the hypothalamus

2. _____ from the hypothalamus stimulate the actions of the anterior pituitary.
   a. Nerve impulses
   b. Exocrine hormones
   c. ADH hormones
   d. Releasing hormones

3. An undersecretion of thyroid hormones can produce _____, characterized by retarded mental and physical development.
   a. cretinism
   b. precocious development
   c. goiter
   d. Graves' disease

4. The hypothalamus responds to decreasing levels of thyroxine by _____.
   a. stimulating the thyroid gland with a nerve impulse
   b. releasing more thyroxine
   c. secreting hormones that stimulate the release of TSH from the anterior pituitary
   d. increasing body temperature

5. _____ is the hormone that stimulates the development of specialized white blood cells.
   a. Parathormone
   b. Estrogen
   c. Thymosin
   d. Aldosterone

6. Which hormone secreted in a daily rhythm is thought to influence sleep/wake cycles?
   a. insulin
   b. melatonin
   c. thymosin
   d. glucagon

7. Why does ordinary table salt prevent the development of simple goiters?
   a. Salt is required to stimulate the feedback mechanism that controls the amount of thyroxine produced.
   b. Salts and other minerals inhibit the feedback mechanism, thereby creating the conditions that allow goiters to develop.
   c. Table salt is iodized.
   d. Ordinary table salt cannot prevent the development of simple goiters.

8. Identify the series of events that are initiated when thyroxine levels are low.
   a. The anterior pituitary causes the hypothalamus to secrete TSH, which inhibits the continued production of thyroxine.
   b. The hypothalamus secretes releasing hormones that cause the anterior pituitary to secrete TSH, which stimulates the thyroid to secrete thyroxine.
   c. The thyroid gland produces increased thyroxine when it stimulates the posterior pituitary to secrete its releasing hormones.
   d. The posterior pituitary stimulates the anterior pituitary, which responds by stimulating the thyroid to secrete TSH.

9. Which of the following statements is a correct description of why a particular gland is very large when we are young, but much smaller when we reach adulthood?
   a. The thyroid is most active when we are young to prevent the development of conditions such as cretinism.
   b. The thymus gland is large during youth and decreases with age as our immune system matures.
   c. The pituitary decreases in size after we reach adult stature and growth hormone is no longer needed to stimulate growth.
   d. The pancreas is most active when we are young and decreases in size as less insulin is required when we mature.

10. Gigantism occurs when there is an oversecretion of hormone that causes exceptionally rapid growth. In some cases, tumor growth can cause oversecretion of hormones. Where would the tumor have to be to give rise to gigantism?
    a. thyroid gland   b. anterior pituitary
    c. pancreas   d. adrenal medulla

11. How do peptide hormones exert their specific actions since they circulate throughout the entire body?
    a. The cell secreting the hormone and the cell receiving the hormone are very close together.
    b. The cell receiving the hormone has transmembrane protein receptors that bind to the extracellular hormone.
    c. All cells in the body possess receptors for all circulating hormones, but not all are functional.
    d. None of the answers is correct.

12. How do steroid hormones elicit their biological effect?
    a. They bind to receptors embedded within the cell membrane.
    b. They employ a sequence of intracellular messengers like cAMP.
    c. They are able to diffuse across the cell and nuclear membranes to bind to their nuclear receptor.
    d. none of the above

13. Which of the following is characteristic of exocrine glands?
    a. The secretions are released into the bloodstream.
    b. The secretions are not released through a small tube.
    c. They produce hormones.
    d. none of the above

14. Which of the following statements about the role of the hypothalamus is (are) true?
    a. The hypothalamus controls the release and synthesis of hormones by the anterior pituitary through a combination of several hormones, in part because of a unique linking of capillary beds—one in the hypothalamus, and one in the anterior pituitary.
    b. The hypothalamic hormones affect the anterior pituitary by stimulating or inhibiting other hormones synthesized by the anterior pituitary.
    c. Modified neurons (neurosecretory cells) with their cell bodies in the hypothalamus and their endings in the anterior pituitary release hormones that enter a capillary bed and blood carried to the rest of the body.
    d. The first two answers are both correct.
    e. All of the above statements are true.
    f. None of these statements is true.

15. How is the concentration of thyroxine in the bloodstream regulated?
    a. by negative feedback mechanisms
    b. It is inhibited by the presence of thyroid-stimulating hormone (TSH).
    c. It is inhibited by the presence of thyroid-releasing hormone (TRH).
    d. by the parathyroid gland

16. Which of the following statements about the adrenal gland is true?
    a. The adrenal glands are similar to the pancreas and pituitary in being composed of two different tissues, and therefore the two parts of the adrenal gland have very different functions.
    b. The adrenal cortex secretes adrenaline.
    c. The hormones produced by the adrenal cortex are substances that are important in the "fight or flight" response.
    d. The adrenal medulla produces three very different functional classes of hormones.

17. _____ are chemical messages produced by specialized cells and released into the bloodstream where they can be distributed to distant or nearby cells.

18. _____ is released from the posterior pituitary and triggers the milk let-down reflex and causes uterine contractions during birth.

19. Secretions of hormones by the _____ is controlled directly by the sympathetic nervous system.

20. The _____ is a gland that produces both exocrine and endocrine secretions.

21. _____ and _____ are two types of steroid hormones produced and secreted from the ovaries that play a role in controlling the menstrual cycle and pregnancy.

22. The adrenal cortex releases _____ in response to a drop in blood sodium levels.

23. Label the organs of the endocrine system on the diagram below.

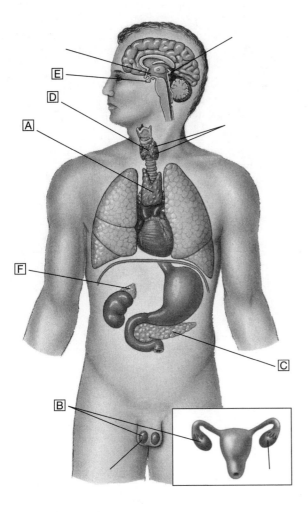

24. Label the structures of the neck as they appear in the illustration below.

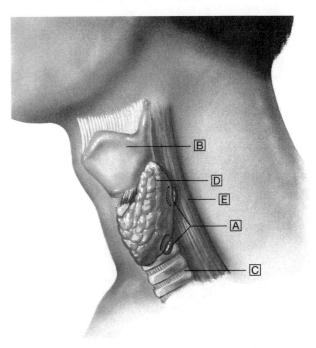

25. The adrenal glands have two distinct regions. Label these regions on the diagram below.

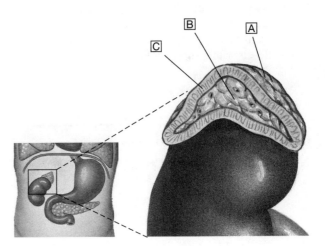

26. You have just discovered a new hormone. When you break the hormone apart to study its structure, you find that it is composed of many amino acids. Which of the following classes of hormones would your new hormone fit into?
   a. steroid
   b. amino acid
   c. peptide
   d. prostaglandin

27. Which of the following are based on the structure of cholesterol?
   a. testosterone
   b. glucocorticoids
   c. oxytocin
   d. A and B only
   e. A and C only
   f. all of the above

28. Ibuprofen is often prescribed for relief of menstrual cramps. Why?
   a. Ibuprofen blocks electrical signals from pain nerves to the brain.
   b. Ibuprofen acts directly on the muscle cells in the uterus to cause relaxation.
   c. Ibuprofen blocks production of prostaglandins.
   d. None of the answers is a correct description of how ibuprofen stops menstrual cramps.

29. Why are positive feedback loops much more rare than negative feedback loops?
   a. Positive feedback loops amplify the initial response that triggered them, so without a self-limiting end result, they would be "explosive."
   b. Negative feedback loops control a single variable, while positive feedback loops can control more than one variable. Thus, negative feedback loops are simpler and use less energy.
   c. Negative feedback loops act to negate the response that triggers them, which helps to keep important variables like body temperature or blood sugar levels within acceptable ranges.
   d. both A and B
   e. both A and C

30. If you are resting and your heart rate slows down, which of the following types of communication would be most affected?
   a. paracrine
   b. endocrine
   c. exocrine
   d. autocrine

31. Insulin and glucagon from the pancreas work in concert to keep blood sugar levels under tight control. In addition, hormones from other glands such as thyroxine and the glucocorticoids also play a role in keeping glucose levels in the appropriate range. Why are so many different hormones used to regulate blood glucose levels?
   a. because glucose is used exclusively for energy by all the tissues of the body
   b. because, unlike other tissues of the body that can use proteins or fats for energy, the brain has to have glucose for energy
   c. because glucose plays a role in keeping ions inside and outside of cells in balance
   d. because glucose is used to help carry oxygen in the blood

32. Androgen insensitivity is a rare condition where a genetic (XY) male develops as a female except that the individual has testes that remain in the body cavity and no uterus or ovaries. Blood samples show that the levels of testosterone and other androgens are normal for a male body. Based on this, where do you think the defect in hormonal signaling is likely to be in this condition?
   a. LH levels from the anterior pituitary must be below average.
   b. FSH levels from the anterior pituitary must be below average.
   c. Androgen receptors must not be functioning properly and are unable to respond to the circulating androgens.
   d. The cAMP intracellular second messenger pathway must not be functioning properly.

ESSAY CHALLENGE

1. List and describe the four types of vertebrate hormones.

2. Compare and contrast endocrine and exocrine glands.

3. Suppose you have ridden your bicycle a few miles on a hot day and have lost a lot of water through perspiration. What will your pituitary gland do in response to this situation?

4. What general types of hormones does the hypothalamus secrete and what do these hormones do?

5. Since thyroxine regulates metabolic rate, it affects most cells of the body. Its levels in the blood are tightly controlled. Explain how thyroxine can shut off its own release.

6. What are the two main hormones secreted by the islet cells of the pancreas? Under what conditions are these hormones secreted and what are their effects on blood glucose levels?

7. What are the steps, starting with hormone release by the anterior pituitary, that are involved with the development of secondary sexual characteristics during puberty?

8. Many college students get sick during or following final exams. Give a possible explanation of this phenomenon based on what you know about how stress affects the endocrine system.

MEDIA ACTIVITIES

To access a Media Activity visit http://www.prenhall.com/audesirk7. Log in to the Web site selected by your instructor, navigate to this chapter, and select the appropriate Media Activity number.

33.1 Hypothalamic Control of the Pituitary
Estimated time: 5 minutes

The hypothalamus and the pituitary gland work together to coordinate many actions of the endocrine system. In this activity, you will learn how the hypothalamus controls hormonal release by the pituitary gland.

33.2 Modes of Action of Hormones
Estimated time: 5 minutes

Explore two ways hormones act to affect cells throughout the body.

33.3 Web Investigation: Losing on Artificial Hormones
Estimated time: 30 minutes

For centuries athletes have searched for performance-enhancing drugs that would guarantee victory. The modern pharmacopoeia is full of enticing alternatives, but the long-term effects can be devastating. Can a drug-free athlete win in the modern world?

1. Different substances have different physiological effects. What are the seven performance enhancement (http://www.howstuffworks.com/athletic-drug-test1.htm) goals?

2. Two of the most frequently abused groups of drugs are anabolic steroids (http://165.112.78.61/ResearchReports/Steroids/anabolicsteroids2.html#what) and steroidal supplements. What are the differences between the two?

3. Abuse of anabolic steroids can have varying effects depending on gender. What are some of the common health hazards (http://165.112.78.61/SteroidAlert/Steroidalert.html#Anchor-Health-56611) of anabolic steroid abuse regardless of age or gender?

4. At the center of the blood doping scandal at the 2002 Winter Olympics, where two Olympic skiers were stripped of their medals, was a new drug called darbepoietin (http://www.swisstox.net/en/news_e.php?st_lang_key= en&st_news_id=926). In the past, blood doping required removing blood from the athlete, freezing it, and then reinjecting it right before competition. This increases the number of red blood cells, thus increasing the oxygen-carrying capacity of the blood. Recently, use of drugs like darbepoietin and erythropoietin (EPO) (http://www.tirgan.com/procrit.htm) are making it easier for athletes to blood-dope. What natural substance in the body are these drugs mimicking and how does that affect red blood cell numbers? For what purpose were these drugs originally created?

ISSUES IN BIOLOGY

Environmental Estrogens

Since the 1940s, ecologists have documented dwindling natural populations of many species. This decline in populations, due to a reduction in fertility of eagles, otters, gulls, alligators, and other species, was traced to pesticide contamination of the food chain. Metabolites of pesticides apparently acted like the female sex hormone, estrogen. Young males exposed to high levels of environmental estrogens became "feminized" and, consequently, sterile. These environmental estrogens, also called xenoestrogens (http://e.hormone.tulane.edu/edc.html), could be a problem for human populations too. They may play a role in the decline in human sperm counts observed since the 1950s.

Pesticides aren't the only source of xenoestrogens. Environmental estrogens are all around us from both synthetic and natural sources. Synthetic xenoestrogens enter the environment from pesticides, herbicides, plastics, and by-products of manufacturing processes. Phytoestrogens (http://e.hormone.tulane.edu/learning/phytoestrogens.html), xenoestrogens that occur naturally in many plants and fungi, have always been a part of the human diet. Phytoestrogens occur in high concentrations in soybean, alfalfa and bean sprouts, leguminous tubers (yams, cassava, potato), flaxseed, and unrefined grain products. Populations that have diets rich in phytoestrogens have significantly lower risks of developing estrogen-related cancers of breast, ovary, endometrium, and prostate. For example, the traditional Asian diet is rich in phytoestrogens, and Asian women have lower levels of plasma estrogen and a lower incidence of breast cancer than women in Western countries. Are phytoestrogens responsible for these health benefits? Clinical studies will be required to answer that question, particularly because intake of phytoestrogens is only one of many differences in diet and lifestyle between Asian and Western cultures.

So why is exposure to some types of environmental estrogens harmful and to other types seemingly helpful? The answer to that question is not completely understood, but there is some evidence that it has to do with how the estrogens bind to estrogen receptors. Binding by some phytoestrogens is thought to weaken the estrogen response while binding by some synthetic xenoestrogens might strengthen the estrogen response.

Many phytoestrogen supplements are now being marketed for relief of symptoms of menopause. Since recent studies show that long-term use of estrogen and progesterone by post-menopausal women increases the incidence of many estrogen-related cancers, women are turning to phytoestrogens as the answer. However, studies (http://nutrition.tufts.edu/magazine/2002spring/soy3.html) that have tested specific phytoestrogens show no relief of the symptoms of menopause, such as hot flashes and night sweats. Also, since phytoestrogens are considered to be food supplements, many haven't been tested, so we do not know about the possible side effects of long-term use. In fact, some phytoestrogens may bind the estrogen receptor just as tightly as estrogen and have the same deleterious effects as of some of the synthetic xenoestrogens. Can certain phytoestrogens provide relief from the symptoms of menopause or even some protection against cancer? Only further research will tell.

1. How do estrogens exert their effects in the body?

2. How do xenoestrogens differ from phytoestrogens?

3. Should women use phytoestrogen supplements to prevent cancer or the symptoms of menopause?

BIZARRE FACTS IN BIOLOGY

Sex Reversal in Fish

Always the bridesmaid, never the bride? Why not be the groom? With certain species of fish, this is an option.

Fish that can alter their sex are known as successive hermaphrodites (http://www.sciencenews.org/sn_edpik/ls_4.htm). Normally the sex reversal occurs only once. For example, a sexually mature female reproduces and then becomes a male. The ovaries shrink, the fish develops testes, and male hormones are released. These physiological changes also alter the animal's behavior. These new males become aggressive, defend territory, and court females.

Normally, sex reversal occurs in response to changes in the environment. For example, in a species of coral reef fish, *Labroides dimidiatus* (http://www.aquariumofthebay.com/bluestreakcleanerwrasse.html), the basic social group is a dominant male with three to six females living in his territory. If the dominant male dies, within days one of the female fish will become male to take his place. It is only when the male is absent that the sex change can occur. This suppression of sex reversal is critical for maintaining the social structure of the group. In other species, sex reversal may occur in response to a skewed sex ratio in the group. If there are more females than males, a female may change sex to increase its chance of mating.

Sex reversal allows fish to adapt to changes in their social environment. Sexual flexibility increases reproductive fitness and genetic diversity in these populations.

References

Alder, T. 1995. Fishy sex: Uncovering the wild ways of fish. *Science News* 148:266–7.
Robertson, D. R. 1972. Social control of sex reversal in a coral-reef fish. *Science*, 1007–9.

1. Why do scientists study sex reversal in fish? In other words, what can we learn that is applicable to other species, including humans?

2. What are some of the reasons fish do not reverse their sex more often?

KEY TERMS

adrenal cortex
adrenal gland
adrenal medulla
adrenocorticotropic
    hormone (ACTH)
aldosterone
amino acid based hormone
androgen
angiotensin
anterior pituitary
antidiuretic
    hormone (ADH)
atrial natriuretic
    peptide (ANP)
calcitonin
cholecystokinin
cortisol
cyclic AMP
diabetes mellitus

duct
endocrine disrupter
endocrine gland
endocrine hormone
endocrine system
environmental estrogen
epinephrine
erythropoietin
estrogen
exocrine gland
follicle-stimulating
    hormone (FSH)
gastrin
glucagon
glucocorticoid
goiter
growth hormone
hypothalamus
inhibiting hormone

insulin
islet cell
leptin
local hormone
luteinizing hormone (LH)
melanocyte-stimulating
    hormone (MSH)
melatonin
neurosecretory cell
norepinephrine
ovary
oxytocin
pancreas
parathyroid gland
parathyroid hormone
peptide hormone
pineal gland
pituitary gland
posterior pituitary

progesterone
prolactin
prostaglandin
receptor
releasing hormone
renin
second messenger
secretin
steroid hormone
target cell
testis
testosterone
thymosin
thymus
thyroid gland
thyroid-stimulating
    hormone (TSH)
thyroxine

ANSWER KEY

SELF TEST

1. a
2. d
3. a
4. c
5. c
6. b
7. c
8. b
9. b
10. b
11. b
12. c
13. d
14. d
15. a
16. a
17. hormones
18. oxytocin
19. adrenal medulla
20. pancreas
21. estrogen, progesterone
22. aldosterone
23. A. thymus gland
    B. gonads
    C. pancreas
    D. thyroid gland
    E. pituitary gland
    F. adrenal gland

24. A. parathyroid glands
    B. larynx
    C. trachea
    D. thyroid gland
    E. esophagus
25. A. adrenal capsule
    B. adrenal medulla
    C. adrenal cortex
26. c
27. d
28. a, c
29. e
30. b
31. b
32. c

ESSAY CHALLENGE

1. 1) peptide hormones, made from chains of amino acids; 2) amino acid–based hormones, made from single amino acids; 3) steroid hormones, which resemble cholesterol; 4) prostaglandins, which are made from fatty acids
2. Exocrine glands secrete substances outside the body or into the digestive tract through ducts, while endocrine glands secrete substances into the body and are ductless.
3. The pituitary gland will release ADH in order to cause the kidneys to reabsorb water.
4. The hypothalamus secretes releasing hormones and inhibiting hormones which either stimulate or

inhibit, respectively, the release of hormones from the anterior pituitary.

5. When there are sufficient amounts of circulating thyroxin, this will inhibit the release of a specific TSH-releasing hormone from the hypothalamus and also inhibit the release of TSH (thyroid stimulating hormone) from the anterior pituitary. Both of these will lead to a reduction in the amount of TSH, which will decrease the release of thyroxine from the thyroid gland.

6. Insulin and glucagon are secreted by the islet cells of the pancreas. Insulin is secreted in response to a rise in blood glucose levels and causes cells to take up glucose and use it or store it as glycogen or fat, thus decreasing blood glucose. Glucagon is secreted in response to a drop in blood glucose and stimulates glycogen breakdown and glucose release by liver cells, thus increasing blood glucose levels.

7. The anterior pituitary begins to secrete higher levels of both luteinizing hormone (LH) and follicle-stimulating hormone (FSH). Increased levels of LH and FSH stimulate the ovaries and testes to produce more sex hormones. Increased levels of sex hormones, such as estrogen and testosterone, bind to receptors on many different target tissues to develop secondary sexual characteristics in females and males, respectively.

8. In response to stress, releasing hormones from the hypothalamus stimulate the anterior pituitary to release ACTH. ACTH causes the release of glucocorticoids by the adrenal cortex. Among other effects, the glucocorticoids cause suppression of the immune response, which would allow microorganisms to get a foot in the door to cause an infection.

MEDIA ACTIVITIES

33.3   Web Investigation: Losing on Artificial Hormones

1. 1. Build mass and strength of muscles and/or bones 2. Increase delivery of oxygen to exercising tissues 3. Mask pain 4. Stimulate the body 5. Relax 6. Reduce weight 7. Hide use of other drugs

2. Anabolic steroids are synthetic versions of male sex hormones (androgens) that are known to mimic the effects of the endogenous hormones. Steroid supplements are substances that can be converted into androgens or androgen-like substances in the body. Since these are considered dietary supplements, they can be bought without prescription and have not been widely tested. Therefore, it is not known whether these substances actually lead to increases in levels of endogenous steroids, or whether they have long-term deleterious side effects.

3. Abuse of anabolic steroids can lead to potentially fatal liver cysts and liver cancer; blood clotting,

cholesterol changes, and hypertension, each of which can promote heart attack and stroke; and acne. Also, some scientists believe that increases in aggression and aggressive behaviors may accompany anabolic steroid use.

4. These drugs mimic the hormone erythropoietin, normally released from the kidneys, which stimulates the production of red blood cells by the bone marrow. These drugs were originally created to alleviate anemia caused by cancer, kidney disease, or other chronic illnesses.

ISSUES IN BIOLOGY

1. Estrogens are produced primarily by the ovaries in females and to a much lesser extent by the testes in males. Estrogens are released starting from the fetal stages onward and influence development, behavior, and cognition in addition to driving development of secondary sexual characteristics during puberty and regulating various aspects of reproduction, such as egg cell maturation, menstruation, and pregnancy.

2. Xenoestrogens, also called environmental estrogens, are any of a variety of natural or synthetic compounds, not produced in the animal body, that mimic the effects of natural estrogen hormones produced by animals. Phytoestrogens are xenoestrogens specifically produced by plants or fungi.

3. Recent studies have shown that certain phytoestrogens do not alleviate symptoms of menopause such as hot flashes. Other studies have shown that women from cultures with diets high in phytoestrogens have lower circulating levels of estrogen, which may play a role in lower risk of certain cancers. While these studies suggest a possible link between phytoestrogens and lowered risk for certain cancers, this link has not yet been proven and possible side effects of long-term use of phytoestrogen supplements are unknown. Therefore, women should rely on a diet rich in fruits and vegetables to supply their phytoestrogens, instead of using supplements.

BIZARRE FACTS IN BIOLOGY

1. Research on fish may shed light on how different variables such as social interactions, environment, and stress might affect human reproduction and sexuality. These studies might also give insight into the role of the brain and various signalling molecules like hormones or neurotransmitters in shaping human sexuality and sexual preference.

2. While the reasons are not entirely known, it is thought that the fish change sexes only in response to environmental/social pressures because sex reversal exacts a toll on the fish. Sex reversal uses energy and causes loss of reproductive days and possibly a decreased ability to defend against predators or competitors.

CHAPTER 34: THE NERVOUS SYSTEM AND THE SENSES

AT-A-GLANCE

1. Which portion of a neuron will conduct impulses toward the cell body?
   a. axon
   b. Schwann cells
   c. dendrites
   d. synaptic terminals

2. The point at which the action potential is triggered is called _____.
   a. resting potential
   b. threshold
   c. repolarization

3. Depending on the type of synapse, the effect of the neurotransmitter can be _____ to the postsynaptic membrane, making the membrane _____.
   a. excitatory; more negative
   b. inhibitory; less negative
   c. excitatory; less negative

4. Which of these divisions of the peripheral nervous system will innervate skeletal muscle?
   a. autonomic nervous system
   b. sympathetic nervous system
   c. somatic nervous system

5. Which of these areas of the brain is part of the limbic system?
   a. thalamus
   b. cerebral cortex
   c. medulla oblongata
   d. hypothalamus

6. If a drug causes the neuron's membrane to become a little more permeable to all ions, what will happen to the resting and threshold potentials?
   a. The resting and threshold potentials will be unchanged.
   b. The resting potential will move closer to the threshold potential.
   c. The resting potential will move further from the threshold potential.

7. What would be the effect at a synapse if the neurotransmitter was allowed to remain in the synaptic cleft bound to receptors?
   a. The size of the synaptic signal would remain the same.
   b. The size of the synaptic signal would be smaller.
   c. The size of the synaptic signal would be larger.

8. You are looking at a cross section of the human spinal cord. The gray, butterfly-shaped area is made up mostly of _____.
   a. myelinated axons
   b. cell bodies
   c. meninges

9. Your patient has suffered a small stroke and reports that he can no longer feel the touch of his hand on a surface. He knows he is touching the surface, but only because he sees his hand there. In which region of the brain did this stroke occur?
   a. frontal lobe
   b. occipital lobe
   c. parietal lobe
   d. hippocampus

10. How does Prozac act as an antidepressant?
    a. Prozac acts as a postsynaptic excitatory neurotransmitter.
    b. Prozac prevents the destruction of serotonin.
    c. Prozac enhances the action of serotonin as a co-neurotransmitter.
    d. Prozac acts to block reuptake of serotonin, enhancing its actions as an antidepressant.

11. True or False: Neurons are both structurally polar and functionally polar cells.
    a. True
    b. False

12. How can you distinguish between a light touch and a moderate poke to the arm?
    a. The action potentials are different sizes depending upon the strength of the stimulus.
    b. The frequency of action potentials changes with the strength of the stimulus.
    c. There are different neurotransmitters released depending upon the strength of the stimulus.

13. What part of the brain might you suspect had suffered a stroke if a person's basic emotions and behaviors suddenly change?
    a. limbic system
    b. corpus callosum
    c. occipital lobe
    d. cerebellum

14. Where does the ear convert the mechanical energy called sound into electrical signals that are sent to the brain?
    a. outer ear
    b. middle ear
    c. inner ear
    d. Eustachian tube

15. What happens when an image (or a portion of an image) falls on the spot where the ganglion cell axons exit the eye?
    a. Transduction of light into an electrical signal by rods and cones still occurs.
    b. Transduction of light energy to electrical energy does not occur here.
    c. This is the site of greatest visual acuity, and it allows you to see great detail.
    d. Only black and white vision exists at this point.

16. The _____ is the fundamental unit of the nervous system.

17. The _____ is the electrical impulse used to convey signals within neurons.

18. A _____ is a specific chemical released by the synaptic terminal.

19. The _____ controls voluntary functions.

20. The _____ is part of the hindbrain that controls several automatic functions, such as breathing and heart rate.

21. The _____ is involved in coordinating movements of the body.

22. In the diagram below, there are structures that are not labeled. Please complete the diagram by providing these labels.

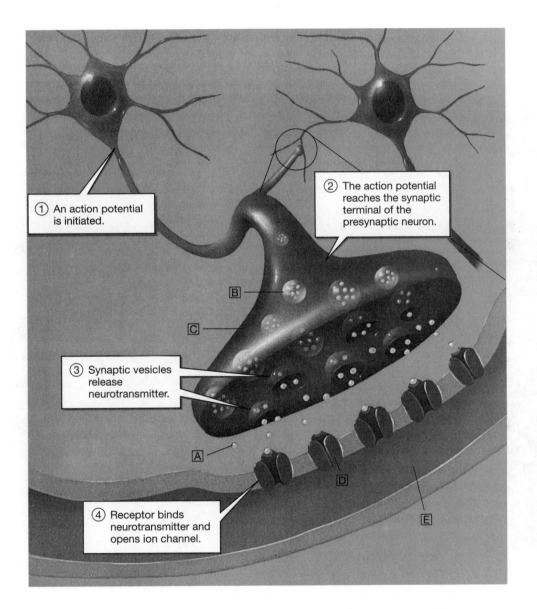

① An action potential is initiated.

② The action potential reaches the synaptic terminal of the presynaptic neuron.

③ Synaptic vesicles release neurotransmitter.

④ Receptor binds neurotransmitter and opens ion channel.

B

C

A

D

E

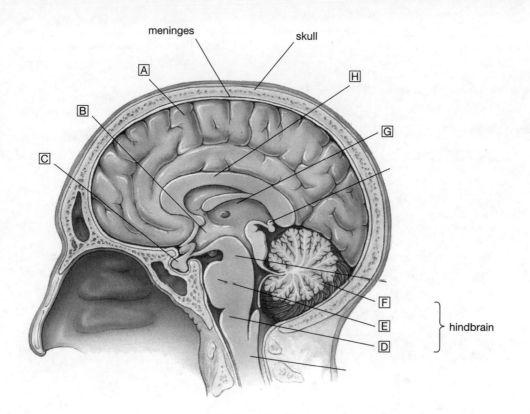

meninges   skull

A

B   H

C   G

F

E   } hindbrain

D

23. Label the structures seen on the cross section of the human brain above.

24. Label the indicated structures associated with the ear shown on the image below.

25. Arthropod eyes are composed of many light-receptive ommatidia. Label the structures present on an ommatidium below.

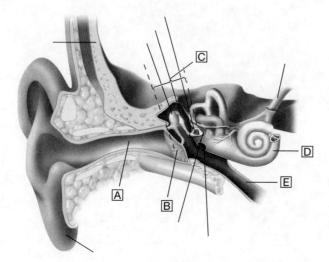

C

D

E

A   B

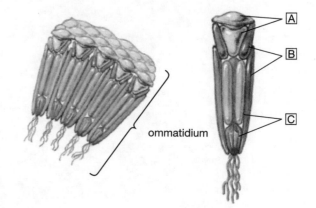

ommatidium

A

B

C

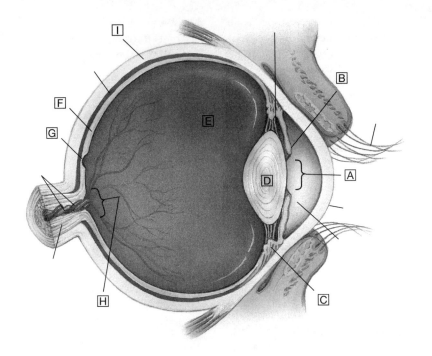

26. Label the indicated structures of the human eye on the image above.

27. Label the indicated structures on the diagram of the cells of the human retina below.

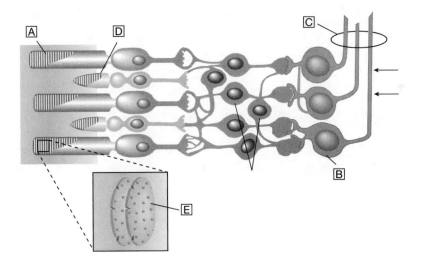

28. You are recording from a neuron with an electrode and determine that the resting membrane potential is around –70 millivolts. What would happen to the membrane potential if you added 3 times more sodium to the extracellular solution?
   a. The membrane potential will stay the same.
   b. The membrane potential will become more positive.
   c. The membrane potential will become more negative.

29. You've just discovered a new terrestrial species. It is tube-shaped, like an earthworm, but it moves at a right angle to the long axis of its body by rolling (like a rolling pin rolling across a table). It has chemoreceptors all over its body, but no obvious eyes or other sensory structures. What type of nervous system do you suppose this new species has?
   a. centralized   b. nerve net
   c. none

30. If you compared fMRI brain scans from two patients, one with Alzheimer's and one without, what would you expect to see?
   a. The Alzheimer's brain would be all red and yellow, and the normal brain would be black.
   b. The normal brain would be all red and yellow, and the Alzheimer's brain would be black.
   c. The normal brain would have more red and yellow areas.
   d. The Alzheimer's brain would have more red and yellow areas.

31. Which of the following does the brain use to interpret information about sensory inputs from the peripheral nervous system?
   a. amplitude of receptor potentials
   b. amplitude of action potentials
   c. frequency of action potentials
   d. where the sensory signals originate from in the body
   e. Both the amplitude of receptor potentials and action potentials are used.
   f. Both the frequency of action potentials and where the signals originate are used.

32. Does having only one tongue present the same disadvantages as if you had only one eye or one ear?
   a. Yes, because having two ears allows us to localize sound.
   b. Yes, because having two eyes gives us a bigger visual range and binocular vision, which again gives us the ability to accurately localize objects in our environment.
   c. Yes, because having two tongues would allow us to better locate food sources in our environment.
   d. No, having two tongues would not allow us to better locate food sources in our environment.

ESSAY CHALLENGE

1. How do working memory and long-term memory develop?

2. Compare and contrast the sympathetic and parasympathetic division of the autonomic nervous system.

3. How is sound converted into nerve impulses?

4. How do rods and cones differ in the perception of light?

5. How do you explain the fact that, until this question mentioned it, you were unaware of the buzz of the fluorescent lamp overhead or the feeling of the chair under your tush?

6. Is your "picture" of the world an exact replica? Why or why not?

7. Why does loss of the myelin sheath around axons impair the ability to conduct electrical signals, as seen in victims of multiple sclerosis?

8. How can a hard poke to the eye cause you to "see stars"?

9. How can the pain from a punch in the arm be categorized as a chemical sense?

MEDIA ACTIVITIES

To access a Media Activity visit http://www.prenhall.com/audesirk7. Log in to the Web site selected by your instructor, navigate to this chapter, and select the appropriate Media Activity number.

34.1 The Nervous System: Electrical Signals
Estimated time: 10 minutes

Neurons send electrical signals called an action potential. Review the events that generate an action potential in a neuron.

34.2 The Nervous System: Synapses
Estimated time: 5 minutes

Review signals are transferred from neuron to neuron across the synapses.

34.3 Reflex Arc
Estimated time: 5 minutes

Watch how the reflex arc allows us to react quickly to pain.

34.4 Brain Structure
Estimated time: 5 minutes

Review the basic structures of the brain and their function.

34.5 The Vertebrate Eye
Estimated time: 5 minutes

Review the structure of the eye and how it captures light and sends visual signals to the brain.

34.6 Web Investigation: From Tragedy to Triumph
Estimated time: 30 minutes

Before WWII, spinal cord injuries were usually lethal. Today many survivors live in wheelchairs, some only with the support of complex and expensive medical apparatus. Scientific researchers are looking for new treatments and developing experimental spinal repair protocols. Since his paralysis in 1995, Christopher Reeve (http://www.christopherreeve.com/) has brought national attention to spinal cord injury and has inspired and funded research into new treatments. At this time there is no cure for SCI, but there are several promising leads.

1. In most cases the initial spinal cord trauma (usually crushing) is aggravated by secondary physiological events. What happens (http://science-education.nih.gov/nihHTML/ose/snapshots/multimedia/ritn/spinal/happens.html) within the first few hours? What effects are not observed for several weeks?

2. Acute spinal injuries are now immediately treated with methylprednisolone. Why?

3. Recent developments in treatment of spinal cord injury have fallen into three basic categories: 1) drugs, like methylprednisolone, that help to reduce the effects of secondary damage to the spinal cord; 2) drugs or treatments that promote activity in the nerves or regrowth of injured nerves; or 3) rehabilitation interventions to maintain the health of the nerves and muscles past the point of the injury. Following are several examples of possible new therapies for spinal cord injury. Into which of the above categories does each therapy fall?

3a. Transplants/neurotrophic factors (http://www.nih.gov/news/pr/dec2001/ninds-01.htm)

3b. Functional electrical stimulation (http://www.mech.gla.ac.uk/~henrik/fes-intro.html)

3c. 4-AP (http://www.vet.purdue.edu/cpr/research.html#Drug)

3d. GM-1 ganglioside (http://www.ncbi.nlm.nih.gov/entrez/query.fcgi?cmd=Retrieve&db=PubMed&list_uids=9770243&dopt=Abstract)

4. An old proverb states, "an ounce of prevention is worth a pound of cure." What is the #1 cause of spinal cord injuries (http://www.cureparalysis.org/statistics/index.html)?

ISSUES IN BIOLOGY

What Is Alzheimer's Disease?

Alzheimer's disease is the leading cause of dementia, a reduction in cognitive abilities, in older people. It is estimated that greater than four million Amercans suffer from this disease. Before you are disheartened by these statistics, recognize that they are a result of our accomplishments in medicine. First, improved understanding of diseases allow for accurate identification, which sets the stage for finding cures. Second, we see more age-related illnesses in our society in part because advances in medicine have allowed our population as a whole to live longer. Alzheimer's disease was first described in the medical literature in 1907 by Dr. Alois Alzheimer. At that time, all forms of dementia were grouped together. This grouping continued until recently, which is probably why the name seems recent even though the disease has been identified for over 95 years. The dementia associated with Alzheimer's disease is caused by a progressive loss of neurons in the brain that produce the neurotransmitter acetylcholine. Memory loss is the most common symptom linked to this disease, but it can affect a variety of areas, such as language skills, sense of time and space, comprehension, and awareness. As the disease progresses, patients experience personality changes, emotional instability, and will eventually become unable to care for themselves.

Autopsy of postmortem brains, which at present is the only way to confirm a diagnosis of this disease, reveals two characteristic features: amyloid plaques, which are aggregations of amyloid beta peptide, and neurofibrillary tangles, which are twisted masses of the tau protein. We do not know what causes these plaques and tangles, or whether they cause the death of neurons or are a result of it. The majority of research (http://web.sfn.org/content/Publications/BrainBriefings/alzheimers_disease_plaques.html) into this disease is attempting to answer just those questions.

Because Alzheimer's disease has no known cause, it is difficult to identify who is at risk. The most accurate way to diagnose a living patient with Alzheimer's is with a thorough clinical exam, including laboratory and neuropsychological tests and brain imaging, by a doctor experienced with Alzheimer's disease. Among other things, an early diagnosis can rule out other causes for the dementia and allow for suitable treatment of symptoms. Some of the symptoms, such as depression, sleeplessness, and agitation, can be treated with medicines that are already available. All four of the FDA-approved (http://www.alzforum.org/dis/tre/drt/default.asp) drugs now available for Alzheimer's inhibit the breakdown of acetylcholine. This helps diminish some of the symptoms of dementia by increasing the amount of acetylcholine available from the neurons that remain. Many drugs that are now in clinical trials target prevention or destruction of plaques and tangles in hopes that this will spare neurons. As research brings us closer to understanding the cause of this disease, it will also bring us closer to finding a cure.

1. What percentage of Americans over the age of 65 have Alzheimer's disease? Over the age of 85?

2. Since there is no cure for Alzheimer's disease, what is the benefit of getting an early diagnosis?

3. Your grandfather has just been diagnosed with Alzheimer's disease. You are concerned that you and other family members could be future Alzheimer's patients. What steps would or could you take to discover those at risk?

BIZARRE FACTS IN BIOLOGY

A Real Shocker

Common among the folklore originating throughout the Amazon River drainage basin of South America is the story of an electric fish so powerful that it can stun and even kill large animals such as horses. This is no myth: the ability to generate and use electricity is a well-documented phenomenon in biology.

All animals release some electrical energy. Muscle movement and nerve conduction are two examples of biochemical processes that release electrical energy. Therefore, it should not be too surprising that some organisms have adaptations that take advantage of this phenomenon. Strongly electric fish, such as the electric eel (http://www.aip.org/radio/html/electric_eels.html) (*Electrophorus*) of the Amazon River, have electric organs that make up about half of the muscle mass of the body. These electric organs are composed of multinucleated cells called electrocytes (electric cells). Electrocytes are stacked in a coinlike fashion with as many as 10,000 cells in each of 70 or more columns. Although each cell produces only a small current, the large stacks of electrocytes are discharged simultaneously, producing a powerful discharge. The voltage produced in an ordinary muscle cell is no greater than 0.1 volt, but the electric eel's current has been measured at 550 volts—enough to stun a prey organism and certainly enough to discourage any predator with an appetite for electric eel. Tourists to South America are regularly warned about wading through muddy water where electric eels are common.

Weakly electric fish (http://soma.npa.uiuc.edu/labs/nelson/electric_fish.html) use the electrical field to sense rather than shock. Some fish like sharks, skates, and rays are called electroreceptive, because even though they can't generate an electric field, they have the ability to sense the electric fields generated by other animals. It has been well documented that these fish can sense prey buried in the sand even when all visual, olfactory, and auditory cues are eliminated.

Individual recognition is a specialized use of the electroreceptive organs. Animals with eyesight use vision to aid in mate recognition, courtship displays, and social interactions. The electroreceptive organs of electric fish might serve the same function as eyes in habitats where vision is poor or not possible. For mate recognition, males of some species of weakly electric fish can determine the mating status of females simply by sensing the character of her electrical field. Much research is still required to determine the extent to which these cartilaginous fish can use their electrosensing ability.

1. How is a catfish different from a knifefish (http://www.tiscali.co.uk/reference/encyclopaedia/hutchinson/m0007334.html)?

2. What purpose (http://www.exploratorium.edu/xref/exhibits/electric_fish.html), other than mate recognition, do weak electric fields serve for fish that inhabit murky or muddy waters?

3. How would you expect an electric fish to react (http://www.hhmi.org/biointeractive/neurophysiology/click.html) to an aluminum rod in its environment? How about a plastic rod?

KEY TERMS

action potential
amygdala
aqueous humor
association neuron
auditory canal
auditory tube
autonomic nervous
    system
axon
basilar membrane
binocular vision
blind spot
blood–brain barrier
brain
cell body
central nervous system
cephalization
cerebellum
cerebral cortex
cerebral hemisphere
cerebrospinal fluid
cerebrum
choroid
cochlea
compound eye
cone

convergence
convolution
cornea
corpus callosum
dendrite
divergence
dorsal root ganglion
echolocation
effector
electrolocation
external ear
farsighted
forebrain
fovea
ganglion
ganglion cell
gray matter
hair cell
hindbrain
hippocampus
hypothalamus
inner ear
intensity
iris
lens
limbic system

long-term memory
medulla
meninges
midbrain
middle ear
motor neuron
myelin
nearsighted
nerve
nerve net
neuron
neurotransmitter
ommatidium
optic nerve
outer ear
pain receptor
parasympathetic division
peripheral nerve
peripheral nervous
    system
photopigment
pons
postsynaptic neuron
postsynaptic potential
    (PSP)
presynaptic neuron

pupil
receptor
receptor potential
reflex
resting potential
reticular formation
retina
rod
sclera
sensory neuron
sensory receptor
somatic nervous system
smell
spinal cord
sympathetic division
synapse
synaptic terminal
taste
taste bud
tectorial membrane
thalamus
threshold
tympanic membrane
vitreous humor
white matter
working memory

ANSWER KEY

SELF TEST

1. c
2. b
3. c
4. c
5. d
6. b
7. c
8. b
9. c
10. d
11. a
12. b
13. a
14. c
15. b
16. neuron
17. action potential
18. neurotransmitter
19. somatic nervous system
20. medulla
21. cerebellum
22. A. neurotransmitter
    B. synaptic vesicle
    C. presynaptic terminal
    D. neurotransmitter receptor
    E. dendrite of postsynaptic neuron
23. A. cerebral cortex
    B. hypothalamus
    C. pituitary gland
    D. medulla oblongata
    E. pons
    F. cerebellum
    G. thalamus
    H. corpus callosum
24. A. auditory canal
    B. tympanic membrane
    C. middle ear
    D. cochlea
    E. Eustachian tube
25. A. lenses
    B. pigmented cells
    C. receptor cells
26. A. pupil
    B. iris
    C. lens muscle
    D. lens
    E. vitreous humor
    F. retina
    G. fovea
    H. blind spot
    I. sclera
27. A. rods
    B. ganglion cells
    C. optic nerve

D. cones
E. photopigment molecules
28. a
29. b
30. c
31. f
32. d

ESSAY CHALLENGE

1. These processes are poorly understood, but working memory seems to be electrical in nature, involving the repeated activity of a particular neural circuit. As long as the circuit is active, the memory stays. Long-term memory seems to be structural, the result of persistent changes in the expression of certain genes.

2. The sympathetic division acts on organs in ways that prepare the body for stressful activity during the "fight-or-flight" response. The parasympathetic division does the exact opposite. It dominates during maintenance activities such as digestion. Each system counteracts the other.

3. When sound enters the ear and vibrates the tympanic membrane, it is carried into the cochlea where the basilar membrane vibrates in response to the sound. Movement of the basilar membrane causes hair cells attached to the membrane to bend and produce receptor potentials. The receptor potentials stimulate the release of neurotransmitters onto neurons of the auditory nerve. This causes the generation of action potentials in the auditory nerve that conveys these signals to the brain.

4. There are three varieties of cones that respond to three different wavelengths of light (red, green, and blue). Therefore, they allow for color vision. Rods, on the other hand, dominate peripheral vision and are more sensitive to light than cones. They are important for vision in dim light.

5. While the selectivity seems to be set by cortical areas of the brain, the reticular formation in the midbrain filters incoming sensory information before it reaches consciousness, which allows us to focus our attention for activities like reading.

6. Our "picture" of the world is shaped by the types of sensory receptors that we possess and the ranges and sensitivities of those receptors. For instance, we can see only visible light, while many insects, bees in particular, can see ultraviolet light.

7. Myelin is similar to the rubber coating on an electrical wire; it acts as an insulator so that the wave of depolarization underlying the action potential doesn't dissipate across the membrane. When the myelin is gone, some of the positive charge dissipates, so that the next region of the axon doesn't get to threshold and the action potential dies out.

8. The brain interprets action potentials from the optic nerve as visual signals, regardless of what causes them. This system works well most of the time, because the receptors that send signals along the optic nerve respond to light. But, on occasion, a traumatic event such as a poke to the eye or a blow to the head can cause the generation of action potentials in the optic nerve that have nothing to do with visual stimuli.

9. Most pain is caused by tissue damage which releases chemicals, like potassium and enzymes that produce bradykinin, into the extracellular fluid. So, while the stimulus (the punch) is mechanical in nature, the pain it causes comes from stimulation of nerve cells by the chemicals released when cells are broken open.

MEDIA ACTIVITIES

34.6 Web Investigation: From Tragedy to Triumph

1. Within hours after the injury, disrupted blood flow leads to oxygen deprivation and death of cells. Also, bleeding into the area increases swelling, further compressing nerves and cells, and leads to a destructive chemical environment. Free radicals and macrophages can cause damage to uninjured cells. In addition, astrocytes begin to divide, forming scar tissue that can block regrowth of nerves. Within weeks, cerebrospinal fluid–filled cysts begin to form. Scar tissue surrounds these and they can elongate and cause further cell damage or blockage to axon growth. Also, undamaged axons start to lose their myelin coverings, which also disrupts the flow of information to and from the brain.

2. Researchers believe that the two main effects of methylprednisolone are: 1) suppression of the immune system's inflammatory response, which can further damage tissue in the area; and 2) reduction of free radicals, which can also kill cells that were not damaged by the initial injury.

3. Transplants, neurotrophic factors, and the drug 4-AP (4-amino pyridine) all fall within category 2, because they promote activity in nerves or stimulate regrowth of nerves. Functional electrical stimulation falls into the second category because it is used to maintain the health of muscles and to allow people with spinal cord injuries to regain some behaviors, like grasping, by directly electrically stimulating the muscles. GM-1 ganglioside, falls into the first category, because, like methylprednisolone, it seems to help protect the spinal cord from secondary damage.

4. Motor vehicle accidents, which are responsible for almost half of all spinal cord injuries, are the number-one cause of spinal cord injuries.

ISSUES IN BIOLOGY

1. Approximately 10% of Americans over the age of 65 and 50% of Americans over the age of 85 have Alzheimer's disease.

2. An early diagnsosis can serve four important functions: 1) it can rule out other, treatable, causes of the dementia; 2) it can lead to appropriate treatments, because even though there is no drug that can stop progression of the disease, there are treatments that can alleviate or diminish some of the symptoms; 3) plans can be made about the type of caregiving and disease management that will be employed; and 4) it allows the person time to deal with legal matters, like writing a will or assigning power of attorney, while they are still competent.

3. There are two genetic tests for rare, inherited forms of Alzheimer's that may be advised by a physician if there is a clear family pattern of one of these two types. Otherwise, there aren't really any good, pre-symptom indicators of Alzheimer's disease. At present, this isn't a huge disadvantage because available treatments are for symptoms of the disease and don't do anything to delay its onset.

BIZARRE FACTS IN BIOLOGY

1. Catfish can only sense, but not generate, electric fields, so they are considered to be electroreceptive, while knifefish can both produce and sense electrical fields and are thus called electric fish.

2. Weakly electric fish could use electric fields for navigation, prey localization, and communication with their own species over territory.

3. The aluminum rod will affect the electric field differently than the plastic rod, but the fish should be able to detect the presence of both.

CHAPTER 35: ACTION AND SUPPORT: THE MUSCLES AND SKELETON

AT-A-GLANCE

SELF TEST

1. Which muscle tissue type is also called *striated muscle,* due to its appearance under the microscope?
   a. smooth muscle
   b. cardiac muscle
   c. skeletal muscle

2. The bending of the _____ cross bridges when the energy of ATP is available provides the force of contraction at the molecular level.
   a. myosin
   b. actin
   c. accessory proteins

3. The nervous system controls the strength and degree of muscle contraction due to _____.
   a. the number of fibers stimulated
   b. the frequency of action potentials
   c. The first two answers are both correct.

4. Which muscle cell type produces slow, sustained, wavelike contractions?
   a. smooth
   b. cardiac
   c. skeletal

5. This type of bone tissue is the site of muscle attachment for skeletal muscle.
   a. spongy
   b. compact

6. If the sliding filament model of contraction is dependent upon ATP molecules being available, then why would a dead body undergo a condition called *rigor mortis*?
   a. Cross-bridges of myosin cannot pull actin toward the midline of the sarcomere without ATP.
   b. A dead body's cells cannot make ATP.
   c. Cross-bridges cannot turn loose the binding sites on actin, and thus the muscle cells cannot return to a relaxed state.

7. Why would a person still be able to maintain a functional level of calcium in the muscle sarcoplasmic reticulum even if they had a diet very low in or devoid of calcium?

   a. Increased osteoclastic activity due to low blood calcium levels will remove the needed calcium from the bones.

   b. Calcium needed for the sarcoplasmic reticulum will be reabsorbed from the filtrate in the kidneys.

8. The rate of contraction of smooth muscle is very slow compared to the rate of contraction of cardiac or skeletal muscle. What cellular characteristic of smooth muscle cells could account for this difference in rates?

   a. Contraction of smooth muscle is involuntary.

   b. Smooth muscle may be stimulated by hormones.

   c. Smooth muscle lacks a sarcoplasmic reticulum in each cell; the calcium must come into the cell from the surrounding interstitial fluids. This takes time.

9. Osteoporosis is a disease in which calcium is removed from bone with a resultant loss of bone mass and strength. Women are eight times more likely to suffer from this disease. Why would that be so?

   a. Women are smaller.

   b. Women consume less calcium.

   c. Estrogen is reduced after menopause.

   d. All of the above.

10. Skeletal designs include exoskeletons and endoskeletons. You can see that the exoskeletal design is limited to the smaller animals. Even a lobster is smaller than many other animals with an endoskeleton. Why is there a size limitation for the exoskeletal design?

   a. An exoskeleton is lighter.

   b. An exoskeleton covers the entire body of the animal.

   c. The force inward will increase faster than the strength of the exoskeleton to resist such forces. At some point the skeleton becomes increasingly massive and too heavy.

11. You are examining microscopic slides of tissues from parts of a body found after an explosion. How could you tell if the skeletal muscle you are looking at is from a thigh?

   a. The motor neuron you are viewing appears to innervate only a few muscle cells.

   b. You see one motor neuron, one muscle fiber being innervated.

   c. The motor neuron appears to innervate many muscle fibers.

12. What is the smallest functional skeletal muscle structure?

   a. a muscle fiber

   b. a myofibril

   c. a thin and thick filament

   d. a sarcomere

13. Which of the following is a function of neuromuscular junctions that is NOT shared by neuron-to-neuron synapses?

   a. Summation of electrical stimulation in the postsynaptic cell always occurs.

   b. Changes in postsynaptic cells may be either excitatory or inhibitory.

   c. Postsynaptic cells will always respond with an excitatory postsynaptic potential when stimulated.

   d. Postsynaptic cells do not require summation to generate an AP.

   e. The first two answers are both correct.

   f. The third and fourth answers are correct.

14. What type of skeleton is found outside the body at the body surface?

   a. hydrostatic skeleton

   b. endoskeleton

   c. exoskeleton

   d. all of the above

15. What cell type directly participates in the remodeling of bone during the growth of an individual?

   a. osteocytes

   b. osteoclasts

   c. osteoblasts

   d. The first two answers are both correct.

   e. The second and third answers are both correct.

16. What is the name of the attachment that binds one bone to another?

   a. joint

   b. tendon

   c. ligament

   d. lever

17. What do you call the muscle attachment on the hip bone (pelvis) if the other end of the muscle is attached to the femur near the knee? Assume the knee is elevated when the muscle contracts.

   a. flexor

   b. extensor

   c. insertion

   d. origin

18. John has fallen and broken his femur. Which of the following will deposit new bone to mend the fracture?

    a. osteocytes

    b. osteoblasts

    c. osteoclasts

    d. chondrocytes

19. If you were examining a microscope slide of an unknown muscle tissue type and did not see any striations (striping) in the cells, which muscle type would you be looking at?

    a. skeletal muscle

    b. cardiac muscle

    c. smooth muscle

20. Why do you think your muscles contract uncontrollably when exposed to a strong electric shock? Don't try this at home!

    a. The electric shock directly causes myosin cross-bridges to bind with actin.

    b. The electric shock is carried throughout the muscle fibers and stimulates the sarcoplasmic reticula to release their calcium stores.

    c. The electric shock speeds up the rate at which ATP binds to myosin cross-bridges.

21. If you broke your hip and were confined to a bed for several months, what would you predict would happen to your bone density?

    a. Your bone density would increase.

    b. Your bone density would decrease.

    c. Your bone density would not be affected.

22. Which skeleton type would be most desirable if you were a small animal who needed to change its body shape to squeeze into/through small cracks and crevices in the ground?

    a. endoskeleton

    b. exoskeleton

    c. hydrostatic

23. How would a torn biceps muscle impair the ability of your arm to move?

    a. It would keep you from flexing your forearm.

    b. It would keep you from moving your arm at the shoulder.

    c. It would keep you from extending your forearm.

24. If a person had significantly reduced or absent cartilage pads in their knees, how do you think this would affect joint function?

    a. The bones of the joint would move more easily because cartilage tissues would not be in the way.

    b. Joint movements would be painful because there is no cartilage keeping the bones from grinding together.

    c. Joint movement would not be affected.

25. Functionally speaking, why would it be inappropriate to say that smooth muscle could be used to generate skeletal movements?

    a. Smooth muscle contractions could be too slow for an animal to react to changes in its environment.

    b. Smooth muscle contractions would not allow an animal to generate voluntary movements.

    c. Smooth muscle contractions are generally best at producing wavelike contractions, which are inefficient for forceful skeletal movements.

    d. All of the above are correct.

26. Why do you think a muscle produces a stronger contraction after extensive weight training, even though the number of muscle cells doesn't change?

    a. The number of thick and thin filaments increases in each muscle cell, allowing a sarcomere to form more cross-bridges and thus a stronger contraction.

    b. A greater number of action potentials is sent to a trained muscle, thus generating stronger contractions.

    c. A trained muscle has more motor units than an untrained one, resulting in the potential for stronger contractions.

    d. All of the above are correct.

27. The poison, tetrodotoxin, interferes with the body's ability to transmit action potentials. Which of the following would be affected by this?

    a. beating of the heart

    b. contraction of the diaphragm

    c. walking

    d. All of the above would be affected.

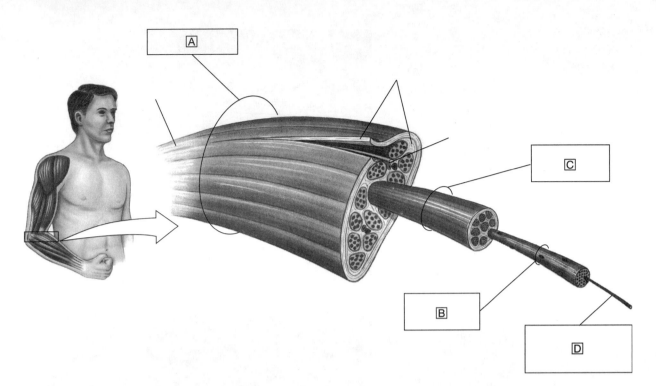

28. Skeletal muscle has many layers of organization. Label these structures as indicated on the diagram above.

29. Label the indicated structures on the image of a muscle fiber below.

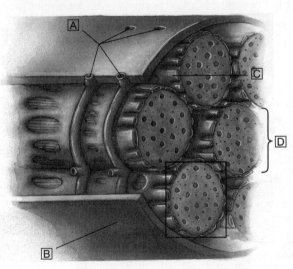

30. Label the indicated portions of the myofibrils found within the skeletal muscle fibers shown below.

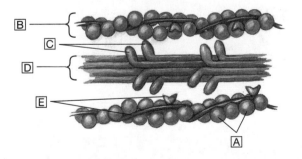

31. Label the indicated bones of the human skeleton shown below.

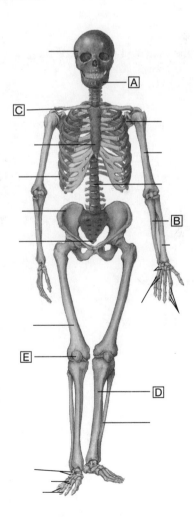

403

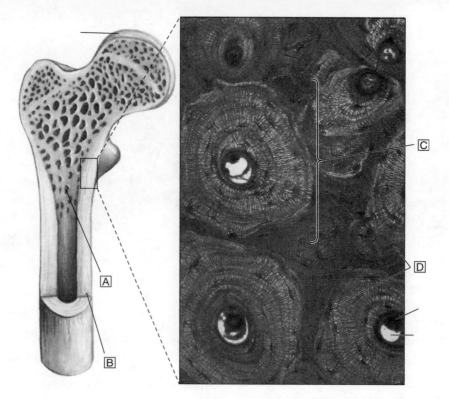

(Credit: Peter Arnold, Inc.)

32. Label the indicated portions of the bone shown in the figure above.

33. Label the indicated portions of the knee joint shown below.

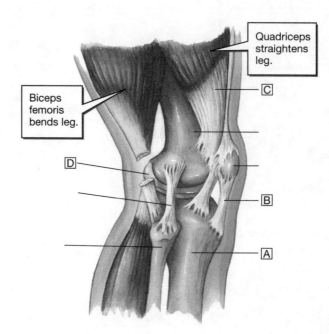

Quadriceps straightens leg.

Biceps femoris bends leg.

ESSAY CHALLENGE

1. How do accessory proteins and calcium regulate muscle contraction?

2. Compare and contrast the three forms of skeletons in the animal kingdom.

3. What are the various functions of the human skeleton?

4. How do osteoclasts and osteoblasts remodel bone?

MEDIA ACTIVITIES

To access a Media Activity visit http://www.prenhall.com/audesirk7. Log in to the Web site selected by your instructor, navigate to this chapter, and select the appropriate Media Activity number.

35.1 Muscle Structure
Estimated time: 5 minutes

In this animation, you will explore the various levels of structure found within skeletal muscles.

35.2 Muscle Contraction
Estimated time: 10 minutes

The contraction of skeletal muscles is described as a sliding-filament mechanism. Here you will review the mechanism and the molecular processes that produce a muscle contraction.

35.3 Web Investigation: Hidden Hazards of Space Travel
Estimated time: 30 minutes

Although weightlessness may seem like an enjoyable experience, prolonged periods can have a profound effect on muscle and skeletal physiology. Specifically, the removal of a resistant force (i.e., gravity) on the body can affect bones and muscles in several negative ways. Take a closer look at the effects of weightlessness on the human body and get a new appreciation of the problems that astronauts encounter in space.

1. Generally speaking, what are some of the changes (http://www.nsbri.org/HumanPhysSpace/introduction/intro-bodychanges.html) the human body experiences when in space?

2. What changes occur in the body with regard to skeletal muscle composition (http://jem.tksc.nasda.go.jp/med/index_e.html) (i.e., slow-twitch [Type I] and fast-twitch [Type II] fibers) and function (http://paperairplane.mit.edu/16.423J/Space/SBE/muscle/muscle_background.html)?

3. What countermeasures can be taken to minimize the effects of weightlessness on human muscle?

4. What changes occur in the body with regard to bone tissue composition?

5. What countermeasures can be taken to minimize the effects of weightlessness on the human skeleton?

ISSUES IN BIOLOGY

Part-Time Athletes; Full-Time Injuries?

Estimated Time: 30 minutes

The list of activities available to a weekend athlete is extensive—soccer, softball, football, skiing, running, weight training, and so on. These activities, coupled with increased leisure time, offer the certainty of injury to the ill-trained athlete. In addition, athletic superstores and extensive equipment are now widely available. All of these factors have supported an increase in "shopping-mall physical therapy centers"—a sure sign that Americans are hurting themselves in increasing numbers each year.

The injuries of professional athletes are reported daily in the news media. We follow the rise and fall of sports teams through a season on the basis of their injuries (http://www.aaos.org/wordhtml/prevspor.htm). Success or failure is connected to joint and muscle injuries for these professionals. From a gold medalist in the Olympics to a local sports hero, all are subject to injuries. If these well-trained people are hurting, what does this suggest about the untrained, poorly equipped amateur who has not warmed up and cooled down properly? Joints are subject to great stress as a result of the variety of functions they perform in differing body motions. A dislocation involves the displacement of bones at a joint due to abnormal contact, which overcomes the ligaments', tendons', and muscles' ability to maintain normal joint composition. Sprains are the results of stretching or tearing the ligaments at a joint without the dislocation of bones. Bursitis is commonly caused by the excessive use of joints in repeated motions, such as in tennis ("tennis elbow"). Arthritis (a joint disease that has more than 100 varieties) can lead to inflamed, swollen, and painful joints. Osteoarthritis most commonly results from wear and tear on the joints over time. Sports early in life can reduce the "athletic life" of an individual.

The knee joint allows the leg to swing and, to some degree, bend and twist. (See section 35.5, "How Does the Body Move?") Because the force applied to the joint can be up to seven times the weight of the individual, repeated stress can cause distortions and disruptions of the bones, cartilage, and ligaments of the knee. The number of Americans who suffer yearly from knee injuries is unknown, but that number is certainly increasing, as shown by the increased need for physical therapy each year. Torn cartilage is removed from the knee by orthopedic surgeons. Torn ligaments must be repaired. Knees get rebuilt. More than 50,000 pieces of torn cartilage are removed each year from football players alone. There seems to be no end to the demand for sports medicine. See "Health Watch: How Bones Heal" in your textbook.

1. For one week, take notice of the skeletal-muscular injuries to sports figures reported in your local news media. How would you find out the number of injuries for the same period of time for amateur athletes in your area?

2. What actions can the coach of a Little League team take to lessen the possibilities of skeletal-muscular injuries to the players?

3. As we age, why would recovery from skeletal-muscular injuries become a longer and more complicated event? Consider the effects of aging on all the systems of the body.

BIZARRE FACTS IN BIOLOGY

When Is a Leg Like a Garden Hose?

If you were to walk across the room right now, it would involve the use of antagonistic muscle pairs; flexor and extensor muscles that work together to produce deliberate limb movements. Imagine what locomotion would be like if you had only flexors or extensors! Although you would be able to produce movements, it would be difficult for you to coordinate them in any fashion that would allow you to move from place to place. This interaction between antagonistic muscles is so important that most animals with skeletons (endoskeletons or exoskeletons) use it. However, the spiders (Order Araneae http://www.amonline.net.au/spiders/resources/index.htm) buck this trend. Spiders are one of the few animal groups that, in addition to the use of muscles, require the use of a hydrostatic skeleton to move. Muscles attached to the inside of the spider limb exoskeleton act only as flexors; extensor muscles simply do not exist! Spiders are able to extend their legs in spite of this by using their circulatory system. Their circulatory system increases blood pressure in specific limbs, resulting in the limb straightening out in a fashion similar to when you send water through an empty hose. It is the coordinated interplay between flexor muscles and hydraulic pressure buildup that allows a spider to control its limb movements.

Some spiders, namely the jumping spiders (http://tolweb.org/tree?group=Salticidae&contgroup=Dionycha), have perfected this system to great effect. Jumping spiders are known for their ability to jump long distances to surprise and capture prey. They accomplish this feat by contracting a muscle in their cephalothorax that sends blood under high pressure to their hindmost pair of legs. This results in a powerful extension of the hind legs that allows jumping spiders to jump up to fifty times their own length!

1. Speculate on how dehydration would affect the ability of a spider to move.

2. What advantage might a spider have by using a hydrostatic skeleton for movement, rather than relying exclusively on muscle? Compare the size of grasshopper limbs (particularly the hind limbs) to equivalently sized spider limbs as an aid.

KEY TERMS

actin
antagonistic muscles
appendicular skeleton
axial skeleton
ball-and-socket joint
bone
cardiac muscle
cartilage
chondrocyte
compact bone
endoskeleton

exoskeleton
extensor
flexor
hinge joint
hydrostatic skeleton
insertion
intervertebral disc
joint
ligament
motor unit
muscle fiber

myofibril
myosin
myosin head
neuromuscular junction
origin
osteoblast
osteoclast
osteocyte
osteon
osteoporosis
sarcomere

sarcoplasmic reticulum
skeletal muscle
skeleton
smooth muscle
spongy bone
tendon
thick filament
thin filament
T tubule
Z line

ANSWER KEY

SELF TEST

1. c
2. a
3. c
4. a
5. b
6. c
7. a
8. c
9. d
10. c
11. c
12. d
13. f
14. c
15. e
16. c

17. d
18. b
19. c
20. b
21. b
22. c
23. a
24. b
25. d
26. a
27. d
28. A. skeletal muscle
    B. muscle fiber
    C. bundle of muscle fibers
    D. myofibril
29. A. T tubules
    B. muscle fiber membrane

C. sarcoplasmic reticulum

D. myofibril

30. A. actin
    B. thin filament
    C. crossbridge
    D. thick filament
    E. accessory proteins
31. A. mandible
    B. ulna
    C. clavicle
    D. tibia
    E. patella
32. A. spongy bone
    B. compact bone
    C. osteon
    D. osteocytes
33. A. bone
    B. ligament
    C. tendon
    D. cartilage

ESSAY CHALLENGE

1. Calcium ions cause contraction to occur when they are released from the sarcoplasmic reticulum. They bind to the small accessory protein (troponin), which pulls the larger protein (tropomyosin) away from the myosin binding sites. Myosin and actin can then bind and cause muscle contraction. See Section 35.2B, "Muscle Contraction Results from Thick and Thin Filaments Sliding Past One Another."

2. 1) hydrostatic skeletons of worms and other organisms consist of a fluid-filled sac and are quite flexible; 2) exoskeletons encase the bodies of arthropods and vary in thickness, and also are flexible; 3) endoskeletons are found only in echinoderms and vertebrates, and are internal. See section 35.3 "What Does the Skeleton Do?" for details.

3. 1) provides a rigid framework for the body; 2) aids in locomotion; 3) produces red blood cells; 4) serves as a storage site for calcium and phosphorus; 5) participates in sensory transduction. See section 35.3A, "The Vertebrate Skeleton Serves Many Functions" for details.

4. Osteoclasts dissolve bone by secreting acids and enzymes that dissolve the hard matrix, forming a tunnel. Osteoblasts fill in the tunnel with concentric deposits of new bone matrix. See section 35.4B, "Bone Provides a Strong, Rigid Framework for the Body" for details.

MEDIA ACTIVITIES

35.3 Web Investigation: Hidden Hazards of Space Travel

1. space motion sickness, a headward shift of blood distribution, a reduction in body fluid composition, muscle and bone atrophy, and cardiovascular deconditioning

2. a shift in muscle composition from Type I to Type II fibers, a general decrease in muscle strength, a flexor muscle bias, and a brief period of movement overcompensation due to the absence of gravity

3. Regular exercise has been shown to minimize the effects of weightlessness on human muscle.

4. excessive loss of calcium and phosphorus in the urine, resulting in a reduction of bone density and a greater chance of kidney stones

5. Exercise and dietary supplementation have been suggested as countermeasures to slow down this process.

ISSUES IN BIOLOGY

1. Contact all of the local public and private schools in your area and inquire (with their athletics office) about injury frequency in a given time period.

2. Ensure all the children are of adequate physical fitness before participation in sports, wear proper protective gear, warm-up/stretch, and have proper pre-game training/practice.

3. Tissues do not repair themselves as rapidly with age and injuries can compound themselves over time, resulting in more complicated recovery.

BIZARRE FACTS IN BIOLOGY

1. Dehydration would result in a reduction in blood pressure, and would impact the ability of a dehydrated spider to straighten its legs. In fact, extremely dehydrated spiders can be found curled up on their backs because they lack sufficient pressure to straighten their legs.

2. Weight reduction may be an advantage for the use of hydrostatic skeletons.

CHAPTER 36: ANIMAL REPRODUCTION

AT-A-GLANCE

SELF TEST

1. The interstitial cells produce _____.
   a. sperm
   b. ova
   c. testosterone
   d. estrogen

2. The _____ secretes LH and FSH.
   a. anterior pituitary
   b. hypothalamus
   c. posterior pituitary
   d. ovary

3. Which hormone stimulates the ovulation event?
   a. estrogen
   b. LH
   c. chorionic gonadotropin
   d. progesterone

4. Which male reproductive structure maintains the optimum temperature required for sperm production?
   a. vas deferens   b. scrotum
   c. epididymis   d. seminiferous tubules

5. The ovarian structure that secretes both progesterone and estrogen is _____.
   a. primary oocyte
   b. secondary oocyte
   c. corpus luteum
   d. immature follicle

6. The average number of sperm released per ejaculation is between _____.
   a. 300,000,000 to 400,000,000
   b. 30,000,000 to 40,000,000
   c. 3,000,000 to 4,000,000
   d. 300,000 to 400,000

7. Which of the birth control techniques is the most effective?
   a. birth control pills
   b. IUD
   c. Norplant
   d. abstinence

8. Regarding human female fertility, which of the following is NOT a characteristic?

   a. It is possible to produce more than one ovum per menstrual cycle.

   b. A human female does not produce more ova than those potential ova present at her birth.

   c. Females produce more ova over a lifetime than males produce sperm.

   d. In the ovaries, the potential ova are in an arrested state of division.

9. Of the following sexually transmitted diseases, which is (are) incurable?

   a. chlamydia

   b. herpes

   c. syphilis

   d. gonorrhea

10. Permanent contraception in a male involves _____.

   a. removal of the prostate

   b. severing the seminiferous tubules

   c. severing the vas deferens

   d. blocking the urethra

11. During a 28-day female menstrual cycle, pituitary hormones, ovarian hormones, and hormones of the hypothalamus interact with each other to drive the cyclic changes in the uterine lining. What might be the outcome if the ovaries of a young woman were removed during a surgical procedure?

   a. There would be increases in GnRH from the hypothalamus and FSH and LH from the pituitary.

   b. GnRH from the hypothalamus would decrease, while the FSH and LH from the pituitary would increase.

   c. GnRH from the hypothalamus would increase, while the FSH and LH from the pituitary would decrease.

   d. GnRH from the hypothalamus and FSH and LH from the pituitary would decrease.

12. What type of asexual reproduction involves haploid eggs maturing into haploid adults?

   a. budding

   b. regeneration

   c. fission

   d. parthenogenesis

13. Which of the following events must occur to maximize the likelihood of a successful mating, if the mating is outside the bodies of the parents?

   a. A special spermatophore must be produced by the male.

   b. Sperm and eggs must be released at the same time.

   c. A single individual must release both eggs and sperm.

   d. Sperm and eggs must be released within the same limited area.

   e. Both the second and fourth answers are correct.

14. Enzymes from the sperm digest protective layers that surround the egg. Where are these enzymes housed in the sperm?

   a. in the nucleus

   b. in the acrosome

   c. in the midpiece

   d. in the tail

15. Where is the egg (normally) when fertilization occurs?

   a. in one of the ovaries

   b. in the cervix

   c. in one of the uterine tubes

   d. in the uterus

16. Which of the following would be considered to be a barrier against sperm reaching the egg?

   a. follicle cells

   b. zona pellucida

   c. acrosomal enzymes

   d. The first two answers are both correct.

   e. none of the above

17. Which of the following contraceptive methods is considered to be the LEAST effective?

   a. IUDs

   b. hormonal regulation of ovulation

   c. removal of the penis from the vagina prior to ejaculation

   d. condoms

18. Parthenogenesis, budding, and regeneration are examples of _____.

19. In _____, sperm and egg fuse outside the body of the female.

20. The _____ are the central structures of the male reproductive system.

21. The _____ are the paired gonads of the female reproductive system.

22. _____ is the union of haploid gametes to form a diploid zygote.

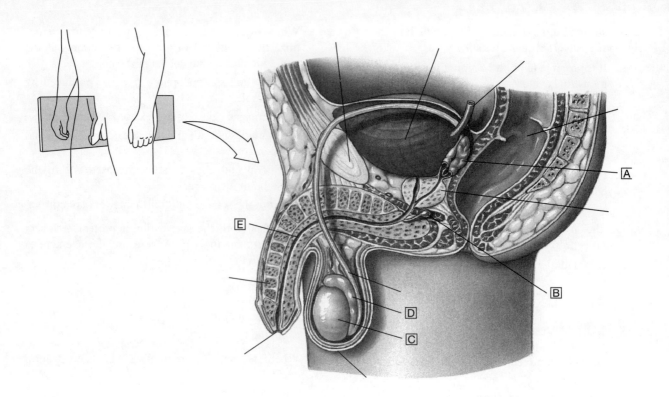

23. Label the indicated structures on the image of the male reproductive system above.

24. The male reproductive structures that are found within the scrotal sac are responsible for the formation of sperm. Label these structures on the image below.

25. Sperm are the male gametes of humans. Label the structures indicated on the diagram of a single sperm below.

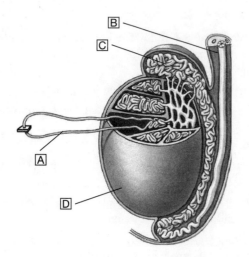

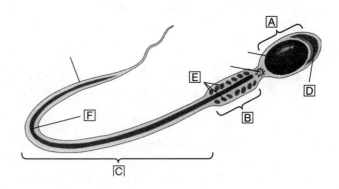

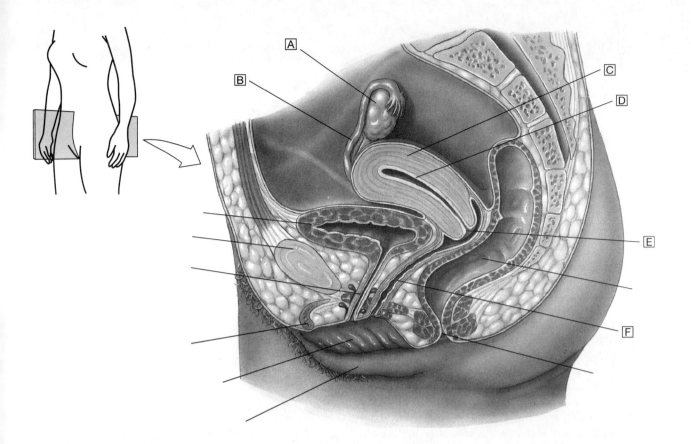

26. Label the indicated structures of the female reproductive system shown above.

27. The ovary is the site of egg production in the female. Label the indicated structures on the diagram of an ovary below.

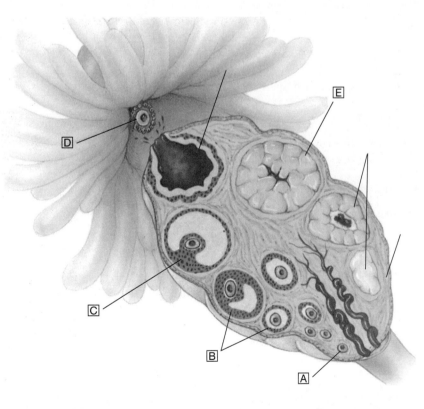

28. Compared to sexual reproduction, which is an advantage of asexual reproduction?

   a. There is no need to find a mate.

   b. Competition for mates is unnecessary.

   c. There is no waste of sperm or eggs.

   d. All of the above are advantages.

29. Given the obvious advantages of asexual reproduction, why do you think so many animals have evolved the capacity for sexual reproduction?

   a. Sexual reproduction is easier than asexual reproduction.

   b. Offspring are larger, and thus are better able to survive in the environment.

   c. Offspring produced through sexual reproduction have the advantage of possessing genetic variability, thus enhancing natural selection processes for the species.

   d. None of the responses are correct.

30. Hormonally speaking, what is the difference between a child and a person who is going through puberty?

   a. concentrations of gonadotropin-releasing hormone (GnRH)

   b. concentrations of FSH

   c. concentrations of testosterone or estrogen

   d. concentrations of insulin

   e. The first three responses are correct.

31. If, during spermatogenesis, defective sperm were produced due to cell division errors in mitosis, which cells would most likely be to blame?

   a. interstitial cells

   b. spermatogonia

   c. primary spermatocytes

   d. secondary spermatocytes

32. The inhibition of the production of which hormone would be an effective means of preventing sperm production WITHOUT affecting testosterone production?

   a. LH

   b. FSH

   c. estrogen

   d. GnRH

33. If, during oogenesis, defective oocytes were produced due to cell division errors in meiosis II, which structures would most likely be to blame?

   a. oogonia

   b. primary oocyte

   c. secondary oocyte

   d. spermatids

34. During oogenesis, what would you predict is the functional advantage of the production of only one "large" viable egg, as opposed to four "small" viable eggs?

   a. A large egg is easier for sperm to penetrate.

   b. It takes less energy to produce one large viable egg.

   c. A large egg has more cytoplasm and nutrients, increasing the chance that a fertilized egg will complete development.

   d. None of the above responses are correct.

35. Which of the following physiological situations describes what occurs during an erection?

   a. Penis arterioles are constricted while the veins are dilated, resulting in increased blood flow to the penis.

   b. Penis arterioles are dilated while the veins are constricted, resulting in decreased blood flow to the penis.

   c. Penis arterioles are constricted while the veins are dilated, resulting in decreased blood flow to the penis.

   d. Penis arterioles are dilated while the veins are constricted, resulting in increased blood flow to the penis.

36. Which of the following STDs would be unaffected by antibiotics?

   a. syphilis

   b. chlamydia

   c. gonorrhea

   d. crab lice

37. If a woman were interested in an effective form of contraception, but did not want to affect the physiology of her endocrine system, which of the following choices should she consider?

   a. birth control pills

   b. an IUD

   c. Depo-Provera

   d. Norplant

ESSAY CHALLENGE

1. How are spermatogenesis and oogenesis similar and different?

2. Compare and contrast sexual and asexual reproduction.

3. Briefly describe the menstrual cycle.

4. What are the three general approaches to temporary contraception?

MEDIA ACTIVITIES

To access a Media Activity visit http://www.prenhall.com/audesirk7. Log in to the Web site selected by your instructor, navigate to this chapter, and select the appropriate Media Activity number

36.1 Human Reproductive System
Estimated time: 10 minutes

In this activity, you will explore the structure and function of the human reproductive system and the formation of sperm in the male and an egg in the female.

36.2 Hormonal Control of the Menstrual Cycle
Estimated time: 10 minutes

Here you will explore the interplay of hormones and physical events during the course of the menstrual cycle.

36.3 Web Investigation: The Frozen Zoo
Estimated time: 30 minutes

The development of "Frozen Zoos" (http://www.auduboninstitute.org/rcenter/res_fzoo.htm) (also called Genome Resource Banks http://natzoo.si.edu/ConservationAndScience/ReproductiveScience/GenomeResTech/default.cfm) has provided a powerful tool for biologists to combat the extinction of endangered species. However, this is not without controversy. Although there have been reproductive successes and useful applications of these technologies, there are a number of ethical arguments (http://net.unl.edu/newsFeat/med_eth/me_cloning3.html) that must be considered before frozen zoos become mainstream. In addition, the evolution of conservation techniques over several decades have caused traditional zoos to rethink their approach (http://www.emagazine.com/march-april_2002/0302feat1.html) to wildlife conservation. Investigate the presented links and explore this topic in more detail!

1. What is an inherent problem in storing tissues at such low temperatures? How do researchers get around this problem?

2. What kind of biological materials are stored in "frozen zoos" and Genome Resource Banks?

3. What are some examples of successes using these reproductive technologies?

4. Aside from the potential to produce offspring of endangered species, what are other applications of frozen zoos?

5. Why do some conservationists think that frozen zoos are not such a good idea?

6. How are traditional zoos reconsidering their role in animal conservation?

ISSUES IN BIOLOGY

Why Are Sexually Transmitted Diseases So Harmful?

Sexual activity provides an opportunity for passing along agents of disease from one partner to another. Although this has always been possible, only in the twentieth century have sexually transmitted diseases (STDs) reached epidemic levels. The Centers for Disease Control and Prevention in Atlanta reports that millions of young adults have STDs, the cost of health care related to these diseases is now in the billions, and that the U.S. health care system is overwhelmed by the demand for services. One of every 20 babies born in the United States has a chlamydial infection, and the type

II herpes virus infects 1 out of every 10,000 newborns. Each year 1 million female Americans contract pelvic inflammatory disease. Of every 200,000 individuals that are hospitalized for this disease, more than 100,000 become permanently sterile.

Acquired immune deficiency syndrome (AIDS) is a group of chronic disorders that can follow infection by the human immunodeficiency virus (HIV). Because HIV cripples the immune system, the body becomes highly vulnerable to otherwise non-life-threatening diseases. AIDS is mainly a sexually transmitted disease that passes the virus through semen, blood, and vaginal fluid. AIDS has reached epidemic proportions mainly due to sexual transmission. The tests to identify a nonsymptomatic individual were not available until a few years ago. That behavioral changes could affect the rate of transmission was not realized until well after many individuals had progressed to AIDS. Public education about the disease was very sparse, and the general public was slow to understand the true nature of AIDS. Now public education (http://www.thebody.com/) is the most important tool in the control of this disease.

Gonorrhea (http://www.cdc.gov/ncidod/dastlr/gcdir/gono.html) is a sexually transmitted disease that can be cured by prompt diagnosis and treatment. The Centers for Disease Control and Prevention ranks gonorrhea first among reported communicable diseases in the United States. The rise in gonorrhea rate has paralleled the increased use of the birth control pill and increased sexual permissiveness.

Syphilis is caused by the bacterium *Treponema pallidum*, which is transmitted by sexual contact. After penetrating exposed tissue, the bacterium produces a localized ulcer. From there the treponemes move into the bloodstream and lymphatic system. Women who have been infected typically have miscarriages, stillbirths, or sickly and syphilitic infants. Pelvic inflammatory disease affects more than 14 million women in the United States each year. It is one of the serious complications of gonorrhea, chlamydial infections, and other STDs; this disease can also arise when microbes that normally inhabit the vagina ascend into the pelvic region. The oviducts may be scarred, which can lead to abnormal pregnancies as well as sterility.

Sexual contact with various partners poses risks that must be considered. An individual can have no symptoms but may still be capable of passing an STD to his or her partner. Information concerning these diseases, along with suggested safeguards, is widely available. The fact that sexual contact could lead to sterility, illness, and even death should provide more than enough motivation for responsible behavior.

1. Why would some medical authorities consider that there is no way to have truly safe sex—that is, to avoid contracting a sexually transmitted disease?

2. A woman had spent her youth in wild behaviors, but now she has married and wishes to have a family. What could be the serious long-term effects of STDs on her or her spouse's ability to have children?

3. After years of hard work and dedicated service to your country, you are appointed United States AIDS Czar. It is your goal to eliminate the HIV virus from the population. Discuss your plans of action to accomplish this end.

BIZARRE FACTS IN BIOLOGY

One Too Many for the Road?

Making and drinking alcoholic beverages (http://www.drugabuse.com/drugs/alcohol/) is almost as old as human culture itself. For ancient people, alcohol was a significant source of calories, like fat, and it was safer to drink the wine than the water, when you consider the bacterial contamination of the water supplies due to the lack of sanitation. Modern sanitation practices have made the water safe to drink (in most places), but alcohol remains a fixture of human social interaction.

For men, alcohol consumption has a particularly undesirable side effect. Normal, healthy males consuming a "social" amount of alcohol, enough to be mildly to moderately intoxicating, experience a 20% drop in their serum levels of testosterone (http://www.encyclopedia.com/searchpool.asp?target=@DOCTITLE%20testosterone). Chronic alcohol consumption (http://www.hosppract.com/issues/1999/04/cekick.htm), as in alcoholics, can reduce serum testosterone levels 50%. Chronic alcoholic men can become feminized; they lose facial and pubic hair, and they start to deposit fat beneath their nipples. Many become impotent. Why does a change in testosterone levels have such a dramatic effect?

Testosterone controls the development of male sexual characteristics, such as facial hair, muscle and bone mass, and sexual behavior. Men need a constant, stable supply of testosterone to maintain "maleness." Chronically high levels of alcohol in the body cause less testosterone synthesis and increase the rate of testosterone clearance from the body, reducing the maleness signal.

Fortunately, feminization is observed only in chronic alcohol abusers with extensive liver damage. Severe liver damage disrupts many metabolic pathways; feminization is just one long-term consequence of liver destruction. However, recent studies suggest that even healthy, nonalcoholic men show a transient decrease in blood testosterone levels with frequent, heavy alcohol consumption (binge drinking)—just one more thing to think about before you tie one on.

References

Gordon, G. G., Altman, K, Souther, A. L., Rubin, E., and Lieber, C. S. 1976. Effect of alcohol (ethanol) administration on sex-hormone metabolism in normal men. *N Eng J Med* 295:793–7.

Lieber, C. S. 1998. Hepatic and other medical disorders of alcoholism: From pathogenesis to treatment. *J Stud Alcohol* 59:9–25.

Mendelson, J. H., Mello, N. K., and Ellingboe, J. 1977. Effects of acute alcohol intake on pituitary-gonadal hormones in normal human males. *J Phar Exp Thera* 202:676–82.

Ruusa, J., Bergman, B., and Sundell, M. L. 1997. Sex hormones during alcohol withdrawal: A longitudinal study of 29 male alcoholics during detoxification. *Alcohol and Alcoholism* 32:591–7.

1. Are the effects of alcohol on testosterone synthesis reversible?

2. For hunter-gatherer societies, would the benefits of consuming significant amounts of alcohol outweigh the risks? Why or why not?

3. Would chronic alcohol consumption have a similar effect on women?

KEY TERMS

acquired immune deficiency syndrome (AIDS)
acrosome
asexual reproduction
budding
bulbourethral gland
cervix
chlamydia
clitoris
contraception
copulation
corona radiata
corpus luteum
crab lice
egg
embryo
endometrium
epididymis
estrogen
external fertilization
fertilization

fetus
fission
follicle
follicle-stimulating hormone (FSH)
genital herpes
genital wart
gonad
gonadotropin-releasing hormone (GnRH)
gonorrhea
hermaphrodite
internal fertilization
interstitial cell
labia
luteinizing hormone (LH)
menstrual cycle
menstruation
oogenesis
oogonia
ovary
ovulation

parthenogenesis
penis
pheromone
placenta
polar body
primary oocyte
primary spermatocyte
progesterone
prostate gland
puberty
regeneration
scrotum
secondary oocyte
secondary spermatocyte
semen
seminal vesicle
seminiferous tubule
Sertoli cells
sexually transmitted disease (STD)
sexual reproduction
spawning

sperm
spermatid
spermatogenesis
spermatogonia
spermatophore
sterilization
syphilis
testes
testosterone
trichomoniasis
urethra
uterine tube
uterus
vagina
vas deferens
zona pellucida
zygote

ANSWER KEY

SELF TEST

1. c
2. a
3. b
4. b
5. c
6. a
7. d
8. c
9. b
10. c
11. a
12. d
13. e
14. b
15. c
16. d
17. c
18. asexual reproduction
19. external fertilization
20. testes
21. ovaries
22. fertilization
23. A. seminal vesicle
    B. bulbourethral gland
    C. testis
    D. epididymis
    E. urethra
24. A. seminiferous tubule

    B. vas deferens
    C. epididymis
    D. testis
25. A. head
    B. midpiece
    C. tail
    D. acrosome
    E. mitochondria
    F. flagellum
26. A. ovary
    B. uterine tube
    C. uterus
    D. endometrium
    E. cervix
    F. vagina
27. A. new follicle
    B. developing follicle
    C. mature follicle with secondary oocyte
    D. ovulated secondary oocyte (egg)
    E. corpus luteum
28. d
29. c
30. e
31. b
32. b
33. c
34. c
35. d
36. d
37. b

419

ESSAY CHALLENGE

1. Spermatogenesis forms sperm through meiosis in the testes. This process is capable of producing millions of sperm every time it happens. Oogenesis forms oocytes through meiosis in the ovaries but only results in one viable egg each time it happens.

2. In asexual reproduction, mitosis produces offspring, which are identical to the parent. This requires only one parent. In sexual reproduction, which requires two parents usually, gametes (sperm and egg) fuse to form the offspring, which will be different from the parent.

3. During the menstrual cycle, hormones stimulate the development of follicles, as well as changes in the wall of the uterus. As a follicle matures, a hormonal signal triggers ovulation. If the ooctye is fertilized and implants in the uterus, development will ensue. If fertilization does not occur, the developed wall of the uterus is sloughed off and released in menstruation.

4. 1) synthetic hormones (birth control pills) can prevent ovulation; 2) a barrier method such as the diaphragm, cervical cap, and condom prevent the sperm from reaching the egg; 3) intrauterine devices and "morning after" pills prevent implantation of the fertilized egg in the uterus.

MEDIA ACTIVITIES

36.3   Web Investigation: The Frozen Zoo

1. Ice formation inside the cell will destroy it. This can be prevented by removing the water from the cells and replacing it with cryoprotectant fluid.

2. sperm, embryos, tissues, blood products, and DNA

3. An African wildcat kitten, cheetah cubs, black-footed ferrets, and Caracal cats have all been produced through use of these technologies.

4. (1) ease of transport of embryos and genetic material, as opposed to a living animal, (2) the ability to increase the genetic diversity of small populations, (3) the ability to research the genetics of an endangered species without having to search for the animal in the wild, (4) prevention of inbreeding of

individuals, and (5) better comprehension of reproductive cycles and development of endangered animals

5. (1) lack of adequate habitat for endangered offspring, (2) possible reintroduction of pathogens that may have contributed to their decline, (3) lack of genetic diversity to sustain breeding populations

6. Zoos are moving from their "display of endangered animals" approach to that of trying to ensure the survival of endangered species, through propagation efforts and conservation of genetic material.

ISSUES IN BIOLOGY

1. Regardless of the "safe sex" method, there is no 100% effective way of ensuring that bodily fluids (and thus bacteria and viruses) are not being exchanged between partners.

2. If the woman was unaware of having an STD during her youth, pelvic inflammatory disease could have scarred her oviducts, which can lead to sterility and/or abnormal pregnancies. In addition, an STD, left untreated, can be transmitted to her partner.

3. A variety of responses may apply, but could include the development of an AIDS vaccine, education on AIDS transmission, encouraging/rewarding condom use and/or abstinence, improve blood bank virus screening, and the development of a cure for those currently with the disease.

BIZARRE FACTS IN BIOLOGY

1. Only in cases where casual drinking has occurred. For chronic alcohol consumers with liver damage, there is no mechanism for them to restore testosterone back to normal levels.

2. This is debatable. The benefit of alcohol intake comes from the calories that are consumed, but if too much is consumed, then it would be difficult for individuals to effectively carry out hunter-gatherer activities.

3. No, because the female source of testosterone (androgens) comes from the adrenal glands.

CHAPTER 37: ANIMAL DEVELOPMENT

AT-A-GLANCE

SELF TEST

1. Cells constantly receive chemical messages from other cells of the body. These messages can alter developmental life by _____.
   a. altering cell membrane function
   b. alteration of carbohydrates and fat metabolism
   c. altering the transcription of genes and thus of proteins made by the cell

2. This form of development results in animals that, generally, live for a longer period of time.
   a. indirect development
   b. direct development

3. The first stage of cleavage is called the _____.
   a. gastrulation
   b. blastula stage
   c. morula

4. Which of these germinal layers will develop from the process of gastrulation?
   a. mesoderm
   b. ectoderm
   c. endoderm

5. Which of these germinal layers will form the skin and the nervous system in development?
   a. mesoderm
   b. endoderm
   c. ectoderm

6. After the end of the _____ month of development, the embryo is called a *fetus*.
   a. fifth
   b. first
   c. second

7. In an embryonic disc of cells, you change the position of one of the cells so that it is now between two different cells. Will it develop in this new position as it would in the old position?
   a. No, as the cell-to-cell communication could now be different.
   b. Yes, as these are the same cells from the same embryonic disc as before.

8. What type of organism could develop if it did not go through gastrulation? What could it do?
   a. It would be the same as if it did go through gastrulation.
   b. It would lack muscles and bones, at least.
   c. It would lack a nervous system.

9. If an insect requires a specific temperature to become sexually active and El Niño has kept the temperature below average, then the insect would _____.
   a. develop normally as there is no relationship between temperature and development
   b. develop earlier to make up for the lost time waiting to develop by others of its kind
   c. delay sexual activity until the proper temperature is reached in its environment

10. If the level of progesterone must be kept high to keep the endometrium intact, and the hormone HCG is needed to maintain the corpus luteum, which produces progesterone, suggest a means of inducing spontaneous abortion.
   a. introduce a foreign substance into the uterus
   b. reduce the size of the corpus luteum
   c. block the action of progesterone on the endometrium and it will be lost from the uterus, as does RU486

11. The greatest difference between "indirect" and "direct" development is that _____.
   a. the body form that emerges from an egg of a species that will follow "indirect" development looks very different from the sexually mature adult form
   b. the body form that emerges from an egg of a species that will follow "direct" development looks very different from the sexually mature adult form
   c. species that exhibit the "indirect" line of development are typified by extraembryonic membranes
   d. none of the above

12. What is a morula?
   a. a series of mitotic cell divisions of the fertilized egg
   b. a solid ball of small cells about the size of fertilized egg
   c. a hollow space surrounded by cells
   d. none of the above

13. What embryonic layer gives rise to muscle tissue?
   a. endoderm
   b. ectoderm
   c. mesoderm

14. How can the fate of embryonic cells be determined by chemical messages received from still other embryonic cells?
   a. induction
   b. Specific surface proteins recognize chemical trails or pathways, causing the cells that bear them to migrate along these pathways.
   c. Cells may adopt different developmental fates, depending upon their response to a concentration gradient of a regulatory substance.
   d. all of the above

15. Which of the following hormones stimulates the secretion of milk, a process called *lactation?*
   a. estrogen   b. progesterone
   c. prolactin   d. oxytocin

16. Which of the following provides experimental evidence that aging is controlled by DNA?
   a. The number of mitotic divisions that a cell can undergo is directly proportional to the shortening of the telomeres.
   b. An increased ability to repair DNA (e.g., by combating the deleterious effects of reactive oxygen species) is directly proportional to increased life span for a cell.
   c. Some "immortal" cancer cell lines have reproduced for decades while maintaining genetically identical cells, indicating that they have found a way to bypass the regulatory mechanisms in the life span of a cell.
   d. all of the above

17. _____ is a series of mitotic divisions of the fertilized egg.

18. _____ is the process by which embryonic cells specialize into different cell types.

19. The _____ is the structure in a mammal that supports and nourishes the developing embryo.

20. Label the indicated parts on the diagram of a developing embryo below.

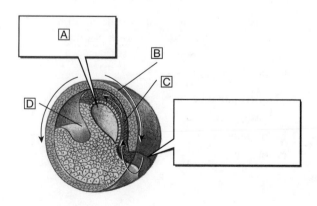

21. As the embryo develops, the neural tube begins to appear. Label these structures on this more advanced embryo.

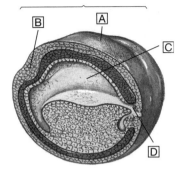

23. Identify the indicated structures on this cross section through a 22- to 25-day-old embryo.

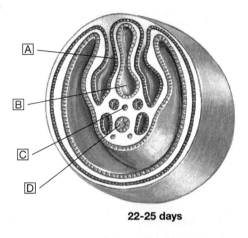

22-25 days

22. As the embryo implants, it continues to develop. On the image below, label the structures that appear during this time.

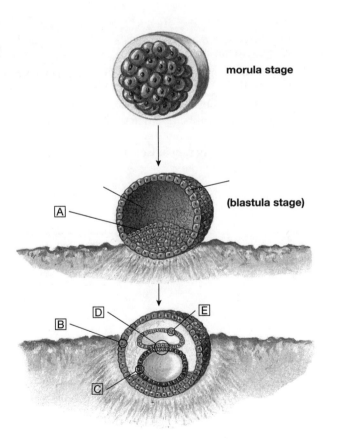

morula stage

(blastula stage)

24. Label the structures of the female breast seen in the diagram below.

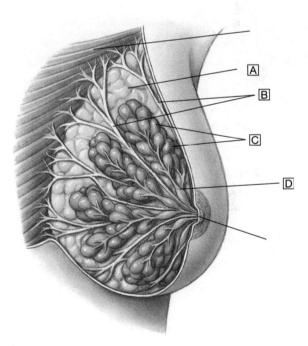

25. Which of the following animals would you predict utilizes indirect development?
- **a.** a duck
- **b.** an iguana
- **c.** an ostrich
- **d.** a frog

26. Which of the following statements about reptilian extraembryonic membranes is NOT true?
- **a.** The chorion helps regulate the exchange of water between the environment and the embryo.
- **b.** The amnion encloses the embryo in fluid.
- **c.** The allantois carries blood between the embryo and the placenta.
- **d.** The yolk sac contains food for use by the embryo.

27. Developmentally speaking, what problems would occur in an embryo if gastrulation DID NOT happen?
- **a.** The embryo could not form a small, solid, ball of cells.
- **b.** Cleavage would not occur.
- **c.** The embryo could not form a hollow, spherical, ball of cells.
- **d.** Organs would not form.

28. If you were to stop induction within a developing embryo, which of the following processes would be most affected?
- **a.** cleavage
- **b.** blastula formation
- **c.** gastrulation
- **d.** organogenesis
- **e.** Both answers c and d are correct.

29. If you wanted to prove that most cells in the human body contain sufficient DNA to produce a clone, from which of the following cells might you harvest DNA?
- **a.** a sperm cell
- **b.** a brain cell
- **c.** an egg cell
- **d.** a skin cell
- **e.** Both b and d are correct.

30. If you wanted to inject embryonic cells into a person in an effort to help repair their spinal cord injury, which of the following types would give you the greatest chance of success?
- **a.** bone cells
- **b.** liver cells
- **c.** skin cells
- **d.** stem cells

31. Reptile embryos (and their extraembryonic membranes) differ from those of humans in that _____.
- **a.** reptile embryos have an extra membrane, the allantois, not found in human embryos
- **b.** human embryos have no yolk sac
- **c.** the reptile chorion exchanges gases between the embryo and the air

32. All of the following are true about the fetal umbilical vein except _____.
- **a.** it carries nutrient-poor blood
- **b.** it carries blood from the fetus to the placenta
- **c.** it is located in the umbilical cord
- **d.** it carries oxygen-rich blood

33. If a woman were unable to produce milk due to an endocrine gland disorder, she might consider prescribed injections of _____ to alleviate the problem.
- **a.** oxytocin
- **b.** prolactin
- **c.** growth hormone

34. Colostrum is particularly beneficial to a newborn baby because _____.
- **a.** it is especially rich in fat
- **b.** it provides antibodies to the baby which bolsters its immune system
- **c.** it is especially rich in lactose
- **d.** it is high in protein
- **e.** Both b and d are correct.

ESSAY CHALLENGE

1. List and describe the four extraembryonic membranes and their functions.

2. What are the three tissue layers formed during gastrulation and what do they become?

3. What are the two major functions of the placenta?

4. How do labor and birth occur?

MEDIA ACTIVITIES

To access a Media Activity visit http://www.prenhall.com/audesirk7. Log in to the Web site selected by your instructor, navigate to this chapter, and select the appropriate Media Activity number.

37.1 Stages of Animal Development
Estimated time: 5 minutes

Explore the process of animal development and gastrulation in an animal embryo.

37.2 Control of Development
Estimated time: 5 minutes

Observe how genes, gene regulating substances, and proteins coordinate to control embryonic development.

37.3 Human Development
Estimated time: 10 minutes

Explore the key events that occur during each stage of human embryonic development.

37.4 Web Investigation: Far-Reaching Choices
Estimated time: 30 minutes

Think about the chemicals you are exposed to every day: caffeine, alcohol, cigarette smoke, over-the-counter drugs, formaldehyde from carpets, paint fumes, gas. The list goes on and on. Some are generally harmless, others are not. In a few cases, even a short exposure can have devastating effects on a developing fetus. Answer the questions to learn more about chemicals, drugs, and pregnancy.

1. Fetal alcohol syndrome (caused by maternal consumption of alcohol) is the leading cause of mental retardation in the United States. What are the symptoms (http://www.marchofdimes.com/professionals/681_1170.asp)? Is there a cure? During pregnancy, how much alcohol is too much?

2. What effects does maternal smoking have on a fetus?

3. Most people have heard of the limb abnormalities caused by thalidomide. What developmental abnormalities are associated with the acne medicine Accutane? What steps has the manufacturer taken to prevent Accutane-related birth defects?

4. As an expecting mother, painting the nursery may not be a good idea. Why?

5. Look at the long list of drugs (http://www.betterhealth.vic.gov.au/bhcv2/bhcarticles.nsf/(Pages)/Birth_defects_can_be_caused_by_drugs?OpenDocument) known to cause birth defects. How many have you taken in the last six months? Make a list of questions a woman who is or might be pregnant should consider before exposing herself to unknown drugs or chemicals.

ISSUES IN BIOLOGY

What's Happening to Me?

Temper outbursts, fatigue, depression, crying spells, night sweats, nightmares, food cravings, confusion, hair loss, abdominal bloating, bruising, headaches, loss of sexual desire, and more, *much* more (http://www.menopause-treatment.com/). These are among the many symptoms of an unavoidable, incurable condition that strikes women between the ages of 40 and 50, lasts 1 to 3 years, and then is over. The prognosis is good—but those afflicted (and close family members) may doubt their survival. Combine all this with other, more familiar symptoms of hot flashes, muscle aches, breast tenderness, and irregular, heavy menstrual bleeding, and the diagnosis becomes apparent: menopause (http://www.mayoclinic.com/invoke.cfm?id=DS00119).

Menopause is the cessation of monthly hormonal menstrual cycles that, during the preceding years, produced an ovulatory event. As part of the normal aging process or as a result of the surgical removal of both ovaries, these monthly cycles gradually change, then stop. During the changes, a woman's body is adjusting to losses of hormone levels that have managed the biological components of her reproductive life for decades. For many women these changes come easily; for others the changes bring misery. There is great variety in the collection of symptoms women may experience.

Some women experience serious medical disorders as a result of menopause. More than 28 million Americans currently have the bone-weakening condition called osteoporosis; 80 percent of them are women. The loss of estrogen leads to the accelerated loss of bone and to the disabling symptoms of osteoporosis. Fifty percent of women over the age of 50 will have osteoporosis-related bone fractures. Each year 50,000 people die after fracture-related complications, at an annual cost of $13.8 billion. The loss of estrogen also increases the risk of heart disease due to potential increases in LDL blood cholesterol levels, coronary spasms, and the loss of elasticity in arteries.

Fortunately, through research and education, women are becoming aware of nutritional and medical options that will greatly reduce the potential health risks of menopause. Simply increasing milk consumption during adolescence may protect young girls against osteoporosis later in life by increasing their bone mass. Dietary calcium increases during and after menopause are also recommended. Weight-bearing exercise contributes to overall increases in bone mass. Many women are replacing their diminished estrogen with hormones that they take orally or absorb through skin patches. Estrogen replacement therapy eliminates most, if not all, of the nuisance menopause symptoms and can also counteract the more serious cardiovascular conditions and osteoporosis. There are, however, possible side effects (http://www.nia.nih.gov/menopause2003/) to hormone replacement therapy. A woman who is considering this option should discuss all these issues with her physician.

1. Many women have hormonal problems before menopause especially at certain times during the monthly menstrual cycle. One collection of symptoms is called premenstrual syndrome (PMS). Do you think a person with PMS might have more problems during menopause?

2. What is the relationship between estrogen and osteoporosis?

3. There are many questions and concerns about estrogen replacement therapy. Some studies indicate that it increases a woman's risk for uterine and breast cancers. Other studies report that estrogen replacement therapy protects against these cancers. If you had to choose between the apparent benefits of this treatment before these questions are answered conclusively, would you choose to use estrogen replacement therapy?

BIZARRE FACTS IN BIOLOGY

Temperature and Sex Determination

Can you imagine this scenario? Parents who want to have a girl need only adjust the thermostat in their home. It might sound crazy, but for some types of organisms, particularly reptiles, the sex of offspring can be determined by environmental cues, such as temperature (http://news.nationalgeographic.com/news/2001/08/0815_lizardsex.html), after fertilization. In many species of reptiles, gender is determined in response to environmental temperature. For example, in the American alligator—*Alligator mississippiensis* (http://www.flmnh.ufl.edu/NatSci/herpetology/brittoncrocs/csp_amis.htm)—all eggs incubated at a constant temperature of 30 °C (86 °F) and below produce females, whereas all eggs incubated at 33 °C (91 °F) produce males. The temperature varies within the nest, so some eggs will develop into males and some into females due to these small variations in temperature.

The molecular mechanisms of sex determination are still not well understood, but hormones appear to play a key role. One hypothesis is that temperature affects the genes that control which hormones are produced in such species. Another hypothesis is that temperature may influence the rates of transcription and translation of sex-determining genes. Because many reptilian species are in danger of extinction, research is being conducted to better understand the critical role of temperature in sex determination and development.

1. Why would understanding the role of temperature in sex determination potentially be an important part of restoring endangered species?

2. How might global warming be particularly devastating to reptiles that practice temperature-dependent sex determination?

Stem Cells: Whither Goest Thou?

During development, the cells of the embryo turn off the activity of some genes and begin the process of differentiation. Differentiation (http://www.ultranet.com/~jkimball/BiologyPages/S/Spemann.html) creates the cells that will become the specialized tissues of the body. Once a cell has begun the path of differentiation, it cannot turn back; a cell destined to become a liver cell cannot "change its mind" and become skin.

Or so we thought. Recently, scientists have detected a population of undifferentiated cells, called adult stem cells (AS cells -http://www.accessexcellence.org/WN/SU/stemcell4299.html), in tissues that don't regenerate rapidly, such as muscle, liver, pancreas, and even the brain. These AS cells don't appear to be limited in their ability to differentiate either, since brain AS cells injected into bone-marrow-deprived hosts have been shown to differentiate to make blood cells. It is not yet known whether or not AS cells are simply multipotent—able to differentiate into a variety of cell types—or totipotent—able to differentiate into any cell type, like embryonic cells. The surrounding cells affect the differentiation pathway because brain AS cells don't normally become blood cells.

Finding AS cells in these organs suggests that they may have a limited ability to replace damaged cells by signaling the AS cells to differentiate. Recent work with stem cells injected into rat brains has shown that these cells can hone in on areas damaged by stroke, trauma, or disease states like Alzheimer's and repair some of the damage. If we can understand how these injected stem cells learn where to go, it may be possible to trigger the AS cells already present within tissues to do the same. Much work remains to determine where AS cells are located, whether these AS cells can migrate within a tissue, what signals are needed to trigger differentiation, and if the AS cells can repair the damage well enough to restore normal function.

References

Helmuth, L. 2000. Stem cells hear call of injured tissue. *Science* 290:1479–80.
Morrison, S. J. 2001. Stem cell potential: Can anything make anything? *Curr Bio* 11:R7–R9
van der Kooy, D., and Weiss, S. 2000. Why stem cells? *Science* 287:1439–41.

1. What does the discovery of AS cells in various organs tell us about the process of differentiation?

2. Why would stem cell therapy be preferred over a transplant to repair damaged tissue?

3. Is it appropriate to test stem cell therapies in patients with incurable disease before we fully understand the system?

KEY TERMS

aging	development	gastrula	metamorphosis
allantois	differentiation	gastrulation	morula
amnion	direct development	implantation	notochord
amniotic egg	ectoderm	indirect development	organogenesis
blastocyst	embryonic disc	induction	placenta
blastopore	embryonic stem cells	inner cell mass	yolk
blastula	endoderm	labor	yolk sac
chorion	extraembryonic membrane	lactation	
chorionic villus	fetal alcohol syndrome	larva	
cleavage	(FAS)	mammary glands	
colostrum	fetus	mesoderm	

ANSWER KEY

SELF TEST

1. c
2. b
3. c
4. a
5. c
6. c
7. a
8. b
9. c
10. c
11. a
12. b
13. c
14. d
15. c
16. d
17. cleavage
18. differentiation
19. placenta

20. A. primitive gut
    B. ectoderm
    C. mesoderm
    D. blastocoel
21. A. neural fold
    B. neural plate
    C. primitive gut
    D. blastopore
22. A. inner cell mass
    B. chorion
    C. amnion
    D. embryonic disc
    E. yolk sac
23. A. future umbilical cord
    B. digestive tract
    C. notochord
    D. neural tube
24. A. fat
    B. suspensory ligaments
    C. mammary gland
    D. milk duct

25. d
26. c
27. d
28. e
29. e
30. d
31. c
32. b
33. b
34. e

ESSAY CHALLENGE

1. (1) the chorion exchanges oxygen and carbon dioxide; (2) the amnion encloses the embryo in a watery environment; (3) the allantois surrounds wastes; and (4) the yolk sac contains the stored food

2. The endoderm will form the digestive tract, the ectoderm will form the skin and nervous system, and the mesoderm will form the muscles and skeleton.

3. (1) It secretes hormones that stimulate the growth of the mother's uterus and mammary glands, and (2) it allows selective exchange of materials between the mother and fetus.

4. The full-term fetus produces steroid hormones that cause increased estrogen and prostaglandin production by the placenta and uterus. These hormones make the uterus more likely to contract. When contractions are strong enough, the baby's head enters the cervix, which stimulates stretch receptors that ultimately trigger oxytocin release. Oxytocin causes the uterus to contract more forcefully, and the baby is born.

MEDIA ACTIVITIES

37.4   Web Investigation: Far-Reaching Choices

1. Symptoms include low birth weight, small eyes and brain, and poorly formed organs. There is no cure. ANY amount of alcohol is too much.

2. Symptoms can include low birth weight, mental retardation, learning disabilities, and increased risk of complications as a newborn.

3. Abnormalities include hydrocephaly, microcephaly, mental retardation, ear and eye abnormalities, cleft lip, palate, and other facial abnormalities, and heart defects. The manufacturer has attempted to address these issues by placing warning labels on the drug for physicians and patients, providing patient information kits that include consent forms for the patient to sign stating she understands the serious risk of birth defects, and offering to refer the patient for a free pregnancy test and birth control counseling session.

4. Some of the substances in paint, or in materials used while painting, can cause birth defects and miscarriages.

5. The questions created by students will be varied, but should all address the issue presented.

ISSUES IN BIOLOGY

1. Because women with PMS are especially sensitive to fluctuations of sex hormones, they may be more sensitive to the symptoms of menopause.

2. Bone loss accelerates at the onset of menopause due to decreased estrogen levels.

3. This question is free-form and will have many possible responses.

BIZARRE FACTS IN BIOLOGY

Temperature and Sex Determination

1. Knowing whether a species practices temperature dependent sex determination would help determine the location of where a new population might be established. Were the proposed habitat too warm or too cold, all males or females would result.

2. If global temperatures increase significantly, this could skew the male/female ratios of populations of these animals, making it difficult for them to reproduce.

Stem Cells: Whither Goest Thou?

1. The same basic parts are used to generate different tissues. It is the way that the stem cells are stimulated to produce various specific cell types that differs.

2. If a patient could harvest their own stem cells to repair or replace damaged tissue, they wouldn't have to worry about rejection of tissue transplants.

3. This is an opinion-based question whose answer depends on the personal feelings of the student.

CHAPTER 38: ANIMAL BEHAVIOR

AT-A-GLANCE

SELF TEST

1. Innate behavior is _____.
   a. any observable response to external or internal stimuli
   b. a behavior performed reasonably completely the first time
   c. behavior that is changed on the basis of experience
   d. a change in the speed of random movements
   e. a directed movement toward or away from a stimulus

2. Learned behavior is _____.
   a. any observable response to external or internal stimuli
   b. a behavior performed reasonably completely the first time
   c. behavior that is changed on the basis of experience
   d. a change in the speed of random movements
   e. a directed movement toward or away from a stimulus

3. Which of the following is NOT a type of innate behavior?

   a. kineses

   b. fixed action patterns

   c. taxes

   d. habituation

4. Territoriality _____.

   a. is a behavior in which an animal shares resources with another of its species

   b. increases the aggressive encounters an individual is likely to have

   c. usually leads to a reduction in fitness

   d. involves the active defense of an area containing important resources

5. Which of the following is NOT an important function of mating behaviors?

   a. communicate species identity

   b. communicate gender

   c. communicate sexual receptivity

   d. defuse aggressive responses

   e. All of the above are important functions of mating behaviors.

6. Which of the following is unlikely to be a consequence of sociality?

   a. conservation of energy

   b. ease of finding mates

   c. increased access to limited resources such as food or nest sites

   d. an increase in foraging efficiency

   e. an increased ability to deter predators

7. Grasshopper mice (genus *Onychomys*) are insectivores. Among their prey are beetles that, when threatened, elevate their rear ends and eject a spray of acetic acid into the faces of potential predators. Adult grasshopper mice avoid this by plunging the beetle's rear end into the ground and biting off its head. Juvenile grasshopper mice, when first exposed to these beetles, perform the "jam and bite" behavior but don't always get the right end of the beetle up! Which of the following is the best explanation for this feeding behavior?

   a. The "jam and bite" behavior is innate but modified by learning.

   b. The behavior is a fixed action pattern.

   c. The behavior is completely learned.

8. Which of the following is NOT a likely example of one animal attempting to alter another's behavior?

   a. When threatened, a water moccasin (cottonmouth snake) opens its mouth in a wide gape, exposing the bright white lining of the mouth.

   b. A common flicker (a form of woodpecker) spends significant amounts of time drumming its beak on an aluminum sculpture.

   c. Kangaroo rats living in the desert Southwest rub oils from their skin into the soil at communal sand-bathing areas.

   d. A male spider vibrates a female's web in a specific sequence prior to attempting to mate.

   e. All of the above are likely examples of one animal attempting to alter another's behavior.

9. The rove beetle lays its eggs in the nest of a particular species of ant. Beetle larvae produce a scent that causes the ants to carry the larvae into the ants' brood chamber, where the larvae proceed to eat ant eggs and larvae. Later, the adult beetles mimic the ants themselves in order to get food. An adult beetle approaches an ant and touches the ant with its antennae. Then, it touches its forelegs to the ant's mandibles. This causes the ant to regurgitate sweet, nutritious fluids for the beetle to eat. The adult beetle behavior is an example of _____.

   a. the use of pheromones to evoke a fixed action pattern

   b. the use of touch to evoke habituation

   c. the use of touch to evoke classical conditioning

   d. the use of touch to evoke a fixed action pattern

10. Male white-crowned sparrows have distinctive songs that identify not only their species but also the general region in which they live. In the wild, male birds first begin singing a soft "sub-song" at 150 to 200 days after hatching; over time, this develops into the full song characteristic of the species and region in which they live. Experiments with lab-reared birds reveal that males can only learn the song of white-crowned sparrows—they cannot learn even similar songs of closely related species. And, in order for full song to develop properly, males must be exposed to the songs of other white-crowned sparrows between 10 and 50 days after hatching and they must be able to hear themselves sing when they start producing sub-songs at 150 to 200 days after hatching (if they are deafened before they begin producing sub-song, their full song will not develop).

    Based on this information, which of the following is correct? Justify your answer.

    a. The song is a fixed action pattern.

    b. The song is an innate behavior modified by experience.

    c. Song development is an example of unconstrained learning.

    d. Song development requires imprinting.

11. The ability to change a behavior as a result of new experiences (i.e., learning) is most closely associated with which of the following behaviors?
    a. innate behaviors
    b. habituation
    c. operant conditioning
    d. all of the above

12. Which of the following forms of communication would be the most likely to be effective over long distances?
    a. communication by sound
    b. communication by touch
    c. communication by visual cues
    d. communication using chemical cues
    e. Both b and c answers are correct.
    f. Both a and d answers are correct.

13. The basis for viewer interest in the popular television shows, *Survivor* and *Survivor: The Australian Outback*, stems from our fascination with which of the following behaviors?
    a. territoriality
    b. dominance hierarchy
    c. aggression
    d. all of the above
    e. none of the above

14. Which of the following characteristics would NOT need to be communicated in order to find a mate?
    a. the sex of the individual searching
    b. the species of the individual searching
    c. the "attractiveness" or "fitness" of the individual searching
    d. environmental or meteorological conditions

15. Which of the following conditions would be most likely to force animals to associate into loosely organized social groupings?
    a. when weather conditions are extreme
    b. when prey numbers are low but predator numbers are high
    c. when predator numbers decrease but prey numbers remain high
    d. Both of the first two answers are correct.
    e. All of the above are correct.
    f. None of the above is correct.

16. Which of the following is NOT likely to be a behavior that can be explained in biological terms?
    a. similar behaviors in identical human twins
    b. responses to pheromones among members of the same species
    c. avoidance of mating with closely related individuals
    d. all of the above
    e. none of the above

17. _____ is any observable activity of a living animal.

18. In _____, animals acquire new and appropriate responses to stimuli through experience.

19. _____ is a special form of learning in which learning is rigidly programmed to occur only at a certain period of development.

20. _____ are chemical substances produced by an individual that influence the behavior of another.

21. In a _____, each animal establishes a rank that determines its access to resources.

22. _____ is the defense of an area where important resources are located.

23. Without thinking about it, some mothers begin lactating when they hear a baby crying. This indicates that lactation in humans is _____.
    a. a learned behavior
    b. an innate response to a specific stimulus
    c. triggered by any vocal stimulation
    d. a maladaptive behavior
    e. the result of imprinting

24. A female bird will continue to feed a parasitic cuckoo chick in its nest even after the chick has killed the bird's own offspring and grown larger than its foster parent. All the cuckoo needs to do is open its mouth and food is inserted. This indicates that feeding of a gaping mouth by an adult bird is _____.
    a. a behavior easily modified by experience
    b. a purely learned behavior
    c. a behavior that has equally large innate and learned components
    d. an innate behavior not easily modified by experience
    e. No conclusion can be reached based on the information provided.

25. Small birds will often mob large predatory birds like owls and hawks. This behavior involves the smaller birds gathering or flying near the larger bird, calling loudly, and even striking the larger bird, and may result in the larger bird leaving the area. This behavior is risky for the smaller birds but is commonly seen. From this description we can reasonably conclude that _____.
    a. birds are not intelligent enough to know what is good for them
    b. there must be some advantage of this behavior, such as protecting their chicks, that makes the risks worthwhile
    c. these birds must have learned this behavior by operant conditioning
    d. this behavior is clearly maladaptive and should be eliminated by natural selection

26. Bears often scratch the bark on trees located near the outer edges of their range. This behavior is most likely done to _____.

 a. attract potential prey to the area

 b. mark the limits of their territory to keep other bears out

 c. induce sap to flow so they can feed on the sugary fluid

 d. attract potential mates to the area

 e. control the menstrual cycle of female bears in the area

27. Insect pests such as gypsy moths and Japanese beetles can be effectively controlled by setting out traps baited with synthetic sex pheromones of the species in question. This type of control is considered better than using chemical pesticides because _____.

 a. the pheromones are cheaper than chemical pesticides

 b. the pheromone traps will kill a broad range of pest species

 c. the pheromones are very species-specific, so no useful insects are affected

 d. the pheromone traps will kill both males and females, while chemical pesticides kill only females

 e. all of the above

28. Fish hatchery workers know that if they want artificially spawned salmon to return to a specific stream to spawn when they reach adulthood, the workers have to raise the fry (baby salmon) in water from that stream during a certain critical time in their early development. This is a clear demonstration of _____.

 a. operant conditioning

 b. trial-and-error learning

 c. habituation

 d. imprinting

 e. none of the above

29. The hybrid offspring produced by mating a member of the eastern European population of blackcaps (a bird) to a member of the western European population of the same species follow a migration route intermediate between that of their parents. This occurs even if the offspring are raised in isolation. From this information we can reasonably conclude that migration in this species _____.

 a. uses the stars to determine direction

 b. is a purely learned behavior

 c. is controlled entirely by a single gene pair

 d. is imprinted on the birds when they are very young

 e. has a genetic component

30. If you trim the feathers on the left side of a peacock's tail but leave the right side unaltered, this treatment is expected to _____ the male's chance of mating.

 a. increase

 b. decrease

 c. have no effect on

ESSAY CHALLENGE

1. How might innate and learned behaviors differ? Are they truly different?

2. Describe some of the ways that animals communicate.

3. How is territoriality beneficial and detrimental to an organism?

4. What are the advantages and disadvantages to group living?

5. Explain why females of many of the species studied to date appear to increase the fitness of their offspring when they choose symmetrical males as their mates.

6. Rutting male elk produce a number of signals to attract mates and repel rivals. These include 1) loud bugling calls, 2) visual displays, and 3) the release of pheromones. Compare and contrast these three types of signals based on 1) the distance over which they are effective in attracting females, 2) how long the signal is expected to persist after it has stopped being emitted, and 3) how much detailed information can be encoded in each signal.

MEDIA ACTIVITIES

To access a Media Activity visit http://www.prenhall.com/audesirk7. Log in to the Web site selected by your instructor, navigate to this chapter, and select the appropriate Media Activity number.

38.1 Observing Behavior: Homing in Digger Wasps
Estimated time: 15 minutes

Repeat some of Niko Tinbergen's famous experiments with digger wasps on innate versus learned behaviors.

38.2 Communication in Honeybees
Estimated time: 10 minutes

Social animals often have to communicate with each other to survive. This activity explores one of the most sophisticated and well-studied examples of communication in non-vertebrate animals, the dancing "language" of honeybees.

38.3 Web Investigation: Sex and Symmetry
Estimated time: 20 minutes

In his 1871 treatise, *On The Origin Of Species*, Charles Darwin not only proposed natural selection as a driving force for evolutionary change but also identified sexual selection as an important special case thereof. Darwin noted that it is not sufficient for sexually reproducing animals just to live to reproductive age, they must also find mates and convince them that they are suitable partners. Since females invest more in reproduction than males (eggs are larger than sperm, females often carry and/or feed young, etc.), they are usually the pickier sex when it comes to choosing mates. They should select mates based on characteristics that are good predictors of the fitness of the other's genes, but what might those traits be? Several hypotheses have been put forth, with facial and bodily symmetry being one of the most interesting.

1. In Nosil and Reimchen's (http://www.sfu.ca/~pnosila/fafitness.html) studies of water boatman tarsal length, what other effect (besides female mate choice) do they indicate might cause asymmetrical males to leave fewer offspring than symmetrical males? Which effect of this asymmetry do you think is larger, the one on sexual selection or the one on natural selection?

2. In the paper by Molly Morris and Kenneth Casey (http://www.sciencedirect.com/science?_ob=MImg&_imagekey=B6W9W45KKVHH5F1&_cdi=6693&_orig=browse&_coverDate=01%2F31%2F1998&_sk=999449998&view=c&wchp=dGLbVlzlSztA&_acct=C000037421&_version=1&_userid=681903&md5=0d2675359a670a01de92ee1eb2ab1cfa&), what species was examined? What male characteristic did they change the symmetry of? How did they accomplish this manipulation?

3. In the abstract of the paper by Swaddle (http://www.sciencedirect.com/science?_ob=MImg&_imagekey=B6W9W45N4RHG7V1&_cdi=6693&_orig=browse&_coverDate=01%2F31%2F1996&_sk=999489998&view=c&wchp=dGLbVtblSzBk&_acct=C000037421&_version=1&_userid=681903&md5=6885244c54203c606db97676a8ad4eb0&), what species was used? What characteristic was manipulated to test the effects of symmetry? How was reproductive success measured in this experiment? Do you think this is a valid indicator?

4. Jennisons (http://asab.icapb.ed.ac.uk/exercises/alevel_psych/zebra_finch.html) used the same species and characteristic as Swaddle (above). However, Jennisons measured female mate choice differently. How did Jennisons do this? Do you think this measure was a better predictor of mating success than that used by Swaddle? Explain?

5. In Renee Borges's (http://www.ias.ac.in/jbiosci/june2000/clipboard.pdf) critique of the fluctuating asymmetry hypothesis, what does the author say about the magnitude of asymmetries produced in some studies versus those seen in nature? Do you think this is a valid criticism of published studies?

ISSUES IN BIOLOGY

What Is New About the Nature vs. Nurture Debate?

In 1975 Harvard biologist Edward O. Wilson published a textbook entitled *Sociobiology: The New Synthesis*. This book linked new theoretical advances in the study of evolution and genetics with the field of animal behavior in an attempt to construct a theoretical framework for the study of how social behavior has evolved in a variety of animals. In his provocative last chapter Wilson turns his attention to humans. The controversy over whether human behavior—especially complex behaviors that must surely owe at least some of their expression to culture—follows the same rules as does behavior of other species is still alive and well. With your introduction to animal behavior and your understanding of the complex relationships between genes and environment, you are ready to be introduced to some of the important issues that arise when we attempt to investigate humans in the same way that we investigate other species.

Studies of human behavior take two seemingly separate but related forms. On the one hand are scientists adding the tools of modern molecular genetics to those of more traditional genetic analyses to determine the extent of genetic influences on complex human behaviors. Identifying a genetic influence and perhaps even locating specific genes that contribute to such pressing human problems as schizophrenia, alcohol dependency (http://www.niaaa.nih.gov/publications/aa18.htm), and obesity will surely help us develop new and better ways to help those who suffer from these conditions. But are our attempts (and our successes, such as they are) to understand the genetic underpinnings of complex human behaviors a mixed blessing?

On the other hand are scientists in the field of evolutionary psychology (http://www.psych.ucsb.edu/research/cep/), who are concerned with the evolution of complex human behaviors, especially social behaviors. On the basis of the premise that all behavior has at least some genetic basis and that human behavior is no less subject to natural selection than is behavior in other species, evolutionary psychologists use cross-cultural and other kinds of studies to ask whether some "universal elements" of human nature really do exist. Are men, like males in other species, more promiscuous than women? If so, does that difference reflect reproductive advantages favored by natural selection over our evolutionary history? Is beauty really "in the eye of the beholder," or do we develop universal standards of beauty to help us assess the quality of potential mates? Scientists (http://www.mindship.org/moller.htm) have addressed these kinds of questions in other species without controversy; should we accept this kind of investigation into ourselves?

One danger of both approaches is that they lead to the misperception that all of human behavior is genetically programmed. A gene that may help contribute, even in a small way, to a complex behavior suddenly becomes, to the public mind, a gene "for" that behavior—ignoring the virtually infinite complexity of gene/environment/culture interactions that are always involved in even relatively simple social behaviors. Suddenly, we are faced with a number of troubling questions. Especially important, does knowing that a behavior has a genetic basis or has been shaped by evolution over long periods of time change our evaluation of that behavior or change the degree of responsibility we assign to individuals expressing it? This and other questions are posed in the essay "Genetics and Genethics" (http://www.counterbalance.org/genetics6.html).

1. The essay "Genetics and Genethics" argues that the view of simple biological determinism is misguided. On the basis of your understanding of the complex interplay among genetics, development, and the environment (including culture), how would you explain the fallacy of the argument that "we are what our genes make us"? Develop a written/verbal analogy or diagram to explain this fallacy.

2. "Genetics and Genethics" introduces the question of whether sexual orientation may have at least a partial genetic basis. Review the evidence summarized by Keith Bell (http://hamp.hampshire.edu/~kebF92/genetics.html), and compare this evidence with that for a genetic contribution to alcoholism. How strong is the evidence for each case? Is one stronger than the other? Justify your answer. What additional information might we realistically expect to find (without performing unethical human experiments) that would make either case stronger?

3. Fortunately or unfortunately, the people who will be making individual and public policy decisions on the basis of new information about human behavior are unlikely to be biologists (or even biology students) who understand the complexity of the science involved. What kinds of problems might arise if the idea that "we are what our genes make us" were to become widespread among leaders of business, industry, and government? Are those dangers sufficiently great that research in this area should be halted or slowed? Why or why not?

BIZARRE FACTS IN BIOLOGY

The Journey Ends in Lovers Meeting

Ever feel like you do all the work in your relationship—that your significant other is always leeching off you? For the female anglerfish (http://ramseydoran.com/anglerfish/deep_sea.htm), this is the way romance works in the depths of the ocean. Living in the ocean from 3000 to 10,000 feet below the surface poses problems for deep-sea organisms such as the anglerfish. At these depths, marine life is widely dispersed. This makes finding a mate extremely difficult. What's a young, single anglerfish to do?

Some species of anglerfish have evolved a unique mating system in which the male attaches to a female for life. After he attaches to her, the vascular systems of the two fish fuse, and the male becomes dependent on the female for nourishment. Although the male anglerfish might be thought of as a parasite, he still retains his ability to breathe, pump blood to his tissues, and excrete wastes, independently of the female. In some species, the males will lose organs, including their eyes. However, the male is not truly parasitic on the female as he provides her a crucial resource she needs to reproduce—his sperm.

This reproductive strategy has also been found in parasitic species. Parasites, like deep-sea organisms, have trouble finding mates, because they are spread out among different hosts. In the molluscan parasite *Enteroxenos bonnevie*, which lives in the gut of sea cucumbers, the males attach to the female and degenerate into little more than a sac of sperm. Both the male and the female benefit from this arrangement, because they can pass on their genes to the next generation.

References

Gage, J., and Tyler, P. 1991. *Deep Sea Biology: A Natural History of Organisms at the Deep Sea Floor*. New York: Cambridge.

Gould, S. J. 1983. *Hen's Teeth and Horse's Toes: Further Reflections in Natural History*. New York: W.W. Norton & Company.

Lutzen, J. 1979. Studies on the life history of *Enteroxenos bonnevie*, a gastropod endoparasitic in aspidochirote holotherians. *Ophelia* 18:1-51.

1. Can you think of other environments that would make finding a mate difficult?

2. In many other types of organisms, the male is larger than the female. What purpose does this difference in body size serve? Why is this not necessary for anglerfish?

3. How does the male receive nourishment from the food ingested by the female? (You may need to review material about digestion and circulation to answer this question.)

4. What prevents the female anglerfish from eating the male when he approaches her?

A Trip of a Lifetime ... on Gossamer Wings

When considering a 2000-mile journey from Mexico to Canada, most of us would board an aircraft capable of flying at 600 mph. Now imagine that you are a butterfly and had to make this same journey. Having wintered in a temperate environment, you leave on your northward journey in early spring, following the ever-increasing abundance of sprouting milkweed (*Asclepias*) plants. This is an enormous distance to cover, especially when you weigh only a fraction of an ounce and fly at an average of 5 mph.

Monarch butterflies (*Danaus plexippus* L.) (http://www.mbsf.org/frame.html) are one of the few migratory (http://butterflywebsite.com/) butterflies in the Northern Hemisphere. Migration is a seasonal movement from one location to another due to changing environmental conditions and food resources. It implies a return to the original area as conditions improve. However, it really is a one-way trip for the original departing monarch butterflies, because they never reach Canada. Their progeny replace these dying elders. Utilizing this multigenerational relay, the monarchs hand off the "migration baton" to several generations along the way and each succeeding generation continues its quest for milkweed plants ever farther northward.

Female monarchs lay their eggs on milkweed plants. The eggs hatch into colorful caterpillars and feed on the toxic foliage. The toxin (cardiac glycoside) in the foliage of the milkweed deters most large herbivores from eating the leaves, but the monarch caterpillar is immune to this toxin and sequesters the toxin unaltered in its tissues.

As the caterpillars mature and change into adults, the unaltered toxin is concentrated in their wings. If an "uneducated" predator, such as a bird, does pluck a monarch in flight, the ingested toxin will induce severe vomiting; the predator is now "educated" to avoid other monarchs. Thus, a plant toxin that protects the plant from predators also protects the monarch butterflies on their migration across North America.

In late summer to early fall, cooling temperatures and the loss of feeding and egg-laying sites cause millions of these orange-winged insects to fly southward to their ancestors' overwintering roosts. No relay is used in this journey; this long flight is conducted by the most-recent generations hatched in the northern ranges. These butterflies must seek conditions that provide above-freezing temperatures at night and high relative humidity in order to retain their fat reserves for the long trip back. Whereas a small population of monarchs overwinter along the Gulf Coast, hundreds of thousands complete the journey back to Mexico by October. Can you imagine the sight of this cloud of color as it moves southward?

1. Monarch butterflies are believed to use the sun as a compass to aid them in their migration. If they use a sun compass to migrate from their northern ranges to their summer breeding grounds, how do they find their way back? As you formulate your answer, remember that several generations are required to complete the migrations. Those individuals beginning the southward journey will have died along the way. How do the butterflies "know" to switch directions once they've reached their goal?

2. Design a technique for capturing, marking, and recapturing butterflies to determine the distance that monarchs travel. Keep in mind the size and fragility of these animals.

3. How can logging practices and pesticide applications in Mexico affect monarch populations?

Light from Life

Some of the coolest lights ever produced occur in an array of life-forms, ranging from bacteria to fish. "Cool" is an accurate description because nearly 100% of the energy produced by this biochemical reaction is released as light, compared with only 10% of the energy released by an electric lightbulb. This "cool" reaction is called bioluminescence (http://lifesci.ucsb.edu/~biolum/index.shtml).

The biochemical reaction that produces bioluminescence is similar among the various organisms that use it. The protein luciferin is broken down by the enzyme luciferinase in the presence of ATP, calcium or magnesium, and oxygen. Some scientists speculate that bioluminescence may have evolved when Earth's atmosphere began to accumulate oxygen. The free oxygen was toxic to some of the early inhabitants, and bioluminescence might have provided a pathway for detoxification.

Although the significance of bioluminescence is not always apparent in a particular organism, many uses have been demonstrated. For example, click beetles in the tropics and fireflies (which are also beetles) use their light-producing capabilities for courtship and for mate recognition. Bioluminescence can be used to startle or confuse, perhaps by temporarily blinding a potential predator. The flashlight fish (http://www.animalnation.com/Archive/aqua/flashfis.html) has small cavities under its eyes that are jam-packed with bioluminescent bacteria.

Some fungi use bioluminescence to advertise their presence. One type of fungus glows in the dark, attracting insects to lay their eggs within the fungi. The larvae devour the fungi, but the spores are dispersed by the adult and juvenile insects. In certain parts of the southern Appalachian Mountains, this glowing of fungi at night is termed fox-fire (http://www.bioart.co.uk/lux/arm.html).

These cool lights can also be deceptive. Female fireflies of the genus *Photuris* prey on males of other firefly genera by mimicking their flashing mating signals. When the amorous male responds to a female's return flash and arrives for the mating, he becomes her meal instead. Bioluminescence is the latest tool in the genetic engineer's arsenal (http://www.chem.msu.su:8081/eng/group/biolum.html). The gene for luciferinase can be used as marker for tracking other biologic processes, such as cellular infection by viruses or the transfer of antibiotic resistance among bacteria, making bioluminescence very "cool" indeed.

1. What explanations could be presented for the evolution of bioluminescence in such diverse types of organisms?

2. Bioluminescence is known to play a role in sexual selection—for example, in fireflies and click beetles. How does bioluminescence play a part in natural selection?

3. Krill, which are marine crustaceans, use bioluminescence for purposes of recognition. Krill have organs of light reception called photophores by which they can detect the light of another krill. Explain why a species without photophores—for example, a species of fungus—would use bioluminescence.

4. In the symbiotic relationship between flashlight fish and bioluminescent bacteria, what is the benefit to the bacteria? To the fish?

KEY TERMS

aggression	ethology	kin selection	trial-and-error learning
altruism	habituation	learning	waggle dance
behavior	imprinting	operant conditioning	
communication	innate	pheromone	
dominance hierarchy	insight learning	territoriality	

ANSWER KEY

SELF TEST

1. b
2. c
3. d
4. d
5. e
6. c
7. a
8. e
9. d
10. d
11. b
12. f
13. d
14. d
15. d
16. e
17. behavior
18. trial-and-error learning
19. imprinting
20. pheromones
21. dominance hierarchy
22. territoriality
23. b
24. d
25. b
26. b
27. c
28. d
29. e
30. b

ESSAY CHALLENGE

1. Innate behaviors are performed reasonably complete the first time, whereas learned behaviors typically involve some experiences. Learning may influence the type of innate behavior an organism exhibits. There is really no sharp distinction between these two types of behaviors.

2. 1) visual communication may involve some sort of specific movement that conveys a message; 2) communication by sound involves animals making specific types of noise to convey messages; 3) chemical messages such as pheromones influence behavior of other organisms; and 4) communication by touch can convey messages and establish social bonds.

3. Territoriality is beneficial because it can help an organism establish an attractive range with many resources. It can then attract mates to its range. Territoriality can be detrimental because it requires a large energy expenditure by an organism, and in the process of defense, an organism may become injured or die.

4. Disadvantages include 1) competition for limited resources, 2) increased risk of contagious diseases, 3) risk that offspring will be killed by other members of the group, and 4) increased risk of being spotted by predators. Advantages include 1) increased ability to defend against predators, 2) increased hunting efficiency, 3) division of labor, and 4) increased likelihood of finding mates.

5. Symmetry appears to be a reliable indicator of "good genes." In particular, it seems to show that the individual has withstood onslaughts from parasites, diseases, and other hardships without them causing differences in the development of the two sides of the body that would cause asymmetry. As a result, when she mates with a symmetrical male, she increases the chances of matching her genes with good genes that will increase the survival chances of her offspring.

6. The sound (bugling) and chemical (pheromone) signals are likely to attract females over greater distances than do the visual displays. However, the visual and sound signals, being almost instantaneous, do not persist long after the male stops emitting them. The visual and sound signals can also carry more information and be updated or changed far more rapidly than can the chemical signals.

MEDIA ACTIVITIES

38.3   Web Investigation: Sex and Symmetry

1. The authors indicate that an asymmetrical water boatman may not be able to feed as well, leading to poorer physical condition and survival. It is unclear from the information provided which effect would be bigger, that on sexual selection (i.e., female mate choice, not addressed here) or that on natural selection (on feeding ability).

2. The species examined was the swordtail, *Xiphophorus cortezi*. They studied the effects of asymmetry in the vertical bars on the sides of males on female mate choice. They removed bars on one side by freeze branding.

3. The zebra finch, *Taeniopygia guttata*, was used in this study. Colored leg bands were applied symmetrically or asymmetrically to males. Reproductive success was measured as the number of offspring surviving past the period of parental care. This is probably a good measure of reproductive success, though reaching mating age would be better still.

4. Jennisons used the amount of time the female spent on a perch in front of chambers containing four different males. This is probably a poorer predictor of mating success, as no mating actually takes place. (A female may spend most of her time with one male but mate with another, for example.)

5. The author indicates that some of the experimental studies produced asymmetries that were much larger than any seen in nature. If this is indeed true, it may mean that any findings made cannot necessarily be applied to nature.

ISSUES IN BIOLOGY

1. All the genes we possess together comprise our genotype, which can be viewed as a set of instructions for constructing "us," just as blueprints are instructions for building a house. However, in going from the blueprints to the finished house (or from our genotype to our phenotype), a number of environmental factors can intervene. For example, some materials specified to construct certain structures may be in short supply when they are built, necessitating substitutions of other, similar materials, such as steel roof tiles for those made of lead. And intentional alterations may be made to make the house better fit its specific site, such as more insulation for colder climates or larger windows facing a scenic view. As a result, even identical twins with the same genotype may differ if they are raised under different circumstances, such as being fed different foods (raw materials—e.g., one may have more magnesium in his/her bones) or being raised in different climates (physical influences on development—e.g., one may have more subcutaneous fat). It is not unreasonable, then, that social systems (such as being raised by alcoholic or homosexual parents) might also influence our phenotypes.

2. The report by Keith Bell indicates that about 50% of identical twins of gay or lesbian individuals share their sibling's sexual orientation, which is greater than that for non-identical twins (20% in one study) or for adopted siblings (10% in the same study). Since similar results were reported for alcoholism in the linked NIAAA report, but no percentages were given, we can conclude that the evidence for each "behavior" is similarly strong. Also, it is safe to say that there is a genetic component (i.e., a predisposition) to both behaviors, but other factors are also important—i.e., there is no indication of genetic determinism. Studies of sexual orientation of children of gay versus straight biological parents raised by gay versus straight adoptive parents, would strengthen the case for a genetic component to homosexuality. We could even gain some insight into critical periods ("imprinting?") by investigating the age at which adopted children are relocated. Ethical considerations make adoption by alcoholic parents more controversial.

3. On the business front, people who are found to have genes that predispose them to certain diseases may be denied health or life insurance or even be shunned by employers as they are "bad risks." This raises questions of equal opportunities and equal rights. Industry will focus on genetic treatments for diseases and conditions like alcoholism whose causes are only partly genetic. They may price a genetic "cure" such that only the rich can afford it, leading to a greater social divide between the haves and have-nots. And this work may come at the expense of addressing environmental factors known to contribute to alcoholism such as unemployment, neighborhood decay, lack of social services, etc. Governments will have to decide if individuals that possess genes that predispose them to criminal activities are responsible for their illegal actions. Should they be treated medically or incarcerated? While the dangers are real and serious, the potential rewards are great. So rather than slowing or stopping the rate of research, we need to step up the rate of social and ethical discourse to keep pace of new scientific developments and possibilities.

BIZARRE FACTS IN BIOLOGY
The Journey Ends in Lovers Meeting

1. Many organisms that are fixed in one place as adults have trouble finding mates. Many flowering plants have come to rely on insects to carry sperm (inside pollen grains) from "males" to "females" (though these sexes may both be found in different flowers on the same plant or even different parts of the same flower). Among invertebrates attached to substrates in the intertidal zone or coral reefs, synchronized "broadcast spawning" is the rule, as all members of a species expel their eggs and/or sperm into the water at the same time, fertilization occurring at random. However, some barnacles (crustaceans attached as adults) possess "parasitic" males while others have the longest penises (relative to body size) known.

2. Larger body size in males often reflects competition between males for mates. They may either have to fight for access to females or mating sites, or females may choose larger may size as it may reflect overall male fitness. Since anglerfish are so scarce and encounters are so rare, these advantages are unlikely to be important. Rather, a premium is placed on males' abilities to find females, which may be enhanced by smaller size.

3. The female ingests a food item (prey individual) and her digestive system breaks it down into smaller molecules that can be absorbed across the walls of her gut and into her blood. Her circulatory system transports some of these molecules to the male's circulation, which is fused to the female's. His circulation transports the molecules to his cells, which absorb and use them.

443

4. The female's lure is a species-specific signal to attract only males of the same species. It is possible that the male somehow signals to the female that he is a male of the same species and she'd do better if she didn't eat him! He then attaches to her skin by biting her and begins to metamorphose immediately.

A Trip of a Lifetime . . . on Gossamer's Wings

1. Monarch butterflies traveling north might rely on a magnetic compass, orienting to the Earth's magnetic North Pole. The switch from migrating south (towards Mexico) to migrating back to the north (towards their "summering grounds") might be triggered by changing day length.
2. Monarch butterflies can be captured (or recaptured) using lightweight nets such as "mist nets" of handheld butterfly nets. They should be handled with great care to avoid injury. Individualized markings may be applied to the wings or abdomen using small drops of permanent paint. A record of location and time of capture/release should be made for each individual. Recapture later on will allow individuals to be identified, and their subsequent locations and times of recapture compared to the initial values to calculate distance and speed traveled.
3. Since huge numbers of monarchs from across North America are concentrated in small forested areas in Mexico for part of the year, losses of habitat due to deforestation or mortality due to pesticide use may severely reduce populations of these insects.

Light From Life

1. The explanation presented involves the reaction evolving to detoxify oxygen as that gas first appeared in the atmosphere long ago. So organisms that are relatively closely related may simply have inherited the trait from a common ancestor. But the presence of the same reaction in very distantly related organisms points at multiple origins of the reaction, indicating that "raw materials" (substrates and enzymes that could be easily modified to give the bioluminescent reaction) were widely available and easily altered.
2. Bioluminescence may increase survival rates (i.e., as "counter shading" organs on the lower surface of fishes makes their shadow less visible to potential predators) and/or birth rates (i.e., as deep sea and nocturnal animals may more readily find and identify mates). Both will increase fitness.
3. Fungi might employ bioluminescence to attract animals that might excrete in their vicinity, providing nourishment. Conversely, their light might repel negatively phototactic fungivores or be an advertisement of their distastefulness.
4. The fish gain the ability to attract or find food and mates. The bacteria gain a relatively safe home and constant supply of nutrients.

CHAPTER 39: POPULATION GROWTH AND REGULATION

AT-A-GLANCE

SELF TEST

1. Which of the following processes would contribute to an increase in population size?
   a. birth
   b. death
   c. immigration
   d. emigration
   e. Both a and c are correct.

2. The rate at which a population reproduces and grows under ideal or optimal conditions is known as the _____.
   a. replacement-level fertility
   b. biotic potential
   c. carrying capacity
   d. environmental resistance
   e. survivorship curve

3. A clan of spotted hyenas in Ngorongoro Crater (Africa), gobbling down the carcass of a zebra from which they have chased a lone lioness, exhibit _____ competition among themselves.
   a. contest competition
   b. scramble competition
   c. intraspecific competition
   d. interspecific competition
   e. Both b and c are correct.

4. The number of individuals of a particular species that the local environment will support is called _____.
   a. biotic limit
   b. trophic level
   c. biotic potential
   d. carrying capacity
   e. ecological maximum

5. Currently, what is the approximate human population of the United States?
   a. 125 million
   b. 290 million
   c. 376 million
   d. 433 million
   e. 528 million

6. Which of the following areas has the highest human population growth rate, with a fertility rate of more than 2.5%?
   a. Africa
   b. China
   c. Central and South America
   d. North America
   e. Asia (excluding China)

7. If the number of births in a population is greater than the number of deaths, which of the following is correct?
   a. The population is increasing in size.
   b. The population is decreasing in size.
   c. The value for the rate of growth (r) is positive.
   d. The value for the rate of growth (r) is negative.
   e. Both a and c are correct.

8. The biotic potential of a species depends on which of the following factors?
   a. the age at which the organism first reproduces
   b. the chance of survival to the age of reproduction
   c. the frequency with which reproduction occurs
   d. the average number of offspring produced each time
   e. the length of the reproductive life span of the organism
   f. all of the above

9. Which of the following factors is least likely to influence population size in a density-dependent way?
   a. predation
   b. competition
   c. emigration
   d. climate and weather
   e. parasitism and disease

10. The biotic potential of a population is most likely to be achieved _____.
   a. when the population is declining
   b. when the population exceeds the carrying capacity
   c. when the population is increasing but is near carrying capacity
   d. when the population is small compared to the carrying capacity
   e. a and b are both correct.

11. Assuming that birth rate and death rate for a population were equal, what would happen to population numbers if emigration exceeded immigration?
   a. Population numbers would decrease.
   b. Population numbers would increase.
   c. Abiotic components would dwindle.
   d. Abiotic components would flourish

12. Which of the following examples illustrates the principle of exponential growth?
   a. a population of aphids whose population numbers decrease consistently from year to year
   b. a population of spiders whose population numbers increase one year but decrease in other years
   c. a population of spider mites whose population numbers double every two weeks for the course of the summer
   d. a population of purseweb tarantulas whose population numbers remain essentially unchanged over time

13. Which of the following would NOT decrease the carrying capacity of an ecosystem?
   a. depletion of nonrenewable resources
   b. depletion of renewable resources occurring at a slower rate than the ability of a particular renewable resource to recover
   c. depletion of renewable resources occurring at a rate that exceeds the ability of a particular renewable resource to recover
   d. none of the above

14. How have humans been able to expand the carrying capacity over the course of recorded history?
   a. through advances in technology and medicine
   b. by co-opting the resources of other species
   c. by exploiting renewable resources faster than they can be replaced and nonrenewable resources that cannot be replaced
   d. all of the above

15. Why is the U.S. population rate growing as rapidly as it is despite the fact that its fertility rate is 2.03, below the replacement-level fertility of 2.1 children per female?
   a. Even though our fertility rate is below RLF = 2.1, for many years after World War II the fertility rate exceeded the replacement level; therefore, the population is still going up because more women are reproducing.
   b. emigration
   c. immigration
   d. Both a and c are correct.

16. Dividing 0.693 by the value r calculates a population's _____.

17. If a population displays exponential growth for a short period, followed by a rapid die-off, that population is experiencing a _____-and-bust cycle.

18. A graph of population growth that initially has an exponential phase, followed by a leveling off, is called a _____ curve.

19. An ecological effect that limits population size regardless of the population density is called a(n) _____ factor.

20. A graph of population that shows the distribution of males and females of each age group is called the _____ of the population.

21. RLF means _____.

22. Using the graph of bacteria population growth below, label each line according to the death rate.

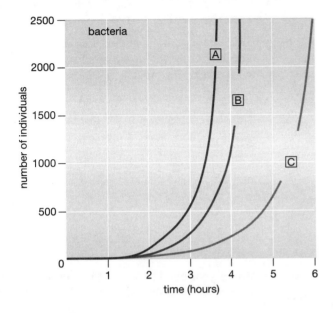

23. Label the portions of the S-curve of population growth graph below.

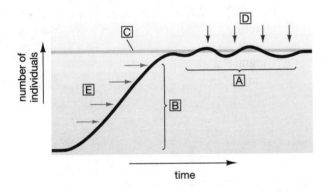

24. Another way to look at populations is through survivorship curves. Label each of the curves below as to survivorship.

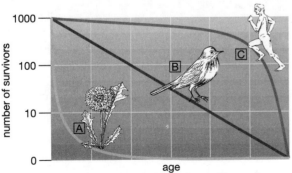

25. Age-structure diagrams indicate the overall health of the population. Label the three diagrams below as to how the population is changing.

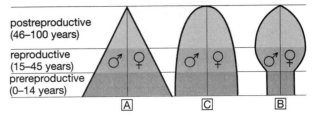

26. Which of the following would NOT be a suitable research project for an ecologist?

  a. the effect of parasitic worms on death rates of people in tropical Africa

  b. the recovery of the forest community around Mount St. Helens following its eruption in 1980

  c. adaptations of deep-sea fish that allow them to live under such high pressures

  d. how predation by feral cats on ground-nesting birds on an island affects the numbers of each species

  e. how the three-dimensional structure of the active site of an enzyme involved in converting glucose to glycogen in the liver affects its activity

27. An ecologist studying a population of ostriches records 1000 individuals at the start of a one-year study. Over the course of the year he records 100 births and 60 deaths. What is the growth rate, r, for this population?

  a. 0.04

  b. 0.1

  c. 0.4

  d. 40

  e. 100

28. A population of pocket gophers has a growth rate (r) of 0.2 per year. If there are initially 100 individuals, how many pocket gophers do you expect at the end of the first and second years?

  a. 120; 144

  b. 120; 140

  c. 20; 4

  d. 120.2; 120.4

  e. 200; 400

29. Once established, exotic species introduced into a new area often increase dramatically in numbers for quite some time. This increase is believed to occur because _____.

a. they lack many of the natural enemies (predators, parasites, etc.) that would keep their numbers in check in their native range

b. exotic species always have very high population growth rates (r)

c. there are many vacant niches in most ecosystems that exotic species can readily fill

d. exotic species always have very high carrying capacities

e. all of the above

30. Developing countries like Pakistan that have passed only halfway through the demographic transition _____.

a. have high growth rates as death rates have already dropped but birth rates remain high

b. have high growth rates as birth rates have already risen but have not yet fallen back down

c. have low growth rates as birth rates have already dropped but death rates remain high

d. have low growth rates as death rates have already risen but birth rates remain low

e. have unchanged growth rates as both birth and death rates have declined simultaneously

31. As the size of a snowshoe hare population rises, the number of deaths due to predation by lynx often also rises because _____.

a. the number of encounters between predators and prey will increase when there are more prey around

b. some of the lynx will switch from other prey like grouse to seeking out snowshoe hares as the latter's numbers increase

c. the increased food available to lynx will eventually increase the numbers of lynx by increasing their birth rate

d. all of the above

32. Which of the following is an example of contest competition?

a. A pack of hyenas chase a lone lion away from a dead zebra so they can feed on it instead.

b. A hawk eats a white-footed mouse during the day and as a result that mouse is not available to an owl the following night.

c. A gypsy moth eats leaves of an oak tree.

d. An ant colony protects an acacia tree from plant-eating insects and receives a place to live and food in return.

e. A pair of robins use a maple tree as a platform on which to build their nest.

33. Your personal "ecological footprint" depends on _____.

a. the size of your house, how well it is insulated, and the climate in the region where you live

b. the types of transportation you use, how much you travel, and whether you travel alone or with a group

c. the types and amounts of foods you eat and how much you waste

d. how many goods you consume and the waste you produce

e. all of the above

ESSAY CHALLENGE

1. What are the three factors that determine how much a population changes?

2. Identify some of the factors that influence biotic potential.

3. Why does delaying childbirth slow population growth?

4. Describe some of the differences between density-dependent and density-independent factors.

5. Describe the differences between predators and parasites.

6. Which of the three main types of survivorship curves ("early loss," "constant loss," and "late loss") do you expect to see in species that produce the largest numbers of offspring? In which do you expect to see the greatest parental care given to the young? From a population standpoint, is one strategy better than the others?

7. In southern Africa, HIV and AIDS are rampant among children and young adults. Social mores dictate that young men are promiscuous, resulting in the rapid spread of the disease among their lovers and wives. And since many women are destitute and have little access to health care and contraceptives, they are easily pressured into unsafe sex. As many as one third of women aged 15 to 24 years are infected in some areas. Also, mothers frequently pass the virus on to their offspring *in utero*, during delivery, or by breastfeeding, causing infant infection rates to skyrocket. It is predicted that death rates among children and young adults will increase manyfold in the next decade. What are the predicted effects of this epidemic on the age structure diagrams of the populations involved? What are the expected economic impacts? How might society have to change due to this preferential mortality among the young?

MEDIA ACTIVITIES

To access a Media Activity visit http://www.prenhall.com/audesirk7. Log in to the Web site selected by your instructor, navigate to this chapter, and select the appropriate Media Activity number.

39.1 Population Growth and Regulation
Estimated time: 10 minutes

Ecologists describe the growth of populations using models, which can be very simple or very complicated equations or sets of equations. In this activity, you'll examine two types of models: density-independent growth and density-dependent growth. Both models are important in understanding the dynamics of populations in nature.

39.2 Human Population Growth and Regulation
Estimated time: 5 minutes

This activity allows you to explore some of the many parameters influencing human population growth and the potential issues associated with unrestrained growth.

39.3 Web Investigation: Acorns, Mice, Moths, Deer, and Disease
Estimated time: 10 minutes

It seems like a very straightforward experiment. Add acorns to forest tracts and observe the effects on gypsy moth and mouse populations. But behind this apparently simple protocol lies extensive biological knowledge. This exercise will explore the facts and theories used to design the Lyme disease experiment.

1. Lyme disease is spread to humans and domestic animals by black-legged deer ticks. What are the preferred hosts (http://www.riaes.org/resources/ticklab/lyme3.html) of the adult and immature ticks (http://www.ag.ohio-state.edu/~ohioline/hyg-fact/2000/2147.html)?

2. Gypsy moth (http://www.fs.fed.us/ne/morgantown/4557/gmoth/home.html) caterpillars eat oak leaves and other foliage. What are their natural enemies? Would increasing the gypsy moth population be a good way to control Lyme disease?

3. White-footed mice are an important part of the Lyme disease ecological chain. What are their primary food sources (http://www.ukans.edu/~mammals/pero-leuco.html) (aside from acorns and moth pupae)? What are their major predators?

4. Deer also play a role in the spread of Lyme disease. What are their food and habitat requirements (http://www.fs.fed.us/database/feis/animals/mammal/odvi/biological_data_and_habitat_requirements.html)? Do they have any predators?

5. Government researchers are looking at nematodes (http://www.ars.usda.gov/is/AR/archive/mar98/tick0398.htm), fungi, and pesticides as potential anti-Lyme-disease agents. Pick one. Use your ecological knowledge to design an experiment that would test its effectiveness in a natural environment.

ISSUES IN BIOLOGY

Are Zebra Mussels Still Spreading?

In the mid-1980s a new species found its way to North America. The zebra mussel (http://www.seagrant.umn. edu/exotics/zmid.html) (*Dreissena polymorpha*), a small, clamlike mollusk that grows to about 25 centimeters as an adult, was introduced into the waters of the Great Lakes (http://www.great-lakes.net/envt/flora-fauna/invasive/zebra. html), probably carried in the bilge of a Russian freighter. The zebra mussel can reproduce in less than a year, and a single female can release 1 million eggs each year. In the absence of their natural pathogens, parasites, and predators, the zebra mussel populations in the Great Lakes has grown enormously and are now invading eight major river systems, including the St. Lawrence, Hudson, Mississippi, Ohio, Illinois, Tennessee, Susquehanna, and Arkansas rivers. The mussels are spread from one body of water to another by natural flow, carried on the feathers or feet of migrating waterfowl, or by human transport in bait buckets or on trailered boats. Most of the freshwater systems in North America are now threatened by invasion of the zebra mussel.

The zebra mussels grow in massive colonies, where nearly a half million individuals may grow on each square meter of substrate. These colonies encrust the hulls and rudders of ships and the hinges of lock gates and block the drains and intake ducts used by industries and power stations. In 1990, for example, Detroit Edison spent more than $500,000 to remove zebra mussels from the intake pipes of its power plants.

The zebra mussels also have severe negative effects on the local ecosystem. As filter-feeders, they take in water and filter out algae as food, excreting their waste as sediment. A single individual can filter 1 liter of water each day, and a colony covering 1 square meter of substrate can filter 180 million liters of water per year. Enormous colonies of zebra mussels can reduce the algal populations of lakes and rivers, thus removing a significant portion of the base of the food chain and resulting in a decline in the fish populations. Thus, these mussels are a threat to the local biodiversity.

The tremendous filtering capacity of these organisms may have some positive consequences. Zebra mussels have been a major factor in cleaning Lake Erie after a century of pollution from fertilizers and sewage. After the first 10 years of zebra mussel existence in Lake Erie, light penetration in the water has increased from only a few centimeters to nearly 10 meters. If these organisms could be controlled, they could become a useful tool in the treatment of sewage and pollution.

(Adapted from: Bush, Mark B. 1997. *Ecology of a Changing Planet*. Upper Saddle River, NJ: Prentice Hall.)

1. Explain why organisms introduced into regions where they did not evolve can have devastating effects on the biological communities there.

2. Explain how zebra mussels might spread from one freshwater system to another. In what ways would this dispersal be natural, and in what ways might it be assisted by humans?

3. What difficulties might zebra mussels have in establishing themselves in a new freshwater ecosystem as they disperse across North America? In what ways is their biology well suited to making the necessary adaptations?

4. How might zebra mussels prove to be beneficial to humans?

BIZARRE FACTS IN BIOLOGY

When the Pressure's On, It's Frog-Eat-Frog

For many animals that don't practice parental care, growing up is a very risky proposition. You start out very small, which exposes you to predation by a host of animals. Due to your large surface-to-volume ratio, you're also more prone to drying out, absorbing toxic levels of pollutants, etc. And mommy and daddy aren't there to protect you. To compensate for your low probability of reaching maturity, your parents also gave you a multitude of siblings, with which you may have to compete for food (Sound familiar? This is Darwin's "struggle for survival.").

As if growing up isn't hard enough, some species also face tremendous time pressure to do so. For example, many amphibians lay their eggs in temporary ponds or puddles, requiring the hatching larvae to grow and metamorphose into terrestrial adults (frogs, toads, or salamanders) before their first home dries up. And to make it a real crapshoot, there's no way of predicting how long they'll have or how much competition for resources they'll face. If the spring is dry, the pond may dry up before any adults emerge. And if many females lay their eggs in the same pond, competition for food such as algae and detritus may be so intense that growth and development rates are slowed, so none may mature in time even in a normal spring.

To increase the odds that at least some individuals mature even in years when resources are scarce due to overpopulation (i.e., when the population greatly exceeds its carrying capacity), a few amphibian species have evolved a novel strategy. Basically, a small number of individuals develop into cannibals! Not only do they acquire a taste for their own species' flesh, but they also develop into a distinctly different "morph" (form). Cannibal morphs have larger heads and bigger teeth that make them better at capturing and consuming their own kind. This process has been extensively studied in the spadefoot toad (http://www.bio.unc.edu/faculty/pfennig/lab/pfennig_files/research_interests.htm) (*Scaphiopus* spp.) and tiger salamander (http://lsweb.la.asu.edu/jcollins/) (*Ambystoma tigrinum*). One curious finding is that becoming a cannibal is *not* genetically programmed, but brought on by an environmental cue such as crowding. So the cannibals differ phenotypically but not genotypically from the "normal" herbivorous or omnivorous morph. Also, cannibals can identify their own brothers and sisters, preferentially feeding on other families' members if given the chance. The benefits of this strategy are obvious. Not only is the resource base available to these lucky cannibals increased (and, by virtue of being biochemically identical, species-mates are also highly nutritious), but the number of their competitors is decreased. This brings the population below carrying capacity, speeding growth and development and increasing the chance of maturing in time. As a result, the population becomes more stable as well. Is there a downside to this behavior? Eating your own kind may make you more likely to acquire diseases (http://www.biology.gatech.edu/professors/labsites/jones/pdfs/PfennigHo&Hoffman1998.pdf) from your food than if you eat more distantly related species. This is because conspecifics are more likely to carry diseases to which you are susceptible. It has even been suggested that prion diseases (http://www.eurekalert.org/pub_releases/2003-04/aaft-wcm040403.php) like "mad cow disease" in cattle and Creutzfeldt-Jakob disease in humans owe their existence to cannibalism. One such disease, Kuru (http://www.as.ua.edu/ant/bindon/ant270/lectures/kuru/kuru.htm), was first described in humans in the Fore tribe in New Zealand, which practiced ritualized cannibalism until the practice was outlawed.

Nobody is suggesting humans adopt cannibalism as a means of population control (Jonathan Swift's satirical *A Modest Proposal* (http://art-bin.com/art/omodest.html#hit) aside), but for some species (http://www.sciencedaily.com/releases/1998/12/981216075921.htm) under some circumstances, cannibalism makes perfect sense.

References

Cowley, G., et al. 2001. Cannibals to cows: the path of a deadly disease. *Newsweek* March 12 2001:52-61.

Fox, L. R. 1975. Cannibalism in natural populations. *Annual Review of Ecology and Systematics* 6:87-106.

Pfennig, D. W. 2000. Effect of predator-prey phylogenetic similarity on the fitness consequences of predation: a trade-off between nutrition and disease? *American Naturalist* 155:335-345.

Polis, G. A. 1981. The evolution and dynamics of intraspecific predation. *Annual Review of Ecology and Systematics* 12:225-251.

1. While separate cannibal morphs have been described in relatively few species, at least 1300 species have been shown to practice cannibalism at some time or another (Polis, 1981). Under what circumstances is cannibalism favored? When would it be detrimental?

2. Bovine spongiform encephalopathy (http://www.ivu.org/hrv/madcownw.html) ("mad cow disease") spread rapidly through the cattle population of Britain before it was identified and understood. How did this disease spread so rapidly despite the fact that cattle are not cannibals by nature? How was its spread halted?

KEY TERMS

abiotic	demographic transition	exotic	population
age structure	density-dependent	exponential growth	population cycle
biotic	density-independent	growth rate	predator
biotic potential	doubling time	host	prey
boom-and-bust cycle	ecological footprint	immigration	replacement-level fertility
carrying capacity	ecology	interspecific competition	(RLF)
community	ecosystem	intraspecific competition	scramble competition
competition	emigration	J-curve	S-curve
contest competition	environmental resistance	parasite	survivorship curve

ANSWER KEY

SELF TEST

1. e
2. b
3. e
4. d
5. b
6. a
7. e
8. f
9. d
10. d
11. a
12. c
13. c
14. d
15. d
16. doubling time
17. boom
18. S or S-shaped
19. density-independent
20. age structure diagram or age pyramid
21. replacement level fertility

22. A. no deaths
    B. 10% die between doublings
    C. 25% die between doublings
23. A. equilibrium
    B. exponential growth
    C. carrying capacity
    D. environmental resistance
    E. biotic potential
24. A. early loss
    B. constant loss
    C. late loss
25. A. expanding population
    B. shrinking population
    C. stable population
26. e
27. a
28. a
29. a
30. a
31. d
32. a
33. e

ESSAY CHALLENGE

1. Births, deaths, and migration (both into and out of a population) are the three factors.

2. Reproductive age, reproductive frequency, the number of offspring born in each birth, the organism's life span, and the death rate of individuals were all factors identified in the textbook.

3. If the teen is 19 at first birth, the generation time (between her being born and giving birth) is 19. For the woman in her thirties, the generation time is 30+ years. The population will increase more rapidly in the first case.

4. Density-dependent factors are those that act on individuals based on the number of individuals in a given space. Some examples are famine and disease. Population-independent factors act on individuals regardless of population density. Some examples are droughts and floods.

5. A predator eats (kills) its prey. A parasite gets its food from a host without killing it.

6. For the population to be relatively stable over time, species with large numbers of offspring must suffer large losses before maturity (i.e., be "early loss"). Otherwise, numbers would increase dramatically from generation to generation. Since parental care usually reduces infant (i.e., early) mortality, species with "late loss" curves would be likely to show the greatest parental care, though "constant loss" species may have significant parental care as well. Since reproduction and mortality are expected to balance out in each case, none of these strategies can be considered best from a population standpoint.

7. The age structure pyramids should show a progressive constriction of the base, and children and women of childbearing age suffer high mortality. Since younger adults are the most productive members of the society, economic productivity will likely be greatly affected. Death of younger adults will also result in many elderly persons without children to care for them and many orphaned infants and children, with a greater burden on the state to care for these individuals.

MEDIA ACTIVITIES

39.3 Web Investigation: Acorns, Mice, Moths, Deer, and Disease

1. The preferred hosts of adult ticks are white-tailed deer, though at least 13 species may serve as hosts. Immature ticks (larvae and nymphs) are less host-specific, infecting dozens of species of mammals and birds, but white-footed mice are preferred. (Recall it is the nymph that typically infects humans with the Lyme disease bacterium.)

2. The natural enemies of gypsy moth caterpillars include small mammals, insect parasitoids and predators, birds, and at least one virus and one species of fungus. Increasing the gypsy moth population alone would likely have no effect on Lyme disease. If the increase in gypsy moths is accomplished by reducing white-footed mouse numbers, however, say by reducing the numbers of acorns available, this will reduce the transmission of the Lyme disease bacterium from the mice to the ticks. However, the costs may be too high as oaks and other plants would suffer serious defoliation as a result.

3. The primary food sources for white-footed mice are green plants, grasses, fruits, nuts, and some insects. The principal predators on white-footed mice are owls, weasels, skunks, foxes, coyotes, and snakes.

4. Deer are primarily browsers on a tremendous variety of plants, including leaves, twigs, and stems of woody plants, as well as mast (i.e., infrequently produced large crops of nuts and seeds), fruits, cultivated crops, and sometimes grasses and forbs. They are most frequently found in riparian habitats but also frequent mixed deciduous and coniferous forests. Humans, coyotes, dogs, wolves, black and grizzly bears, mountain lions, lynx, and bobcats are their most important predators.

5. For any of these potential anti-Lyme-disease agents, select a number of similar field plots and randomly assign half as unmanipulated "control plots." The other half, the "experimental plots," receive the appropriate treatment (i.e., spraying with nematodes or fungal spores or application of the pesticide to deer at feeding stations). After waiting the appropriate period of time (recall it can take two years for adult ticks on deer to produce nymphs that can infect humans), compare the numbers of Lyme-disease-bacterium-infected tick nymphs or cases of human Lyme disease on the control plots to those on the experimental plots. Did the treatment significantly reduce the number of disease-carrying nymphs or incidence of disease?

ISSUES IN BIOLOGY

1. Their natural enemies, including pathogens, parasites, and predators, are absent. Since these normally keep species' numbers in check by increasing death rates and/or decreasing birth rates, their absence allows species to increase dramatically in numbers, causing much damage in the process.

2. Natural spread of zebra mussels might occur via flow of water downstream or attached to the feathers or feet of waterfowl. Human-assisted spread might occur in bait buckets or trailered boats transferred between water bodies.

3. As they spread, zebra mussels will encounter new environmental conditions like different temperatures, water chemistries, flow regimes, etc. Given that they produce huge numbers of offspring sexually, chances are good that at least some of their genetically diverse offspring will possess characteristics that allow them to survive under most conditions.

4. Given their high filtering rates, zebra mussels might be employed to clear waters of particulate sewage and pollution.

BIZARRE FACTS IN BIOLOGY

1. Cannibalism may be favorable whenever the size of a population greatly exceeds the food resources available to support it, i.e., when a population exceeds its carrying capacity. It would likely be detrimental under all other circumstances.

2. Cattle were fed meal containing ground-up cattle parts infected with the prions that cause the disease. The spread of BSE was halted by stopping the practice of using cattle remains in cattle feed and destroying all infected and suspect cattle.

CHAPTER 40: COMMUNITY INTERACTIONS

AT-A-GLANCE

SELF TEST

1. When groups of species that interact with each other in a given area are considered together, the level of organization is called the _____.
   a. biome
   b. biosphere
   c. population
   d. community
   e. ecosystem

2. No two species can occupy the same ecological niche in the same place at the same time. This statement is known as _____.
   a. mutualism
   b. a premating isolating mechanism
   c. Darwin's theory of natural selection
   d. the Hardy-Weinberg principle
   e. the competitive exclusion principle

3. The close interaction between organisms of different species over an extended period of time, in which one individual benefits while the other individual neither benefits nor is harmed by the relationship, is known as _____.
   a. predation
   b. competition
   c. parasitism
   d. mutualism
   e. commensalism

4. The structural change in a community and the abiotic environment over time, in which assemblages of plants and animals replace one another in a relatively predictable sequence, is called _____.
   a. evolution
   b. radiation
   c. selection
   d. succession
   e. symbiosis

5. Honeyguides are African birds that excitedly lead the way to a bee's nest, and ratels are the honey- and bee-eating mammals that open up and scatter the contents of the bee's nests, allowing both the ratels and the honeyguides to feed on the contents. This relationship is an example of _____.
   a. predation
   b. competition
   c. parasitism
   d. mutualism
   e. commensalism

6. The rattles of rattlesnakes would be similar in function to which of the following?
   a. camouflage
   b. warning coloration
   c. startle coloration
   d. aggressive mimicry
   e. Both b and c are correct.

7. On many coral reefs in the Pacific, large fish bearing parasites will visit "cleaning stations" where species of small fish, known as *cleaner wrasses,* remove parasites and loose scales from the larger fish. The cleaner fish may even enter the mouth and gills of the larger fish to clean parasites from the soft tissues. The cleaner fish are recognized by their coloration, black with a bright blue or yellow stripe, and by a little "dance" that invites the larger fish in to be cleaned. Also on the reef, however, is a small fish known as the *saber-tooth blenny.* Looking and acting very much like the cleaner wrasse, the blenny also attracts the larger fish, but instead of cleaning away parasites, the blenny bites small bits of flesh from the larger fish. The interactions among the larger fish, the cleaner wrasse, and the saber-tooth blenny represent all but which of the following?
   a. mutualism
   b. parasitism
   c. aggressive mimicry
   d. warning coloration

8. In the rocky intertidal zone, along the coast of the state of Washington, space on the substrate (rocks) is a critical resource for sessile (attached) organisms, such as algae, barnacles, and mussels, and also for other organisms that graze the algae or prey on the sessile animals. For example, limpets graze the algae, and three species of barnacle dominate the algae for space. Among them they form a dominance hierarchy, with the larger *Semibalanus* dominating *Balanus,* which in turn dominates the smaller *Chthamalus.* The mussel, *Mytilus,* is at the top of this hierarchy. A large thaid snail feeds on *Balanus* and *Chthamalus* but cannot take the larger Semibalanus or the mussel. The starfish, *Pisaster,* however, prefers to feed on mussels and the large barnacle *Semibalanus.* Thus, if the starfish is present in this community, the community will be a diverse assemblage of nearly all of the species described here; but if the starfish is absent, the dominant mussel will take over most of the available space. In this example we see _____.
   a. predation
   b. intraspecific competition
   c. interspecific competition
   d. a keystone species
   e. all of the above

9. Trypanosoma is a protozoan (single-celled organism) that lives and reproduces for an extended period in the blood of a mammalian host (e.g., a human, native antelope, or introduced cattle). Newly introduced cattle generally die from this infection if they are not treated, whereas the native antelope, or cattle that have been exposed to this protozoan for several generations, are less severely affected. This relationship is an example of _____.
   a. predation
   b. competition
   c. parasitism
   d. mutualism
   e. commensalism

10. The ability of termites and cattle to live on diets high in cellulose, without actually digesting cellulose themselves, is the result of a symbiotic relationship with microbes in their guts. The microbes have a favorable environment in which to live and a ready source of food, and they provide the host with the products of digested cellulose. This relationship is an example of _____.
    a. predation
    b. competition
    c. parasitism
    d. mutualism
    e. commensalism

11. Why are community interactions so important?
    a. Interspecies interactions affect the ability of species to survive and reproduce.
    b. Coevolution has shaped the behaviors and form of interacting species.
    c. Neither a nor b are correct.
    d. Both a and b are correct.

12. What is the term for the situation in which two or more species cannot live in the same exact regional habitat exhibiting the same behaviors at the same time of day?
    a. resource partitioning
    b. an ecological niche
    c. competitive exclusion principle
    d. none of the above

13. A poisonous frog with bright and colorful body markings is an example of _____.
    a. camouflage
    b. mimicry
    c. warning coloration
    d. aggressive mimicry

14. What is the term for a situation in which one organism benefits from its close association with a second species, but the second species is harmed in the process?

    a. commensalism

    b. mutualism

    c. parasitism

    d. Both a and b are correct.

15. What is a "keystone species?"

    a. any species that is found in the state of Pennsylvania

    b. a species that plays a key role in determining community structure that is greater than its abundance alone would predict

    c. a type of symbiosis between two species in which one species lives inside another

    d. any species that plays an important role in the community

    e. none of the above

16. Plants and animals invade a region recently scoured clean by a retreating glacier and over time are replaced by other species. This statement describes _____.

    a. pioneer species

    b. a climax community

    c. primary succession

    d. secondary succession

    e. Both a and c are correct.

    f. Both b and d are correct.

17. Water treatment plants on Lake Erie became clogged with _____ that were introduced into the lake accidentally by cargo ships discharging ballast water.

18. When two interacting species act as agents of natural selection on one another over evolutionary time, the process is called _____.

19. The term that describes how similar species can share a small, common range without driving each other to extinction is _____.

20. _____ is the situation where species evolve to resemble other organisms.

21. When a predator looks like a nonthreatening species to trick prey into coming close enough to be captured, it is called _____.

22. A _____ community is at the end of succession when a stable level of interaction between species is reached.

23. Competitive exclusion states that only one organism can occupy a niche at a time. Label the two graphs below, indicating which one shows this phenomenon.

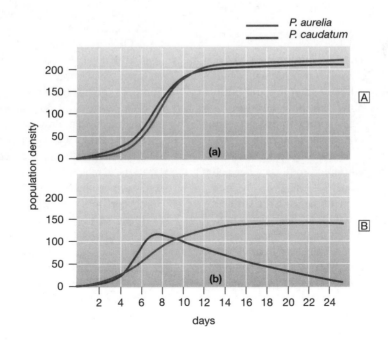

time (years)

0 ————————————————————————————————→ 200

24. Label the stages of succession seen in the image above.

25. Often, when exotic species like purple loosestrife and zebra mussels are introduced into a new environment, their numbers initially increase exponentially but eventually level off. The leveling off of their numbers could be due to _____.
  a. the population reaching its carrying capacity
  b. the predators, competitors, and parasites already present in their new home finally "learning" (or evolving) how to combat them and control their numbers
  c. the predators, competitors, and parasites that controlled their numbers in their native range finally catching up with them as they too arrive in the new home
  d. all of the above

26. Within a year of abandoning agriculture on a plot of prairie, the previously bare soil is overrun with annual weeds. Light, carbon dioxide, and mineral nutrients are readily available, but soil moisture is limiting. Still, some species appear to coexist very close to one another. Upon closer examination, two such species, smartweed and bristly foxglove, are observed to have very different root systems and ways of managing water. Smartweed has a very deep taproot, extending about a meter beneath the surface, tapping (literally) into a continuous deep water supply. Bristly foxtail has a much shallower and spreading fibrous root system, reaching less than 20 cm down. However, the latter plant is able to tolerate periods of drought and rapidly take up water after a rain. This example is a clear case of _____.
  a. resource partitioning
  b. competitive exclusion
  c. intraspecific competition
  d. commensalism
  e. a keystone species

27. In many ways, parasitism and predation are very similar types of interactions between species. Which of the following is NOT true about their differences?
  a. Parasites are usually much smaller than their hosts, but predators are usually larger than their prey.
  b. Parasites are usually much more numerous than their hosts, but predators are usually less numerous than their prey.
  c. Parasites usually don't immediately kill their hosts, but predators do usually immediately kill their prey.
  d. Parasites usually have no effect on their hosts, but predators usually harm their prey.

28. Following applications of insecticides to agricultural fields to control pest insects, sometimes the crops suffer MORE insect damage than if no pesticides were applied. Knowing what you know about interactions between species and the factors that regulate population sizes, what is the most likely explanation for this?
  a. The insecticides probably killed off most of the predators that previously kept the size of the plant-eating insect population from exploding. The insects then increased in number and did more damage to the plants.
  b. The insecticides probably killed off most of the competitors that previously kept the size of the plant-eating insect population from exploding. The insects then increased in number and did more damage to the plants.
  c. The insecticides probably weakened the defenses of the plants, making them more vulnerable to attack by the surviving plant-eating insects.
  d. The insecticides probably inhibited the growth of mycorrhizae and nitrogen-fixing bacteria on which the plants rely for nutrients. The plants were therefore weakened and more prone to attack by insects.

460

29. Corals are polyps of colenterates (cnidarians) that contain numerous algae in their tissues. The algae contain photopigments which give the corals their color. When stressed by high temperatures, water pollution, or similar shocks, many corals expel their algae and turn white, a process called "coral bleaching." This appears to help the coelenterates survive the initial shock, but if they do not recover their native algae quickly, they soon die. Similarly, the algae cannot live for long outside of the coelenterates' bodies. Based on this information, the relationship between the two organisms is most likely _____.

a. a mutualism

b. interspecific competition

c. a commensalism

d. a parasitism

e. a predation

30. Rabbits were first introduced from their native Europe into Australia in 1859. Lacking natural enemies in their new home they rapidly increased in numbers, spreading throughout the island nation. Their excessive grazing devastated many native plants, and they outcompeted many native animals as well. To control this menace, the myxoma virus, which infects only rabbits, was introduced from South America in 1950. In short order it reduced the rabbit population by an estimated 99%. However, after a few years the virus ceased to be an effective control of rabbit numbers. Closer examination indicated that, not only had the rabbits become more resistant to the virus, but the virus had also become less virulent. How would you describe this change in the relationship between the virus and the rabbit?

a. coevolution

b. convergent evolution

c. adaptive radiation

d. resource partitioning

31. The beaver, *Castor canadensis*, seldom reaches densities anywhere near those achieved by most other rodents. However, its effect on ecosystems can be enormous. By damming streams it creates ponds and wetlands. This can kill trees in the midst of an otherwise continuous stand of climax forest, making room for many aquatic and semiaquatic species. When the beaver moves on and the pond fills in, the meadow left behind also represents a new and different habitat type suitable for yet other species. In short, the beaver can dramatically increase the complexity of ecosystems, leaving behind a mosaic of habitat types that supports enormous biodiversity. It is clear from this description that the beaver is _____ in the forest ecosystem.

a. a keystone species   b. a pioneer species

c. a climax species   d. a dominant species

32. Boulders are often overturned by wave action during storms along the lower reaches of the rocky intertidal shore. Along the coast of Southern California, there is a fairly predictable sequence of species that colonize the bare rock as spores and then replace each other. This starts with the green algae *Ulva*, which is replaced after a year or so by various red algae and so on. This is an example of _____.

a. primary succession   b. secondary succession

c. aggressive mimicry   d. a keystone species

33. Fireflies use their amazing bioluminescence to find mates of the right species. Males fly around and emit a series of flashes in a pattern that differs from all other species. A female, perched nearby, may respond with her own species-specific signal. The male immediately flies towards her and, after a few more exchanges, it's wedded bliss! Well, not always. Females of a few species have learned to imitate other species' signals and, when their males arrive, they eat them. These *femme fatales* are exhibiting a form of _____.

a. aggressive mimicry   b. startle coloration

c. camouflage   d. warning coloration

e. chemical warfare

ESSAY CHALLENGE

1. Describe what an ecological niche is and why it is important to organisms.

2. Describe the competitive exclusion principle.

3. What is the intertidal zone?

4. What are some of the counteracting behaviors that moths and bats have evolved, and what are the implications of these behaviors?

5. Why do so many different types of butterflies have similar coloration as monarch butterflies?

6. What is mutualism?

7. You are studying the community of a small pond and discover two similar, small species of fish in your samples. You believe they may be competitors, but want scientific evidence to support or refute this "gut feeling." Briefly describe how you would go about this, including the types of studies you might conduct and kinds of findings you would expect if your hypothesis is true.

MEDIA ACTIVITIES

To access a Media Activity visit http://www.prenhall.com/audesirk7. Log in to the Web site selected by your instructor, navigate to this chapter, and select the appropriate Media Activity number.

40.1 Competition
Estimated time: 10 minutes

Explore what competition is and the different types of competition between and within species.

40.2 The Importance of Keystone Species
Estimated time: 5 minutes

Explore how the loss of a keystone species affects the community in which it lives.

40.3 Primary Succession: Glacier Bay Alaska
Estimated time: 10 minutes

Explore the process of succession in Glacier Bay, Alaska. View scientific data to determine how the pattern of succession by numerous tree species varies through the bay.

40.4 Web Investigation: Invasion of the Zebra Mussels
Estimated time: 30 minutes

As this chapter's *Case Study* in the textbook has pointed out, the zebra mussel has had profound effects on the economy and ecology of freshwater habitats in eastern and midwestern North America following its lightning-fast spread across the continent. We have already detailed a number of topics related to this species in the *Issues in Biology* feature from the previous chapter. Is there anything more to say? You betcha!

1. The huge reproductive potential, planktonic larvae, and desiccation-resistant adults (that survive for days attached to boats and inside the cooling pipes of their motors) of zebra mussels have allowed them to spread rapidly throughout the Great Lakes and nearby waters. However, several authors in the late 1980s, noting that the species' distribution was limited to cooler waters in Eurasia, predicted that it would not spread into the lower reaches of the Mississippi River due to its presumed intolerance of higher temperatures. Examining this animated map (http://www.nationalatlas.gov/zmussels1.html) showing the species spread across North America between 1988 and 1999, do you think this prediction was correct? How might the greater-than-expected genetic diversity of the species discussed in the Web link for the next question (below) contribute to this?

2. Studies have indicated that the original native range of the zebra mussel was limited to the Black Sea and Caspian Sea area of Russia and the Ukraine. The species spread westward throughout Europe in the late 1700s and early 1800s when a series of canals was built, linking these regions. It apparently jumped the Atlantic Ocean sometime around 1985 or 1986, appearing in Lake St. Claire (on the river connecting Lake Huron and Lake Erie), apparently brought across in the ballast water of transatlantic cargo ships. While several researchers initially presumed the invaders came over just once from the species' native range in Asia, recent genetic studies (http://www. sg.ohio-state.edu/PDFS/PUBLICATIONS/TWINELINE/2001/tl-ja-01.PDF) (summarized on page 3 of the linked document) suggest otherwise. Where does this study suggest the North American populations came from? Was it likely a single invasion or multiple invasions?

3. The *Case Study Revisited* in Chapter 40 of the textbook tells us that the round goby, another recent import from the Black and Caspian Sea area, feeds on zebra mussels both in its native range and in North America. However, it goes on to explain that this fish also has a nasty habit of eating the eggs of native fish. In what other ways (http://www.uwm.edu/Dept/GLWI/people/jjanssen/goby/) does this species negatively impact populations of other fish in the Great Lakes?

4. Zebra mussels are extremely efficient filter feeders. They strain small particles, including microscopic algae and detritus, from the water as they pump it across their gills. They are so good at this, in fact, that they have been credited with increasing water clarity in Lake Erie by reducing suspended algae concentrations. Some authorities have even proposed using zebra mussels to "clean up" murky "hyper-eutrophic" (literally, "overfed") lakes and ponds that have frequent blooms of nuisance blue-green algae (cyanobacteria). These blooms occur when there is an oversupply of nutrients to the waterbodies from agricultural and sewage runoff. However, one recent study has indicated that feeding by zebra mussels may actually help *cause* blooms of *Microcystis* (http://www.glerl.noaa.gov/res/Task_rpts/nsvander10-1.html), one of these nuisance species. How do the authors say this can happen?

5. Introduced species like the zebra mussel often explode in numbers initially as their natural enemies are left behind in the old country and potential enemies in their new range have not yet "evolved" ways of utilizing them. The linked document (http://sgnis.org/publicat/proceed/1994/515.pdf) provides evidence that which class of natural enemies (predator, parasites, or competitors) had begun interacting with zebra mussels in North America as early as 1993? Do the authors seem surprised by how rapidly these enemies apparently adapted to interacting with this foreign invader?

ISSUES IN BIOLOGY

What Is Happening to the Red-cockaded Woodpecker?

The red-cockaded woodpecker (http://www.tpwd.state.tx.us/nature/endang/animals/birds/rcw.htm) is an 8-inch-long, black-and-white striped woodpecker found only in the pinewoods of the southeastern United States. It is one of 21 species of woodpeckers found in North America, north of Mexico, and one of nine species in a guild of woodpeckers found in the southeastern United States. The red-cockaded woodpecker is an endangered species perched on the brink of extinction. In the words of Robert McFarlane, "It is a specialist competing in a world of generalists, a featherweight thrown headlong into the path of giant economic and management forces, clogging up the machinery, thanks to the Endangered Species Act." To understand the plight of the red-cockaded woodpecker and its importance to the southern pines ecosystem, we must examine the role that it plays in its community.

In a general sense, woodpeckers make their living by excavating nesting and roosting cavities in trees and foraging for insects on and under the bark of trees. However, each species has a unique way of going about this business—each species has a unique niche. Woodpeckers have evolved special adaptations in the structure of their feet, bill, skull, tongue, and even tail feathers to assist them in this excavating/foraging. Some species, such as the red-headed and downy woodpeckers, are more general in what they eat and in where and how they feed, whereas the red-cockaded woodpeckers (especially the females) and sapsuckers are much more specialized. Although other woodpeckers may forage more broadly among different kinds of trees, the red-cockaded woodpecker tends to limit its foraging to pine trees and takes a higher proportion of animal food, mostly ants, than does any other woodpecker. Specialization confers the advantage of superior ability to exploit one specific resource, but it also carries the greater risk of extinction when that resource declines or disappears.

The red-cockaded woodpecker (https://ecos.fws.gov/species_profile/SpeciesProfile?spcode=B04F) is a specialist, limited to the belt of southern pinewoods that stretch across the southern tier of states, from Texas through the deep south to Virginia. But it is not only a specialist in its feeding, it is also a specialist in the construction of nesting/roosting cavities. All woodpeckers excavate cavities in trees, but only the red-cockaded woodpecker regularly excavates cavities in living trees; the other species take advantage of the less resistant wood of dead trees. Excavating the wood of living trees is not an easy task, so the red-cockaded woodpeckers gain an advantage by choosing older trees, normally more than 60 to 80 years old. A fungus causing "red heart" (heartrot) infects the mature trees, its enzymes digesting the wood and making the heartwood more easily excavated. Excavating cavities in living trees, even infected trees, takes a long time, 6 months to 2 years, compared with the 6 to 10 days usually required by other species that work on dead trees. Thus, the cavities excavated in living trees by red-cockaded woodpeckers represent a very significant investment of time and energy and are, therefore, very valuable. Even though live trees represent a more costly investment for the red-cockaded woodpeckers, there is an advantage to using live trees. Live trees produce a resin when they are injured, and this resin surrounds the wound of the cavity opening where excavation has occurred. In fact, red-cockaded woodpeckers actually drill holes around the cavity opening to increase the flow of resin. The advantage is that this sticky resin apparently deters predation by snakes, which feed on nestlings in cavities. These cavities are also very important to other cavity-nesting animals, including other woodpeckers, other cavity-nesting birds, and mammals such as squirrels, as it is much easier to take over and perhaps enlarge, if necessary, an existing cavity than it is to excavate one from scratch.

Red-cockaded woodpeckers tend to live in clans, consisting of a breeding pair and a few offspring, normally males, who remain at home to help the parents raise more young. This system of young remaining to help their parents, rather than leaving to establish their own territories and find mates, is known as cooperative breeding; it usually arises when opportunities for establishing a territory and mating are in short supply. Thus, it appears that good territories are hard to find for these birds. To survive and reproduce, the average clan requires 175 to 250 acres of pinewoods to provide their specialized food requirements and their need for mature trees for nesting and roosting cavities.

The fate of the red-cockaded woodpecker is entangled in the economics of the southeastern United States, where timber is a major industry. The southern pinewoods once extended as a relatively unbroken expanse across the southeast, but our civilization has rendered this ecosystem into a patchwork of smaller, more isolated, managed forests. These forests, many managed by the U.S. Forest Service, are a major source of trees for the commercial timber industry. Timber companies prefer to harvest younger trees (less than 60 to 80 years old) before they mature and succumb to red heart; they prefer to harvest these trees in the most economical way, which usually means clear-cutting. One of the major problems for the forest industry in the southeast is the southern pine beetle. Although many insects feed on the green foliage of trees, the pine beetle lays its eggs under the bark of the trees, where the hatching larvae burrow through and feed on the soft cambium tissue. In this part of the country, pine beetles reach epidemic populations every 10 years or so, becoming a serious problem for the timber industry. To control pine beetle outbreaks, the Forest Service often allows clear-cutting of large areas of trees, including surrounding areas of noninfested trees to act as a buffer to the spread of the beetle. The beetle is a main item in the diet of many woodpecker species, including the red-cockaded, so healthy populations of woodpeckers might offer effective control over pine beetle outbreaks.

The southern pinewoods is a fire-maintained ecosystem, in which regular periodic fires are necessary to remove deadwood and prevent the saplings of hardwood species from overgrowing and replacing the pines in succession. These fires are most likely to occur in mature stands of forest where deadwood has accumulated and is another problem for the timber industry. But, fire is important in both nutrient cycling and in maintaining the community at a subclimax stage of the successional sequence, as the textbook points out in section 40.6, "Succession: How Do Community Interactions Cause Change over Time?" So, here lies the dilemma. How should the forests be managed (http://www.ur.ku.edu/News/97N/JanNews/Jan27/Biodiver.html): Should they be managed in a way that maintains an intact ecosystem, where red-cockaded woodpeckers and other species that depend on the woodpeckers can survive? Or should the forests be allowed to become the cheapest source of timber to support the needs of a growing human population? The result of forestry practices to date has been the reduction of the quantity and quality of southern pinewoods necessary to sustain healthy populations of the red-cockaded woodpecker; it is now threatened with extinction.

(Adapted from McFarlane, Robert W. 1992. *A Stillness in the Pines: The Ecology of the Red-Cockaded Woodpecker.* New York: W.W. Norton & Co.)

1. How would being a generalist or specialist make a species more or less likely to go extinct?

2. In what ways are red-cockaded woodpeckers important to other species of woodpeckers and to other animals in this community?

3. How is fire important to the ecology of the pinewoods ecosystem, and what issues does the importance of fire raise with respect to management of this ecosystem?

BIZARRE FACTS IN BIOLOGY

Gut and Run!

You are trapped in a dark corner, surrounded by enemies. You aren't carrying a weapon—how can you escape? What if you ripped open your body, covered your enemies with your guts, and ran off? This may sound like a scene from a science-fiction or horror film, but it is just another stressful day in the life of certain species of sea cucumbers (http://www.ucmp.berkeley.edu/echinodermata/holothuroidea.html).

Sea cucumbers are members of the phylum Echinodermata, which also includes sea urchins and sea stars. They are sluggish animals, creeping or burrowing along the bottom of the ocean. This slow mode of locomotion prevents sea cucumbers from quickly fleeing predators. Because they cannot outrun their enemies, sea cucumbers have developed a clever trick to buy time. When attacked by a predator, the sea cucumber expels some of its major organs, such as the respiratory tract, gonads, and intestines (http://www.calacademy.org/research/izg/echinoderm/conference/abst082.htm). The predator becomes entangled in the organs and will die if it cannot free itself.

Expelling major organs, a phenomenon known as evisceration (http://people.hofstra.edu/faculty/peter_c_daniel/Animal_Physiology/special_topics_spring2002/Sarah_Petrario/Autotomy_and_Eviseration.htm), would kill most organisms. However, sea cucumbers have the ability to regenerate. Undifferentiated cells in the damaged area multiply rapidly. The body signals the cells to organize and differentiate into the pattern of the lost limb or organ. If you cut a sea cucumber into many small pieces, you might expect each piece to develop into an independent organism. On the contrary, only a few of these pieces are capable of regeneration. One end of the sea cucumber acts as the center of regeneration, signaling the body to repair damaged limbs or organs. In some species, this center lies at the anterior end of the animal, near the mouth. If you cut such a sea cucumber in half, only the top (anterior) half would regenerate. The bottom (posterior) half would die, cut off from the signals vital for regeneration. This fact has practical importance to some Pacific Islanders who cut sea cucumbers in half to harvest their intestines (http://www.spc.org.nc/coastfish/News/BDM/13/04.Lambeth.html), which are subsequently eaten! They throw the remaining body wall halves back assuming they will both regenerate lost parts, but this may not be so.

Regeneration has a lot to offer. For many invertebrates, regeneration allows organisms to replace lost limbs. For sea cucumbers, it offers a unique way to escape predators. In other types of organisms, regeneration is a means of asexual reproduction. Scientists believe that studying animals who regenerate may offer insight into the regulation of cell differentiation in development as well as how the body provides the signals to repair damaged tissues.

References

Barnes, R. D. 1980. *Invertebrate Zoology*. Philadelphia: W. B. Saunders.

Barnes, R. S. K., Calow, P., and Olive, P. J. W. 1993. *Invertebrates: A New Synthesis*. Oxford: Blackwell Scientific.

1. Describe how the ability to regenerate limbs comes at the cost of reproductive fitness.

2. Compare the regeneration process with the process of normal development and cell differentiation.

3. Why do echinoderm species other than sea cucumbers, such as sea urchins and sea stars, not need to use the expulsion of tubules and/or evisceration for defense?

Twelve-Legged Frogs: A Serious Warning or Nothing New?

Twelve-legged frogs! Ever since 1996, when middle school students in Minnesota noticed an alarming proportion of deformed frogs, scientists have been debating (http://www.hartwick.edu/biology/def_frogs/) the cause (http://www.npsc.nbs.gov/narcam/backgrnd/backgrnd.htm) of these deformities.

Evidence suggests that a naturally occurring parasite (http://www.im.nbs.gov/naamp3/papers/54/54df.html) can explain many, but perhaps not all, of the abnormalities. Dr. Stan Sessions showed that the cyst stage of a type of fluke (a trematode) was sufficient to induce the development of extra legs in both frogs and salamanders. Look at this image (http://www.im.nbs.gov/naamp3/papers/54/54df_f5.html), and notice the fluke cysts on the left-hand side of the tadpole and the absence of cysts on the right-hand side. The left leg has been split in two, but the right leg looks normal. Sessions hypothesized that the cyst was acting as a physical disruption of the developing limb field. Using resin beads (http://www.hartwick.edu/biology/def_frogs/trem/new.html) to simulate the fluke cyst, he duplicated in his lab the limb deformities associated with the fluke infection.

Limb duplication deformities have recently been induced by fluke infections in the laboratory (Stopper *et al.*, 2002), adding credence to flukes as a cause of at least some of the deformities seen in nature. But chemicals may also play a part in fluke infection. Johnson and Sutherland (2003) "... suggest that exogenous agents (e.g., pesticides, nutrient run-off, introduced fishes) might be interacting with Ribeiroia [a fluke], resulting in elevated infection levels, and ... highlight the need for studies incorporating multiple stressor[s]." The recent (apparent) rise in the incidence of amphibian deformities could then be interpreted as increasing pesticide levels making the amphibians more susceptible to trematode infection (Kiesecker, 2002). However, other deformities, like missing and reduced limbs, may be due to pesticides or other chemicals alone. And increased UV-B levels, due to the breakdown of the ozone layer, could increase conversion of photo-sensitive pesticides into more toxic products.

While the situation is obviously quite complex, it is clear that fluke infections cause at least some of the reported amphibian deformities. And Johnson and Sutherland (2003) go on to indicate that all of this might make perfectly sound evolutionary sense, as "Under natural conditions, malformations might promote parasite transmission by increasing the susceptibility of infected amphibians to predation by definitive hosts [water birds]." As a result, these deformities may allow the trematodes to increase the chances of completing their complex life cycle, which includes stages parasitizing two intermediate hosts (snails and amphibians) before moving on to mature inside their definitive host.

References

Benno Meyer-Rochow, V., and Koebke, J. 1986. A study of the extra extremity in a five-legged rana temporaria. *Zoologischer Anzeiger* 217:1–13.

Bishop, D. W., and Hamilton, R. 1947. Polydactyly and limb duplication occurring naturally in the tiger salamander, ambystoma tigrinum. *Science* 106:641–42.

Johnson, P. T. J., and Sutherland, D. R. 2003. Amphibian deformities and Ribeiroia infection: An emerging helminthiasis. *Trends in Parasitology* 19:332-335.

Kiesecker, J. M. 2002. Synergism between trematode infection and pesticide exposure: A link to amphibian limb deformities in nature? *Proceedings of the National Academy of Sciences of the United States of America* 99:9900-9904.

Muneoka, K., Holler-Dinsmore, G. V., and Bryant, S. V. 1986. Pattern discontinuity, polarity and directional intercalation in axolotl limbs. *Journal of Embryology and Experimental Morphology* 93:51-72.

Sessions, S. K. "Evidence That Trematodes Cause Deformities, Including Extra Limbs, in Amphibians." (http://www.im.nbs.gov/naamp3/papers/54/54df.html)*The North American Amphibian Monitoring Program Third Annual Meeting 1997*. Sessions, S. K., and Ruth, S. B. 1990. An explanation for naturally occurring supernumerary limbs in amphibians. *Journal of Experimental Zoology* 245:38–47.

Stopper G. F, Hecker, L., and Franssen, R A., and Sessions, S. K. 2002. How trematodes cause limb deformities in amphibians. *Journal of Experimental Zoology* 294:252-263.

1. How could you design an experiment that would falsify the claim that the flukes are responsible for the increase in frog deformities recently observed, if indeed the hypothesis was wrong?

2. Some of the deformities involve limbs growing out of the frogs' chests. Could the fluke hypothesis explain this type of deformity? If so, how? If not, why not?

3. If the fluke hypothesis story is correct, how could you explain why frogs are growing more limbs but other animals in the same area are not?

KEY TERMS

aggressive mimicry	competitive exclusion	intraspecific competition	resource partitioning
biome	principle	keystone species	secondary succession
camouflage	disturbance	mimicry	startle coloration
climax community	ecological niche	mutualism	subclimax
coevolution	exotic species	parasite	succession
commensalism	interspecific competition	pioneer	symbiosis
community	intertidal zone	primary succession	warning coloration

ANSWER KEY

SELF TEST

1. d
2. e
3. e
4. d
5. d
6. e
7. d
8. e
9. c
10. d
11. d
12. c
13. c
14. c
15. b
16. e
17. zebra mussels
18. coevolution
19. resource partitioning
20. Mimicry
21. aggressive mimicry
22. climax
23. A. grown in separate flasks
    B. grown in the same flask
24. A. empty field
    B. grasses
    C. sedges
    D. bramble, bushes
    E. pines
    F. hardwoods, climax forest
25. d
26. a
27. d
28. a
29. a
30. a
31. a
32. a
33. a

ESSAY CHALLENGE

1. An ecological niche encompasses an organism's entire way of life, from where it lives to the kinds of foods it eats to the range of environmental conditions it tolerates.
2. If two organisms share the same ecological niche, one of them will eventually outcompete the other, if forced to live together.
3. The intertidal zone is the small area of shoreline that is sometimes covered with salt water and sometimes dry, depending on whether the tide is high or low.
4. Bats have evolved echolocation to find the moths, and some moths have developed the ability to hear the echolocation from bats. When the moths hear these clicks, they take evasive action by flying erratically. To counter this, bats may switch frequencies to avoid detection. Moths may produce their own clicks to confuse bats. Bats may then stay silent to listen for moths.
5. Monarchs take up some poison from the milkweed plants they eat during their caterpillar stage. This poison makes birds sick if they eat monarch butterflies. Monarchs are thus somewhat immune from predation by birds. Other butterflies who happen to look enough like monarchs also benefit from this immunity from predation.
6. A mutualistic interaction benefits both individuals.
7. First, the two must utilize the same (limiting) resources, so you should collect data on their niches to see if they overlap. Are they eating the same types and sizes of foods in the same parts of the pond, selecting the same breeding sites at the same time of the year, etc.? Second, you have to demonstrate that the presence of each is having a harmful impact on the other. You could do this by setting up duplicate ponds and removing one or the other species from each pond and recording the effects on the other, comparing your results to unaltered controls. If they do compete, removing either should benefit the other (increasing the size of the population, their growth rate, etc.). Also, you could add individuals of one or the other and record the effect on the other similarly. If they do compete, this should harm the other.

MEDIA ACTIVITIES

40.4 Web Investigation: Invasion of the Zebra Mussels

1. Since zebra mussels did expand their range into the lower Mississippi River by the mid 1990s, it is clear that they can tolerate the higher water temperatures there. The high genetic diversity found in the North American populations of zebra mussels makes it more likely that at least some of the individuals will possess tolerance to warmer temperatures.
2. The results of this study indicate that North American zebra mussels probably came from many sources in northwestern and northcentral Europe. The evidence suggests there were multiple invasions of the species into this continent.
3. The round goby's territorial behavior has allowed them to outcompete native fish species for food, shelter, and spawning areas. Predation by round gobies can also significantly depress the abundances of crustaceans like amphipods and isopods in an area, which many young of native fish species rely on for food.
4. The authors suggest that *Microcystis* may actually increase in importance as a result of zebra mussel

grazing as the mollusks selectively reject these toxic algae in their pseudofeces (particles that were filtered but not ingested). Since they ingest and hence destroy less noxious phytoplankton (literally "plant drifters") like green algae and diatoms, they can actually shift these systems towards dominance by blue-greens.

5. This study looked at parasite infestations in zebra mussels collected from the St. Lawrence River. The authors did seem surprised that these parasites, which must normally undergo an extended period of coevolution with their hosts to utilize them fully, had already infested them just a few years after they arrived at the study sites.

ISSUES IN BIOLOGY

1. As specialists depend on just one or a few resources to survive, they are more likely to go extinct if those resources decline. Generalists can simply switch to other resources and survive.

2. Red-cockaded woodpeckers excavate cavities in living pine trees that can be taken over by other woodpeckers, other cavity-nesting birds, or mammals such as squirrels.

3. Fire recycles nutrients and destroys saplings of encroaching hardwood species that would otherwise replace the pines in succession. As a result, it maintains the community in a subclimax stage. If fires are suppressed, the pines will decline and this crucial resource for red-cockaded woodpeckers will be lost.

BIZARRE FACTS IN BIOLOGY

Gut and Run!

1. If you have to utilize stored materials to rebuild lost body parts, those materials are not available to produce gametes. Therefore, reproductive output will decline.

2. In normal development, undifferentiated stem cells multiply and most of the "daughter" cells differentiate to make up all of the varied cell types in the adult organism. Regeneration is similar, as undifferentiated cells in the area of the lost body part also multiply and differentiate to replace lost cells, tissues, and organs.

3. They have spiny skin and other defenses that sea cucumbers lack.

Twelve-Legged Frogs: A Serious Warning or Nothing New?

1. It is hard to prove a negative, i.e., that trematodes are not causing the deformities; though, finding deformed tadpoles with no sign of infection would support that hypothesis. However, you can prove that other factors may (also) be causing these problems, as was done after the initial discovery of deformed frogs in Minnesota. Researchers took water from the pond in question and made serial dilutions of it with "pure" water. As expected, if it were a chemical agent, the samples that contained the highest concentrations of pond water also produced the most deformities in the laboratory.

2. The fluke hypothesis requires flukes be present at the site of the deformity to mechanically interfere with normal development. If flukes are observed during limb formation in those areas, those deformities could be caused by flukes. If they are absent, some other cause must be considered.

3. Other animals might not be subjected to parasitism by the same or similar parasites, they might not be made more susceptible to infection by the same chemical agents, or they might simply have a sufficiently different developmental pattern to make them immune to these deformities.

CHAPTER 41: HOW DO ECOSYSTEMS WORK?

AT-A-GLANCE

SELF TEST

1. The base of the energy pyramid represents _____.

   a. producers
   b. decomposers
   c. primary consumers
   d. secondary consumers
   e. tertiary consumers

2. Which of the following are heterotrophic?

   a. producers
   b. decomposers
   c. primary consumers
   d. secondary consumers
   e. b, c, and d are all correct.

3. Of the following trophic levels, which would support the fewest organisms?

   a. producer
   b. decomposer
   c. primary consumer
   d. secondary consumer
   e. tertiary consumer

4. Which of the following trophic levels is always the final link in the food chain?

   a. producer
   b. decomposer
   c. primary consumer
   d. secondary consumer
   e. tertiary consumer

5. In the carbon cycle, carbon (C) is returned to the atmosphere by _____.

   a. photosynthesis
   b. evaporation of water
   c. burning of fossil fuels
   d. respiration of plants and animals
   e. c and d are both correct.

6. For which of the following nutrients is rock a major reservoir?

   a. water
   b. oxygen
   c. carbon
   d. nitrogen
   e. phosphorus

7. Which of the following is/are a major contributor to the problem of acid deposition?
   a. oxygen
   b. carbon dioxide
   c. sulfur dioxide
   d. nitrogen oxides
   e. Both c and d are correct.

8. DDT and other substances that undergo biological magnification are dangerous because they are _____.
   a. biodegradable
   b. not biodegradable
   c. fat soluble
   d. water soluble
   e. Both b and c are correct.

9. Which of the following nutrients remains chemically the same as it is cycled through the food chain and is generally not used in the synthesis of new molecules?
   a. water
   b. carbon
   c. nitrogen
   d. phosphorus
   e. Both c and d are correct.

10. Which of the following materials cycle through an ecosystem: 1) carbon, 2) nitrogen, 3) oxygen, 4) water, and 5) energy?
    a. 1 through 5
    b. 1 through 4
    c. 1 through 3
    d. only 1 and 2
    e. only 4 and 5

11. Although the textbook suggests that organisms remove nutrients from the reservoirs (where nutrients are stored), some biologists distinguish between the "reservoir," where nutrients are stored but not directly available to living organisms, and the "exchange pool," where nutrients are directly available, in usable form, to living organisms. For example, atmospheric carbon dioxide would be considered to be in the exchange pool for plants. Using this distinction, for plants, atmospheric nitrogen would be in the _____.
    a. reservoir
    b. exchange pool
    c. biotic community
    d. all of the above

12. What term describes a photosynthetic alga?
    a. producer
    b. autotroph
    c. consumer
    d. heterotroph
    e. Either a or b is correct.
    f. Either c or d is correct.

13. A spider that feeds on an aphid that in turn feeds on germinating blades of wheat would belong to what consumer category?
    a. herbivore
    b. primary consumer
    c. secondary consumer
    d. tertiary consumer

14. What are macronutrients?
    a. large molecules that provide a source of energy when ingested
    b. molecules that are required in large quantities for an organism to survive
    c. protein molecules
    d. all of the above

15. How is nitrogen released back to the atmosphere once it has been incorporated into the body of an organism?
    a. nitrogen fixation
    b. through a process involving a symbiotic association with a legume
    c. by decomposers and denitrifying bacteria
    d. Both a and b are correct.

16. Why is acid rain, or acid deposition, considered to be harmful?
    a. Moisture in the air becomes acidified and then falls on plants and the soil below, harming them.
    b. Acid rain leeches essential nutrients out of the soil (e.g., potassium and calcium), and kills decomposers in the soil.
    c. Dead, or weakened, plants make the soil much more susceptible to erosion.
    d. all of the above

17. Which of the following is NOT considered to be a greenhouse gas?

    a. oxygen   **b.** water vapor

    c. methane   **d.** carbon dioxide

18. Primary, secondary, and tertiary consumers are all names for different _____ levels.

19. Organisms that eat the remnants of other living things, such as leaves, deceased animals, and other "litter," are called _____ feeders.

20. The law that dictates how much energy passes between trophic levels (such as between primary consumers and secondary consumers) is called the _____ law.

21. Cyanobacteria can turn the nitrogen in the atmosphere into a usable form for other organisms. This is called _____.

22. The water cycle is also called the _____ cycle.

23. Bald eagle eggshells became dangerously brittle because the eagles had eaten fish from water polluted by the insecticide _____.

24. The image below indicates the different levels of productivity in the various ecosystems. Label these systems correctly.

25. Food chains are typically discussed in terms of trophic level. Using the image below, label the trophic levels for the terrestrial food chain.

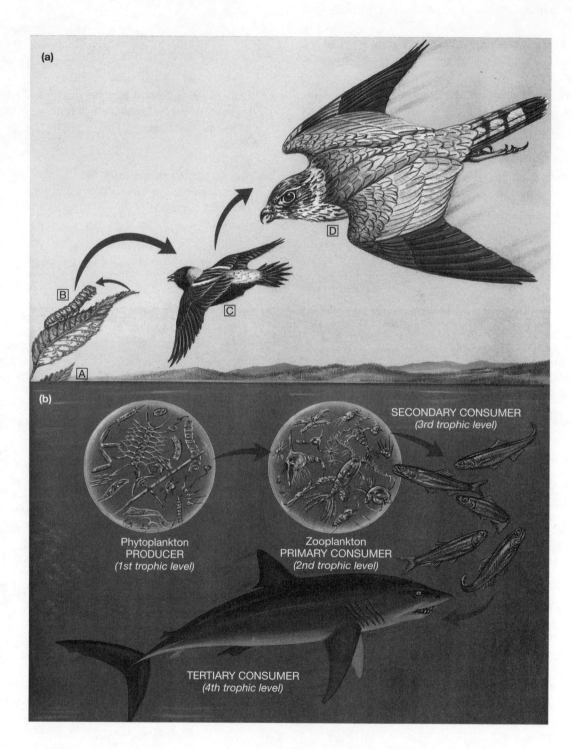

26. The image above indicates an energy pyramid. Complete the pyramid by providing the correct labels and the correct caloric equivalents.

27. Water is essential to life on Earth. The diagram below is meant to demonstrate the hydrologic cycle. Fill in the boxes with the appropriate labels.

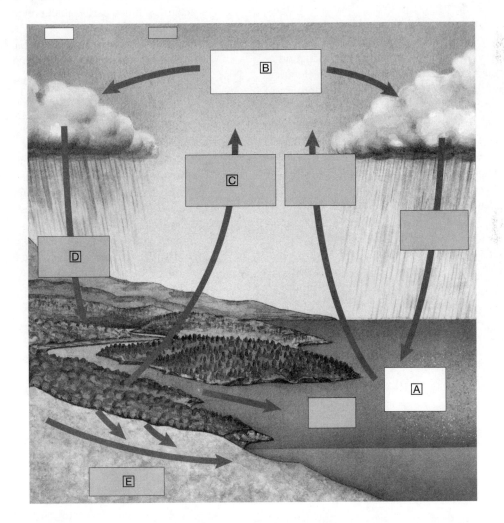

475

28. An ecologist studying a plot of ground in the tundra excludes all herbivores from her study area and estimates the plant biomass at 530 grams per square meter. She comes back to the same plot one year later and estimates that the biomass has increased to 670 grams per square meter. The difference in these two values, 140 grams, represents the _____ for that year.
   a. biological magnification
   b. food chain length
   c. food web complexity
   d. net primary productivity
   e. trophic transfer efficiency

29. As one moves from the equator towards the poles, the net primary productivity of forest ecosystems generally _____.
   a. decreases
   b. increases
   c. remains the same
   d. first decreases and then increases
   e. first increases and then decreases

30. Conserving electricity by using fluorescent lights instead of incandescent lights and turning off lights and appliances when not in use _____.
   a. actually increases greenhouse gas production as the predominant fossil fuel–powered electrical generating plants consume large quantities of carbon dioxide when they are operating
   b. has no effect on greenhouse gas production because nearly all electricity in this country is produced by nuclear reactors and renewable wind and solar generating stations
   c. helps reduce greenhouse gas production because the majority of electricity in this country is still produced by fossil fuel–powered generating plants. Since these plants produce carbon dioxide when they operate, conserving electricity reduces greenhouse gas production.

31. Of the solar energy that strikes the outer reaches of the Earth's atmosphere, approximately what percentage ends up in carbohydrate molecules produced by photosynthetic organisms?
   a. 0.03%   b. 1%
   c. 3%   d. 10%
   e. 90%

32. Earthworms are _____.
   a. detritus feeders
   b. herbivores
   c. primary consumers
   d. producers
   e. secondary consumers

33. So far, global warming has been documented to be causing _____.
   a. changes in precipitation patterns on land, with some areas subjected to more severe and frequent droughts, and other areas more frequent and severe floods
   b. melting of ice sheets and retreat of glaciers at unprecedented rates
   c. shifts in the distribution and abundance of a number of plant and animal species
   d. shifts in the timing of spring events, which are occurring much earlier than previously
   e. all of the above
   f. None of the above. To date, global warming has had no effects on any of the things mentioned above.

34. Since the Clean Air Act Amendments of 1990 went into effect, acid precipitation has _____.
   a. ceased to be a problem anywhere in the United States
   b. declined somewhat in many areas but is still a problem, even continuing to get worse in some areas like the Adirondack Mountains of New York
   c. continued on as before, unabated as the regulations are not being enforced
   d. actually gotten much worse, as the controls were poorly planned and implemented and exacerbated the problem

ESSAY CHALLENGE

1. What are the two underlying laws of ecosystem function?

2. Describe the differences between primary, secondary, and tertiary consumers.

3. Describe the 10% law and how it explains the ratio of primary consumers to secondary (or tertiary) consumers.

4. Explain why the largest nutrient reservoirs are typically found in the abiotic, or nonliving, parts of ecosystems.

5. What makes the hydrologic cycle different from other types of nutrient cycles?

6. Explain how a global temperature rise of 0.5 to 1.0 degrees C can have such a large effect on life on this planet.

7. Explain how the demise of the salmon population in a stream in the Pacific Northwest can impact the surrounding forest.

8. Despite large reductions in sulfur dioxide emissions after the Clean Air Act Amendments were passed in 1990, acid rain continues to damage ecosystems in several areas such as the Adirondack Mountains of New York State. Explain why this is and what it tells us about acid rain.

9. While few of us operate large fossil fuel-powered generating plants, we can all decrease the production of greenhouse gases we necessitate by our lifestyles. List a few of the things you can do to reduce your "ecological footprint" with respect to global warming.

MEDIA ACTIVITIES

To access a Media Activity visit http://www.prenhall.com/audesirk7. Log in to the Web site selected by your instructor, navigate to this chapter, and select the appropriate Media Activity number.

41.1 Ecology Models—Building a Food Web
Estimated time: 10 minutes

Explore how energy and nutrients are transferred in a food web and the roles that organisms play within the ecosystem.

41.2 The Global Carbon Cycle and Greenhouse Effect
Estimated time: 10 minutes

Explore how carbon moves between the atmosphere, oceans, rocks, and living organisms. See how the accumulation of carbon in the atmosphere leads to a rise in the earth's temperature.

41.3 Web Investigation: When the Salmon Return
Estimated time: 30 minutes

This chapter's case study documents the plight of salmon populations in the Pacific Northwest, and indicates how the Endangered Species Act (http://www.nwr.noaa.gov/1salmon/salmesa/pubs/esabrochure.html) has been used as a weapon to help preserve their dwindling wild stocks. It also outlines the importance of the salmon for the productivity of forests (http://web.uvic.ca/~reimlab/reimchen_ecoforestry.pdf) along the rivers and streams in which they spawn.

1. Dams form obvious barriers for adult salmon migrating upstream to spawn, and fish ladders have been developed to help them bypass these hurdles. But dams are also significant obstacles for juveniles migrating downstream to the sea. Many are killed as they pass through the turbines of hydroelectric generators, and others become disoriented by water pooling behind the dams and never reach the sea. To alleviate this, the U.S. Army Corps of Engineers has for years transported millions of juvenile salmon downstream in trucks and barges (http://www.defenders.org/wildlife/new/marine/salmon/dam.html). However, many critics have called this a costly boondoggle that doesn't work. What are the four harmful effects (http://www.wildsalmon.org/library_files/barging_trucking_pr.pdf) of this practice listed in the linked article? Also, dams on the Snake River hold water in the river longer, allowing it to warm more. How does this factor alone impact salmon?

2. Much of the Pacific Northwest gets a large percentage of its energy from hydroelectric dams. A proposal to breach the four dams on the lower Snake River to allow endangered native salmon stocks to recover has been criticized by some as environmentally and economically unsound. They claim that this move would necessitate increased burning of fossil fuels to supply the region's energy needs, which would increase greenhouse gas production and the cost of energy. However, a recent study by the RAND Corporation has indicated that removing those dams would actually benefit both the environment and the region's economy, as well as help save the salmon. What percentage of the region's energy does the report claim is produced by these four dams, and what does the report propose to replace this?

3. A published study of salmon in a hatchery in British Columbia, Canada, has documented a 25% decrease in egg size over just a few generations (http://www.helsinki.fi/ml/ekol/egru/pdf/science299.pdf). While this allows females to lay more eggs in a single clutch, it is considered maladaptive for fish spawning in the wild, and hence potentially disastrous if these fish pass the trait on to endangered wild salmon stocks. Why is small egg size such a risk in the wild? What advantage does larger egg size carry with it?

4. Some have argued that conservation of wild salmon stocks is unnecessary because fish farmed in screened enclosures in nearshore marine and estuarine habitats can replace them as a human food source. However, what five problems with farmed salmon (http://www.sierraclub.org/e-files/wild_salmon.asp) are identified in the linked article?

ISSUES IN BIOLOGY

What Are Bioaccumulation and Endocrine-disrupting Chemicals?

Energy moves through Earth's ecosystems in one direction, from the sun, entering food webs through photosynthesis, passing from one trophic level to another, and ultimately back out into space as heat. The second law of thermodynamics and section 41.2 of your textbook tell us that these energy transfers are inefficient. In contrast, matter remains on Earth, usually within a single ecosystem, where it is constantly cycled between the biotic and abiotic components in one of the biogeochemical cycles. One example is the carbon cycle [http://www.arm.gov/docs/education/globwarm/carbcyexpert.html (See section 41.3 of your textbook, "How Do Nutrients Move Within and Among Ecosystems?")].

Biological magnification, or bioaccumulation, which has been recognized in human and wildlife populations for years, occurs because of these different fates of matter and energy in ecosystems and because some materials (especially heavy metals and organic chlorine chemicals) are poorly metabolized or not metabolized by consumers and are stored in fat. Rachel Carson (http://www.rachelcarson.org/) discussed the process (without using these terms) in *Silent Spring*, published in 1962. The discovery of high DDT concentrations in human breast milk in the late 1960s was probably a major factor leading to the banning of DDT in the United States in 1972. Other examples are described in the textbook.

Despite these findings, we know relatively little about the effects of the accumulation of toxic materials in humans and wildlife. Environmental toxicologists recognize at least 50 chemicals, mostly pesticides, that are widely distributed in ecosystems and are reported to have disruptive effects on reproductive and endocrine function in wildlife and humans (*Envir. Health Perspec.* 101:378–384). For several reasons, the potential for adverse health effects exists even when these toxins are present in the environment at exceedingly low concentrations. Natural hormones in living vertebrates are found in concentrations of tenths of a part per billion. Significant developmental effects have been demonstrated for embryonic mice experiencing hormone concentration differences of a few tenths of parts per trillion. Perhaps most importantly, animals feeding at higher trophic levels in an ecosystem may bioaccumulate these toxins to levels 3 billion times the environmental level (for example, polar bears in the Arctic).

The term endocrine disrupters (http://e.hormone.tulane.edu/) is preferred, rather than environmental estrogens, because in addition to the estrogenic (feminizing) effect of certain of these toxins, androgenizing (masculinization) and growth effects have also been documented. These effects include such wildlife impacts as thyroid dysfunction, decreased fertility, decreased hatching success, gross birth deformities, and behavioral abnormalities. The synthetic hormone DES has had some of the same effects on humans. The effects differ on embryos and adults; more typically affect embryos (and at lower concentrations) and may appear long after exposure to the environmental toxin. Given the proven effects of DES on humans, and the similarities of chemical structure or function of these materials, the possibility (some scientists would say probability) that they might affect humans is very real. Recent evidence of decreased sperm counts (http://ehpnet1.niehs.nih.gov/docs/1997/105-11/swan.html) among males of industrialized countries as compared with those in nonindustrialized countries further raises concerns.

(From Colborn, T., D. Dumanoski, and J. P. Myers. 1996. *Our Stolen Future.* New York: Plume/Penguin Books.)

1. How do matter and energy act differently in ecosystems?

2. How does this difference lead to biomagnification in organisms at the top of the food chain/food web?

3. Why is the widespread occurrence of endocrine disruptive chemicals a concern for humans?

BIZARRE FACTS IN BIOLOGY

Giant Worms

As you travel down toward the bottom of the ocean, you are startled to learn that the temperature outside the submarine is more than 100 degrees Celsius and that the pressure is extremely high. Without your submarine light source, the area would be in total darkness. Scanners also sense that the water is full of toxic chemicals. This is definitely not the most hospitable environment that you have encountered on your journey, yet a diverse array of organisms call this place home. You look out of the submarine window and see an amazing landscape. Some of the organisms are somewhat familiar to you—crabs, sea anemones, giant clams, shrimps, and a few fish (http://people.whitman.edu/~yancey/realindex.html). However, the most conspicuous object you see really catches your attention. Large, white tubes project up from the seafloor. Bright red plumes extend out from the top of the tubes. Are they plants or animals?

The tube creature (http://www.ucmp.berkeley.edu/annelida/pogonophora.html) is a giant worm. On closer inspection, you cannot find anything resembling a mouth or digestive system. The bright red color turns out to be the protein hemoglobin. In the worm, the hemoglobin carries hydrogen sulfide throughout its body. The tube worm uses the hydrogen sulfide to make the energy it needs to make glucose but not directly. Rather, a bacterium living in all of the worm's cells uses hydrogen sulfide as an energy source to convert water and carbon dioxide into glucose. The worm gets food and the bacteria get a safe place to live.

It turns out that the worm and bacterium are interdependent. Two organisms that interact to the benefit of both organisms exist in a mutualistic symbiotic relationship (http://www.baylorhealth.com/proceedings/13_3/13_3_dimijian.html). If either member of the mutualistic relationship dies, the other organism will likely perish as well.

1. What could be the evolutionary benefits of a mutualistic relationship such as the one observed between the tube worm and bacteria?

2. What would be the impact on the ecosystem if the hydrothermal vent sealed shut and no more gases (hydrogen sulfide) were emitted?

3. Compare and contrast the way photosynthetic organisms and chemoautotrophic bacteria obtain energy.

KEY TERMS

acid deposition	decomposer	greenhouse effect	omnivore
autotroph	deforestation	greenhouse gas	primary consumer
biodegradable	detritus feeder	herbivore	producer
biogeochemical cycle	energy pyramid	heterotroph	reservoir
biological magnification	food chain	hydrologic cycle	secondary consumer
biomass	food web	net primary productivity	tertiary consumer
carnivore	fossil fuel	nitrogen fixation	trophic level
consumer	global warming	nutrient cycle	

ANSWER KEY

SELF TEST

1. a
2. e
3. e
4. b
5. e
6. e
7. e
8. e
9. a
10. b
11. a
12. e
13. c
14. b
15. c
16. d
17. a

18. trophic
19. detritus
20. 10%
21. nitrogen fixation
22. hydrologic
23. DDT
24. A. open ocean
    B. estuary
    C. tropical rain forest
    D. tundra
    E. continental shelf
    F. coniferous forest
    G. grassland
    H. deciduous forest
    I. desert
25. A. first trophic level
    B. second trophic level
    C. third trophic level
    D. fourth trophic level
26. A. secondary consumer (10 calories)
    B. producer (1000 calories)
    C. primary consumer (100 calories)
    D. tertiary consumer (1 calorie)
27. A. water in ocean (reservoir)
    B. water vapor in atmosphere
    C. evaporation
    D. precipitation
    E. groundwater seepage
28. d
29. a
30. c
31. a
32. a
33. e
34. b

ESSAY CHALLENGE

1. One of the laws indicates that energy moves in a one-way direction through communities within ecosystems. The other indicates that nutrients constantly cycle and recycle within and among ecosystems.

2. Primary consumers are often the most numerous and eat plants; they are herbivores. Secondary consumers are the organisms that eat herbivores; they are carnivores. When carnivores eat other carnivores, they are considered tertiary consumers.

3. The 10% law suggests that only 10% of the energy produced at one trophic level actually is transferred to the next higher trophic level.

4. The main building blocks of life are often inorganic molecules. For example, carbon atoms are found in carbon dioxide gas in the atmosphere and oceans and also found in fossil fuels.

5. In the hydologic cycle, water does not change its chemical form. (Carbon, nitrogen, and sulfur all change chemical forms in their respective cycles.)

6. Rising average temperatures can mean that the polar ice caps can melt, flooding many large population areas, as well as putting huge selection pressure on many species that require colder conditions to live.

7. During their life at sea, the salmon acquire large quantities of nitrogen and other nutrients (like phosphorus and calcium) that they bring into the forest locked up inside their tissues when they return to the stream to spawn. When they die after spawning, these nutrients are released by predators, decomposers, and/or detritus feeders into the nearby forests. When the salmon populations crash, this fertilizer effect is lost, resulting in decreased production in the forest.

8. While the legislation reduced sulfur dioxide emissions, emissions of nitrogen oxides, primarily from fuels for transportation, actually increased dramatically. As a result, the acid rain problem persists downwind of these emissions where bedrock and soils cannot buffer these acid inputs. To truly stop acid rain, further reductions, especially in nitrogen oxide emissions, are needed.

9. You can choose more fuel-efficient transportation, car pool, and/or take public transportation to reduce your personal production of greenhouse gases. Also, since most electricity is still produced by burning fossil fuels, conserving electricity will also reduce greenhouse gases produced on your behalf. Insulating your home and turning down the thermostat also helps. Planting trees can actually take greenhouse gases out of the air.

MEDIA ACTIVITIES

41.3   Web Investigation: When the Salmon Return

1. The four harmful effects of transporting juveniles listed in the article are: 1) the stressful, crowded conditions can spread disease and sap strength; 2) disruption of homing instincts; 3) increased predation by birds and other fish when disoriented salmon are dumped from the barges; and 4) disruption of the normal changes that prepare the young for the transition to salt water. Also, the dams increase water temperatures to levels these cold-water fish cannot tolerate.

2. The report claims that less than 5% of the region's energy is produced by these four dams. It goes on to predict that investment in increased energy efficiency and clean, renewable energy alternatives could easily and cheaply replace this lost potential.

3. Larger eggs give rise to larger juveniles with larger reserves of energy. In wild salmon, this can mean the difference between surviving the perils of early life or dying of starvation. So salmon that produce many, smaller eggs may have far fewer offspring reaching maturity than those that produce fewer, larger eggs.

4. The article claims that farming salmon cannot replace declining wild stocks because: 1) farming creates intense pollution as wastes accumulate; 2) escaping farmed fish are often exotics which compete with or displace native stock; 3) farmed salmon are expensive; 4) farmed salmon are contaminated with antibiotics and are less nutritious; and 5) farmed salmon do not taste as good.

ISSUES IN BIOLOGY

1. Matter is constantly cycled and recycled within and among ecosystems, never leaving the Earth. Energy, however, is constantly supplied to Earth's ecosystems from the sun in the form of electromagnetic radiation, enters the food chain during photosynthesis, and is passed from one organism to another, constantly being degraded. Ultimately, all of the energy is lost back to space, but now in the form of heat.

2. As the herbivores are eating large quantities of plants, and carnivores are eating large quantities of herbivores, etc., in order to obtain enough energy to run their lives, they are also accumulating any fat-soluble, degradation-resistant chemical toxins their prey have in their systems. As a result, the further up the trophic pyramid you go, the higher the concentration of these materials you find in their bodies.

3. These chemicals are known to cause reproductive problems, birth deformities, and behavioral abnormalities in humans, and suspected to cause cancers as well, even when present only in small quantities.

BIZARRE FACTS IN BIOLOGY

1. In mutualistic relationships both species benefit. Usually, at least one gains access to resources it would otherwise be unable to acquire. In the relationship described here, the worm benefits as it gains access to an energy and nutrient (material) source in the form of the glucose produced by the bacteria, some of which is passed on to the worm. The bacteria gain a safe place to live close to their energy source (the hydrogen sulfide coming out of the thermal vent), so both benefit.

2. The most obvious impact would be that the bacteria would be unable to synthesize glucose, which is at the base of the entire food web. As a result, the ecosystem would rapidly run out of usable energy and collapse. Also, because the vent releases superheated gas into an otherwise frigid region, many organisms would probably die due to the cold.

3. Both use carbon dioxide as a reactant and produce glucose as the primary product. However, photosynthetic organisms obtain the energy to link carbon atoms together from photons of light, absorbed by photopigments like chlorophyll, while chemosynthetic bacteria get their energy from hydrogen sulfide.

CHAPTER 42: EARTH'S DIVERSE ECOSYSTEMS

AT-A-GLANCE

SELF TEST

1. Which of these terrestrial biomes is the driest?
   a. chaparral
   b. coniferous forest
   c. deciduous forest
   d. desert
   e. grassland
   f. rain forest

2. Low-nutrient freshwater lakes are termed _____.
   a. eutrophic
   b. oligotrophic

3. Biological diversity is greatest in which terrestrial biome?
   a. chaparral
   b. desert
   c. grassland
   d. taiga
   e. tropical rain forest
   f. tundra

4. Because of reduced evaporation due to fog, many coastal regions bordering deserts are characterized by small woody plants with adaptations to conserve water. What is the name of this biome?
   a. chaparral
   b. savanna
   c. steppe
   d. taiga
   e. tundra

5. In what terrestrial biome would you expect the most precipitation?
   a. chaparral
   b. grassland
   c. northern coniferous forest
   d. temperate deciduous forest
   e. tropical rain forest

6. The Great Basin Desert in Nevada and Utah is a result of _____.
   a. a lack of drainage
   b. overgrazing
   c. a permanent high barometric pressure zone
   d. poor soil
   e. a rain shadow

7. Based on what you know about winds and air pressure zones, at which latitude(s) would you expect to find deserts?

   a. the equator

   b. 30 degrees

   c. 40 degrees

   d. 60 degrees

   e. 80 degrees

8. Which of the following factors naturally influences Earth's climate?

   a. distribution of land and water

   b. elevation of land

   c. angle at which sunlight strikes the planet

   d. air currents

   e. All of these are factors that influence climate.

9. In what terrestrial biome would you expect the climate to allow the most biological productivity?

   a. chaparral

   b. grassland

   c. northern coniferous forest

   d. temperate deciduous forest

   e. temperate rain forest

   f. tropical rain forest

10. Why are so many desert animals active only at night (nocturnal)?

    a. Reflection of light from the bright sun makes it too difficult for visual predators to hunt.

    b. The surface temperature of the ground would be too hot to walk on.

    c. Temperatures are lower and humidity is higher at night.

11. On which side of a mountain range would you expect the total annual rainfall to be the greatest?

    a. on the side first struck by the prevailing winds (i.e., wind that would be forced to travel up the mountains)

    b. on the side of the mountains where the air is flowing toward sea level

12. Which of the following is NOT one of the four fundamental resources required for life?

    a. nutrients

    b. energy

    c. water vapor

    d. suitable temperature

13. Which of the biomes is home to the greatest concentration of biodiversity on the planet?

    a. savannas

    b. tropical deciduous forests

    c. tropical rain forests

    d. temperate deciduous forests

14. Which of the following freshwater life zones does not support photosynthetic life-forms?

    a. limnetic zones

    b. littoral zones

    c. profundal zones

15. What type of freshwater lake contains few nutrients?

    a. oligotrophic lakes

    b. eutrophic lakes

16. Where would you most likely have to go to encounter a geothermal vent that spews hydrogen sulfide that is ingested by sulfur bacteria?

    a. photic zone

    b. aphotic zone

17. Distances north and south from the equator are measured in degrees of _____.

18. The roughly circular patterns characteristic of many ocean currents are called _____.

19. Mountains can create rain _____, which can lead to the formation of desert biomes.

20. Large land areas with similar environmental conditions and similar plant communities are called _____.

21. The zone of water found closest to the shore with abundant plant life is called the _____ zone.

22. In the ocean, there is a zone that subsists solely on the excrement and bodies of other organisms that sink down from above. This is called the _____ zone.

23. Both depth and proximity to the shore determine the distribution of life in the ocean. Label the resulting life regions on the image above.

24. The image below describes the airflow over the globe. These flow patterns result in predictable winds. Label these winds correctly.

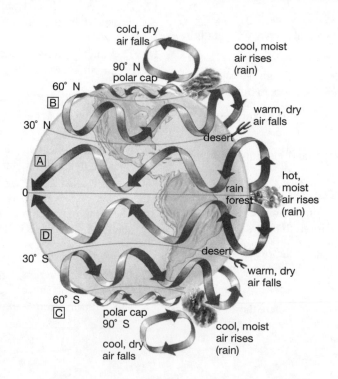

cold, dry
air falls

cool, moist
air rises
(rain)

90° N
polar cap

60° N

warm, dry
air falls

B

30° N

desert

A

hot,
moist
air rises
(rain)

rain
forest

0

D

desert

30° S

warm, dry
air falls

60° S

C

polar cap
90° S

cool, moist
air rises
(rain)

cool, dry
air falls

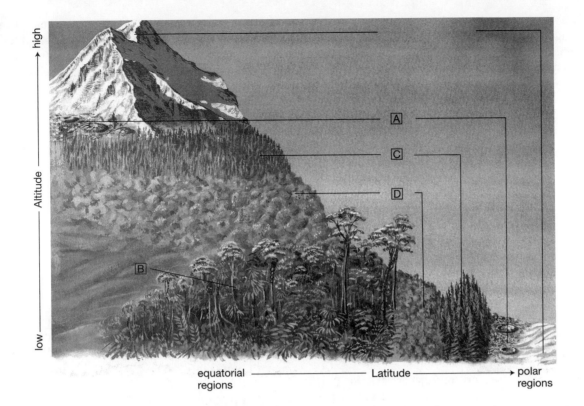

25. Temperature drops and biome types change with both increasing altitude (elevation) and increasing latitude. Label the biomes found at the elevations and latitudes indicated above.

26. Freshwater bodies exhibit distinct life zones similar to those seen in the ocean. Label these zones in the diagram below.

27. Man-made chemicals called _____ destroy stratospheric ozone, which normally absorbs harmful ultraviolet radiation from the sun.
   a. chlorofluorocarbons
   b. greenhouse gases
   c. nitrogen oxides
   d. radionuclides
   e. sulfur dioxide and methane

28. Every few years the Tradewinds die down, allowing warm surface waters to flow back eastward in the southern Pacific Ocean. This causes winter rains in Peru, droughts in Indonesia and South Africa, and a reduction in the anchovy harvest off the coast of Peru. This phenomenon is called _____.
   a. El Niño
   b. La Niña
   c. the Gulf Stream
   d. eutrophication
   e. upwelling

29. Which biome contains soils that are extremely rich in nutrients due to the accumulation of dead organic matter over many centuries?
   a. prairie
   b. tropical rain forest
   c. desert
   d. taiga
   e. temperate deciduous forest

30. Extensive, shallow root systems that can quickly soak up water after infrequent rainstorms and spiny leaves and waxy coatings to reduce water loss are adaptations seen in most plants in which biome?
   a. desert
   b. prairie
   c. tropical rain forest
   d. tundra
   e. temperate deciduous forest

31. Atlantic cod were once phenomenally abundant in the shallow waters off the coast of New England and the Maritime Provinces of eastern Canada. In fact, it has been said that this fishery alone fed the early European colonists to North America for the first century or more they were here. In the last half-century, however, the Atlantic cod fishery has almost completely collapsed. This decline has been due to _____.
   a. overfishing taking far more fish than could be replaced by normal reproduction
   b. acid rain causing the marine food web to collapse
   c. the death of eggs and fry as the ozone hole has increased UV damage
   d. global warming
   e. overpopulation exceeding the carrying capacity of the system for the cod, causing massive starvation

32. Damage due to sediments and excess nutrients from logging, farming, and development on land and rising water temperatures due to global warming are critically endangering which marine ecosystem?
   a. coral reefs
   b. intertidal zones
   c. estuaries
   d. open oceans
   e. hydrothermal vent communities

33. The largest expanses of undisturbed and uncut forests exist in the _____.
   a. taiga
   b. tropical rain forest
   c. temperate deciduous forest
   d. temperate rain forest
   e. tropical deciduous forest

34. _____ biomes are dominated by grasses but have scattered trees and thorny bushes. They have distinct wet and dry seasons. In Africa, this biome type supports huge herds of migrating large mammals.
   a. Savanna
   b. Tropical rain forest
   c. Taiga
   d. Prairie
   e. Tundra

ESSAY CHALLENGE

1. How are weather and climate similar? Different?

2. In the Northern Hemisphere, why are there often deserts to the east of large mountains?

3. What is biodiversity?

4. Why do the ocean currents follow nearly circular patterns?

5. What are the four fundamental resources required for life?

6. Describe some of the ways that humans have affected most ecosystems.

7. Of the four fundamental resources required for life, which two are generally readily available in almost all terrestrial environments? Which two are very unevenly distributed, producing the distribution patterns of the different biomes, which contain dominant plants with specific adaptations to those factors?

8. Explain why primary productivity is often very low in the deep waters of the open ocean, even in the Tropics.

MEDIA ACTIVITIES

To access a Media Activity visit http://www.prenhall.com/audesirk7. Log in to the Web site selected by your instructor, navigate to this chapter, and select the appropriate Media Activity number.

42.1 Tropical Atmospheric Circulation and World Biomes
Estimated time: 5 minutes

In this activity you will learn the effect of solar radiation on air circulation in the earth's atmosphere. Examine how the circulation of air effects the distribution of Earth's biomes.

42.2 Web Investigation: Wings of Hope
Estimated time: 30 minutes

The Kipepeo Butterfly Project (http://www.kipepeo.org/index.htm) in the coastal dry forests of Kenya is an example of one strategy being employed to save forest ecosystems throughout the world. (A similar project in the tropical rain forest of Costa Rica is called Mariposario del Bosque Nuevo http://www.elbosquenuevo.org/butterflies/.) By promoting renewable, non-timber forest products (http://www.ntfp.org/definition.html) like butterflies, collected fruits and nuts, and rattan, indigenous people can earn an income from intact forests, alleviating the financial pressure to convert them to agriculture or clear-cut them for a one-time windfall. It can also help reduce the demand for wood for fuel and construction and increases their investment in conserving the ecosystem.

1. The Kipepeo Butterfly Project has involved farmers in areas surrounding the Arabuko-Sokoke Forest. How many endemic (i.e., found nowhere else) and endangered species of birds and mammals occur in this forest? What new income-generating initiative was added to butterfly collecting in recent years? What problems have plagued the butterfly project?

2. The Liana Project (http://www.cnr.berkeley.edu/~austint/lianas/) is an effort by the Brazilian government to organize a non-timber forest products industry based in its dwindling tropical rain forests. What products are they promoting? (See the Introduction to the Report and check out the "Photos" section.) What two traditional staple non-timber forest products, which have become unprofitable due to falling prices on the international market, is the Liana Project trying to replace? (See the Forward to the Report; follow the "Project Report (English)" link, then the "FORWARD BY RAN AND CNPT" link.)

3. One variation on the non-timber forest products theme is called agroforestry. This involves manipulating the forest to favor one or more specific crops but keeping much of the character of the forest intact. One example of this approach is the production of traditional shade coffee (http://nationalzoo.si.edu/ConservationAndScience/ MigratoryBirds/Fact_Sheets/default.cfm?fxsht=1). How does shade coffee production differ from the newer method of producing "sun coffee?" What are the benefits of sun coffee over shade coffee? How is shade coffee production better environmentally?

4. Creating a non-timber forest products industry involving indigenous people is not an easy task. One of the most infamous failures involves Ben & Jerry's Rainforest Crunch (http://www.betterworld.com/BWZ/9512/cover2. htm#1) ice cream. The idea was simple. Sell an ice cream that features a Brazil nut brittle, the nuts coming from a cooperative of indigenous peoples who collect and process the nuts in the Brazilian rain forest, and return some of the profits to the cooperative. In this way, the people could afford not to sell the rights to their lands to clear-cutters or miners. However, it didn't work out that way. What went wrong? How did the system fall apart?

ISSUES IN BIOLOGY

Why Should We Be Concerned About Biodiversity Loss and Deforestation?

Biodiversity (http://ceres.ca.gov/biodiv/bioregions.html), short for biological diversity, is not an easy term to define. Definitions tend to limit concepts, whereas the concept of biodiversity, especially as a conservation biology issue (http://conbio.net/scb/), may never be sufficiently broad. Your textbook's authors consider biodiversity to be the "richness" of an ecosystem, based upon the number of species therein. (See Chapter 41's feature, "Earth Watch: Food Chains Magnify Toxic Substances.") This is a reasonable starting point but fails to adequately describe the extent of the important genetic variation that Harvard biologist E. O. Wilson considers our most important heritage (for the loss of which our children will fault us the most). The discussions of the mechanisms of evolution in Chapter 15 are fertile ground for a more inclusive concept. Evolution and adaptation require genetic variability in order to operate; "all genotypes are not equally adaptive." Genetic diversity within a species, which is possibly visible as geographic races or subspecies, declines when the population size of a species decreases substantially, or when races or subspecies are driven to extinction. Thus, to be a useful conservation biology concept, biodiversity must include the range of genetic diversity found among and within the diversity of species found in our biosphere.

Tropical forests of all types constitute just more than half of all forest cover on the planet. Rain forest (http://www. ran.org/ran/) is the most common type of forest in the Tropics. The destruction of tropical rain forest is the form of deforestation most widely discussed by the popular media. This destruction is dramatic when seen by way of the photos of the Amazonian forests burning in the late 1980s and early 1990s, or the Indonesian forest fires spread by the droughts of El Niño in 1997 and 1998. Representing only about 1/20 of terrestrial habitat, tropical forests are home to an estimated 50% to 67% of the planet's species. Loss of tropical forest, therefore, has a disproportionate effect on total biodiversity. Between 1960 and 1990, approximately 20% of tropical forests were lost worldwide; Asia lost almost one-third of its tropical forest during this period. Think of the economic, ecosystem, cultural, and aesthetic value lost with all of the species displaced by such activity! The U.N. Food and Agricultural Organization (FAO) (http://www.fao.org/) defines deforestation in a very restrictive way to include only forests converted to other use (i.e., logged or clear-cut forests left to regrow if they can would not be included). By such a measure, the decade of the 1980s saw a 2% decline worldwide, and almost all of that was in the Tropics (3.6% of 1980 tropical forests). More than 7% of tropical forest land was changed in this decade, however. Of this lost or degraded tropical forest, 45% was converted to agriculture or tree plantations, 25% was "severely" degraded, and 12% was fragmented. Since numerous studies have shown that fragmentation is nearly as destructive of biodiversity as more complete destruction, this means that almost 6% of tropical forest lands became lost to biodiversity in one decade.

Deforestation (http://www.wri.org/biodiv/index.html), however, is a problem that exists on the planet wherever forests occur naturally. Temperate wooded land cover actually increased by 0.1% in the 1980s but only because of significant increases in tree plantations. The United States suffered a loss of 1.1% of its forest cover during this time, despite increasing plantations. Apparently, 90% to 95% of the old growth forests of the U.S. Pacific Northwest have been logged (thus the controversies over protecting the northern spotted owl and various salmon stocks). Regrowth or replanting there, as throughout the continent and the world, produces forests that are less diverse and less complex. Such forests are often vulnerable to invasion by numerous exotic species, which compound the problems for declining species. In the United States, the Endangered Species Act is left to sort out the problems. Other temperate forest is declining, too. Between 35% and 50% of the trees in Germany and Switzerland are dead or dying from pollution. It is no wonder that the FAO estimates that, worldwide, more than 11 times as much land is being deforested each year as is being replanted to trees. A problem, indeed!

1. What reasons can you describe for either a narrow or a broad definition of biodiversity?

2. Where is the current "hot spot" for deforestation?

3. What is being done about forest and biodiversity loss in the United States?

BIZARRE FACTS IN BIOLOGY

The Unfortunate (Double) Legacy of Thomas Midgley, Jr.

Time can dramatically alter our opinion of events. This is clearly demonstrated by the two primary career accomplishments of mechanical engineer-turned-industrial chemist Thomas J. Midgley, Jr. (1889-1944): the discovery that tetraethyl lead can stop internal combustion engines from knocking; and the development of chlorofluorocarbons (CFCs) as refrigerants.

In 1921, Midgley discovered that adding a small quantity of tetraethyl lead (TEL) to gasoline prevented engine "knock." This engine-damaging malfunction is caused by premature ignition of some of the fuel in the cylinder as it is being compressed. Adding TEL to gasoline eliminated this problem, allowing manufacturers to increase the engine's compression ratio, yielding more power and greater fuel efficiency. To sell the additive to gasoline refiners, a new company called the Ethyl Corporation (http://www.ethyl.com/) was formed as a joint venture of General Motors, Du Pont, and Standard Oil of New Jersey, and gasoline with the additive was called "Ethyl."

In 1928, Midgley was called on to solve another problem. The refrigerants of the day, gases that were cyclically compressed to a liquid and then allowed to vaporize, absorbing heat, were either very toxic or highly flammable, or both. And since many were also corrosive, they tended to leak, resulting in many deaths. Midgley sought a gas that avoided these problems and, reportedly in just three days, found one. It was dichlorofluoromethane, the first of the chlorofluorocarbons or "CFCs," a group later trademarked "Freons." Midgley demonstrated dichlorofluoromethane's benign properties at a meeting of the American Chemical Society in 1930 by inhaling a lung-full of the gas and gently blowing it over a lit candle, which was extinguished. Other CFCs followed quickly, and they were also used for aerosol propellants, for expanding foams, in air conditioners, etc.

For his efforts, Midgley received many honors during his lifetime, but after his death in 1944 his legacy began to unravel. Lead, whose neurotoxicity had been known since antiquity, was increasingly seen as a public health problem, causing learning disorders in children, kidney failure, hypertension and heart disease, and some cancers. In fact, within a year of the start of Ethyl production in 1923 a number of workers on the Ethyl production line went insane and died from acute lead poisoning, prompting a ban on the sale of TEL-based gasoline until an inquiry could be conducted. To alleviate fears, Midgley held a press conference during which he poured TEL over his hands and inhaled the vapor. Despite protests by many prominent scientists, the ban on sales of Ethyl was quickly lifted. Only recently has it been discovered that Midgley, suffering from severe lead poisoning, subsequently took a prolonged leave of absence in 1924 to recover. Over the next several decades nearly all the research on the effects of TEL was funded by the Ethyl Corporation. Not surprisingly, the researchers failed to find conclusive evidence that leaded gasoline posed a public health risk. The U.S. EPA began phasing out leaded gasoline use in the 1970s, a process that was completed in 1996. But this was as much because lead fouled the newly mandated catalytic converters as it was due to concerns over lead contamination of the environment. (Catalytic converters reduce emissions of nitrogen oxides, hydrocarbons, and carbon monoxide from exhaust, alleviating smog.) It has been estimated that over the 60-some years of its use, 7 million tons of lead were released into the environment from the burning of leaded gasoline in the U.S. alone. This increased our average lead exposure to 300 to 500 times that of "normal" (pre-Midgley) levels. As many as 68 million young children are believed to have received toxic levels of lead between 1927 and 1987 and as many as 5,000 deaths per year may have been caused by lead-related heart disease before TEL use was phased out. But lead burdens in humans have already declined dramatically since the phase-out.

Midgley's other major "invention," CFCs, favored just as poorly. In 1974, Mario Molina and F. Sherwood Rowland published a paper describing how stratospheric ozone gas, which absorbs harmful ultraviolet radiation from the sun, was being destroyed by chlorine released during the breakdown of CFCs. They, along with Paul Crutzen, shared the 1995 Nobel Prize in Chemistry (http://www.nobel.se/chemistry/laureates/1995/index.html) "for their work in atmospheric chemistry, particularly concerning the formation and decomposition of ozone." While ozone levels worldwide were soon shown to be dropping fast, of particular concern was the vast reduction in ozone levels noted each year in the Southern Hemisphere around Antarctica in the so-called "ozone hole" (http://toms.gsfc.nasa.gov/multi/epanim97.html). Before long a sharp rise in skin cancer rates was noticed in the area, presumably due to elevated UV levels. It turns out that the stability of CFCs, a plus for their role as refrigerants, worked against them in the environment as it allowed many molecules to reach the stratosphere before being split by the intense ultraviolet radiation there. To make matters worse, CFCs were discovered to be greenhouse gases with Earth-warming potentials thousands of times as great as carbon dioxide. Given the serious health and climate implications, industrialized nations signed the Montreal Protocol (1987) and subsequent treaties to phase out CFC production and use.

In light of these two rather dubious (in hindsight) inventions, historian John McNeill remarked in his book on the environmental history of the twentieth century that Midgley "had more impact on the atmosphere than any other single organism in earth history." Midgley's changing legacy can be summed up by a line from a poem by James Russell Lowell; "Time makes ancient good uncouth."

References

Bryson, Bill. 2003. *A Short History of Nearly Everything*. New York: Broadway Books.
Kitman, J. L. 2000. The Secret History of Lead. (http://thenation.com/doc.mhtml?i=20000320&s=kitman) *The Nation*, March 20, 2000.
McNeill, J.R. 2001. *Something New Under the Sun: An Environmental History of the Twentieth-Century World*. New York: Norton.

1. What does the linked ad for ethyl gasoline (http://www.uwsp.edu/geo/courses/geog100/Icons&Photos/Ethyl10-27.jpg) from October 1927 tell you that Ethyl gasoline will do for your car's performance? What does the ad tell you about the nature of the Ethyl additive? This ad for ethyl gasoline, from February 1929, introduces the modern working woman "Ethyl" as a symbol of Ethyl gasoline. What does this ad inform you Ethyl gasoline will do for your car's performance? What does it tell you about the nature of the additive?

2. The Ethyl Corporation often portrayed TEL as the only way to stop engines from knocking and boost power. However, recently uncovered documents and exhaustive investigative reporting indicate that a second engine additive, also nicknamed "ethyl," (http://www.radford.edu/~wkovarik/lead/)was known early on to provide the same performance benefits as TEL without the toxicity, and it was a renewable resource to boot! What was "the other ethyl?" How much of the final fuel mixture had to be this other ethyl to give the same performance as TEL-laced Ethyl gasoline? What was the Ethyl Corporations motive in covering up the finding of the other ethyl? Which "early auto industry pioneer," (http://www.radford.edu/~wkovarik/papers/fuel.html) viewed the other ethyl as the fuel of the future?

3. The Ethyl Corporation also produces another anti-knock gasoline additive called MMT (http://home.ica.net/~fresch/ndp/ethylmmt.htm). What does the MMT stand for? Which heavy metal does it contain? What are its known health effects? Which North American country uses MMT, and was sued by the Ethyl Corporation for violation of NAFTA provisions when it tried to ban MMT use in 1997?

4. MTBE (http://www.ethanol.org/mtbe_information.htm) is an additive designed to make gasoline burn cleaner. However, its use has been controversial and has been banned in some areas because of its unusual behavior in the environment. What does MTBE stand for? What is this unusual behavior in the environment? Why does MTBE make gasoline burn cleaner? What other additive, also used in reformulated gasolines (RFGs), serves the same role as MTBE but without the latter's problems?

KEY TERMS

aphotic zone
biodiversity
biome
chaparral
climate
coral reef
desert
El Niño
estuary
eutrophic lake

grassland
gyre
hydrothermal vent
   community
intertidal zone
La Niña
limnetic zone
littoral zone
nearshore zone
northern coniferous forest

oligotrophic lake
ozone layer
pelagic
permafrost
photic zone
phytoplankton
plankton
prairie
profundal zone
rain shadow

savanna
taiga
temperate deciduous forest
temperate rain forest
tropical deciduous forest
tropical rain forest
tundra
upwelling
weather
zooplankton

ANSWER KEY

SELF TEST

1. d
2. b
3. e
4. a
5. e
6. e
7. b
8. e
9. f
10. c
11. a
12. c
13. c
14. c
15. a
16. b
17. latitude
18. gyres
19. shadows
20. biomes
21. littoral
22. aphotic
23. A. intertidal zone
    B. nearshore zone
    C. photic zone
    D. aphotic zone
24. A. N.E. tradewinds
    B. westerlies
    C. polar easterlies
    D. S.E. tradewinds
25. A. tundra
    B. tropical forest
    C. coniferous forest
    D. deciduous forest
26. A. littoral zone
    B. limnetic zone
    C. profundal zone
27. a
28. a
29. a
30. a
31. a
32. a
33. a
34. a

ESSAY CHALLENGE

1. Weather is a short-term fluctuation in the temperature, humidity, and cloud cover, to name just three effects. Climate is a description of long-term trends in the weather.

2. Mountains produce a rain shadow, which means that the air going over a mountain range drops its moisture as the air temperature drops. On the other side of the mountain, the air is dry and can often remove water from the ground, creating a desert.

3. Biodiversity indicates the total number of species that an ecosystem supports and the complexity of the interactions among the species.

4. Earth's rotation, winds, and direct heating of the water by the sun can affect these currents.

5. Nutrients, energy, liquid water, and appropriate temperatures are the four fundamental resources.

6. Human-dominated ecosystems are often simpler, rely on nonrenewable energy sources, tend to lose nutrients, tend to pollute water, tend to be too simple to be stable, and are continuously growing.

7. Nutrients and energy (coming from the soil and sunlight, respectively, for photosynthetic organisms) are readily available in most terrestrial ecosystems. However, the distribution of liquid water and appropriate temperatures are very uneven, varying with latitude, altitude, locations of mountains and continents, etc.

8. In the upper waters of the photic zone, energy (from sunlight) is abundant; but nutrients are often limiting, and they are constantly sinking into deeper waters. In the deeper waters of the aphotic zone, nutrients are abundant but energy from sunlight is scarce, as the water readily absorbs solar energy. As a result, the entire water column is limited by one or the other of these two fundamental resources.

MEDIA ACTIVITIES

42.2 Web Investigation: Wings of Hope

1. Six species of birds and three species of mammals in the forest are either endemic or endangered. In recent years, honey production has been added as a new income-generating activity. Some problems facing the butterfly project have included: the seasonality of butterfly supply and demand, making income erratic; diseases and parasites afflicting the butterflies; and the losses and delays associated with export.

2. The Liana Project is an attempt to develop an industry in rattan-like furniture, baskets, and trays, made locally by artisans using native Brazilian vines collected in a non-destructive manner from the rain forest. It is an effort to replace non-timber forest product industries

in Brazil nuts and rubber, which have become unprofitable due to falling prices of those commodities.

3. In shade coffee production, an overstory (canopy) of other tree species, some of which are nitrogen fixers, is maintained above the coffee plants. In sun coffee production, all other plants are removed. Sun coffee systems are more productive than shade coffee operations. However, they require a greater investment of capital in the form of inorganic fertilizers, pesticides, etc., and degrade the soils quickly, often leading to abandonment of sites after just a few years.

4. Due to the intense demand created by the success of the ice cream, the cooperative could not supply all of the nuts needed. As a result, 95% or more of the nuts were purchased from commercial agribusinesses, which flooded the market, causing prices to fall. This resulted in reduced profits for the cooperative, which was forced to get out of the nut business altogether. Some nut collectors were even forced to sell the rights to their lands to grazers and miners.

ISSUES IN BIOLOGY

1. Narrowly defining biodiversity as the number of species in an ecosystem increases comprehension and may simplify scientific study. Broadly defining biodiversity to also include genetic diversity within each species adds an evolutionary perspective. This is important in conservation biology because it tells us that smaller populations with less diversity are less likely to be able to adapt to new or changing conditions.

2. Deforestation is currently greatest in tropical forests, which include the biodiversity riches of the tropical rain forests.

3. Forest loss has been combated by regrowth and replanting, but the latter typically results in less diverse tree plantations that are subject to invasion by exotic species, etc. Conservation efforts centered around the northern spotted owl and salmon stocks help preserve not only those species but forest biodiversity as well.

BIZARRE FACTS IN BIOLOGY

1. The 1927 ad promises greater performance (more power, faster pick-up), as well as greater economy (lessened depreciation). It only tells you that Ethyl gasoline contains "Ethyl brand of anti-knock compound." The 1929 ad tells you that "Ethyl" will increase power and efficiency, but gives no information whatsoever about the nature of the additive.

2. The other ethyl was ethyl alcohol or ethanol. Adding just 15% ethanol by volume gave the same performance boost as adding three grams per gallon of TEL. The Ethyl Corporation covered up the viability of ethanol as an alternative anti-knock additive purely out of greed, as they could control the market of TEL but not of ethanol. Henry Ford believed ethyl alcohol was the fuel of the future, and he and others viewed TEL as simply a temporary solution until ethanol production could be scaled up to supply the nation's automotive needs.

3. MMT stands for methylcyclopentadienyl manganese tricarbonyl. It contains the heavy metal manganese which, like lead, is a known neurotoxin. It has been linked to Parkinson's disease-like symptoms, psychosis, severe neurological disease, and premature death. Canada has used MMT since 1977 and was sued by the Ethyl corporation for NAFTA violations when it tried to ban MMT in 1997.

4. MTBE stands for methyl tertiary butyl ether. It is unusual in that it moves easily through soils and groundwater, showing up in drinking and recreational waters. It serves as a source of oxygen to help gasoline burn more completely and hence cleaner. This same role can be accomplished by adding ethyl alcohol (ethanol) to the gasoline.